MW00700541

THE NEW TESTAMENT

JOURNAL EDITION

SALT LAKE CITY, UTAH

Visit us at deseretbook.com

ISBN 978-1-63993-038-8 (hardbound)

Printed in China
RR Donnelley, Dongguan, China

10 9 8 7 6 5 4 3 2 1

THE NEW TESTAMENT

OF OUR LORD AND SAVIOUR

JESUS CHRIST

TRANSLATED OUT OF THE
ORIGINAL GREEK: AND WITH THE
FORMER TRANSLATIONS DILIGENTLY COMPARED
AND REVISED, BY HIS MAJESTY'S
SPECIAL COMMAND

AUTHORIZED KING JAMES VERSION
WITH EXPLANATORY NOTES AND
CROSS-REFERENCES TO THE STANDARD WORKS
OF THE CHURCH OF JESUS CHRIST
OF LATTER-DAY SAINTS

ABBREVIATIONS

Old Testament

Gen.	Genesis
Ex.	Exodus
Lev.	Leviticus
Num.	Numbers
Deut.	Deuteronomy
Josh.	Joshua
Judg.	Judges
Ruth	Ruth
1 Sam.	1 Samuel
2 Sam.	2 Samuel
1 Kgs.	1 Kings
2 Kgs.	2 Kings
1 Chr.	1 Chronicles
2 Chr.	2 Chronicles
Ezra	Ezra
Neh.	Nehemiah
Esth.	Esther
Job	Job
Ps.	Psalms
Prov.	Proverbs
Eccl.	Ecclesiastes
Song	Song of Solomon
Isa.	Isaiah
Jer.	Jeremiah
Lam.	Lamentations
Ezek.	Ezekiel
Dan.	Daniel
Hosea	Hosea
Joel	Joel
Amos	Amos
Obad.	Obadiah
Jonah	Jonah
Micah	Micah
Nahum	Nahum
Hab.	Habakkuk
Zeph.	Zephaniah
Hag.	Haggai
Zech.	Zechariah
Mal.	Malachi

New Testament

Matt.	Matthew
Mark	Mark
Luke	Luke
John	John
Acts	Acts
Rom.	Romans
1 Cor.	1 Corinthians
2 Cor.	2 Corinthians
Gal.	Galatians
Eph.	Ephesians
Philip.	Philippians
Col.	Colossians
1 Thes.	1 Thessalonians
2 Thes.	2 Thessalonians
1 Tim.	1 Timothy
2 Tim.	2 Timothy
Titus	Titus
Philem.	Philemon
Heb.	Hebrews
James	James
1 Pet.	1 Peter
2 Pet.	2 Peter
1 Jn.	1 John
2 Jn.	2 John
3 Jn.	3 John
Jude	Jude
Rev.	Revelation

Book of Mormon

1 Ne.	1 Nephi
2 Ne.	2 Nephi
Jacob	Jacob
Enos	Enos
Jarom	Jarom
Omni	Omni
W of M	Words of Mormon
Mosiah	Mosiah
Alma	Alma
Hel.	Helaman
3 Ne.	3 Nephi
4 Ne.	4 Nephi
Morm.	Mormon
Ether	Ether
Moro.	Moroni

Doctrine and Covenants

D&C	Doctrine and Covenants
OD	Official Declaration

Pearl of Great Price

Moses	Moses
Abr.	Abraham
JS—M	Joseph Smith—Matthew
JS—H	Joseph Smith—History
A of F	Articles of Faith

Other Abbreviations and Explanations

JST	Joseph Smith Translation
TG	Topical Guide
BD	Bible Dictionary
HEB	An alternate translation from the Hebrew
GR	An alternate translation from the Greek
IE	An explanation of idioms and difficult wording
OR	Alternate words that clarify the meaning of an archaic expression
HC	History of the Church

Italics in biblical text. Following the traditional format, italics in Bible verses indicate words that are not found in the original text (Hebrew, Aramaic, or Greek) but have been added for clarification in the translation.

THE NAMES AND ORDER OF ALL THE

BOOKS OF THE NEW TESTAMENT

THE GOSPEL ACCORDING TO

ST MATTHEW

CHAPTER 1

Christ is born of Mary—She conceives by the power of the Holy Ghost—Our Lord is named Jesus.

THE book of the generation of Jesus Christ, the son of [a]David, the son of Abraham.
2 [a]Abraham begat Isaac; and Isaac begat Jacob; and Jacob begat [b]Judas and his brethren;
3 And Judas begat [a]Phares and [b]Zara of Thamar; and Phares begat [c]Esrom; and Esrom begat Aram;
4 And Aram begat Aminadab; and Aminadab begat Naasson; and [a]Naasson begat Salmon;
5 And Salmon begat [a]Booz of Rachab; and Booz begat Obed of Ruth; and Obed begat Jesse;
6 And Jesse begat David the king; and David the king begat [a]Solomon of her *that had been the wife* of Urias;
7 And Solomon begat Roboam; and Roboam begat Abia; and Abia begat Asa;
8 And Asa begat Josaphat; and Josaphat begat Joram; and Joram begat Ozias;
9 And Ozias begat Joatham; and Joatham begat Achaz; and Achaz begat Ezekias;
10 And Ezekias begat Manasses; and Manasses begat Amon; and Amon begat Josias;
11 And Josias begat Jechonias and his brethren, about the time they were carried away to [a]Babylon:
12 And after they were brought to Babylon, Jechonias begat Salathiel; and Salathiel begat [a]Zorobabel;
13 And Zorobabel begat Abiud; and Abiud begat Eliakim; and Eliakim begat Azor;
14 And Azor begat Sadoc; and Sadoc begat Achim; and Achim begat Eliud;
15 And Eliud begat Eleazar; and Eleazar begat Matthan; and Matthan begat Jacob;
16 And Jacob begat [a]Joseph the husband of [b]Mary, of whom was born [c]Jesus, [d]who is called [e]Christ.
17 So all the generations from Abraham to David *are* fourteen generations; and from David until the carrying away into Babylon *are* fourteen generations; and from the carrying away into Babylon unto Christ *are* fourteen [a]generations.
18 ¶ [a]Now the [b]birth of Jesus Christ was [c]on this wise: When as his mother Mary was espoused to

Title: JST entitles this book "The Testimony of St. Matthew."
1 1*a* TG Jesus Christ, Davidic Descent of.
2*a* Gen. 25:19.
b TG Israel, Judah, People of.
3*a* Ruth 4:18; 1 Chr. 2:4 (4–15).
b Gen. 38:30.
c 1 Chr. 2:9.
4*a* Num. 1:7.
5*a* Ruth 4:21.
6*a* 2 Sam. 12:24 (24–25); 1 Chr. 3:5.
11*a* TG Israel, Bondage of, in Other Lands.
12*a* 1 Chr. 3:19 (17–19); Ezra 2:2 (1–2); Hag. 1:1.
16*a* Luke 3:23 (23–38).
b 1 Ne. 11:18 (14–21); Mosiah 3:8.
c Luke 20:14; D&C 93:14 (3–17).
d JST Matt. 1:4 . . . *as the prophets have written*, who is called Christ.
e The Greek title "Christ" and the Hebrew title "Messiah" are synonymous, meaning "Anointed One."
17*a* TG Book of Remembrance.
18*a* JST Matt. 2:1 Now, *as it is written*, the birth of . . .
b D&C 20:1.
c GR in this way.

Joseph, before they came together,
she was found with child of the
Holy Ghost.
19 Then Joseph her husband, being a just *man*, and not willing to
make her a publick [a]example, [b]was
minded to [c]put her away privily.
20 But while he thought on these
things, behold, the angel of the Lord
appeared unto him in a [a]dream,
saying, Joseph, thou son of [b]David,
fear not to take unto thee Mary thy
wife: for that which is conceived in
her is of the [c]Holy Ghost.
21 And she shall bring forth a
son, and thou shalt call his [a]name
[b]JESUS: for he shall [c]save his people
from their sins.
22 Now all this was done, that it
might be fulfilled which was spoken
of the Lord by the prophet, saying,
23 [a]Behold, a [b]virgin shall be with
child, and shall bring forth a son,
and they shall call his [c]name [d]Em-
manuel, which being interpreted
is, God with us.
24 Then Joseph being raised from
sleep did as the angel of the Lord
had bidden him, and took unto him
his [a]wife:
25 And knew her not till she had
brought forth her [a]firstborn son: and
he called his name JESUS.

CHAPTER 2

The wise men are directed by a star to Jesus—Joseph takes the child to Egypt—Herod slays the children in Bethlehem—Jesus is taken to Nazareth to dwell.

NOW when Jesus was [a]born in Bethlehem of Judæa in the days of Herod
the king, behold, there came wise
men from the east to Jerusalem,
2 Saying, [a]Where is he that is born
[b]King of the Jews? for we have seen
his [c]star in the east, and are come
to [d]worship him.
3 When Herod the king had heard
these things, he was troubled, and all
Jerusalem with him.
4 [a]And when he had gathered all
the chief priests and scribes of the
people together, he [b]demanded of
them where Christ should be born.
5 And they said unto him, In Bethlehem of Judæa: for thus it is written by the prophet,
6 And thou [a]Bethlehem, *in* the land
of [b]Juda, art not the least among
the princes of Juda: for out of thee
shall come a [c]Governor, that shall
[d]rule my people Israel.
7 Then Herod, when he had privily called the wise men, inquired
of them diligently what time the
star appeared.
8 And he sent them to Bethlehem,
and said, Go and search diligently
for the young child; and when ye
have found *him*, bring me word
again, that I may come and worship
him also.
9 When they had heard the king,
they departed; and, lo, the star,
which they saw in the east, went

19*a* TG Example.
b IE desired to release or divorce her secretly.
c Deut. 24:1.
20*a* TG Dream.
b 2 Ne. 19:7.
c Luke 1:35; Alma 7:10.
21*a* TG Jesus Christ, Prophecies about.
b Luke 2:21.
c TG Forgive; Jesus Christ, Atonement through; Jesus Christ, Mission of; Jesus Christ, Redeemer; Jesus Christ, Savior; Redemption; Salvation.
23*a* Isa. 7:14.
b TG Jesus Christ, Birth of.
c TG Name.
d TG Jesus Christ, Prophecies about.
24*a* Luke 2:5.
25*a* TG Firstborn.
2 1*a* TG Jesus Christ, Birth of.
2*a* JST Matt. 3:2 . . . Where is *the child* that is born, *the Messiah* of the Jews? . . .
b Isa. 6:5; Jer. 23:5; 2 Ne. 10:14; Alma 5:50; D&C 128:22 (22–23); Moses 7:53.
c Hel. 14:5 (1–2, 5); 3 Ne. 1:21.
d TG Worship.
4*a* JST Matt. 3:4–6 (Appendix).
b GR inquired.
6*a* TG Jesus Christ, Prophecies about.
b TG Israel, Judah, People of.
c 1 Chr. 5:2; Micah 5:2; John 7:42.
d GR tend, protect, nurture.

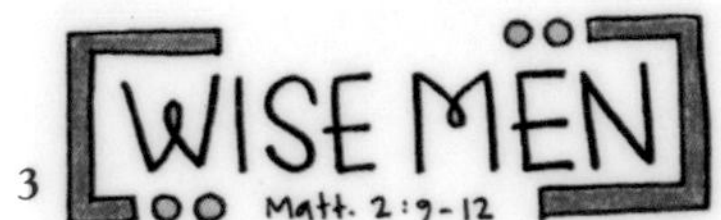

before them, till it came and stood
over where the young child was.
10 When they saw the star, they
rejoiced with exceeding great joy.
11 ¶ And when they were come
into the house, they saw the young
child with Mary his mother, and
fell down, and worshipped him:
and when they had opened their
treasures, they presented unto him
gifts; gold, and [a]frankincense, and
myrrh.
12 And being warned of God in a
[a]dream that they should not return
to Herod, they departed into their
own country another way.
13 And when they were departed,
behold, the angel of the Lord appeareth to Joseph in a dream, saying, Arise, and take the young child
and his mother, and flee into Egypt,
and be thou there until I bring thee
word: for Herod will seek the young
child to destroy him.
14 When he arose, he took the
young child and his mother by night,
and departed into Egypt:
15 And was there until the death
of Herod: that it might be fulfilled
which was spoken of the Lord by
the prophet, saying, Out of [a]Egypt
have I called my son.
16 ¶ Then Herod, when he saw
that he was [a]mocked of the wise
men, [b]was exceeding wroth, and
sent forth, and [c]slew all the children that were in Bethlehem, and
in all the [d]coasts thereof, from two
years old and under, according to
the time which he had diligently
inquired of the wise men.
17 Then was fulfilled that which
was spoken by [a]Jeremy the prophet,
saying,
18 In [a]Rama was there a voice
heard, lamentation, and weeping,
and great [b]mourning, Rachel weeping *for* her [c]children, and would not
be comforted, because they are not.
19 ¶ But when Herod was dead, behold, an angel of the Lord appeareth
in a [a]dream to Joseph in Egypt,
20 Saying, Arise, and take the young
child and his mother, and go into
the [a]land of Israel: for they are dead
which sought the young child's life.
21 And he arose, and took the
young child and his mother, and
came into the land of Israel.
22 But when he heard that Arche-
laus did reign in Judæa in the [a]room
of his father Herod, he was afraid
to go thither: notwithstanding, being warned of God in a [b]dream, he
turned aside into the parts of Galilee:
23 And he came and dwelt in a
city called [a]Nazareth: that it might
be fulfilled which was [b]spoken by
the prophets, He shall be called a
[c]Nazarene.

CHAPTER 3

John the Baptist preaches in Judæa—Jesus is baptized, and the Father acclaims Him as His Beloved Son.

IN those days came [a]John the Baptist, preaching in the wilderness
of Judæa,
2 And saying, [a]Repent ye: for the
[b]kingdom of heaven [c]is at hand.
3 For this is he that was spoken
of by the prophet [a]Esaias, saying,
The [b]voice of one crying in the

11*a* Lev. 2:1.
12*a* TG Dream.
15*a* TG Jesus Christ, Prophecies about.
16*a* GR deceived by.
b GR became extremely angry.
c TG Tyranny.
d GR surrounding regions.
17*a* IE Jeremiah.
18*a* Jer. 31:15.
b TG Mourning.
c Jer. 40:1.
19*a* JST Matt. 3:19 . . . *vision* . . .
TG Dream.
20*a* TG Israel, Land of.
22*a* GR place.
b TG Dream.
23*a* 1 Ne. 11:13.
b TG Scriptures, Lost.
c JST Matt. 3:24–26 (Appendix).
3 1*a* JS—H 1:72.
2*a* The Greek word denotes "a change of heart or mind," i.e., "a conversion."
Alma 7:9; 9:25 (25–26); Hel. 5:32;
D&C 33:10.
b Luke 10:9.
TG Kingdom of God, in Heaven; Kingdom of God, on Earth.
c GR has come.
Isa. 56:1; Matt. 4:17; D&C 39:19.
3*a* See JST Luke 3:4–11 (Appendix).
TG Foreordination.
b Isa. 40:3; Mark 1:3; Luke 3:4; John 1:23; D&C 65:3; 88:66.

wilderness, [c]Prepare ye the way of the Lord, make his [d]paths straight.

4 And the same John had his [a]raiment of [b]camel's hair, and a leathern girdle about his loins; and his meat was [c]locusts and wild honey.

5 Then went out to him Jerusalem, and all Judæa, and all the region round about Jordan,

6 And were baptized of him in Jordan, [a]confessing their sins.

7 ¶ But when he saw many of the Pharisees and Sadducees come to his [a]baptism, he said unto them, O [b]generation of vipers, who hath [c]warned you to flee from the wrath to come?

8 [a]Bring forth therefore fruits [b]meet for [c]repentance:

9 And think not to say within yourselves, We have Abraham [a]to *our* father: for I say unto you, that God is able of these stones to raise up children unto Abraham.

10 And now also the axe is laid unto the root of the trees: therefore every tree which [a]bringeth not forth good fruit is [b]hewn down, and cast into the fire.

11 [a]I indeed [b]baptize you with water unto [c]repentance: but [d]he that cometh after me is mightier than I, whose shoes I am not [e]worthy to bear: he shall [f]baptize you with the Holy Ghost, and *with* [g]fire:

12 Whose [a]fan *is* in his hand, and he will throughly purge his floor, and gather his wheat into the [b]garner; but he will burn up the chaff with unquenchable [c]fire.

13 ¶ Then cometh Jesus from Galilee to Jordan unto John, to be [a]baptized of him.

14 But John forbad him, saying, I have need to be baptized of thee, and comest thou to me?

15 [a]And Jesus answering said unto him, [b]Suffer *it to be so* now: for thus it [c]becometh us to [d]fulfil all [e]righteousness. Then he suffered him.

16 And Jesus, when he was [a]baptized, went up [b]straightway out of the water: and, lo, the heavens were opened unto him, and he saw the [c]Spirit of God descending like a [d]dove, and lighting upon him:

17 And lo a [a]voice from heaven, saying, This is my [b]beloved [c]Son, in whom I am well pleased.

CHAPTER 4

Jesus fasts forty days and is tempted—He begins His ministry, calls disciples, and heals the sick.

THEN was Jesus [a]led up of the Spirit into the wilderness [b]to be [c]tempted of the devil.

2 And when he had [a]fasted [b]forty

3*c* 1 Ne. 10:8 (7–10); D&C 34:6; 65:1 (1–2); 84:26.
d Alma 7:19 (9, 19).
4*a* GR garment. See also 2 Kgs. 1:8.
b Zech. 13:4.
c Lev. 11:22.
6*a* TG Confession.
7*a* See JST Matt. 9:18–21 (Appendix). Luke 7:29 (29–30).
b GR crop of serpents. Matt. 12:34; 23:33; Alma 9:8; 10:17 (17–25).
c TG Warn.
8*a* JST Matt. 3:34–36 (Appendix).
b GR appropriate to, worthy of.
c TG Baptism, Qualifications for; Repent.
9*a* GR as our father.
10*a* Alma 5:36 (36–41); 3 Ne. 14:19; D&C 52:18; 97:7.
b Luke 13:7; Jacob 5:42 (42–66).
11*a* JST Matt. 3:38–40 (Appendix).
b Acts 19:3 (1–7); 2 Ne. 31:5 (5–10).
c TG Baptism, Qualifications for.
d See JST John 1:27–34 (Appendix).
e TG Worthiness.
f TG Holy Ghost, Baptism of.
g D&C 19:31.
12*a* Jer. 51:2.
b GR storehouse.
c D&C 43:32; 63:34 (33–34); 101:66.
13*a* TG Jesus Christ, Baptism of.
15*a* JST Matt. 3:43–46 (Appendix).
b GR Permit it now.
c GR is fitting for us.
d TG Baptism, Essential.
e TG Jesus Christ, Mission of; Righteousness.
16*a* TG Baptism; Baptism, Immersion.
b GR immediately.
c TG God, Spirit of.
d TG Holy Ghost, Dove, Sign of.
17*a* Mark 9:7; Luke 9:35 (34–36). TG God, Body of, Corporeal Nature; God, Manifestations of.
b Matt. 17:5; 3 Ne. 11:7; JS—H 1:17. TG Witness of the Father.
c TG Godhead; God the Father, Elohim; Jesus Christ, Divine Sonship.
4 1*a* TG Guidance, Divine.
b JST Matt. 4:1 . . . to be *with God.*
c TG Jesus Christ, Temptation of; Temptation; Test.
2*a* Mosiah 3:7. TG Fast, Fasting.
b Ex. 24:18.

days and forty nights, [c]he was afterward an hungred.
3 And when the [a]tempter came to
him, he said, If thou be the Son of
God, command that these stones be
made [b]bread.
4 But he answered and said, It
is written, [a]Man shall not [b]live by
[c]bread alone, but by every [d]word
that proceedeth out of the [e]mouth
of God.
5 [a]Then the devil taketh him up
into the [b]holy city, and setteth him
on a pinnacle of the temple,
6 [a]And saith unto him, [b]If thou be
the Son of God, cast thyself down:
for it is written, He shall give his
angels charge concerning thee: and
in *their* hands they shall bear thee
up, lest at any time thou dash thy
foot against a stone.
7 Jesus said unto him, It is written
again, Thou shalt not [a]tempt the
Lord thy God.
8 [a]Again, the devil taketh him up
into an exceeding high mountain,
and sheweth him all the [b]king-
doms of the world, and the glory of
them;
9 [a]And saith unto him, All these
things will I give thee, if thou wilt
fall down and worship me.
10 Then saith Jesus unto him, Get
thee hence, [a]Satan: for it is written,
Thou shalt [b]worship the Lord thy
God, and him only shalt thou serve.
11 Then the devil leaveth him,
[a]and, behold, [b]angels came and
ministered unto him.
12 ¶ Now when Jesus had heard
that John was cast into prison, he
departed into [a]Galilee;
13 And leaving Nazareth, he came
and dwelt in Capernaum, which is
upon the sea coast, in the borders
of Zabulon and Nephthalim:
14 That it might be [a]fulfilled which
was spoken by Esaias the prophet,
saying,
15 The land of [a]Zabulon, and the
land of Nephthalim, *by* the way of
the sea, beyond Jordan, Galilee of
the Gentiles;
16 The people which sat in [a]dark-
ness saw great [b]light; and to them
which sat in the region and shadow
of death light is sprung up.
17 ¶ From that time Jesus began
to [a]preach, and to say, [b]Repent: for
the [c]kingdom of heaven [d]is at hand.
18 ¶ And Jesus, walking by the
sea of Galilee, saw two brethren,
Simon called Peter, and Andrew his
brother, casting a net into the sea:
for they were [a]fishers.
19 And he saith unto them, [a]Follow
me, and I will make you [b]fishers
of men.

2*c* JST Matt. 4:2 . . . *and had communed with God,* he was afterwards an hungered, *and was left to be tempted of the devil.*
3*a* TG Devil.
b TG Bread.
4*a* Deut. 8:3; D&C 84:44 (43–44).
b TG Mortality.
c TG Bread.
d TG Revelation.
e TG God, Body of, Corporeal Nature.
5*a* JST Matt. 4:5 Then *Jesus was taken* up into the holy city, and *the Spirit* setteth him on *the* pinnacle of the temple.
b Neh. 11:1.
6*a* JST Matt. 4:6 *Then the devil came unto him and said,* If . . .
b Matt. 27:40; D&C 20:22.
7*a* D&C 10:29; 24:13 (13–14). TG Jesus Christ, Temptation of; Test.
8*a* JST Matt. 4:8 *And* again, *Jesus was in the Spirit, and it* taketh him . . .
b D&C 10:19. TG Kings, Earthly.
9*a* JST Matt. 4:9 And *the devil came unto him again, and said,* All . . .
10*a* TG Devil.
b TG Worship.
11*a* JST Matt. 4:11–12 *And now Jesus knew that John was cast into prison, and he sent angels,* and, behold, *they* came and ministered unto him [John]. *And Jesus* departed into Galilee . . .
b TG Angels.
12*a* Luke 4:14.
14*a* D&C 24:14.
15*a* Isa. 9:1 (1–2).
16*a* D&C 57:10.
b TG Jesus Christ, Light of the World; Jesus Christ, Prophecies about.
17*a* TG Preaching.
b TG Repent.
c TG Kingdom of God, in Heaven.
d GR has come. Isa. 56:1; Matt. 3:2.
18*a* TG Skill.
19*a* JST Matt. 4:18 . . . *I am he of whom it is written by the prophets;* follow me . . . TG Jesus Christ, Exemplar.
b TG Apostles; Missionary Work.

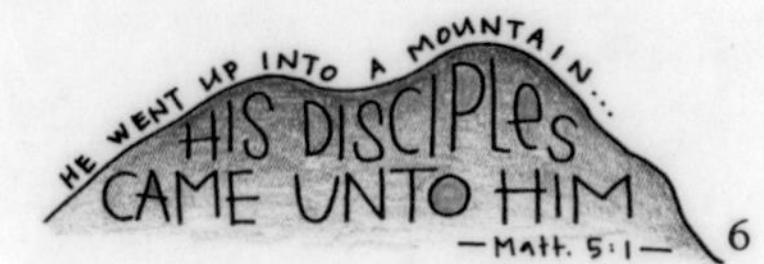

20 And they straightway left *their* nets, and [a]followed him.

21 And going on from thence, he saw other two brethren, James *the son* of [a]Zebedee, and John his brother, in a ship with Zebedee their father, mending their nets; and he [b]called them.

22 And they immediately left the ship and their father, and followed him.

23 ¶ And Jesus went about all [a]Galilee, [b]teaching in their synagogues, and [c]preaching the gospel of the kingdom, and [d]healing all manner of [e]sickness and all manner of disease among the [f]people.

24 And his fame went throughout all Syria: and they brought unto him all sick people that were taken with divers diseases and torments, and those which were possessed with [a]devils, and those which were lunatic, and those that had the [b]palsy; and he [c]healed them.

25 And there followed him great multitudes of people from Galilee, and *from* Decapolis, and *from* Jerusalem, and *from* Judæa, and *from* beyond Jordan.

CHAPTER 5

Jesus preaches the Sermon on the Mount—Its teachings replace and transcend some aspects of the law of Moses—All are commanded to be perfect like their Father in Heaven.

[a]AND seeing the multitudes, he went up into a mountain: and when he was set, his disciples came unto him:

2 And he opened his mouth, and taught them, saying,

3 [a]Blessed *are* the [b]poor in spirit: for theirs is the [c]kingdom of heaven.

4 Blessed *are* they that [a]mourn: for they shall be [b]comforted.

5 Blessed *are* the [a]meek: for they shall inherit the [b]earth.

6 Blessed *are* they which do [a]hunger and thirst after [b]righteousness: for they shall be filled.

7 Blessed *are* the [a]merciful: for they shall obtain mercy.

8 Blessed *are* the [a]pure in [b]heart: for they shall [c]see God.

9 Blessed *are* the [a]peacemakers: for they shall be called the [b]children of God.

10 Blessed *are* they which are [a]persecuted for [b]righteousness' sake: for [c]theirs is the kingdom of heaven.

11 Blessed are ye, when *men* shall [a]revile you, and persecute *you*, and shall say all manner of [b]evil against you falsely, [c]for my sake.

12 [a]Rejoice, and be exceeding glad: for great *is* your [b]reward in heaven:

20*a* TG Commitment.
21*a* John 21:2.
b TG Called of God.
23*a* Luke 4:44.
b Matt. 9:35.
c D&C 71:1.
d TG Heal; Miracle.
e TG Sickness.
f JST Matt. 4:22 . . . people *which believed on his name.*
24*a* Matt. 8:16 (16, 28, 33); 9:32 (32–34).
b GR paralysis.
c Mosiah 3:5 (5–6).
5 1*a* 3 Ne. 12:1 (1–48).
3*a* The Latin *beatus* is the basis of the English "beatitude," meaning "to be fortunate," "to be happy," or "to be blessed." TG Blessing.
b IE poor in pride, humble in spirit; 3 Ne. 12:3 reads ". . . the poor in spirit who come unto me." James 2:5 (1–9); D&C 56:18 (18–20); 88:17. TG Contrite Heart; Humility; Poor in Spirit.
c TG Kingdom of God, in Heaven.
4*a* TG Mourning; Sorrow.
b TG Comfort.
5*a* GR gentle, forgiving, or benevolent; the Hebrew in Ps. 37:11 characterizes as the humble those who have suffered. TG Meek.
b TG Earth, Destiny of.
6*a* 3 Ne. 12:6. TG Teachable.
b TG Good Works; Righteousness.
7*a* TG Mercy.
8*a* TG Chastity; Cleanliness; Purity.
b TG Heart.
c TG God, Presence of; God, Privilege of Seeing.
9*a* TG Contentment; Peace; Peacemakers.
b TG Sons and Daughters of God.
10*a* TG Affliction; Persecution.
b TG Righteousness.
c D&C 6:37; 10:55.
11*a* TG Malice; Reviling.
b TG Backbiting; Slander.
c GR on account of me.
12*a* 2 Ne. 9:18. TG Joy.
b D&C 84:38. TG Reward.

for so [c]persecuted they the prophets
which were before you.
13 ¶ Ye are the [a]salt of the earth:
but if the salt have lost his savour,
wherewith shall it be salted? it is
thenceforth good for nothing, but
to be cast out, and to be trodden
under foot of men.
14 Ye are the [a]light of the world.
A city that is set on an hill cannot
be hid.
15 Neither do men light a [a]candle,
and put it under a bushel, but on a
candlestick; and it giveth light unto
all that are in the house.
16 Let your [a]light so shine before
men, that they may see your good
[b]works, and [c]glorify your Father
which is in heaven.
17 ¶ Think not that I am come to
[a]destroy the [b]law, or the prophets:
I am not come to destroy, but to
fulfil.
18 For verily I say unto you, Till
heaven and earth pass, one jot or
one tittle shall in no wise pass from
the [a]law, till all be [b]fulfilled.
19 [a]Whosoever therefore shall
[b]break one of these least commandments, and shall [c]teach men so,
he shall be called the least in the
kingdom of heaven: but whosoever
shall do and [d]teach *them,* the same
shall be called great in the kingdom
of heaven.
20 For I say unto you, That except
your [a]righteousness shall exceed
the righteousness of the [b]scribes and
Pharisees, ye shall in no case enter
into the kingdom of heaven.
21 ¶ Ye have heard that it was said
by them of old time, Thou [a]shalt not
[b]kill; and whosoever shall kill shall
be [c]in danger of the judgment:
22 But I say unto you, That whosoever is [a]angry with his brother
[b]without a cause shall be [c]in danger of the judgment: and whosoever shall say to his brother, [d]Raca,
shall be [e]in danger of the council:
but whosoever shall say, Thou fool,
shall be in danger of hell fire.
23 Therefore if thou bring thy
gift to the altar, and there remem-
berest that thy brother hath ought
against thee;
24 Leave there thy gift before the
altar, and go thy way; first be [a]rec-
onciled to thy brother, and then
come and offer thy gift.
25 [a]Agree with thine adversary
quickly, whiles thou art in the way
with him; lest at any time the adversary deliver thee to the judge,
and the judge deliver thee to the
officer, and thou be cast into prison.
26 Verily I say unto thee, Thou
shalt by no means come out thence,
till thou hast paid [a]the uttermost
farthing.
27 ¶ Ye have heard that it was said
by them of old time, Thou shalt not
commit [a]adultery:
28 But I say unto you, That

12*c* TG Persecution.
13*a* See Lev. 2:13 and Num. 18:19, where salt is a token of the covenant and was part of sacrificial ritual. TG Salt.
14*a* TG Mission of Early Saints.
15*a* Luke 11:33 (33–34).
16*a* 3 Ne. 18:24. TG Children of Light; Example; Light [noun].
b 1 Pet. 2:12. TG Good Works.
c John 15:8.
17*a* D&C 10:52 (52, 54).
b TG Law of Moses.
18*a* TG Law of Moses.
b D&C 1:38.
19*a* JST Matt. 5:21 (Appendix).
b TG Sin.
c 2 Ne. 28:15 (12, 15).
d TG Missionary Work.
20*a* TG Righteousness.
b TG Scribe.
21*a* TG Commandments of God.
b TG Blood, Shedding of; Murder.
c GR subject to condemnation.
22*a* Prov. 29:22 (21–23); 3 Ne. 12:22 (21–24). TG Anger; Rashness.
b JST Matt. 5:24 and 3 Ne. 12:22 omit the words "without a cause."
c GR subject to condemnation.
d A word suggesting contempt or derision in both Aramaic and Greek.
e IE subject to the Sanhedrin.
24*a* Matt. 18:15 (15–18). TG Forgive; Reconciliation.
25*a* GR Quickly have kind thoughts for, or be well disposed toward. TG Communication; Disputations.
26*a* GR the last penny.
27*a* D&C 42:22 (22–26).

whosoever [a]looketh on a [b]woman to
[c]lust after her hath committed [d]adul-
tery with her already in his heart.
29 And if thy right eye [a]offend thee,
pluck it out, and cast *it* from thee:
for it is profitable for thee that one
of thy members should perish, and
not *that* thy whole body should be
cast into [b]hell.
30 And if thy right [a]hand offend
thee, cut it off, and cast *it* from thee:
for it is profitable for thee that one
of thy members should perish, and
not *that* thy whole body should be
cast into [b]hell.
31 It hath been said, Whosoever
shall put away his wife, let him
give her a writing of [a]divorcement:
32 But I say unto you, That whosoever shall [a]put away his [b]wife,
saving for the cause of [c]fornication,
causeth her to commit adultery: and
whosoever shall marry her that is
divorced committeth adultery.
33 ¶ Again, ye have heard that it
hath been said by them of old time,
Thou shalt not [a]forswear thyself,
but shalt [b]perform unto the Lord
thine [c]oaths:
34 But I say unto you, [a]Swear not
at all; neither by heaven; for it is
God's [b]throne:
35 Nor by the earth; for it is his
[a]footstool: neither by Jerusalem;
for it is the [b]city of the great King.
36 Neither shalt thou swear by thy
head, because thou canst not make
one hair white or black.
37 But let your [a]communication be,
Yea, yea; Nay, nay: for whatsoever
is more than these cometh [b]of evil.
38 ¶ Ye have heard that it hath
been said, An [a]eye for an eye, and
a tooth for a tooth:
39 But I say unto you, That ye resist not [a]evil: but whosoever shall
smite thee on thy right [b]cheek, [c]turn
to him the other also.
40 And if any man will sue thee
at the law, and take away thy coat,
let him have *thy* cloak also.
41 And whosoever shall compel
thee to go a mile, go with him twain.
42 [a]Give to him that asketh thee,
and from him that would [b]borrow
of thee turn not thou away.
43 ¶ Ye have heard that it hath
been said, Thou shalt [a]love thy
[b]neighbour, and hate thine enemy.
44 But I say unto you, [a]Love your
[b]enemies, [c]bless them that [d]curse
you, do [e]good to them that [f]hate you,
and [g]pray for them which despitefully use you, and [h]persecute you;
45 That ye [a]may be the [b]children
of your Father which is in heaven:
for he maketh his sun to rise on
the evil and on the good, and sendeth [c]rain on the just and on the
unjust.

28*a* D&C 63:16 (16–17).
b TG Body, Sanctity of; Woman.
c Mosiah 4:30 (29–30). TG Carnal Mind; Chastity; Fornication; Lust; Motivations; Sensuality.
d TG Adulterer; Sexual Immorality.
29*a* GR cause to stumble; see also Matt. 18:6–9. TG Offense.
b TG Damnation; Hell.
30*a* Matt. 18:8; JST Matt. 18:9 (Matt. 18:9 note *a*).
b JST Matt. 5:33–34 . . . hell. *And now this I speak, a parable concerning your sins; wherefore, cast them from you, that ye may not be hewn down and cast into the fire.*
31*a* TG Divorce.
32*a* Ezek. 44:22.
b D&C 42:74.
c 1 Cor. 7:10 (10–11). TG Fornication.
33*a* GR break your oath, or perjure yourself. Ps. 139:20.
b TG Dedication.
c Deut. 23:21. TG Oath.
34*a* TG Honesty; Profanity; Swearing.
b Isa. 66:1.
35*a* Isa. 60:13; Ezek. 43:7.
b Ps. 48:2.
37*a* TG Communication.
b GR from the evil one.
38*a* Lev. 24:20; 3 Ne. 12:38 (38–40). TG Punish.
39*a* TG Evil.
b Lam. 3:30. TG Patience.
c TG Forbear.
42*a* TG Almsgiving; Generosity; Poor.
b TG Borrow; Debt.
43*a* D&C 112:11.
b TG Neighbor.
44*a* TG Love.
b TG Enemies; Opposition.
c TG Retribution.
d TG Curse.
e TG Benevolence.
f TG Hate.
g Job 42:10; Acts 7:60 (55–60). TG Prayer.
h TG Persecution.
45*a* GR may become; see Mosiah 5:7.
b TG Sons and Daughters of God.
c Job 2:10; 2 Ne. 2:11; Alma 60:13; D&C 5:22; 29:39; 122:7 (5–9).

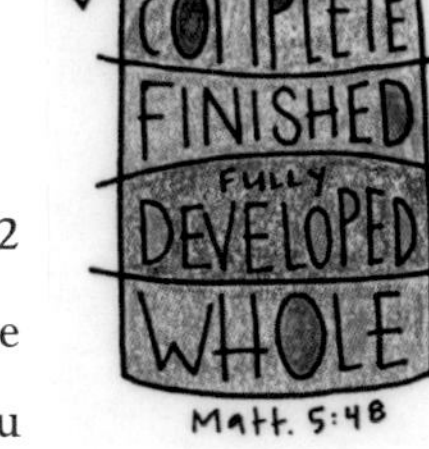

46 For if ye [a]love them which love you, what reward have ye? do not even the publicans the same?

47 And if ye salute your brethren only, what do ye more *than others?* do not even the publicans so?

48 [a]Be ye therefore [b]perfect, even as your [c]Father which is in heaven is [d]perfect.

CHAPTER 6

Jesus continues the Sermon on the Mount—He teaches the disciples the Lord's Prayer—They are commanded to seek first the kingdom of God and His righteousness.

[a]TAKE heed that ye do not your [b]alms before men, to be seen of them: otherwise ye have no reward of your Father which is in heaven.

2 Therefore when thou doest *thine* alms, do not sound a trumpet before thee, as the [a]hypocrites do in the synagogues and in the streets, that they may have [b]glory of men. Verily I say unto you, They have their reward.

3 But when thou doest alms, let not thy left hand know what thy right hand doeth:

4 That thine [a]alms may be in secret: and thy Father which seeth in secret himself shall [b]reward thee openly.

5 ¶ And when thou prayest, thou shalt not be as the [a]hypocrites *are:* for they love to pray standing in the synagogues and in the corners of the streets, that they may be seen of men. Verily I say unto you, They have their reward.

6 But thou, when thou prayest, enter into thy [a]closet, and when thou hast [b]shut thy door, [c]pray to thy Father which is in [d]secret; and thy Father which [e]seeth in secret shall [f]reward thee openly.

7 But when ye pray, use not vain [a]repetitions, as the [b]heathen *do:* for they think that they shall be heard for their much speaking.

8 Be not ye therefore like unto them: for your Father [a]knoweth what things ye have [b]need of, before ye ask him.

9 [a]After this manner therefore [b]pray ye: Our [c]Father which art in heaven, [d]Hallowed be thy [e]name.

10 Thy [a]kingdom come. Thy [b]will be done [c]in earth, as *it is* in heaven.

11 Give us this day our daily [a]bread.

12 And forgive us our [a]debts, as we [b]forgive our debtors.

46*a* Prov. 19:6.
48*a* JST Matt. 5:50 *Ye are* therefore *commanded to be* perfect . . .
b GR complete, finished, fully developed. D&C 67:13. TG God, the Standard of Righteousness; Godliness; Man, New, Spiritually Reborn; Man, Potential to Become like Heavenly Father; Mission of Early Saints; Objectives; Perfection.
c TG God the Father, Elohim.
d TG God, Perfection of.
6 1*a* JST Matt. 6:1 *And it came to pass that, as Jesus taught his disciples, he said unto them,* Take heed . . . 3 Ne. 13:1 (1–34).
b GR righteousness, acts of religious devotion. TG Almsgiving; Generosity; Motivations; Poor.
2*a* GR pretenders; the Greek word means "a play actor," or "one who feigns, represents dramatically, or exaggerates a part." TG Hypocrisy.
b D&C 121:35 (34–35).
4*a* TG Welfare.
b Luke 14:14.
5*a* Alma 31:14 (14–22).
6*a* Alma 33:7 (4–11); 34:26 (17–27).
b 2 Kgs. 4:33.
c TG Prayer.
d TG Meditation.
e TG God, Omniscience of.
f TG Reward.
7*a* Eccl. 5:2; Alma 31:20; 3 Ne. 19:24.
b TG Heathen.
8*a* D&C 84:83 (81–86). TG God, Intelligence of; God, Omniscience of.
b Ps. 23:1.
9*a* IE It is in this way that you ought to pray.
b TG Prayer.
c TG God the Father, Elohim.
d GR Let Thy name be sanctified.
e TG Name.
10*a* TG Kingdom of God, on Earth; Millennium.
b TG God, Will of.
c GR on earth.
11*a* TG Bread.
12*a* GR debts, offenses, faults, or sins. TG Debt.
b TG Forgive.

13 [a]And [b]lead us not into [c]temptation, [d]but deliver us from evil: For thine is the kingdom, and the power, and the [e]glory, for ever. Amen.

14 For if ye [a]forgive men their trespasses, your heavenly Father will also forgive you:

15 But if ye [a]forgive not men their trespasses, neither will your Father forgive your trespasses.

16 ¶ Moreover when ye fast, be not, as the hypocrites, of a sad countenance: for they disfigure their faces, that they may appear unto men to [a]fast. Verily I say unto you, They [b]have their reward.

17 But thou, when thou fastest, anoint thine head, and wash thy face;

18 That thou appear not unto men to [a]fast, but unto thy Father which is in secret: and thy Father, which seeth in secret, shall [b]reward thee openly.

19 ¶ Lay not up for yourselves [a]treasures upon earth, where moth and rust doth corrupt, and where thieves [b]break through and steal:

20 But lay up for yourselves [a]treasures in heaven, where neither moth nor rust doth corrupt, and where thieves do not break through nor [b]steal:

21 For where your treasure is, there will your heart be also.

22 The light of the body is the eye: if therefore thine [a]eye be [b]single, thy whole body shall be full of [c]light.

23 But if thine eye be evil, thy whole body shall be full of darkness. If therefore the light that is in thee be darkness, how great *is* that [a]darkness!

24 ¶ [a]No man can [b]serve two [c]masters: for either he will [d]hate the one, and love the other; or else he will hold to the one, and despise the other. Ye cannot serve God and [e]mammon.

25 [a]Therefore I say unto you, Take no [b]thought for your life, what ye shall eat, or what ye shall drink; nor yet for your body, what ye shall put on. Is not the life more than meat, and the body than raiment?

26 Behold the fowls of the air: for they sow not, neither do they reap, nor gather into barns; yet your heavenly Father feedeth them. Are ye not much better than they?

27 Which of you by taking thought can add one cubit unto his stature?

28 And why take ye thought for raiment? [a]Consider the lilies of the field, how they grow; they toil not, neither do they spin:

29 And yet I say unto you, That even Solomon in all his glory was not arrayed like one of these.

30 Wherefore, if God so clothe the grass of the field, which to day is, and to morrow is cast into the oven, [a]*shall he* not much more *clothe* you, O ye of little [b]faith?

31 Therefore take no thought, saying, What shall we eat? or, What

13*a* JST Matt. 6:14 And *suffer* us not *to be led* into temptation . . .
b Syriac: do not let us enter into temptation.
c TG Temptation; Test.
d GR but protect us from the evil one. TG Deliver; Evil.
e 1 Chr. 29:11. TG Glory.
14*a* TG Forbear.
15*a* TG Forgive.
16*a* Zech. 7:5 (5–6).
b GR receive.
18*a* TG Fast, Fasting; Motivations.
b TG Reward.
19*a* TG Family, Managing Finances in.
b GR dig through (as an earthen wall).
20*a* Heb. 10:34; 1 Pet. 1:4 (1–16). TG Treasure.
b TG Stealing.
22*a* 3 Ne. 13:22; Morm. 8:15; D&C 4:5; 59:1 (1–2).
b GR healthy, sincere, without guile. JST Matt. 6:22 . . . single *to the glory of God* . . . TG Dedication.
c D&C 93:28 (28, 36–38).
23*a* TG Darkness, Spiritual.
24*a* TG Loyalty.
b TG Service.
c Alma 5:39 (39–42).
d TG Hate.
e TG Idolatry; Treasure; Worldliness.
25*a* JST Matt. 6:25–27 (Appendix).
b GR anxious concern. Ps. 55:22; Prov. 16:3; Luke 12:22; Philip. 4:6; 3 Ne. 13:25; D&C 84:81. TG Self-Sacrifice.
28*a* TG Meditation.
30*a* JST Matt. 6:34 . . . *how much more will he not provide for you, if ye are not of little faith?*
b TG Fa

shall we drink? or, Wherewithal
shall we be clothed?
32 (For after all these things do
the Gentiles seek:) for your heavenly Father [a]knoweth that ye have
need of all these things.
33 [a]But [b]seek ye first the [c]kingdom
of God, and his [d]righteousness; and
all these [e]things shall be [f]added
unto you.
34 Take therefore no thought for
the morrow: for the morrow shall
take [a]thought for the things of itself. Sufficient unto the day *is* the
evil thereof.

CHAPTER 7

Jesus concludes the Sermon on the Mount—He commands, Judge not; ask of God; beware of false prophets—He promises salvation to those who do the will of the Father.

[a]JUDGE not, that ye be not [b]judged.
2 For with what [a]judgment ye
judge, ye shall be judged: and with
what [b]measure ye mete, it shall be
[c]measured to you again.
3 [a]And why beholdest thou the
[b]mote that is in thy brother's eye,
but considerest not the [c]beam that
is in thine own eye?
4 Or how wilt thou say to thy
brother, Let me pull out the mote
out of thine eye; and, behold, a beam
is in thine own eye?
5 Thou [a]hypocrite, first cast out
the beam out of thine own eye; and
then shalt thou see clearly to cast
out the mote out of thy brother's
eye.
6 ¶ [a]Give not that which is [b]holy
unto the dogs, neither cast ye your
[c]pearls before swine, lest they trample them under their feet, and turn
again and rend you.
7 ¶ [a]Ask, and it shall be [b]given you;
[c]seek, and ye shall find; [d]knock, and
it shall be opened unto you:
8 For every one that asketh receiveth; and he that [a]seeketh findeth;
and to him that knocketh it shall
be opened.
9 Or what man is there of you,
whom if his son ask [a]bread, will he
give him a stone?
10 Or if he ask a fish, will he give
him a serpent?
11 If ye then, [a]being evil, know
how to give good gifts unto your
children, how much more shall your
Father which is in heaven give good
things to them that ask him?
12 Therefore all things [a]whatsoever

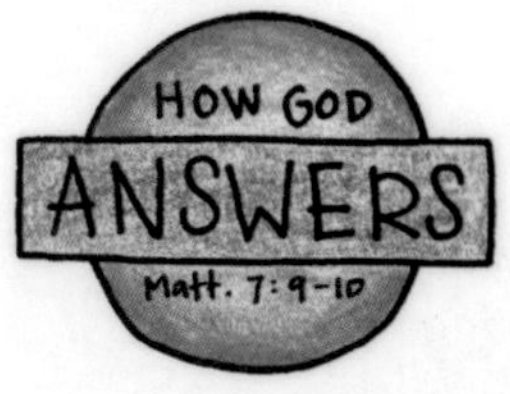

32*a* Hel. 8:8; D&C 84:83.
33*a* JST Matt. 6:38 *Wherefore, seek not the things of this world* but seek ye first *to build up* the kingdom of God, and *to establish* his righteousness . . .
b 1 Kgs. 3:13; Alma 39:14 (12–14); D&C 6:7 (6–7); 11:23; 68:31 (31–32); 106:3. TG Commitment; Dedication; Priesthood, Magnifying Callings within.
c Col. 3:2. TG Mission of Early Saints; Objectives.
d Prov. 21:21. TG God, the Standard of Righteousness; Righteousness.
e Prov. 28:10. TG Blessing.
f 2 Ne. 5:11 (10–13); Mosiah 2:41. TG Abundant Life.
34*a* D&C 84:84.
7 1*a* JST Matt. 7:1–2 *Now these are the words which Jesus taught his disciples that they should say unto the people.* Judge not *unrighteously,* that ye be not judged; *but judge righteous judgment.* Alma 41:14 (14–15); 3 Ne. 14:1 (1–27); D&C 11:12.
b TG Accountability.
2*a* TG Judgment.
b Prov. 11:25; D&C 1:10.
c Esth. 7:10; 1 Ne. 14:3; D&C 10:26 (25–27).
3*a* JST Matt. 7:4–8 (Appendix).
b GR speck, chip, or splinter. TG Gossip.
c The Greek word refers to a wooden beam used in constructing houses.
5*a* TG Hypocrisy.
6*a* JST Matt. 7:9–11 (Appendix).
b TG Holiness; Sacred; Sacrilege.
c Prov. 23:9; Matt. 15:26 (26–28); D&C 6:12 (10–12); 10:37 (36–37); 41:6.
7*a* JST Matt. 7:12–17 (Appendix). Isa. 58:9 (8–9); Hel. 10:5 (4–11); D&C 6:5. TG Faith; God, Access to; Prayer; Problem-Solving.
b TG Revelation.
c TG Meditation; Objectives; Study.
d TG Learn.
8*a* TG Education.
9*a* TG Bread.
11*a* GR although you are wicked.
12*a* TG Good Works.

ye would that [b]men should [c]do to
you, [d]do ye even so to them: for this
is the [e]law and the prophets.
13 ¶ Enter ye in at the [a]strait [b]gate:
for wide *is* the gate, and broad *is* the
way, that leadeth to [c]destruction, and
many there be which go in thereat:
14 Because [a]strait *is* the [b]gate, and
narrow *is* the way, which leadeth
unto [c]life, and few there be that
find it.
15 ¶ Beware of [a]false prophets,
which come to you in [b]sheep's
clothing, but [c]inwardly they are
ravening [d]wolves.
16 Ye shall [a]know them by their
[b]fruits. Do men gather grapes of
thorns, or figs of thistles?
17 Even so every good tree bringeth
forth [a]good [b]fruit; but a [c]corrupt tree
bringeth forth [d]evil fruit.
18 A good tree cannot bring forth
evil fruit, neither *can* a corrupt tree
bring forth good fruit.
19 Every tree that bringeth not
forth good [a]fruit is [b]hewn down,
and cast into the fire.
20 Wherefore by their [a]fruits ye
shall know them.
21 ¶ Not every one that [a]saith unto
me, [b]Lord, Lord, shall enter into the
kingdom of heaven; but he that [c]do-
eth the [d]will of my Father which is
in [e]heaven.
22 Many will say to me in that day,
Lord, Lord, have we not [a]prophesied
in thy name? and in thy [b]name have
cast out devils? and in thy name
done many wonderful works?
23 [a]And then will I profess unto
them, I never knew you: [b]depart
from me, ye that work [c]iniquity.
24 ¶ Therefore whosoever [a]heareth
these sayings of mine, and [b]doeth
them, [c]I will liken him unto a [d]wise
man, which [e]built his house upon
[f]a rock:
25 And the [a]rain descended, and
the floods came, and the winds
blew, and [b]beat upon that house;
and it fell not: for it was founded
upon a [c]rock.
26 And every one that heareth
these sayings of mine, and doeth
them not, shall be likened unto a
[a]foolish man, which built his house
upon the sand:
27 And the rain descended, and

12*b* TG Marriage, Continuing Courtship in.
c Deut. 15:15 (12–15); Prov. 24:29. TG Citizenship; Courtesy; Kindness.
d TG Benevolence.
e TG Law of Moses.
13*a* GR narrow; see also 2 Ne. 31:17–21.
b Luke 13:24; 3 Ne. 27:33; D&C 22:4 (1–4); 43:7.
c D&C 132:25. TG Hell.
14*a* Mosiah 3:17.
b 1 Ne. 8:20 (19–24); 2 Ne. 33:9. TG Baptism, Essential.
c Jer. 21:8.
15*a* TG False Prophets.
b TG Sheep.
c TG Hypocrisy.
d TG Guile.
16*a* GR recognize, detect. TG Discernment, Spiritual.
b Prov. 20:11; Jer. 28:9 (8–9); Luke 6:44; Moro. 7:6 (5–17). TG Good Works.
17*a* The Greek wording carries the meaning of beautiful, precious fruit without blemish.
b Matt. 12:33; 3 Ne. 14:20 (17–20).
c GR decayed, rotten, stale.
d GR bad, spoiled, degenerate.
19*a* Luke 3:9; John 15:2 (1–6); Jacob 5:26 (26–60); Alma 5:36; D&C 97:7.
b Luke 13:7.
20*a* James 2:18 (14–26); 1 Jn. 3:10 (10–18).
21*a* Titus 1:16. TG Hypocrisy; Sincere.
b Hosea 8:2 (1–4); Luke 6:46.
c Luke 8:21 (9–21); D&C 138:4. TG Duty; Good Works; Obedience.
d TG God, Will of.
e JST Matt. 7:30–31 . . . heaven. *For the day soon cometh, that men shall come before me to judgment, to be judged according to their works.*
22*a* Jer. 23:25 (25–32). TG Unrighteous Dominion.
b D&C 84:67. TG Name.
23*a* JST Matt. 7:33 And then will I *say, Ye* never knew *me* . . . Ps. 101:4; Matt. 25:12; Mosiah 26:27 (23–27); 3 Ne. 14:23.
b Ps. 119:115. TG Judgment, the Last.
c GR lawlessness. TG Sin.
24*a* Mosiah 4:10; Hel. 5:12 (9–12); D&C 41:5.
b TG Commitment; Obedience.
c GR he will resemble.
d TG Wisdom.
e D&C 6:34; 11:24.
f GR the rock. 3 Ne. 11:39 (39–40).
25*a* D&C 90:5.
b TG Adversity.
c TG Rock.
26*a* TG Foolishness.

the floods came, and the winds blew,
and beat upon that [a]house; and it
[b]fell: and great was the fall of it.
28 And it came to pass, when Jesus
had ended [a]these sayings, the people
were [b]astonished at his [c]doctrine:
29 For he taught them as *one* having
[a]authority, and not as [b]the scribes.

CHAPTER 8

Jesus heals a leper, cures the centurion's servant and others, stills the tempest, and casts out devils—The devils enter a herd of swine.

WHEN he was come down from the
mountain, great multitudes followed him.
2 And, behold, there came a [a]leper
and worshipped him, saying, Lord,
if thou wilt, thou canst make me
clean.
3 And Jesus put forth *his* hand, and
touched him, saying, I will; be thou
clean. And immediately his leprosy
was [a]cleansed.
4 And Jesus saith unto him, See
thou tell no man; but go thy way,
shew thyself to the priest, and offer
the gift that Moses commanded, for
a testimony unto them.
5 ¶ And when Jesus was entered
into Capernaum, there came unto
him a centurion, beseeching him,
6 And saying, Lord, my [a]servant
lieth at home sick of the [b]palsy,
grievously tormented.
7 And Jesus saith unto him, I will
come and heal him.
8 The centurion answered and said,
Lord, I am not [a]worthy that thou
shouldest come under my roof: but
speak the word only, and my servant shall be [b]healed.
9 For I am a man under [a]authority,
having soldiers under me: and I say
to this *man,* Go, and he goeth; and
to another, Come, and he cometh;
and to my servant, Do this, and he
doeth *it.*
10 [a]When Jesus heard *it,* he marvelled, and said to them that followed, Verily I say unto you, I have
not found so great [b]faith, no, not
in Israel.
11 And I say unto you, That [a]many
shall come from the east and west,
and shall sit down with Abraham,
and Isaac, and Jacob, in the kingdom of heaven.
12 But the [a]children of the kingdom shall be cast out into [b]outer
darkness: there shall be [c]weeping
and gnashing of teeth.
13 And Jesus said unto the centurion, Go thy way; and as thou hast
believed, *so* be it done unto thee.
And his servant was healed in the
selfsame hour.
14 ¶ And when Jesus was come
into Peter's house, he saw his [a]wife's
mother [b]laid, and sick of a fever.
15 And he [a]touched her hand, and
the fever left her: and she arose, and
ministered unto them.
16 ¶ When the even was come, they
brought unto him many that were
possessed with [a]devils: and he cast
out the [b]spirits with *his* word, and
[c]healed all that were sick:

27*a* Prov. 14:11.
b TG Apostasy of Individuals.
28*a* JST Matt. 7:36 . . . these sayings *with his disciples,* the people . . .
b Matt. 13:54.
c John 7:16; 2 Ne. 31:21.
29*a* JST Matt. 7:37 . . . authority *from God,* and not as *having authority from* the scribes.
TG Jesus Christ, Authority of; Jesus Christ, Teaching Mode of; Teaching with the Spirit.
b GR their scribes.
TG Scribe.
8 2*a* TG Leprosy.
3*a* TG Miracle.
6*a* GR child, servant, son; see John 4:43–54.
b GR paralysis.
8*a* GR fit, qualified.
b TG Heal.
9*a* TG Authority.
10*a* JST Matt. 8:9 *And when they that followed him, heard this, they marveled. And* when Jesus . . .
b 3 Ne. 17:8 (5–20).
11*a* Luke 13:29 (28–30); Acts 10:45; 2 Ne. 10:18 (9–18); D&C 45:9.
12*a* 2 Ne. 30:2.
b Matt. 22:13 (1–14); D&C 77:8; 133:72.
c Isa. 65:14; Matt. 13:42; Rev. 19:20; D&C 112:24.
14*a* 1 Cor. 9:5; 1 Tim. 4:3.
b GR lying sick and feverish.
15*a* GR took hold of.
16*a* Matt. 4:24; 9:32 (32–34).
b TG Spirits, Evil or Unclean.
c TG Heal.

17 That it might be fulfilled which
was spoken by Esaias the prophet,
saying, [a]Himself took our [b]infirmi-
ties, and bare *our* [c]sicknesses.
18 ¶ Now when Jesus saw great
multitudes about him, he gave
commandment to depart unto the
other side.
19 And a certain scribe came, and
said unto him, Master, I will [a]follow
thee whithersoever thou goest.
20 And Jesus saith unto him, The
foxes have holes, and the birds of
the air *have* nests; but the Son of
man hath not where to lay *his* head.
21 And another of his disciples said
unto him, Lord, [a]suffer me first to
go and bury my father.
22 But Jesus said unto him, [a]Fol-
low me; and let the [b]dead bury
their dead.
23 ¶ And when he was entered into
a ship, his disciples followed him.
24 And, behold, there arose a great
[a]tempest in the sea, insomuch that
the ship was covered with the waves:
but he was asleep.
25 And his disciples came to *him*,
and awoke him, saying, Lord, save
us: we perish.
26 And he saith unto them, Why
are ye [a]fearful, O ye of little faith?
Then he arose, and [b]rebuked the
winds and the sea; and there was a
great calm.
27 But the men marvelled, saying, What manner of man is this,
that even the winds and the [a]sea
obey him!
28 ¶ And when he was come to
the other side into the country of
the Gergesenes, there met him two
possessed with [a]devils, coming out
of the tombs, exceeding fierce, so
that no man might pass by that way.
29 And, behold, they cried out,
saying, What have we to do with
thee, Jesus, thou Son of God? art
thou come hither to torment us before [a]the time?
30 And there was a good way off
from them an herd of many swine
feeding.
31 So the devils besought him,
saying, If thou cast us out, suffer us
to go away into the herd of swine.
32 And he said unto them, Go.
And when they were come out, they
went into the herd of swine: and,
behold, the whole herd of swine ran
violently down a steep place into
the sea, and perished in the waters.
33 And they that kept them fled,
and went their ways into the city, and
told every thing, and what was be-
fallen to the possessed of the devils.
34 And, behold, the whole city
came out to [a]meet Jesus: and when
they saw him, they besought *him* that
he would depart out of their [b]coasts.

CHAPTER 9

Jesus forgives sins, heals a paralytic, and calls Matthew—Jesus eats with sinners, heals a woman who touches His garments, and raises Jairus's daughter to life—He opens the eyes of the blind, casts out a devil, and preaches the gospel.

AND he entered into a ship, and
passed over, and came into his own
city.
2 And, behold, they brought to him
a man sick of the [a]palsy, lying on
a bed: and Jesus seeing their [b]faith
said unto the sick of the palsy; Son,
be of good [c]cheer; thy [d]sins be forgiven thee.
3 And, behold, certain of the
scribes said within themselves, This
man blasphemeth.
4 And Jesus [a]knowing their

17*a* GR He Himself.
b TG Jesus Christ, Atonement through.
c TG Sickness.
19*a* Luke 9:57; 2 Ne. 31:10 (10–13); Moro. 7:11; D&C 4:3; 56:2.
21*a* GR let, allow.
22*a* TG Commitment.
b TG Death.
24*a* Jonah 1:4; 1 Ne. 18:13 (9–13).
26*a* TG Courage; Fearful.
b Ps. 65:7; 89:9; 107:29. TG God, Power of.
27*a* Hel. 12:16 (8–17).
28*a* TG Spirits, Evil or Unclean.
29*a* GR the appointed hour.
34*a* John 12:18.
b GR lands, regions.
9 2*a* GR stroke, paralysis.
b Luke 7:50.
c D&C 68:6; 112:4.
d D&C 25:3; 62:3.
4*a* TG God, Omniscience of.

- fill your days with -
COMPASSIONATE DETOURS
Matt. 9

thoughts said, Wherefore think ye
evil in your hearts?
5 [a]For whether is easier, to say,
Thy sins be forgiven thee; or to
say, Arise, and walk?
6 But that ye may know that the
[a]Son of man hath [b]power on earth
to [c]forgive sins, (then saith he to
the sick of the palsy,) Arise, take up
thy bed, and go unto thine house.
7 And he arose, and departed to
his house.
8 But when the multitudes saw
it, they marvelled, and glorified
God, which had given such power
unto men.
9 ¶ And as Jesus passed forth
from thence, he saw a man, named
[a]Matthew, sitting at the [b]receipt of
custom: and he saith unto him, Follow me. And he arose, and followed
him.
10 ¶ And it came to pass, as Jesus sat
at meat in the house, behold, many
publicans and sinners came and sat
down with him and his disciples.
11 And when the Pharisees saw *it*,
they said unto his disciples, [a]Why
eateth your Master with publicans
and sinners?
12 But when Jesus heard *that*, he
said unto them, They that be whole
need not a physician, but they that
are sick.
13 But go ye and learn what *that*
meaneth, [a]I [b]will have [c]mercy, and
not sacrifice: for I am not come to
[d]call the [e]righteous, but sinners to
[f]repentance.
14 ¶ Then came to him the disciples of John, saying, Why do we
and the Pharisees fast oft, but thy
disciples fast not?
15 And Jesus said unto them, Can
the children of the bridechamber
mourn, as long as the bridegroom
is with them? but the days will
come, when the bridegroom shall
be taken from them, [a]and then shall
they fast.
16 [a]No man putteth a piece of [b]new
cloth unto an old garment, for that
which is put in to fill it up taketh
from the garment, and the rent is
made worse.
17 Neither do men put new wine
into old bottles: else the bottles
break, and the wine runneth out,
and the bottles perish: but they put
new wine into new bottles, and both
are preserved.
18 ¶ While he spake these things
unto them, behold, there came a
certain [a]ruler, and worshipped him,
saying, [b]My daughter is even now
dead: but come and lay thy [c]hand
upon her, and she shall [d]live.
19 And Jesus arose, and followed
him, and *so did* his disciples.
20 ¶ And, behold, a woman, which
was diseased with an [a]issue of [b]blood
twelve years, came behind *him*, and
touched the hem of his garment:
21 For she said within herself, If I
may but touch his garment, I shall
be [a]whole.
22 But Jesus turned him about,
and when he saw her, he said,
Daughter, be of good comfort; thy
faith hath made thee [a]whole. And
the woman was made whole from
that hour.
23 And when Jesus came into the
ruler's house, and saw the minstrels
and the people making a noise,
24 He said unto them, Give place:
for the maid is not dead, but sleepeth.
And they [a]laughed him to scorn.

5*a* JST Matt. 9:5 For is *it not* easier to say, Thy sins be forgiven thee, *than* to say, Arise and walk?
6*a* TG Jesus Christ, Son of Man.
b GR authority. TG Jesus Christ, Authority of.
c TG Forgive.
9*a* Luke 5:27 (27–32).
b GR tax office.
11*a* See JST Mark 3:21–25 (Appendix).
Isa. 53:3 (1–3); 65:5.
13*a* Hosea 6:6.
b GR desire.
c TG Mercy.
d 1 Tim. 1:15.
e TG Righteousness.
f TG Repent.
15*a* TG Fast, Fasting.
16*a* JST Matt. 9:18–21 (Appendix).
b GR unshrunken.
18*a* Luke 8:41.
b JST Matt. 9:24 . . . My daughter is even now *dying* . . .
c TG Administrations to the Sick; Hands, Laying on of.
d D&C 66:9.
20*a* GR hemorrhage.
b Lev. 15:25.
21*a* GR free from disease.
22*a* TG Heal.
24*a* GR ridiculed Him. 1 Ne. 8:27 (26–27). TG Laughter.

25 But when the people were put
forth, he went in, and took her by
the hand, and the maid arose.
26 And the fame hereof went
abroad into all that land.
27 ¶ And when Jesus departed
thence, two blind men followed
him, crying, and saying, *Thou* Son
of David, have mercy on us.
28 And when he was come into the
house, the [a]blind men came to him:
and Jesus saith unto them, [b]Believe
ye that I am able to do this? They
said unto him, Yea, Lord.
29 Then touched he their eyes,
saying, According to your [a]faith be
it unto you.
30 And their [a]eyes were [b]opened;
and Jesus [c]straitly charged them,
saying, See *that* no man know *it*.
31 But they, when they were departed, [a]spread abroad his [b]fame in
all that country.
32 ¶ As they went out, behold,
they brought to him a dumb man
possessed with a [a]devil.
33 And when the devil was cast
out, the dumb spake: and the multitudes marvelled, saying, It was
never so seen in Israel.
34 But the Pharisees said, He
casteth out devils through the prince
of the devils.
35 And Jesus went about all the
cities and villages, [a]teaching in
their synagogues, and preaching
the [b]gospel of the kingdom, and
[c]healing every sickness and every
disease among the people.
36 ¶ But when he saw the multitudes, he was moved with [a]compas-
sion on them, because [b]they fainted,
and were scattered abroad, as [c]sheep
having no [d]shepherd.
37 Then saith he unto his disciples,
The [a]harvest truly *is* plenteous, but
the [b]labourers *are* few;
38 Pray ye therefore the Lord of
the harvest, that he will send forth
labourers into his harvest.

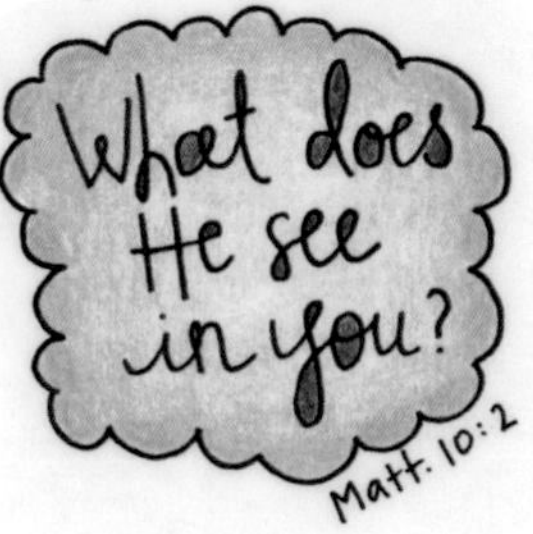

CHAPTER 10

Jesus instructs and empowers the Twelve Apostles and sends them forth to preach, minister, and heal the sick—Those who receive the Twelve receive the Lord.

AND when he had [a]called unto *him*
his [b]twelve disciples, he gave them
[c]power *against* [d]unclean spirits, to
cast them out, and to [e]heal all manner of [f]sickness and all manner of
disease.
2 Now the names of the twelve
apostles are these; The first, Simon,
who is called Peter, and Andrew his
brother; James *the son* of Zebedee,
and John his brother;
3 Philip, and Bartholomew; Thomas,
and Matthew the [a]publican; James
the son of Alphæus, and Lebbæus,
whose surname was Thaddæus;
4 Simon the Canaanite, and Judas
Iscariot, who also [a]betrayed him.
5 These twelve Jesus [a]sent forth,
and commanded them, saying, Go
not into the way of the Gentiles,
and into *any* city of the [b]Samaritans
enter ye not:

28*a* Matt. 20:30 (30–34); John 9:1 (1–4); Mosiah 3:5; 3 Ne. 17:9 (7–10); D&C 84:69.
b GR Do you have faith that.
29*a* TG Faith.
30*a* Ps. 146:8 (1–10).
b TG Heal; Miracle.
c GR warned them sternly.
31*a* Mark 7:36.
b John 12:19.
32*a* Matt. 4:24; 8:16 (16, 28, 33).
35*a* Matt. 4:23.
b D&C 84:80 (79–80); JS—M 1:31.
c Mosiah 3:5.
36*a* TG Compassion.
b GR they were harassed.
c TG Sheep.
d TG Jesus Christ, Good Shepherd; Shepherd.
37*a* Luke 10:2. TG Harvest.
b Jacob 5:70.
10 1*a* 1 Ne. 12:7 (6–7); Moro. 2:2 (1–3). TG Delegation of Responsibility.
b TG Apostles.
c GR authority over. D&C 50:32. TG Authority; Jesus Christ, Power of; Priesthood, Power of.
d TG Spirits, Evil or Unclean; Uncleanness.
e TG Heal.
f TG Sickness.
3*a* GR tax collector.
4*a* TG Jesus Christ, Betrayal of.
5*a* 3 Ne. 28:34; D&C 107:35.
b Luke 9:52.

6 But go rather to the [a]lost [b]sheep
of the house of Israel.
7 And as ye go, preach, saying,
The kingdom of heaven [a]is at hand.
8 [a]Heal the sick, cleanse the [b]lep-
ers, raise the dead, [c]cast out devils:
[d]freely ye have received, freely [e]give.
9 Provide neither gold, nor silver,
nor brass in your [a]purses,
10 Nor [a]scrip for *your* journey, neither two coats, neither shoes, nor yet
staves: for the workman is [b]worthy
of his [c]meat.
11 And into whatsoever city or
town ye shall [a]enter, inquire who
in it is worthy; and there abide till
ye go thence.
12 And when ye come into an
house, salute it.
13 And if the house be worthy,
let your peace come upon it: but
if it be not worthy, let your peace
return to you.
14 And whosoever shall not receive
you, nor hear your words, when ye
depart out of that house or city,
shake off the [a]dust of your [b]feet.
15 Verily I say unto you, It shall
be more tolerable for the land of
[a]Sodom and Gomorrha in the day
of judgment, than for that city.
16 ¶ Behold, I send you forth as
[a]sheep in the midst of wolves: be
ye therefore [b]wise as serpents, and
[c]harmless as doves.
17 But beware of men: for they
will deliver you up to the councils,
and they will scourge you in their
synagogues;
18 And ye shall be brought before
governors and [a]kings [b]for my sake,
for a [c]testimony against them and
the Gentiles.
19 But when they deliver you up,
[a]take no thought how or what ye
shall speak: for it shall be given
you in that same hour what ye shall
[b]speak.
20 For it is not ye that speak, but
the [a]Spirit of your Father which
speaketh in you.
21 And the brother shall deliver
up the brother to death, and the
father the child: and the children
shall rise up against *their* parents,
and cause them to be put to death.
22 And ye shall be [a]hated of all *men*
[b]for my [c]name's sake: but he that
[d]endureth to the end shall be saved.
23 But when they persecute you
in this city, flee ye into another: for
verily I say unto you, Ye shall not
have gone over the cities of Israel,
till the Son of man be come.
24 The [a]disciple is not above *his*
master, nor the servant above his
lord.
25 It is enough for the disciple [a]that
he be as his master, and the servant
as his lord. If they have called the
master of the house Beelzebub, how
much more *shall they call* them of
his household?
26 Fear them not therefore: for

6*a* TG Missionary Work.
b TG Sheep.
7*a* GR has come.
8*a* Luke 9:2; D&C 84:68.
b TG Leprosy.
c D&C 84:67.
d GR without payment. Isa. 55:1.
e TG Generosity.
9*a* Luke 10:4; 22:35 (35–36); D&C 24:18; 84:78.
10*a* GR traveling bag or beggar's bag. Mark 6:8.
b 1 Cor. 9:14.
c Num. 18:31; Luke 10:7.
11*a* D&C 24:15.
14*a* Luke 10:11 (11–12); Acts 13:51; D&C 75:20 (19–22).
b Acts 18:6 (5–6); D&C 60:15; 84:92 (92–93).
15*a* Ezek. 16:48.
16*a* Luke 10:3.
b Jacob 6:12; Alma 18:22; Morm. 9:28; D&C 111:11.
c GR guileless.
18*a* Ps. 119:46; Acts 9:15; D&C 1:23; 124:3 (3, 16, 107).
b GR on account of me.
c GR witness to.
19*a* GR do not be anxiously concerned. Dan. 3:16; Acts 20:24.
b Ex. 4:12 (12–15); Mark 13:11; Luke 21:15 (14–15); D&C 24:6. TG Teaching.
20*a* TG God, Spirit of; Teaching with the Spirit.
22*a* 1 Ne. 22:5. TG Hate; Martyrdom; Persecution.
b GR because of my name.
c TG Name.
d Mark 13:13; 3 Ne. 15:9; D&C 10:4; 53:7. TG Perseverance; Steadfastness.
24*a* John 15:20.
25*a* GR that he become.

there is nothing [a]covered, that shall
not be revealed; and hid, that
shall not be known.
27 What I tell you in darkness, *that*
speak ye in light: and what ye hear
in the ear, *that* preach ye upon the
housetops.
28 And [a]fear not them which kill
the body, but are not able to kill the
soul: but rather [b]fear him which
is able to [c]destroy both [d]soul and
body in [e]hell.
29 Are not two [a]sparrows sold for
a farthing? and one of them shall
not fall on the ground without your
Father.
30 But the very [a]hairs of your head
are all numbered.
31 Fear ye not therefore, ye are of
more [a]value than many [b]sparrows.
32 Whosoever therefore shall
[a]confess me before men, him will I
confess also before my Father which
is in heaven.
33 But whosoever shall [a]deny me
before men, him will I also deny before my Father which is in heaven.
34 Think not that I am come to
send [a]peace on earth: I came not
to send peace, but a sword.
35 For I am come to set a man at
variance against his father, and the
daughter against her mother, and
the daughter in law against her
mother in law.
36 And a man's [a]foes *shall be* they
of his own [b]household.
37 He that [a]loveth father or mother
[b]more than me is not worthy of me:
and he that [c]loveth son or daughter
more than me is not worthy of me.
38 And he that taketh not his
[a]cross, and followeth after me, is
not [b]worthy of me.
39 [a]He that findeth his life shall
[b]lose it: and he that [c]loseth his [d]life
for my sake shall find it.
40 ¶ He that [a]receiveth you [b]receiv-
eth me, and he that receiveth me
receiveth him that sent me.
41 He that [a]receiveth a prophet
in the name of a prophet shall receive a prophet's [b]reward; and he
that receiveth a righteous man in
the name of a righteous man shall
receive a righteous man's reward.
42 And whosoever shall give to
drink unto one of these little ones
a cup of cold *water* only in the
[a]name of a disciple, verily I say unto
you, he shall in no wise [b]lose his
reward.

CHAPTER 11

Jesus acclaims John as more than a prophet—The cities of Chorazin, Bethsaida, and Capernaum are rebuked for unbelief—The Son reveals the Father—The yoke of Christ is easy, and His burden is light.

AND it came to pass, when Jesus
had made an end of commanding
his twelve disciples, he departed
thence to teach and to [a]preach in
their cities.

26*a* Morm. 5:8.
28*a* Isa. 51:7; Jer. 1:8 (7–8); Luke 12:4 (4–5).
b Deut. 13:8 (6–11); D&C 3:7 (6–8).
c TG Devil.
d TG Soul.
e TG Hell.
29*a* TG God, Omniscience of.
30*a* Luke 21:18 (17–18).
31*a* Gen. 39:3 (1–6); Ps. 37:25; Rom. 8:39 (35–39); 1 Ne. 17:3 (1–5, 12–14); Mosiah 2:41; D&C 121:33.
b TG Nature, Earth.
32*a* GR solemnly covenant with, promise me. TG Witness.
33*a* Rom. 1:16 (15–18); 2 Tim. 2:12 (10–15); 2 Ne. 31:14 (12–21); D&C 101:5 (1–5).
34*a* John 7:43. TG Peace.
36*a* TG Persecution.
b Micah 7:6.
37*a* TG Love.
b Luke 14:26.
c 1 Sam. 2:29.
38*a* Matt. 16:24; Luke 9:23; 14:27; 3 Ne. 12:30; D&C 23:6.
b TG Worthiness.
39*a* JST Matt. 10:34 He *who seeketh to save* his life . . .
b GR sacrifice.
c Luke 9:24 (23–26). TG Loyalty.
d TG Martyrdom; Self-Sacrifice.
40*a* Luke 9:48; 10:16; D&C 84:36 (36–38). TG Priesthood, Magnifying Callings within; Teachable.
b Ex. 16:8. TG Hospitality.
41*a* TG Sustaining Church Leaders.
b TG Reward.
42*a* TG Name.
b Mark 9:41; D&C 84:90.
11 1*a* TG Missionary Work.

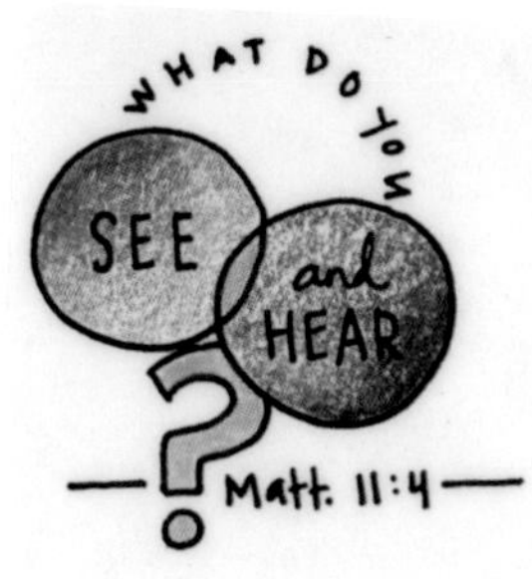

2 Now when [a]John had heard in
the prison the works of Christ, he
sent two of his disciples,
3 And said unto him, Art thou he
that should come, or do we look for
another?
4 Jesus answered and said unto
them, Go and shew John again those
[a]things which ye do hear and see:
5 The [a]blind receive their [b]sight,
and the lame walk, the [c]lepers are
cleansed, and the deaf hear, the
dead are raised up, and the [d]poor
have the gospel preached to them.
6 And blessed is *he,* whosoever shall
not be [a]offended in me.
7 ¶ And as they departed, Jesus
began to say unto the multitudes
concerning John, What went ye out
into the wilderness to see? A reed
shaken with the wind?
8 But what went ye out for to see?
A man clothed in soft raiment? behold, they that wear soft *clothing* are
in [a]kings' houses.
9 But what went ye out for to see?
A prophet? yea, I say unto you, and
more than a [a]prophet.
10 For this is *he,* of whom it is written, Behold, I send my [a]messenger
before thy face, which shall [b]pre-
pare thy way before thee.
11 Verily I say unto you, Among
them that are born of [a]women there
hath not risen a greater than [b]John
the Baptist: [c]notwithstanding he that
is least in the kingdom of heaven is
greater than he.
12 And from the days of John the
Baptist until now the kingdom of
heaven suffereth violence, and [a]the
violent take it by force.
13 [a]For all the [b]prophets and the
law [c]prophesied until John.
14 And if ye will receive *it,* this is
[a]Elias, which was for to come.
15 He that hath ears to [a]hear, let
him hear.
16 ¶ But whereunto shall I liken
this generation? It is like unto children sitting in the markets, and
calling unto their fellows,
17 And saying, We have piped
unto you, and ye have not danced;
we have mourned unto you, and ye
have not lamented.
18 For John came neither eating
nor drinking, and they say, He hath
a devil.
19 The Son of man came eating
and drinking, and they say, Behold
a man gluttonous, and [a]a winebibber, a friend of [b]publicans and sinners. But wisdom is justified [c]of
her children.
20 ¶ Then began he to upbraid the
[a]cities wherein most of his mighty
works were done, because they repented not:
21 Woe unto thee, Chorazin! woe
unto thee, Bethsaida! for if the
mighty works, which were done
in you, had been done in Tyre and
Sidon, they would have [a]repented
long ago in sackcloth and [b]ashes.
22 But I say unto you, It shall be
more [a]tolerable for Tyre and Sidon
at the day of judgment, than for
you.
23 And thou, Capernaum, which
art [a]exalted unto heaven, shalt be
brought down to [b]hell: for if the
mighty works, which have been
done in thee, had been done in

2*a* Luke 7:18 (18–35).
4*a* John 5:36.
5*a* Ps. 146:8; Isa. 42:7.
b TG Sight.
c TG Leprosy.
d D&C 35:15.
6*a* Isa. 8:14 (14–15); Matt. 24:10.
8*a* TG Kings, Earthly.
9*a* Matt. 14:5; 21:26; Luke 20:6.
10*a* Mal. 3:1; Mark 1:2; 1 Ne. 11:27; D&C 35:4; 45:9.
b Isa. 40:3.
11*a* TG Woman.
b John 5:35 (32–35).
c GR but he who is less important. Luke 7:28; D&C 50:26.
12*a* GR violent men are seizing control of it, or plundering it.
13*a* JST Matt. 11:13–15 (Appendix).
b Zech. 7:12; 1 Ne. 3:20; Mosiah 15:13. TG Jesus Christ, Prophecies about.
c IE The law and prophets foretold such violence.
14*a* Luke 1:17.
15*a* Ezek. 33:31 (30–33); Heb. 5:11 (11–14); 2 Ne. 9:31; D&C 1:14.
19*a* GR a drunkard.
b GR tax collectors.
c GR by her deeds, works.
20*a* Alma 34:31 (31–36); 3 Ne. 9:3; D&C 84:114.
21*a* Ezek. 3:6.
b Job 2:8; 42:6.
22*a* D&C 45:54; 75:22.
23*a* TG Haughtiness.
b TG Hell.

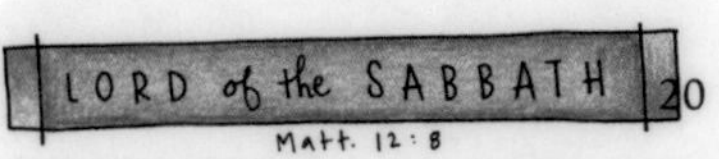

Sodom, it would have remained
until this day.
24 But I say unto you, That it shall
be more tolerable for the land of
[a]Sodom in the day of judgment,
than for thee.
25 ¶ At that time Jesus answered
and said, I [a]thank thee, O Father,
Lord of heaven and earth, because
thou hast [b]hid these things from
the wise and [c]prudent, and hast
[d]revealed them unto [e]babes.
26 Even so, Father: for so it seemed
good in thy sight.
27 All [a]things are delivered unto
me of my Father: and no man
knoweth the Son, but the Father; neither [b]knoweth any man the Father,
save the Son, [c]and *he* to whomsoever
the Son will [d]reveal *him.*
28 ¶ [a]Come unto me, all *ye* that
[b]labour and are heavy laden, and I
will give you [c]rest.
29 Take my [a]yoke upon you, and
[b]learn of me; for I am [c]meek and
[d]lowly in [e]heart: and ye shall find
[f]rest unto your souls.
30 For my yoke *is* [a]easy, and my
burden is light.

CHAPTER 12

Jesus proclaims Himself Lord of the Sabbath and heals on the Sabbath day—He is accused of casting out devils through the power of Beelzebub—He speaks of blasphemy against the Holy Ghost and says that an evil and adulterous generation seeks signs.

AT that time Jesus went on the [a]sab-
bath day through the [b]corn; and
his disciples were an hungred, and
began to pluck the [c]ears of corn,
and to eat.
2 But when the Pharisees saw *it,*
they said unto him, Behold, thy disciples do that which is not lawful
to do upon the sabbath day.
3 But he said unto them, Have ye
not [a]read what [b]David did, when
he was an hungred, and they that
were with him;
4 How he entered into the house
of God, and did eat the [a]shewbread,
which was not lawful for him to eat,
neither for them which were with
him, but only for the priests?
5 Or have ye not read in the law,
how that on the [a]sabbath days the
priests in the temple profane the
sabbath, and are blameless?
6 But I say unto you, That in this
place is *one* greater than the [a]temple.
7 But if ye had known what *this*
meaneth, I will have [a]mercy, and
not sacrifice, ye would not have
condemned the guiltless.
8 For the Son of man is Lord even
of the [a]sabbath day.
9 And when he was departed
thence, he went into their synagogue:
10 ¶ And, behold, there was a man
which had *his* hand withered. And
they asked him, saying, Is it lawful
to heal on the sabbath days? that
they might accuse him.
11 And he said unto them, What
man shall there be among you,

24*a* Ezek. 16:48.
25*a* GR praise.
Luke 10:21.
b Matt. 13:11;
D&C 6:11 (11–12).
c TG Prudence.
d Alma 32:23;
D&C 133:58.
e GR innocent people.
2 Ne. 9:42 (42–43);
Alma 32:23;
3 Ne. 26:16 (14–16);
D&C 128:18.
27*a* TG Jesus Christ,
Messiah.
b TG Knowledge.
c JST Matt. 11:28 . . . and *they* to *whom* the Son will reveal *himself; they shall see the Father also.*
d Luke 10:22;
John 14:6 (6–14).
TG God, Privilege of
Seeing.
28*a* Ps. 55:22;
Isa. 55:3;
D&C 10:67.
TG Problem-Solving.
b TG Labor.
c TG Rest.
29*a* 1 Jn. 2:6.
TG Jesus Christ, Taking
the Name of.
b D&C 32:1.
TG Learn.
c GR gentle and humble.
TG Humility;
Meek.
d TG Contrite Heart.
e TG Heart.
f Mosiah 2:41;
Alma 37:34 (33–34);
D&C 54:10; 59:23.
TG Comfort.
30*a* 1 Jn. 5:3 (1–5);
Alma 37:46 (43–47).
12 1*a* John 5:9.
b GR grain.
c Deut. 23:25.
3*a* TG Jesus Christ,
Teaching Mode of.
b 1 Sam. 21:6 (3–6).
4*a* TG Bread, Shewbread.
5*a* Num. 28:9 (9–10).
6*a* TG Temple.
7*a* Hosea 6:6.
8*a* TG Sabbath.

that shall have one sheep, and if it fall into a pit on the sabbath day, will he not lay hold on it, and lift *it* out?

12 How much then is a man better than a sheep? Wherefore it is lawful to do well on the sabbath days.

13 Then saith he to the man, Stretch forth thine hand. And he stretched *it* forth; and it was restored whole, like as the other.

14 ¶ Then the Pharisees went out, and held a council against him, how they might destroy him.

15 But [a]when Jesus knew *it,* he withdrew himself from thence: and great multitudes followed him, and he healed them all;

16 And charged them that they should not make him known:

17 That it might be fulfilled which was spoken by [a]Esaias the prophet, saying,

18 Behold my [a]servant, whom I have [b]chosen; my [c]beloved, in whom my soul is well pleased: I will put my spirit upon him, and he shall shew judgment to the Gentiles.

19 He shall not strive, nor [a]cry; neither shall any man hear his voice in the streets.

20 A bruised reed shall he not break, and smoking flax shall he not quench, till he send forth [a]judgment unto victory.

21 And in his [a]name shall the [b]Gentiles trust.

22 ¶ Then was brought unto him one possessed with a devil, blind, and dumb: and he healed him, insomuch that the blind and dumb both spake and saw.

23 And all the people were amazed, and said, Is not this the son of [a]David?

24 But when the Pharisees heard *it,* they said, This *fellow* doth not cast out devils, but by [a]Beelzebub the prince of the devils.

25 And Jesus knew their [a]thoughts, and said unto them, Every [b]kingdom divided against itself is brought to desolation; and every city or house divided against itself shall not stand:

26 And if [a]Satan cast out Satan, he is divided against himself; how shall then his kingdom stand?

27 And if I by Beelzebub cast out devils, by whom do your children cast *them* out? therefore they shall be your judges.

28 But if I cast out [a]devils by the [b]Spirit of God, then the kingdom of God is come unto [c]you.

29 Or else how can one enter into a strong man's house, and [a]spoil his goods, except he first bind the strong man? and then he will spoil his house.

30 He that is not with me is against me; and he that gathereth not [a]with me scattereth abroad.

31 ¶ Wherefore I say unto you, All manner of sin and blasphemy shall be forgiven [a]unto men: but the [b]blasphemy *against* the *Holy* Ghost shall [c]not be forgiven unto men.

32 And whosoever speaketh a word against the Son of man, it shall be forgiven him: but whosoever speaketh against the Holy Ghost, it shall not be [a]forgiven him, neither

---

15*a* JST Matt. 12:13 . . . *Jesus knew when they took counsel, and* he withdrew . . .
17*a* Isa. 42:1–3.
18*a* GR son.
b TG Jesus Christ, Authority of.
c TG Witness of the Father.
19*a* GR cry for help.
20*a* D&C 52:11.
21*a* TG Jesus Christ, Taking the Name of; Name.
b GR nations.
2 Ne. 10:18 (9, 11, 18).
23*a* TG Jesus Christ, Davidic Descent of.
24*a* 2 Kgs. 1:2 (2–6).
25*a* Ps. 139:2; Luke 11:17; John 2:25; Mosiah 24:12; D&C 6:16.
b TG Governments.
26*a* TG Spirits, Evil or Unclean.
28*a* TG Devil.
b TG God, Spirit of.
c JST Matt. 12:23 . . . you. *For they also cast out devils by the Spirit of God, for unto them is given power over devils, that they may cast them out.*
29*a* GR plunder.
30*a* Mark 9:40; Luke 9:50; 2 Ne. 10:16.
31*a* JST Matt. 12:26 . . . unto men *who receive me and repent;* but . . .
b TG Blaspheme; Holy Ghost, Unpardonable Sin against.
c TG Holy Ghost, Loss of.
32*a* TG Death, Spiritual, Second; Forgive.

It is lawful to do well.
— Matt. 12:12 —

in this world, neither in the *world*
to come.
33 Either make the tree good, and
his [a]fruit good; or else make the
tree corrupt, and his fruit corrupt:
for the tree is known by *his* [b]fruit.
34 O [a]generation of vipers, how can
ye, being evil, [b]speak good things?
for out of the abundance of the
heart the mouth speaketh.
35 A good man out of the good
[a]treasure of the heart bringeth forth
good things: and an evil man out
of the evil treasure bringeth forth
[b]evil things.
36 But I say unto you, That every
[a]idle [b]word that men shall [c]speak,
they shall give [d]account thereof in
the day of [e]judgment.
37 For by thy [a]words thou shalt
be justified, and by thy words thou
shalt be condemned.
38 ¶ Then certain of the scribes
and of the Pharisees answered, saying, Master, we would see a [a]sign
from thee.
39 But he answered and said
unto them, An evil and adulterous
generation seeketh after a [a]sign;
and there shall no sign be given
to it, but the sign of the prophet
Jonas:
40 For as Jonas was three days and
three nights in the whale's belly;
so shall the Son of man be [a]three
days and three nights in the heart
of the earth.
41 The men of [a]Nineveh shall rise
in judgment with this generation,
and shall condemn it: because they
[b]repented at the preaching of Jonas;
and, behold, a greater than Jonas
is here.
42 The [a]queen of the south shall
rise up in the judgment with this
generation, and shall condemn it: for
she came from the uttermost parts
of the earth to hear the wisdom of
Solomon; and, behold, a greater than
Solomon *is* here.
43 [a]When the [b]unclean spirit is
gone out of a man, he walketh
through dry places, seeking rest,
and findeth none.
44 Then he saith, I will return into
my house from whence I came out;
and when he is come, he findeth *it*
empty, swept, and garnished.
45 Then goeth [a]he, and taketh with
himself seven other [b]spirits more
wicked than himself, and they enter in and dwell there: and the last
[c]*state* of that man is [d]worse than the
first. Even so shall it be also unto
this wicked generation.
46 ¶ While he yet talked to the
people, behold, *his* mother and his
[a]brethren stood [b]without, desiring
to speak with him.
47 Then one said unto him, Behold,
thy mother and thy brethren stand
without, desiring to speak with thee.
48 But he answered and said
unto him that told him, Who is my
mother? and who are my brethren?
49 And he stretched forth his hand
toward his disciples, and said, Behold my [a]mother and my brethren!
50 For whosoever shall do the [a]will
of my Father which is in heaven,
the same is my [b]brother, and sister,
and mother.

33*a* Matt. 7:17 (16–20); 3 Ne. 14:20 (17–20).
b Moro. 7:16 (5–19).
34*a* Matt. 3:7; 23:33; D&C 121:23.
b Luke 6:45; James 3:10 (10–12).
35*a* TG Treasure.
b TG Evil.
36*a* Eccl. 5:2; Eph. 5:4.
b TG Gossip.
c TG Profanity.
d TG Accountability.
e Alma 11:43 (43–44). TG Judgment, the Last.
37*a* Prov. 18:21.
38*a* John 6:30.
39*a* TG Miracle; Signs; Sign Seekers.
40*a* TG Jesus Christ, Death of; Jesus Christ, Types of, in Anticipation.
41*a* Jonah 3:5.
b TG Repent.
42*a* 1 Kgs. 10:1 (1–10).
43*a* JST Matt. 12:37–38 (Appendix).
b TG Uncleanness.
45*a* JST Matt. 12:39 . . . *the evil spirit,* and taketh . . .
b TG Spirits, Evil or Unclean.
c TG Apostasy of Individuals.
d Alma 24:30.
46*a* John 7:3 (3, 5, 10); 1 Cor. 9:5. TG Jesus Christ, Family of.
b GR outside.
49*a* Mosiah 5:7. TG Marriage, Motherhood.
50*a* Mark 3:35. TG God, Will of.
b TG Brotherhood and Sisterhood.

CHAPTER 13

Jesus explains why He teaches with parables—He gives the parables of the sower, the wheat and the tares, the grain of mustard seed, the leaven, the treasure hidden in the field, the pearl of great price, and the net cast into the sea—A prophet is not honored by his own people.

THE same day went Jesus out of the
house, and sat by the [a]sea side.
2 And great multitudes were gathered together unto him, so that he
went into a ship, and sat; and the
whole multitude stood on the shore.
3 And he spake many things unto
them in parables, saying, Behold, a
sower went forth to sow;
4 And when he sowed, some *seeds*
fell by the way side, and the fowls
came and devoured them up:
5 Some fell upon [a]stony places,
where they had not much earth: and
forthwith they sprung up, because
they had no deepness of earth:
6 And when the sun was up, they
were scorched; and because they
had no root, they withered away.
7 And some fell among [a]thorns;
and the thorns sprung up, and
choked them:
8 But other fell into good ground,
and [a]brought forth fruit, some an
hundredfold, some sixtyfold, some
thirtyfold.
9 Who hath ears to hear, let him
hear.
10 And the disciples came, and
said unto him, Why speakest thou
unto them in [a]parables?
11 He answered and said unto
them, Because it is given unto you
to know the [a]mysteries of the kingdom of heaven, but to them it is
not given.
12 [a]For whosoever hath, to him
shall be [b]given, and he shall have
more [c]abundance: but whosoever
hath not, from him shall be taken
away even that he hath.
13 Therefore speak I to them in
parables: because they seeing see
not; and hearing they hear not, neither do they understand.
14 And in them is fulfilled the
prophecy of Esaias, which saith, By
hearing ye shall [a]hear, and shall not
understand; and seeing ye shall see,
and shall not perceive:
15 For this people's [a]heart is waxed
gross, and *their* ears are dull of
hearing, and their [b]eyes they have
[c]closed; lest at any time they should
see with *their* eyes, and hear with
their ears, and should understand
with *their* heart, and should be converted, and I should [d]heal them.
16 But blessed *are* your [a]eyes, for
they see: and your ears, for they hear.
17 For verily I say unto you, That
many [a]prophets and righteous *men*
have desired to see *those things* which
ye see, and have not seen *them*; and
to hear *those things* which ye hear,
and have not heard *them*.
18 ¶ [a]Hear ye therefore the parable of the sower.
19 When any one heareth the word
of the kingdom, and [a]understandeth
it not, then cometh the wicked *one*,
and [b]catcheth away that which was
sown in his heart. This is he which
received seed by the way side.

13 1*a* Mark 4:1 (1–12).
5*a* IE rocky land over which a thin layer of soil is spread.
7*a* Jer. 4:3 (3–18).
8*a* GR began to bring forth.
10*a* Dan. 12:10. TG Jesus Christ, Teaching Mode of.
11*a* Matt. 11:25; D&C 6:11 (11–12); 19:8. TG Mysteries of Godliness.
12*a* JST Matt. 13:10–11 For whosoever *receiveth*, to him shall be given, and he shall have more abundance; but whosoever *continueth not to receive*, from him shall be taken away even that he hath.
b Matt. 25:29.
c Prov. 9:9.
14*a* Jer. 5:21; Rom. 11:8; 2 Ne. 9:31; 16:10.
15*a* TG Apostasy of Israel; Hardheartedness.
b TG Spiritual Blindness.
c TG Unbelief.
d 3 Ne. 9:13; 18:32.
16*a* Luke 10:23.
17*a* Heb. 11:13; 1 Pet. 1:10 (10–11).
18*a* GR Learn, Understand.
19*a* 1 Ne. 8:23 (20–23).
b D&C 84:50 (49–53); 93:39 (38–39).

20 But he that received the seed
into [a]stony places, the same is he
that heareth the word, and anon
with joy receiveth it;
21 Yet hath he not root in himself,
but dureth for a while: for when
[a]tribulation or [b]persecution ariseth
because of the word, by and by [c]he
is offended.
22 He also that received seed
among the thorns is he that heareth
the word; and the care of this [a]world,
and the [b]deceitfulness of [c]riches,
choke the word, and he becometh
unfruitful.
23 But he that received seed into
the good ground is he that [a]heareth
the word, and [b]understandeth
it; which also beareth [c]fruit, and
bringeth forth, some an hundredfold, some sixty, some thirty.

SOWER
Matt. 13:24

24 ¶ Another [a]parable put he forth
unto them, saying, The [b]kingdom of
heaven is likened unto a man which
sowed good [c]seed in his field:
25 But while men slept, his enemy
came and sowed [a]tares among the
wheat, and went his way.
26 But when the blade was sprung
up, and brought forth fruit, then
appeared the tares also.
27 So the servants of the householder came and said unto him,
Sir, didst not thou sow good seed in
thy field? from whence then hath
it tares?
28 He said unto them, An enemy
hath done this. The servants said
unto him, Wilt thou then that we
go and gather them up?
29 But he said, Nay; lest while ye
gather up the tares, ye root up also
the wheat with them.
30 Let both grow together until
the [a]harvest: and in the time of
harvest I will say to the reapers,
Gather ye together [b]first the tares,
and bind them in bundles to [c]burn
them: but gather the wheat into
my barn.
31 ¶ Another parable put he forth
unto them, saying, The kingdom of
heaven is like to a [a]grain of mustard
seed, which a man took, and sowed
in his field:
32 Which indeed is the least of
all seeds: but when it is grown, it
is the greatest among herbs, and
becometh a tree, so that the [a]birds
of the air come and lodge in the
branches thereof.
33 ¶ Another parable spake he
unto them; The kingdom of heaven
is like unto [a]leaven, which a woman
took, and hid in three measures of
meal, till the whole was leavened.
34 All these things spake Jesus
unto the multitude in parables;
and without a parable spake he not
unto them:
35 That it might be fulfilled
which was spoken by the prophet,
saying, I will open my mouth in
[a]parables; I will utter things which
have been kept [b]secret from the
foundation of the world.
36 Then Jesus sent the multitude
away, and went into the house: and
his disciples came unto him, saying,
Declare unto us the parable of the
[a]tares of the field.
37 He answered and said unto
them, He that soweth the good [a]seed
is the Son of man;
38 The field is the world; the good
seed are the children of the kingdom;

20*a* Zech. 7:12.
21*a* TG Test; Tribulation.
b D&C 40:2 (1–3). TG Persecution.
c GR he stumbles, falls away. TG Apostasy of Individuals; Offense.
22*a* Hel. 7:5; D&C 39:9. TG Worldliness.
b TG Deceit.
c TG Treasure.
23*a* TG Teachable.
b JST Matt. 13:21 . . . understandeth *and endureth;* which . . .
c Alma 32:42 (41–43). TG Good Works.
24*a* D&C 86:1 (1–11).
b TG Kingdom of God, on Earth.
c Matt. 13:37 (36–43).
25*a* TG Apostasy of the Early Christian Church.
30*a* TG Harvest.
b JST Matt. 13:29 . . . first the *wheat* into my barn; *and the tares are bound* in bundles *to be burned.*
c D&C 38:12.
31*a* Isa. 60:22.
32*a* TG Nature, Earth.
33*a* GR yeast. TG Leaven.
35*a* Ps. 78:2; Mark 4:11 (11–12).
b D&C 35:18.
36*a* D&C 86:1 (1–7); 101:65 (65–67).
37*a* Matt. 13:24 (24–30).

but the [a]tares are the children of the wicked *one;*

39 The enemy that sowed them is the devil; [a]the [b]harvest is the end of the world; and the reapers are the angels.

40 As therefore the tares are gathered and burned in the fire; so shall it be in the [a]end of this world.

41 The Son of man shall send forth his [a]angels, and they shall gather out of his kingdom all things that [b]offend, and them which do iniquity;

42 And shall cast them into a furnace of fire: there shall be [a]wailing and [b]gnashing of teeth.

43 Then shall the [a]righteous [b]shine forth as the [c]sun in the kingdom of their Father. Who hath ears to hear, let him hear.

44 ¶ Again, the kingdom of heaven is like unto [a]treasure hid in a field; the which when a man hath found, he hideth, and for joy thereof goeth and selleth all that he hath, and buyeth that field.

45 ¶ Again, the kingdom of heaven is like unto a merchant man, seeking goodly pearls:

46 Who, when he had found one [a]pearl of great price, went and sold [b]all that he had, and bought it.

47 ¶ Again, the kingdom of heaven is like unto a net, that was cast into the sea, and [a]gathered of every kind:

48 Which, when it was full, they drew to shore, and sat down, and gathered the good into vessels, but cast the bad away.

49 So shall it be at the [a]end of the [b]world: the angels shall come forth, and [c]sever the wicked from among the [d]just,

50 [a]And shall cast them into the furnace of fire: there shall be wailing and gnashing of teeth.

51 Jesus saith unto them, Have ye understood all these things? They say unto him, Yea, Lord.

52 Then said he unto them, Therefore every [a]scribe [b]*which is* instructed unto the kingdom of heaven is like unto a man *that is* an householder, which bringeth forth out of his treasure *things* new and old.

53 ¶ And it came to pass, *that* when Jesus had finished these parables, he departed thence.

54 And when he was come into his own country, he taught them in their synagogue, insomuch that they were [a]astonished, and said, Whence hath this *man* this [b]wisdom, and *these* mighty works?

55 Is not this the carpenter's [a]son? is not his mother called Mary? and his [b]brethren, James, and Joses, and Simon, and Judas?

56 And his sisters, are they not all with us? Whence then hath this *man* all these things?

57 And they were offended in him. But Jesus said unto them, A prophet is not without [a]honour, save in his own country, and in his own house.

58 And he did not many mighty works there because of their [a]unbelief.

38*a* D&C 88:94. TG Devil, Church of.
39*a* JST Matt. 13:39–44 (Appendix).
b TG Harvest.
40*a* TG World, End of.
41*a* TG Angels.
b TG Offense.
42*a* Matt. 8:12; Rev. 19:20; D&C 19:5; 29:15; 112:24.
b TG Pain.
43*a* Ps. 68:3; Alma 40:25. TG Righteousness.
b TG Celestial Glory.
c D&C 76:70.
44*a* TG Treasure.
46*a* Rev. 3:18.
b Alma 22:15.
47*a* Matt. 22:10 (1–14).
49*a* TG World, End of.
b JST Matt. 13:49–51 . . . world. *And the world is the children of the wicked.* The angels . . .
c GR separate.
d TG Righteousness.
50*a* JST Matt. 13:51 . . . and shall cast them *out into the world to be burned.* There shall be wailing . . .
52*a* TG Scribe.
b GR which has become a disciple in.
54*a* Matt. 7:28.
b TG God, Wisdom of; Jesus Christ, Teaching Mode of.
55*a* Mark 6:3.
b TG Jesus Christ, Family of.
57*a* TG Prophets, Rejection of.
58*a* Luke 4:23 (23–27); Ether 12:12 (6–19); Moro. 7:37 (33–39).

CHAPTER 14

John the Baptist is beheaded—Jesus feeds the five thousand and walks on the sea—Those who touch the hem of His garment are made whole.

AT that time [a]Herod the tetrarch
heard of the fame of Jesus,
2 And said unto his servants, This is
John the Baptist; he is risen from the
dead; and therefore mighty works
do shew forth themselves in him.
3 ¶ For Herod had laid hold on
John, and bound him, and put *him*
in prison for Herodias' sake, his
brother Philip's wife.
4 For John said unto him, It is not
[a]lawful for thee to have her.
5 And [a]when he would have put
him to death, he feared the multitude, because they counted him as
a [b]prophet.
6 But when Herod's birthday was
kept, the daughter of Herodias
danced before them, and pleased
Herod.
7 Whereupon he [a]promised with
an oath to give her whatsoever she
would ask.
8 And she, being before instructed
of her mother, said, Give me here
John Baptist's head in a [a]charger.
9 And the king was sorry: nevertheless for the oath's sake, and
them which sat with him at meat,
he commanded *it* to be given *her*.
10 And he sent, and [a]beheaded
John in the prison.
11 And his head was brought in
a charger, and given to the damsel:
and she brought *it* to her mother.
12 And his disciples came, and
took up the body, and buried it, and
went and told Jesus.
13 ¶ When Jesus heard *of it*, he departed thence by ship into a desert
place apart: and when the people
had heard *thereof*, they followed him
on foot out of the cities.
14 And Jesus went forth, and saw
a great multitude, and was moved
with [a]compassion toward them, and
he healed their [b]sick.
15 ¶ And when it was evening, his
disciples came to him, saying, This
is a desert place, and the time is now
past; send the multitude away, that
they may go into the villages, and
buy themselves [a]victuals.
16 But Jesus said unto them, They
need not depart; give ye them to eat.
17 And they say unto him, We have
here but five loaves, and two fishes.
18 He said, Bring them hither to me.
19 And he commanded the multitude to sit down on the grass, and
took the five loaves, and the two
fishes, and looking up to heaven,
he blessed, and [a]brake, and gave
the loaves to *his* disciples, and the
disciples to the multitude.
20 And they did all eat, and were
filled: and they [a]took up of the
fragments that remained twelve
baskets full.
21 And they that had eaten were
about [a]five thousand men, beside
women and children.
22 ¶ And straightway Jesus constrained his disciples to get into a
ship, and to go before him unto the
other side, while he sent the multitudes away.
23 And when he had sent the multitudes away, he went up into a mountain apart to [a]pray: and when the evening was come, he was there alone.
24 But the ship was now in the
midst of the sea, tossed with waves:
for the wind was contrary.
25 And [a]in the fourth watch of the
night Jesus went unto them, walking on the sea.
26 And when the disciples saw

---

14 1*a* Luke 9:7.
4*a* Lev. 18:16; 20:21. TG Divorce.
5*a* GR although he desired to kill him.
b Matt. 11:9; 21:26; Luke 20:6.
7*a* TG Vow.
8*a* GR platter.
10*a* TG Tyranny.
14*a* TG Compassion.
b TG Sickness.
15*a* GR food.
19*a* 3 Ne. 18:5 (4–5); 20:6 (6–7).
20*a* 2 Kgs. 4:44 (42–44); Matt. 15:37 (36–38).
21*a* Mark 6:44 (32–44); Luke 9:14 (10–17); John 6:10 (1–13).
23*a* Matt. 26:36; Luke 6:12; 9:28.
25*a* IE between three and six in the morning.

HE WALKED ON THE WATER!
Matt. 14:29

him walking on the sea, they were
troubled, saying, It is a spirit; and
they cried out for fear.
27 But straightway Jesus spake
unto them, saying, Be of good [a]cheer;
it is I; be not afraid.
28 And Peter answered him and
said, Lord, if it be thou, bid me come
unto thee on the water.
29 And he said, Come. And when
Peter was come down out of the
ship, he walked on the water, to go
to Jesus.
30 But when he saw the wind boister-
ous, he was [a]afraid; and beginning to
sink, he cried, saying, Lord, save me.
31 And immediately Jesus stretched
forth *his* hand, and caught him, and
said unto him, O thou of little [a]faith,
wherefore didst thou [b]doubt?
32 And when they were come into
the ship, the wind ceased.
33 Then they that were in the ship
came and worshipped him, saying,
Of a truth thou art the Son of God.
34 ¶ And when they were gone
over, they came into the land of
Gennesaret.
35 And when the men of that place
[a]had knowledge of him, they sent
out into all that country round
about, and brought unto him all
that were diseased;
36 And besought him that they
might only touch the [a]hem of his
garment: and as many as touched
were made perfectly [b]whole.

CHAPTER 15

The scribes and Pharisees contend against Jesus—He heals the daughter of a gentile woman—He feeds the four thousand.

THEN came to Jesus [a]scribes and
Pharisees, which were of Jerusalem, saying,
2 Why do thy disciples transgress
the [a]tradition of the elders? for they
wash not their hands when they
eat bread.
3 But he answered and said unto
them, Why do ye also transgress the
commandment of God by your [a]tra-
dition?
4 For God commanded, saying,
[a]Honour thy father and mother: and,
He that curseth father or mother,
[b]let him die the death.
5 But ye say, Whosoever shall say
to *his* father or *his* mother, *It is* a
[a]gift, by whatsoever thou mightest
be profited by me;
6 And honour not his father or his
mother, *he shall be free*. Thus have ye
made the commandment of God of
none effect by your tradition.
7 *Ye* hypocrites, well did Esaias
prophesy of you, saying,
8 This people draweth nigh unto
me with their [a]mouth, and [b]hon-
oureth me with *their* lips; but their
[c]heart is far from me.
9 But in vain they do [a]worship me,
teaching *for* [b]doctrines the [c]com-
mandments of men.
10 ¶ And he called the multitude,
and said unto them, Hear, and understand:
11 Not that which goeth into the
mouth [a]defileth a man; but that
which cometh out of the [b]mouth,
this defileth a man.
12 Then came his disciples, and
said unto him, Knowest thou that
the Pharisees were offended, after
they heard this saying?
13 But he answered and said,
Every [a]plant, which my heavenly

27*a* TG Cheerful.
30*a* TG Courage; Fearful.
31*a* Mark 4:40; 16:14; Luke 24:25.
b TG Doubt.
35*a* GR recognized Him.
36*a* Mark 5:27 (25–34).
b TG Heal.
15 1*a* TG Scribe.
2*a* Alma 24:7; D&C 123:7 (7–8).
3*a* TG Traditions of Men.
4*a* TG Honor; Honoring Father and Mother; Respect.
b GR he shall surely die. TG Capital Punishment.
5*a* Mark 7:11.
8*a* Jer. 12:2.
b Isa. 29:13; Titus 1:16 (15–16); 2 Ne. 27:25 (24–25). TG Hypocrisy.
c Ezek. 33:31; Alma 34:28; D&C 45:29.
9*a* Isa. 1:13.
b Matt. 16:12; Col. 2:22 (18–22); Titus 1:14 (13–14); 2 Ne. 28:9.
c TG Apostasy of Israel.
11*a* TG Cleanliness.
b TG Gossip; Profanity.
13*a* John 15:2 (1–2). TG Vineyard of the Lord.

Father hath not planted, shall be
rooted up.
14 Let them alone: they be [a]blind
[b]leaders of the blind. And if the
blind lead the blind, both shall fall
into the ditch.
15 Then answered Peter and
said unto him, Declare unto us this
parable.
16 And Jesus said, Are ye also yet
without understanding?
17 Do not ye yet understand, that
whatsoever entereth in at the mouth
goeth into the belly, and is cast out
into the draught?
18 But those things which proceed
out of the [a]mouth come forth from
the heart; and they defile the man.
19 For out of the [a]heart proceed
evil thoughts, [b]murders, [c]adulteries,
[d]fornications, thefts, [e]false witness,
[f]blasphemies:
20 These are *the things* which [a]defile
a man: but to eat with unwashen
hands defileth not a man.
21 ¶ Then Jesus went thence, and
departed into the [a]coasts of Tyre
and Sidon.
22 And, behold, a woman of Canaan
came out of the same coasts,
and cried unto him, saying, Have
mercy on me, O Lord, *thou* Son of
David; my daughter is grievously
vexed with a devil.
23 But he answered her not a word.
And his disciples came and besought
him, saying, Send her away; for she
crieth after us.
24 But he answered and said, I am
not [a]sent but unto the lost sheep of
the house of [b]Israel.
25 Then came she and worshipped
him, saying, Lord, help me.
26 But he answered and said, It
is not meet to take the children's
bread, and to cast *it* to [a]dogs.
27 And she said, Truth, Lord: yet
the dogs eat of the crumbs which
fall from their masters' table.
28 Then Jesus answered and said
unto her, O woman, great *is* thy
[a]faith: be it unto thee even as thou
wilt. And her daughter was made
whole from that very hour.
29 And Jesus departed from thence,
and came nigh unto the sea of Galilee;
and went up into a mountain,
and sat down there.
30 And great multitudes came unto
him, having with them *those that
were* lame, blind, dumb, maimed,
and many others, and cast them
down at Jesus' feet; and he healed
them:
31 Insomuch that the multitude
wondered, when they saw the dumb
to speak, the maimed to be whole,
the lame to walk, and the blind to
see: and they glorified the God of
Israel.
32 ¶ Then Jesus called his disciples
unto him, and said, I have compassion
on the multitude, because
they continue with me now three
days, and have nothing to eat: and
I will not send them away fasting,
lest they faint in the way.
33 And his disciples say unto him,
Whence should we have so much
bread in the wilderness, as to fill
so great a multitude?
34 And Jesus saith unto them, How
many loaves have ye? And they said,
Seven, and a few little fishes.
35 And he commanded the multitude
to sit down on the ground.
36 And he took the seven [a]loaves
and the fishes, and gave thanks,
and brake *them*, and gave to his
disciples, and the disciples to the
multitude.
37 And they did all eat, and were

14*a* TG Spiritual Blindness.
b TG Governments; Leadership.
18*a* Mosiah 4:30 (29–30).
19*a* Gen. 6:5; Heb. 3:12; Hel. 12:4. TG Chastity.
b TG Blood, Shedding of; Murder.
c TG Adulterer; Sexual Immorality.
d TG Fornication.
e Ps. 27:12; Hel. 7:21 (21–22).
f GR slanderous statements. TG Blaspheme.
20*a* TG Pollution.
21*a* GR regions.
24*a* 3 Ne. 15:23. TG Jesus Christ, Messenger of the Covenant.
b TG Israel, Scattering of.
26*a* Prov. 23:9; Matt. 7:6; D&C 6:12 (10–12); 10:37 (36–37); 41:6.
28*a* James 5:15 (14–15).
36*a* TG Bread.

filled: and they [a]took up of the
[b]broken *meat* that was left seven
baskets full.
38 And they that did eat were four
thousand men, beside women and
children.
39 And he sent away the multitude, and took ship, and came into
the coasts of Magdala.

CHAPTER 16

Jesus warns against the doctrine of the Pharisees and Sadducees—Peter testifies that Jesus is the Christ and is promised the keys of the kingdom—Jesus foretells His death and resurrection.

THE Pharisees also with the Sadducees came, and tempting desired
him that he would shew them a
sign from [a]heaven.
2 He [a]answered and said unto them,
When it is evening, ye say, *It will be*
fair weather: for the sky is red.
3 And in the morning, *It will be*
foul weather to day: for the sky is
red and [a]lowring. O *ye* [b]hypocrites,
ye can discern the face of the sky;
but can ye not *discern* the [c]signs of
the [d]times?
4 A wicked and [a]adulterous generation seeketh after a [b]sign; and there
shall no sign be given unto it, but
the [c]sign of the prophet [d]Jonas. And
he left them, and departed.
5 And when his disciples were
come to the other side, they had
forgotten to take bread.
6 ¶ Then Jesus said unto them,
Take heed and beware of the [a]leaven
of the Pharisees and of the Sadducees.
7 And they reasoned among themselves, saying, *It is* because we have
taken no bread.
8 [a]*Which* when Jesus perceived,
he said unto them, O ye of little
faith, why reason ye among yourselves, because ye have brought no
bread?
9 Do ye not yet understand, neither remember the five loaves of
the five thousand, and how many
baskets ye took up?
10 Neither the seven loaves of the
four thousand, and how many baskets ye took up?
11 How is it that ye do not understand that I spake *it* not to you
concerning bread, that ye should
beware of the leaven of the Pharisees and of the Sadducees?
12 Then understood they how that
he bade *them* not beware of the
leaven of bread, but of the [a]doc-
trine of the Pharisees and of the
[b]Sadducees.
13 ¶ When Jesus came into the
coasts of Cæsarea Philippi, he asked
his disciples, saying, Whom do men
say that I the Son of man am?
14 And they said, Some *say that thou*
art John the Baptist: some, [a]Elias;
and others, Jeremias, or one of the
prophets.
15 He saith unto them, But whom
say [a]ye that I am?
16 And Simon Peter answered and
said, Thou art the [a]Christ, the [b]Son
of the [c]living God.
17 And Jesus answered and said
unto him, Blessed art thou, Simon
[a]Bar-jona: for flesh and blood hath
not [b]revealed *it* unto thee, but my
Father which is in heaven.
18 And I say also unto thee, That

37*a* 2 Kgs. 4:44 (42–44); Matt. 14:20 (19–21).
b GR excess food.
16 1*a* TG Heaven.
2*a* Prov. 26:5.
3*a* GR dark, gloomy.
b TG Hypocrisy.
c 2 Pet. 3:4 (3–10).
d Esth. 1:13.
4*a* TG Adulterer.
b Mark 8:12 (11–21).
c Jonah 1:17.
d TG Jesus Christ, Death of.
6*a* TG Leaven.
8*a* JST Matt. 16:9 *And* when *they reasoned among themselves,* Jesus perceived *it . . .*
12*a* Matt. 15:9.
b Matt. 22:23 (23–33).
14*a* IE Elijah.
15*a* IE The plural pronoun used here in the Greek indicates that Jesus asked this question of all the apostles and not just one of them.
16*a* TG Loyalty.
b TG Jesus Christ, Divine Sonship.
c TG God, Body of, Corporeal Nature.
17*a* IE Son of Jonah.
b TG Revelation; Testimony; Witness.

thou art Peter, and upon this [a]rock I
will build my [b]church; and the gates
of [c]hell shall not [d]prevail against it.
19 And I will [a]give unto thee the
[b]keys of the [c]kingdom of heaven:
and whatsoever thou shalt [d]bind
on earth shall be bound in heaven:
and whatsoever thou shalt loose
on earth shall be loosed in heaven.
20 Then charged he his disciples
that they should tell no man that
he was Jesus the [a]Christ.
21 ¶ From that time forth began
Jesus to shew unto his disciples,
how that he must go unto Jerusalem, and suffer many things of the
elders and chief priests and scribes,
and be killed, and be [a]raised again
the third day.
22 Then Peter took him, and began
to rebuke him, saying, Be it far from
thee, Lord: this shall not be unto thee.
23 But he turned, and said unto
Peter, Get thee behind me, Satan:
thou art an offence unto me: for
thou [a]savourest not the things that
be of God, but those that be of men.
24 ¶ [a]Then said Jesus unto his disciples, If any *man* will come after
me, let him [b]deny himself, and take
up his [c]cross, and [d]follow [e]me.
25 For whosoever will save his life
shall lose it: and whosoever will [a]lose
his life for my sake shall [b]find it.
26 For what is a man [a]profited, if
he shall [b]gain the whole [c]world, and
[d]lose his own [e]soul? or what shall a
man give in exchange for his soul?
27 For the [a]Son of man shall come
in the [b]glory of his Father with
his angels; and then he shall [c]re-
ward every man according to his
[d]works.
28 Verily I say unto you, There be
some standing here, which shall not
taste of [a]death, till they see the Son
of man coming in his [b]kingdom.

CHAPTER 17

Jesus is transfigured before Peter, James, and John on the mount—Jesus heals a lunatic, tells of His coming death, and pays taxes in a miraculous manner.

AND after six days Jesus taketh
[a]Peter, James, and John his brother,
and bringeth them up into an high
mountain apart,
2 And was [a]transfigured before
them: and his face did shine as the
sun, and his raiment was white as
the light.

18*a* Here is a subtle wordplay upon "Peter" (Greek *petros* = small rock) and "rock" (Greek *petra* = bedrock). Christ is the Stone of Israel. John 1:42; 1 Cor. 3:11 (9–11); 10:4; D&C 50:44; 128:10. TG Rock.
b TG Church Organization; Jesus Christ, Head of the Church.
c TG Hell.
d D&C 17:8; 21:6.
19*a* D&C 7:7; 27:13. TG Delegation of Responsibility; God, Gifts of.
b TG Apostles; Priesthood; Priesthood, Authority; Priesthood, History of; Priesthood, Keys of.
c TG Kingdom of God, on Earth.
d Hel. 10:7 (5–11); D&C 138:58 (58–60). TG Genealogy and Temple Work; Marriage, Celestial; Salvation for the Dead; Sealing.
20*a* TG Jesus Christ, Messiah.
21*a* TG Jesus Christ, Resurrection.
23*a* Hel. 10:4 (4–5).
24*a* JST Matt. 16:25–29 (Appendix).
b TG Self-Mastery.
c Matt. 10:38; 3 Ne. 12:30.
d Philip. 3:17 (13–21); 2 Ne. 31:12 (12–13).
e JST Matt. 16:25–26 . . . me. *And now for a man to take up his cross, is to deny himself all ungodliness, and every worldly lust, and keep my commandments.*
25*a* TG Self-Mastery; Self-Sacrifice.
b TG Abundant Life.
26*a* 1 Sam. 12:21; Prov. 13:7; Eccl. 1:3 (2–3).
b Job 27:8. TG Selfishness; Treasure.
c TG Worldliness.
d Luke 9:25.
e TG Mortality; Soul.
27*a* TG Jesus Christ, Son of Man.
b TG Glory; Jesus Christ, Glory of; Jesus Christ, Second Coming.
c TG Jesus Christ, Judge; Judgment, the Last; Retribution; Reward.
d Prov. 24:12. TG Good Works.
28*a* TG Translated Beings.
b TG Millennium.
17 1*a* D&C 128:20.
2*a* Mark 9:2 (2–13); Luke 9:29 (28–36); John 1:14; 2 Pet. 1:16 (16–19). TG Jesus Christ, Glory of; Transfiguration.

3 And, behold, there appeared
unto them [a]Moses and [b]Elias talking with him.
4 Then answered Peter, and said
unto Jesus, Lord, it is good for us
to be here: if thou wilt, let us make
here three tabernacles; one for thee,
and one for Moses, and one for Elias.
5 While he yet spake, behold, a
bright [a]cloud overshadowed them:
and behold a [b]voice out of the cloud,
which said, This is my [c]beloved
[d]Son, in whom I am well pleased;
hear ye him.
6 And when the disciples heard
it, they fell on their face, and were
sore [a]afraid.
7 And Jesus came and touched
them, and said, Arise, and be not
afraid.
8 And when they had lifted up
their eyes, they saw no man, save
Jesus only.
9 And as they came down from
the mountain, Jesus charged them,
saying, Tell the [a]vision to no [b]man,
until the Son of man be risen again
from the [c]dead.
10 And his disciples asked him,
saying, Why then say the scribes
that Elias must first come?
11 [a]And Jesus answered and said
unto them, Elias truly shall first
come, and [b]restore all things.
12 But I say unto you, That Elias is
come already, and they knew him
not, but have done unto him whatsoever they [a]listed. Likewise shall
also the Son of man suffer of them.
13 Then the disciples understood
that he spake unto them of John
the Baptist.
14 ¶ And when they were come to
the multitude, there came to him a
certain man, kneeling down to him,
and saying,
15 Lord, have mercy on my son:
for he is lunatic, and sore vexed:
for ofttimes he [a]falleth into the fire,
and oft into the water.
16 And I brought him to thy disciples, and they could not cure him.
17 Then Jesus answered and said,
O [a]faithless and [b]perverse generation, how long shall I be with you?
how long shall I suffer you? bring
him hither to me.
18 And Jesus rebuked the devil;
and he departed out of him: and the
child was cured from that very hour.
19 Then came the disciples to Jesus
apart, and said, Why could not we
cast him out?
20 And Jesus said unto them, Because of your [a]unbelief: for verily
I say unto you, If ye have [b]faith as
a grain of mustard seed, ye shall
say unto this [c]mountain, Remove
hence to yonder place; and it shall
remove; and nothing shall be [d]im-
possible unto you.
21 Howbeit this [a]kind goeth not
out but by prayer and [b]fasting.
22 ¶ And while they abode in Galilee, Jesus said unto them, The Son
of man shall be [a]betrayed into the
hands of men:
23 And they shall kill him, and the
third day he shall be [a]raised again.
And they were exceeding sorry.
24 ¶ And when they were come to
Capernaum, they that received tribute *money* came to Peter, and said,
Doth not your master pay [a]tribute?

3*a* D&C 63:21; 110:11. TG Priesthood, Keys of; Translated Beings.
b IE Elijah. 1 Kgs. 17:1; Luke 4:25; D&C 110:13 (13–16).
5*a* Ex. 24:15.
b TG God, Body of, Corporeal Nature.
c Matt. 3:17; 3 Ne. 11:7; JS—H 1:17. TG Witness of the Father.
d TG God; Godhead; God the Father, Elohim; Jesus Christ, Divine Sonship.
6*a* Ex. 3:6; Deut. 5:5.
9*a* TG Vision.
b Mark 9:9 (9–13).
c TG Death.
11*a* JST Matt. 17:10–14 (Appendix).
b D&C 27:6; 77:14; 110:13–16. TG Dispensations; Restoration of the Gospel.
12*a* GR desired.
15*a* GR throws himself.
17*a* TG Unbelief.
b Deut. 32:5.
20*a* GR little faith. TG Doubt.
b TG Faith.
c Ether 12:30; Moses 7:13.
d TG God, Power of.
21*a* D&C 84:67 (65–73).
b TG Fast, Fasting.
22*a* TG Jesus Christ, Betrayal of.
23*a* TG Jesus Christ, Resurrection.
24*a* D&C 58:21 (21–22).

25 He saith, Yes. And when he was come into the house, Jesus [a]prevented him, saying, What thinkest thou, Simon? of whom do the [b]kings of the earth take custom or tribute? of their own children, or of strangers?

26 Peter saith unto him, Of strangers. Jesus saith unto him, Then are the children free.

27 Notwithstanding, lest we should offend them, go thou to the sea, and cast an hook, and take up the fish that first cometh up; and when thou hast opened his mouth, thou shalt find a piece of [a]money: that take, and [b]give unto them for me and thee.

CHAPTER 18

Jesus explains how we are to treat our offending brethren—The Son of Man came to save that which was lost—All of the Twelve receive the keys of the kingdom—Jesus explains why we should forgive.

AT the same time came the disciples unto Jesus, saying, Who is the [a]greatest in the kingdom of heaven?

2 And Jesus called a little child unto him, and set him in the midst of them,

3 And said, Verily I say unto you, Except ye be converted, and become as little [a]children, ye shall not enter into the kingdom of heaven.

4 Whosoever therefore shall [a]humble himself as this little [b]child, the same is greatest in the kingdom of heaven.

5 And whoso shall receive one such little child in my [a]name receiveth me.

6 But whoso shall [a]offend one of these little ones which believe in me, it were better for him that a millstone were hanged about his neck, and *that* he were drowned in the depth of the sea.

7 ¶ Woe unto the world because of [a]offences! for it must needs be that offences come; but woe to that man by whom the offence cometh!

8 Wherefore if thy hand or thy foot offend thee, cut them off, and cast *them* from thee: it is better for thee to enter into life halt or maimed, rather than having two hands or two feet to be cast into everlasting fire.

9 And if thine eye offend thee, pluck it out, and cast *it* from thee: it is better for thee to enter into life with one eye, rather than having two eyes to be cast into [a]hell fire.

10 Take heed that ye despise not one of these [a]little ones; for I say unto you, That in heaven their angels do always behold the face of my Father which is in heaven.

11 For the [a]Son of man is come to [b]save that which was [c]lost.

12 How think ye? if a man have an hundred [a]sheep, and one of them be gone astray, doth he not leave the ninety and nine, and goeth into the mountains, and seeketh that which is gone astray?

13 And if so be that he find it, verily I say unto you, he rejoiceth more of that *sheep*, than of the ninety and nine which went not astray.

14 Even so it is not the will of your Father which is in heaven, that one of these [a]little ones should [b]perish.

25*a* GR spoke to him first.
b TG Kings, Earthly.
27*a* Ex. 30:13; 38:26.
b TG Citizenship.
18 1*a* Luke 9:46.
3*a* 1 Cor. 14:20; Mosiah 3:19. TG Children; Salvation of Little Children.
4*a* TG Humility; Meek.
b TG Children.
5*a* TG Name.
6*a* GR cause to stumble. D&C 121:19 (19–22). TG Offense.
7*a* TG Sin.
9*a* JST Matt. 18:8–9 . . . hellfire. *And a man's hand is his friend, and his foot, also; and a man's eye, are they of his own household.*
10*a* TG Children; Family, Children, Responsibilities toward.
11*a* TG Jesus Christ, Son of Man.
b TG Jesus Christ, Mission of; Life, Sanctity of; Worth of Souls.
c JST Matt. 18:11 . . . lost, *and to call sinners to repentance; but these little ones have no need of repentance, and I will save them.*
12*a* TG Sheep.
14*a* TG Children.
b Mosiah 28:3.

15 ¶ Moreover if thy brother shall
[a]trespass against thee, go and [b]tell
him his [c]fault between thee and him
alone: if he shall hear thee, thou
hast gained thy brother.
16 But if he will not hear *thee, then*
take with thee one or two more,
that in the mouth of two or three
[a]witnesses every word may be established.
17 And if he shall neglect to hear
them, tell *it* unto the [a]church: but
if he [b]neglect to hear the [c]church,
let him be unto thee as an heathen
man and a publican.
18 Verily I say unto you, Whatsoever ye shall [a]bind on earth shall
be bound in heaven: and whatsoever ye shall loose on earth shall
be loosed in heaven.
19 Again I say unto you, That if
two of you shall [a]agree on earth as
[b]touching any thing that they shall
[c]ask, it shall be done for them of my
Father which is in heaven.
20 For where two or three are [a]gath-
ered [b]together in my [c]name, there
am I in the [d]midst of them.
21 ¶ Then came Peter to him, and
said, Lord, how oft shall my brother
sin against me, and I [a]forgive him?
till seven times?
22 Jesus saith unto him, I say not
unto thee, Until seven times: but,
Until [a]seventy times seven.
23 ¶ Therefore is the kingdom of
heaven likened unto a certain king,
which would [a]take account of his
[b]servants.
24 And when he had begun to
reckon, one was brought unto him,
which owed him ten thousand
talents.
25 But forasmuch as he had not to
pay, his lord commanded him to be
[a]sold, and his wife, and children,
and all that he had, and payment
to be made.
26 The servant therefore fell down,
and worshipped him, saying, Lord,
have patience with me, and I will
pay thee all.
27 Then the lord of that servant
was moved with compassion, and
loosed him, and forgave him the
debt.
28 But the same servant went out,
and found one of his fellowservants,
which owed him [a]an hundred pence:
and he laid hands on him, and took
him by the throat, saying, Pay me
that thou owest.
29 And his fellowservant fell down
at his feet, and besought him, saying, Have patience with me, and I
will pay thee all.
30 And he would not: but went and
cast him into prison, till he should
pay the debt.
31 So when his fellowservants
saw what was done, they were very
[a]sorry, and came and told unto their
lord all that was done.
32 Then his lord, after that he had
called him, said unto him, O thou
wicked servant, I forgave thee all
that [a]debt, because thou desiredst
me:
33 [a]Shouldest not thou also have
had [b]compassion on thy fellowservant, even as I had [c]pity on thee?
34 And his lord was wroth, and
delivered him to the tormentors,
till he should pay all that was due
unto him.
35 So likewise shall my heavenly

15*a* TG Offense.
b TG Reproof.
c Matt. 5:24 (23–24); Luke 17:3 (3–4); D&C 42:88 (88–92).
16*a* 2 Ne. 29:8. TG Witness.
17*a* 1 Cor. 6:1; D&C 42:81.
b Titus 3:10.
c TG Church.
18*a* TG Apostles; Priesthood, Keys of; Sealing.
19*a* TG Common Consent.
b D&C 6:32; 42:3.
c TG Prayer.
20*a* TG Church.
b TG Unity.
c TG Name.
d D&C 29:5; 32:3; 45:59; 49:27.
21*a* TG Forbear.
22*a* D&C 98:40 (39–48). TG Patience.
23*a* GR settle accounts with. TG Accountability; Stewardship.
b TG Servant.
25*a* 2 Kgs. 4:1.
28*a* IE approximately three months' wages of a poor working man.
31*a* GR distressed.
32*a* TG Debt.
33*a* TG Ingratitude.
b TG Compassion; Mercy.
c GR compassion.

Father do also unto you, if ye from
your hearts [a]forgive not every one
his brother their trespasses.

CHAPTER 19

Jesus teaches about marriage and divorce—Eternal life is for those who keep the commandments—The Twelve Apostles will judge the house of Israel.

AND it came to pass, *that* when
Jesus had finished these sayings,
he departed from Galilee, and came
into the coasts of Judæa beyond
Jordan;
2 And great multitudes followed
him; and he healed them there.
3 ¶ The Pharisees also came unto
him, tempting him, and saying
unto him, Is it lawful for a man to
[a]put away his wife for every cause?
4 And he answered and said unto
them, Have ye not read, that he
which [a]made *them* at the beginning
made them male and female,
5 And said, For this cause shall a
man leave father and mother, and
shall [a]cleave to his wife: and they
twain shall be one flesh?
6 Wherefore they are no more
twain, but one flesh. What therefore God hath [a]joined together, let
not man [b]put asunder.
7 They say unto him, Why did
Moses then command to give a
[a]writing of [b]divorcement, and to
put her away?
8 He saith unto them, Moses because of the [a]hardness of your hearts
suffered you to put away your [b]wives:
but from the beginning it was not so.
9 And I say unto you, Whosoever
shall put away his wife, except *it*
be for [a]fornication, and shall marry
another, committeth [b]adultery: and
whoso marrieth her which is put
away doth commit adultery.
10 ¶ His disciples say unto him, If
the case of the man be so with *his*
wife, it is not good to marry.
11 But he said unto them, All *men*
cannot receive this saying, save *they*
to whom it is given.
12 For there are some eunuchs,
which were so born from *their* mother's womb: and there are some eunuchs, which were made eunuchs of
men: and there be eunuchs, which
have made themselves eunuchs for
the kingdom of heaven's sake. He
that is able to receive *it*, let him
receive *it*.
13 ¶ Then were there brought unto
him little children, that he should
put *his* [a]hands on them, and pray:
and the disciples rebuked [b]them.
14 But Jesus said, [a]Suffer little
[b]children, and forbid them not, to
come unto me: for of such is the
kingdom of heaven.
15 And he laid *his* hands on them,
and departed thence.
16 ¶ And, behold, one came and
said unto him, Good Master, what
good thing shall I do, that I may
have [a]eternal life?
17 And he said unto him, Why
callest thou me good? *there is* none
[a]good but one, *that is*, God: but if
thou wilt enter into [b]life, keep the
[c]commandments.
18 He saith unto him, Which? Jesus
said, Thou shalt do no [a]murder,
Thou shalt not commit [b]adultery,
Thou shalt not [c]steal, Thou shalt
not bear [d]false witness,

35*a* TG Forgive.
19 3*a* GR divorce.
4*a* TG Man, Physical Creation of.
5*a* TG Family, Love within; Marriage, Celestial.
6*a* TG Marriage, Marry.
b GR divide, separate.
7*a* GR certificate of divorce.
b TG Divorce.
8*a* TG Hardheartedness.
b TG Family, Eternal.
9*a* TG Fornication.
b TG Sexual Immorality.
13*a* TG Hands, Laying on of.
b JST Matt. 19:13 . . . them, *saying, There is no need, for Jesus hath said, Such shall be saved.*
14*a* GR Allow, Permit.
b D&C 137:10.
TG Children; Salvation of Little Children.
16*a* TG Eternity.
17*a* TG God, Perfection of.
b Prov. 4:22.
c 1 Ne. 22:31.
18*a* TG Blood, Shedding of; Murder.
b TG Adulterer.
c TG Stealing.
d Prov. 25:18.

19 [a]Honour thy father and *thy* mother: and, Thou shalt [b]love thy [c]neighbour as thyself.

20 The young man saith unto him, All these things have I kept from my youth up: what lack I yet?

21 Jesus said unto him, If thou wilt be [a]perfect, go *and* sell that thou hast, and [b]give to the [c]poor, and thou shalt have [d]treasure in heaven: and come *and* [e]follow me.

22 But when the young man heard that saying, he went away sorrowful: for he had [a]great possessions.

23 ¶ Then said Jesus unto his disciples, Verily I say unto you, That a [a]rich man shall [b]hardly enter into the kingdom of heaven.

24 And again I say unto you, It is easier for a camel to go through the eye of a needle, than for a [a]rich man to enter into the kingdom of God.

25 When his disciples heard *it*, they were exceedingly amazed, saying, Who then can be saved?

26 [a]But Jesus beheld *them*, and said unto them, With men this is impossible; but with God all things are [b]possible.

27 ¶ Then answered Peter and said unto him, Behold, we have forsaken all, and followed thee; what shall we have therefore?

28 And Jesus said unto them, Verily I say unto you, That ye which have followed me, in the [a]regeneration when the Son of man shall sit in the throne of his glory, ye also shall sit upon twelve thrones, [b]judging the twelve tribes of Israel.

29 And every one that hath [a]forsaken houses, or brethren, or sisters, or father, or mother, or wife, or children, or lands, for my [b]name's sake, shall receive an hundredfold, and shall inherit [c]everlasting life.

30 But many *that are* [a]first shall be last; and the last *shall be* first.

CHAPTER 20

Jesus gives the parable of the laborers in the vineyard—He foretells His crucifixion and resurrection—He came to give His life as a ransom for many.

FOR the kingdom of heaven is like unto a man *that is* an householder, which went out early in the morning to hire [a]labourers into his vineyard.

2 And when he had agreed with the labourers for a penny a day, he sent them into his [a]vineyard.

3 And he went out about the third hour, and saw others standing [a]idle in the marketplace,

4 And said unto them; Go ye also into the vineyard, and whatsoever is right I will give you. And they went their way.

5 Again he went out about the sixth and ninth hour, and did likewise.

6 And about the [a]eleventh hour he went out, and found others standing idle, and saith unto them, Why stand ye here all the day idle?

7 They say unto him, Because no man hath hired us. He saith unto them, Go ye also into the vineyard; and whatsoever is right, *that* shall ye receive.

8 So when even was come, the lord

19*a* TG Family, Children, Duties of; Honoring Father and Mother.
b TG Citizenship; Love.
c TG Fellowshipping; Neighbor.
21*a* TG Commitment; Perfection.
b TG Almsgiving; Sacrifice.
c TG Poor.
d TG Treasure.
e Alma 22:15.
22*a* GR many.
23*a* 2 Ne. 9:30; Jacob 2:19 (16–19); D&C 6:7 (5–7).
b GR with difficulty.
24*a* Prov. 18:11.
26*a* JST Matt. 19:26 But Jesus beheld *their thoughts*, and said unto them, With men this is impossible; but *if they will forsake all things for my sake*, with God *whatsoever things I speak* are possible.
b Job 42:2. TG God, Power of.
28*a* JST Matt. 19:28 . . . *resurrection* . . .
b Morm. 3:18 (18–20); D&C 29:12. TG Apostles; Judgment, the Last.
29*a* D&C 19:36. TG Self-Sacrifice.
b TG Name.
c TG Exaltation.
30*a* D&C 29:30.
20 1*a* TG Labor.
2*a* TG Vineyard of the Lord.
3*a* Alma 38:12.
6*a* D&C 33:3 (1–3).

of the vineyard saith unto his steward, Call the [a]labourers, and give them *their* [b]hire, beginning from the last unto the first.

9 And when they came that *were hired* about the eleventh hour, they received every man a penny.

10 But when the first came, they supposed that they should have received more; and they likewise received every man a penny.

11 And when they had received *it,* they murmured against the goodman of the house,

12 Saying, These last have wrought *but* one hour, and thou hast made them equal unto us, which have borne the burden and heat of the day.

13 But he answered one of them, and said, Friend, I do thee no wrong: didst not thou agree with me for a penny?

14 Take *that* thine *is,* and go thy way: I will give unto this last, even as unto thee.

15 Is it not lawful for me to do what I will with mine own? Is thine eye evil, because I am good?

16 So the [a]last shall be first, and the first last: for many be [b]called, but few chosen.

17 ¶ And Jesus going up to Jerusalem took the twelve disciples apart in the way, and said unto them,

18 Behold, we go up to Jerusalem; and the Son of man shall be [a]betrayed unto the chief priests and unto the scribes, and they shall condemn him to [b]death,

19 And shall deliver him to the Gentiles to [a]mock, and to scourge, and to [b]crucify *him:* and the third day he shall [c]rise again.

20 ¶ Then came to him the mother of Zebedee's children with her sons, worshipping *him,* and desiring a certain thing of him.

21 And he said unto her, What wilt thou? She saith unto him, Grant that these my two sons may sit, the one on thy right hand, and the other on the left, in thy kingdom.

22 But Jesus answered and said, Ye know not what ye ask. Are ye able to drink of the cup that I shall drink of, and to be baptized with the baptism that I am baptized with? They say unto him, We are able.

23 And he saith unto them, Ye shall drink indeed of my cup, and be baptized with the baptism that I am baptized with: but to sit on my right hand, and on my left, is not mine to give, but *it shall be given to them* for whom it is prepared of my [a]Father.

24 And when the ten heard *it,* they were moved with indignation against the two brethren.

25 But Jesus called them *unto him,* and said, Ye know that the princes of the Gentiles exercise dominion over them, and they that are great exercise authority upon them.

26 But it shall not be so among you: but whosoever will be [a]great among you, let him be your [b]minister;

27 And whosoever [a]will be chief among you, let him be your [b]servant:

28 Even as the [a]Son of man came not to be ministered unto, but to minister, and to [b]give his life a [c]ransom for many.

29 And as they departed from Jericho, a great multitude followed him.

30 ¶ And, behold, two [a]blind men

8*a* D&C 39:13.
b TG Wages.
16*a* Jacob 5:63.
b TG Called of God; Foreordination.
18*a* TG Jesus Christ, Betrayal of.
b TG Jesus Christ, Death of.
19*a* TG Mocking.
b TG Jesus Christ, Crucifixion of; Martyrdom.
c TG Jesus Christ, Resurrection.
23*a* TG Godhead.
26*a* TG Leadership.
b TG Priesthood, Magnifying Callings within.
27*a* GR desires to be.
b TG Humility; Self-Sacrifice; Servant; Service.
28*a* Moses 6:57.
b TG God, Gifts of.
c D&C 138:2 (2–4). TG Jesus Christ, Atonement through; Jesus Christ, Redeemer; Redemption.
30*a* Matt. 9:28 (28–31); Mark 10:46 (46–52); John 9:1 (1–4); Mosiah 3:5; 3 Ne. 17:9 (7–10); D&C 84:69.

sitting by the way side, when they
heard that Jesus passed by, cried
out, saying, Have mercy on us, O
Lord, *thou* Son of David.
31 And the multitude rebuked
them, because they should hold
their peace: but they cried the more,
saying, Have mercy on us, O Lord,
thou Son of David.
32 And Jesus stood still, and called
them, and said, What will ye that I
shall do unto you?
33 They say unto him, Lord, that
our eyes may be opened.
34 So Jesus had [a]compassion *on*
them, and touched their eyes: and
immediately their eyes received
[b]sight, and they followed him.

CHAPTER 21

Jesus rides in triumph into Jerusalem—He cleanses the temple, curses the fig tree, and discusses authority—He gives the parables of the two sons and the wicked husbandmen.

AND when they drew nigh unto Jerusalem, and were come to Bethphage, unto the mount of Olives,
then sent Jesus two disciples,
2 Saying unto them, Go into the village [a]over against you, and straightway ye shall find an ass tied, and a
colt with her: loose *them,* and bring
them unto me.
3 And if any *man* say ought unto
you, ye shall say, The Lord hath
need of them; and straightway he
will send them.
4 All this was done, that it might
be fulfilled which was spoken by
the prophet, saying,
5 Tell ye the daughter of Sion, Behold, thy [a]King cometh unto thee,
meek, and sitting upon an ass, and
a colt the foal of an ass.
6 And the disciples went, and did
as Jesus commanded them,
7 [a]And brought the ass, and the
colt, and put on them their clothes,
and they set *him* thereon.
8 And a very great multitude
spread their garments in the way;
others cut down branches from the
trees, and strawed *them* in the way.
9 And the multitudes that went
before, and that followed, cried,
saying, [a]Hosanna to the Son of
David: [b]Blessed *is* he that cometh
in the name of the Lord; Hosanna in
the highest.
10 And when he was come into
Jerusalem, all the city was moved,
saying, Who is this?
11 And the [a]multitude said, This
is Jesus the prophet of Nazareth of
Galilee.
12 ¶ And Jesus went into the temple
of God, and cast out all them that
sold and bought in the temple, and
overthrew the tables of the moneychangers, and the seats of them that
sold doves,
13 And said unto them, It is written, My [a]house shall be called the
house of [b]prayer; but ye have made
it a [c]den of thieves.
14 And the blind and the lame
came to him in the temple; and he
healed them.
15 And when the chief priests and
scribes saw the wonderful things
that he did, and the [a]children crying
in the temple, and saying, Hosanna
to the Son of David; they were sore
displeased,
16 And said unto him, Hearest thou
what these say? And Jesus saith unto
them, Yea; have ye never read, Out
of the mouth of babes and sucklings
thou hast perfected praise?
17 ¶ And he left them, and went
out of the city into Bethany; and
he lodged there.
18 Now in the morning as he returned into the city, he hungered.

34*a* TG Compassion.
b TG Sight.
21 2*a* GR in front of you.
5*a* Isa. 62:11; Zech. 9:9 (9–11).
7*a* JST Matt. 21:5 . . . and brought the *colt,* and put on *it* their clothes; *and Jesus took the colt and sat* thereon; *and they followed him.*
9*a* Luke 19:40.
b Ps. 118:25–26.
11*a* GR crowds kept saying.
13*a* Ps. 27:4. TG Temple.
b TG Prayer.
c Jer. 7:11.
15*a* JST Matt. 21:13 . . . children *of the kingdom* crying . . .

19 And when he saw a fig tree [a]in
the way, he came to it, and found
nothing thereon, but leaves only,
and said unto it, Let no [b]fruit grow
on thee henceforward for ever. And
[c]presently the fig tree withered
away.
20 And when the disciples saw *it*,
they marvelled, saying, How soon
is the fig tree withered away!
21 Jesus answered and said unto
them, Verily I say unto you, If ye
have [a]faith, and [b]doubt not, ye shall
not only do this *which is done* to the
fig tree, but also if ye shall say unto
this [c]mountain, Be thou removed,
and be thou cast into the sea; it
shall be done.
22 And all [a]things, whatsoever ye
shall [b]ask in [c]prayer, believing,
ye shall receive.
23 ¶ And when he was come into
the temple, the chief priests and the
elders of the people came unto him
as he was teaching, and said, By
what [a]authority doest thou these
things? and who gave thee this
authority?
24 And Jesus answered and said
unto them, I also will ask you one
thing, which if ye tell me, I in like
wise will tell you by what [a]author-
ity I do these things.
25 The baptism of John, whence
was it? from heaven, or of men? And
they reasoned with themselves, saying, If we shall say, From heaven;
he will say unto us, Why did ye not
then believe him?
26 But if we shall say, Of men; we
fear the people; for all hold John
as a [a]prophet.
27 And they answered Jesus, and
said, We cannot tell. And he said
unto them, Neither tell I you by
what authority I do these things.
28 ¶ But what think ye? A *certain*
man had two sons; and he came to
the first, and said, Son, go [a]work to
day in my vineyard.
29 He answered and said, [a]I will
not: but afterward he repented,
and went.
30 And he came to the second, and
said likewise. And he answered
and said, I *go*, sir: and [a]went [b]not.
31 Whether of them twain did the
will of *his* father? They say unto
him, The first. Jesus saith unto them,
Verily I say unto you, That the publicans and the harlots go into the
kingdom of God before you.
32 For John came unto you in the
way of [a]righteousness, and ye [b]be-
lieved him not: but the [c]publicans
and the harlots believed him: [d]and
ye, when ye had seen *it*, repented
not afterward, that ye might believe him.
33 ¶ [a]Hear another parable: There
was a certain householder, which
planted a vineyard, and hedged it
round about, and digged a winepress
in it, and built a tower, and let it
out to [b]husbandmen, and went into
a far country:
34 And when the time of the fruit
drew near, he sent his servants to
the husbandmen, that they might
receive the fruits of it.

19*a* GR by the road.
b TG Vineyard of the Lord.
c GR immediately; see also Mark 11:20–24.
21*a* TG Faith.
b TG Doubt.
c TG God, Power of.
22*a* TG Blessing.
b 3 Ne. 18:20; Morm. 9:21.
c TG Prayer.
23*a* TG Authority.
24*a* TG Jesus Christ, Authority of.
26*a* Matt. 11:9; 14:5; Luke 20:6.
28*a* Jacob 5:71 (70–71).
29*a* GR I don't desire to go.
30*a* TG Hypocrisy.
b D&C 41:5.
32*a* TG Righteousness.
b TG Unbelief.
c Luke 3:12; 7:29 (28–30).
d JST Matt. 21:32–34 . . . and ye, *afterward*, when ye had seen *me*, repented not, that ye might believe him. *For he that believed not John concerning me, cannot believe me, except he first repent. And except ye repent, the preaching of John shall condemn you in the day of judgment* . . .
33*a* JST Matt. 21:34–35 . . . *And again,* hear another parable; *for unto you that believe not, I speak in parables; that your unrighteousness may be rewarded unto you. Behold,* there was . . .
b TG Stewardship; Watchman.

35 And the husbandmen took his
[a]servants, and [b]beat one, and killed
another, and stoned another.
36 Again, he sent other servants
more than the first: and they did
unto them likewise.
37 But last of all he sent unto them
his son, saying, They will reverence
my son.
38 But when the husbandmen saw
the son, they said among themselves,
This is the [a]heir; come, let us kill him,
and let us seize on his inheritance.
39 And they caught him, and cast
him out of the vineyard, and slew *him*.
40 When the lord therefore of the
vineyard cometh, what will he do
unto those husbandmen?
41 They say unto him, He will
miserably destroy those wicked
men, and will let out *his* [a]vineyard
unto other husbandmen, which
shall render him the fruits in their
seasons.
42 Jesus saith unto them, Did ye
never read in the scriptures, The
[a]stone which the builders [b]rejected,
the same is become the head of the
[c]corner: this is the Lord's doing, and
it is marvellous in our eyes?
43 Therefore say I unto you, The
[a]kingdom of God shall be [b]taken
from you, and [c]given to a [d]nation
bringing forth the fruits thereof.
44 [a]And whosoever shall fall on
this stone shall be broken: but on
whomsoever it shall fall, it will grind
him to powder.
45 [a]And when the chief priests and
Pharisees had heard his parables,
they perceived that he spake of
them.
46 But when they sought to lay
hands on him, they feared the multitude, because they took him for a
prophet.

CHAPTER 22

Jesus gives the parable of the marriage of the king's son—Pay tribute to Cæsar and to God—Worldly marriages endure in this life only—The first commandment is to love the Lord—Jesus asks, What think ye of Christ?

AND Jesus answered and spake unto
them again by parables, and said,
2 The kingdom of heaven is like
unto a certain king, which [a]made
a [b]marriage for his son,
3 And sent forth his servants to
call them that were bidden to the
wedding: and [a]they would not come.
4 Again, he sent forth other servants, saying, Tell them which are
bidden, Behold, I have prepared my
dinner: my oxen and *my* fatlings
are killed, and all things *are* ready:
come unto the marriage.
5 But they made light of *it*, and
went their ways, one to his farm,
another to his merchandise:
6 And the remnant took his servants, and entreated *them* spitefully,
and slew *them*.
7 But when the king heard *thereof*,
he was wroth: and he sent forth his
armies, and destroyed those murderers, and burned up their city.
8 Then saith he to his servants, The
wedding is ready, but they which
were bidden were not worthy.
9 Go ye therefore into the highways, and as many as ye shall find,
bid to the marriage.
10 So those servants went out into
the highways, and [a]gathered together all as many as they found,

35*a* Matt. 23:30 (29–38).
b TG Prophets, Rejection of.
38*a* John 11:53 (47–53); Heb. 1:2.
41*a* TG Vineyard of the Lord.
42*a* TG Cornerstone; Jesus Christ, Prophecies about; Rock.
b Luke 9:22; 1 Pet. 2:7.
c Zech. 10:4.
43*a* Isa. 5:5 (1–7); Luke 14:24 (21–24); Acts 13:46; 1 Ne. 13:26; D&C 90:3 (1–5).
b Dan. 2:44.
c Isa. 48:11.
d TG Nations.
44*a* Isa. 8:14 (13–15); Luke 2:34; Rom. 9:32 (28–33); 1 Pet. 2:8 (6–8).
45*a* JST Matt. 21:47–56 (Appendix).
22 2*a* GR gave a wedding celebration.
b Luke 5:34; Rev. 19:7 (7–9); 21:2; D&C 65:3.
3*a* GR they did not want to come.
10*a* Matt. 13:47 (47–53).

both bad and good: and the wedding
was furnished with guests.
11 ¶ And when the king came in
to see the guests, he saw there a
man which had not on a wedding
[a]garment:
12 And he saith unto him, Friend,
how camest thou in hither not having a wedding garment? And he was
speechless.
13 Then said the king to the servants, Bind him hand and foot,
and take him away, and cast *him*
into [a]outer darkness; there shall
be weeping and gnashing of teeth.
14 For many are [a]called, but few
are [b]chosen.
15 ¶ Then went the Pharisees, and
took counsel how they might [a]en-
tangle him in *his* talk.
16 And they sent out unto him
their disciples with the Herodians,
saying, Master, we know that thou
art true, and teachest the way of
God in truth, [a]neither carest thou
for any *man:* for thou [b]regardest not
the person of men.
17 Tell us therefore, What thinkest
thou? Is it [a]lawful to give tribute
unto Cæsar, or not?
18 But Jesus perceived their wickedness, and said, Why [a]tempt ye me,
ye hypocrites?
19 Shew me the tribute money.
And they brought unto him a penny.
20 And he saith unto them, Whose
is this image and superscription?
21 They say unto him, Cæsar's.
Then saith he unto them, [a]Render
therefore unto [b]Cæsar the things
which are Cæsar's; and unto God
the things that are God's.
22 When they had heard *these*
words, they marvelled, and left him,
and went their way.
23 ¶ The same day came to him
the [a]Sadducees, which say that there
is no resurrection, and asked him,
24 Saying, Master, Moses said, If
a man die, having no children, his
[a]brother shall [b]marry his wife, and
raise up seed unto his brother.
25 Now there were with us seven
brethren: and the first, when he
had married a wife, deceased, and,
having no issue, left his wife unto
his brother:
26 Likewise the second also, and
the third, unto the seventh.
27 And last of all the woman died
also.
28 Therefore in the resurrection
whose wife shall she be of the seven?
for they all had her.
29 Jesus answered and said unto
them, Ye do err, not knowing the
[a]scriptures, nor the [b]power of God.
30 For in the [a]resurrection they
neither [b]marry, nor are given in
marriage, but are as the [c]angels of
God in heaven.
31 But as touching the resurrection of the dead, have ye not read
that which was spoken unto you by
God, saying,
32 I am the [a]God of Abraham, and
the God of Isaac, and the God of Jacob? God is not the God of the dead,
but of the living.
33 And when the multitude heard
this, they were astonished at his
doctrine.
34 ¶ But when the Pharisees had
heard that he had put the Sadducees to silence, they were gathered
together.

11*a* Rev. 19:8.
13*a* Matt. 8:12 (11–12); D&C 77:8; 133:72 (71–73).
14*a* D&C 121:34 (34–40).
b JST Matt. 22:14 . . . chosen; *wherefore all do not have on the wedding garment.*
15*a* Mark 12:13 (13–17); Luke 11:54; 20:20 (19–26).
16*a* IE you court no man's favor.
b Prov. 24:23.
17*a* D&C 58:22 (20–23).
18*a* GR are you testing. TG Test.
21*a* TG Citizenship.
b TG Governments.
23*a* Matt. 16:12 (1, 6, 11–12); Acts 23:8.
24*a* Deut. 25:5; Mark 12:19.
b Ruth 3:13.
29*a* D&C 138:1 (1–4). TG Jesus Christ, Teaching Mode of; Scriptures, Study of.
b TG God, Power of.
30*a* TG Resurrection.
b TG Marriage, Marry; Marriage, Temporal.
c D&C 131:4 (1–4); 132:16 (15–17).
32*a* Gen. 32:9; 1 Ne. 19:10; D&C 136:21.

35 Then one of them, *which was* a lawyer, asked *him a question,* [a]tempting him, and saying,
36 Master, which *is* the great commandment in the law?
37 Jesus said unto him, Thou shalt [a]love the Lord thy God with all thy [b]heart, and with all thy soul, and with all thy [c]mind.
38 This is the first and great [a]commandment.
39 And the second *is* like unto it, Thou shalt [a]love thy neighbour as thyself.
40 On these two commandments hang all the [a]law and the prophets.
41 ¶ While the Pharisees were gathered together, Jesus asked them,
42 Saying, What think ye of Christ? whose son is he? They say unto him, *The Son* of [a]David.
43 He saith unto them, How then doth David in spirit call him Lord, saying,
44 The LORD said unto my Lord, Sit thou on my right hand, till I make thine enemies thy footstool?
45 If David then call him Lord, how is he his son?
46 And no man was able to answer him a word, neither [a]durst any *man* from that day forth ask him any more *questions.*

CHAPTER 23

Jesus pronounces woes upon the scribes and Pharisees—They will be held responsible for killing the prophets—They will not escape the damnation of hell.

THEN spake Jesus to the multitude, and to his disciples,
2 Saying, The [a]scribes and the Pharisees sit in Moses' [b]seat:
3 All therefore whatsoever they bid you observe, *that* observe and do; but do not ye after their works: for they say, and do not.
4 For they bind heavy burdens and grievous to be borne, and lay *them* on men's shoulders; but they *themselves* will not move them with one of their fingers.
5 But all their works they do for to be seen of men: they [a]make broad their [b]phylacteries, and enlarge the [c]borders of their garments,
6 And love the [a]uppermost rooms at feasts, and the chief seats in the synagogues,
7 And greetings in the markets, and to be called of men, Rabbi, [a]Rabbi.
8 But be not ye called [a]Rabbi: for one is your [b]Master, *even* Christ; and all ye are brethren.
9 [a]And call no *man* your father upon the earth: for one is your Father, which is in heaven.
10 Neither be ye called masters: for one is your Master, [a]*even* Christ.
11 But he that is [a]greatest among you shall be your [b]servant.
12 And whosoever shall [a]exalt himself shall be [b]abased; and he that shall [c]humble himself shall be exalted.

35*a* TG Test.
37*a* TG Dedication; God, Love of; Love.
b TG Heart.
c TG Mind.
38*a* TG Commandments of God.
39*a* TG Love.
40*a* Mark 12:33 (13–37); Rom. 13:10 (8–10). TG Law of Moses.
42*a* TG Jesus Christ, Davidic Descent of.
46*a* GR dared.
23 2*a* TG Scribe.
b The Greek word connotes a chair of judgment and instruction.
5*a* GR enlarge their phylacteries.
b Ex. 13:9 (9, 16); Deut. 6:8.
c Num. 15:38.
6*a* Luke 11:43; 14:7.
7*a* JST Matt. 23:4 . . . Rabbi, *(which is master).*
8*a* Hebrew and Aramaic: Master, or, My master.
b Col. 4:1 (1–11).
9*a* JST Matt. 23:6 And call no *one* your *creator* upon the earth, *or your heavenly Father;* for one is your *creator and heavenly* Father, *even he who* is in heaven.
10*a* JST Matt. 23:7 . . . even *he whom your heavenly Father sent, which is Christ; for he hath sent him among you that ye might have life.*
11*a* Mark 10:44 (42–45); Luke 22:24 (24–30). TG Leadership.
b TG Servant.
12*a* TG Haughtiness; Pride.
b D&C 49:10.
c James 1:9 (8–16); D&C 112:3; 124:114. TG Humility.

13 ¶ But woe unto you, [a]scribes and
[b]Pharisees, [c]hypocrites! for ye shut
up the kingdom of heaven against
men: for ye neither go in *yourselves,*
neither suffer ye them that are entering to go in.
14 Woe unto you, scribes and
Pharisees, hypocrites! for ye [a]devour
widows' houses, and for a pretence
make long prayer: therefore ye shall
receive the greater [b]damnation.
15 Woe unto you, scribes and Pharisees, hypocrites! for ye compass sea
and land to make one proselyte,
and when he is made, ye make him
twofold more the child of hell [a]than
yourselves.
16 Woe unto you, *ye* [a]blind guides,
which say, Whosoever shall swear
by the temple, it is nothing; but
whosoever shall swear by the gold
of the temple, he is a debtor!
17 *Ye* fools and blind: for whether
is greater, the gold, or the temple
that sanctifieth the gold?
18 And, Whosoever shall swear
by the altar, it is nothing; but whosoever sweareth by the gift that is
upon it, he is guilty.
19 *Ye* fools and blind: for whether
is greater, the gift, or the altar that
sanctifieth the gift?
20 Whoso therefore shall swear by
the altar, sweareth by it, and by all
things thereon.
21 And whoso shall swear by the
temple, sweareth by it, and by him
that dwelleth therein.
22 And he that shall swear by
heaven, sweareth by the throne of
God, and by him that sitteth thereon.
23 Woe unto you, scribes and Pharisees, [a]hypocrites! for ye pay [b]tithe of
mint and [c]anise and cummin, and
have [d]omitted the weightier *matters*
of the law, [e]judgment, [f]mercy, and
faith: these ought ye to have done,
and not to leave the other undone.
24 *Ye* blind guides, which strain at
a gnat, and swallow a [a]camel.
25 Woe unto you, scribes and Pharisees, hypocrites! for ye make clean
the outside of the cup and of the
platter, but within they are full of
[a]extortion and [b]excess.
26 *Thou* blind Pharisee, [a]cleanse
first that *which is* within the cup
and platter, that the outside of them
may be clean also.
27 Woe unto you, scribes and Pharisees, hypocrites! for ye are like unto
[a]whited [b]sepulchres, which indeed
appear [c]beautiful outward, but are
within full of dead *men's* bones, and
of all [d]uncleanness.
28 Even so ye also outwardly appear
[a]righteous unto men, but within ye
are full of [b]hypocrisy and iniquity.
29 Woe unto you, scribes and
Pharisees, hypocrites! because ye
build the tombs of the prophets,
and garnish the sepulchres of the
righteous,
30 And say, If we had been in the
days of our fathers, we would not
have been partakers with them in
the blood of the [a]prophets.
31 Wherefore ye be witnesses unto
yourselves, that ye are the children
of them which [a]killed the [b]prophets.
32 Fill ye up then the [a]measure of
your [b]fathers.

13*a* TG Scribe.
b TG Apostasy of Israel.
c GR actors.
14*a* TG Injustice.
b TG Damnation.
15*a* JST Matt. 23:12 . . . than *he was before, like unto* yourselves.
16*a* TG Spiritual Blindness.
23*a* TG Hypocrisy.
b TG Tithing.
c GR dill.
d GR abandoned.
e TG Justice.
f TG Mercy.
24*a* JST Matt. 23:21 . . . camel; *who make yourselves appear unto men that ye would not commit the least sin, and yet ye yourselves, transgress the whole law.*
25*a* GR rapacity, greediness.
b GR self-indulgence, lack of self-control. TG Temperance.
26*a* TG Purification; Wash.
27*a* GR whitewashed tombs. Acts 23:3.
b Luke 11:44.
c TG Beauty.
d TG Cleanliness.
28*a* D&C 10:37.
b TG Guile.
30*a* Matt. 21:35 (33–42).
31*a* TG Martyrdom.
b TG Prophets, Rejection of.
32*a* Judg. 2:19.
b Acts 7:51 (51–52); Hel. 13:25 (25–29).

33 Ye serpents, *ye* [a]generation of
vipers, how can ye escape the [b]dam-
nation of hell?
34 ¶ Wherefore, behold, I send unto
you [a]prophets, and wise men, and
[b]scribes: and *some* of them ye shall
kill and crucify; and *some* of them
shall ye scourge in your synagogues,
and persecute *them* from city to city:
35 That upon you may come all
the righteous [a]blood shed upon the
earth, from the blood of [b]righteous
Abel unto the blood of Zacharias
son of Barachias, whom ye slew
between the [c]temple and the altar.
36 Verily I say unto you, All these
things shall come upon this [a]gen-
eration.
37 O [a]Jerusalem, Jerusalem, *thou*
that [b]killest the prophets, and stonest them which are sent unto thee,
how often [c]would I have [d]gathered
thy children together, even as a hen
gathereth her chickens under *her*
wings, and ye [e]would not!
38 Behold, your house is left unto
you [a]desolate.
39 [a]For I say unto you, Ye shall not
see me henceforth, till ye shall say,
[b]Blessed *is* he that cometh in the
name of the Lord.

CHAPTER 24

Jesus foretells the doom of Jerusalem and the destruction of the temple—Great calamities will precede His Second Coming—He gives the parable of the fig tree.

AND Jesus went out, and departed
from the temple: and his disciples
came to *him* for to [a]shew him the
buildings of the [b]temple.
2 And Jesus said unto them, [a]See
ye not all these things? verily I say
unto you, There shall not be left
here one [b]stone upon another, that
shall not be thrown down.
3 ¶ And as he sat upon the mount
of Olives, the disciples came unto
him privately, saying, Tell us, when
shall these things be? and what *shall*
be the [a]sign of thy coming, and of
the end of the [b]world?
4 And Jesus answered and said
unto them, Take heed that no man
[a]deceive you.
5 For many shall come in my
[a]name, saying, I am [b]Christ; and
shall [c]deceive many.
6 And ye shall hear of [a]wars and
rumours of wars: see that ye be not
[b]troubled: for all *these things* must
come to pass, but the end is not yet.
7 For [a]nation shall rise against
nation, and kingdom against kingdom: and there shall be [b]famines,
and pestilences, and earthquakes,
in divers places.
8 All these *are* the beginning of
[a]sorrows.

33*a* Matt. 3:7; 12:34.
b TG Damnation; Punish.
34*a* D&C 1:38; 43:25.
b TG Scribe.
35*a* TG Martyrdom.
b TG Righteousness.
c Luke 11:51.
36*a* JST Matt. 23:33–35 . . . generation. Ye *bear testimony against your fathers, when ye, yourselves, are partakers of the same wickedness. Behold your fathers did it through ignorance, but ye do not; wherefore, their sins shall be upon your heads.*
37*a* TG Jerusalem.
b TG Prophets, Rejection of.
c GR have I desired to gather.
d 3 Ne. 10:6 (4–6); D&C 29:2; 43:24 (24–25). TG Israel, Gathering of.
e D&C 138:21 (21–22). TG Rebellion; Stubbornness.
38*a* Ps. 69:25; Jer. 12:7; 22:5.
39*a* JS—M 1:1.
b Ps. 118:26.
24 1*a* JS—M 1:2.
b D&C 45:20 (15–21). TG Temple.
2*a* D&C 45:18.
b Luke 19:44 (41–44); JS—M 1:3 (1–55).
3*a* Luke 21:7 (7–36); D&C 45:16 (16–75).
b JS—M 1:4 adds "or the destruction of the wicked, which is the end of the world." D&C 45:22. TG Last Days; World, End of.
4*a* Col. 2:18 (16–23); D&C 49:23 (22–24). TG Lying.
5*a* TG Name.
b TG False Christs.
c Mark 13:6. TG Apostasy of the Early Christian Church.
6*a* TG War.
b GR frightened. D&C 45:35 (34–35).
7*a* TG Last Days; Nations.
b TG Drought.
8*a* TG Sorrow.

9 Then shall they deliver you up
to be afflicted, and shall [a]kill you:
and ye shall be [b]hated of all nations
[c]for my name's sake.
10 And then shall many be [a]of-
fended, and shall betray one another, and shall hate one another.
11 And many [a]false prophets shall
rise, and shall deceive many.
12 And because [a]iniquity shall
abound, the love of many shall
wax [b]cold.
13 But he that shall [a]endure unto
the end, the same shall be saved.
14 And this [a]gospel of the [b]kingdom
shall be preached in all the world
for a witness unto all nations; and
then shall the [c]end come.
15 When ye therefore shall see the
[a]abomination of desolation, spoken
of by Daniel the prophet, stand in
the [b]holy place, (whoso readeth, let
him [c]understand:)
16 Then let them which be in
Judæa [a]flee into the mountains:
17 Let him which is on the housetop not come down to take any thing
out of his house:
18 Neither let him which is in the
field return back to take his clothes.
19 And [a]woe unto them that are
with child, and to them that give
suck in those days!
20 But pray ye that your flight be
not in the winter, neither on the
sabbath day:
21 For then shall be great [a]trib-
ulation, such as was not since the
beginning of the world to this time,
no, nor ever shall be.
22 And except those days should be
shortened, there should no flesh be
saved: but for the elect's sake those
[a]days shall be shortened.
23 Then if any man shall say unto
you, Lo, here *is* Christ, or there; [a]be-
lieve *it* not.
24 For there shall arise [a]false
[b]Christs, and [c]false prophets, and
shall shew great [d]signs and wonders;
insomuch that, if *it were* possible,
they shall [e]deceive the very [f]elect.
25 Behold, I have told you before.
26 Wherefore if they shall say unto
you, Behold, he is in the desert; go
not forth: behold, *he is* in the [a]secret
chambers; believe *it* not.
27 For as the [a]lightning cometh out
of the [b]east, and shineth even unto
the west; so shall also the coming
of the Son of man be.
28 For wheresoever the carcase is,
there will the eagles be [a]gathered
together.
29 ¶ Immediately after the tribulation of those [a]days shall the [b]sun
be [c]darkened, and the moon shall
not give her light, and the stars shall
fall from heaven, and the powers of
the heavens shall be shaken:
30 And then shall appear the [a]sign
of the Son of man in [b]heaven: and
then shall all the tribes of the earth
[c]mourn, and they shall see the [d]Son

9*a* TG Martyrdom.
b TG Persecution.
c GR on account of my name.
10*a* Isa. 8:14 (14–15); Matt. 11:6.
11*a* TG Apostasy of the Early Christian Church; False Prophets.
12*a* D&C 45:27.
b TG Apostasy of Individuals.
13*a* TG Perseverance; Steadfastness.
14*a* TG Gospel; Restoration of the Gospel.
b TG Kingdom of God, on Earth.
c D&C 29:23; 43:31.
15*a* TG Abomination of Desolation.
b TG Jerusalem.
c D&C 57:9.
16*a* TG Israel, Scattering of.
19*a* Luke 23:29.
21*a* JS—M 1:18. TG Tribulation.
22*a* TG Time.
23*a* D&C 49:22.
24*a* TG Apostasy of the Early Christian Church.
b TG False Christs.
c TG False Prophets.
d Rev. 16:14 (13–14). TG Signs; Sign Seekers.
e Rev. 13:14 (11–18). TG Deceit.
f D&C 29:7 (7–8); 84:34 (33–34).
26*a* D&C 49:22 (22–23).
27*a* D&C 45:36 (36–44).
b Ezek. 43:2.
28*a* D&C 29:8 (7–8); JS—M 1:27.
29*a* TG Day of the Lord.
b TG Astronomy.
c Isa. 13:10; Ezek. 32:7; 34:12 (11–19); Joel 2:10; Rev. 6:12.
30*a* D&C 88:93. TG Jesus Christ, Second Coming.
b TG Heaven.
c Zech. 12:12; Rev. 1:7 (7–8).
d TG Jesus Christ, Son of Man.

of man coming in the clouds of
heaven with [e]power and great [f]glory.
31 And he shall send his [a]angels
with a great sound of a [b]trumpet,
and they shall gather together his
[c]elect from the four winds, from one
end of [d]heaven to the other.
32 Now learn a parable of the [a]fig
tree; When his branch is yet tender,
and putteth forth leaves, ye know
that summer *is* nigh:
33 So likewise ye, when ye shall
see all these things, know that [a]it
is near, *even* at the [b]doors.
34 Verily I say unto you, This [a]gen-
eration shall not pass, till all these
[b]things be [c]fulfilled.
35 Heaven and earth shall [a]pass
away, but my [b]words shall not
[c]pass away.
36 ¶ But of that [a]day and [b]hour
knoweth no *man,* no, not the [c]an-
gels of heaven, but my Father only.
37 But as the days of [a]Noe *were,*
so shall also the coming of the Son
of man be.
38 For as in the days that were
before the [a]flood they were eating
and drinking, marrying and giving
in marriage, until the day that Noe
entered into the ark,
39 And knew not until the flood
came, and took them all away; so
shall also the coming of the Son of
man be.
40 Then shall two be in the field;
the one shall be taken, and the
other left.
41 Two *women shall be* grinding at
the mill; the one shall be taken, and
the other left.
42 ¶ [a]Watch therefore: for ye know
not what hour your Lord doth
come.
43 But know this, that if the goodman of the house had known in
what watch the thief would come,
he would have watched, and would
not have suffered his house to be
[a]broken up.
44 Therefore be ye also [a]ready: for
in such an [b]hour [c]as ye think not
the Son of man cometh.
45 Who then is a [a]faithful and [b]wise
[c]servant, whom his lord hath made
ruler over his household, to give
them meat in due season?
46 Blessed *is* that [a]servant, whom
his lord when he cometh shall find
so doing.
47 Verily I say unto you, That he
shall make him ruler over all his
goods.
48 But and if that evil servant shall
say in his heart, My lord [a]delayeth
his coming;
49 And shall begin to smite *his* fellowservants, and to eat and drink
with the drunken;
50 The lord of that servant shall
come in a day when he looketh not
for *him,* and in an hour that he is
not aware of,
51 And shall cut him asunder, and
appoint *him* his portion with the
hypocrites: there shall be weeping
and gnashing of teeth.

CHAPTER 25

Jesus gives the parables of the ten virgins, the talents, and the sheep and the goats.

30*e* TG Jesus Christ, Power of.
f TG Jesus Christ, Glory of.
31*a* TG Angels.
b Isa. 27:13; 1 Thes. 4:16; D&C 49:23 (23–28).
c Ps. 147:2 (1–20); JS—M 1:27. TG Election.
d Deut. 30:4.
32*a* D&C 35:16.
33*a* GR He is near.
b D&C 45:63.
34*a* JS—M 1:34 (31–35).
b Isa. 10:22 (21–34); D&C 1:7.
c D&C 45:21.
35*a* D&C 29:23 (22–29).
b D&C 1:38 (37–39).
c Josh. 21:45; 1 Kgs. 8:56; D&C 45:23.
36*a* D&C 39:21; 49:7.
b TG Jesus Christ, Second Coming.
c TG Angels.
37*a* IE Noah. Gen. 7:1; Luke 17:27 (26–27); 3 Ne. 22:9.
38*a* TG Worldliness.
42*a* TG Millennium, Preparing a People for; Watch.
43*a* Ex. 22:2 (1–4).
44*a* TG Procrastination.
b Luke 12:40; D&C 45:2; 51:20.
c GR when you do not expect Him.
45*a* D&C 51:19.
b D&C 72:4.
c D&C 58:26 (26–29); 84:86 (85–86); 107:100 (99–100). TG Stewardship.
46*a* TG Servant.
48*a* D&C 45:26.

[a]THEN shall the kingdom of heaven
be likened unto ten [b]virgins, which
took their [c]lamps, and went forth to
meet the bridegroom.
2 And five of them were wise, and
five *were* foolish.
3 They that *were* foolish took their
lamps, and took no oil with them:
4 But the wise took oil in their
vessels with their lamps.
5 While the bridegroom tarried,
they all [a]slumbered and [b]slept.
6 And at midnight there was a
cry made, Behold, the [a]bridegroom
cometh; go ye out to meet him.
7 Then all those virgins arose, and
trimmed their [a]lamps.
8 And the foolish said unto the
wise, Give us of your oil; for our
lamps [a]are gone out.
9 But the wise answered, saying,
Not so; lest there be not enough for
us and you: but go ye rather to them
that sell, and buy for yourselves.
10 And while they went to buy,
the bridegroom came; and they
that were [a]ready went in with him
to the marriage: and the door was
[b]shut.
11 Afterward came also the other
virgins, saying, Lord, Lord, open
to us.
12 But he answered and said, [a]Ver-
ily I say unto you, I [b]know you not.
13 [a]Watch therefore, for ye know
neither the day nor the hour wherein
the Son of man cometh.
14 ¶ For *the kingdom of heaven is* as
a man travelling into a far country,
who called his own servants, and
delivered unto them his goods.
15 And unto one he [a]gave five [b]tal-
ents, to another two, and to another
one; to every man according to his
several ability; and straightway took
his journey.
16 Then he that had received the
five talents went and traded with
the same, and made *them* other five
talents.
17 And likewise he that *had received*
two, he also gained other two.
18 But he that had received one
went and digged in the earth, and
hid his lord's money.
19 After a long time the lord of
those servants cometh, and [a]reck-
oneth with them.
20 And so he that had received
five talents came and brought
other five talents, saying, Lord, thou
[a]deliveredst unto me five talents:
behold, I have gained beside them
five talents more.
21 His lord said unto him, Well
done, *thou* good and faithful [a]ser-
vant: thou hast been [b]faithful over
a few things, I will make thee [c]ruler
over many things: enter thou into
the [d]joy of thy lord.
22 He also that had received two
talents came and said, Lord, thou
deliveredst unto me two talents:
behold, I have gained two other
talents beside them.
23 His lord said unto him, Well
done, good and [a]faithful servant;
thou hast been faithful over a few
things, I will make thee ruler over
many things: enter thou into the
joy of thy lord.
24 Then he which had received
the one talent came and said, Lord,
I knew thee that thou art an [a]hard
man, reaping where thou hast not
sown, and gathering where thou
hast not strawed:
25 And I was [a]afraid, and went and

25 1*a* JST Matt. 25:1 *And* then, *at that day, before the Son of man comes,* the kingdom of . . .
b D&C 45:56 (56–59); 63:54.
c Lev. 24:2.
5*a* D&C 35:21.
b TG Sleep.
6*a* D&C 88:92; 133:10.
7*a* Luke 12:35; D&C 33:17.
8*a* GR are going out.
10*a* TG Millennium, Preparing a People for; Procrastination.
b GR locked.
12*a* JST Matt. 25:11 . . . Verily I say unto you, Ye know *me* not.
b Matt. 7:23.
13*a* TG Watch.
15*a* Mark 4:24 (23–25).
b TG Talents; Work, Value of.
19*a* GR settled accounts. D&C 72:3 (3–5).
20*a* GR entrustedst.
21*a* TG Servant.
b Luke 16:10; D&C 132:53.
c Rev. 3:21; D&C 132:20. TG Leadership; Stewardship.
d TG Joy.
23*a* D&C 52:13. TG Trustworthiness.
24*a* GR strict.
25*a* D&C 60:2 (2–3, 13).

hid thy talent in the earth: lo, *there* thou hast *that is* thine.

26 His lord answered and said unto him, *Thou* wicked and [a]slothful servant, thou knewest that I [b]reap where I sowed not, and gather where I have not strawed:

27 Thou oughtest therefore to have put my money to the exchangers, and *then* at my coming I should have received mine own with [a]usury.

28 Take therefore the [a]talent from him, and give *it* unto him which hath ten talents.

29 For unto every one that hath shall be [a]given, and he shall have [b]abundance: but from him that hath not shall be [c]taken away even that which he hath.

30 And cast ye the unprofitable servant into outer darkness: there shall be weeping and gnashing of teeth.

31 ¶ When the [a]Son of man shall come in his [b]glory, and all the holy angels with him, then shall he sit upon the throne of his glory:

32 And before him shall be gathered all [a]nations: and he shall [b]separate them one from another, as a [c]shepherd divideth *his* [d]sheep from the goats:

33 And he shall set the sheep on his [a]right hand, but the goats on the left.

34 Then shall the King say unto them on his [a]right hand, Come, ye [b]blessed of my Father, [c]inherit the [d]kingdom prepared for you from the foundation of the world:

35 For I was an [a]hungred, and ye [b]gave me meat: I was thirsty, and ye gave me drink: I was a [c]stranger, and ye took me in:

36 Naked, and ye clothed me: I was sick, and ye [a]visited me: I was in [b]prison, and ye came unto me.

37 Then shall the righteous answer him, saying, Lord, when saw we thee an hungred, and fed *thee*? or thirsty, and gave *thee* drink?

38 When saw we thee a stranger, and took *thee* in? or naked, and clothed *thee*?

39 Or when saw we thee [a]sick, or in prison, and came unto thee?

40 And the King shall answer and say unto them, Verily I say unto you, Inasmuch as ye have [a]done *it* unto one of the [b]least of these my [c]brethren, ye have done *it* unto me.

41 Then shall he say also unto them on the [a]left hand, [b]Depart from me, ye [c]cursed, into everlasting [d]fire, [e]prepared for the devil and his angels:

42 For I was an [a]hungred, and ye gave me no meat: I was thirsty, and ye gave me no drink:

43 I was a stranger, and ye took me not in: naked, and ye clothed me not: sick, and in prison, and ye visited me not.

44 Then shall they also answer him, saying, Lord, when saw we thee an hungred, or athirst, or a stranger, or naked, or sick, or in prison, and did not minister unto thee?

45 Then shall he answer them, saying, Verily I say unto you, Inasmuch

26*a* TG Laziness.
b TG Harvest.
27*a* TG Usury.
28*a* D&C 82:18.
29*a* Matt. 13:12.
b D&C 82:3.
c Alma 12:11 (9–11); D&C 1:33; 60:3 (2–3).
31*a* TG Jesus Christ, Son of Man.
b TG Jesus Christ, Second Coming; Millennium.
32*a* TG Nations.
b TG Jesus Christ, Judge; Judgment, the Last; Separation.
c TG Shepherd.
d TG Sheep.
33*a* D&C 29:27.
34*a* Moses 7:56 (56–57).
b TG Blessing.
c TG Exaltation; Reward.
d Luke 12:32; Rev. 22:5.
35*a* TG Poor.
b TG Almsgiving; Generosity.
c TG Hospitality; Stranger.
36*a* GR took care of, cared for.
b Heb. 13:3.
39*a* TG Health.
40*a* Mosiah 2:17; D&C 42:38.
b TG Good Works; Neighbor; Poor.
c TG Welfare.
41*a* D&C 19:5.
b D&C 29:28.
c GR who have come under a curse. (See also 2 Ne. 9:16; D&C 76:31–38, 43–48.) TG Curse.
d TG Hell.
e GR which has been prepared.
42*a* Job 22:7 (6–7).

as ye did *it* not to one of the [a]least
of these, ye did *it* not to me.
46 And these shall go away into
[a]everlasting [b]punishment: but the
[c]righteous into [d]life [e]eternal.

CHAPTER 26

Jesus is anointed—He keeps the Pass-
over and institutes the sacrament—He
suffers in Gethsemane, is betrayed by
Judas, and is taken before Caiaphas—
Peter denies that he knows Jesus.

AND it came to pass, when Jesus had
finished all these sayings, he said
unto his disciples,
2 Ye know that after two days
is *the feast of* the [a]passover, and
the Son of man is [b]betrayed to be
[c]crucified.
3 Then assembled together the
chief priests, and the scribes, and
the elders of the people, unto the
palace of the high priest, who was
called [a]Caiaphas,
4 And [a]consulted that they might
take Jesus by [b]subtilty, and [c]kill
him.
5 But they said, Not on the feast
day, lest there be an [a]uproar among
the people.
6 ¶ Now when Jesus was in Bethany, in the house of Simon the leper,
7 There came unto him a woman
having an alabaster box of very precious [a]ointment, and poured it on
his head, as he sat *at meat.*
8 But when his disciples saw *it,*
they had indignation, saying, To
what purpose *is* this [a]waste?
9 For this ointment might have
been sold for much, and given to
the poor.
10 When Jesus understood *it,* he
said unto them, Why trouble ye
the woman? for she hath [a]wrought
a good work upon me.
11 For ye have the poor always
with you; but me ye have not always.
12 For in that she hath poured
this ointment on my body, she did
it [a]for my burial.
13 Verily I say unto you, Wheresoever this gospel shall be preached
in the whole world, *there* shall also
this, that this woman hath done, be
told for a memorial of her.
14 ¶ Then one of the twelve, called
Judas Iscariot, went unto the chief
priests,
15 And said *unto them,* What will
ye give me, and I will deliver him
unto you? And they covenanted
with him for [a]thirty pieces of silver.
16 And from that time he sought
opportunity to [a]betray him.
17 ¶ Now the first *day* of the *feast*
of [a]unleavened bread the disciples
came to Jesus, saying unto him,
Where wilt thou that we prepare
for thee to eat the [b]passover?
18 And he said, Go into the city [a]to
such a man, and say unto him, The
Master saith, My [b]time is at hand; I
will keep the passover at thy house
with my disciples.
19 And the disciples did as Jesus
had appointed them; and they made
ready the [a]passover.
20 Now when the even was come,
he sat down with the twelve.
21 And as they did eat, he said,
Verily I say unto you, that one of
you shall betray me.
22 And they were exceeding sorrowful, and began every one of them
to say unto him, Lord, is it I?
23 And he answered and said, He

45*a* Prov. 14:31.
46*a* D&C 19:11 (6–12).
b TG Damnation; Punish.
c TG Righteousness.
d TG Resurrection.
e TG Eternal Life.
26 2*a* TG Passover.
b TG Jesus Christ, Betrayal of.
c TG Martyrdom.
3*a* John 11:49 (47–52).
4*a* GR plotted.
b GR treachery, cunning. Matt. 27:20 (11–26).
c Mark 14:1 (1–2); Luke 22:2 (1–2).
5*a* TG Rioting and Reveling.
7*a* John 11:2.
8*a* TG Waste.
10*a* TG Benevolence.
12*a* GR to prepare me for my burial.
15*a* Ex. 21:32 (28–32).
16*a* TG Jesus Christ, Betrayal of.
17*a* TG Bread, Unleavened.
b TG Passover.
18*a* GR to a certain man.
b John 7:6.
19*a* Ex. 12:27 (1–51).

that dippeth *his* hand with me in
the dish, the same shall betray me.
24 The Son of man goeth as it is
[a]written of him: but woe unto that
man by whom the [b]Son of man is
betrayed! [c]it had been good for that
man if he had not been [d]born.
25 Then Judas, which betrayed
him, answered and said, Master, is it
I? He said unto him, Thou hast said.
26 ¶ [a]And as they were eating,
Jesus took [b]bread, [c]and blessed
it, and brake *it,* and gave *it* to the
disciples, and said, Take, eat; this
is my [d]body.
27 And he took the [a]cup, and gave
thanks, and gave *it* to them, saying,
[b]Drink ye all of it;
28 For this is my [a]blood of the new
[b]testament, which is shed for many
for the [c]remission of sins.
29 But I say unto you, I will not
[a]drink henceforth of this fruit of the
vine, until that day when I [b]drink
it new with you in my Father's
kingdom.
30 And when they had sung an
[a]hymn, they went out into the mount
of Olives.
31 Then saith Jesus unto them,
All ye shall be [a]offended because
of me this night: for it is written, I
will [b]smite the [c]shepherd, and the
sheep of the flock shall be scattered
abroad.
32 But after I am [a]risen again, I will
go before you into Galilee.
33 Peter answered and said unto
him, Though all *men* shall be offended because of thee, *yet* will I
never be [a]offended.
34 Jesus said unto him, Verily I
say unto thee, That this night, before the cock crow, thou shalt deny
me thrice.
35 Peter said unto him, Though I
should die with thee, yet will I not
deny thee. Likewise also said all
the disciples.
36 ¶ Then cometh Jesus with
them unto a place called [a]Gethsem-
ane, and saith unto the disciples,
Sit ye here, while I go and [b]pray
yonder.
37 And he took with him Peter
and the two sons of Zebedee, and
[a]began to be sorrowful and very
heavy.
38 Then saith he unto them, My
soul is [a]exceeding sorrowful, even
unto death: tarry ye here, and [b]watch
with me.
39 And he went a little further,
and fell on his face, and [a]prayed,
saying, O my [b]Father, if it be possible, let this [c]cup pass from me:
nevertheless not as I [d]will, but as
[e]thou [f]*wilt.*
40 And he cometh unto the disciples, and findeth them [a]asleep, and

---

24*a* TG Jesus Christ, Prophecies about.
b TG Jesus Christ, Son of Man.
c GR it would have been good.
d Luke 22:22; Acts 2:23.
26*a* JST Matt. 26:22, 24–25 (Appendix).
b TG Bread; Bread of Life; Jesus Christ, Types of, in Memory.
c JST Matt. 26:22 . . . and *brake* it, and *blessed* it, and gave to *his* disciples, and said, Take, eat; this is *in remembrance of* my body *which I give a ransom for you.*
d TG Sacrament.
27*a* 1 Cor. 10:16 (16–17).
b GR All of you drink from it. TG Sacrament.
28*a* Ex. 24:8 (3–8); Deut. 32:14; Heb. 9:16 (15–22). TG Jesus Christ, Atonement through.
b GR covenant. TG Covenants.
c TG Jesus Christ, Redeemer; Remission of Sins.
29*a* Mark 14:25; Luke 22:18.
b JST Matt. 26:26 . . . *shall come and* drink it . . . D&C 27:5 (5–14).
30*a* TG Singing.
31*a* TG Offense.
b GR strike, hit, slay.
c Zech. 13:7.
32*a* TG Jesus Christ, Resurrection.
33*a* Luke 22:33–34, 56–62.
36*a* TG Jesus Christ, Atonement through.
b Matt. 14:23; Luke 6:12; 9:28.
37*a* GR began to be distressed and troubled.
38*a* GR deeply grieved. TG Pain; Sorrow.
b GR stay awake.
39*a* Heb. 5:7. TG Prayer.
b TG God the Father, Elohim.
c Mark 14:36 (32–42); Mosiah 3:7; D&C 19:18 (16–19).
d GR wish, desire. Isa. 50:5. TG Agency.
e TG Godhead.
f TG Obedience; Self-Mastery.
40*a* TG Sleep.

saith unto Peter, What, [b]could ye not
watch with me one hour?
41 [a]Watch and [b]pray, that ye enter
not into [c]temptation: the spirit indeed *is* willing, but the flesh *is* weak.
42 He went away again the sec-
ond time, and prayed, saying, O
my Father, if this cup may not pass
away from me, except I drink it, thy
[a]will be done.
43 And he came and found them
asleep again: for their eyes were
heavy.
44 And he left them, and went
away again, and prayed the third
time, saying the same words.
45 Then cometh he to his disciples,
and saith unto them, Sleep on now,
and take *your* rest: behold, the hour
is at hand, and the Son of man is
[a]betrayed into the hands of sinners.
46 Rise, let us be going: behold,
he is at hand that doth betray me.
47 ¶ And while he yet spake, lo,
Judas, one of the twelve, came, and
with him a great multitude with
swords and staves, from the chief
priests and elders of the people.
48 Now he that betrayed him gave
them a sign, saying, Whomsoever
I shall kiss, that same is he: hold
him fast.
49 And [a]forthwith he came to
Jesus, and said, Hail, master; and
kissed him.
50 And Jesus said unto him, Friend,
wherefore art thou come? Then
came they, and laid hands on Jesus,
and took him.
51 And, behold, one of them which
were with Jesus stretched out *his*
hand, and drew his sword, and
struck a [a]servant of the high priest's,
and smote off his ear.
52 Then said Jesus unto him, Put
up again thy sword into his place:
for all they that take the sword shall
[a]perish with the sword.
53 Thinkest thou that I cannot
now pray to my Father, and he shall
presently give me more than twelve
legions of angels?
54 But how then shall the [a]scrip-
tures be fulfilled, that thus it must
be?
55 In that same hour said Jesus to
the multitudes, Are ye come out
as against a thief with swords and
staves for to take me? I sat daily
with you [a]teaching in the temple,
and ye laid no hold on me.
56 But all this was done, that the
scriptures of the prophets might
be fulfilled. Then all the disciples
forsook him, and fled.
57 ¶ And they that had laid hold
on Jesus led *him* away to [a]Caiaphas
the high priest, where the scribes
and the elders were assembled.
58 But Peter followed him afar off
unto the high priest's palace, and
went in, and sat with the servants,
to see the end.
59 Now the chief priests, and elders, and all the council, sought
false [a]witness against Jesus, [b]to put
him to death;
60 But found none: yea, though
many false witnesses came, *yet*
found they none. At the last came
two false [a]witnesses,
61 And said, This *fellow* said, I am
able to destroy the [a]temple of God,
and to build it in three days.
62 And the high priest arose, and
said unto him, Answerest thou nothing? what *is it which* these witness
against thee?
63 But Jesus [a]held his [b]peace.
And the high priest answered and

40*b* GR are you so powerless that you could not stay awake with me . . .
41*a* TG Watch.
b TG Prayer.
c TG Temptation.
42*a* Acts 21:14.
TG God, Will of.
45*a* TG Jesus Christ, Betrayal of.
49*a* GR immediately.
51*a* John 18:10.
52*a* TG Punish; Retribution.
54*a* 2 Ne. 9:7 (5–10); Mosiah 3:15 (11–17).
55*a* Luke 21:37; John 8:2 (1–2).
TG Teaching.
57*a* John 18:13 (13, 24).
TG Jesus Christ, Trials of.
59*a* TG Slander.
b GR so that they might put Him to death.
60*a* Deut. 19:15 (15–19).
61*a* Matt. 27:40; Mark 14:58; John 2:19 (18–22).
63*a* GR was silent, "kept silent."
b Isa. 53:7.

said unto him, I [c]adjure thee by
the [d]living God, that thou tell us
whether thou be the Christ, the
Son of God.
64 Jesus saith unto him, Thou hast
said: nevertheless I say unto you,
Hereafter shall ye see the [a]Son of
man sitting on the right hand of
[b]power, and [c]coming in the clouds
of heaven.
65 Then the high priest rent his
clothes, saying, He hath spoken
[a]blasphemy; what further need
have we of witnesses? behold, now
ye have heard his blasphemy.
66 What think ye? They answered
and said, He is [a]guilty [b]of [c]death.
67 Then did they [a]spit in his
face, and buffeted him; and others
smote *him* with the palms of their
hands,
68 Saying, Prophesy unto us, thou
Christ, Who is he that [a]smote thee?
69 ¶ Now Peter sat without in the
palace: and a [a]damsel came unto
him, saying, Thou also wast with
Jesus of Galilee.
70 But he denied before *them* all,
saying, I know not what thou sayest.
71 And when he was gone out into
the porch, another *maid* saw him,
and said unto them that were there,
This *fellow* was also with Jesus of
Nazareth.
72 And again he denied with an
oath, I do not know the man.
73 And after a while came unto *him*
they that stood by, and said to Peter,
Surely thou also art *one* of them; for
thy speech [a]bewrayeth thee.
74 Then began he to curse and to
swear, *saying,* I know not the man.
And immediately the [a]cock crew.
75 And Peter remembered the
word of Jesus, which said unto him,
Before the cock crow, thou shalt
[a]deny me thrice. And he went out,
and wept bitterly.

CHAPTER 27

Jesus is accused and condemned before Pilate—Barabbas is released—Jesus is mocked, crucified, and buried in the tomb of Joseph of Arimathæa.

WHEN the morning was come, all
the chief priests and elders of the
people took counsel against Jesus
to put him to death:
2 And when they had bound him,
they led *him* away, and delivered
him to [a]Pontius Pilate the governor.
3 ¶ Then Judas, which had betrayed him, when he saw that he
was condemned, repented himself,
and brought again the thirty pieces
of silver to the chief priests and
elders,
4 Saying, I have sinned in that I
have [a]betrayed the innocent [b]blood.
And they said, What *is that* to us?
[c]see thou *to that.*
5 And he cast down the pieces of
silver in the temple, and departed,
and went [a]and [b]hanged himself.
6 And the chief priests took the silver pieces, and said, It is not lawful
for to put them into the treasury,
because it is the price of blood.
7 And they took counsel, and
bought with them the [a]potter's field,
to bury [b]strangers in.
8 Wherefore that field was called,
The field of blood, unto this day.
9 Then was fulfilled that which
was spoken by Jeremy the prophet,

63*c* GR charge (you) under oath ("cause you to swear").
d TG Oath; Swearing.
64*a* TG Jesus Christ, Son of Man.
b TG Celestial Glory.
c TG Jesus Christ, Second Coming.
65*a* TG Blaspheme.
66*a* TG Guilt.
b JST Matt. 26:67 . . . *and worthy* of death.
c TG Jesus Christ, Death of.
67*a* Isa. 50:6.
68*a* Luke 22:64.
69*a* GR servant-girl.
73*a* GR reveals you.
74*a* GR rooster crowed.
75*a* TG Honesty.
27 2*a* TG Jesus Christ, Trials of.
4*a* TG Jesus Christ, Betrayal of.
b TG Blood, Shedding of.
c GR that is your affair. JST Matt. 27:5 . . . See thou to *it; thy sins be upon thee.*
5*a* JST Matt. 27:6 . . . and hanged himself *on a tree. And straightway he fell down, and his bowels gushed out, and he died.*
b Acts 1:18 (15–20).
7*a* Zech. 11:13 (12–13).
b TG Stranger.

saying, And they took the [a]thirty
pieces of silver, the price of him
that was valued, whom they of the
children of Israel did value;
10 And gave them for the potter's
field, as the Lord appointed me.
11 And Jesus stood before the
governor: and the governor asked
him, saying, Art thou the King of
the Jews? And Jesus said unto him,
[a]Thou sayest.
12 And when he was accused of
the chief priests and elders, he answered [a]nothing.
13 Then said Pilate unto him, Hearest thou not how many things they
witness against thee?
14 And he answered him to never
a word; insomuch that the governor
marvelled greatly.
15 Now at *that* feast the governor
was [a]wont to [b]release unto the people a prisoner, whom they [c]would.
16 And they had then a notable
prisoner, called Barabbas.
17 Therefore when they were
gathered together, Pilate said unto
them, Whom will ye that I release
unto you? Barabbas, or Jesus which
is called Christ?
18 For he knew that for [a]envy they
had [b]delivered him.
19 ¶ When he was set down on the
judgment seat, his wife sent unto
him, saying, Have thou nothing to
do with that just man: for I have
suffered many things this day in a
[a]dream because of him.
20 But the chief [a]priests and elders [b]persuaded the multitude that
they should [c]ask Barabbas, and destroy Jesus.
21 The governor answered and said
unto them, Whether of the twain
will ye that I release unto you? They
said, Barabbas.
22 Pilate saith unto them, What
shall I do then with Jesus which is
called Christ? *They* all say unto him,
Let him be [a]crucified.
23 And the governor said, Why,
what evil hath he done? But they
cried out [a]the more, saying, Let him
be crucified.
24 ¶ When Pilate saw that he [a]could
prevail nothing, but *that* rather a
[b]tumult was made, he took water,
and washed *his* hands before the
multitude, saying, I am innocent
of the blood of this [c]just person:
see ye *to it*.
25 Then answered all the people,
and said, His [a]blood *be* on us, and
on our children.
26 ¶ Then released he Barabbas unto them: and when he had
[a]scourged Jesus, he delivered *him*
to be crucified.
27 Then the soldiers of the governor
took Jesus into the [a]common hall,
and gathered unto him the whole
band *of soldiers*.
28 And they stripped him, and put
on him a [a]scarlet robe.
29 ¶ And when they had [a]plaited
a crown of thorns, they put *it* upon
his head, and a [b]reed in his right
hand: and they bowed the knee before him, and mocked him, saying,
Hail, King of the Jews!
30 And they [a]spit upon him, and
took the reed, and smote him on
the head.
31 And after that they had mocked
him, they took the robe off from him,
and put his own raiment on him,
and led him away to crucify *him*.
32 And as they came out, they

9*a* TG Jesus Christ, Betrayal of.
11*a* JST Matt. 27:12 . . . Thou sayest *truly; for thus it is written of me.*
12*a* TG Jesus Christ, Trials of.
15*a* GR accustomed.
b Luke 23:17.
c GR desired.
18*a* TG Envy.
b TG Jesus Christ, Betrayal of.
19*a* TG Dream.
20*a* TG Priestcraft.
b Matt. 26:4 (3–4); Acts 3:13; 13:28; 2 Ne. 10:5 (3–6).
c GR request.
22*a* 2 Ne. 10:3.
23*a* GR exceedingly, beyond measure.
24*a* GR was accomplishing.
b TG Rioting and Reveling.
c John 18:38 (28–38).
25*a* Ps. 69:27; Acts 5:28; 2 Ne. 6:10 (8–11).
26*a* Isa. 50:6. TG Cruelty.
27*a* GR governor's house, residence.
28*a* JST Matt. 27:30 . . . *purple* . . .
29*a* GR woven.
b GR stalk, staff.
30*a* 1 Ne. 19:9.

found a man of Cyrene, Simon by
name: him they compelled to bear
his cross.
33 And when they were come unto
a place called Golgotha, that is to
say, a place of [a]a skull,
34 ¶ They gave him [a]vinegar to
drink mingled with gall: and when
he had tasted *thereof*, he would not
drink.
35 And they [a]crucified him, and
[b]parted his garments, casting lots:
that it might be fulfilled which was
spoken by the prophet, They parted
my [c]garments among them, and
upon my vesture did they cast lots.
36 And sitting down they watched
him there;
37 And set up over his head his
accusation written, THIS IS JESUS
THE KING OF THE JEWS.
38 Then were there two thieves
crucified with him, one on the right
hand, and another on the left.
39 ¶ And they that passed by [a]re-
viled him, wagging their heads,
40 And saying, Thou that destroyest the [a]temple, and buildest *it* in
three days, save thyself. If thou be
the [b]Son of God, come down from
the cross.
41 Likewise also the chief priests
mocking *him*, with the scribes and
elders, said,
42 He saved others; himself he cannot save. If he be the King of Israel,
let him now come down from the
cross, and we will believe him.
43 He [a]trusted in God; let him [b]de-
liver him now, if he will have him:
for he said, I am the [c]Son of God.
44 The thieves also, which were
crucified with him, [a]cast the same
in his teeth.
45 Now from the sixth hour there
was [a]darkness over all the land unto
the ninth hour.
46 And about the ninth hour Jesus
cried with a loud voice, saying, Eli,
Eli, lama sabachthani? that is to say,
[a]My God, my God, why hast thou
[b]forsaken me?
47 Some of them that stood there,
when they heard *that*, said, This *man*
calleth for [a]Elias.
48 And straightway one of them
ran, and took a sponge, and filled *it*
with [a]vinegar, and put *it* on a reed,
and gave him to drink.
49 The rest said, Let be, let us see
whether Elias will come to save him.
50 ¶ Jesus, when he had cried
again with [a]a loud voice, yielded
up the ghost.
51 And, behold, the [a]veil of the
temple was [b]rent in twain from the
top to the bottom; and the earth did
[c]quake, and the rocks rent;
52 And the [a]graves were opened;
and many [b]bodies of the [c]saints
[d]which slept [e]arose,
53 And came out of the graves after
his resurrection, and went into the
[a]holy city, and appeared unto many.
54 Now when the centurion, and
they that were with him, watching
Jesus, saw the earthquake, and those
things that were done, they feared
greatly, saying, Truly this was the
Son of God.
55 And many [a]women were there
beholding afar off, which followed

33*a* JST Matt. 27:35 . . . *burial* . . .
34*a* Ps. 69:21.
35*a* TG Jesus Christ, Crucifixion of.
b IE they divided His clothes among themselves.
c Ps. 22:18.
39*a* TG Reviling.
40*a* Matt. 26:61; Mark 14:58; John 2:19 (18–22).
b Matt. 4:6; D&C 20:22.
43*a* Ps. 22:8.
b TG Deliver.
c TG Jesus Christ, Divine Sonship.
44*a* GR insulted, reproached Him.
45*a* TG Darkness, Physical.
46*a* Ps. 22:1.
b D&C 121:1 (1–8).
47*a* IE Elijah.
48*a* TG Jesus Christ, Prophecies about.
50*a* JST Matt. 27:54 . . . a loud voice, *saying, Father, it is finished, thy will is done,* yielded up the ghost.
51*a* TG Jesus Christ, Types of, in Anticipation; Veil.
b GR torn into two pieces.
c 3 Ne. 8:6 (5–12); Moses 7:56 (55–56).
52*a* TG Jesus Christ, Prophecies about.
b D&C 129:1.
c TG Saints.
d GR who had died.
e TG Resurrection.
53*a* Neh. 11:1.
55*a* TG Woman.

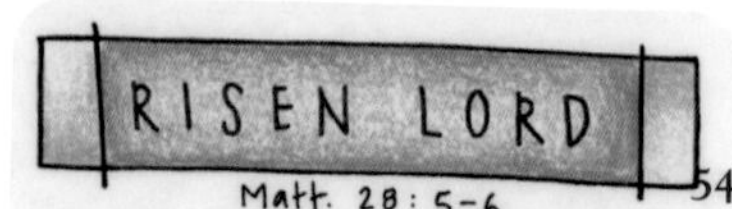

Jesus from Galilee, ministering
unto him:
56 Among which was Mary Magdalene, and Mary the mother of
James and [a]Joses, and the mother
of Zebedee's children.
57 When the even was come, there
came a rich man of Arimathæa,
named [a]Joseph, who also himself
was Jesus' [b]disciple:
58 He went to Pilate, and [a]begged
the body of Jesus. Then Pilate commanded the body to be delivered.
59 And when Joseph had taken
the body, he wrapped it in a clean
linen cloth,
60 And laid it in his own new tomb,
which he had hewn out in the rock:
and he rolled a great [a]stone to the
door of the [b]sepulchre, and departed.
61 And there was Mary Magdalene,
and the other Mary, sitting [a]over
against the sepulchre.
62 ¶ Now the next day, that followed the day of the [a]preparation,
the chief priests and Pharisees came
together unto Pilate,
63 Saying, Sir, we remember that
that [a]deceiver said, while he was
yet alive, After three days I will
rise again.
64 Command therefore that the
sepulchre be made sure until the
third day, lest his disciples come by
night, and steal him away, and say
unto the people, He is risen from
the dead: so the last [a]error shall be
worse than the first.
65 Pilate said unto them, Ye have
a watch: go your way, make *it* as
sure as ye can.
66 So they went, and made the
sepulchre sure, sealing the stone,
and setting a watch.

CHAPTER 28

Christ the Lord is risen—He appears to many—He has all power in heaven and earth—He sends the Apostles to teach and baptize all nations.

[a]IN the end of the [b]sabbath, as it began to dawn toward the first *day* of
the week, came Mary Magdalene and
the other Mary to see the sepulchre.
2 And, behold, there was a great
earthquake: for [a]the [b]angel of the
Lord descended from heaven, and
came and rolled back the stone from
the door, and sat upon it.
3 [a]His [b]countenance was like lightning, and his raiment white as snow:
4 And for fear of him the keepers
did shake, and became as dead *men*.
5 [a]And the angel answered and
said unto the women, Fear not ye:
for I know that ye seek Jesus, which
was crucified.
6 He is not here: for he is [a]risen, as
he said. Come, see the place where
the [b]Lord lay.
7 And go quickly, and tell his
disciples that he is risen from the
dead; and, behold, he goeth before
you into Galilee; there shall ye see
him: lo, I have told you.
8 And they departed quickly from
the sepulchre with fear and great
joy; and did run to bring his disciples word.
9 ¶ And as they went to tell his
disciples, behold, [a]Jesus met them,
saying, All hail. And they came
and held him by the feet, and worshipped him.
10 Then said Jesus unto them, Be
not afraid: go tell my brethren that
they go into Galilee, and there shall
they see me.

56*a* GR Joseph.
57*a* John 19:38.
b John 8:31.
58*a* GR asked for, requested.
60*a* John 11:38 (37–40); 20:1.
b 1 Ne. 19:10.
61*a* GR in front of, before.
62*a* TG Passover.
63*a* John 2:19.
64*a* GR deception.
28 1*a* GR After the sabbath.
b TG Sabbath.
2*a* JST Matt. 28:2 . . . *two angels* . . .
b TG Angels.
3*a* JST Matt. 28:3 *And their* countenance was like lightning, and *their* raiment white as snow . . .
b D&C 20:6.
5*a* JST Matt. 28:4 And the *angels* answered and said unto the women, Fear not ye; for *we* know . . .
6*a* TG Jesus Christ, Resurrection; Resurrection.
b TG Jesus Christ, Lord.
9*a* TG Jesus Christ, Appearances, Postmortal.

11 ¶ Now when they were going,
behold, some of the [a]watch came into
the city, and [b]shewed unto the chief
priests all the things that were done.
12 And when they were assembled
with the elders, and had taken counsel, they gave [a]large money unto
the soldiers,
13 Saying, Say ye, His disciples
came by night, and stole him *away*
while we slept.
14 And if this come to the governor's ears, we will persuade him,
and [a]secure you.
15 So they took the money, and did
as they were taught: and this saying
is commonly reported among the
Jews until this day.
16 ¶ Then the eleven disciples went
away into Galilee, into a mountain where Jesus had appointed
them.
17 And when they saw him, they
worshipped him: but some [a]doubted.
18 And [a]Jesus came and spake
unto them, saying, All [b]power is
given unto me in heaven and in
earth.
19 ¶ Go ye therefore, and [a]teach
all [b]nations, [c]baptizing them in the
name of the [d]Father, and of the Son,
and of the Holy Ghost:
20 [a]Teaching them to [b]observe
all things whatsoever I have [c]com-
manded you: and, lo, [d]I am with
you alway, *even* unto the [e]end of the
world. Amen.

THE GOSPEL ACCORDING TO
ST MARK

CHAPTER 1

Jesus is baptized by John—He preaches the gospel, calls disciples, casts out devils, heals the sick, and cleanses a leper.

THE beginning of the [a]gospel
of Jesus Christ, the Son of
God;
2 As it is written in the prophets,
Behold, I send my [a]messenger before thy face, which shall prepare
thy way before thee.
3 The [a]voice of one crying in the
wilderness, Prepare ye the way of
the Lord, make his paths straight.
4 John did baptize in the wilderness, and [a]preach the [b]baptism of

11*a* GR guard.
b GR reported.
12*a* GR much money.
14*a* GR keep you out of trouble.
17*a* TG Doubt.
18*a* TG Jesus Christ, Appearances, Postmortal.
b Heb. 2:8; 1 Ne. 9:6. TG God, Power of; Jesus Christ, Messiah; Jesus Christ, Power of; Priesthood, Power of.
19*a* GR preach to, make disciples of (meaning "make Christians in all nations"). TG Apostles; Israel, Mission of; Missionary Work; Mission of Early Saints; Mission of Latter-day Saints; Teaching.
b TG Nations.
c TG Baptism; Baptism, Essential.
d TG Godhead.
20*a* The Greek text suggests this would be post-baptismal teaching. TG Prophets, Mission of.
b TG Baptism, Qualifications for.
c Jer. 1:7 (7–10).
d D&C 30:11; 31:13; 61:10; 62:9. TG Guidance, Divine; Protection, Divine.
e D&C 24:8; 132:49. TG World, End of.

[MARK]
Title: JST entitles this book "The Testimony of St. Mark."
1 1*a* TG Gospel.
2*a* Mal. 3:1; Matt. 11:10.
3*a* Matt. 3:3; Luke 3:4; John 1:23.
4*a* TG Missionary Work.
b TG Baptism.

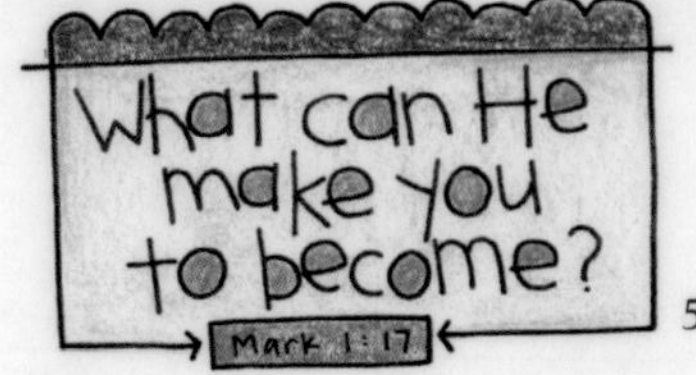

[c]repentance for the [d]remission of
sins.
5 And there went out unto him
all the land of Judæa, and they of
Jerusalem, and were all [a]baptized
of him in the river of Jordan, [b]con-
fessing their sins.
6 And John was [a]clothed with
[b]camel's hair, and with a girdle of
a skin about his loins; and he did
eat [c]locusts and wild honey;
7 And preached, saying, There
cometh one mightier than I after me,
the latchet of whose shoes I am not
worthy to stoop down and unloose.
8 I indeed have baptized you
with water: [a]but he shall baptize
you with the Holy Ghost.
9 And it came to pass in those days,
that Jesus came from Nazareth of
Galilee, and was [a]baptized of John
in Jordan.
10 And straightway coming [a]up
out of the water, he saw the heavens
opened, and the Spirit like a [b]dove
descending upon him:

11 And there came a voice from
heaven, *saying,* Thou art my beloved
Son, in whom I am well pleased.
12 [a]And immediately the Spirit
driveth him into the [b]wilderness.
13 And he was there in the wilderness forty days, tempted of Satan;
and was with the wild beasts; and
the angels ministered unto him.
14 Now after that John was put
in prison, Jesus came into Galilee,
[a]preaching the gospel of the kingdom of God,
15 And saying, The [a]time is fulfilled, and the [b]kingdom of God [c]is
at hand: [d]repent ye, and [e]believe
the gospel.
16 Now as he walked by the sea of
Galilee, he saw Simon and Andrew
his brother casting a net into the
sea: for they were fishers.
17 And Jesus said unto them, Come
ye after me, and I will make you to
become [a]fishers of men.
18 And straightway they forsook
their nets, and followed him.
19 And when he had gone a little
further thence, he saw James the *son*
of Zebedee, and John his brother,
who also were in the ship mending
their nets.
20 And straightway he called them:
and they left their father Zebedee
in the ship with the hired servants,
and went after him.
21 And they went into Capernaum;
and straightway on the sabbath day
he entered into the synagogue, and
[a]taught.
22 And they were astonished at
his doctrine: for he taught them as
one that had [a]authority, and not as
the [b]scribes.
23 And there was in their synagogue a man with an [a]unclean spirit;
and he cried out,
24 Saying, Let *us* alone; [a]what have
we to do with thee, thou Jesus of
Nazareth? art thou come to destroy
us? I know thee who thou art, the
[b]Holy One of God.
25 And Jesus [a]rebuked him, saying,
Hold thy peace, and come out of
him.

4*c* TG Repent.
d TG Remission of Sins.
5*a* TG Baptism, Immersion.
b TG Baptism, Qualifications for.
6*a* TG Clothing.
b 2 Kgs. 1:8.
c Lev. 11:22.
8*a* JST Mark 1:6 . . . but he shall *not only* baptize you with *water, but with fire, and* the Holy Ghost.
9*a* TG Baptism; Baptism, Essential; Jesus Christ, Baptism of.
10*a* TG Baptism, Immersion.
b TG Holy Ghost, Dove, Sign of.
12*a* JST Mark 1:10–11 And immediately the Spirit *took* him into the wilderness. And he was there in the wilderness forty days, *Satan seeking to tempt him;* and was with . . .
b GR desert.
14*a* TG Jesus Christ, Teaching Mode of.
15*a* TG Time.
b D&C 33:10 (1–18). TG Kingdom of God, in Heaven.
c GR has arrived.
d TG Repent.
e TG Faith.
17*a* TG Apostles; Missionary Work.
21*a* TG Jesus Christ, Teaching Mode of.
22*a* TG Authority; Jesus Christ, Authority of.
b TG Scribe.
23*a* TG Spirits, Evil or Unclean.
24*a* GR what business do you have with us . . .
b TG Holiness.
25*a* TG Heal.

26 And when the unclean spirit
had [a]torn him, and cried with a loud
voice, he came out of him.
27 And they were all amazed, insomuch that they questioned among
themselves, saying, What thing is this?
what new doctrine *is* this? for with
[a]authority commandeth he even the
unclean spirits, and they do obey him.
28 And immediately his fame
spread abroad throughout all the
region round about Galilee.
29 And forthwith, when they were
come out of the synagogue, they
entered into the house of Simon
and Andrew, with James and John.
30 But Simon's wife's mother lay
sick of a fever, and [a]anon they tell
him of her.
31 And he came and took her by
the hand, and [a]lifted her up; and
immediately the fever left her, and
she ministered unto them.
32 And at even, when the sun did
set, they brought unto him all that
were diseased, and them that were
possessed with devils.
33 And all the city was gathered
together at the door.
34 And he [a]healed many that were
sick of divers diseases, and cast out
many [b]devils; and [c]suffered not the
devils to speak, because they knew
him.
35 And in the morning, rising up
a great while before day, he went
out, and departed into a solitary
place, and there prayed.
36 And Simon and they that were
with him followed after him.
37 And when they had found him,
they said unto him, All *men* seek for
thee.
38 And he said unto them, Let us
go into the next towns, that I may
[a]preach there also: for therefore
came I forth.
39 And he preached in their synagogues throughout all Galilee, and
cast out [a]devils.
40 And there came a [a]leper to him,
beseeching him, and kneeling down
to him, and saying unto him, If thou
wilt, thou canst make me [b]clean.
41 And Jesus, moved with [a]com-
passion, put forth *his* hand, and
touched him, and saith unto him,
I will; be thou clean.
42 And as soon as he had spoken,
immediately the leprosy departed
from him, and he was cleansed.
43 And he [a]straitly charged him,
and forthwith sent him away;
44 And saith unto him, See thou
say nothing to any man: but go thy
way, shew thyself to the priest, and
offer for thy cleansing those things
which Moses commanded, for a testimony unto them.
45 But he went out, and began
to publish *it* much, and to [a]blaze
abroad the matter, insomuch that
Jesus could no more openly enter
into the city, but was without in
desert places: and they came to him
from every quarter.

CHAPTER 2

Jesus forgives sins, heals a paralytic, eats with tax gatherers and sinners, and announces that He is Lord of the Sabbath.

AND again he entered into Capernaum after *some* days; and it was
noised that he was [a]in the house.
2 And straightway many were gathered together, insomuch that there
was no room to receive *them*, no,
not so much as about the door: and
he [a]preached the word unto them.
3 And they come unto him, bringing one sick of the palsy, which was
[a]borne of four.

26*a* Mark 9:20 (14–29).
27*a* TG Authority; Jesus Christ, Authority of.
30*a* GR immediately.
31*a* TG Heal.
34*a* TG Heal; Miracle.
b Mosiah 3:6 (5–6).
TG Spirits, Evil or Unclean.
c GR did not allow.
38*a* TG Jesus Christ, Mission of; Teaching.
39*a* Luke 4:36 (31–37); D&C 35:9 (6–12).
40*a* TG Leprosy.
b GR pure.
41*a* TG Compassion.
43*a* GR warned him sternly.
45*a* GR spread widely.
2 1*a* OR at home.
2*a* TG Jesus Christ, Teaching Mode of.
3*a* GR carried.

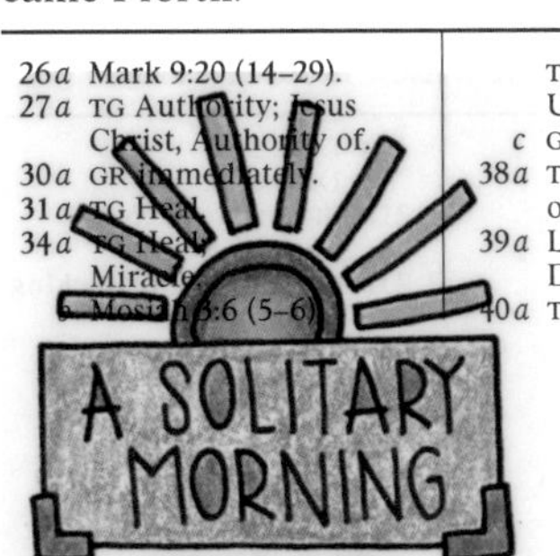

4 And when they could not come
nigh unto him for the press, they
uncovered the roof where he was:
and when they had broken *it* up,
they let down the bed wherein the
sick of the palsy lay.
5 When Jesus saw their faith, he
said unto the sick of the palsy, Son,
thy sins be [a]forgiven thee.
6 But there were certain of the
scribes sitting there, and reasoning
in their hearts,
7 Why doth this *man* thus speak
[a]blasphemies? who can forgive sins
but God only?
8 And immediately when Jesus
perceived in his spirit that they so
reasoned within themselves, he said
unto them, Why reason ye these
things in your hearts?
9 Whether is it easier to say to the
sick of the palsy, *Thy* sins be forgiven
thee; or to say, Arise, and take up
thy bed, and walk?
10 But that ye may know that the
[a]Son of man hath power on earth
to forgive sins, (he saith to the sick
of the palsy,)
11 I say unto thee, [a]Arise, and take
up thy [b]bed, and go thy way into
thine house.
12 And immediately he arose, took
up the bed, and went forth before
them all; insomuch that they were
all amazed, and glorified God,
saying, We never saw it on this
fashion.
13 And he went forth again by the
sea side; and all the multitude resorted unto him, and he taught them.
14 And as he passed by, he saw
Levi the *son* of Alphæus sitting at
the [a]receipt of custom, and said unto
him, Follow me. And he arose and
followed him.
15 And it came to pass, that, as
Jesus sat at meat in his house, many
publicans and sinners sat also together with Jesus and his disciples:
for there were many, and they
followed him.
16 And when the scribes and
Pharisees saw him eat with [a]publi-
cans and sinners, they said unto his
disciples, How is it that he eateth
and drinketh with publicans and
sinners?
17 When Jesus heard *it*, he saith
unto them, They that are [a]whole
have no need of the physician, but
they that are sick: I came not to
call the righteous, but sinners to
repentance.
18 And the disciples of John and
of the Pharisees used to [a]fast: and
they come and say unto him, Why
do the disciples of John and of the
Pharisees fast, but thy disciples
fast not?
19 And Jesus said unto them, Can
the children of the bridechamber fast, while the [a]bridegroom is
with them? as long as they have
the [b]bridegroom with them, they
cannot fast.
20 But the days will come, when
the bridegroom shall be taken away
from them, and then shall they fast
in those days.
21 No man also seweth a piece of
[a]new cloth on an old garment: else
the new piece that filled it up taketh
away from the old, and the rent is
made worse.
22 And no man putteth new
wine into old bottles: else the
new wine doth burst the bottles, and
the wine is spilled, and the bottles
will be marred: but new wine must
be put into new bottles.
23 And it came to pass, that he
went through the corn fields on
the sabbath day; and his disciples
began, as they went, [a]to pluck the
ears of corn.
24 And the Pharisees said unto him,
Behold, why do they on the sabbath
day that which is not lawful?

5*a* Luke 7:48; James 5:15 (14–15).
7*a* TG Blaspheme.
10*a* TG Jesus Christ, Son of Man.
11*a* Alma 15:10 (4–11); 3 Ne. 9:13 (10–22).
b 3 Ne. 7:22.
14*a* GR tax office.
16*a* Luke 15:1 (1–2).
17*a* Moro. 8:8 (8–27).
18*a* Luke 5:33 (33–38).
19*a* Luke 5:35.
b D&C 65:3.
21*a* GR unshrunken or unsized.
23*a* GR occasionally picking some grain.

25 And he said unto them, Have ye
never read what David did, when
he had need, and was an hungred,
he, and they that were with him?
26 How he went into the house of
God in the days of Abiathar the high
priest, and did eat the shewbread,
which is not lawful to eat but for
the priests, and gave also to them
which were with him?
27 And he said unto them, The
[a]sabbath was made for man, and
not man for the sabbath:
28 [a]Therefore the [b]Son of man is
Lord also of the sabbath.

CHAPTER 3

Jesus heals on the Sabbath day—He chooses and ordains the Twelve Apostles—He asks, Can Satan cast out Satan?—Jesus speaks of blasphemy against the Holy Ghost and identifies those who believe as being members of His family.

AND he entered again into the synagogue; and there was a man there
which had a withered hand.
2 And they [a]watched him, whether
he would heal him on the sabbath
day; that they might accuse him.
3 And he saith unto the man which
had the withered hand, Stand forth.
4 And he saith unto them, Is it
lawful to do good on the [a]sabbath
days, or to do evil? to save life, or
to kill? But they [b]held their peace.
5 And when he had looked round
about on them with [a]anger, being
grieved for the [b]hardness of their
hearts, he saith unto the man,
Stretch forth thine hand. And he
stretched *it* out: and his hand was
restored whole as the other.
6 And the Pharisees went forth, and
straightway took [a]counsel with the
Herodians against him, how they
might destroy him.
7 But Jesus withdrew himself with
his disciples to the sea: and a great
multitude from Galilee followed
him, and from Judæa,
8 And from Jerusalem, and from
Idumæa, and *from* beyond Jordan;
and they about Tyre and Sidon, a
great multitude, when they had
heard what great things he did,
came unto him.
9 And he spake to his disciples,
that a small [a]ship should wait on
him because of the multitude, lest
they should throng him.
10 For he had healed many; insomuch that they [a]pressed upon him
for to touch him, as many as had
plagues.
11 And [a]unclean spirits, when they
saw him, fell down before him, and
cried, saying, Thou art the Son of
God.
12 And he straitly charged them
that they should not make him
known.
13 And he goeth up into a mountain, and calleth *unto him* whom he
[a]would: and they came unto him.
14 And he [a]ordained twelve, that
they should be with him, and that
he might send them forth to [b]preach,
15 And to have [a]power to heal
[b]sicknesses, and to cast out [c]devils:
16 And Simon he surnamed Peter;
17 And James the *son* of Zebedee,
and John the brother of James; and
he surnamed them Boanerges, which
is, The sons of [a]thunder:
18 And Andrew, and Philip, and
Bartholomew, and Matthew, and
Thomas, and James the *son* of
Alphæus, and Thaddæus, and Simon the Canaanite,

27*a* TG Sabbath.
28*a* JST Mark 2:26–27 (Appendix).
b TG Jesus Christ, Son of Man.
3 2*a* GR watched carefully, maliciously.
4*a* TG Sabbath.
b GR remained silent.
5*a* TG God, Indignation of.
b GR insensibility, dullness.
TG Cruelty.
6*a* TG Counsel.
9*a* GR boat.
10*a* GR impetuously rushed at Him.
11*a* TG Spirits, Evil or Unclean.
13*a* GR desired.
14*a* TG Apostles; Jesus Christ, Authority of; Priesthood, Authority; Priesthood, History of; Priesthood, Ordination.
b TG Missionary Work.
15*a* GR authority.
TG Priesthood; Priesthood, Power of.
b TG Sickness.
c TG Devil.
17*a* Luke 9:54.

19 And Judas Iscariot, which also
betrayed him: and they [a]went into
an house.
20 And the multitude cometh together again, so that they could not
so much as [a]eat bread.
21 And when his friends heard *of*
it, they went out to lay hold on him:
for they said, He is [a]beside himself.
22 ¶ And the scribes which came
down from Jerusalem said, He hath
Beelzebub, and by the prince of the
devils casteth he out devils.
23 And he called them *unto him,*
and said unto them in parables, How
can Satan cast out Satan?
24 And if a kingdom be divided
against itself, that kingdom cannot stand.
25 And if a house be divided against
itself, that house cannot stand.
26 And if Satan rise up against
himself, and be divided, he cannot
stand, but hath an end.
27 No man can enter into a strong
man's house, and spoil his goods,
except he will first bind the strong
man; and then he will spoil his
house.
28 [a]Verily I say unto you, All sins
shall be forgiven unto the sons of
men, and blasphemies [b]wherewith
soever they shall blaspheme:
29 But he that shall [a]blaspheme
against the Holy Ghost hath never
[b]forgiveness, but is in danger of
[c]eternal damnation:
30 Because they said, He hath an
unclean spirit.
31 ¶ There came then his [a]breth-
ren and his mother, and, standing
[b]without, sent unto him, calling
him.
32 And the multitude sat about
him, and they said unto him, Behold, thy mother and thy brethren
without seek for thee.
33 And he answered them, saying,
Who is my mother, or my brethren?
34 And he looked round about on
them which sat about him, and said,
Behold my mother and my brethren!
35 For whosoever shall do the [a]will
of God, the same is my brother, and
my sister, and mother.

CHAPTER 4

Jesus gives the parables of the sower, the candle under a bushel, the seed growing secretly, and the mustard seed—He stills the tempest.

AND he began again to teach by the
[a]sea side: and there was gathered
unto him a great multitude, so that
he entered into a ship, and sat in
the sea; and the whole multitude
was by the sea on the land.
2 And he taught them many things
by parables, and said unto them in
his [a]doctrine,
3 Hearken; Behold, there went out
a [a]sower to sow:
4 And it came to pass, as he sowed,
some fell by the way side, and the
fowls of the air came and devoured
it up.
5 And some fell on stony ground,
where it had not much earth; and
immediately it sprang up, because
it had no depth of earth:
6 But when the sun was up, it was
scorched; and because it had no root,
it withered away.
7 And some fell among thorns, and
the thorns grew up, and choked it,
and it yielded no fruit.
8 And other fell on good ground,
and did yield fruit that sprang up
and increased; and brought forth,
some thirty, and some sixty, and
some an hundred.
9 And he said unto them, He that
hath ears to hear, let him hear.

19*a* OR went home.
20*a* Mark 6:31 (30–36).
21*a* GR out of his senses.
28*a* JST Mark 3:21–25 (Appendix).
b GR however so many.
29*a* TG Holy Ghost, Unpardonable Sin against.
b TG Forgive.
c TG Damnation; Eternity; Punish.
31*a* TG Jesus Christ, Family of.
b OR outside.
35*a* Matt. 12:50.
4 1*a* Matt. 13:1.
2*a* 3 Ne. 11:39 (31–41).
3*a* D&C 86:2 (2–3).

10 And when he was [a]alone, they
that were about him with the twelve
asked of him the parable.
11 And he said unto them, Unto you
it is given to know the [a]mystery of
the kingdom of God: but unto them
that are without, all *these* things are
done in [b]parables:
12 That seeing they may see, and
not [a]perceive; and hearing they may
hear, and not understand; lest at any
time they should be converted, and
their sins should be [b]forgiven them.
13 And he said unto them, Know
ye not this parable? and how then
will ye know all parables?
14 ¶ The sower soweth the word.
15 And these are they by the
way side, where the word is sown;
but when they have heard, [a]Satan
cometh immediately, and taketh
away the word that was sown in
their hearts.
16 And these are they likewise
which are sown on stony ground;
who, when they have heard the
word, immediately [a]receive it with
gladness;
17 And have no root in themselves,
and so endure but for a time: afterward, when [a]affliction or [b]persecu-
tion ariseth for the word's sake, immediately they are offended.
18 And these are they which are
sown among thorns; such as hear
the word,
19 And the cares of this world, and
the deceitfulness of [a]riches, and the
[b]lusts of other things entering in,
choke the word, and it becometh
unfruitful.
20 And these are they which are
sown on good ground; such as hear
the word, and receive *it*, and bring
forth fruit, some thirtyfold, some
sixty, and some an hundred.
21 ¶ And he said unto them, Is a
[a]candle brought to be put under a
bushel, or under a bed? and not to
be set on a candlestick?
22 For there is nothing hid, which
shall not be manifested; neither
was any thing kept secret, but that
it should come abroad.
23 [a]If any man have ears to hear,
let him hear.
24 And he said unto them, Take
heed what ye hear: with what measure ye mete, it shall be measured to
you: [a]and unto you that hear shall
more be [b]given.
25 [a]For he that hath, to him shall
be given: and he that hath not, from
him shall be [b]taken even that which
he hath.
26 ¶ And he said, So is the kingdom of God, as if a man should cast
seed into the ground;
27 And should sleep, and rise night
and day, and the seed should spring
and [a]grow up, he knoweth not how.
28 For the earth bringeth forth
[a]fruit of herself; first the blade,
then the ear, after that the full corn
in the ear.
29 But when the fruit is brought
forth, immediately he putteth in the
sickle, because the [a]harvest is come.
30 ¶ And he said, Whereunto shall
we liken the kingdom of God? or
with what comparison shall we
compare it?
31 *It is* like a grain of mustard
seed, which, when it is sown in the
earth, is less than all the seeds that
be in the earth:
32 But when it is sown, it groweth up, and becometh greater than

10*a* JST Mark 4:9 . . . alone *with the twelve, and they that believed in him,* they that were . . .
11*a* TG Mysteries of Godliness.
b Matt. 13:35 (34–35); Luke 8:10. TG Jesus Christ, Teaching Mode of.
12*a* TG Spiritual Blindness.
b TG Forgive.
15*a* TG Devil.
16*a* D&C 40:2.
17*a* 1 Ne. 8:28 (24–28). TG Affliction.
b TG Persecution.
19*a* TG Treasure.
b TG Lust.
21*a* 3 Ne. 18:24.
23*a* See JST Isa. 42:19–23 (Appendix).
24*a* JST Mark 4:20 . . . and unto you that *continue to receive,* shall more be given . . .
b Matt. 25:15; Luke 8:18.
25*a* JST Mark 4:20 . . . for he that *receiveth,* to him shall be given; *but* he that *continueth not to receive,* from him shall . . .
b D&C 43:10; 60:3.
27*a* 1 Cor. 3:6 (6–7).
28*a* TG Nature, Earth.
29*a* TG Harvest.

all herbs, and shooteth out great
branches; so that the fowls of the air
may lodge under the shadow of it.
33 And with many such parables
spake he the word unto them, as
they were [a]able to hear *it*.
34 But without a parable spake he
not unto them: and when they were
alone, he expounded all things to
his disciples.
35 And the same day, when the
even was come, he saith unto them,
Let us pass over unto the other side.
36 And when they had sent away
the multitude, they took him even
as he was in the ship. And there
were also with him other little
ships.
37 And there arose a great storm of
wind, and the waves beat into the
ship, so that it was now full.
38 And he was in the hinder part
of the ship, asleep on a pillow: and
they awake him, and say unto him,
Master, carest thou not that we
perish?
39 And he arose, and rebuked the
wind, and said unto the sea, [a]Peace,
be still. And the wind ceased, and
there was a great [b]calm.
40 And he said unto them, Why
are ye so [a]fearful? how is it that ye
have no [b]faith?
41 And they feared exceedingly,
and said one to another, What manner of man is this, that even the
wind and the sea obey him?

CHAPTER 5

Jesus casts out a legion of devils, who then enter the swine—A woman is healed by touching Jesus' clothes—He raises Jairus's daughter from the dead.

AND they came over unto the other
side of the sea, into the country of
the Gadarenes.
2 And when he was come out of
the ship, immediately there met
him out of the tombs a man with
an unclean spirit,
3 Who had *his* dwelling among the
tombs; and no man could bind him,
no, not with chains:
4 Because that he had been often
bound with fetters and chains, and
the chains had been [a]plucked asunder by him, and the fetters broken
in pieces: neither [b]could any *man*
tame him.
5 And always, night and day, he
was in the mountains, and in the
tombs, crying, and cutting himself
with stones.
6 But when he saw Jesus afar off,
he ran and worshipped him,
7 And cried with a loud voice, and
said, What have I to do with thee,
Jesus, *thou* Son of the most high
God? I [a]adjure thee by God, that
thou torment me not.
8 For he said unto him, Come out
of the man, *thou* [a]unclean [b]spirit.
9 And he asked him, What *is* thy
name? And he answered, saying, My
name *is* Legion: for we are many.
10 And he besought him much that
he would not send them away out
of the country.
11 Now there was there nigh unto
the mountains a great herd of swine
feeding.
12 And all the devils besought him,
saying, Send us into the swine, that
we may enter into them.
13 And forthwith Jesus gave them
leave. And the unclean spirits went
out, and entered into the swine: and
the herd ran violently down a steep
place into the sea, (they were about
two thousand;) and were [a]choked
in the sea.
14 And they that fed the swine
fled, and told *it* in the city, and in
the country. And they went out to
see what it was that was done.
15 And they come to Jesus, and
see him that was possessed with the

33*a* JST Mark 4:26 . . . able to *bear;* but without . . .
39*a* TG Peace.
b Ps. 89:9.
40*a* Matt. 14:31; Mark 16:14; Luke 24:25.
b Alma 44:4 (1–5); D&C 4:5 (1–7).
5 4*a* GR broken, taken apart.
b GR was any man strong enough to tame him.
7*a* OR implore.
8*a* TG Spirits, Evil or Unclean.
b TG Heal.
13*a* OR drowned.

[a]devil, and had the legion, sitting, and clothed, and in his right [b]mind: and they were afraid.

16 And they that saw *it* told them how it befell to him that was possessed with the devil, and *also* concerning the swine.

17 And they began to pray him to depart out of their coasts.

18 And when he was come into the ship, he that had been possessed with the devil prayed him that he might be with him.

19 Howbeit Jesus suffered him not, but saith unto him, Go home to thy friends, and tell them how great things the Lord hath done for thee, and hath had [a]compassion on thee.

20 And he departed, and began to [a]publish in Decapolis how great things Jesus had done for him: and all *men* did marvel.

21 And when Jesus was passed over again by ship unto the other side, much people gathered unto him: and he was nigh unto the sea.

22 And, behold, there cometh one of the rulers of the synagogue, Jairus by name; and when he saw him, he fell at his feet,

23 And besought him greatly, saying, My little daughter lieth at the point of death: *I pray thee,* come and lay thy [a]hands on her, that she may be healed; and she shall live.

24 And *Jesus* went with him; and much people followed him, and thronged him.

25 And a certain woman, which had an [a]issue of blood twelve years,

26 And had suffered many things of many physicians, and had spent all that she had, and was nothing bettered, but rather grew worse,

27 When she had heard of Jesus, came in the press behind, and touched his [a]garment.

28 For she said, If I may touch but his clothes, I shall be whole.

29 And straightway the fountain of her blood was dried up; and she felt in *her* body that she was healed of that plague.

30 And Jesus, immediately knowing in himself that [a]virtue had gone out of him, turned him about in the press, and said, Who touched my clothes?

31 And his disciples said unto him, Thou seest the multitude thronging thee, and sayest thou, Who touched me?

32 And he looked round about to see her that had done this thing.

33 But the woman fearing and trembling, knowing what was done in her, came and fell down before him, and told him all the truth.

34 And he said unto her, Daughter, thy [a]faith hath made thee whole; go in [b]peace, and be whole of thy plague.

35 While he yet spake, there came from the ruler of the synagogue's *house certain* which said, Thy daughter is dead: why troublest thou the Master any further?

36 As soon as Jesus heard the word that was spoken, he saith unto the ruler of the synagogue, Be not afraid, only [a]believe.

37 And he suffered no man to follow him, save Peter, and James, and John the brother of James.

38 And he cometh to the house of the ruler of the synagogue, and seeth the tumult, and them that wept and wailed greatly.

39 And when he was come in, he saith unto them, Why make ye this [a]ado, and weep? the damsel is not dead, but sleepeth.

40 And they [a]laughed him to scorn. But when he had put them all out, he taketh the father and the mother of the damsel, and them that were with him, and entereth in where the damsel was lying.

15*a* 1 Ne. 11:31; Morm. 9:24.
b TG Mind.
19*a* TG Compassion.
20*a* Luke 8:39.
23*a* TG Administrations to the Sick; Hands, Laying on of.
25*a* OR hemorrhage.
27*a* Matt. 14:36.
30*a* GR power, strength. Luke 6:19 (17–19); 8:46 (41–48).
34*a* Hel. 15:9 (9–10); D&C 46:19.
b TG Peace of God.
36*a* GR exercise faith.
39*a* OR uproar, tumult.
40*a* OR ridiculed Him.

41 And he took the damsel by the
hand, and said unto her, Talitha
cumi; which is, being interpreted,
Damsel, I say unto thee, [a]arise.
42 And straightway the damsel
[a]arose, and walked; for she was *of
the age* of twelve years. And they
were astonished with a great astonishment.
43 And he [a]charged them straitly
that no man should know it; and
commanded that something should
be given her to eat.

CHAPTER 6

Jesus sends forth the Twelve—John the Baptist is beheaded by Herod—Our Lord feeds the five thousand, walks on the water, and heals multitudes.

AND he went out from thence, and
came into his own country; and his
disciples follow him.
2 And when the sabbath day was
come, he began to teach in the synagogue: and many hearing *him* were
astonished, saying, From whence
hath this *man* these things? and what
[a]wisdom *is* this which is given unto
him, that even such mighty works
are wrought by his hands?
3 Is not this the [a]carpenter, the son
of Mary, the [b]brother of James, and
Joses, and of Juda, and Simon? and
are not his sisters here with us?
And they were offended at him.
4 But Jesus said unto them, A
prophet is not without honour, but
in his own country, and among his
own kin, and in his own house.
5 And he could there do no [a]mighty
work, save that he [b]laid his [c]hands
upon a few sick folk, and healed *them*.
6 And he marvelled because of
their [a]unbelief. And he went round
about the villages, teaching.
7 ¶ And he called *unto him* the
[a]twelve, and began to send them
forth by [b]two and two; and gave
them power over unclean spirits;
8 And commanded them that they
should take nothing for *their* journey, save a staff only; no [a]scrip, no
bread, no money in *their* purse:
9 But *be* shod with sandals; and
not put on two coats.
10 And he said unto them, In what
place soever ye enter into an house,
there abide till ye depart from that
place.
11 And whosoever shall not receive
you, nor hear you, when ye depart
thence, shake off the [a]dust under
your feet for a testimony against
them. Verily I say unto you, It shall
be more tolerable for Sodom and
Gomorrha in the day of judgment,
than for that city.
12 And they went out, and
[a]preached that men should repent.
13 And they cast out many devils,
and [a]anointed with oil many that
were sick, and healed *them*.
14 And king [a]Herod heard *of him*;
(for his name was spread abroad:)
and he said, That John the Baptist
was risen from the dead, and therefore mighty works do shew forth
themselves in him.
15 Others said, That it is Elias. And
others said, That it is a prophet, or
as one of the prophets.
16 But when Herod heard *thereof*,
he said, It is John, whom I beheaded:
he is risen from the dead.
17 For Herod himself had sent
forth and laid hold upon John, and
bound him in prison for Herodias'
sake, his brother Philip's wife: for
he had married her.
18 For John had said unto Herod,
It is not lawful for thee to have thy
brother's wife.
19 Therefore Herodias had a

41*a* TG Death, Power over.
42*a* TG Heal.
43*a* GR strongly warned them.
6 2*a* Eccl. 9:16.
3*a* Matt. 13:55.
b TG Jesus Christ, Family of.
5*a* Morm. 9:18 (18–21).
b TG Hands, Laying on of.
c TG Administrations to the Sick.
6*a* OR lack of faith.
7*a* TG Apostles.
b Luke 10:1; D&C 42:6.
8*a* Matt. 10:10 (9–11).
11*a* Luke 10:11; D&C 24:15.
12*a* TG Preaching.
13*a* Ex. 31:11. TG Administrations to the Sick; Anointing.
14*a* Luke 9:7 (7–9).

quarrel against him, and would
have killed him; but she could not:
20 For Herod feared John, knowing that he was a [a]just man [b]and an
holy, and [c]observed him; and when
he heard him, he did many things,
and heard him gladly.
21 And when a convenient day was
come, that Herod on his birthday
made a supper to his [a]lords, high
captains, and chief *estates* of Galilee;
22 And when the daughter of the
said Herodias came in, and danced,
and pleased Herod and them that
sat with him, the king said unto the
damsel, Ask of me whatsoever thou
wilt, and I will give *it* thee.
23 And he [a]sware unto her, Whatsoever thou shalt ask of me, I will
give *it* thee, unto the [b]half of my
kingdom.
24 And she went forth, and said
unto her mother, What shall I ask?
And she said, The head of John the
Baptist.
25 And she came in straightway
with [a]haste unto the king, and asked,
saying, I will that thou give me [b]by
and by in a [c]charger the head of
[d]John the Baptist.
26 And the king was exceeding
sorry; *yet* for his [a]oath's sake, and
for their sakes which sat with him,
[b]he would not reject her.
27 And immediately the king sent
an executioner, and commanded his
head to be brought: and he went
and beheaded him in the prison,
28 And brought his head in a
charger, and gave it to the damsel:
and the damsel gave it to her mother.
29 And when his disciples heard *of*
it, they came and took up his corpse,
and laid it in a tomb.
30 And the apostles gathered themselves together unto Jesus, and told
him all things, both what they had
done, and what they had taught.
31 And he said unto them, Come
ye yourselves apart into a [a]desert
place, and rest a while: for there were
many coming and going, and they
had no [b]leisure so much as to eat.
32 And they departed into a [a]des-
ert place by ship privately.
33 And the people saw them departing, and many knew him, and
ran afoot thither out of all cities,
and outwent them, and came together unto him.
34 And Jesus, when he came out,
saw much people, and was moved
with [a]compassion toward them, because they were as sheep not having
a [b]shepherd: and he began to [c]teach
them many things.
35 And when the day was now far
spent, his disciples came unto him,
and said, [a]This is a desert place, and
now the time *is* far passed:
36 Send them away, that they may
go into the country round about, and
into the villages, and buy themselves
bread: for they have nothing to eat.
37 He answered and said unto
them, Give ye them to eat. And they
say unto him, Shall we go and buy
two hundred [a]pennyworth of bread,
and give them to eat?
38 He saith unto them, How many
loaves have ye? go and see. And
when they knew, they say, Five,
and two fishes.
39 And he commanded them to

20*a* GR righteous and holy man.
b JST Mark 6:21 . . . and a holy *man, and one who feared God* and observed *to worship* him; and when he heard him he did many things *for him*, and heard . . .
c GR protected.
21*a* GR nobles, military commanders, and prominent men.
23*a* TG Swearing.
b Esth. 5:3.
25*a* TG Haste.
b GR at once.
c OR platter.
d TG Martyrdom.
26*a* TG Vow.
b GR he did not desire to refuse.
31*a* JST Mark 6:32 . . . *solitary* . . .
b Mark 3:20.
32*a* JST Mark 6:33 . . . *solitary* . . .
34*a* TG Compassion.
b TG Shepherd.
c TG Jesus Christ, Teaching Mode of.
35*a* JST Mark 6:36 . . . This is a *solitary* place, and now the time *for departure* is *come* . . .
37*a* GR *denarii;* one *denarius* was a workman's daily wage.

make all sit down by companies
upon the green grass.
40 And they sat down in ranks, by
hundreds, and by fifties.
41 And when he had taken the
five loaves and the two fishes, he
looked up to heaven, and blessed,
and brake the loaves, and gave *them*
to his disciples to set before them;
and the two fishes divided he among
them all.
42 And they did all eat, and were
filled.
43 And they took up twelve baskets full of the fragments, and of
the fishes.
44 And they that did eat of the
loaves were about [a]five thousand
men.
45 And straightway he constrained
his disciples to get into the ship,
and to go to the other side before
unto Bethsaida, while he sent away
the people.
46 And when he had [a]sent them
away, he departed into a mountain
to pray.
47 And when even was come, the
ship was in the midst of the sea,
and he alone on the land.
48 And he saw them [a]toiling in
rowing; for the wind was contrary
unto them: and about the fourth
watch of the night he cometh unto
them, walking upon the sea, and
would have passed by them.
49 But when they saw him walking
upon the sea, they supposed it had
been a spirit, and cried out:
50 For they all saw him, and were
[a]troubled. And immediately he
talked with them, and saith unto
them, Be of good cheer: it is I; be
not afraid.
51 And he went up unto them into
the ship; and the wind ceased: and
they were sore amazed in themselves
beyond measure, and wondered.
52 For they [a]considered not *the*
miracle of the loaves: for their heart
was [b]hardened.
53 And when they had passed over,
they came into the land of Gennesaret, and drew to the shore.
54 And when they were come out
of the ship, straightway they knew
him,
55 And ran through that whole
region round about, and began to
carry about in beds those that were
sick, where they heard he was.
56 And whithersoever he entered,
into villages, or cities, or country,
they laid the sick in the streets, and
besought him that they might touch
if it were but the border of his garment: and as many as touched him
were made whole.

CHAPTER 7

Jesus reproves the Pharisees for their false traditions and ceremonies—He casts a devil out of the daughter of a Greek woman—He opens the ears and loosens the tongue of a person with an impediment.

THEN came together unto him the
Pharisees, and certain of the scribes,
which came from Jerusalem.
2 And when they saw some of his
disciples eat bread with defiled,
that is to say, with unwashen, hands,
they found fault.
3 For the Pharisees, and all the
Jews, except they [a]wash *their* hands
oft, eat not, holding the tradition
of the elders.
4 And *when they come* from the
market, except they wash, they eat
not. And many other things there
be, which they have received to
hold, *as* the washing of cups, and
pots, brasen vessels, and of tables.
5 Then the Pharisees and scribes
asked him, Why walk not thy disciples according to the tradition of
the elders, but eat bread with [a]un-
washen hands?
6 He answered and said unto
them, Well hath Esaias prophesied
of you hypocrites, as it is written,

44*a* Matt. 14:21 (13–21); Luke 9:14 (10–17); John 6:10 (1–13).
46*a* GR bid them farewell.
48*a* GR struggling at their oars.
50*a* OR terrified.
52*a* OR did not understand. 1 Cor. 2:11.
b TG Hardheartedness.
7 3*a* TG Purification.
5*a* TG Wash.

This people [a]honoureth me with *their* lips, but their heart is far from me.

7 Howbeit in vain do they worship me, teaching *for* doctrines the commandments of men.

8 For laying aside the commandment of God, ye hold the [a]tradition of men, *as* the washing of pots and cups: and many other such like things ye do.

9 And he said unto them, Full well ye reject the commandment of God, that ye may keep your own tradition.

10 [a]For Moses said, Honour thy father and thy mother; and, Whoso [b]curseth father or mother, let him die the death:

11 But ye say, If a man shall say to his father or mother, *It is* [a]Corban, that is to say, a gift, by whatsoever thou mightest be profited by me; *he shall be free.*

12 And ye suffer him no more to do ought for his father or his mother;

13 Making the word of God of none effect through your tradition, which ye have delivered: and many such like things do ye.

14 ¶ And when he had called all the people *unto him,* he said unto them, Hearken unto me every one *of you,* and understand:

15 There is nothing from without a man, that entering into him can [a]defile him: but the things which come out of him, those are they that [b]defile the man.

16 If any man have ears to hear, let him hear.

17 And when he was entered into the house from the people, his disciples asked him concerning the parable.

18 And he saith unto them, Are ye so without understanding also? Do ye not perceive, that whatsoever thing from without entereth into the man, *it* cannot defile him;

19 Because it entereth not into his heart, but into the belly, and goeth out into the draught, purging all meats?

20 And he said, That which cometh out of the man, that [a]defileth the man.

21 For from within, out of the [a]heart of men, proceed evil thoughts, [b]adulteries, fornications, murders,

22 [a]Thefts, [b]covetousness, [c]wickedness, [d]deceit, lasciviousness, an evil eye, blasphemy, pride, foolishness:

23 All these [a]evil things come from within, and [b]defile the man.

24 ¶ And from thence he arose, and went into the borders of Tyre and Sidon, and entered into an house, [a]and would have no man know *it:* but he could not be hid.

25 For a *certain* woman, whose young daughter had an unclean spirit, heard of him, and came and fell at his feet:

26 The woman was a Greek, a Syrophenician by nation; and she besought him that he would cast forth the devil out of her daughter.

27 But Jesus said unto her, Let the [a]children first be filled: for it is not meet to take the children's bread, and to cast *it* unto the [b]dogs.

28 And she answered and said unto him, Yes, Lord: yet the dogs under the table eat of the children's crumbs.

6*a* TG Apostasy of Israel; Hypocrisy.
8*a* TG Traditions of Men.
10*a* JST Mark 7:10–12 (Appendix).
b TG Curse; Honoring Father and Mother.
11*a* Matt. 15:5.
15*a* JST Mark 7:15 . . . defile him, *which is food;* but the things which come out of him; those are they that defile the man, *that proceedeth forth out of the heart.*
b Titus 1:15; 2 Ne. 19:17; D&C 93:35.
20*a* James 3:6; D&C 88:121.
21*a* 1 Jn. 2:16.
b TG Adulterer.
22*a* TG Stealing.
b TG Covet.
c TG Wickedness.
d TG Deceit; Fraud.
23*a* TG Motivations.
b Mosiah 4:30.
24*a* JST Mark 7:22–23 . . . and would *that* no man *should come unto him.* But he could not *deny them; for he had compassion upon all men.*
27*a* JST Mark 7:26 . . . children *of the kingdom* first . . .
b D&C 41:6.

29 And he said unto her, For this
saying go thy way; the devil is gone
out of thy daughter.
30 And when she was come to her
house, she found the [a]devil gone
out, and her daughter laid upon the
bed.
31 ¶ And again, departing from the
coasts of Tyre and Sidon, he came
unto the sea of Galilee, through the
midst of the coasts of Decapolis.
32 And they bring unto him one
that was deaf, and had an impediment in his speech; and they beseech
him to put his [a]hand upon him.
33 And he took him aside from the
multitude, and put his fingers into
his ears, and he spit, and touched
his tongue;
34 And looking up to heaven, he
sighed, and saith unto him, Eph-
phatha, that is, Be opened.
35 And straightway his ears were
[a]opened, and the string of his tongue
was loosed, and he spake plain.
36 And he charged them that they
should tell no man: but the more he
charged them, so much the more a
great deal they [a]published *it;*
37 And were beyond measure astonished, saying, He hath done all
things well: he maketh both the
deaf to hear, and the dumb to speak.

CHAPTER 8

Jesus feeds the four thousand—He counsels, Beware of the leaven of the Pharisees—He heals a blind man in Bethsaida—Peter testifies that Jesus is the Christ.

In those days the multitude being
very great, and having nothing to
eat, Jesus called his disciples *unto*
him, and saith unto them,
2 I have compassion on the multitude, because they have now been
with me three days, and have nothing to eat:
3 And if I send them away fasting
to their own houses, they will faint
by the way: for [a]divers of them came
from far.
4 And his disciples answered him,
From whence can a man satisfy
these *men* with bread here in the
wilderness?
5 And he asked them, How many
loaves have ye? And they said, Seven.
6 And he commanded the people to
sit down on the ground: and he took
the seven loaves, and gave thanks,
and brake, and gave to his disciples
to set before *them;* and they did set
them before the people.
7 And they had a few small fishes:
and he blessed, and commanded to
set them also before *them.*
8 So they did eat, and were filled:
and they took up of the broken *meat*
that was left seven baskets.
9 And they that had eaten were
about four thousand: and he sent
them away.
10 ¶ And straightway he entered
into a ship with his disciples, and
came into the parts of Dalmanutha.
11 And the Pharisees came forth,
and began to question with him,
seeking of him a [a]sign from heaven,
tempting him.
12 And he sighed deeply in his
spirit, and saith, Why doth this generation seek after a [a]sign? verily I
say unto you, There shall no sign be
given unto this generation.
13 And he left them, and entering
into the ship again departed to the
other side.
14 ¶ Now *the disciples* had forgotten to take bread, neither had they
in the ship with them more than
one loaf.
15 And he charged them, saying,
Take heed, beware of the leaven of
the Pharisees, and *of* the leaven
of Herod.
16 And they reasoned among themselves, saying, *It is* because we have
no bread.
17 And when Jesus knew *it,* he saith
unto them, Why reason ye, because

30*a* 1 Ne. 11:31.
32*a* TG Administrations to the Sick; Hands, Laying on of.
35*a* TG Miracle.
36*a* Matt. 9:31.
8 3*a* GR some.
11*a* D&C 46:9; 63:7 (7–11).
12*a* Matt. 16:4 (1–12).

ye have no bread? perceive ye not yet, neither understand? [a]have ye your heart yet [b]hardened?
18 Having eyes, see ye not? and having ears, hear ye not? and do ye not remember?
19 When I brake the five loaves among five thousand, how many baskets full of fragments took ye up? They say unto him, Twelve.
20 And when the seven among four thousand, how many baskets full of fragments took ye up? And they said, Seven.
21 And he said unto them, How is it that ye do not understand?
22 ¶ And he cometh to Bethsaida; and they bring a blind man unto him, and besought him to touch him.
23 And he took the blind man by the hand, and led him out of the town; and when he had spit on his eyes, and put his [a]hands upon him, he asked him if he saw [b]ought.
24 And he looked up, and said, I see men as trees, walking.
25 After that he put *his* hands again upon his eyes, and made him look up: and he was restored, and saw [a]every man clearly.
26 And he sent him away to his house, saying, Neither go into the town, nor tell *it* to any in the town.
27 ¶ And Jesus went out, and his disciples, into the towns of Cæsarea Philippi: and by the way he asked his disciples, saying unto them, Whom do men say that I am?
28 And they answered, John the Baptist: but some *say*, Elias; and others, One of the prophets.
29 And he saith unto them, But whom say ye that I am? And Peter answereth and saith unto him, Thou art the [a]Christ.
30 And he charged them that they should [a]tell no man of him.
31 And he began to [a]teach them, that the Son of man must suffer many things, and be rejected of the elders, and *of* the chief priests, and scribes, and be killed, and after three days rise again.
32 And he spake that saying openly. And Peter took him, and began to rebuke him.
33 But when he had turned about and looked on his disciples, he rebuked Peter, saying, Get thee behind me, [a]Satan: for [b]thou savourest not the things that be of God, but the things that be of men.
34 ¶ And when he had called the people *unto him* with his disciples also, he said unto them, Whosoever will come after me, let him [a]deny himself, and take up his cross, and [b]follow me.
35 [a]For whosoever will save his life shall lose it; but whosoever shall [b]lose his [c]life for my sake and the gospel's, the same shall save it.
36 For what shall it profit a man, if he shall [a]gain the whole world, and lose his own soul?
37 Or what shall a man give in exchange for his [a]soul?
38 Whosoever therefore shall be [a]ashamed of me and of my words in this adulterous and sinful generation; of him also shall the [b]Son of man be ashamed, when he cometh in the glory of his Father with the holy [c]angels.

17*a* GR do you still have hardened hearts?
b TG Hardheartedness.
23*a* TG Administrations to the Sick; Hands, Laying on of.
b OR anything.
25*a* OR everything.
29*a* TG Jesus Christ, Messiah.
30*a* Luke 9:21.
31*a* TG Jesus Christ, Teaching Mode of.
33*a* Alma 12:5 (5–6, 34).
b GR you do not consider, cherish.
34*a* TG Self-Mastery.
b TG Jesus Christ, Exemplar.
35*a* JST Mark 8:37–38 (Appendix).
b Luke 9:24; JST Luke 9:24–25 (Appendix).
c Heb. 11:35; JST Heb. 11:35 (Heb. 11:35 note *b*); D&C 103:28 (27–28). TG Martyrdom.
36*a* Jer. 45:5.
37*a* JST Mark 8:39–40 . . . soul? *Therefore deny yourselves of these, and be not ashamed of me.*
38*a* 1 Ne. 8:28 (24–28). TG Shame.
b TG Jesus Christ, Son of Man.
c JST Mark 8:42–43 (Appendix).

CHAPTER 9

Jesus is transfigured on the mountain—He casts out an unclean spirit—He teaches concerning His death and resurrection, who will be greatest, and the condemnation of those who offend His little ones.

AND he said unto them, Verily I say
unto you, That there be some of
them that stand here, which shall
not taste of death, till they have
seen the kingdom of God come with
power.
2 ¶ And after [a]six days Jesus taketh
with him Peter, and James, and John,
[b]and leadeth them up into an high
mountain apart by themselves:
and he was [c]transfigured before
them.
3 And his raiment became shining,
exceeding white as snow; so as
no fuller on earth can white them.
4 And there appeared unto them
Elias with [a]Moses: and they were
talking with Jesus.
5 And Peter answered and said
to Jesus, Master, it is good for us to
be here: and let us make three tabernacles;
one for thee, and one for
Moses, and one for Elias.
6 For he wist not what to say; for
they were sore afraid.
7 And there was a cloud that overshadowed
them: and a [a]voice came
out of the cloud, saying, This is my
[b]beloved Son: hear him.
8 And suddenly, when they had
looked round about, they saw no
man any more, save Jesus only with
themselves.
9 And as they came down from
the mountain, he charged them that
they should tell no [a]man what things
they had seen, till the Son of man
were risen from the dead.
10 And they kept that saying with
themselves, questioning one with
another what the [a]rising from the
dead should mean.
11 ¶ And they asked him, saying,
Why say the scribes that Elias must
first come?
12 And he answered and told
them, Elias verily cometh first, [a]and
[b]restoreth all things; and how it is
written of the [c]Son of man, that he
must [d]suffer many things, and be
set at [e]nought.
13 But I say unto you, That Elias
is indeed come, and they have done
unto him whatsoever they [a]listed,
as it is written of [b]him.
14 ¶ And when he came to *his*
disciples, he saw a great multitude
about them, and the scribes questioning
with them.
15 And straightway all the people,
when they beheld him, were
greatly amazed, and running to *him*
saluted him.
16 And he asked the scribes, What
question ye with them?
17 And one of the multitude answered
and said, Master, I have
brought unto thee my son, which
hath a dumb spirit;
18 And wheresoever he taketh him,
he [a]teareth him: and he foameth, and
gnasheth with his teeth, and pineth
away: and I spake to thy disciples
that they should cast him out; and
they could not.
19 He answereth him, and saith,
O faithless generation, how long
shall I be with you? how long shall
I suffer you? bring him unto me.
20 And they brought him unto

---

9 2*a* Luke 9:28 (28–36).
b JST Mark 9:1 . . . *who asked him many questions concerning his sayings;* and *Jesus* leadeth them . . .
c Matt. 17:2 (1–13); Luke 9:29 (28–36).
4*a* JST Mark 9:3 . . . Moses, *or in other words, John the Baptist and Moses* . . .
7*a* TG God, Manifestations of.
b Matt. 3:17; Luke 9:35 (34–36).
9*a* Matt. 17:9 (9–12).
10*a* John 20:9.
12*a* JST Mark 9:10 . . . and *prepareth* all things; and *teacheth you of the prophets;* how . . .
b TG Dispensations.
c TG Jesus Christ, Prophecies about.
d TG Jesus Christ, Crucifixion of.
e Isa. 53:3.
13*a* GR willed, chose, intended.
b JST Mark 9:11 . . . him; *and he bore record of me, and they received him not. Verily this was Elias.*
18*a* GR dashes on the ground, convulses, lacerates.

him: and when he saw him, straightway the spirit [a]tare him; and he
fell on the ground, and wallowed
foaming.
21 And he asked his father, How
long is it ago since this came unto
him? And he said, Of a child.
22 And ofttimes it hath cast him
into the fire, and into the waters,
to destroy him: but if thou canst do
any thing, have [a]compassion on us,
and help us.
23 Jesus said unto him, If thou canst
believe, all things *are* [a]possible to
him that [b]believeth.
24 And straightway the father of
the child cried out, and said with
tears, Lord, I believe; help thou mine
[a]unbelief.
25 When Jesus saw that the people came running together, he [a]re-
buked the [b]foul spirit, saying unto
him, *Thou* dumb and deaf spirit, I
charge thee, come out of him, and
enter no more into him.
26 And *the spirit* cried, and rent
him sore, and came out of him: and
he was as one dead; insomuch that
many said, He is dead.
27 But Jesus took him by the hand,
and [a]lifted him up; and he arose.
28 And when he was come into
the house, his disciples asked him
privately, Why could not we cast
him out?
29 And he said unto them, This
kind can come forth by nothing,
but by prayer and [a]fasting.
30 ¶ And they departed thence,
and passed through Galilee; and
he would not that any man should
know *it*.
31 For he taught his disciples, and
said unto them, The [a]Son of man is
delivered into the hands of men,
and they shall kill him; and after
that he is killed, he shall [b]rise the
third day.
32 But they understood not that
saying, and were afraid to ask him.
33 ¶ And he came to Capernaum:
and being in the house he asked
them, What was it that ye [a]disputed
among yourselves by the way?
34 But they held their peace: for
by the way they had [a]disputed
among themselves, who *should be*
the [b]greatest.
35 And he sat down, and called the
twelve, and saith unto them, If any
man desire to be [a]first, *the same* shall
be last of all, and [b]servant of all.
36 And he took a child, and set him
in the midst of them: and when he
had taken him in his arms, he said
unto them,
37 [a]Whosoever shall receive one
of such [b]children in my name, receiveth me: and whosoever shall
receive me, receiveth not me, but
him that sent me.
38 ¶ And John answered him, saying, Master, we saw one [a]casting out
devils in thy name, and he followeth
not us: and we forbad him, because
he followeth not us.
39 But Jesus said, Forbid him not:
for there is no man which shall do
a [a]miracle in my [b]name, that can
lightly speak evil of me.
40 For he that is not against us is
[a]on our part.
41 For whosoever shall give you a
cup of water to drink in my name,

20*a* Mark 1:26.
22*a* TG Compassion.
23*a* Dan. 3:29. TG God, Power of.
b TG Faith.
24*a* TG Doubt.
25*a* TG Heal.
b TG Spirits, Evil or Unclean.
27*a* Acts 3:7.
29*a* TG Problem-Solving.
31*a* TG Jesus Christ, Son of Man.
b TG Jesus Christ, Resurrection.
33*a* GR reasoned, disputed, pondered.
34*a* TG Disputations.
b Luke 9:46.
35*a* Prov. 18:17.
b TG Meek.
37*a* JST Mark 9:34–35 Whosoever shall *humble himself like one of these children, and receiveth me, ye shall receive in my name.* And whosoever shall receive me, receiveth not me *only*, but him that sent me, *even the Father*.
b TG Children; Salvation of Little Children.
38*a* Luke 11:19; Acts 19:13.
39*a* TG Miracle.
b TG Name.
40*a* Matt. 12:30; Luke 9:50.

because ye belong to Christ, verily
I say unto you, he shall not [a]lose
his [b]reward.
42 And whosoever shall [a]offend
one of *these* little ones that believe
in me, it is better for him that a
millstone were hanged about his
neck, and he were cast into the sea.
43 [a]And if thy hand offend thee,
[b]cut it off: it is better for thee to enter into life maimed, than having
two hands to go into [c]hell, into the
fire that never shall be quenched:
44 Where their worm dieth not,
and the fire is not quenched.
45 And if thy foot [a]offend thee, cut
it off: it is better for thee to enter
halt into life, than having two feet
to be cast into hell, into the fire that
never shall be quenched:
46 Where their worm dieth not,
and the fire is not quenched.
47 And if thine eye offend thee,
pluck it out: it is better for thee to
enter into the kingdom of God with
one eye, than having two eyes to be
cast into hell fire:
48 Where their [a]worm dieth not,
and the fire is not quenched.
49 For every one shall be [a]salted
with fire, and every sacrifice shall
be salted with salt.
50 Salt *is* good: but if the salt have
lost his saltness, wherewith will ye
season it? Have salt in yourselves,
and have [a]peace one with another.

CHAPTER 10

Jesus teaches the higher law of marriage—He blesses little children—Jesus counsels the rich young man, foretells His own death, and heals blind Bartimæus.

AND he arose from thence, and
cometh into the coasts of Judæa by
the farther side of Jordan: and the
people resort unto him again; and,
as he was wont, he taught them
again.
2 ¶ And the Pharisees came to him,
and asked him, Is it lawful for a
man to put away *his* wife? tempting
him.
3 And he answered and said unto
them, What did Moses command
you?
4 And they said, Moses suffered to
write a bill of divorcement, and to
put *her* away.
5 And Jesus answered and said unto
them, For the hardness of your heart
he wrote you this precept.
6 But from the beginning of the
creation God made them male and
female.
7 For this cause shall a [a]man leave
his father and mother, and cleave
to his [b]wife;
8 And they twain shall be one flesh:
so then they are no more twain, but
one flesh.
9 What therefore God hath [a]joined
together, let not man put [b]asunder.
10 And in the house his disciples
asked him again of the same *matter*.
11 And he saith unto them, Whosoever shall put away his wife, and
marry another, committeth adultery
against her.
12 And if a woman shall put away
her husband, and be married to
another, she committeth adultery.
13 ¶ And they brought young children to him, that he should touch
them: and *his* disciples rebuked
those that brought *them*.
14 But when Jesus saw *it*, he was
much displeased, and said unto
them, Suffer the little [a]children to
come unto me, and forbid them not:
for of such is the kingdom of God.
15 Verily I say unto you, Whosoever shall not receive the kingdom
of God as a little [a]child, he shall not
enter therein.

41*a* Matt. 10:42; D&C 84:90.
b TG Reward.
42*a* TG Offense.
43*a* JST Mark 9:40–48 (Appendix).
b TG Self-Mastery.
c TG Hell.
45*a* GR cause thee to stumble.
48*a* Isa. 66:24; D&C 76:44.
49*a* TG Salt.
50*a* 1 Thes. 5:13. TG Peace.
10 7*a* TG Marriage, Husbands.
b TG Marriage, Wives.
9*a* TG Family, Eternal; Genealogy and Temple Work; Marriage, Marry.
b TG Divorce.
14*a* Moro. 8:8 (5–9). TG Example.
15*a* TG Meek.

16 And he took them up in his
arms, put *his* hands upon them, and
[a]blessed them.
17 ¶ And when he was gone forth
into the way, there came one running, and kneeled to him, and asked
him, Good Master, what shall I do
that I may inherit eternal life?
18 And Jesus said unto him, Why
callest thou me good? *there is* none
[a]good but one, *that is*, God.
19 Thou knowest the commandments, Do not commit [a]adultery, Do
not [b]kill, Do not [c]steal, Do not bear
false witness, [d]Defraud not, [e]Honour
thy father and mother.
20 And he answered and said unto
him, Master, all these have I observed
from my youth.
21 Then Jesus beholding him loved
him, and said unto him, One thing
thou lackest: go thy way, sell whatsoever thou hast, and [a]give to the
poor, and thou shalt have treasure
in heaven: and come, take up the
cross, and [b]follow me.
22 And he was sad at that saying,
and went away grieved: for he had
great possessions.
23 ¶ And Jesus looked round about,
and saith unto his disciples, How
hardly shall they that have riches
enter into the kingdom of God!
24 And the disciples were astonished at his words. But Jesus answereth again, and saith unto them,
Children, how hard is it for them
that [a]trust in [b]riches to enter into
the kingdom of God!
25 It is easier for a camel to go
through the eye of a needle, than
for a rich man to enter into the
kingdom of God.
26 And they were astonished out of
measure, saying among themselves,
Who then can be saved?
27 And Jesus looking upon them
saith, [a]With men *it is* impossible,
but not with God: for with God all
things are [b]possible.
28 ¶ Then Peter began to say unto
him, Lo, we have left all, and have
followed thee.
29 And Jesus answered and said,
Verily I say unto you, There is no
man that hath left house, or brethren, or sisters, or father, or mother,
or wife, or children, or lands, for
my sake, and the gospel's,
30 But he shall receive an [a]hun-
dredfold now in this time, houses,
and brethren, and sisters, and mothers, and children, and lands, with
persecutions; and in the world to
come eternal life.
31 [a]But many *that are* [b]first shall
be last; and the last first.
32 ¶ And they were in the way
going up to Jerusalem; and Jesus
went before them: and they were
amazed; and as they followed, they
were afraid. And he took again the
twelve, and began to tell them what
things should happen unto him,
33 *Saying,* Behold, we go up to Jerusalem; and the [a]Son of man shall
be delivered unto the chief priests,
and unto the [b]scribes; and they shall
condemn him to death, and shall
deliver him to the Gentiles:
34 And they shall [a]mock him, and
shall scourge him, and shall spit

16*a* 3 Ne. 17:21.
TG Salvation of Little Children.
18*a* Ether 4:12 (11–12).
19*a* D&C 66:10.
b TG Murder.
c TG Stealing.
d TG Fraud.
e TG Honoring Father and Mother.
21*a* TG Charity; Generosity.
b TG Jesus Christ, Exemplar.
24*a* Jacob 2:18 (17–19).
b TG Treasure.
27*a* JST Mark 10:26 . . . With men *that trust in riches,* it is impossible; but not *impossible with men who trust in God and leave all for my sake,* for with *such* all *these* things are possible.
b TG God, Power of.
30*a* TG Reward.
31*a* JST Mark 10:30–31 But *there are* many *who make themselves* first, *that* shall be last, and the last first. *This he said, rebuking Peter . . .*
b Jacob 5:63; Ether 13:12 (10–12).
33*a* TG Jesus Christ, Son of Man.
b TG Scribe.
34*a* TG Mocking.

upon him, and shall kill him: and
the third day he shall [b]rise again.
35 ¶ And James and John, the sons
of Zebedee, come unto him, saying,
Master, we would that thou shouldest do for us whatsoever we shall
desire.
36 And he said unto them, What
would ye that I should do for you?
37 They said unto him, Grant unto
us that we may sit, one on thy right
hand, and the other on thy left hand,
in thy glory.
38 But Jesus said unto them, Ye
know not what ye ask: can ye drink
of the cup that I drink of? and be
baptized with the [a]baptism that I
am baptized with?
39 And they said unto him, We
can. And Jesus said unto them, Ye
shall indeed drink of the cup that
I drink of; and with the baptism
that I am baptized withal shall ye
be baptized:
40 But to sit on my right hand and
on my left hand is not mine to give;
but *it shall be given to them* for whom
it is prepared.
41 And when the ten heard *it,* they
began to be much displeased with
James and John.
42 But Jesus called them *to him,*
and saith unto them, Ye know that
they which are accounted to rule
over the Gentiles exercise lordship
over them; and their great ones exercise authority upon them.
43 But so shall it not be among
you: but whosoever will be [a]great
among you, shall be your minister:
44 And whosoever of you will be
the [a]chiefest, shall be servant of all.
45 For even the Son of man came
not to be ministered unto, but to
minister, and to give his life a [a]ran-
som for many.
46 ¶ And they came to Jericho:
and as he went out of Jericho with
his disciples and a great number of
people, blind [a]Bartimæus, the son
of Timæus, sat by the highway side
begging.
47 And when he heard that it was
Jesus of Nazareth, he began to cry
out, and say, Jesus, *thou* Son of David, have mercy on me.
48 And many charged him that he
should hold his peace: but he cried
the more a great deal, *Thou* Son of
David, have mercy on me.
49 And Jesus stood still, and commanded him to be called. And they
call the [a]blind man, saying unto
him, Be of good comfort, rise; he
calleth thee.
50 And he, casting away his garment, rose, and came to Jesus.
51 And Jesus answered and said
unto him, What wilt thou that I
should do unto thee? The blind man
said unto him, Lord, that I might
receive my sight.
52 And Jesus said unto him, Go
thy way; thy faith hath [a]made thee
whole. And immediately he received his sight, and followed Jesus
in the way.

CHAPTER 11

Jesus rides into Jerusalem amid shouts of hosanna—He curses a fig tree, drives the money changers from the temple, and confounds the scribes on the matter of authority.

AND when they came nigh to Jerusalem, unto Bethphage and Bethany,
at the mount of Olives, he sendeth
forth two of his disciples,
2 And saith unto them, Go your way
into the village over against you: and
as soon as ye be entered into it, ye
shall find a colt tied, whereon never
man sat; loose him, and bring *him.*
3 And if any man say unto you,
Why do ye this? say ye that the Lord
hath need of him; and straightway
he will send him hither.
4 And they went their way, and
found the colt tied by the door

34*b* TG Jesus Christ, Resurrection.
38*a* TG Jesus Christ, Baptism of.
43*a* D&C 50:26 (26–27).
44*a* Matt. 23:11; Luke 22:24 (24–30); 2 Ne. 9:5.
45*a* Rom. 4:25.
46*a* Matt. 20:30 (29–34).
49*a* 1 Ne. 17:51.
52*a* GR saved, preserved, healed thee.

without in a place where two ways
met; and they loose him.
5 And certain of them that stood
there said unto them, What do ye,
loosing the colt?
6 And they said unto them even
as Jesus had commanded: and they
let them go.
7 And they brought the [a]colt to
Jesus, and cast their garments on
him; and he sat upon him.
8 And many spread their garments
in the way: and others cut down
branches off the trees, and strawed
them in the way.
9 And they that went before, and
they that followed, cried, saying,
Hosanna; [a]Blessed *is* he that cometh
in the name of the Lord:
10 [a]Blessed *be* the kingdom of our
father David, that cometh in the
name of the Lord: Hosanna in the
highest.
11 And Jesus entered into Jerusalem, and into the temple: and when
he had looked round about upon all
things, and now the eventide was
come, he went out unto Bethany
with the twelve.
12 ¶ And on the morrow, when
they were come from Bethany, he
was hungry:
13 And seeing a fig tree afar off
having leaves, he came, if haply
he might find any thing thereon:
and when he came to it, he found
nothing but leaves; for the time of
figs was not *yet*.
14 And Jesus answered and said
unto it, No man eat fruit of thee
hereafter for ever. And his disciples heard *it*.
15 ¶ And they come to Jerusalem:
and Jesus went into the temple, and
began to cast out them that sold and
bought in the temple, and overthrew
the tables of the moneychangers,
and the seats of them that sold
doves;
16 And would not suffer that any
man should carry *any* vessel through
the temple.
17 And he taught, saying unto
them, Is it not written, My house
shall be called of all nations the
house of prayer? but ye have made
it a den of thieves.
18 And the scribes and chief priests
heard *it*, and sought how they might
[a]destroy him: for they feared him,
because all the people was astonished at his doctrine.
19 And when even was come, he
went out of the city.
20 ¶ And in the morning, as they
passed by, they saw the fig tree dried
up from the roots.
21 And Peter calling to remembrance saith unto him, Master, behold, the fig tree which thou cursedst
is withered away.
22 And Jesus answering saith unto
them, Have [a]faith in God.
23 For verily I say unto you, That
whosoever shall say unto this mountain, Be thou removed, and be thou
cast into the sea; and shall not [a]doubt
in his heart, but shall believe that
those things which he saith shall
come to pass; he shall have whatsoever he saith.
24 Therefore I say unto you, What
things soever ye desire, when ye
[a]pray, [b]believe that ye receive *them*,
and ye shall have *them*.
25 And when ye stand [a]praying,
forgive, if ye have ought against
any: that your Father also which is
in heaven may [b]forgive you your
trespasses.
26 But if ye do not [a]forgive, neither
will your Father which is in heaven
forgive your trespasses.
27 ¶ And they come again to Jerusalem: and as he was walking in
the temple, there come to him the
chief priests, and the scribes, and
the elders,

---

11 7*a* Zech. 9:9.
9*a* Ps. 118:26.
10*a* JST Mark 11:11–12 *That bringeth* the kingdom of our father David; *Blessed is he* that cometh in the name of the Lord . . .
18*a* TG Jesus Christ, Betrayal of.
22*a* TG Faith.
23*a* TG Doubt.
24*a* TG Prayer.
b 3 Ne. 18:20; D&C 29:6.
25*a* TG Prayer.
b TG Forgive.
26*a* D&C 64:9 (7–10).

28 And say unto him, By what [a]authority doest thou these things? and who gave thee this authority to do these things?
29 And Jesus answered and said unto them, I will also ask of you one question, and answer me, and I will tell you by what authority I do these things.
30 The baptism of John, was *it* from heaven, or of men? answer me.
31 And they reasoned with themselves, saying, If we shall say, From heaven; he will say, Why then did ye not believe him?
32 But if we shall say, Of men; they feared the people: for all *men* counted John, that he was a prophet indeed.
33 And they answered and said unto Jesus, We cannot tell. And Jesus answering saith unto them, Neither do I tell you by what authority I do these things.

CHAPTER 12

Jesus gives the parable of the wicked husbandmen—He speaks of paying taxes, celestial marriage, the two great commandments, the divine sonship of Christ, and the widow's mites.

AND he began to speak unto them by parables. A *certain* man planted a vineyard, and set an hedge about *it,* and digged *a place for* the winefat, and built a tower, and let it out to husbandmen, and went into a far country.
2 And at the season he sent to the husbandmen a servant, that he might receive from the husbandmen of the fruit of the vineyard.
3 And they caught *him,* and beat him, and sent *him* away empty.
4 And again he sent unto them another servant; and at him they cast stones, and wounded *him* in the head, and sent *him* away shamefully handled.
5 And again he sent another; and him they killed, and many others; beating some, and killing some.
6 Having yet therefore one son, his wellbeloved, he sent him also last unto them, saying, They will reverence my son.
7 But those husbandmen said among themselves, This is the heir; come, let us kill him, and the inheritance shall be ours.
8 And they took him, and killed *him,* and cast *him* out of the vineyard.
9 What shall therefore the lord of the vineyard do? he will come and destroy the husbandmen, and will give the [a]vineyard unto others.
10 And have ye not read this scripture; The [a]stone which the builders rejected is become the head of the corner:
11 This was the Lord's doing, and it is marvellous in our eyes?
12 And they sought to lay hold on him, but feared the people: for they knew that he had spoken the parable against them: and they left him, and went their way.
13 ¶ And they send unto him certain of the Pharisees and of the Herodians, to [a]catch him in *his* words.
14 And when they were come, they say unto him, Master, we know that thou art true, and carest for no man: for thou regardest not the person of men, but teachest the way of God in truth: Is it lawful to give tribute to Cæsar, or not?
15 Shall we give, or shall we not give? But he, knowing their hypocrisy, said unto them, Why [a]tempt ye me? bring me a penny, that I may see *it.*
16 And they brought *it.* And he saith unto them, Whose *is* this image and superscription? And they said unto him, Cæsar's.
17 And Jesus answering said unto them, Render to Cæsar the things that are Cæsar's, and to God the things that are God's. And they marvelled at him.

28*a* TG Priesthood, Authority.
12 9*a* TG Vineyard of the Lord.
10*a* TG Cornerstone.
13*a* Matt. 22:15 (15–22); Luke 11:54 (53–54); 20:20 (19–26).
15*a* TG Test.

18 ¶ Then come unto him the Sadducees, which say there is no resurrection; and they asked him, saying,

19 Master, Moses wrote unto us, If a man's brother die, and leave *his* wife *behind him,* and leave no children, that his [a]brother should take his wife, and raise up seed unto his brother.

20 Now there were seven brethren: and the first took a wife, and dying left no seed.

21 And the second took her, and died, neither left he any seed: and the third likewise.

22 And the seven had her, and left no seed: last of all the woman died also.

23 In the resurrection therefore, when they shall rise, whose wife shall she be of them? for the seven had her to wife.

24 And Jesus answering said unto them, [a]Do ye not therefore err, because ye know not the scriptures, neither the power of God?

25 For when they shall rise from the dead, they neither [a]marry, nor are given in marriage; but are as the angels which are in heaven.

26 And as touching the dead, that they [a]rise: have ye not read in the book of Moses, how in the bush God [b]spake unto him, saying, I *am* the [c]God of Abraham, and the God of Isaac, and the God of Jacob?

27 [a]He is not the God of the dead, but the God of the living: ye therefore do greatly err.

28 ¶ And one of the [a]scribes came, and having heard them reasoning together, and perceiving that he had answered them well, asked him, Which is the first commandment of all?

29 And Jesus answered him, The first of all the commandments *is,* [a]Hear, O Israel; The Lord our God is one Lord:

30 And thou shalt [a]love the Lord thy God with all thy [b]heart, and with all thy soul, and with all thy mind, and with all thy [c]strength: this *is* the first commandment.

31 And the second *is* like, *namely* this, Thou shalt love thy neighbour as thyself. There is none other commandment greater than these.

32 And the scribe said unto him, Well, Master, thou hast said the truth: for there is one God; and there is none other but he:

33 And to love him with all the heart, and with all the understanding, and with all the soul, and with all the strength, and to love *his* neighbour as himself, is more than all whole burnt [a]offerings and sacrifices.

34 And when Jesus saw that he answered discreetly, he said unto him, Thou art not far from the kingdom of God. And no man after that durst ask him *any question.*

35 ¶ And Jesus answered and said, while he taught in the temple, How say the scribes that Christ is the Son of David?

36 For David himself said by the Holy Ghost, The [a]LORD said to my Lord, Sit thou on my right hand, till I make thine enemies thy footstool.

37 David therefore himself calleth him Lord; and whence is he *then* his son? And the common people heard him gladly.

38 ¶ And he said unto them in his doctrine, Beware of the [a]scribes, which love to go in long clothing, and *love* [b]salutations in the marketplaces,

---

19*a* Deut. 25:5; Matt. 22:24; Luke 20:28.
24*a* JST Mark 12:28 . . . *Ye do err therefore,* because ye know not, *and understand not* the scriptures . . .
25*a* TG Marriage, Marry.
26*a* TG Resurrection.
b TG God, Manifestations of.
c Ex. 3:6.
27*a* JST Mark 12:32 He is not *therefore* the God of the dead, but the God of the living; *for he raiseth them up out of their graves.* Ye therefore . . .
28*a* TG Scribe.
29*a* Deut. 6:4.
30*a* Deut. 6:5.
b TG Commitment.
c TG Strength.
33*a* Matt. 22:40 (15–40). TG Sacrifice.
36*a* Ps. 110:1.
38*a* TG Pride.
b John 12:43 (42–43).

39 And the chief seats in the synagogues, and the uppermost rooms at feasts:
40 Which devour widows' houses, and for a pretence make long prayers: these shall receive greater [a]damnation.
41 ¶ And Jesus sat over against the treasury, and beheld how the people cast money into the treasury: and many that were rich cast in much.
42 And there came a certain [a]poor widow, and she threw in two [b]mites, which make a farthing.
43 And he called *unto him* his disciples, and saith unto them, Verily I say unto you, That this [a]poor widow hath cast more in, than all they which have cast into the treasury:
44 For all *they* did cast in of their [a]abundance; but she of her [b]want did [c]cast in [d]all that she had, *even* all her living.

CHAPTER 13

Jesus tells of the calamities and signs preceding the Second Coming—There will be false Christs and false prophets—He gives the parable of the fig tree.

[a]AND as he went out of the temple, one of his disciples saith unto him, Master, see what manner of stones and what buildings *are here!*
2 And Jesus answering said unto him, Seest thou these great buildings? there shall not be left one stone upon another, that shall not be thrown down.
3 And as he sat upon the mount of Olives over against the temple, Peter and James and John and Andrew asked him privately,
4 Tell us, when shall these things be? and what *shall be* the [a]sign when all these things shall be fulfilled?
5 And Jesus answering them began to say, Take heed lest any *man* deceive you:
6 For many shall come in my name, saying, I am *Christ;* and shall [a]deceive many.
7 And when ye shall hear of wars and rumours of wars, be ye not troubled: for *such things* must needs be; but the end *shall* not *be* yet.
8 For [a]nation shall rise against nation, and kingdom against kingdom: and there shall be earthquakes in divers places, and there shall be famines and troubles: these *are* the beginnings of sorrows.
9 ¶ But take heed to yourselves: for they shall deliver you up to councils; and in the synagogues ye shall be beaten: and ye shall be brought before rulers and [a]kings for my sake, for a testimony against them.
10 And the [a]gospel must first be [b]published among all nations.
11 But when they shall lead *you,* and deliver you up, take no thought beforehand what ye shall speak, neither do ye premeditate: but whatsoever shall be given you in that hour, that [a]speak ye: for it is not ye that speak, but the [b]Holy Ghost.
12 Now the brother shall betray the brother to death, and the father the son; and children shall rise up against *their* parents, and shall cause them to be put to death.
13 And ye shall be [a]hated of all *men* for my name's sake: but he that shall [b]endure unto the end, the same shall be saved.
14 ¶ But when ye shall see the abomination of desolation, spoken of by Daniel the prophet, standing where it ought not, (let him that readeth understand,) then let them that be in Judæa flee to the mountains:

40*a* TG Damnation.
42*a* TG Poor.
b Deut. 16:17.
43*a* TG Almsgiving.
44*a* TG Treasure.
b 2 Cor. 8:2 (2–12).
c Mosiah 4:24 (16–27).
d TG Generosity.
13 1*a* The text of JST Mark 13 is the same as JST Matthew 24. See Pearl of Great Price, JS—M.
4*a* TG Signs.
6*a* Matt. 24:5.
8*a* 1 Ne. 14:15; D&C 87:6.
9*a* TG Kings, Earthly.
10*a* TG Gospel.
b 1 Ne. 13:37; 3 Ne. 20:40; D&C 19:29.
11*a* Matt. 10:19 (19–20).
b TG Holy Ghost, Mission of.
13*a* 1 Ne. 11:34.
b Matt. 10:22 (22–33); 3 Ne. 15:9.

15 And let him that is on the housetop not go down into the house, neither enter *therein,* to take any thing
out of his house:
16 And let him that is in the field
not turn back again for to take up
his garment.
17 But woe to them that are with
child, and to them that give suck
in those days!
18 And pray ye that your flight be
not in the winter.
19 For *in* those days shall be [a]af-
fliction, such as was not from the
beginning of the creation which
God created unto this time, neither
shall be.
20 And except that the Lord had
shortened those days, no flesh
should be saved: but for the [a]elect's
sake, whom he hath chosen, he hath
shortened the days.
21 And then if any man shall say
to you, Lo, here *is* Christ; or, lo, *he*
is there; believe *him* not:
22 For [a]false Christs and [b]false
prophets shall rise, and shall shew
[c]signs and wonders, to seduce, if *it*
were possible, even the elect.
23 But take ye heed: behold, I have
foretold you all things.
24 ¶ But in those days, after that
tribulation, the sun shall be darkened, and the moon shall not give
her light,
25 And the [a]stars of heaven shall
fall, and the powers that are in
heaven shall be shaken.
26 And then shall they see the [a]Son
of man coming in the clouds with
great power and glory.
27 And then shall he send his
angels, and shall gather together
his elect from the four winds, from
the uttermost part of the earth to the
uttermost part of heaven.
28 Now learn a parable of the [a]fig
tree; When her branch is yet tender,
and putteth forth leaves, ye know
that summer is near:
29 So ye in like manner, when ye
shall see these things come to pass,
know that it is nigh, *even* at the doors.
30 Verily I say unto you, that this
[a]generation shall not pass, till all
these things be done.
31 Heaven and earth shall pass
away: but my [a]words shall not
pass away.
32 ¶ But of that [a]day and *that* hour
knoweth no man, no, not the angels
which are in heaven, neither the
Son, but the Father.
33 Take ye heed, [a]watch and [b]pray:
for ye know not when the time is.
34 *For the Son of man is* as a man
taking a far journey, who left his
house, and gave [a]authority to his
servants, and to every man his work,
and commanded the porter to watch.
35 Watch ye therefore: for ye know
not when the master of the house
cometh, at even, or at midnight, or at
the cockcrowing, or in the morning:
36 Lest coming suddenly he find
you [a]sleeping.
37 And what I say unto you I say
unto all, Watch.

CHAPTER 14

Jesus is anointed with oil—He eats the Passover, institutes the sacrament, suffers in Gethsemane, and is betrayed by Judas—Jesus is falsely accused, and Peter denies that he knows Him.

AFTER two days was *the feast of*
the passover, and of unleavened
bread: and the chief priests and
the [a]scribes sought how they might
take him by craft, and put *him* to
[b]death.
2 But they said, Not on the feast
day, lest there be an uproar of the
people.

19*a* TG Affliction.
20*a* D&C 29:7; 84:34.
22*a* TG False Christs.
b TG False Prophets.
c TG Signs.
25*a* TG World, End of.
26*a* TG Jesus Christ, Son of Man.
28*a* D&C 45:37.
30*a* D&C 45:21.
31*a* D&C 64:31.
32*a* TG Day of the Lord.
33*a* See JST Luke 12:41–57 (Appendix). D&C 45:44. TG Watch.
b TG Prayer.
34*a* TG Authority.
36*a* TG Procrastination; Sleep.
14 1*a* TG Scribe.
b Matt. 26:4 (2–5); Luke 22:2 (1–2).

3 ¶ And being in Bethany in the
house of Simon the leper, as he sat at
meat, there came a woman having an
alabaster box of ointment of spikenard very precious; and she brake
the box, and poured *it* on his head.
4 And there were some that had
indignation within themselves, and
said, Why was this [a]waste of the
ointment made?
5 For it might have been sold for
more than three hundred pence,
and have been given to the poor.
And they murmured against her.
6 And Jesus said, Let her alone; why
trouble ye her? she hath wrought a
good work on me.
7 For ye have the [a]poor with you
always, and whensoever ye will ye
may do them good: but me ye have
not always.
8 She hath done what she could:
[a]she is come aforehand to anoint
my body to the burying.
9 Verily I say unto you, Wheresoever this gospel shall be preached
throughout the whole world, *this* also
that [a]she hath done shall be spoken
of for a memorial of her.
10 ¶ And Judas Iscariot, one of the
twelve, went unto the chief priests,
[a]to betray him unto them.
11 And when they heard *it*, they
were glad, and promised to give him
money. And he sought how he might
conveniently betray him.
12 ¶ And the first day of unleavened
bread, when they killed the passover,
his disciples said unto him, Where
wilt thou that we go and prepare
that thou mayest eat the [a]passover?
13 And he sendeth forth two of
his [a]disciples, and saith unto them,
Go ye into the city, and there shall
meet you a man bearing a pitcher
of water: follow him.
14 And wheresoever he shall go
in, say ye to the goodman of the
house, The Master saith, Where is
the guestchamber, where I shall eat
the passover with my disciples?
15 And he will shew you a large
upper room furnished *and* prepared:
there make ready for us.
16 And his disciples went forth,
and came into the city, and found
as he had said unto them: and they
made ready the passover.
17 And in the evening he cometh
with the twelve.
18 And as they sat and did eat,
Jesus said, Verily I say unto you,
One of you which eateth with me
shall betray me.
19 And they began to be sorrowful,
and to say unto him one by one, *Is*
it I? and another *said, Is* it I?
20 And he answered and said unto
them, *It is* one of the twelve, that
dippeth with me in the dish.
21 The Son of man indeed goeth,
as it is written of him: but woe to
that man by whom the Son of man
is betrayed! good were it for that
man if he had never been born.
22 ¶ [a]And as they did eat, Jesus
took [b]bread, and blessed, and brake
it, and gave to them, and said, Take,
eat: this is my [c]body.
23 And he took the cup, and when
he had given [a]thanks, he gave *it* to
them: and they all drank of it.
24 And he said unto them, This
is my blood of the new testament,
which is shed for many.
25 Verily I say unto you, I will
[a]drink no more of the fruit of the
vine, until that day that I drink it
new in the kingdom of God.
26 ¶ And when they had sung an
hymn, they went out into the mount
of Olives.
27 And Jesus saith unto them, All
ye shall be offended because of me

4*a* D&C 117:4 (4–7).
7*a* TG Poor.
8*a* JST Mark 14:8 . . . *and this which she has done unto me, shall be had in remembrance in generations to come, wheresoever my gospel shall be preached; for verily she has come beforehand . . .*
9*a* John 12:7 (7–8).
10*a* JST Mark 14:31 . . . to betray *Jesus* unto them; *for he turned away from him, and was offended because of his words.*
12*a* TG Passover.
13*a* Luke 22:8 (7–13).
22*a* JST Mark 14:20–26 (Appendix).
b TG Bread, Unleavened; Jesus Christ, Types of, in Memory; Passover.
c Luke 22:19; John 6:53.
23*a* TG Thanksgiving.
25*a* Matt. 26:29; Luke 22:18; D&C 27:5.

this night: for it is written, I will
smite the [a]shepherd, and the sheep
shall be scattered.
28 But after that I am risen, I will
go before you into Galilee.
29 But Peter said unto him, Although all shall be offended, yet
will not I.
30 And Jesus saith unto him, Verily
I say unto thee, That this day, *even*
in this night, before the cock crow
twice, thou shalt deny me thrice.
31 But he spake the more vehemently, If I should die with thee,
I will not deny thee in any wise.
Likewise also said they all.
32 [a]And they came to a place which
was named Gethsemane: and he
saith to his disciples, Sit ye here,
while I shall pray.
33 And he taketh with him Peter
and James and John, and began to be
[a]sore amazed, and to be [b]very [c]heavy;
34 And saith unto them, My soul
is exceeding sorrowful unto death:
tarry ye here, and watch.
35 And he went forward a little,
and fell on the ground, and prayed
that, if it were possible, the hour
might pass from him.
36 And he said, Abba, Father, all
things *are* possible unto thee; [a]take
away this [b]cup from me: nevertheless
not what I will, but what thou wilt.
37 And he cometh, and findeth
them sleeping, and saith unto Peter,
Simon, sleepest thou? couldest not
thou watch one [a]hour?
38 [a]Watch ye and pray, lest ye enter
into [b]temptation. The spirit truly *is*
ready, but the flesh *is* weak.
39 And again he went away, and
prayed, and spake the same words.
40 And when he returned, he found
them asleep again, (for their eyes
were heavy,) neither wist they what
to answer him.
41 And he cometh the third time,
and saith unto them, Sleep on now,
and take *your* rest: it is enough, the
hour is come; behold, the Son of
man is betrayed into the hands of
sinners.
42 Rise up, let us go; lo, he that
betrayeth me is at hand.
43 ¶ And immediately, while he
yet spake, cometh Judas, one of the
twelve, and with him a great multitude with swords and staves, from
the chief priests and the scribes and
the elders.
44 And he that [a]betrayed him had
given them a token, saying, Whomsoever I shall kiss, that same is he;
take him, and lead *him* away safely.
45 And as soon as he was come, he
goeth straightway to him, and saith,
Master, master; and kissed him.
46 ¶ And they laid their hands on
him, and took him.
47 And one of them that stood by
drew a sword, and smote a servant
of the high priest, and cut off his ear.
48 And Jesus answered and said
unto them, Are ye come out, as
against a thief, with swords and
with staves to take me?
49 I was daily with you in the
temple teaching, and ye took me not:
but the scriptures must be fulfilled.
50 And they all forsook him, and
fled.
51 And there followed him a certain young man, [a]having a linen
cloth cast about *his* naked *body;* and
the young men laid hold on him:
52 And he left the linen cloth, and
fled from them naked.
53 ¶ And they led Jesus away to
the high priest: and with him were
assembled all the chief priests and
the elders and the scribes.
54 And Peter followed him afar
off, even into the palace of the high
priest: and he sat with the servants,
and warmed himself at the fire.
55 And the chief priests and all the
council sought for witness against

27*a* Zech. 13:7.
32*a* JST Mark 14:36–38 (Appendix).
33*a* GR amazed, awestruck, astonished.
b GR depressed, dejected, in anguish.
c Ps. 69:20.
36*a* 3 Ne. 11:11.
b Matt. 26:39 (36–46); D&C 19:17 (13–20).
37*a* D&C 76:107; 122:8 (7–8).
38*a* TG Watch.
b D&C 20:33; 23:1; 31:12.
44*a* TG Jesus Christ, Betrayal of.
51*a* JST Mark 14:57 . . . *a disciple,* having . . .

Jesus to put him to [a]death; and
found none.
56 For many bare [a]false witness
against him, but their witness agreed
not together.
57 And there arose certain, and
bare false witness against him,
saying,
58 We heard him say, I will destroy this [a]temple that is made
with hands, and within three days
I will build another made without
hands.
59 But neither so did their witness
agree together.
60 And the high priest stood up
in the midst, and asked Jesus, saying, Answerest thou nothing? what
is it which these witness against
thee?
61 But he held his peace, and [a]an-
swered nothing. Again the high
priest asked him, and said unto
him, Art thou the [b]Christ, the Son
of the Blessed?
62 And Jesus said, I am: and ye shall
see the [a]Son of man sitting on the
right hand of power, and coming in
the clouds of heaven.
63 Then the high priest rent his
clothes, and saith, What need we
any further witnesses?
64 Ye have heard the blasphemy:
what think ye? And they all [a]con-
demned him to be [b]guilty of death.
65 And some began to spit on him,
and to cover his face, and to buffet
him, and to say unto him, Prophesy:
and the servants did strike him with
the palms of their hands.
66 ¶ And as Peter was beneath in
the palace, there cometh one of the
maids of the high priest:
67 And when she saw Peter warm-
ing himself, she looked upon him,
and said, And thou also wast with
Jesus of Nazareth.
68 But he denied, saying, I know
not, neither understand I what thou
sayest. And he went out into the
porch; and the cock crew.
69 And a maid saw him again, and
began to say to them that stood by,
This is *one* of them.
70 And he denied it again. And a
little after, they that stood by said
again to Peter, Surely thou art *one* of
them: for thou art a Galilæan, and
thy speech agreeth *thereto*.
71 But he began to curse and to
swear, *saying*, I know not this man
of whom ye speak.
72 And the second time the cock
crew. And Peter called to mind
the word that Jesus said unto him,
Before the cock crow twice, thou
shalt deny me thrice. And when he
thought thereon, he wept.

CHAPTER 15

Pilate decrees the death of Jesus—Jesus is mocked and crucified between two thieves—He dies and is buried in the tomb of Joseph of Arimathæa.

AND straightway in the morning
the chief priests held a consultation
with the elders and scribes and the
whole council, and bound Jesus, and
carried *him* away, and delivered *him*
to Pilate.
2 And [a]Pilate asked him, Art thou
the King of the Jews? And he answering said unto him, [b]Thou sayest *it*.
3 And the chief priests accused
him of many things: but he [a]an-
swered nothing.
4 And Pilate asked him again,
saying, Answerest thou nothing?
behold how many things they witness against thee.
5 But Jesus yet answered nothing;
so that Pilate marvelled.
6 Now at *that* feast he [a]released
unto them one prisoner, whomsoever they desired.

55*a* TG Jesus Christ, Death of.
56*a* TG Lying.
58*a* Matt. 26:61; 27:40; John 2:19 (18–22); Heb. 9:11.
61*a* Isa. 53:7 (7–8).
b TG Jesus Christ, Messiah.
62*a* TG Jesus Christ, Son of Man.
64*a* TG Jesus Christ, Trials of.
b TG Guilt.
15 2*a* TG Jesus Christ, Trials of.
b JST Mark 15:4 . . . *I am, even as* thou sayest.
3*a* Isa. 53:7 (7–8); Mosiah 14:7 (6–8).
6*a* GR usually released.

7 And there was *one* named Barabbas, *which lay* bound with them
that had made insurrection with
him, who had committed murder
in the insurrection.
8 And the multitude crying aloud
began to desire *him to do* as he had
ever done unto them.
9 But Pilate answered them, saying, Will ye that I release unto you
the [a]King of the Jews?
10 For he knew that the chief
priests had delivered him for [a]envy.
11 But the chief priests moved the
people, that he should rather release
Barabbas unto them.
12 And Pilate answered and said
again unto them, What will ye then
that I shall do *unto him* whom ye
call the King of the Jews?
13 And they cried out again, Crucify him.
14 Then Pilate said unto them,
Why, what evil hath he done? And
they cried out the more exceedingly,
Crucify him.
15 ¶ And *so* Pilate, willing to content the people, released Barabbas
unto them, and delivered Jesus,
when he had scourged *him,* to be
crucified.
16 And the soldiers led him away
into the hall, called Prætorium; and
they call together the whole band.
17 And they clothed him with purple, and plaited a crown of [a]thorns,
and put it about his *head,*
18 And began to salute him, Hail,
King of the Jews!
19 And they [a]smote him on the
head with a reed, and did spit upon
him, and bowing *their* knees worshipped him.
20 And when they had [a]mocked
him, they took off the purple from
him, and put his own clothes on
him, and led him out to crucify him.
21 And they compel one Simon a
Cyrenian, who passed by, coming out
of the country, the father of Alexander and Rufus, to bear his cross.
22 And they bring him unto the
place Golgotha, which is, being interpreted, The place of a skull.
23 And they gave him to drink
wine mingled with myrrh: but he
received *it* not.
24 And when they had crucified
him, they parted his [a]garments,
casting lots upon them, what every
man should take.
25 And it was the third hour, and
they crucified him.
26 And the superscription of his
accusation was written over, THE
KING OF THE JEWS.
27 And with him they crucify two
[a]thieves; the one on his right hand,
and the other on his left.
28 And the scripture was [a]fulfilled,
which saith, And he was numbered
with the transgressors.
29 And they that passed by railed
on him, wagging their heads, and
saying, Ah, thou that destroyest the
temple, and buildest *it* in three days,
30 Save thyself, and come down
from the cross.
31 Likewise also the chief priests
mocking said among themselves
with the scribes, He saved others;
himself he cannot save.
32 Let Christ the King of Israel
descend now from the cross, that
we may see and believe. And they
that were crucified with him [a]re-
viled him.
33 And when the sixth hour was
come, there was [a]darkness over the
whole land until the ninth hour.
34 And at the ninth hour Jesus
cried with a loud voice, saying,
[a]Eloi, Eloi, lama sabachthani? which
is, being interpreted, My God, my
God, why hast thou [b]forsaken me?
35 And some of them that stood by,
when they heard *it,* said, Behold, he
calleth Elias.

9*a* Luke 23:22 (17–25).
10*a* TG Envy.
17*a* TG Jesus Christ, Trials of.
19*a* 1 Ne. 11:32.
20*a* TG Mocking.
24*a* Ps. 22:18.
27*a* Mosiah 14:9.
28*a* Isa. 53:12.
32*a* TG Malice; Reviling.
33*a* TG Darkness, Physical.
34*a* Aramaic: My God, my God, why hast thou forsaken me?
b TG Jesus Christ, Crucifixion of.

SIMON

MARK 15:21

36 And one ran and filled a sponge
full of [a]vinegar, and put *it* on a reed,
and gave him to drink, saying, Let
alone; let us see whether Elias will
come to take him down.
37 And Jesus cried with a loud
voice, and gave up the [a]ghost.
38 And the veil of the temple was
rent in twain from the top to the
bottom.
39 ¶ And when the centurion,
which stood over against him, saw
that he so cried out, and gave up the
ghost, he said, Truly this man was
the Son of God.
40 There were also women looking
on afar off: among whom was Mary
Magdalene, and Mary the mother
of James the less and of Joses, and
Salome;
41 (Who also, when he was in Galilee, followed him, and ministered
unto him;) and many other women
which came up with him unto
Jerusalem.
42 ¶ And now when the even was
come, because it was the [a]preparation,
that is, the day before the sabbath,
43 Joseph of Arimathæa, an honourable [a]counsellor, which also
waited for the kingdom of God,
came, and went in boldly unto Pilate, and [b]craved the body of Jesus.
44 And Pilate marvelled if he were
already dead: and calling *unto him*
the centurion, he asked him whether
he had been any while dead.
45 And when he knew *it* of the centurion, he gave the body to Joseph.
46 And he bought fine linen, and
took him down, and wrapped him in
the linen, and laid him in a [a]sepul-
chre which was hewn out of a rock,
and rolled a stone unto the door of
the sepulchre.
47 And Mary Magdalene and Mary
the mother of Joses beheld where he
was laid.

CHAPTER 16

Christ is risen—He appears to Mary Magdalene, then to others—He sends the Apostles to preach and promises that signs will follow faith—He ascends into heaven.

AND when the sabbath was past,
Mary Magdalene, and Mary the
mother of James, and Salome, had
bought sweet spices, that they might
come and anoint him.
2 And very early in the morning
the [a]first *day* of the week, they came
unto the sepulchre at the [b]rising of
the sun.
3 And they said among themselves,
Who shall roll us away the stone
from the door of the sepulchre?
4 [a]And when they looked, they saw
that the stone was rolled away: for
it was very great.
5 And entering into the sepulchre,
they saw a young man sitting on the
right side, [a]clothed in a long white
garment; and they were [b]affrighted.
6 And he saith unto them, Be not
affrighted: Ye seek Jesus of Nazareth,
which was crucified: he is [a]risen; he
is not here: behold the place where
they laid him.
7 But go your way, tell his disciples
and Peter that he goeth before you
into Galilee: there shall ye see him,
as he said unto you.
8 And they went out quickly, and
fled from the sepulchre; for they
trembled and were amazed: neither
said they any thing to any *man*; for
they were afraid.
9 ¶ Now when *Jesus* was [a]risen
early the first *day* of the week, he
[b]appeared first to [c]Mary Magdalene,
out of whom he had cast seven devils.
10 *And* she went and told them
that had been with him, as they
mourned and wept.
11 And they, when they had heard

36*a* Ps. 69:21.
37*a* TG Spirits, Disembodied.
42*a* TG Passover.
43*a* TG Counselor.
b GR requested, desired.
46*a* Mosiah 14:9.
16 2*a* TG Jesus Christ, Types of, in Memory.
b John 20:1.
4*a* JST Mark 16:3–6 (Appendix).
5*a* TG Clothing.
b GR amazed, astonished.
6*a* TG Immortality.
9*a* TG Jesus Christ, Resurrection.
b TG Jesus Christ, Appearances, Postmortal.
c Luke 8:2.

that he was alive, and had been seen
of her, believed not.
12 ¶ After that he appeared in
another form unto two of them,
as they walked, and went into the
country.
13 And they went and told *it* unto
the residue: neither believed they
them.
14 ¶ Afterward he appeared unto
the [a]eleven as they sat at meat, and
upbraided them with their [b]unbe-
lief and [c]hardness of heart, because
they believed not them which had
seen him after he was risen.
15 And he said unto them, Go ye
into all the world, and [a]preach the
[b]gospel to every [c]creature.
16 He that [a]believeth and is [b]bap-
tized shall be saved; but he that believeth not shall be [c]damned.
17 And these [a]signs shall [b]follow
them that believe; In my [c]name shall
they [d]cast out [e]devils; they shall
speak with new [f]tongues;
18 They shall take up [a]serpents;
and if they drink any deadly thing,
it shall not [b]hurt them; they shall
lay [c]hands on the [d]sick, and they
shall recover.
19 ¶ So then after the [a]Lord had
spoken unto them, he was received
up into heaven, and sat on the right
hand of God.
20 And they went forth, and
preached every where, the Lord
working with *them,* and confirming
the word with signs following. Amen.

THE GOSPEL ACCORDING TO

ST LUKE

CHAPTER 1

Gabriel promises Zacharias that Elisabeth will bear a son, whom they will name John—He also tells Mary that she will be the mother of the Son of God—Mary visits Elisabeth and utters a psalm of praise—John the Baptist is born—Zacharias prophesies of John's mission.

[a]FORASMUCH as [b]many have
taken in hand to set forth in
order a declaration of those
things [c]which are most surely believed among us,
2 Even as they delivered them
unto us, which from the beginning
were [a]eyewitnesses, and ministers
of the word;
3 It seemed good to me also, having

14*a* TG Apostles.
b Matt. 14:31; Mark 4:40; Luke 24:25.
c TG Stiffnecked.
15*a* John 20:21 (19–31); Acts 6:4 (1–4); D&C 66:5. TG Israel, Mission of.
b TG Gospel.
c Acts 11:18 (1–18); D&C 68:8; 124:128. TG Missionary Work.
16*a* TG Baptism, Qualifications for; Faith.
b TG Baptism; Baptism, Essential.
c TG Damnation.
17*a* D&C 84:65 (64–73). TG Holy Ghost, Gifts of; Miracle; Signs.
b D&C 63:9.
c TG Name.
d D&C 24:13; 35:9.
e TG Spirits, Evil or Unclean.
f TG Language.
18*a* Acts 28:3.
b TG Protection, Divine.
c TG Administrations to the Sick; Hands, Laying on of.
d TG Heal.
19*a* TG Jesus Christ, Lord.

[LUKE]

Title: JST entitles this book "The Testimony of St. Luke."
1 1*a* JST Luke 1:1 *As I am a messenger of Jesus Christ, and knowing that* many have . . .
b 2 Tim. 4:13; 1 Ne. 13:26 (24–26).
c GR which have been fulfilled.
2*a* John 1:14; Acts 5:32; 26:16.

had perfect understanding of all
things from the very first, to write
unto thee in order, most excellent
[a]Theophilus,
4 That thou mightest [a]know the
certainty of those things, wherein
thou hast been instructed.
5 ¶ THERE was in the days of
Herod, the king of Judæa,
a certain priest named
[a]Zacharias, of the course of [b]Abia:
and his wife *was* of the daughters of
Aaron, and her name *was* Elisabeth.
6 And they were both righteous
before God, walking in all the commandments and [a]ordinances of the
Lord blameless.
7 And they had no child, because
that Elisabeth was [a]barren, and
they both were *now* well [b]stricken
in years.
8 And it came to pass, that while
he executed the [a]priest's office before God in the order of his [b]course,
9 According to the custom of the
[a]priest's office, his lot was to burn
incense when he went into the
temple of the Lord.
10 And the whole multitude of the
people were praying without at the
time of incense.
11 And there appeared unto him
an angel of the Lord standing on
the right side of the altar of incense.
12 And when Zacharias saw *him,*
he was troubled, and fear fell upon
him.
13 But the angel said unto him,
[a]Fear not, Zacharias: for thy prayer is
heard; and thy wife Elisabeth shall
bear thee a [b]son, and thou shalt call
his name John.
14 And thou shalt have joy and
gladness; and many shall rejoice
at his birth.
15 For he shall be great in the sight
of the Lord, and shall drink neither
[a]wine nor strong drink; and he shall
be [b]filled with the [c]Holy Ghost, even
from his mother's womb.
16 And many of the children of
Israel shall he turn to the Lord
their God.
17 And he shall go before him in
the spirit and power of [a]Elias, to
turn the hearts of the [b]fathers to the
children, and the [c]disobedient to
the wisdom of the just; to make ready
a people [d]prepared for the Lord.
18 And Zacharias said unto the
angel, Whereby shall I [a]know this?
for I am an [b]old man, and my wife
well [c]stricken in years.
19 And the [a]angel answering said
unto him, I am [b]Gabriel, that stand
in the presence of God; and am sent
to speak unto thee, and to shew thee
these glad tidings.
20 And, behold, thou shalt be
[a]dumb, and not able to speak, until
the day that these things shall be
performed, because thou [b]believest
not my words, which shall be fulfilled in their season.
21 And the people waited for
Zacharias, and marvelled that he
tarried so long in the temple.
22 And when he came out, he could
not speak unto them: and they perceived that he had seen a vision in
the temple: for he beckoned unto
them, and remained speechless.
23 And it came to pass, that, as
soon as the [a]days of his ministration

3*a* Acts 1:1.
4*a* John 20:31 (30–31); 1 Ne. 6:4.
5*a* TG Priesthood, Aaronic.
b 1 Chr. 24:10 (5, 10, 19); Neh. 12:4.
6*a* TG Ordinance.
7*a* TG Barren.
b GR advanced.
8*a* TG Priest, Aaronic Priesthood. BD Priests.
b JST Luke 1:8 . . . *priesthood,*
9*a* Lev. 7:35.
13*a* Dan. 10:12.
b TG Foreordination.
15*a* Num. 6:3 (2–8); D&C 89:7 (5, 7).
b D&C 84:27.
c TG Holy Ghost, Gift of; Holy Ghost, Mission of.
17*a* This is the Greek form of the Hebrew name, Elijah. Matt. 11:14; D&C 27:7 (6–8).
b TG Salvation for the Dead.
c TG Disobedience.
d Luke 1:76.
18*a* Gen. 15:8 (7–9).
b Gen. 18:13.
c GR advanced.
19*a* TG Angels.
b Dan. 8:16; D&C 27:7; 128:21.
20*a* Dan. 10:15; Mosiah 27:19; Alma 30:49 (47–52).
b Luke 12:29; 24:25; Morm. 9:11 (9–11, 27).
23*a* Lev. 8:33.

were accomplished, he departed to
his own house.
24 And after those days his wife
Elisabeth conceived, and hid herself five months, saying,
25 Thus hath the Lord dealt with
me in the days wherein he looked
on *me*, to take away my [a]reproach
among men.
26 And in the sixth month the [a]an-
gel Gabriel was sent from God unto
a city of Galilee, named Nazareth,
27 To a [a]virgin espoused to a man
whose name was Joseph, of the
house of David; and the virgin's
name *was* Mary.
28 And the angel came in unto her,
and said, Hail, *thou that art* highly
favoured, the Lord *is* with thee:
blessed *art* thou among [a]women.
29 And when she saw *him*, she was
troubled at his saying, and cast in
her mind what manner of salutation this should be.
30 And the angel said unto her,
[a]Fear not, Mary: for thou hast found
favour with God.
31 And, behold, thou shalt conceive
in thy womb, and bring forth a son,
and shalt call his name [a]JESUS.
32 He shall be great, and shall be
called the [a]Son of the Highest: and
the Lord God shall give unto him
the [b]throne of his father [c]David:
33 And he shall [a]reign over the
house of Jacob for ever; and of his
kingdom there shall be no [b]end.
34 Then said Mary unto the angel,
How shall this be, seeing I [a]know
not a man?
35 And the angel answered and
said unto her, The [a]Holy Ghost shall
come upon thee, and the power of
the Highest shall overshadow thee:
therefore also that holy thing which
shall be born of thee shall be called
the [b]Son of God.
36 And, behold, thy [a]cousin Elisabeth, she hath also conceived a son
in her [b]old age: and this is the sixth
month with her, who was called
barren.
37 For with God nothing shall be
[a]impossible.
38 And Mary said, Behold the
handmaid of the Lord; be it unto
me according to thy word. And the
angel departed from her.
39 And Mary arose in those days,
and went into the hill country with
haste, into a city of Juda;
40 And entered into the house of
Zacharias, and [a]saluted Elisabeth.
41 And it came to pass, that, when
Elisabeth heard the salutation of
Mary, the babe leaped in her womb;
and Elisabeth was [a]filled with the
Holy Ghost:
42 And she spake out with a loud
voice, and said, Blessed *art* thou
among [a]women, and blessed *is* the
fruit of thy womb.
43 And [a]whence *is* this to me, that
the mother of my Lord should come
to me?
44 For, lo, as soon as the voice of
thy salutation sounded in mine ears,
the babe leaped in my womb for joy.
45 And blessed *is* she that believed:
for there shall be a performance of
those things which were told her
from the Lord.
46 And Mary [a]said, My soul doth
[b]magnify the Lord,
47 And my spirit hath [a]rejoiced in
God my [b]Saviour.

25*a* TG Barren; Reproach.
26*a* Moro. 7:29 (29–32).
27*a* 1 Ne. 11:13.
28*a* TG Woman.
30*a* TG Courage; Fearful.
31*a* TG Jesus Christ, Birth of.
32*a* TG Godhead; Jesus Christ, Divine Sonship.
b TG Jesus Christ, Millennial Reign.
c TG Jesus Christ, Davidic Descent of.
33*a* Micah 4:7. TG Jesus Christ, Mission of.
b 2 Sam. 7:16; Isa. 9:7 (6–7).
34*a* 1 Ne. 11:18 (15–20); Alma 7:10 (7–12).
35*a* Matt. 1:20.
b 2 Cor. 1:19.
36*a* GR relative (not necessarily a cousin).
b TG Old Age.
37*a* Gen. 18:14; Rom. 4:21. TG God, Power of.
40*a* GR greeted.
41*a* TG Holy Ghost, Gifts of.
42*a* TG Woman.
43*a* GR how.
46*a* TG Singing.
b 1 Sam. 2:1 (1–10).
47*a* TG Thanksgiving.
b TG Jesus Christ, Savior; Salvation.

48 For he hath regarded the low
estate of his [a]handmaiden: for, behold, from henceforth all generations shall call me [b]blessed.
49 For he that is mighty hath done
to me great [a]things; and [b]holy *is*
his name.
50 And his mercy *is* on them that
fear him from generation to generation.
51 He hath shewed strength with
his arm; he hath scattered the
[a]proud in the imagination of their
hearts.
52 He hath put down the mighty
from *their* seats, and exalted them
of [a]low degree.
53 He hath filled the hungry with
good things; and the rich he hath
sent empty away.
54 He hath [a]holpen his servant Israel, in remembrance of *his* mercy;
55 As he spake to our [a]fathers, to
Abraham, and to his [b]seed for ever.
56 And Mary abode with her about
three months, and returned to her
own house.
57 Now Elisabeth's full time came
that she should be delivered; and
she brought forth a son.
58 And her neighbours and her
[a]cousins heard how the Lord had
shewed great [b]mercy upon her; and
they rejoiced with her.
59 And it came to pass, that on
the [a]eighth day they came to [b]cir-
cumcise the child; and they called
him Zacharias, after the name of
his father.
60 And his mother answered and
said, Not *so;* but he shall be called
John.
61 And they said unto her, There
is none of thy kindred that is called
by this name.
62 And they made signs to his
father, how he would have him
called.
63 And he asked for a [a]writing table, and wrote, saying, His name is
John. And they marvelled all.
64 And his mouth was opened immediately, and his tongue *loosed,* and
he spake, and praised God.
65 And fear came on all that dwelt
round about them: and all these sayings were [a]noised abroad throughout all the hill country of Judæa.
66 And all they that heard *them* laid
them up in their hearts, saying, What
manner of child shall this be! And
the hand of the Lord was with him.
67 And his father Zacharias was
filled with the Holy Ghost, and
[a]prophesied, saying,
68 [a]Blessed *be* the Lord God of
Israel; for he hath [b]visited and
[c]redeemed his people,
69 And hath raised up an horn of
salvation for us in the house of his
servant David;
70 As he [a]spake by the mouth of
his holy [b]prophets, which have been
since the world began:
71 That we should be saved from
our enemies, and from the hand of
all that hate us;
72 To perform the mercy [a]*promised*
to our fathers, and to remember his
holy [b]covenant;
73 The [a]oath which he sware to
our [b]father Abraham,
74 That he would grant unto us,
that we being delivered out of the
hand of our enemies might serve
him without [a]fear,
75 In [a]holiness and righteousness
before him, all the days of our life.
76 And thou, child, shalt be called
the prophet of the Highest: for thou

48*a* 1 Sam. 1:11.
b Ps. 72:17;
Luke 11:27 (27–28).
49*a* Ps. 126:2.
b Ps. 99:3; Isa. 57:15.
51*a* Ex. 18:11.
52*a* Ezek. 21:26.
54*a* OR helped.
55*a* Ps. 132:11; Micah 7:20;
Luke 1:72;
Gal. 3:16.
b TG Seed of Abraham.
58*a* GR relatives.
b TG God, Mercy of.
59*a* D&C 84:28 (27–28).
b TG Circumcision.
63*a* IE writing tablet.
65*a* GR discussed.
67*a* TG Holy Ghost, Gifts of.
68*a* TG Thanksgiving.
b Luke 7:16.
c TG Jesus Christ,
Redeemer.
70*a* TG Prophets, Mission of.
b TG Jesus Christ,
Prophecies about.
72*a* Micah 7:20;
Luke 1:55 (54–55).
b TG Covenants.
73*a* TG Oath; Vow.
b TG Family, Patriarchal.
74*a* Philip. 1:14 (12–17).
75*a* TG Holiness.

shalt go before the face of the Lord
to [a]prepare his ways;
77 To give [a]knowledge of salvation
unto his people by the [b]remission
of their sins,
78 Through the [a]tender mercy of
our God; whereby the [b]dayspring
from on high hath visited us,
79 To give [a]light to them that sit
in [b]darkness and *in* the shadow of
[c]death, to guide our feet into the
way of peace.
80 And the child grew, and waxed
strong in spirit, and was in the
deserts till the day of his shewing
unto Israel.

CHAPTER 2

Heavenly messengers herald the birth of Jesus in Bethlehem—He is circumcised, and Simeon and Anna prophesy of His mission—At twelve years of age, He goes about His Father's business.

AND it came to pass in those days,
that there went out a decree from
Cæsar Augustus, that all [a]the world
should be [b]taxed.
2 (*And* this [a]taxing was first made
when Cyrenius was governor of
Syria.)
3 And all went to be taxed, every
one into his own city.
4 And Joseph also went up from
Galilee, out of the city of Nazareth,
into Judæa, unto the city of David,
which is called [a]Bethlehem; (because he was of the house and lin-
eage of David:)
5 To be taxed with Mary his [a]es-
poused wife, being great with child.
6 And so it was, that, while they
were there, the days were accomplished that she should be delivered.
7 And she brought forth her [a]first-
born son, and wrapped him in
swaddling clothes, and laid him
in a manger; because there was no
room for them in the [b]inn.
8 And there were in the same country shepherds abiding in the field,
keeping watch over their flock by
night.
9 And, lo, the angel of the Lord
came upon them, and the [a]glory of
the Lord shone round about them:
and they were sore afraid.
10 And the angel said unto them,
Fear not: for, behold, I bring you
[a]good tidings of great [b]joy, which
shall be to all people.
11 For unto you is [a]born this day in
the city of David a [b]Saviour, which
is Christ the [c]Lord.
12 And this *shall be* a [a]sign unto
you; Ye shall find the babe wrapped
in swaddling clothes, lying in a
manger.
13 And suddenly there was with
the angel a multitude of the heavenly host praising God, and saying,
14 [a]Glory to God in the highest,
and on earth [b]peace, good will toward men.
15 And it came to pass, as the angels were gone away from them into
heaven, the shepherds said one to
another, Let us now go even unto
Bethlehem, and see this thing which
is come to pass, which the Lord hath
made known unto us.
16 And they came with [a]haste, and
found Mary, and Joseph, and the
babe lying in a manger.
17 And when they had seen *it*,
they made known abroad the saying
which was told them concerning
this child.

FIRSTBORN
Luke 2:7

76*a* Luke 1:17.
77*a* Luke 11:52.
b TG Remission of Sins.
78*a* 1 Ne. 1:20.
b GR dawn; see Mal. 4:2.
79*a* TG Jesus Christ, Light of the World; Jesus Christ, Prophecies about.
b 1 Pet. 3:19 (18–20). TG Darkness, Spiritual.
c D&C 45:17 (16–17); 138:50 (50–51).
2 1*a* JST Luke 2:1 . . . *his empire* should be taxed.
b GR enrolled, registered (also vv. 3, 5).
2*a* GR enrollment.
4*a* 1 Sam. 16:1; Micah 5:2 (1–2); John 7:42 (41–44); Alma 7:10.
5*a* Matt. 1:24 (20–25).
7*a* TG Firstborn.
b JST Luke 2:7 . . . *inns*.
9*a* TG God, Glory of.
10*a* TG Gospel.
b TG Joy.
11*a* TG Jesus Christ, Birth of.
b TG Jesus Christ, Savior.
c TG Jesus Christ, Lord.
12*a* TG Signs.
14*a* Luke 19:38.
b TG Peace.
16*a* TG Haste.

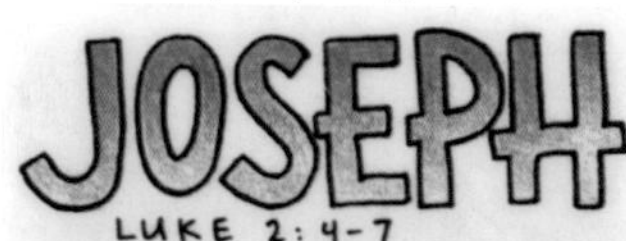

18 And all they that heard *it* [a]won-
dered at those things which were
told them by the shepherds.
19 But Mary kept all these things,
and [a]pondered *them* in her heart.
20 And the shepherds returned,
glorifying and praising God for all
the things that they had heard and
seen, as it was told unto them.
21 And when eight days were accomplished for the [a]circumcising
of the child, his name was called
[b]JESUS, which was so [c]named of
the angel before he was conceived
in the womb.
22 And when the days of her [a]pu-
rification according to the law of
Moses were accomplished, they
brought him to Jerusalem, to present *him* to the Lord;
23 (As it is written in the law of
the Lord, Every male that openeth
the [a]womb shall be called holy
to the Lord;)
24 And to offer a sacrifice according to that which is said in the law
of the Lord, A pair of [a]turtledoves,
or two young pigeons.

25 And, behold, there was a man
in Jerusalem, whose name *was* Simeon; and the same man *was* just and
devout, waiting for the consolation
of Israel: and the Holy Ghost was
upon him.
26 And it was revealed unto him
by the Holy Ghost, that he should
not see death, before he had seen
the Lord's Christ.
27 And he came by the Spirit into
the temple: and when the parents
brought in the child Jesus, to do for
him after the custom of the law,
28 Then took he him up in his arms,
and blessed God, and said,
29 Lord, now lettest thou thy servant depart in peace, according to
thy word:
30 For mine eyes have seen thy
[a]salvation,
31 Which thou hast prepared before the face of all people;
32 A [a]light [b]to lighten the Gentiles,
and the glory of thy people Israel.
33 And Joseph and his mother marvelled at those things which were
spoken of him.
34 And Simeon blessed them, and
said unto Mary his mother, Behold,
this *child* is [a]set for the [b]fall and
rising again of many in Israel; and
for a sign which shall be spoken
against;
35 (Yea, a sword shall [a]pierce
through thy own soul also,) that the
thoughts of many hearts may be
revealed.
36 And there was one Anna,
a [a]prophetess, the daughter of
Phanuel, of the tribe of Aser: she
was of a great age, and had lived
with an husband seven years from
her virginity;
37 And she *was* a widow of about
fourscore and four years, which
departed not from the temple,
but served *God* with [a]fastings and
prayers night and day.
38 And she coming in that instant gave thanks likewise unto
the Lord, and spake of him to all
them that looked for [a]redemption in
Jerusalem.
39 And when they had performed
all things according to the law of
the Lord, they returned into Galilee,
to their own city Nazareth.
40 And the child grew, and [a]waxed
strong in spirit, filled with wisdom:
and the [b]grace of God was upon
him.
41 Now his parents went to Jerusalem every year at the [a]feast of
the passover.
42 And when he was twelve years

18*a* OR marveled.
19*a* TG Meditation.
21*a* TG Circumcision.
b Matt. 1:21.
c TG Jesus Christ, Prophecies about.
22*a* TG Purification.
23*a* Ex. 13:2; 34:19.
24*a* Lev. 1:14; 5:7.
30*a* Ps. 67:2.
32*a* TG Jesus Christ, Light of the World.
b GR for revelation to.
34*a* OR appointed.
b Isa. 8:14 (13–15); Matt. 21:44 (43–45); Rom. 9:32 (28–33); 2 Ne. 18:14; Alma 11:40 (40–41).
35*a* John 19:25.
36*a* TG Woman.
37*a* TG Fast, Fasting.
38*a* D&C 29:42.
40*a* OR became. See JST Matt. 3:24–26 (Appendix).
b TG Grace.
41*a* Deut. 16:1.

old, they went up to Jerusalem after
the custom of the feast.
43 And when they had fulfilled
the days, as they returned, the child
Jesus tarried behind in Jerusalem;
and Joseph and his mother knew
not *of it*.
44 But they, supposing him to have
been in the company, went a day's
journey; and they sought him among
their kinsfolk and acquaintance.
45 And when they found him not,
they turned back again to Jerusalem, seeking him.
46 And it came to pass, that after
three days they found him in the
[a]temple, sitting in the midst of the
[b]doctors, [c]both hearing them, and
[d]asking them questions.
47 And all that heard him were
astonished at his [a]understanding
and answers.
48 And when they saw him, they
were amazed: and his mother said
unto him, Son, why hast thou thus
dealt with us? behold, thy father
and I have sought thee sorrowing.
49 And he said unto them, How is
it that ye sought me? [a]wist ye not
that I must be about my [b]Father's
business?
50 And they understood not the
saying which he spake unto them.
51 And he went down with
them, and came to Nazareth, and
was [a]subject unto them: but his
mother kept all these sayings in her
[b]heart.
52 And Jesus [a]increased in [b]wisdom
and stature, and in [c]favour with
God and man.

CHAPTER 3

John the Baptist preaches and baptizes—Jesus is baptized, and God acclaims Him as His Son—Jesus' genealogy back to Adam is given.

Now in the fifteenth year of the
reign of Tiberius Cæsar, Pontius Pilate being governor of Judæa, and
[a]Herod being tetrarch of Galilee,
and his brother Philip tetrarch of
Ituræa and of the region of Tracho-
nitis, and Lysanias the tetrarch of
Abilene,
2 [a]Annas and Caiaphas being the
[b]high priests, the word of God came
unto John the son of Zacharias in
the wilderness.
3 And he came into all the country
about Jordan, preaching the [a]bap-
tism of repentance for the [b]remis-
sion of sins;
4 [a]As it is written in the book of
the words of Esaias the prophet,
saying, The [b]voice of one crying in
the wilderness, Prepare ye the way
of the Lord, make his paths straight.
5 Every [a]valley shall be filled, and
every mountain and hill shall be
brought low; and the crooked shall
be made straight, and the rough
ways *shall be* made smooth;
6 And all flesh shall see the [a]sal-
vation of God.
7 Then said he to the multitude
that came forth to be baptized of
him, O [a]generation of vipers, who
hath warned you to flee from the
wrath to come?
8 Bring forth therefore [a]fruits
[b]worthy of [c]repentance, and begin

46*a* TG Temple.
b GR teachers.
c JST Luke 2:46 . . . *and they were* hearing *him*, and asking *him* questions.
d John 7:15 (14–15).
47*a* TG Understanding.
49*a* OR knew.
b John 4:34; 6:39 (38–39). TG God the Father, Elohim.
51*a* TG Family, Children, Duties of; Self-Mastery.
b TG Heart.
52*a* 1 Sam. 2:26; 3:19.
b TG God, Wisdom of; Study.
c D&C 93:13 (12–14). TG Jesus Christ, Relationships with the Father.
3 1*a* Luke 9:7.
2*a* John 18:13 (13–24).
b TG Priesthood, Aaronic.
3*a* TG Baptism.
b TG Remission of Sins.
4*a* JST Luke 3:4–11 (Appendix).
b Matt. 3:3; Mark 1:3; John 1:23; D&C 84:28 (26–28); JS—H 1:72 (70–73).
5*a* Isa. 40:4; Hel. 14:23; D&C 109:74.
6*a* TG Salvation.
7*a* GR offspring.
8*a* Alma 13:13 (10–13). TG Baptism, Qualifications for.
b TG Worthiness.
c TG Repent.

not to say within yourselves, [d]We have [e]Abraham to *our* father: for I say unto you, That God is able of these stones to raise up children unto Abraham.

9 And now also the [a]axe is laid unto the root of the trees: every tree therefore which bringeth not forth good [b]fruit is hewn down, and cast into the fire.

10 And the people asked him, saying, What shall we do then?

11 He answereth and saith unto them, He that hath two [a]coats, let him [b]impart to him that hath none; and he that hath meat, let him do likewise.

12 Then came also [a]publicans to be baptized, and said unto him, Master, what shall we do?

13 [a]And he said unto them, Exact no more than that which is appointed you.

14 And the soldiers likewise demanded of him, saying, And what shall we do? And he said unto them, Do violence to no man, neither accuse *any* [a]falsely; and be [b]content with your [c]wages.

15 And as the people were in expectation, and all men [a]mused in their hearts of [b]John, whether he were the Christ, or not;

16 John answered, saying unto *them* all, I indeed baptize you with water; but one mightier than I cometh, the latchet of whose shoes I am not worthy to unloose: he shall [a]baptize you with the Holy Ghost and with fire:

17 Whose [a]fan *is* in his hand, and he will throughly purge his floor, and will gather the wheat into his [b]garner; but the [c]chaff he will burn with fire unquenchable.

18 And many other things in his exhortation preached he unto the people.

19 But [a]Herod the tetrarch, being reproved by him for Herodias his brother Philip's wife, and for all the evils which Herod had done,

20 Added yet this above all, that he shut up John in prison.

21 Now when all the people were baptized, it came to pass, that Jesus also being [a]baptized, and praying, the heaven was opened,

22 And the [a]Holy Ghost descended in a bodily shape like a [b]dove upon him, and a voice came from heaven, which said, Thou art my beloved Son; in thee I am well pleased.

23 And [a]Jesus himself began to be about [b]thirty years of age, being (as was supposed) the son of [c]Joseph, which was *the son* of Heli,

24 Which was *the son* of Matthat, which was *the son* of Levi, which was *the son* of Melchi, which was *the son* of Janna, which was *the son* of Joseph,

25 Which was *the son* of Mattathias, which was *the son* of Amos, which was *the son* of Naum, which was *the son* of Esli, which was *the son* of Nagge,

26 Which was *the son* of Maath, which was *the son* of Mattathias, which was *the son* of Semei, which was *the son* of Joseph, which was *the son* of Juda,

27 Which was *the son* of Joanna, which was *the son* of Rhesa, which

---

8*d* JST Luke 3:13 . . . Abraham *is* our father; *we have kept the commandments of God, and none can inherit the promises but the children of Abraham;* for I say . . .
e TG Abrahamic Covenant.
9*a* Alma 5:52 (51–52); D&C 97:7.
b Matt. 7:19 (15–20); John 15:2 (1–6); Jacob 5:46 (1–77).
11*a* Mosiah 4:16; D&C 104:18 (14–18).
b James 2:16 (14–17); 1 Jn. 3:17 (14–23). TG Generosity.
12*a* Matt. 21:32 (28–32); Luke 7:29 (28–30).
13*a* JST Luke 3:19–20 (Appendix).
14*a* GR for extortion.
b TG Contentment.
c TG Wages.
15*a* TG Meditation.
b John 1:19 (19–27).
16*a* TG Holy Ghost, Gift of.
17*a* OR winnowing fork.
b GR storehouse, granary.
c 2 Ne. 15:24; Mosiah 7:30 (29–31).
19*a* Luke 13:31 (31–34).
21*a* TG Baptism, Essential; Jesus Christ, Baptism of.
22*a* TG Godhead.
b TG Holy Ghost, Dove, Sign of.
23*a* TG Jesus Christ, Davidic Descent of.
b Num. 4:3 (3, 47).
c Matt. 1:16.

was *the son* of Zorobabel, which was *the son* of Salathiel, which was *the son* of Neri,
28 Which was *the son* of Melchi, which was *the son* of Addi, which was *the son* of Cosam, which was *the son* of Elmodam, which was *the son* of Er,
29 Which was *the son* of Jose, which was *the son* of Eliezer, which was *the son* of Jorim, which was *the son* of Matthat, which was *the son* of Levi,
30 Which was *the son* of Simeon, which was *the son* of Juda, which was *the son* of Joseph, which was *the son* of Jonan, which was *the son* of Eliakim,
31 Which was *the son* of Melea, which was *the son* of Menan, which was *the son* of Mattatha, which was *the son* of Nathan, which was *the son* of David,
32 Which was *the son* of Jesse, which was *the son* of Obed, which was *the son* of Booz, which was *the son* of Salmon, which was *the son* of Naasson,
33 Which was *the son* of Aminadab, which was *the son* of Aram, which was *the son* of Esrom, which was *the son* of [a]Phares, which was *the son* of [b]Juda,
34 Which was *the son* of Jacob, which was *the son* of Isaac, which was *the son* of [a]Abraham, which was *the son* of Thara, which was *the son* of Nachor,
35 Which was *the son* of Saruch, which was *the son* of Ragau, which was *the son* of Phalec, which was *the son* of Heber, which was *the son* of Sala,
36 Which was *the son* of Cainan, which was *the son* of Arphaxad, which was *the son* of [a]Sem, which was *the son* of Noe, which was *the son* of Lamech,
37 Which was *the son* of Mathusala, which was *the son* of Enoch, which was *the son* of Jared, which was *the son* of Maleleel, which was *the son* of Cainan,
38 Which was *the* [a]*son* of Enos, which was *the son* of Seth, which was *the son* of [b]Adam, [c]which was *the* [d]*son* of God.

CHAPTER 4

Jesus fasts forty days and is tempted by the devil—Jesus announces His divine sonship in Nazareth and is rejected—He casts out a devil in Capernaum, heals Peter's mother-in-law, and preaches and heals throughout Galilee.

AND Jesus being full of the Holy Ghost returned from Jordan, and was [a]led by the Spirit into the wilderness,
2 [a]Being forty days [b]tempted of the [c]devil. And in those days he did eat nothing: and when they were ended, he afterward hungered.
3 And the devil said unto him, If thou be the Son of God, command this stone that it be made bread.
4 And Jesus answered him, saying, It is written, That [a]man shall not live by bread alone, but by every word of God.
5 [a]And the devil, taking him up into an high mountain, shewed unto him all the kingdoms of the world in a moment of time.
6 And the devil said unto him, All this [a]power will I give thee, and the glory of them: for that is delivered unto me; and to whomsoever I will I give it.
7 If thou therefore wilt worship me, all shall be thine.

33*a* Gen. 38:29 (1–30); Ruth 4:18 (18–22).
b TG Israel, Judah, People of.
34*a* Gen. 11:26 (10–26).
36*a* Gen. 5:32 (3–32).
38*a* TG Family, Patriarchal.
b TG Adam.
c JST Luke 3:45 . . . *who was formed* of God, *and the first man upon the earth.*
d Moses 6:22. TG Man, Physical Creation of.
4 1*a* Ezek. 37:1 (1–2). TG Holy Ghost, Mission of.
2*a* JST Luke 4:2 *And after* forty days, the devil *came unto him, to tempt him.* And in those . . .
b Mosiah 15:5 (4–7); D&C 62:1; Moses 7:24 (24–27).
c TG Devil.
4*a* Deut. 8:3.
5*a* JST Luke 4:5 And the *Spirit taketh* him up into a high mountain, *and he beheld* all the kingdoms . . .
6*a* Rev. 13:2.

8 And Jesus answered and said unto
him, Get thee behind me, Satan: for
it is written, Thou shalt [a]worship the
Lord thy God, and him only shalt
thou [b]serve.
9 [a]And he brought him to Jerusalem, and set him on a pinnacle of
the temple, and said unto him, If
thou be the Son of God, cast thyself
down from hence:
10 For it is written, He shall give his
[a]angels charge over thee, to keep thee:
11 And in *their* hands they shall
bear thee up, lest at any time thou
dash thy foot against a stone.
12 And Jesus answering said unto
him, It is said, Thou shalt not [a]tempt
the Lord thy God.
13 And when the devil had ended
all the temptation, he departed from
him for a season.
14 ¶ And Jesus returned in the
[a]power of the Spirit into [b]Galilee:
and there went out a fame of him
through all the region round about.
15 And he taught in their synagogues, being glorified of all.
16 ¶ And he came to Nazareth,
where he had been brought up: and,
as his custom was, he went into the
synagogue on the sabbath day, and
stood up for to read.
17 And there was delivered unto him
the book of the prophet Esaias. And
when he had opened the book, he
found the place where it was written,
18 The [a]Spirit of the Lord *is* upon
me, because he hath [b]anointed me
to [c]preach the [d]gospel to the [e]poor;
he hath sent me to heal the bro-
kenhearted, to [f]preach [g]deliverance
to the [h]captives, and recovering of
sight to the blind, to set at [i]liberty
them that are bruised,
19 [a]To preach the acceptable year
of the Lord.
20 And he closed the book, and he
gave *it* again to the minister, and
sat down. And the eyes of all them
that were in the synagogue were
fastened on him.
21 And he began to say unto them,
This day is this scripture [a]fulfilled
in your ears.
22 And all bare him witness, and
[a]wondered at the [b]gracious words
which proceeded out of his mouth.
And they said, Is not this [c]Joseph's
son?
23 And he said unto them, Ye will
surely say unto me this proverb,
Physician, heal thyself: whatsoever
we have heard done in [a]Capernaum,
[b]do also here in thy country.
24 And he said, Verily I say unto
you, No prophet is [a]accepted in his
own country.
25 But I tell you of a truth, many
[a]widows were in Israel in the days
of [b]Elias, when the heaven was
shut up three years and six months,
when great famine was throughout
all the land;
26 But unto none of them was Elias
sent, save unto Sarepta, *a city* of Sidon, unto a woman *that was* a widow.
27 And many [a]lepers were in Israel
in the time of Eliseus the prophet;
and none of them was [b]cleansed,
saving Naaman the Syrian.

8*a* TG Worship.
b TG Commitment.
9*a* JST Luke 4:9 And *the Spirit* brought him to Jerusalem, and set him on a pinnacle of the temple. *And the devil came unto him,* and said . . .
10*a* Ps. 91:11 (11–12).
12*a* Deut. 6:16.
14*a* TG Jesus Christ, Power of.
b Matt. 4:12.
18*a* Isa. 61:1 (1–2). TG God, Spirit of.
b TG Anointing; Jesus Christ, Messiah.
c TG Teaching.
d D&C 137:7. TG Gospel.
e TG Poor.
f TG Jesus Christ, Mission of; Preaching.
g GR remission. TG Deliver; Remission of Sins.
h D&C 138:8 (5–10). TG Bondage, Spiritual; Salvation for the Dead; Spirits in Prison.
i TG Liberty.
19*a* John 12:47.
21*a* TG Jesus Christ, Prophecies about.
22*a* OR marveled.
b Ps. 45:2.
c John 6:42.
23*a* John 4:46 (43–54).
b Matt. 13:58.
24*a* TG Prophets, Rejection of.
25*a* 1 Kgs. 17:9 (1, 8–10). TG Widows.
b IE Elijah. 1 Kgs. 17:1; Matt. 17:3 (1–4); D&C 110:13 (13–16).
27*a* TG Leprosy.
b 2 Kgs. 5:14.

28 And all they in the synagogue,
when they heard these things, were
filled with wrath,
29 And rose up, and thrust him
out of the city, and led him unto
the brow of the hill whereon their
city was built, that they might cast
him down headlong.
30 But he [a]passing through the
midst of them went his way,
31 And came down to Capernaum,
a city of Galilee, and taught them
on the sabbath days.
32 And they were astonished at
his doctrine: for his word was with
[a]power.
33 ¶ And in the synagogue there
was a man, which had a spirit of an
unclean devil, and cried out with
a loud voice,
34 Saying, Let *us* alone; what have
we to do with thee, *thou* Jesus of
Nazareth? art thou come to destroy
us? I know thee who thou art; the
Holy One of God.
35 And Jesus rebuked him, saying,
Hold thy peace, and come out of
him. And when the devil had thrown
him in the midst, he came out
of him, and hurt him not.
36 And they were all amazed, and
spake among themselves, saying,
What a word *is* this! for with authority and power he commandeth the
[a]unclean spirits, and they come out.
37 And the fame of him went out
into every place of the country
round about.
38 ¶ And he arose out of the synagogue, and entered into Simon's
house. And Simon's wife's mother
was taken with a great fever; and
they besought him for her.
39 And he stood over her, and [a]re-
buked the fever; and it left her: and
immediately she arose and ministered unto them.
40 ¶ Now when the sun was setting, all they that had any sick
with [a]divers diseases brought them
unto him; and he [b]laid his [c]hands
on every one of them, and healed
them.
41 And devils also came out of
many, crying out, and saying, Thou
art [a]Christ the Son of God. And he
rebuking *them* suffered them not to
speak: for they knew that he was
Christ.
42 And when it was day, he [a]de-
parted and went into a [b]desert place:
and the people sought him, and came
unto him, and [c]stayed him, that he
should not depart from them.
43 And he said unto them, I must
[a]preach the kingdom of God to other
cities also: for therefore am I [b]sent.
44 And he preached in the synagogues of [a]Galilee.

CHAPTER 5

Peter, the fisherman, is called to catch men—Jesus heals a leper—He forgives sins and heals a paralytic—Matthew is called—The sick need a physician—New wine must be put in new bottles.

AND it came to pass, that, as the
people pressed upon him to hear
the word of God, he stood by the
lake of Gennesaret,
2 And saw two ships standing by
the lake: but the fishermen were
gone out of them, and were washing *their* nets.
3 And he entered into one of
the ships, which was Simon's, and
prayed him that he would thrust out
a little from the land. And he sat
down, and taught the people out of
the ship.
4 Now when he had left speaking,
he said unto Simon, Launch out into
the deep, and let down your nets
for a [a]draught.
5 And Simon answering said unto

30*a* John 8:59.
32*a* GR authority.
TG Jesus Christ, Authority of; Jesus Christ, Teaching Mode of; Teaching with the Spirit.
36*a* Mark 1:39 (21–45).
39*a* D&C 84:68 (64–73).
40*a* OR various.
b TG Hands, Laying on of.
c TG Administrations to the Sick.
41*a* TG Jesus Christ, Messiah.
42*a* Luke 5:16; 6:12.
b JST Luke 4:42 . . . *solitary* . . .
c GR detained Him.
43*a* TG Preaching.
b TG Jesus Christ, Messenger of the Covenant.
44*a* Matt. 4:23 (23–25).
5 4*a* GR catch, haul.

him, Master, we have [a]toiled all
the night, and have taken nothing:
nevertheless at thy word I will let
down the net.
6 And when they had this done,
they inclosed a great multitude of
fishes: and their net [a]brake.
7 And they beckoned unto *their*
partners, which were in the other
ship, that they should come and
help them. And they came, and
filled both the ships, so that they
began to sink.
8 When Simon Peter saw *it*, he
fell down at Jesus' knees, saying,
Depart from me; for I am a sinful
man, O Lord.
9 For he was astonished, and all
that were with him, at the draught
of the fishes which they had taken:
10 And so *was* also James, and John,
the sons of Zebedee, which were
partners with Simon. And Jesus said
unto Simon, Fear not; from henceforth thou shalt [a]catch men.
11 And when they had brought
their ships to land, they [a]forsook
all, and [b]followed him.
12 ¶ And it came to pass, when he
was in a certain city, behold a man
full of [a]leprosy: who seeing Jesus
fell on *his* face, and besought him,
saying, Lord, if thou wilt, thou canst
make me clean.
13 And he put forth *his* hand, and
touched him, saying, I will: be thou
clean. And immediately the leprosy
departed from him.
14 And he charged him to tell no
man: but go, and shew thyself to the
[a]priest, and offer for thy cleansing,
according as Moses commanded, for
a testimony unto them.
15 But so much the more went
there a fame abroad of him: and
great multitudes came together to
hear, and to be healed by him of
their infirmities.
16 ¶ And he [a]withdrew himself
into the wilderness, and prayed.
17 And it came to pass on a certain day, as he was teaching, that
there were Pharisees and doctors
of the law sitting by, which were
come out of every town of Galilee,
and Judæa, and Jerusalem: and the
power of the Lord was *present* to heal
them.
18 ¶ And, behold, men brought in
a bed a man which was [a]taken with
a palsy: and they sought *means* to
bring him in, and to lay *him* before
him.
19 And when they could not find
by what *way* they might bring him
in because of the multitude, they
went upon the housetop, and let
him down through the tiling with
his couch into the midst before
Jesus.
20 And when he saw their faith,
he said unto him, Man, thy sins are
[a]forgiven thee.
21 And the scribes and the Pharisees began to reason, saying, Who
is this which speaketh [a]blasphe-
mies? Who can [b]forgive sins, but
God alone?
22 But when Jesus [a]perceived their
thoughts, he answering said unto
them, What reason ye in your hearts?
23 [a]Whether is easier, to say, Thy
sins be forgiven thee; or to say, Rise
up and walk?
24 But that ye may know that the
Son of man hath power upon earth
to [a]forgive sins, (he said unto the
sick of the palsy,) I say unto thee,
Arise, and take up thy couch, and
go into thine house.
25 And immediately he rose up before them, and took up that whereon
he lay, and departed to his own
house, [a]glorifying God.
26 And they were all amazed, and
they glorified God, and were filled

5*a* TG Industry.
6*a* OR was breaking.
10*a* GR capture, take alive. TG Missionary Work.
11*a* Luke 14:33 (28–33).
b TG Apostles.
12*a* TG Leprosy.
14*a* Lev. 14:2 (1–32).
16*a* Luke 4:42; 6:12.
18*a* GR paralyzed.
20*a* TG Forgive.
21*a* TG Blaspheme.
b D&C 64:3 (1–5); 110:5 (4–6). TG Remission of Sins.
22*a* TG Jesus Christ, Teaching Mode of.
23*a* JST Luke 5:23 *Does it require more power to forgive sins than to make the sick* rise up and walk?
24*a* TG Remission of Sins.
25*a* Luke 18:43.

with fear, saying, We have seen
strange things to day.
27 ¶ And after these things he went
forth, and saw a publican, named
[a]Levi, sitting at the receipt of custom:
and he said unto him, Follow me.
28 And he left all, rose up, and
followed him.
29 And Levi made him a great feast
in his own house: and there was a
great company of publicans and
of others that sat down with them.
30 But their scribes and Pharisees
murmured against his disciples, saying, Why do ye eat and drink with
publicans and sinners?
31 And Jesus answering said unto
them, They that are whole need
not a physician; but they that are
sick.
32 I came not to call the righteous,
but [a]sinners to repentance.
33 ¶ And they said unto him, Why
do the disciples of John [a]fast often,
and make prayers, and likewise *the
disciples* of the Pharisees; but thine
eat and drink?
34 And he said unto them, Can ye
make the children of the [a]bride-
chamber fast, while the bridegroom
is with them?
35 But the days will come, when
the [a]bridegroom shall be taken away
from them, and then shall they [b]fast
in those days.
36 ¶ And he spake also a parable
unto them; No man putteth a piece
of a new garment upon an old; if
otherwise, then both the new maketh a rent, and the piece that was
taken out of the new [a]agreeth not
with the old.
37 And no man putteth new wine
into old bottles; else the new wine
will burst the [a]bottles, and be
spilled, and the bottles shall perish.
38 But new wine must be put into
new bottles; and both are preserved.
39 No man also having drunk old
wine [a]straightway desireth new: for
he saith, The old is better.

CHAPTER 6

Jesus heals on the Sabbath—He chooses the Twelve Apostles—He pronounces blessings upon the obedient and woes upon the wicked.

AND it came to pass on the second
sabbath after the first, that he went
through the corn fields; and his disciples plucked the ears of corn, and
did eat, rubbing *them* in *their* hands.
2 And certain of the Pharisees said
unto them, Why do ye that which
is not lawful to do on the [a]sabbath
days?
3 And Jesus answering them said,
Have ye not read so much as this,
what David did, when himself was
an hungred, and they which were
with him;
4 How he went into the house of
God, and did take and eat the [a]shew-
bread, and gave also to them that
were with him; which it is not lawful to eat but for the priests alone?
5 And he said unto them, That
the Son of man is Lord also of the
[a]sabbath.
6 And it came to pass also on another sabbath, that he entered into
the synagogue and taught: and there
was a man whose right hand was
withered.
7 And the scribes and Pharisees
watched him, whether he would heal
on the sabbath day; that they might
find an accusation against him.
8 But he [a]knew their thoughts,
and said to the man which had the
withered hand, Rise up, and stand
forth in the midst. And he arose
and stood forth.
9 Then said Jesus unto them, I will
ask you one thing; Is it lawful on the

LAWGIVER
Luke 6:9

27*a* Matt. 9:9 (9–13).
32*a* John 9:39 (39–41); 1 Tim. 1:15.
33*a* Mark 2:18 (18–22).
34*a* Matt. 22:2 (2–14); Rev. 19:7 (7–9); 21:2.
35*a* Mark 2:19; John 16:5 (4–7).
b Acts 13:2 (2–3).
36*a* GR fits, accords.
37*a* GR leather bags or wineskins.
39*a* GR immediately.
6 2*a* John 5:10 (10–16).
4*a* Ex. 29:33 (32–33); Lev. 24:9 (5–9); 1 Sam. 21:6 (1–6).
5*a* TG Sabbath.
8*a* John 2:24 (23–25).

sabbath days to do good, or to do
evil? to save life, or to destroy *it*?
10 And looking round about upon
them all, he said unto the man,
Stretch forth thy hand. And he did
so: and his hand was restored whole
as the other.
11 And they were filled with madness; and communed one with another what they might do to Jesus.
12 And it came to pass in those
days, that he [a]went out into a mountain to [b]pray, and continued all night
in prayer to God.
13 ¶ And when it was day, he called
unto him his disciples: and of them
he [a]chose [b]twelve, whom also he
named [c]apostles;
14 Simon, (whom he also named
[a]Peter,) and Andrew his brother,
James and John, Philip and Bartholomew,
15 Matthew and Thomas, James the
son of Alphæus, and Simon called
Zelotes,
16 And Judas *the brother* of James,
and Judas [a]Iscariot, which also was
the traitor.
17 ¶ And he came down with
them, and stood in the plain, and
the company of his disciples, and a
great multitude of people out of all
Judæa and Jerusalem, and from the
sea coast of Tyre and Sidon, which
came to hear him, and to be healed
of their diseases;
18 And they that were vexed with
[a]unclean spirits: and they were
healed.
19 And the whole multitude sought
to touch him: for there went [a]virtue
out of him, and [b]healed *them* all.
20 ¶ And he lifted up his eyes on
his disciples, and said, Blessed *be
ye* [a]poor: for yours is the [b]kingdom
of God.
21 Blessed *are ye* that [a]hunger now:
for ye shall be filled. Blessed *are ye*
that weep now: for ye shall [b]laugh.
22 Blessed are ye, when men shall
[a]hate you, and when they shall
[b]separate you *from their company*,
and shall [c]reproach *you*, and [d]cast
out your name as evil, for the Son
of man's sake.
23 [a]Rejoice ye in that day, and
leap for [b]joy: for, behold, your [c]re-
ward *is* great in heaven: for in the
like manner did their fathers unto
the prophets.
24 But woe unto you that are
[a]rich! for ye have [b]received your
consolation.
25 Woe unto you that are full! for
ye shall hunger. Woe unto you that
laugh now! for ye shall mourn and
weep.
26 Woe unto you, when all [a]men
shall speak [b]well of you! for so did
their fathers to the false prophets.
27 ¶ But I say unto you which
hear, [a]Love your enemies, do good
to them which hate you,
28 Bless them that curse you, and
[a]pray for them which despitefully
use you.
29 [a]And unto him that [b]smiteth
thee on the *one* cheek offer also the
other; and him that [c]taketh away
thy cloak forbid not *to take thy*
coat also.
30 [a]Give to every man that [b]ask-
eth of thee; and of him that taketh
away thy goods ask *them* not again.

12*a* Luke 4:42; 5:16.
b Matt. 14:23; 26:36; Luke 9:28.
13*a* 1 Ne. 12:7 (6–7). TG Called of God.
b TG Apostles.
c TG Church Organization.
14*a* John 1:42.
16*a* Josh. 15:25.
18*a* TG Spirits, Evil or Unclean; Uncleanness.
19*a* GR power. Mark 5:30 (25–34); Luke 8:46 (41–48).
b TG Heal.
20*a* James 2:5 (1–9).
b D&C 38:9.
21*a* Isa. 55:1 (1–2).
b TG Laughter.
22*a* 1 Pet. 3:14.
b TG Persecution.
c TG Reproach.
d Isa. 66:5.
23*a* Acts 5:41.
b TG Joy.
c TG Reward.
24*a* TG Treasure.
b Luke 16:25 (19–25).
26*a* TG Trust Not in the Arm of Flesh.
b John 15:19 (18–19); 1 Ne. 22:23; Alma 1:3.
27*a* TG Reconciliation.
28*a* Luke 23:34 (33–34); Acts 7:60 (53–60).
29*a* JST Luke 6:29–30 (Appendix).
b Alma 43:46 (46–47); D&C 98:23 (22–48).
c 1 Cor. 6:7 (6–8).
30*a* TG Generosity.
b Prov. 3:27 (27–28); 21:26 (25–26).

31 And as ye would that men
should do to you, do ye also to them
likewise.
32 For if ye love them which love
you, what thank have ye? for sinners also love those that love them.
33 And if ye do good to them which
do good to you, what thank have
ye? for sinners also do even the
same.
34 And if ye lend *to them* of whom
ye hope to receive, what thank have
ye? for sinners also lend to sinners,
to receive as much again.
35 But [a]love ye your enemies, and
do good, and [b]lend, hoping for nothing again; and your [c]reward shall be
great, and ye shall be the [d]children
of the Highest: for he is kind unto
the [e]unthankful and *to* the evil.
36 Be ye therefore [a]merciful, as
your Father also is [b]merciful.
37 [a]Judge not, and ye shall not be
judged: [b]condemn not, and ye shall
not be condemned: forgive, and ye
shall be [c]forgiven:
38 [a]Give, and it shall be given unto
you; good measure, pressed down,
and shaken together, and running
over, shall men give into your bosom.
For with the same [b]measure that ye
mete withal it shall be measured to
you again.
39 And he spake a parable unto
them, Can the [a]blind [b]lead the
blind? shall they not both fall into
the [c]ditch?
40 The disciple is not above his
master: but every one [a]that is perfect shall be as his master.
41 And why beholdest thou the
[a]mote that is in thy brother's eye,
but perceivest not the beam that is
in thine own eye?
42 Either how canst thou say to
thy brother, Brother, let me pull
out the mote that is in thine eye,
when thou thyself beholdest not the
beam that is in thine own eye? Thou
hypocrite, cast out first the beam
out of thine own eye, and then shalt
thou see clearly to pull out the mote
that is in thy brother's eye.
43 For a good tree bringeth not
forth corrupt [a]fruit; neither doth a
corrupt tree bring forth good fruit.
44 For every tree is known by his
own [a]fruit. For of thorns men do
not gather figs, nor of a bramble
bush gather they grapes.
45 A good man out of the good
treasure of his [a]heart bringeth forth
that which is good; and an evil man
out of the evil treasure of his heart
bringeth forth that which is evil:
for of the abundance of the [b]heart
his [c]mouth [d]speaketh.
46 ¶ And why [a]call ye me, [b]Lord,
Lord, and [c]do not the things which
I say?
47 Whosoever cometh to me, and
heareth my sayings, and [a]doeth
them, I will shew you to whom he
is like:
48 He is like a man which built
an house, and digged deep, and
laid the foundation on a rock: and
when the flood arose, the stream
beat vehemently upon that house,
and could not shake it: for it was
founded upon a rock.
49 But he that [a]heareth, and doeth
not, is like a man that without a
foundation built an house upon the

35*a* TG Charity.
b TG Generosity.
c TG Reward.
d D&C 76:58 (50–62).
e TG Ingratitude.
36*a* TG Mercy.
b TG God, Mercy of.
37*a* Moro. 7:18 (12–19). TG Retribution.
b TG Gossip.
c TG Forgive.
38*a* TG Generosity; Kindness.
b D&C 1:10 (9–10).
39*a* TG Trust Not in the Arm of Flesh.
b TG Leadership.
c GR pit, well, cistern.
40*a* GR having been perfectly prepared. TG Perfection.
41*a* GR chip, splinter.
43*a* 3 Ne. 14:20 (14–20).
44*a* Matt. 7:16 (15–16); Alma 7:24 (23–24); D&C 84:58 (54–58); 97:7 (6–8).
45*a* TG Motivations.
b TG Heart.
c TG Gossip.
d Matt. 12:34; James 3:10 (10–12).
46*a* 1 Ne. 17:41 (40–41); Alma 37:46 (44–47).
b Ezek. 33:31 (30–33); Hosea 8:2 (1–4); Matt. 7:21 (21–23); D&C 112:26; JS—H 1:19.
c TG Disobedience.
47*a* TG Commitment.
49*a* James 1:23 (22–25).

earth; against which the stream did beat vehemently, and immediately it fell; and the ruin of that house was great.

CHAPTER 7

Jesus heals the centurion's servant—Jesus raises from death the son of the widow of Nain—He praises John the Baptist as more than a prophet—A woman anoints Jesus' feet, and He forgives her sins.

NOW when he had ended all his sayings in the audience of the people,
he entered into Capernaum.
2 And a certain centurion's servant,
who was dear unto him, was sick,
and ready to die.
3 And when he heard of Jesus, he
sent unto him the elders of the Jews,
beseeching him that he would come
and heal his servant.
4 And when they came to Jesus,
they besought him [a]instantly, saying, That he was worthy for whom
he should do this:
5 For he loveth our nation, and he
hath built us a synagogue.
6 Then Jesus went with them. And
when he was now not far from the
house, the centurion sent friends to
him, saying unto him, Lord, trouble
not thyself: for I am not worthy that
thou shouldest enter under my roof:
7 Wherefore neither thought I
myself worthy to come unto thee:
but say in a word, and my servant
shall be healed.
8 For I also am a man set under
authority, having under me soldiers,
and I say unto one, Go, and he goeth; and to another, Come, and he
cometh; and to my servant, Do this,
and he doeth *it*.
9 When Jesus heard these things,
he marvelled at him, and turned
him about, and said unto the people
that followed him, I say unto you,
I have not found so great faith, no,
not in [a]Israel.
10 And they that were sent, returning to the house, found the servant
whole that had been sick.
11 ¶ And it came to pass the day
after, that he went into a city called
Nain; and many of his disciples went
with him, and much people.
12 Now when he came nigh to the
gate of the city, behold, there was a
dead man carried out, the only son
of his mother, and she was a widow:
and much people of the city was
with her.
13 And when the Lord saw her, he
had [a]compassion on her, and said
unto her, Weep not.
14 And he came and touched the
bier: and they that bare *him* stood
still. And he said, Young man, I say
unto thee, Arise.
15 And he that was [a]dead sat up,
and began to speak. And he delivered him to his mother.
16 And there came a [a]fear on all:
and they glorified God, saying, That
a great prophet is risen up among
us; and, That God hath [b]visited his
people.
17 And this rumour of him went
forth throughout all Judæa, and
throughout all the region round about.
18 And the disciples of [a]John
shewed him of all these things.
19 ¶ And John calling *unto him* two
of his disciples sent *them* to Jesus,
saying, Art thou he that should
come? or look we for another?
20 When the men were come unto
him, they said, John Baptist hath
sent us unto thee, saying, Art thou
he that should come? or look we for
another?
21 And in that same hour he
[a]cured many of *their* infirmities and
plagues, and of evil spirits; and unto
many *that were* blind he gave [b]sight.
22 Then Jesus answering said unto
them, Go your way, and tell John
what things ye have seen and heard;
how that the blind see, the lame
walk, the lepers are cleansed, the

---

7 4*a* GR earnestly.
9*a* Alma 19:10.
13*a* TG Compassion; Mercy.
15*a* TG Death, Power over.
16*a* Alma 19:25 (24–27); Moses 6:39 (37–40).
b Ex. 3:16; Luke 1:68; D&C 110:7.
18*a* Matt. 11:2 (2–19).
21*a* TG Heal.
b TG Sight.

deaf hear, the dead are raised, to
the [a]poor the gospel is preached.
23 And blessed is *he,* whosoever
shall not be [a]offended in me.
24 ¶ And when the messengers of
John were departed, he began to
speak unto the people concerning
John, What went ye out into the wilderness for to see? A reed shaken
with the wind?
25 But what went ye out for to
see? A man clothed in soft raiment?
Behold, they which are gorgeously
[a]apparelled, and live delicately, are
in kings' courts.
26 But what went ye out for to see?
A prophet? Yea, I say unto you, and
much more than a prophet.
27 This is *he,* of whom it is written,
Behold, I send my [a]messenger before thy face, which shall prepare
thy way before thee.
28 For I say unto you, Among those
that are born of women there is not
a greater prophet than John the
Baptist: but he that is [a]least in the
kingdom of God is greater than he.
29 And all the people that heard
him, and the [a]publicans, justified
God, being baptized with the [b]bap-
tism of John.
30 But the Pharisees and lawyers
[a]rejected the counsel of God [b]against
themselves, being not [c]baptized of
him.
31 ¶ And the Lord said, Whereunto then shall I liken the men of
this generation? and to what are
they like?
32 They are like unto children sitting in the marketplace, and calling one to another, and saying, We
have piped unto you, and ye have
not danced; we have [a]mourned to
you, and ye have not wept.
33 For John the Baptist came neither eating bread nor drinking wine;
and ye say, He hath a devil.
34 The Son of man is come eating
and drinking; and ye say, Behold a
gluttonous man, and a winebibber,
a friend of publicans and sinners!
35 But wisdom is justified of all
her children.
36 ¶ And one of the Pharisees desired him that he would eat with
him. And he went into the Pharisee's house, and sat down to meat.
37 And, behold, a [a]woman in the
city, which was a sinner, when she
knew that *Jesus* sat at meat in the
Pharisee's house, brought an alabaster [b]box of ointment,
38 And stood at his feet behind *him*
weeping, and began to wash his feet
with tears, and did wipe *them* with
the hairs of her head, and kissed
his feet, and [a]anointed *them* with
the ointment.
39 Now when the Pharisee which
had bidden him saw *it,* he spake
within himself, saying, This man,
if he were a prophet, would have
known who and what manner of
woman *this is* that toucheth him:
for she is a sinner.
40 And Jesus answering said unto
him, Simon, I have somewhat to
say unto thee. And he saith, Master, say on.
41 There was a certain creditor
which had two debtors: the one
owed five hundred [a]pence, and the
other fifty.
42 And when they had nothing to
pay, he frankly [a]forgave them both.
[b]Tell me therefore, which of them
will love him most?
43 Simon answered and said, I suppose that *he,* to whom he forgave
most. And he said unto him, Thou
hast rightly judged.
44 And he turned to the woman,
and said unto Simon, Seest thou this
woman? I entered into thine house,
thou gavest me no water for my feet:

22*a* Alma 32:2 (2–6).
23*a* 2 Ne. 18:14 (13–15).
25*a* TG Apparel.
27*a* D&C 45:9.
28*a* Matt. 11:11; D&C 50:26.
29*a* Matt. 21:32 (28–32); Luke 3:12.
b Matt. 3:7 (1–8).
30*a* Alma 5:41.
b GR for.
c TG Baptism, Essential.
32*a* TG Mourning.
37*a* TG Woman.
b GR flask.
38*a* TG Anointing.
41*a* GR *denarii;* one *denarius* was a workman's daily wage.
42*a* TG Forgive.
b TG Jesus Christ, Teaching Mode of.

but she hath washed my feet with
tears, and wiped *them* with the hairs
of her head.
45 Thou gavest me no kiss: but
this woman since the time I came
in hath not ceased to kiss my feet.
46 My head with oil thou didst
not anoint: but this woman hath
anointed my feet with ointment.
47 Wherefore I say unto thee, Her
sins, which are many, are [a]forgiven;
for she loved much: but to whom little is forgiven, *the same* loveth little.
48 And he said unto her, Thy sins
are [a]forgiven.
49 And they that sat at meat with
him began to say within themselves,
Who is this that [a]forgiveth sins also?
50 And he said to the woman, Thy
[a]faith hath saved thee; go in [b]peace.

CHAPTER 8

Jesus gives and interprets the parable of the sower—He stills the tempest; casts out a legion of devils, who then enter the swine; heals a woman of an issue of blood; and raises Jairus's daughter from death.

AND it came to pass afterward, that
he went throughout every [a]city and
village, preaching and shewing the
glad [b]tidings of the kingdom of God:
[c]and the twelve *were* with him,
2 And certain women, which had
been healed of evil spirits and infirmities, [a]Mary called Magdalene,
out of whom went seven devils,
3 And Joanna the wife of Chuza
Herod's steward, and Susanna, and
many others, which ministered unto
him of their substance.

4 ¶ And when much people were
gathered together, and were come
to him out of every city, he spake
by a parable:
5 A sower went out to sow his seed:

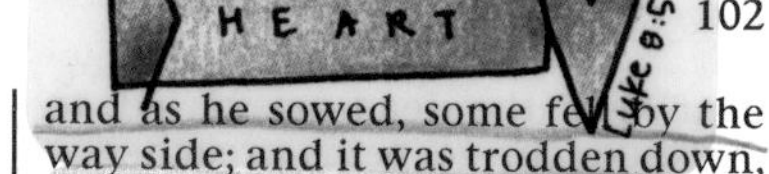

and as he sowed, some fell by the
way side; and it was trodden down,
and the fowls of the air devoured it.
6 And some fell upon a rock; and as
soon as it was sprung up, it withered
away, because it lacked moisture.
7 And some fell among thorns; and
the thorns sprang up with it, and
choked it.
8 And other fell on good ground,
and sprang up, and bare fruit an
hundredfold. And when he had said
these things, he cried, He that hath
ears to hear, let him hear.
9 And his disciples asked him, saying, What might this parable be?
10 And he said, Unto you it is
given to know the [a]mysteries of the
kingdom of God: but to others in
[b]parables; that seeing they might
not see, and hearing they might not
[c]understand.
11 Now the parable is this: The
[a]seed is the word of God.
12 Those by the way side are they
that hear; then cometh the devil,
and taketh away the word out of
their hearts, lest they should believe
and be saved.
13 They on the rock *are they,* which,
when they hear, receive the word
with joy; and these have no root,
which for a while believe, and in
time of [a]temptation fall away.
14 And that which fell among
thorns are they, which, when they
have heard, go forth, and are [a]choked
with [b]cares and [c]riches and [d]plea-
sures of *this* life, and bring no fruit
to [e]perfection.
15 But that on the good ground
are they, which in an [a]honest and
good [b]heart, having heard the word,
keep *it,* and bring forth [c]fruit with
patience.
16 ¶ No man, when he hath lighted

47*a* TG Forgive.
48*a* Mark 2:5.
49*a* TG Remission of Sins.
50*a* Matt. 9:2; Ether 12:4.
b Mosiah 15:18.
8 1*a* Alma 23:4; D&C 66:5; 75:18.
b D&C 76:40.
c JST Luke 8:1 . . . and the twelve *who were ordained of him,* were with him,
2*a* Mark 16:9 (1, 9).
10*a* Alma 26:22.
b Ps. 78:2; Mark 4:11 (11–12).
c Isa. 6:9.
11*a* Alma 32:28 (27–28).
13*a* 1 Ne. 8:28 (24–28). TG Temptation.
14*a* Gal. 6:9 (8–10).
b TG Worldliness.
c TG Treasure.
d TG Pleasure.
e TG Perfection.
15*a* D&C 11:10.
b TG Heart.
c Alma 12:30 (29–30).

a [a]candle, covereth it with a vessel,
or putteth *it* under a bed; but setteth
it on a candlestick, that they which
enter in may see the light.
17 For nothing is [a]secret, that shall
not be made manifest; neither *any
thing* hid, that shall not be known
and come abroad.
18 Take heed therefore how ye
hear: for whosoever [a]hath, to him
shall be [b]given; and whosoever hath
not, from him shall be taken even
that which he seemeth to have.
19 ¶ Then came to him *his* mother
and his [a]brethren, and could not
come at him for the [b]press.
20 And it was told him *by certain*
which said, Thy mother and thy
brethren stand without, desiring
to see thee.
21 And he answered and said unto
them, My [a]mother and my brethren
are these which hear the word of
God, and [b]do it.
22 ¶ Now it came to pass on a certain day, that he went into a ship
with his disciples: and he said unto
them, Let us go over unto the other
side of the lake. And they launched
forth.
23 But as they sailed he fell asleep:
and there came down a storm
of wind on the lake; [a]and they
were filled *with water*, and were in
jeopardy.
24 And they came to him, and
awoke him, saying, Master, master, we perish. Then he arose, and
rebuked the wind and the raging
of the water: and they ceased, and
there was a calm.
25 And he said unto them, Where
is your faith? And they being afraid
wondered, saying one to another,
What manner of man is this! for he
commandeth even the [a]winds and
water, and they obey him.
26 ¶ And they arrived at the country of the Gadarenes, which is [a]over
against Galilee.
27 And when he went forth to
land, there met him out of the city a
certain man, which had devils long
time, and ware no clothes, neither
abode in *any* house, but in the tombs.
28 When he saw Jesus, he cried
out, and fell down before him, and
with a loud voice said, What have
I to do with thee, [a]Jesus, *thou* Son
of God most high? I beseech thee,
torment me not.
29 (For he had commanded the
unclean spirit to come out of the
man. For oftentimes it had caught
him: and he was kept bound with
chains and in fetters; and he brake
the bands, and was driven of the
devil into the wilderness.)
30 And Jesus asked him, saying,
What is thy name? And he said,
[a]Legion: because many devils were
entered into him.
31 And they besought him that he
would not command them to go out
into the [a]deep.
32 And there was there an herd of
many swine feeding on the mountain: and they besought him that
he would suffer them to enter into
them. And he suffered them.
33 Then went the devils out of the
man, and entered into the swine:
and the herd ran violently down a
steep place into the lake, and were
choked.
34 When they that fed *them* saw
what was done, they fled, and went
and told *it* in the city and in the
country.
35 Then they went out to see what
was done; and came to Jesus, and
found the man, out of whom the
devils were departed, sitting at the
feet of Jesus, clothed, and in his
right mind: and they were afraid.
36 They also which saw *it* told them

16*a* 3 Ne. 12:15 (14–16); D&C 60:2 (2–3).
17*a* D&C 1:3.
18*a* 2 Ne. 28:30 (29–31).
b Mark 4:24.
19*a* TG Jesus Christ, Family of.
b GR crowd.
21*a* 3 Ne. 9:17 (13–18).
b Matt. 7:21 (21–23).
23*a* JST Luke 8:23 . . . and they were filled with *fear*, and were in *danger*.
25*a* TG Nature, Earth.
26*a* GR on the other side of.
28*a* James 2:19 (19–20).
30*a* D&C 29:36 (36–38).
31*a* GR abyss. (See also Rev. 9:1; 20:3.)

by what means he that was possessed
of the devils was healed.
37 ¶ Then the whole multitude of
the country of the Gadarenes round
about besought him to depart from
them; for they were taken with great
fear: and he went up into the ship,
and returned back again.
38 Now the man out of whom the
devils were departed besought him
that he might be with him: but Jesus
sent him away, saying,
39 Return to thine own house, and
shew how great things God hath
done unto thee. And he went his
way, and [a]published throughout the
whole city how great things Jesus
had done unto him.
40 And it came to pass, that, when
Jesus was returned, the people *gladly*
received him: for they were all waiting for him.
41 ¶ And, behold, there came a man
named [a]Jairus, and he was a ruler of
the synagogue: and he fell down at
Jesus' feet, and besought him that
he would come into his house:
42 For he had one only daughter,
about twelve years of age, and she
lay a dying. But as he went the people thronged him.
43 ¶ And a woman having an issue
of [a]blood twelve years, which had
spent all her living upon physicians,
neither could be healed of any,
44 Came behind *him,* and touched
the [a]border of his garment: and
immediately her issue of blood
[b]stanched.
45 And Jesus said, Who touched
me? When all denied, Peter and
they that were with him said, Master, the multitude throng thee and
press *thee,* and sayest thou, Who
touched me?
46 And Jesus said, Somebody hath
touched me: for I perceive that [a]vir-
tue is gone out of me.
47 And when the woman saw that
she was not hid, she came trembling,
and falling down before him, she
declared unto him before all the people for what cause she had touched
him, and how she was [a]healed immediately.
48 And he said unto her, Daughter, be of good [a]comfort: thy faith
hath made thee whole; go in peace.
49 ¶ While he yet spake, there
cometh one from the ruler of the
synagogue's *house,* saying to him,
Thy daughter is dead; trouble not
the Master.
50 But when Jesus heard *it,* he answered him, saying, Fear not: believe
only, and she shall be made whole.
51 And when he came into the
house, he suffered no man to go
in, save Peter, and James, and John,
and the father and the mother of
the [a]maiden.
52 And all wept, and bewailed
her: but he said, Weep not; she is
not dead, but sleepeth.
53 And they [a]laughed him to scorn,
knowing that she was dead.
54 And he put them all out, and
took her by the hand, and called,
saying, Maid, arise.
55 And her spirit came again, and
she arose straightway: and he commanded to give her meat.
56 And her parents were astonished: but he charged them that
they should tell no man what was
done.

CHAPTER 9

The Twelve are sent out—Jesus feeds the five thousand—Peter testifies of Christ—Jesus foretells His death and resurrection—He is transfigured on the mount—He heals and teaches.

THEN he called his [a]twelve disciples
together, and gave them power and
[b]authority over all devils, and to
cure diseases.

39*a* Mark 5:20.
41*a* Matt. 9:18 (18–26).
43*a* Lev. 15:25.
44*a* Acts 5:15; 19:12 (11–12).
b GR ceased.
46*a* GR power.
Mark 5:30 (25–34);
Luke 6:19 (17–19).
47*a* TG Heal.
48*a* GR courage, cheer.
51*a* GR child.
53*a* 2 Chr. 30:10;
Alma 26:23.
9 1*a* TG Apostles.
b TG Authority;
Priesthood, Authority.

2 And he sent them to [a]preach
the kingdom of God, and to [b]heal
the sick.
3 And he said unto them, Take
nothing for *your* journey, neither
staves, nor scrip, neither bread,
neither money; neither have two
coats apiece.
4 And whatsoever house ye enter
into, there abide, and thence depart.
5 And whosoever will not receive
you, when ye go out of that city,
[a]shake off the very [b]dust from
your feet for a testimony against
them.
6 And they departed, and went
through the towns, preaching the
[a]gospel, and healing every where.
7 ¶ Now [a]Herod the tetrarch heard
of all that was done by him: and he
was perplexed, because that it was
said of some, that John was risen
from the dead;
8 And of some, that Elias had appeared; and of others, that one of
the old prophets was risen again.
9 And Herod said, John have I beheaded: but who is this, of whom I
hear such things? And he desired
to see him.
10 ¶ And the apostles, when they
were returned, told [a]him all that
they had done. And he took them,
and went aside privately into a
[b]desert place belonging to the city
called Bethsaida.
11 And the people, when they knew
it, followed him: and he received
them, and spake unto them of the
kingdom of God, and healed them
that had need of healing.
12 And when the day began to
wear away, then came the twelve,
and said unto him, Send the multitude away, that they may go into
the towns and country round about,
and lodge, and get victuals: for we
are here in a desert place.
13 But he said unto them, Give
ye them to eat. And they said, We
have no more but five loaves and
two fishes; except we should go and
buy meat for all this people.
14 For they were about [a]five thousand men. And he said to his disciples, Make them sit down by fifties
in a company.
15 And they did so, and made them
all sit down.
16 Then he took the five loaves
and the two fishes, and looking up
to heaven, he blessed them, and
brake, and gave to the disciples to
set before the multitude.
17 And they did eat, and were all
filled: and there was taken up of
fragments that remained to them
twelve baskets.
18 ¶ And it came to pass, as he was
alone praying, his disciples were
with him: and he asked them, saying, Whom say the people that I am?
19 They answering said, John the
Baptist; but some *say,* Elias; and others *say,* that one of the old prophets
is risen again.
20 He said unto them, But whom
say ye that I am? Peter answering
said, The [a]Christ of God.
21 And he straitly charged them,
and commanded *them* to [a]tell no
man that thing;
22 Saying, The Son of man must
suffer many things, and be [a]rejected
of the elders and chief priests and
scribes, and be slain, and be raised
the third day.
23 ¶ And he said to *them* all, If any
man will come after me, let him
deny himself, and take up his [a]cross
daily, and [b]follow me.
24 [a]For whosoever will save his life

2*a* TG Missionary Work; Preaching.
b Matt. 10:8 (7–8).
5*a* D&C 60:15.
b Luke 10:11 (11–12); D&C 84:92.
6*a* TG Gospel.
7*a* Matt. 14:1 (1–3); Mark 6:14 (14–29); Luke 3:1.
10*a* JST Luke 9:10 . . . *Jesus* . . .
b JST Luke 9:10 . . . *solitary* . . .
14*a* Matt. 14:21 (13–21); Mark 6:44 (32–44); John 6:10 (1–13).
20*a* TG Testimony.
21*a* Mark 8:30.
22*a* Matt. 21:42 (42–46); 1 Pet. 2:7.
23*a* See JST Matt. 16:25–26 (Appendix). Matt. 10:38; 3 Ne. 12:30 (29–30).
b TG Jesus Christ, Exemplar.
24*a* JST Luke 9:24–25 (Appendix).

shall [b]lose it: but whosoever will lose his life for my sake, the same shall save it.

25 For what is a man advantaged, if he gain the whole world, and [a]lose himself, or be cast away?

26 For whosoever shall be [a]ashamed of me and of my words, of him shall the [b]Son of man be ashamed, [c]when he shall come in his own glory, and *in his* Father's, and of the holy angels.

27 But I tell you of a truth, there be some standing here, which shall not taste of [a]death, till they see the kingdom of God.

28 ¶ And it came to pass about an [a]eight days after these sayings, he took Peter and John and James, and went up into a [b]mountain to [c]pray.

29 And as he prayed, the fashion of his countenance was [a]altered, and his raiment *was* white *and* [b]glistering.

30 And, behold, there talked with him two men, which were Moses and Elias:

31 Who appeared in glory, [a]and spake of his [b]decease which he should accomplish at Jerusalem.

32 But Peter and they that were with him were heavy with sleep: and when they were awake, they saw his [a]glory, and the two men that stood with him.

33 And it came to pass, as they departed from him, Peter said unto Jesus, Master, it is good for us to be here: and let us make three tabernacles; one for thee, and one for Moses, and one for Elias: not knowing what he said.

34 While he thus spake, there came a cloud, and overshadowed them: and they feared as they entered into the cloud.

35 And there came a voice out of the cloud, saying, This is my [a]beloved Son: hear him.

36 And when the voice was past, Jesus was found alone. And they kept *it* close, and told no man in those days any of those things which they had seen.

37 ¶ And it came to pass, that on the next day, when they were come down from the hill, much people met him.

38 And, behold, a man of the company cried out, saying, Master, I beseech thee, look upon my son: for he is mine only child.

39 And, lo, a spirit taketh him, and he suddenly crieth out; and it teareth him that he foameth again, and bruising him hardly departeth from him.

40 And I besought thy disciples to cast him out; and they could not.

41 And Jesus answering said, O faithless and perverse generation, how long shall I be with you, and suffer you? Bring thy son hither.

42 And as he was yet a coming, the devil threw him down, and tare *him*. And Jesus rebuked the unclean spirit, and healed the child, and delivered him again to his father.

43 ¶ And they were all amazed at the [a]mighty power of God. But while they wondered every one at all things which Jesus did, he said unto his disciples,

44 Let these sayings sink down into your ears: for the Son of man shall be [a]delivered into the hands of men.

45 But they [a]understood not this saying, and it was hid from them,

---

24*b* Matt. 10:39 (34–39); Mark 8:35; D&C 98:13 (13–14); 103:27 (27–28).
25*a* Matt. 16:26.
26*a* D&C 3:7 (6–8).
b TG Jesus Christ, Son of Man.
c JST Luke 9:26 . . . when he shall come in his own *kingdom, clothed in the glory of his Father, with* the holy angels.
27*a* John 21:23 (21–23); 3 Ne. 28:7 (4–10); D&C 7:2 (1–8).
28*a* Mark 9:2 (2–8).
b 2 Pet. 1:18 (10–19).
c Matt. 14:23; 26:36; Luke 6:12.
29*a* Matt. 17:2 (1–13); Mark 9:2 (2–13).
b OR brilliant, glistening.
31*a* JST Luke 9:31 . . . and spake of his *death, and also his resurrection,* which he . . .
b GR departure. TG Jesus Christ, Death of.
32*a* TG Glory.
35*a* Matt. 3:17; Mark 9:7.
43*a* GR majesty, glory.
44*a* 1 Ne. 11:32; 3 Ne. 27:14.
45*a* John 12:16.

that they perceived it not: and they feared to ask him of that saying.

46 ¶ Then there arose a reasoning among them, which of them should be [a]greatest.

47 And Jesus, perceiving the thought of their heart, took a child, and set him by him,

48 And said unto them, Whosoever shall receive this child in my [a]name receiveth me: and whosoever shall [b]receive me receiveth him that sent me: for he that is least among you all, the same shall be [c]great.

49 ¶ And John answered and said, Master, we saw one casting out devils in thy name; and we forbad him, because he followeth not with us.

50 And Jesus said unto him, Forbid *him* not: for he that is not against us is [a]for us.

51 ¶ And it came to pass, when the time was come that he should be received up, he steadfastly set his face to go to Jerusalem,

52 And sent messengers before his face: and they went, and entered into a village of the [a]Samaritans, to make ready for him.

53 And they did not receive him, because his face was as though he would go to Jerusalem.

54 And when his disciples [a]James and John saw *this,* they said, Lord, wilt thou that we command [b]fire to come down from heaven, and consume them, even as Elias did?

55 But he turned, and rebuked them, and said, Ye know not what manner of [a]spirit ye are of.

56 For the [a]Son of man is not come to [b]destroy men's [c]lives, but to [d]save *them.* And they went to another village.

57 ¶ And it came to pass, that, as they went in the way, a certain *man* said unto him, Lord, I will [a]follow thee whithersoever thou goest.

58 And Jesus said unto him, Foxes have holes, and birds of the air *have* nests; but the Son of man hath not where to lay *his* head.

59 And he said unto another, [a]Follow me. But he said, Lord, suffer me first to go and bury my father.

60 Jesus said unto him, Let the dead bury their dead: but go thou and preach the kingdom of God.

61 And another also said, Lord, I will [a]follow thee; but let me first go bid them farewell, which are at home at my house.

62 And Jesus said unto him, No man, having put his hand to the [a]plough, and [b]looking back, is fit for the kingdom of God.

CHAPTER 10

Jesus calls, empowers, and instructs the Seventy—They preach and heal—Those who receive Christ's disciples receive Christ—The Father is revealed by the Son—Jesus gives the parable of the good Samaritan.

AFTER these things the Lord [a]appointed other [b]seventy also, and sent them [c]two and two before his face into every city and place, whither he himself would come.

2 Therefore said he unto them, The [a]harvest truly *is* great, but the labourers *are* few: pray ye therefore the Lord of the harvest, that he would send forth labourers into his harvest.

3 Go your ways: behold, I send you forth as [a]lambs among wolves.

46*a* Matt. 18:1 (1–5); Mark 9:34 (34–37).
48*a* TG Name.
b Matt. 10:40.
c Ether 12:27 (26–27).
50*a* Matt. 12:30; Mark 9:40.
52*a* Matt. 10:5.
54*a* Mark 3:17.
b 2 Kgs. 1:10 (9–16).
55*a* TG Spirits, Evil or Unclean.
56*a* TG Jesus Christ, Son of Man.
b John 3:17 (16–17).
c TG Mortality.
d TG Life, Sanctity of; Worth of Souls.
57*a* Matt. 8:19.
59*a* 2 Ne. 31:12 (12–13). TG Called of God.
61*a* 1 Kgs. 19:20.
62*a* TG Commitment.
b Luke 14:18 (16–24); D&C 133:15.
10 1*a* TG Authority; Called of God; Priesthood, Authority.
b TG Church Organization; Missionary Work; Seventy.
c Mark 6:7.
2*a* Matt. 9:37.
3*a* Matt. 10:16.

4 Carry neither [a]purse, nor scrip,
nor shoes: and [b]salute no man by
the way.
5 And into whatsoever house ye enter, first say, [a]Peace *be* to this house.
6 And if the son of peace be there,
your peace shall rest upon it: if not,
it shall turn to you again.
7 And in the same house remain,
eating and drinking such things as
they give: for the [a]labourer is worthy of his [b]hire. Go not from house
to house.
8 And into whatsoever city ye enter, and they [a]receive you, eat such
things as are set before you:
9 And heal the sick that are therein,
and say unto them, The [a]kingdom
of God is come nigh unto you.
10 But into whatsoever city ye
enter, and they receive you not, go
your ways out into the streets of the
same, and say,
11 Even the very [a]dust of your city,
which cleaveth on us, we do wipe
off against you: notwithstanding be
ye sure of this, that the kingdom of
God is come nigh unto you.
12 But I say unto you, that it shall
be more tolerable in that day for
Sodom, than for that city.
13 Woe unto thee, Chorazin! woe
unto thee, Bethsaida! for if the
mighty works had been done in
Tyre and Sidon, which have been
done in you, they had a great while
ago repented, sitting in sackcloth
and ashes.
14 But it shall be more tolerable
for Tyre and Sidon at the judgment,
than for you.
15 And thou, Capernaum, which
art exalted to heaven, shalt be thrust
down to hell.
16 [a]He that [b]heareth you heareth
me; and he that [c]despiseth you [d]de-
spiseth me; and he that [e]despiseth
me despiseth him that sent me.
17 ¶ And the [a]seventy returned
again with joy, saying, Lord, even the
devils are subject unto us through
thy name.
18 And he said unto them, I beheld
[a]Satan as lightning fall from heaven.
19 Behold, I give unto you [a]power
to [b]tread on serpents and scorpions, and over all the power of the
enemy: and nothing shall by any
means [c]hurt you.
20 Notwithstanding in this [a]rejoice
not, that the spirits are subject unto
you; but rather [b]rejoice, because
your names are [c]written in heaven.
21 ¶ In that hour Jesus [a]rejoiced
in spirit, and said, I thank thee, O
Father, Lord of heaven and earth,
that thou hast hid these things [b]from
the wise and [c]prudent, and hast
revealed them unto [d]babes: even
so, Father; for so it seemed good in
thy sight.
22 All things are [a]delivered to me
of my Father: and no man knoweth
[b]who the Son is, but the Father;
and who the Father is, but the
Son, and *he* to whom the Son will
[c]reveal *him*.
23 ¶ And he turned him unto *his*

4*a* Matt. 10:9.
b 2 Kgs. 4:29.
5*a* 1 Sam. 25:6. TG Peace of God.
7*a* D&C 31:5 (3–7). TG Labor.
b Num. 18:31; Matt. 10:10. TG Wages.
8*a* TG Teachable.
9*a* Matt. 3:2.
11*a* Matt. 10:14 (12–14); Mark 6:11; Luke 9:5; Acts 13:51 (44–52); D&C 24:15; 75:20 (19–22).
16*a* JST Luke 10:17 *And he said unto his disciples,* He that heareth . . .
b Matt. 10:40; Mosiah 15:11.
c GR rejects. D&C 84:36 (35–39).
d 1 Thes. 4:8.
e John 5:23.
17*a* TG Seventy.
18*a* TG Council in Heaven; Devil.
19*a* TG Priesthood, Power of.
b Ps. 91:13.
c Acts 28:5.
20*a* D&C 50:33 (30–34).
b TG Joy.
c Ex. 32:32; Heb. 12:23.
21*a* Matt. 11:25 (25–27).
b JST Luke 10:22 . . . from *them who think they are* wise and prudent . . .
c TG Prudence.
d Alma 32:23; 3 Ne. 26:14 (14–16); D&C 128:18.
22*a* TG Jesus Christ, Authority of.
b JST Luke 10:23 . . . *that* the Son *is* the Father, and the Father *is* the Son, *but him* to whom the Son will reveal *it*.
c Matt. 11:27; John 1:18; 14:6 (6–14).

disciples, and said privately, Blessed *are* the [a]eyes which see the things that ye see:

24 For I tell you, that many [a]prophets and [b]kings have desired to see those things which ye see, and have not seen *them;* and to hear those things which ye hear, and have not heard *them.*

25 ¶ And, behold, a certain lawyer stood up, and tempted him, saying, Master, what shall I do to inherit [a]eternal life?

26 He said unto him, What is written in the law? how readest thou?

27 And he answering said, Thou shalt love the Lord thy God with all thy [a]heart, and with all thy soul, and with all thy strength, and with all thy mind; and thy neighbour as thyself.

28 And he said unto him, Thou hast answered right: this do, and thou shalt [a]live.

29 But he, willing to [a]justify himself, said unto Jesus, And who is my [b]neighbour?

30 And Jesus answering said, A certain *man* went down from Jerusalem to Jericho, and fell among thieves, which stripped him of his raiment, and [a]wounded *him,* and departed, leaving *him* half dead.

31 And by chance there came down a certain priest that way: and when he saw him, he passed by on the other side.

32 And likewise a Levite, when he was at the place, came and looked *on him,* and passed by on the other side.

33 But a certain [a]Samaritan, as he journeyed, came where he was: and when he saw him, he had [b]compassion *on him,*

34 And went to *him,* and bound up his wounds, pouring in oil and wine, and set him on his own beast, and brought him to an inn, and took [a]care of him.

35 And on the morrow when he departed, he took out two pence, and gave *them* to the [a]host, and said unto him, Take care of him; and whatsoever thou spendest more, when I come again, I will repay thee.

36 Which now of these three, thinkest thou, was neighbour unto him that fell among the thieves?

37 And he said, He that shewed mercy on him. Then said Jesus unto him, Go, and do thou likewise.

38 ¶ Now it came to pass, as they went, that he entered into a certain village: and a certain woman named [a]Martha received him into her house.

39 And she had a sister called Mary, which also sat at Jesus' feet, and heard his word.

40 But Martha was cumbered about much serving, and came to him, and said, Lord, dost thou not care that my sister hath left me to serve alone? bid her therefore that she help me.

41 And Jesus answered and said unto her, Martha, Martha, thou art [a]careful and troubled about many things:

42 But one thing is needful: and Mary hath [a]chosen that good part, which shall not be taken away from her.

CHAPTER 11

Jesus gives the Lord's Prayer—He discusses the casting out of devils—He acclaims Himself as greater than Jonah and Solomon—He rebukes the Pharisees and says that the blood of all the prophets may be required of their generation.

AND it came to pass, that, as he was praying in a certain place, when he ceased, one of his disciples said unto him, Lord, [a]teach us to [b]pray, as John also taught his disciples.

2 And he said unto them, When ye pray, say, Our [a]Father which art in

23*a* Matt. 13:16.
24*a* 2 Ne. 25:26 (24–27).
b TG Kings, Earthly.
25*a* Luke 18:18.
27*a* TG Apathy.
28*a* Lev. 18:5.
29*a* Luke 16:15.
b TG Neighbor.
30*a* TG Cruelty.
33*a* John 4:9.
b TG Benevolence; Compassion; Kindness.
34*a* TG Charity; Welfare.
35*a* GR innkeeper.
38*a* John 11:1 (1, 5); 12:2.
41*a* GR worried.
42*a* TG Agency.
11 1*a* TG Teaching.
b TG Prayer.
2*a* TG God the Father, Elohim.

heaven, Hallowed be thy [b]name. Thy
kingdom come. Thy will be done,
as in heaven, so in earth.
3 Give us day by day our daily
bread.
4 And [a]forgive us our sins; for we
also forgive every one that is [b]in-
debted to us. [c]And lead us not into
temptation; but deliver us from
evil.
5 [a]And he said unto them, Which of
you shall have a friend, and shall go
unto him at midnight, and say unto
him, Friend, lend me three loaves;
6 For a friend of mine in his journey is come to me, and I have nothing to set before him?
7 And he from within shall answer
and say, Trouble me not: the door
is now shut, and my children are
with me in bed; I cannot rise and
give thee.
8 I say unto you, Though he will
not rise and give him, because he
is his [a]friend, yet because of his im-
portunity he will rise and give him
as many as he needeth.
9 And I say unto you, Ask, and it
shall be given you; seek, and ye shall
find; knock, and it shall be opened
unto you.
10 For every one that asketh receiveth; and he that seeketh findeth;
and to him that knocketh it shall
be opened.
11 If a son shall ask bread of any
of you that is a father, will he give
him a stone? or if *he ask* a fish, will
he for a fish give him a serpent?
12 Or if he shall ask an egg, will
he offer him a scorpion?
13 If ye then, being evil, know how
to give good gifts unto your children:
how much more shall *your* heavenly
Father give [a]the Holy Spirit to them
that ask him?
14 ¶ And he was casting [a]out a
devil, and it was dumb. And it came
to pass, when the devil was gone
out, the dumb spake; and the people wondered.
15 But some of them said, He
casteth out devils through [a]Beelze-
bub the chief of the devils.
16 And others, tempting *him*,
sought of him a [a]sign from heaven.
17 But he, knowing their [a]thoughts,
said unto them, Every kingdom
divided against itself is brought
to desolation; and a house *divided*
against a house falleth.
18 If Satan also be divided against
himself, how shall his kingdom
stand? because ye say that I cast out
devils through Beelzebub.
19 And if I by Beelzebub cast out
devils, by whom do your sons [a]cast
them out? therefore shall they be
your judges.
20 But if I with the [a]finger of God
cast out devils, no doubt the kingdom of God is come upon you.
21 When a strong man armed
keepeth his palace, his goods are
in peace:
22 But when a stronger than he
shall come upon him, and overcome him, he taketh from him all
his armour wherein he trusted, and
divideth his spoils.
23 He that is not with me is [a]against
me: and he that gathereth not with
me scattereth.
24 When the [a]unclean spirit is gone
out of a man, [b]he walketh through
dry places, seeking rest; and finding

2*b* TG Name.
4*a* TG Forgive.
b TG Debt.
c JST Luke 11:4 . . . And *let us not be led unto* temptation; but deliver us from evil; *for thine is the kingdom and power. Amen.*
5*a* JST Luke 11:5–6 And he said unto them, *Your heavenly Father will not fail to give unto you whatsoever ye ask of him. And he spake a parable, saying,* Which . . .
8*a* TG Brotherhood and Sisterhood; Friendship.
13*a* JST Luke 11:14 . . . *good gifts, through* the Holy Spirit . . .
14*a* JST Luke 11:15 . . . a devil *out of a man,* and *he* was dumb . . .
15*a* Mosiah 3:9 (9–12); Hel. 13:26 (26–27).
16*a* TG Sign Seekers.
17*a* Matt. 12:25; John 2:25.
19*a* Matt. 12:27–28; Mark 9:38 (38–49); Acts 19:13.
20*a* Ex. 8:19; John 3:2; Acts 2:22; 10:38.
23*a* D&C 10:68 (67–68).
24*a* D&C 50:31 (31–33).
b JST Luke 11:25 . . . *it* . . .

none, [c]he saith, I will return unto
my house whence I came out.
25 [a]And when he cometh, he findeth *it* swept and [b]garnished.
26 Then goeth he, and taketh *to*
him seven other spirits more wicked
than himself; and they enter in, and
dwell there: and the last *state* of that
man is worse than the first.
27 ¶ And it came to pass, as he
spake these things, a certain woman
of the company lifted up her voice,
and said unto him, [a]Blessed *is* the
womb that bare thee, and the paps
which thou hast sucked.
28 But he said, Yea rather, [a]blessed
are they that hear the word of God,
and [b]keep it.
29 ¶ And when the people were
gathered thick together, he began
to say, This is an evil generation:
they seek a [a]sign; and there shall
no sign be given it, but the sign of
Jonas the prophet.
30 For as Jonas was a sign unto the
Ninevites, so shall also the Son of
man be to this generation.
31 The [a]queen of the south shall
rise up in the judgment with the
men of this generation, and condemn them: for she came from the
utmost parts of the earth to hear the
wisdom of Solomon; and, behold, a
greater than Solomon *is* here.
32 The men of Nineve shall rise
up in the judgment with this generation, and shall condemn it: for
they repented at the preaching of
Jonas; and, behold, a greater than
Jonas *is* here.
33 No man, when he hath lighted a
[a]candle, putteth *it* in a secret place,
neither under a bushel, but on a
candlestick, that they which come
in may see the light.
34 The light of the body is the [a]eye:
therefore when thine eye is [b]single,
thy whole body also is full of light;
but when *thine eye* is evil, thy body
also *is* full of [c]darkness.
35 Take heed therefore that the
light which is in thee be not darkness.
36 If thy whole body therefore *be*
full of light, having no part dark,
the whole shall be full of light, as
when the bright shining of a candle
doth give thee light.
37 ¶ And as he spake, a certain
Pharisee besought him to dine with
him: and he went in, and sat down
to meat.
38 And when the Pharisee saw *it*,
he marvelled that he had not first
washed before dinner.
39 And the Lord said unto him,
Now do ye Pharisees make [a]clean
the outside of the cup and the platter; but your [b]inward part is full of
[c]ravening and [d]wickedness.
40 *Ye* fools, did not he that made
that which is without make that
which is within also?
41 [a]But rather [b]give [c]alms of such
things as ye have; and, behold, all
things are [d]clean unto you.
42 But woe unto you, Pharisees! for
ye tithe mint and rue and all manner of herbs, and pass over judgment
and the [a]love of God: these ought ye
to have done, and not to leave the
other undone.
43 Woe unto you, Pharisees! for
ye love the [a]uppermost seats in the

24*c* JST Luke 11:25 . . . *it* . . .
25*a* JST Luke 11:26–27 And when *it* cometh, *it* findeth *the house* swept and garnished. Then goeth *the evil spirit,* and taketh seven other spirits . . .
b GR put in order.
27*a* Luke 1:48.
28*a* TG Blessing.
b Prov. 19:16; 29:18. TG Obedience.
29*a* TG Sign Seekers.
31*a* 1 Kgs. 10:1.
33*a* Matt. 5:15 (15–16); 3 Ne. 18:24.
34*a* D&C 88:68 (67–68).
b Morm. 8:15 (13–15); JS—H 1:46.
c TG Darkness, Spiritual.
39*a* TG Purification.
b Titus 1:15 (15–16). TG Hypocrisy.
c GR plunder, spoil.
d TG Wickedness.
41*a* JST Luke 11:42 But *if ye would* rather give alms of such things as ye have; and *observe to do all things which I have commanded you, then would your inward parts be clean also.*
b TG Generosity.
c TG Almsgiving; Charity.
d TG Cleanliness.
42*a* TG Love.
43*a* Matt. 23:6; Luke 20:46.

synagogues, and greetings in the markets.
44 Woe unto you, [a]scribes and Pharisees, hypocrites! for ye are as [b]graves which appear not, and the men that walk over *them* are not aware *of them*.
45 ¶ Then answered one of the lawyers, and said unto him, Master, thus saying thou [a]reproachest us also.
46 And he said, Woe unto you also, *ye* [a]lawyers! for ye lade men with burdens grievous to be borne, and ye yourselves touch not the burdens with one of your fingers.
47 Woe unto you! for ye build the sepulchres of the prophets, and your fathers killed them.
48 Truly ye bear witness that ye [a]allow the deeds of your fathers: for they indeed killed them, and ye build their sepulchres.
49 Therefore also said the wisdom of God, I will send them prophets and apostles, and *some* of them they shall slay and persecute:
50 That the [a]blood of all the prophets, which was [b]shed from the foundation of the world, may be required of this generation;
51 From the blood of Abel unto the blood of Zacharias, which perished between the altar and the [a]temple: verily I say unto you, It shall be required of this generation.
52 Woe unto you, [a]lawyers! for ye have taken away the [b]key of [c]knowledge: ye entered not in yourselves, and them that were entering in ye [d]hindered.
53 And as he said these things unto them, the scribes and the Pharisees began to [a]urge *him* vehemently, and to [b]provoke him to speak of many things:
54 Laying wait for him, and seeking to [a]catch something out of his mouth, that they might accuse him.

CHAPTER 12

Jesus teaches, Beware of hypocrisy; lay up treasures in heaven rather than on earth; prepare for the coming of the Lord; where much is given, much is required; preaching the gospel causes division.

IN the mean time, when there were gathered together an innumerable multitude of people, insomuch that they trode one upon another, he began to say unto his disciples first of all, Beware ye of the [a]leaven of the Pharisees, which is [b]hypocrisy.
2 For there is nothing covered, that shall not be revealed; neither [a]hid, that shall not be known.
3 Therefore whatsoever ye have spoken in [a]darkness shall be heard in the light; and that which ye have [b]spoken in the ear in [c]closets shall be proclaimed upon the housetops.
4 And I say unto you my [a]friends, Be not [b]afraid of them that kill the body, and after that have no more that they can do.
5 But I will forewarn you whom ye shall [a]fear: Fear him, which after he hath killed hath power to cast into [b]hell; yea, I say unto you, Fear him.
6 Are not five sparrows sold for two farthings, and not one of them is [a]forgotten before God?

44*a* TG Scribe.
b Ps. 5:9 (9–10); Matt. 23:27; Acts 23:3.
45*a* TG Reproach.
46*a* Alma 10:27 (12–32).
48*a* GR agree, accord with. Acts 22:20.
50*a* TG Martyrdom.
b TG Prophets, Rejection of.
51*a* Matt. 23:35.
52*a* Alma 10:27 (13–27); 11:20 (20–22).
b Moses 1:23 (23, 41).
c JST Luke 11:53 . . . knowledge, *the fullness of the scriptures;* ye *enter* not in yourselves *into the kingdom;* and *those who* were entering in, ye hindered. Luke 1:77.
d Acts 13:45 (45, 50); 1 Thes. 2:16.
53*a* GR be angry with, be exasperated against.
b TG Provoking.
54*a* Matt. 22:15; Mark 12:13 (13–17); 2 Ne. 27:32 (31–32).
12 1*a* TG Leaven.
b TG Hypocrisy.
2*a* Prov. 28:13.
3*a* D&C 1:3.
b TG Gossip.
c GR places of privacy.
4*a* John 15:15 (13–15).
b Matt. 10:28. TG Peer Influence.
5*a* D&C 122:9 (4–9).
b TG Death, Spiritual, Second; Devil.
6*a* TG God, Omniscience of.

7 But even the very hairs of your
head are all numbered. Fear not
therefore: ye are of more value than
many sparrows.
8 Also I say unto you, Whosoever
shall [a]confess me before men, him
shall the Son of man also confess
before the [b]angels of God:
9 [a]But he that denieth me before
men shall be denied before the angels of God.
10 And whosoever shall speak a
word against the Son of man, it shall
be forgiven him: but unto him that
[a]blasphemeth against the Holy Ghost
it shall not be forgiven.
11 And when they bring you unto
the synagogues, and *unto* magistrates, and [a]powers, [b]take ye no
thought how or what thing ye shall
answer, or what ye shall [c]say:
12 For the [a]Holy Ghost shall [b]teach
you in the same hour what ye ought
to say.
13 ¶ And one of the company
said unto him, Master, speak to my
brother, that he divide the inheritance with me.
14 And he said unto him, Man,
who made me a judge or a divider
over you?
15 And he said unto them, Take
heed, and beware of [a]covetousness:
for a man's life consisteth not in the
abundance of the things which he
possesseth.
16 And he spake a parable unto
them, saying, The ground of a
certain rich man brought forth
plentifully:
17 And he thought within himself,
saying, What shall I do, because I
have no room where to [a]bestow my
fruits?
18 And he said, This will I do: I
will pull down my barns, and build
greater; and there will I bestow all
my fruits and my goods.
19 And I will say to my soul, [a]Soul,
thou hast much goods laid up for
many years; take thine ease, [b]eat,
drink, *and* be merry.
20 But God said unto him, *Thou*
fool, this night thy [a]soul shall be
required of thee: then whose shall
those things be, which thou hast
provided?
21 So *is* he that layeth up [a]trea-
sure for [b]himself, and is not rich
toward God.
22 ¶ And he said unto his disciples,
Therefore I say unto you, [a]Take no
[b]thought for your life, what ye shall
eat; neither for the body, what ye
shall put on.
23 The life is more than meat, and
the body *is more* than raiment.
24 Consider the [a]ravens: for they
neither sow nor reap; which neither
have storehouse nor barn; and God
feedeth them: how much more are
ye better than the fowls?
25 And which of you with taking
thought can add to his stature one
cubit?
26 If ye then be not able to do that
thing which is least, why take ye
thought for the rest?
27 Consider the [a]lilies how they
grow: they toil not, they spin not;
and yet I say unto you, that Solomon
in all his glory was not arrayed like
one of these.
28 If then God so clothe the grass,
which is to day in the field, and to
morrow is cast into the oven; [a]how
much more *will he clothe* you, O ye
of little faith?

8*a* Moro. 7:44 (44–48); D&C 62:3.
b TG Angels.
9*a* JST Luke 12:9–12 (Appendix).
10*a* TG Apostasy of Individuals; Holy Ghost, Unpardonable Sin against.
11*a* GR authorities.
b GR don't worry; don't be anxious about.
c D&C 84:85.
12*a* Ex. 4:12; D&C 24:6.
b TG Holy Ghost, Mission of.
15*a* Ps. 62:10; 119:36. TG Covet.
17*a* GR gather.
19*a* Eccl. 2:24.
b Isa. 22:13; 1 Cor. 15:32.
20*a* TG Soul.
21*a* TG Treasure.
b Hosea 10:1.
22*a* GR Don't worry.
b Matt. 6:25; D&C 84:81.
24*a* Job 38:41.
27*a* TG Nature, Earth.
28*a* JST Luke 12:30 . . . how much more will he *provide for* you, *if ye are not* of little faith?

29 And seek not ye what ye shall
eat, or what ye shall drink, neither
be ye of [a]doubtful mind.
30 For all these things do the nations of the world seek after: and
your Father knoweth that ye have
need of these things.
31 ¶ [a]But rather seek ye the [b]king-
dom of God; and [c]all these things
shall be added unto you.
32 Fear not, little [a]flock; for it is
your Father's good pleasure to give
you the [b]kingdom.
33 Sell that ye have, and give [a]alms;
provide yourselves bags which wax
not old, a [b]treasure in the heavens
that [c]faileth not, where no thief ap-
proacheth, neither moth corrupteth.
34 For where your [a]treasure is,
there will your heart be also.
35 Let your loins be girded about,
and *your* [a]lights burning;
36 And ye yourselves like unto men
that wait for their lord, when he
will return from the wedding; that
when he cometh and knocketh, they
may open unto him immediately.
37 [a]Blessed *are* those servants,
whom the lord when he cometh
shall find [b]watching: verily I say
unto you, that he shall gird himself,
and make them to sit down to meat,
and will come forth and serve them.
38 And if he shall come in the
second watch, or come in the third
watch, and find *them* so, blessed are
those servants.
39 And this know, that if the [a]good-
man of the house had known what
hour the thief would come, he would
have watched, and not have [b]suffered
his house to be broken through.
40 Be ye therefore ready also: for
the Son of man [a]cometh at an [b]hour
when ye think not.
41 ¶ Then Peter said unto him,
Lord, speakest thou this parable
unto us, or even to all?
42 And the Lord said, Who then
is that [a]faithful and wise [b]steward,
whom *his* lord shall make ruler over
his household, to give *them their* portion of meat in due season?
43 Blessed *is* that servant, whom
his lord when he cometh shall find
so [a]doing.
44 Of a truth I say unto you, that
he will make him [a]ruler over [b]all
that he hath.
45 But and if that servant say in his
heart, My lord delayeth his coming;
and shall begin to beat the menservants and [a]maidens, and to eat
and drink, and to be drunken;
46 The lord of that servant will
come in a day when he looketh not
for *him,* and at an hour when he is
not aware, and will cut him in sun-
der, and will appoint him his [a]por-
tion with the unbelievers.
47 And that [a]servant, which knew
his lord's [b]will, and [c]prepared not
himself, neither did according to
his will, shall be beaten with many
stripes.
48 But he that [a]knew not, and did
commit things worthy of stripes,
shall be [b]beaten with few *stripes.* For
unto whomsoever [c]much is [d]given, of
him shall be much [e]required: and to

29*a* Luke 1:20 (19–20); 24:25. TG Doubt.
31*a* JST Luke 12:34 *Therefore* seek ye *to bring forth* the kingdom of God . . .
b 1 Tim. 4:8; Jacob 2:18 (18–19); 3 Ne. 13:33 (25–34); D&C 29:5.
c Deut. 28:8; D&C 24:3 (3–4).
32*a* D&C 35:27.
b Matt. 25:34. TG Kingdom of God, on Earth.
33*a* TG Almsgiving.
b TG Treasure.
c TG Dependability.
34*a* 2 Ne. 9:30; Hel. 13:22 (20–23).
35*a* Matt. 25:7 (7–8).
37*a* JST Luke 12:41–57 (Appendix).
b TG Watch.
39*a* GR master.
b GR allowed, permitted.
40*a* D&C 133:11.
b Matt. 24:44.
42*a* TG Trustworthiness.
b TG Stewardship.
43*a* TG Commitment.
44*a* 1 Pet. 5:4.
b Rom. 8:17 (14–18); 1 Cor. 3:22 (21–23); D&C 76:59 (58–59); 84:38 (35–38).
45*a* GR maidservants.
46*a* TG Punish.
47*a* James 4:17. TG Apostasy of Individuals.
b 2 Ne. 9:27 (25–27).
c TG Accountability; Procrastination.
48*a* Rom. 2:12.
b Deut. 25:2.
c TG Talents.
d TG Stewardship.
e TG Accountability; Duty; Judgment.

whom men have committed much, of him they will ask the more.
49 ¶ I am come to send fire on the earth; and what will I, if it be already kindled?
50 But I have a [a]baptism to be baptized with; and how am I [b]straitened till it be accomplished!
51 Suppose ye that I am come to give peace on earth? I tell you, Nay; but rather division:
52 For from henceforth there shall be five in one house divided, three against two, and two against three.
53 The father shall be divided against the son, and the son [a]against the father; the mother against the daughter, and the daughter against the mother; the mother in law against her daughter in law, and the daughter in law against her mother in law.
54 ¶ And he said also to the people, When ye see a cloud rise out of the west, straightway ye say, There cometh a shower; and so it is.
55 And when *ye see* the south wind blow, ye say, There will be heat; and it cometh to pass.
56 *Ye* hypocrites, ye can discern the face of the sky and of the earth; but how is it that ye do not discern this time?
57 Yea, and why even of yourselves judge ye not what is right?
58 ¶ When thou goest with thine adversary to the magistrate, *as thou art* in the way, give diligence that thou mayest be delivered from him; lest he hale thee to the judge, and the judge deliver thee to the officer, and the officer cast thee into prison.
59 I tell thee, thou shalt not depart thence, till thou hast paid the very last [a]mite.

CHAPTER 13

Jesus teaches, Repent or perish—He gives the parable of the barren fig tree, heals a woman on the Sabbath, and likens the kingdom of God to a mustard seed—He discusses whether few or many are saved and laments over Jerusalem.

THERE were present at that season some that told him of the Galilæans, whose blood Pilate had mingled with their sacrifices.
2 And Jesus answering said unto them, Suppose ye that these Galilæans were [a]sinners above all the Galilæans, because they suffered such things?
3 I tell you, Nay: but, except ye [a]repent, ye shall all likewise [b]perish.
4 Or those eighteen, upon whom the tower in Siloam fell, and slew them, think ye that they were sinners above all men that dwelt in Jerusalem?
5 I tell you, Nay: but, except ye repent, ye shall all likewise perish.
6 ¶ He spake also this parable; A certain *man* had a fig tree planted in his [a]vineyard; and he came and sought fruit thereon, and found none.
7 Then said he unto the dresser of his vineyard, Behold, these three years I come seeking fruit on this fig tree, and find none: [a]cut it down; why cumbereth it the ground?
8 And he answering said unto him, Lord, let it alone this year also, till I shall dig about it, and dung *it:*
9 And if it bear fruit, *well:* and if not, *then* after that thou shalt cut it down.
10 And he was teaching in one of the synagogues on the sabbath.
11 ¶ And, behold, there was a woman which had a spirit of infirmity eighteen years, and was bowed together, and could in no wise lift up *herself.*
12 And when Jesus saw her, he called *her to him,* and said unto her,

---

50*a* Mosiah 3:7.
b GR distressed, hard-pressed.
53*a* Micah 7:6.
59*a* IE the smallest Jewish coin, worth less than half a penny.
13 2*a* TG Suffering.
3*a* D&C 3:11. TG Repent.
b Ether 8:23 (21–24); D&C 19:4.
6*a* TG Vineyard of the Lord.
7*a* Matt. 3:10; 7:19 (19–20); Hel. 14:18 (17–19).

Woman, thou art loosed from thine
infirmity.
13 And he [a]laid *his* [b]hands on her:
and immediately she was made
straight, and glorified God.
14 And the ruler of the synagogue
answered with indignation, because
that Jesus had healed on the sabbath day, and said unto the people,
There are six days in which men
ought to [a]work: in them therefore
come and be healed, and not on the
sabbath day.
15 The Lord then answered him,
and said, *Thou* hypocrite, doth not
each one of you on the sabbath loose
his ox or *his* ass from the stall, and
lead *him* away to watering?
16 And ought not this woman, being a daughter of Abraham, whom
Satan hath bound, lo, these eighteen
years, be loosed from this bond on
the [a]sabbath day?
17 And when he had said these
things, all his adversaries were
ashamed: and all the people rejoiced
for all the glorious things that were
done by him.
18 ¶ Then said he, Unto what is the
kingdom of God like? and whereunto shall I [a]resemble it?
19 It is like a grain of mustard seed,
which a man took, and cast into his
garden; and it grew, and [a]waxed a
great tree; and the fowls of the air
lodged in the branches of it.
20 And again he said, Whereunto
shall I liken the kingdom of God?
21 It is like leaven, which a woman
took and hid in three measures of
meal, till the whole was leavened.
22 And he went through the cities
and villages, teaching, and journeying toward Jerusalem.
23 Then said one unto him, Lord,
are there [a]few that be saved? And
he said unto them,
24 ¶ Strive to enter in at the [a]strait
[b]gate: for many, I say unto you, will
[c]seek to enter in, and shall not be
able.
25 When once the master of the
house is risen up, and hath shut
to the door, and ye begin to stand
without, and to knock at the door,
saying, Lord, [a]Lord, open unto
us; and he shall answer and say
unto you, I know you not whence
ye are:
26 Then shall ye begin to say, We
have eaten and drunk in thy presence, and thou hast taught in our
streets.
27 But he shall say, I tell you,
I know you not whence ye are;
[a]depart from me, all *ye* workers of
iniquity.
28 There shall be [a]weeping and
gnashing of teeth, when ye shall
see Abraham, and Isaac, and Jacob, and all the prophets, in the
[b]kingdom of God, and you *yourselves*
thrust out.
29 And [a]they shall come from
the east, and *from* the west, and
from the north, and *from* the south,
and shall sit down in the kingdom
of God.
30 And, behold, there are last
which shall be first, and there are
[a]first which shall be last.
31 ¶ The same day there came certain of the Pharisees, saying unto
him, Get thee out, and depart hence:
for [a]Herod will kill thee.
32 And he said unto them, Go ye,
and tell that fox, Behold, I cast out
devils, and I do cures to day and to

13*a* TG Hands, Laying on of.
b TG Administrations to the Sick.
14*a* TG Industry.
16*a* TG Sabbath.
18*a* GR compare.
19*a* GR became.
23*a* 3 Ne. 27:33; D&C 121:34.
24*a* GR narrow. 2 Ne. 9:41; Alma 37:13 (13, 44–46); 3 Ne. 14:13 (13–14); D&C 132:22 (22–25).
b Matt. 7:13 (13–14); 3 Ne. 27:33; D&C 22:4 (1–4).
c 1 Ne. 12:17.
25*a* Isa. 55:6.
27*a* Mosiah 26:27 (24–27); 3 Ne. 14:23 (21–23); D&C 29:28 (27–28).
28*a* Mosiah 16:2 (1–2); D&C 133:73 (72–73).
b Alma 5:24 (14–24). TG Exaltation; Kingdom of God, in Heaven.
29*a* Matt. 8:11 (11–12); Acts 10:45; 2 Ne. 10:18 (9–18); D&C 45:9 (7–30).
30*a* 1 Ne. 13:42; Jacob 5:63 (1–77); Ether 13:12 (10–12); D&C 29:30 (30–32).
31*a* Luke 3:19.

morrow, and the third *day* I shall be [a]perfected.
33 Nevertheless I must walk to day, and to morrow, and the *day* following: for it cannot be that a [a]prophet perish out of [b]Jerusalem.
34 O Jerusalem, Jerusalem, which [a]killest the prophets, and stonest them that are sent unto thee; how often would I have gathered thy children together, as a [b]hen *doth gather* her brood under *her* wings, and ye would not!
35 Behold, your house is left unto you [a]desolate: and verily I say unto you, [b]Ye shall not see me, until *the time* come when ye shall say, [c]Blessed *is* he that cometh in the name of the Lord.

CHAPTER 14

Jesus again heals on the Sabbath—He teaches humility and gives the parable of the great supper—Those who follow Him must forsake all else.

AND it came to pass, as he went into the house of one of the chief Pharisees to eat bread on the sabbath day, that they watched him.
2 And, behold, there was a certain man before him which had the dropsy.
3 And Jesus answering spake unto the lawyers and Pharisees, saying, Is it lawful to heal on the sabbath day?
4 And they held their peace. And he took *him*, and healed him, and let him go;
5 And answered them, saying, Which of you shall have an ass or an ox fallen into a pit, and will not straightway pull him out on the [a]sabbath day?
6 And they could not answer him again to these things.
7 ¶ And he put forth a parable to those which were bidden, when he marked how they chose out the [a]chief rooms; saying unto them,
8 When thou art [a]bidden of any *man* to a wedding, sit not down in the highest room; lest a more honourable man than thou be bidden of him;
9 And he that bade thee and him come and say to thee, Give this man place; and thou begin with shame to take the lowest room.
10 But when thou art bidden, go and sit down in the [a]lowest room; that when he that bade thee cometh, he may say unto thee, Friend, go up [b]higher: then shalt thou have [c]worship in the presence of them that sit at meat with thee.
11 For whosoever [a]exalteth himself shall be [b]abased; and he that [c]humbleth himself shall be exalted.
12 ¶ Then said he also to him that bade him, When thou makest a dinner or a supper, call not thy friends, nor thy brethren, neither thy kinsmen, nor *thy* rich neighbours; lest they also bid thee again, and a recompence be made thee.
13 But when thou makest a feast, call the [a]poor, the maimed, the lame, the blind:
14 And thou shalt be [a]blessed; for they cannot recompense thee: for thou shalt be [b]recompensed at the [c]resurrection of the just.
15 ¶ And when one of them that sat at meat with him heard these

32*a* TG Perfection.
33*a* TG Prophets, Rejection of.
b JST Luke 13:33–34 . . . Jerusalem. *This he spake, signifying of his death. And in this very hour he began to weep over Jerusalem,*
34*a* TG Persecution.
b D&C 10:65 (63–65); 43:24 (24–25).
35*a* Jer. 12:7; 22:5; D&C 84:115 (114–15).
b JST Luke 13:36 . . . Ye shall not *know me, until ye have received from the hand of the Lord a just recompense for all your sins;* until the time . . .
c Ps. 118:26.
14 5*a* TG Sabbath.
7*a* GR first places. Matt. 23:6.
8*a* GR invited.
10*a* TG Humility.
b Prov. 25:7 (6–8).
c GR honor, glory, respect.
11*a* TG Haughtiness.
b D&C 101:42. TG Shame.
c D&C 104:82. TG Contrite Heart.
13*a* TG Generosity; Poor.
14*a* TG Blessing.
b Matt. 6:4.
c TG Resurrection.

things, he said unto him, Blessed
is he that shall [a]eat [b]bread in the
kingdom of God.
16 Then said he unto him, A certain man made a great supper, and
bade many:
17 And sent his servant at supper
time to say to them that were bidden,
Come; for all things are now ready.
18 And they all with one *consent*
began to make [a]excuse. The first
said unto him, I have bought a
piece of ground, and I must needs
go and see it: I pray thee have me
excused.
19 And another said, I have bought
five yoke of oxen, and I go to prove
them: I pray thee have me excused.
20 And another said, I have married a wife, and therefore I cannot
come.
21 So that servant came, and
shewed his lord these things. Then
the master of the house being angry
said to his servant, Go out quickly
into the streets and lanes of the
city, and bring in hither the poor,
and the maimed, and the [a]halt, and
the blind.
22 And the servant said, Lord, it
is done as thou hast commanded,
and yet there is room.
23 And the [a]lord said unto the servant, Go out into the highways and
[b]hedges, and [c]compel *them* to come
in, that my house may be filled.
24 For I say unto you, That [a]none
of those men which were bidden
shall taste of my supper.
25 ¶ And there went great multitudes with him: and he turned, and
said unto them,
26 If any *man* come to me, and
[a]hate not his father, and mother,
and wife, and children, and brethren, and sisters, [b]yea, and his own
[c]life also, he cannot be my [d]disciple.
27 And whosoever doth not bear
his [a]cross, and come after me, cannot be my [b]disciple.
28 For which of you, intending to
build a tower, sitteth not down first,
and [a]counteth the [b]cost, whether he
have *sufficient* to [c]finish *it?*
29 Lest [a]haply, after he hath laid
the foundation, and is not able to
finish *it,* all that behold *it* begin to
mock him,
30 Saying, This man began to build,
and was not able to [a]finish.
31 Or what king, going to make
war against another king, sitteth not
down first, and [a]consulteth whether
he be able with ten thousand to
meet him that cometh against him
with twenty thousand?
32 Or else, while the other is yet
a great way off, he sendeth an [a]am-
bassage, and desireth conditions of
peace.
33 So likewise, whosoever he be
of you that [a]forsaketh not all that
he hath, he cannot be my [b]disciple.
34 ¶ [a]Salt *is* good: but if the [b]salt
have lost his savour, wherewith shall
it be seasoned?
35 It is neither fit for the land, nor
yet for the dunghill; *but* men cast
it out. He that hath ears to hear, let
him hear.

15*a* Luke 22:30; Rev. 19:9.
b TG Bread.
18*a* Luke 9:62 (57–62); D&C 121:35 (34–35).
21*a* GR lame.
23*a* 2 Cor. 5:20.
b GR hedged pathways.
c GR urge.
24*a* Matt. 21:43; Acts 13:46.
26*a* Matt. 10:37.
b JST Luke 14:26 . . . *or husband,* yea and his own life also; *or in other words, is afraid to lay down his life for my sake,* he cannot be . . .
c TG Martyrdom.
d TG Self-Mastery.
27*a* See JST Matt. 16:25–26 (Appendix). Matt. 10:38; John 19:17; 2 Ne. 9:18; Jacob 1:8; 3 Ne. 12:30; D&C 56:2.
b JST Luke 14:27–28 . . . disciple. *Wherefore, settle this in your hearts, that ye will do the things which I shall teach, and command you.*
28*a* Prov. 24:27. TG Self-Mastery.
b TG Problem-Solving.
c TG Commitment.
29*a* GR perhaps.
30*a* JST Luke 14:31 . . . finish. *And this he said, signifying there should not any man follow him, unless he was able to continue; saying,*
31*a* Prov. 20:18.
32*a* OR embassy.
33*a* Luke 5:11; D&C 103:27 (27–28).
b D&C 132:50 (49–51).
34*a* JST Luke 14:35–37 (Appendix).
b TG Salt.

CHAPTER 15

Jesus gives the parables of the lost sheep, the piece of silver, and the prodigal son.

THEN drew near unto him all the
[a]publicans and sinners for to hear
him.
2 And the Pharisees and scribes
murmured, saying, This man receiveth sinners, and eateth with them.
3 ¶ And he spake this parable unto
them, saying,
4 What man of you, having an hundred sheep, if he lose one of them,
doth not leave the ninety and nine
[a]in the wilderness, and go after that
which is [b]lost, until he find it?
5 And when he hath found *it,* he
layeth *it* on his shoulders, rejoicing.
6 And when he cometh home, he
calleth together *his* friends and
neighbours, saying unto them, Rejoice with me; for I have found my
sheep which was lost.
7 I say unto you, that likewise
[a]joy shall be in heaven over one
[b]sinner that [c]repenteth, more than
over ninety and nine just persons,
which need no repentance.
8 ¶ Either what woman having
ten pieces of silver, if she lose one
[a]piece, doth not light a candle, and
sweep the house, and seek diligently
till she find *it?*
9 And when she hath found *it,* she
calleth *her* friends and *her* neighbours together, saying, Rejoice with
me; for I have found the piece which
I had lost.
10 Likewise, I say unto you, there is
joy in the presence of the [a]angels of
God over one [b]sinner that repenteth.
11 ¶ And he said, A certain man
had two sons:
12 And the younger of them said
to *his* father, Father, give me the
portion of [a]goods that falleth *to me.*
And he divided unto them *his* living.
13 And not many days after the
younger son gathered all together,
and took his journey into a far country, and there [a]wasted his [b]substance
with [c]riotous living.
14 And when he had spent all,
there arose a mighty famine in that
land; and he began to be in want.
15 And he went and joined himself
to a citizen of that country; and he
sent him into his fields to feed swine.
16 And he [a]would fain have filled
his belly with the [b]husks that the
swine did eat: and no man gave
unto him.
17 And when he [a]came to himself,
he said, How many hired servants of
my father's have bread enough and
to spare, and I perish with hunger!
18 I will [a]arise and go to my father,
and will say unto him, Father, I
have [b]sinned against heaven, and
before thee,
19 And am no more worthy to be
called thy son: make me as one of
thy hired servants.
20 And he arose, and came to his
father. But when he was yet a great
way off, his father saw him, and had
[a]compassion, and ran, and fell on
his neck, and kissed him.
21 And the son said unto him,
Father, I have sinned against heaven,
and in thy sight, and am no more
[a]worthy to be called thy [b]son.
22 But the father said to his servants, Bring forth the best robe, and

---

15 1*a* Mark 2:16 (15–16).
4*a* JST Luke 15:4 . . . *and go into* the wilderness after that which is lost . . .
b Ezek. 34:16 (11–12, 16).
7*a* TG Joy.
b TG Missionary Work.
c TG Repent.
8*a* GR *drachma* (a silver coin equal to the Roman *denarius*—a workman's daily wage).
10*a* TG Angels.
b TG Worth of Souls.
12*a* GR property.
13*a* TG Waste.
b GR property.
c Prov. 28:7. TG Rioting and Reveling.
16*a* GR desired, set the heart upon.
b GR pods (of the carob tree).
17*a* Ps. 119:59. TG Repent.
18*a* Lam. 3:40.
b TG Confession.
20*a* TG Benevolence; Compassion; Family, Love within; Mercy.
21*a* TG Contrite Heart; Worthiness.
b TG Family, Patriarchal.

put *it* on him; and put a ring on his hand, and shoes on *his* feet:

23 And bring hither the fatted calf, and kill *it*; and let us eat, and be merry:

24 For this my son was dead, and is alive again; he was lost, and is found. And they began to be merry.

25 Now his elder son was in the field: and as he came and drew nigh to the house, he heard musick and dancing.

26 And he called one of the servants, and asked what these things meant.

27 And he said unto him, Thy brother is come; and thy father hath killed the fatted calf, because he hath received him safe and sound.

28 And he was angry, and would not go in: therefore came his father out, and entreated him.

29 And he answering said to *his* father, Lo, these many years do I serve thee, neither transgressed I at any time thy commandment: and yet thou never gavest me a kid, that I might make merry with my friends:

30 But as soon as this thy son was come, which hath devoured thy living with harlots, thou hast killed for him the fatted calf.

31 And he said unto him, [a]Son, thou art ever with me, and [b]all that I have is thine.

32 It was [a]meet that we should make merry, and be glad: for this thy brother was dead, and is alive again; and was lost, and is found.

CHAPTER 16

Jesus gives the parable of the unjust steward—He teaches of service and condemns divorce—He gives the parable of the rich man and Lazarus.

AND he said also unto his disciples, There was a certain rich man, which had a steward; and the same was accused unto him that he had [a]wasted his goods.

2 And he called him, and said unto him, How is it that I hear this of thee? give an [a]account of thy [b]stewardship; for thou mayest be no longer steward.

3 Then the steward said within himself, What shall I do? for my lord taketh away from me the stewardship: I cannot dig; to beg I am ashamed.

4 I am resolved what to do, that, when I am put out of the stewardship, they may receive me into their houses.

5 So he called every one of his lord's debtors *unto him*, and said unto the first, How much owest thou unto my lord?

6 And he said, An hundred measures of oil. And he said unto him, Take thy bill, and sit down quickly, and write fifty.

7 Then said he to another, And how much owest thou? And he said, An hundred measures of wheat. And he said unto him, Take thy bill, and write fourscore.

8 And the lord commended the unjust steward, because he had done wisely: for the children of this world are in their generation wiser than the [a]children of [b]light.

9 And I say unto you, Make to yourselves friends of the [a]mammon of unrighteousness; that, when ye fail, they may receive you into everlasting habitations.

10 He that is [a]faithful in that which is least is faithful also in much: and he that is unjust in the least is unjust also in much.

11 If therefore ye have not been faithful in the unrighteous mammon, who will commit to your [a]trust the true [b]*riches*?

12 And if ye have not been faithful in that which is another man's, who shall give you that which is your own?

31*a* TG Family, Love within.
b D&C 84:38.
32*a* GR necessary.
16 1*a* TG Waste.
2*a* TG Accountability.
b TG Stewardship.
8*a* TG Children of Light.
b TG Light [noun].
9*a* D&C 82:22.
10*a* Matt. 25:21; D&C 51:19; 132:44, 53.
11*a* TG Trustworthiness.
b TG Treasure.

13 ¶ No servant can serve two
[a]masters: for either he will hate the
one, and love the other; or else he
will hold to the one, and despise
the other. Ye cannot serve God and
mammon.
14 And the Pharisees also, who
were [a]covetous, heard all these
things: and they derided him.
15 And he said unto them, Ye are
they which [a]justify yourselves before men; but God [b]knoweth your
[c]hearts: for that which is highly esteemed among [d]men is [e]abomination
in the sight of God.
16 [a]The law and the prophets *were*
until John: since that time the kingdom of God is preached, and every
man presseth into it.
17 And it is easier for heaven and
earth to pass, than one tittle of the
[a]law to fail.
18 Whosoever [a]putteth away his
wife, and marrieth another, committeth adultery: and whosoever
marrieth her that is put away from
her husband committeth adultery.
19 ¶ There was a certain rich man,
which was clothed in purple and
fine linen, and fared sumptuously
every day:
20 And there was a certain [a]beggar
named Lazarus, which was laid at
his gate, full of sores,
21 And desiring to be fed with the
crumbs which fell from the rich
man's table: moreover the dogs came
and licked his sores.
22 And it came to pass, that the
beggar died, and was carried by
the [a]angels into [b]Abraham's bosom:
the rich man also died, and was
buried;
23 And in [a]hell he lift up his
eyes, being in torments, and seeth
Abraham afar off, and Lazarus in
his bosom.
24 And he cried and said, Father
Abraham, have mercy on me, and
send Lazarus, that he may dip the
tip of his finger in water, and cool
my tongue; for I am tormented in
this flame.
25 But Abraham said, Son, remember that thou in thy lifetime
[a]receivedst thy good things, and
likewise Lazarus evil things: but
now he is comforted, and thou art
tormented.
26 And beside all this, between
us and you there is a great [a]gulf
fixed: so that they which would pass
from hence to you cannot; neither
can they pass to us, that *would come*
from thence.
27 Then he said, I pray thee therefore, father, that thou wouldest send
him to my father's house:
28 For I have five brethren; that
he may testify unto them, lest they
also come into this place of torment.
29 Abraham saith unto him, They
have [a]Moses and the prophets; let
them hear them.
30 And he said, Nay, father Abraham: but if one went unto them
from the [a]dead, they will repent.
31 And he said unto him, If they
[a]hear not Moses and the [b]prophets,
neither will they be [c]persuaded,
though one rose from the dead.

CHAPTER 17

Jesus speaks of offenses, forgiveness, and faith—Even the faithful are unprofitable servants—Ten lepers are healed—Jesus discourses on the Second Coming.

THEN said he unto the disciples, It
is impossible but that [a]offences will

13*a* Alma 5:39 (38–39).
14*a* Alma 11:24 (20, 24).
15*a* Luke 10:29.
b TG God, Intelligence of; God, Omniscience of.
c Prov. 21:2.
d 2 Ne. 9:28 (28–30).
e TG Man, Natural, Not Spiritually Reborn.
16*a* JST Luke 16:16–23 (Appendix).
17*a* TG Law of Moses.
18*a* TG Divorce.
20*a* TG Poor.
22*a* TG Angels.
b Alma 40:11 (11–21).
23*a* TG Hell; Spirits in Prison.
25*a* Luke 6:24.
26*a* 1 Ne. 15:28 (28–30). TG Separation.
29*a* TG Scriptures, Value of.
30*a* Alma 32:18 (17–18); Ether 12:12 (12, 18); D&C 5:7 (5–10).
31*a* TG Scriptures, Study of; Unbelief.
b 2 Ne. 33:11 (10–14); Hel. 13:26 (24–30).
c D&C 5:8 (7–10); 133:71.
17 1*a* TG Offense.

come: but woe *unto him*, through
whom they come!
2 It were better for him that a
millstone were hanged about his
neck, and he cast into the sea, than
that he should [a]offend one of these
little ones.
3 ¶ Take heed to yourselves: If
thy brother [a]trespass against thee,
rebuke him; and if he repent, [b]for-
give him.
4 And if he trespass against thee
seven times in a day, and seven times
in a day turn again to thee, saying,
I [a]repent; thou shalt forgive him.
5 And the apostles said unto the
Lord, Increase our faith.
6 And the Lord said, If ye had
[a]faith as a grain of mustard seed, ye
might say unto this sycamine tree,
Be thou plucked up by the root, and
be thou planted in the sea; and it
should obey you.
7 But which of you, having a servant plowing or [a]feeding cattle, will
say unto him [b]by and by, when he
is come from the field, Go and sit
down to meat?
8 And will not rather say unto him,
Make ready wherewith I may sup,
and gird thyself, and serve me, till
I have eaten and drunken; and afterward thou shalt eat and drink?
9 Doth he thank that servant because he did the things that were
commanded him? I [a]trow not.
10 So likewise ye, when ye shall
have done all those things which are
commanded you, say, We are [a]un-
profitable servants: we have done
that which was our [b]duty to do.
11 ¶ And it came to pass, as he
went to Jerusalem, that he passed
through the midst of Samaria and
Galilee.
12 And as he entered into a certain
village, there met him ten men that
were [a]lepers, which stood afar off:
13 And they lifted up *their* voices,
and said, Jesus, Master, have mercy
on us.
14 And when he saw *them*, he said
unto them, Go shew yourselves unto
the [a]priests. And it came to pass, that,
as they went, they were cleansed.
15 And one of them, when he saw
that he was healed, turned back,
and with a loud voice glorified God,
16 And fell down on *his* face at his
feet, giving him [a]thanks: and he was
a Samaritan.
17 And Jesus answering said, Were
there not ten [a]cleansed? but where
are the [b]nine?
18 There are not found that returned to give glory to God, save
this stranger.
19 And he said unto him, Arise,
go thy way: thy faith hath made
thee whole.
20 ¶ And when he was demanded
of the Pharisees, when the [a]kingdom
of God should come, he answered
them and said, The kingdom of God
cometh not with observation:
21 Neither shall they say, Lo here!
or, lo there! for, behold, the [a]king-
dom of God [b]is [c]within you.
22 And he said unto the disciples,
The days will come, when ye shall
desire to see one of the days of the
Son of man, and ye shall not see *it*.
23 And they shall say to you, See
here; or, [a]see there: go not after *them*,
nor follow *them*.
24 For as the lightning, that light-
eneth out of the one *part* under
heaven, shineth unto the other *part*
under heaven; so shall also the Son
of man be in his [a]day.

2*a* TG Sin.
3*a* Matt. 18:15 (15–17).
b TG Forgive.
4*a* TG Repent.
6*a* Moses 7:13.
7*a* GR tending a flock.
b GR immediately.
9*a* GR think.
10*a* Rom. 3:12; Mosiah 2:21 (20–26).
TG Humility; Ingratitude.
b TG Duty.
12*a* TG Leprosy.
14*a* Lev. 13:49.
16*a* TG Thanksgiving.
17*a* TG Purification.
b TG Ingratitude.
20*a* TG Kingdom of God, on Earth.
21*a* D&C 65:2.
b JST Luke 17:21 . . . *has already come unto* you.
c Many translations read “among” because the pronoun “you” is plural here in Greek.
23*a* TG False Christs.
24*a* Luke 21:34; 1 Thes. 5:4.

25 But first must he suffer many
things, and be rejected of this generation.
26 And as it was in the days of
[a]Noe, so shall it be also in the days
of the Son of man.
27 They did eat, they drank, they
married wives, they were given in
marriage, until the day that Noe
entered into the ark, and the [a]flood
came, and destroyed them all.
28 Likewise also as it was in the
days of Lot; they did eat, they drank,
they bought, they sold, they planted,
they builded;
29 But the same day that Lot went
out of [a]Sodom it rained fire and
brimstone from heaven, and destroyed *them* all.
30 Even thus shall it be in the day
when the Son of man is revealed.
31 In that day, he which shall be
upon the housetop, and his stuff in
the house, let him not come down
to take it away: and he that is in
the field, let him likewise not return back.
32 Remember [a]Lot's wife.
33 Whosoever shall seek to save
his life shall lose it; and whosoever
shall [a]lose his life shall preserve it.
34 I tell you, in that night there
shall be two *men* in one bed; the
one shall be taken, and the other
shall be left.
35 Two *women* shall be grinding
together; the one shall be taken,
and the other left.
36 Two *men* shall be in the field;
the one shall be taken, and the
other left.
37 [a]And they answered and said
unto him, Where, Lord? And he
said unto them, Wheresoever the
body *is*, thither will the eagles be
gathered together.

CHAPTER 18

Jesus gives the parables of the unjust judge and the Pharisee and publican—He invites little children to come unto Him and teaches how to gain eternal life—He tells of His coming death and resurrection and gives sight to a blind man.

AND he spake a parable unto them
to this end, that men ought [a]always
to [b]pray, and not to [c]faint;
2 Saying, There was in a city a
judge, which feared not God, neither regarded man:
3 And there was a widow in that
city; and she came unto him, saying, Avenge me of mine adversary.
4 And he would not for a while:
but afterward he said within himself, Though I fear not God, nor regard man;
5 Yet because this widow troubleth
me, I will avenge her, lest by her
continual coming she weary me.
6 And the Lord said, Hear what
the [a]unjust judge saith.
7 And shall not God [a]avenge his
own elect, which cry day and night
unto him, though he bear long with
[b]them?
8 [a]I tell you that he will [b]avenge
them speedily. Nevertheless when
the Son of man cometh, shall he
find faith on the earth?
9 And he spake this parable unto
certain which [a]trusted in themselves
that they were righteous, and [b]de-
spised others:
10 Two men went up into the
temple to [a]pray; the one a Pharisee,
and the other a publican.
11 The Pharisee stood and prayed
thus with himself, God, I thank
thee, that I am [a]not as other men
are, extortioners, unjust, adulterers,
or even as this publican.

26*a* TG Earth, Cleansing of; Flood.
27*a* Matt. 24:37 (36–38).
29*a* Gen. 19:24.
32*a* Gen. 19:26.
33*a* TG Sacrifice.
37*a* JST Luke 17:36–40 (Appendix).
18 1*a* TG Perseverance.
b TG Prayer.
c D&C 75:11.
6*a* TG Injustice.
7*a* Num. 31:2; Alma 1:13; D&C 121:5.
b JST Luke 18:7 . . . *men?*
8*a* JST Luke 18:8 I tell you that *he will come, and when he does come,* he will avenge *his saints* speedily. Nevertheless . . .
b TG Justice.
9*a* John 5:44.
b Alma 32:3 (3–5).
10*a* TG Prayer.
11*a* Isa. 65:5; Alma 31:16 (14–18).

12 I [a]fast twice in the week, I give
[b]tithes of all that I [c]possess.
13 And the publican, standing afar
off, would not lift up so much as *his*
eyes unto heaven, but smote upon
his breast, saying, God be merciful
to me a [a]sinner.
14 I tell you, this man went down
to his house justified *rather* than
the other: for every one that [a]ex-
alteth himself shall be abased; and
he that [b]humbleth himself shall be
exalted.
15 And they brought unto him also
infants, that he would touch them:
but when *his* disciples saw *it*, they
rebuked them.
16 But Jesus called them *unto him*,
and said, Suffer little [a]children to
come unto me, and forbid them not:
for of such is the kingdom of God.
17 Verily I say unto you, Whosoever shall not receive the kingdom
of God as a little child shall in no
wise enter therein.
18 And a certain ruler asked him,
saying, Good Master, what shall I do
to inherit [a]eternal life?
19 And Jesus said unto him, Why
callest thou me good? none *is* [a]good,
save one, *that is*, God.
20 Thou knowest the commandments, Do not commit [a]adultery, Do
not [b]kill, Do not steal, Do not bear
[c]false witness, [d]Honour thy father
and thy mother.
21 And he said, All these have I
kept from my youth up.
22 Now when Jesus heard these
things, he said unto him, Yet lackest
thou one thing: sell all that thou hast,
and distribute unto the [a]poor, and
thou shalt have treasure in heaven:
and come, follow me.
23 And when he heard this, he was
very sorrowful: for he was very rich.
24 And when Jesus saw that he
was very sorrowful, he said, How
hardly shall they that have riches
enter into the kingdom of God!
25 For it is easier for a camel to
go through a needle's eye, than for
a rich man to enter into the kingdom of God.
26 And they that heard *it* said, Who
then can be saved?
27 [a]And he said, The things which
are impossible with men are [b]pos-
sible with God.
28 Then Peter said, Lo, we have
left all, and followed thee.
29 And he said unto them, Verily
I say unto you, There is no man
that hath left house, or parents, or
brethren, or wife, or children, for
the kingdom of God's sake,
30 Who shall not [a]receive [b]mani-
fold more in this present time, and
in the world to come life everlasting.
31 ¶ Then he took *unto him* the
twelve, and said unto them, Behold,
we go up to Jerusalem, and all things
that are [a]written by the prophets
concerning the Son of man shall
be accomplished.
32 For he shall be delivered unto
the Gentiles, and shall be [a]mocked,
and spitefully entreated, and spit-
ted on:
33 And they shall scourge *him*, and
put him to death: and the third day
he shall [a]rise again.
34 And they [a]understood none of
these things: and this saying was hid

12*a* Ex. 34:28.
b TG Tithing.
c GR acquire, gain, or possess.
13*a* Alma 38:14 (13–14). TG Contrite Heart.
14*a* 2 Cor. 10:18. TG Haughtiness.
b Ether 12:27; D&C 101:42; 124:114.
16*a* Moro. 8:19 (10–26).
18*a* Luke 10:25.
19*a* TG God, Perfection of.
20*a* D&C 42:24 (23–25).
b D&C 42:79.
c D&C 42:21.
d TG Honoring Father and Mother.
22*a* Mosiah 4:26; Alma 1:27; D&C 42:30 (29–31).
27*a* JST Luke 18:27 And he said *unto them, It is impossible for them who trust in riches, to enter into the kingdom of God; but he who forsaketh the things which are of this world, it is* possible with God, *that he should enter in.*
b TG God, Power of.
30*a* D&C 132:55.
b D&C 104:2.
31*a* 1 Ne. 11:33; 2 Ne. 10:3; Mosiah 3:9 (9–10).
32*a* TG Jesus Christ, Trials of; Mocking.
33*a* TG Jesus Christ, Resurrection.
34*a* John 12:16.

from them, neither knew they the
things which were spoken.
35 ¶ And it came to pass, that as
he was come nigh unto Jericho, a
certain blind man sat by the way
side begging:
36 And hearing the multitude pass
by, he asked what it meant.
37 And they told him, that Jesus
of Nazareth passeth by.
38 And he cried, saying, Jesus,
thou Son of David, have mercy
on me.
39 And they which went before
rebuked him, that he should hold
his peace: but he cried so much
the more, *Thou* Son of David, have
mercy on me.
40 And Jesus stood, and commanded him to be brought unto
him: and when he was come near,
he asked him,
41 Saying, What wilt thou that I
shall do unto thee? And he said,
Lord, that I may receive my sight.
42 And Jesus said unto him, Receive thy [a]sight: thy [b]faith hath
saved thee.
43 And immediately he received
his sight, and followed him, [a]glori-
fying God: and all the people, when
they saw *it*, gave praise unto God.

CHAPTER 19

Jesus came to save souls—He gives the parable of the pounds—He rides in triumph into Jerusalem, weeps over the city, and cleanses the temple again.

AND *Jesus* entered and passed
through Jericho.
2 And, behold, *there was* a man
named Zacchæus, which was the
chief among the publicans, and he
was rich.
3 And he sought to see Jesus who
he was; and could not for the [a]press,
because he was little of stature.
4 And he ran before, and climbed
up into a sycomore tree to see him:
for he was to pass that *way*.
5 And when Jesus came to the
place, he looked up, and saw him,
and said unto him, Zacchæus, make
haste, and come down; for to day I
must abide at thy house.
6 And he made haste, and came
down, and [a]received him joyfully.
7 And when they saw *it*, they all
murmured, saying, That he was
gone to be guest with a man that
is a sinner.
8 And Zacchæus stood, and said
unto the Lord; Behold, Lord, the
half of my goods I give to the poor;
and if I have taken any thing from
any man by false accusation, I restore *him* [a]fourfold.
9 And Jesus said unto him, This
day is salvation come to this house,
forsomuch as he also is a son of
Abraham.
10 For the Son of man is come to
seek and to [a]save that which was
[b]lost.
11 And as they heard these things,
he added and spake a parable, because he was nigh to Jerusalem,
and because they thought that the
kingdom of God should [a]immedi-
ately appear.
12 He said therefore, A certain
nobleman went into a far country
to receive for himself a kingdom,
and to return.
13 And he called his ten servants,
and delivered them ten [a]pounds,
and said unto them, [b]Occupy till
I come.
14 But his [a]citizens hated him, and
sent a [b]message after him, saying,
We will not have this *man* to reign
over us.
15 And it came to pass, that when
he was returned, having received the
kingdom, then he commanded these
[a]servants to be called unto him, to
whom he had given the money, that

42*a* TG Sight.
b 3 Ne. 17:8; D&C 42:48; 58:43.
43*a* Luke 5:25.
19 3*a* GR crowd, multitude.
6*a* TG Hospitality.
8*a* 2 Sam. 12:6.
10*a* TG Life, Sanctity of.
b Ezek. 34:16; 2 Ne. 26:25 (23–29).
11*a* 2 Thes. 2:2 (1–6).
13*a* TG Talents.
b GR Do business.
14*a* TG Citizenship.
b GR ambassador.
15*a* D&C 72:3 (3–4).

he might know how much every
man had gained by trading.
16 Then came the first, saying,
Lord, thy pound hath gained ten
pounds.
17 And he said unto him, Well,
thou good servant: because thou
hast been [a]faithful in a very little,
have thou [b]authority over ten cities.
18 And the second came, saying,
Lord, thy pound hath gained five
pounds.
19 And he said likewise to him, Be
thou also over five cities.
20 And another came, saying, Lord,
behold, *here is* thy pound, which I
have kept laid up in a napkin:
21 For I [a]feared thee, because
thou art an [b]austere man: thou
takest up that thou layedst not
down, and reapest that thou didst
not sow.
22 And he saith unto him, Out of
thine own mouth will I judge thee,
thou wicked servant. Thou knewest
that I was an austere man, taking
up that I laid not down, and reaping that I did not sow:
23 Wherefore then gavest not thou
my money into the bank, that at
my coming I might have [a]required
mine own with [b]usury?
24 And he said unto them that stood
by, Take from him the pound, and
give *it* to him that hath ten pounds.
25 (And they said unto him, Lord,
he hath ten pounds.)
26 For I say unto you, That unto every one [a]which hath shall be given;
and from him that hath not, even
that he hath shall be taken away
from him.
27 But those mine enemies, which
would not that I should reign over
them, bring hither, and slay *them*
before me.
28 ¶ And when he had thus spoken, he went before, ascending up
to Jerusalem.
29 And it came to pass, when he
was come nigh to Bethphage and
Bethany, at the mount called *the*
mount of Olives, he sent two of his
disciples,
30 Saying, Go ye into the village
over against *you;* in the which at
your entering ye shall find a colt
tied, whereon yet never man sat:
loose him, and bring *him hither.*
31 And if any man ask you, Why
do ye loose *him?* thus shall ye say
unto him, Because the Lord hath
need of him.
32 And they that were sent went
their way, and found even as he had
said unto them.
33 And as they were loosing the
colt, the owners thereof said unto
them, Why loose ye the colt?
34 And they said, The Lord hath
need of him.
35 And they brought him to Jesus:
and they cast their garments upon
the [a]colt, and they set Jesus thereon.
36 And as he went, they spread
their clothes in the way.
37 And when he was come nigh,
even now at the descent of the
mount of Olives, the whole multitude of the disciples began to rejoice
and praise God with a loud voice
for all the mighty works that they
had seen;
38 Saying, Blessed *be* the King that
cometh in the name of the Lord:
peace in heaven, and [a]glory in the
highest.
39 And some of the Pharisees from
among the multitude said unto him,
Master, rebuke thy disciples.
40 And he answered and said unto
them, I tell you that, if these should
hold their peace, the [a]stones would
immediately cry out.
41 ¶ And when he was come near,
he beheld the city, and wept over it,
42 Saying, If thou hadst known,
even thou, at least in this thy day,

17*a* TG Stewardship.
b TG Authority.
21*a* TG Courage; Fearful.
b GR harsh, ungenerous.
23*a* GR collected.
b TG Usury.
26*a* JST Luke 19:25 . . . *who occupieth,* shall be given; and from him *who occupieth* not, even that he hath *received* shall be taken away from him.
35*a* Zech. 9:9.
38*a* Luke 2:14.
40*a* Matt. 21:9.

the things *which belong* unto thy
peace! but now they are hid from
thine eyes.
43 For the days shall come upon
thee, that thine [a]enemies shall cast
a [b]trench about thee, and [c]compass
thee round, and keep thee in on
every side,
44 And shall [a]lay thee even with
the ground, and thy children within
thee; and they shall not leave in thee
one [b]stone upon another; because
thou knewest not the time of thy
[c]visitation.
45 And he went into the temple,
and began to cast out them that
sold therein, and them that bought;
46 Saying unto them, It is written,
My house is the [a]house of prayer: but
ye have made it a [b]den of thieves.
47 And he taught daily in the
temple. But the chief priests and the
scribes and the chief of the people
sought to destroy him,
48 And could not find what they
might do: for all the people were
very attentive to hear him.

CHAPTER 20

The chief priests oppose Jesus—He gives the parable of the wicked husbandmen—Render unto Cæsar and God that which is theirs—Jesus teaches the law of marriage.

AND it came to pass, *that* on one of
those days, as he taught the people
in the temple, and preached the gospel, the chief priests and the scribes
came upon *him* with the elders,
2 And spake unto him, saying, Tell
us, by what authority doest thou
these things? or who is he that gave
thee this authority?
3 And he answered and said unto
them, I will also ask you one thing;
and answer me:
4 The baptism of John, was it from
heaven, or of men?
5 And they reasoned with themselves, saying, If we shall say, From
heaven; he will say, Why then believed ye him not?
6 But and if we say, Of men; all
the people will stone us: for they be
persuaded that John was a [a]prophet.
7 And they answered, that they
could not tell whence *it was*.
8 And Jesus said unto them, Neither tell I you by what authority I
do these things.
9 Then began he to speak to the
people this parable; A certain man
planted a [a]vineyard, and let it forth
to [b]husbandmen, and went into a
far country for a long time.
10 And at the season he sent a
servant to the husbandmen, that
they should give him of the fruit
of the vineyard: but the husbandmen beat him, and sent *him* away
empty.
11 And again he sent another servant: and they beat him also, and
entreated *him* shamefully, and sent
him away empty.
12 And again he sent a third: and
they wounded him also, and cast
him out.
13 Then said the lord of the vineyard, What shall I do? I will send
my beloved son: it may be they will
reverence *him* when they see him.
14 But when the husbandmen saw
him, they reasoned among themselves, saying, This is the heir: come,
let us kill him, that the inheritance
may be ours.
15 So they cast him out of the vineyard, and killed *him*. What therefore shall the lord of the vineyard
do unto them?
16 He shall come and destroy
these husbandmen, and shall give
the vineyard to others. And when
they heard *it*, they said, [a]God
forbid.
17 And he beheld them, and said,

43*a* Luke 21:20.
b GR fortification, rampart. Isa. 37:33.
c Deut. 28:52.
44*a* Dan. 9:26.
b Matt. 24:2 (1–51); JS—M 1:3 (1–55).
c Isa. 10:3.
46*a* Isa. 56:7.
b Jer. 7:11; D&C 94:8 (8–9); 109:20 (19–20).
20 6*a* Matt. 11:9; 14:5; 21:26.
9*a* TG Vineyard of the Lord.
b GR farmers.
16*a* GR May it not be.

What is this then that is written,
The [a]stone which the builders rejected, the same is become the head
of the corner?
18 Whosoever shall fall upon that
stone shall be broken; but on whomsoever it shall fall, it will [a]grind him
to powder.
19 ¶ And the chief priests and the
scribes the same hour sought to lay
hands on him; and they feared the
people: for they perceived that he
had spoken this parable against them.
20 And they watched *him*, and
sent forth spies, which should feign
themselves just men, that they might
[a]take hold of his words, that so they
might deliver him unto the power
and authority of the governor.
21 And they asked him, saying,
Master, we know that thou sayest
and teachest rightly, neither ac-
ceptest thou the person *of any*, but
teachest the way of God truly:
22 Is it lawful for us to give [a]trib-
ute unto Cæsar, or no?
23 But he perceived their [a]crafti-
ness, and said unto them, Why
tempt ye me?
24 Shew me a penny. Whose image
and superscription hath it? They
answered and said, Cæsar's.
25 And he said unto them, Render
therefore unto [a]Cæsar the things
which be Cæsar's, and unto God the
things which be God's.
26 And they could not take hold
of his words before the people: and
they marvelled at his answer, and
held their peace.
27 ¶ Then came to *him* certain of the
Sadducees, which deny that there is
any resurrection; and they asked him,
28 Saying, Master, Moses wrote
unto us, If any man's [a]brother die,
having a wife, and he die without
children, that his [b]brother should
take his wife, and raise up seed unto
his brother.
29 There were therefore seven
brethren: and the first took a wife,
and died without children.
30 And the second took her to wife,
and he died childless.
31 And the third took her; and in
like manner the seven also: and they
left no children, and died.
32 Last of all the woman died also.
33 Therefore in the resurrection
whose wife of them is she? for seven
had her to wife.
34 And Jesus answering said unto
them, The children of this world
[a]marry, and are given in marriage:
35 But they which shall be accounted worthy to obtain [a]that
world, and the [b]resurrection from
the dead, neither marry, nor are
given in [c]marriage:
36 Neither can they die any more:
for they are equal unto the [a]angels;
and are the [b]children of God, being
the children of the resurrection.
37 Now that the dead are raised,
even Moses shewed at the [a]bush,
when he calleth the Lord the God
of Abraham, and the God of Isaac,
and the God of Jacob.
38 For he is not a God of the [a]dead,
but of the living: for all live unto
him.
39 ¶ Then certain of the scribes
answering said, Master, thou hast
well said.
40 And after that they durst not
ask him any [a]*question at all*.
41 And he said unto them, How
say they that Christ is David's [a]son?
42 And David himself saith in
the book of Psalms, The LORD said

17*a* TG Rock.
18*a* GR scatter like chaff.
20*a* Matt. 22:15 (15–22); Mark 12:13 (13–17).
22*a* GR taxes. D&C 58:21 (21–22); 98:9 (4–10).
23*a* Alma 10:17; D&C 10:25 (21–27).
25*a* D&C 58:22 (21–23); 63:26 (25–29).
28*a* Deut. 25:5.
b Mark 12:19.
34*a* TG Marriage, Marry; Marriage, Temporal.
35*a* JST Luke 20:35 . . . that world, *through* resurrection from . . .
b TG Objectives; Resurrection.
c D&C 132:16 (7–39).
36*a* D&C 131:2 (1–4); 132:17 (5–17). TG Angels.
b TG Sons and Daughters of God.
37*a* Ex. 3:2 (2–6).
38*a* Rom. 14:9. TG Spirits, Disembodied.
40*a* D&C 84:116.
41*a* Matt. 1:16 (1–16); D&C 93:14 (3–17).

unto my [a]Lord, Sit thou on my right hand,

43 Till I make thine enemies thy footstool.

44 David therefore calleth him Lord, how is he then his son?

45 ¶ Then in the audience of all the people he said unto his disciples,

46 Beware of the [a]scribes, which desire to walk in long robes, and love greetings in the markets, and the [b]highest seats in the synagogues, and the chief rooms at feasts;

47 Which devour widows' houses, and for a shew make long prayers: the same shall receive greater damnation.

CHAPTER 21

Jesus foretells the destruction of the temple and of Jerusalem—He tells of the signs to precede His Second Coming and gives the parable of the fig tree.

AND he looked up, and saw the [a]rich men casting their gifts into the treasury.

2 And he saw also a certain poor widow casting in thither two [a]mites.

3 And he said, Of a truth I say unto you, that this poor widow hath cast in more than they all:

4 For all these have of their abundance cast in unto the offerings of God: but she of her penury hath cast in all the living that she had.

5 ¶ And as some spake of the temple, how it was adorned with goodly stones and gifts, he said,

6 *As for* these things which ye behold, the days will come, in the which there shall not be left one [a]stone upon another, that shall not be thrown down.

7 And they asked him, saying, Master, but when shall these things be? and what [a]sign *will there be* when these things shall come to pass?

8 And he said, Take heed that ye be not deceived: for many shall come in my name, saying, I am *Christ;* and the time draweth near: go ye not therefore after them.

9 But when ye shall hear of wars and commotions, be not terrified: for these things must first come to pass; but the end *is* not by and by.

10 Then said he unto them, [a]Nation shall rise against nation, and kingdom against kingdom:

11 And great earthquakes shall be in divers places, and famines, and [a]pestilences; and fearful sights and great signs shall there be from heaven.

12 But before all these, they shall lay their hands on you, and [a]persecute *you,* delivering *you* up to the synagogues, and into prisons, being brought before kings and rulers for my name's sake.

13 And it shall turn to you for a testimony.

14 Settle *it* therefore in your hearts, not to [a]meditate before what ye shall [b]answer:

15 For I will give you a mouth and [a]wisdom, which all your adversaries shall not be able to [b]gainsay nor resist.

16 And ye shall be betrayed both by parents, and brethren, and kinsfolks, and friends; and *some* of you shall they cause to be put to death.

17 And ye shall be hated of all *men* for my name's [a]sake.

18 But there shall not an [a]hair of your head perish.

19 In your [a]patience [b]possess ye your souls.

42*a* Ps. 110:1.
46*a* 2 Ne. 28:16; Alma 10:27.
b GR first or most honorable. Luke 11:43.
21 1*a* Mosiah 4:23; D&C 56:16.
2*a* D&C 64:34 (22, 34).
6*a* D&C 45:20.
7*a* Matt. 24:3 (3–46); D&C 45:16 (16–75); JS—M 1:4 (4–55).
10*a* 1 Ne. 22:14 (13–14).
11*a* 2 Ne. 6:15; Mosiah 12:4; D&C 97:26 (22–26).
12*a* TG Persecution.
14*a* GR practice, prepare. TG Meditation.
b D&C 84:85.
15*a* Isa. 50:4; Matt. 10:19 (16–20); Acts 6:10; D&C 11:21. TG Wisdom.
b GR speak against, oppose, contradict.
17*a* D&C 98:13; 101:35.
18*a* Matt. 10:30 (29–31); Alma 40:23; D&C 29:25.
19*a* TG Patience.
b GR preserve, win mastery over.

20 And when ye shall see [a]Jerusa-
lem compassed with [b]armies, then
know that the [c]desolation thereof
is nigh.
21 Then let them which are in
Judæa flee to the mountains; and
let them which are in the midst
of it depart out; and let not them
that are in the [a]countries enter
thereinto.
22 For these be the days of vengeance, that all things which are
written may be fulfilled.
23 But woe unto them that are
with child, and to them that give
suck, in those days! for there shall
be great distress in the land, and
wrath upon this people.
24 And they shall fall by the edge
of the sword, and shall be [a]led away
[b]captive into all [c]nations: and Jerusalem shall be [d]trodden down of
the [e]Gentiles, until the times of the
Gentiles be fulfilled.
25 ¶ [a]And there shall be signs
in the sun, and in the [b]moon, and in
the stars; and upon the earth distress
of nations, with perplexity; the sea
and the waves roaring;
26 Men's hearts [a]failing them for
fear, and for looking after those
things which are coming on the
earth: for the powers of heaven shall
be [b]shaken.
27 And then shall they see the Son
of man coming in a [a]cloud with
power and great glory.
28 And when these things begin to
come to pass, then look up, and lift
up your heads; for your [a]redemption
draweth nigh.
29 And he spake to them a parable; Behold the [a]fig tree, and all
the trees;
30 When they now shoot forth, ye
see and know of your own selves
that summer is now nigh at hand.
31 So likewise ye, when ye see
these things come to pass, know ye
that the kingdom of God is nigh
at hand.
32 Verily I say unto you, [a]This generation shall not pass away, till all
be fulfilled.
33 Heaven and earth shall pass
away: but my words shall not
pass away.
34 ¶ And take heed to yourselves,
lest at any time your hearts be
overcharged with [a]surfeiting, and
drunkenness, and [b]cares of this life,
and *so* that [c]day come upon you
[d]unawares.
35 For as a [a]snare shall it come on
all them that dwell on the face of
the whole earth.
36 [a]Watch ye therefore, and [b]pray
always, [c]that ye may be accounted
[d]worthy to escape all these things
that shall come to pass, and to stand
before the [e]Son of man.
37 And in the day time he was
[a]teaching in the temple; and at night
he went out, and abode in the mount
that is called *the mount* of Olives.
38 And all the people came early in
the morning to him in the temple,
for to hear him.

20*a* Luke 19:43.
b Ezek. 38:16 (15–16); Rev. 16:16.
c D&C 45:19 (18–21). TG Abomination of Desolation.
21*a* GR districts or regions.
24*a* Dan. 12:7. TG Israel, Scattering of.
b TG Israel, Bondage of, in Other Lands.
c TG Israel, Twelve Tribes of.
d Dan. 9:27 (24–27).
e D&C 45:25. TG Gentiles.
25*a* JST Luke 21:24–26 (Appendix).
b TG Astronomy.
26*a* D&C 45:26; 88:91.
b Isa. 34:4.
27*a* Dan. 7:13; D&C 34:7.
28*a* D&C 35:26.
29*a* D&C 35:16 (15–16); 45:37 (34–38).
32*a* JST Luke 21:32 . . . this generation, *the generation when the times of the Gentiles be fulfilled,* shall not . . .
34*a* GR debauchery. TG Rioting and Reveling.
b TG Worldliness.
c Luke 17:24; 1 Thes. 5:4.
d TG Procrastination.
35*a* Rev. 3:3; 16:15; D&C 63:15.
36*a* TG Watch.
b TG Prayer.
c JST Luke 21:36 . . . *and keep my commandments,* that ye . . .
d TG Worthiness.
e JST Luke 21:36 . . . Son of man *when he shall come clothed in the glory of his Father.*
37*a* Matt. 26:55; John 8:2 (1–2).

CHAPTER 22

Jesus institutes the sacrament—He suffers in Gethsemane and is betrayed and arrested—Peter denies knowing Him—Jesus is smitten and mocked.

Now the feast of unleavened bread
drew nigh, which is called the
[a]Passover.
2 And the chief [a]priests and [b]scribes
sought how they might [c]kill him; for
they feared the people.
3 ¶ Then entered Satan into Judas surnamed Iscariot, being of the
number of the twelve.
4 And he went his way, and [a]com-
muned with the chief priests and
captains, how he might betray him
unto them.
5 And they were glad, and covenanted to give him [a]money.
6 And he promised, and sought opportunity to betray him unto them
in the absence of the multitude.
7 ¶ Then came the day of [a]unleav-
ened bread, when the [b]passover
must be killed.
8 And he sent [a]Peter and John, saying, Go and prepare us the passover,
that we may eat.
9 And they said unto him, Where
wilt thou that we prepare?
10 And he said unto them, Behold,
when ye are entered into the city,
there shall a man meet you, bearing a pitcher of water; follow him
into the house where he entereth in.
11 And ye shall say unto the [a]good-
man of the house, The Master saith
unto thee, Where is the guestchamber, where I shall eat the passover
with my disciples?
12 And he shall shew you a large
upper room furnished: there make
ready.
13 And they went, and found as
he had said unto them: and they
made ready the passover.
14 And when the hour was come,
he sat down, and the twelve apostles with him.
15 And he said unto them, With
desire I have desired to eat this
passover with you before I suffer:
16 For I say unto you, I will not
any more eat thereof, [a]until it be
fulfilled in the kingdom of God.
17 And he took the cup, and gave
thanks, and said, Take this, and divide *it* among yourselves:
18 For I say unto you, I will not
[a]drink of the fruit of the vine, until the kingdom of God shall come.
19 ¶ And he took [a]bread, and gave
thanks, and brake *it*, and gave unto
them, saying, This is my [b]body which
is [c]given for you: this do in [d]remem-
brance of me.
20 Likewise also the [a]cup after
supper, saying, This cup *is* the new
[b]testament in my blood, which is
shed for you.
21 ¶ But, behold, the hand of him
that betrayeth me *is* with me on
the table.
22 And truly the Son of man goeth,
as it was [a]determined: but woe unto
that man by whom he is [b]betrayed!
23 And they began to inquire
among themselves, which of them
it was that should do this thing.
24 ¶ And there was also a [a]strife
among them, which of them should
be accounted the [b]greatest.
25 And he said unto them, The

---

22 1*a* TG Passover.
2*a* 2 Ne. 10:5. TG Priestcraft.
b TG Scribe.
c Matt. 26:4 (2–5); Mark 14:1 (1–2); 2 Ne. 10:3 (3–6).
4*a* GR talked, conferred.
5*a* Zech. 11:12.
7*a* TG Bread, Unleavened.
b TG Passover.
8*a* Mark 14:13 (12–16).
11*a* GR master; i.e., head of house or family.
16*a* JST Luke 22:16 . . . until it be fulfilled *which is written in the prophets concerning me. Then I will partake with you,* in the . . .
18*a* Matt. 26:29; Mark 14:25; D&C 27:5.
19*a* D&C 20:77.
b Mark 14:22; JST Mark 14:20–25 (Appendix); John 6:53. TG Jesus Christ, Atonement through.
c TG Jesus Christ, Redeemer.
d TG Jesus Christ, Types of, in Memory.
20*a* D&C 20:78.
b GR covenant.
22*a* GR appointed, decreed. TG Foreordination.
b Matt. 26:24; Acts 2:23.
24*a* TG Strife.
b Matt. 23:11; Mark 10:44 (42–45); D&C 50:26.

[a]kings of the Gentiles exercise lordship over them; and they that exercise authority upon them are called
benefactors.
26 But ye *shall* not *be* so: but he
that is greatest among you, let him
be as the younger; and he that is
chief, as he that doth [a]serve.
27 For whether *is* greater, he that
sitteth at meat, or he that serveth?
is not he that sitteth at meat? but I
am among you as he that [a]serveth.
28 Ye are they which have [a]con-
tinued with me in my [b]temptations.
29 And I appoint unto you a kingdom, as my Father hath [a]appointed
unto me;
30 That ye may [a]eat and drink at
my table in my kingdom, and sit on
thrones [b]judging the twelve tribes
of Israel.
31 ¶ And the Lord said, Simon,
Simon, behold, [a]Satan hath desired
to [b]*have* you, that he may sift *you*
as wheat:
32 But I have [a]prayed for thee,
that thy faith fail not: and when
thou art [b]converted, [c]strengthen thy
brethren.
33 And he said unto him, Lord, I
am [a]ready to go with thee, both into
prison, and to death.
34 And he said, I tell thee, Peter,
the cock shall not crow this day,
before that thou shalt [a]thrice deny
that thou knowest me.
35 And he said unto them, When I
sent you without [a]purse, and scrip,
and shoes, lacked ye any thing? And
they said, Nothing.
36 Then said he unto them, But
now, he that hath a purse, let him
take *it*, and likewise *his* scrip: and
he that hath no sword, let him sell
his garment, and buy one.
37 For I say unto you, that this that
is written must yet be accomplished
in me, And he was reckoned among
the [a]transgressors: for the things
concerning me have an end.
38 And they said, Lord, behold,
here *are* two swords. And he said
unto them, It is enough.
39 ¶ And he came out, and went,
as he was [a]wont, to the mount of
Olives; and his disciples also followed him.
40 And when he was at the place,
he said unto them, Pray that ye enter not into [a]temptation.
41 And he was withdrawn from
them about a stone's cast, and
kneeled down, and prayed,
42 Saying, Father, if thou be willing, [a]remove this cup from me: nevertheless not my [b]will, but thine,
be done.
43 And there appeared an [a]angel
unto him from heaven, strengthening him.
44 And being in an [a]agony he
prayed more earnestly: [b]and his
sweat was as it were great drops of
[c]blood falling down to the ground.
45 And when he rose up from
prayer, and was come to his disciples,
he found them sleeping for sorrow,
46 And said unto them, Why sleep
ye? rise and pray, lest ye enter into
temptation.
47 ¶ And while he yet spake, behold a multitude, and he that was

25*a* TG Kings, Earthly.
26*a* Mosiah 2:18 (14, 18–19).
27*a* TG Meek; Self-Sacrifice.
28*a* TG Perseverance.
b TG Jesus Christ, Temptation of; Test.
29*a* TG Authority.
30*a* Luke 14:15; Rev. 19:9.
b Morm. 3:18 (18–20); D&C 29:12. TG Apostles.
31*a* JST Luke 22:31 . . . Satan hath desired you, that he may sift *the children of the kingdom* as wheat. TG Devil.
b TG Test.
32*a* TG Prayer.
b Mosiah 3:19. TG Conversion.
c D&C 108:7. TG Fellowshipping; Missionary Work; Sustaining Church Leaders.
33*a* Matt. 26:33.
34*a* Matt. 26:34 (30–35).
35*a* Matt. 10:9 (9–10); D&C 84:78.
37*a* Isa. 53:12.
39*a* GR accustomed.
40*a* TG Temptation.
42*a* D&C 19:18.
b Moses 4:2 (1–4). TG God, Will of.
43*a* TG Angels.
44*a* TG Pain.
b JST Luke 22:44 . . . and *he sweat as it were* great drops of blood . . .
c Mosiah 3:7; D&C 19:18. TG Jesus Christ, Atonement through.

called Judas, one of the twelve, went before them, and drew near unto Jesus to kiss him.

48 But Jesus said unto him, [a]Judas, [b]betrayest thou the Son of man with a [c]kiss?

49 When they which were about him saw what would follow, they said unto him, Lord, shall we smite with the sword?

50 ¶ And one of them smote the servant of the high priest, and cut off his right ear.

51 And Jesus answered and said, Suffer ye thus far. And he touched his ear, and [a]healed him.

52 Then Jesus said unto the chief priests, and captains of the temple, and the elders, which were come to him, Be ye come out, as against a thief, with swords and staves?

53 When I was daily with you in the temple, ye stretched forth no hands against me: but this is your hour, and the power of [a]darkness.

54 ¶ Then took they him, and led *him*, and brought him into the high priest's house. And Peter followed afar off.

55 And when they had kindled a fire in the midst of the [a]hall, and were set down together, Peter sat down among them.

56 But a certain maid beheld him as he sat by the fire, and earnestly looked upon him, and said, This man was also with him.

57 And he denied him, saying, Woman, I know him not.

58 And after a little while another saw him, and said, Thou art also of them. And Peter said, Man, I am not.

59 And about the space of one hour after another confidently affirmed, saying, Of a truth this *fellow* also was with him: for he is a Galilæan.

60 And Peter said, Man, I know not what thou sayest. And immediately, while he yet spake, the cock crew.

61 And the [a]Lord turned, and looked upon Peter. And Peter remembered the word of the Lord, how he had said unto him, Before the cock crow, thou shalt deny me thrice.

62 And Peter went out, and wept bitterly.

63 ¶ And the men that held Jesus [a]mocked him, and smote *him*.

64 And when they had [a]blindfolded him, they struck him on the face, and asked him, saying, Prophesy, who is it that smote thee?

65 And many other things blasphemously spake they against him.

66 ¶ And as soon as it was day, [a]the elders of the people and the chief priests and the scribes came together, and led him into their council, saying,

67 Art thou the [a]Christ? tell us. And he said unto them, If I tell you, ye will not believe:

68 And if I also ask *you*, ye will not answer me, nor let *me* go.

69 [a]Hereafter shall the [b]Son of man sit on the right hand of the power of God.

70 Then said they all, Art thou then the Son of God? And he said unto them, Ye say that I am.

71 And they said, What need we any further [a]witness? for we ourselves have heard of his own mouth.

CHAPTER 23

Jesus is taken before Pilate, then to Herod, and then to Pilate again—Barabbas is released—Jesus is crucified between two thieves—He is buried in the tomb of Joseph of Arimathæa.

AND the whole multitude of them arose, and led him unto Pilate.

2 And they began to accuse him,

48*a* Acts 1:16.
b TG Jesus Christ, Betrayal of.
c Prov. 27:6.
51*a* TG Heal.
53*a* TG Darkness, Spiritual.
55*a* GR courtyard.
61*a* TG Jesus Christ, Lord.
63*a* TG Jesus Christ, Trials of; Mocking.
64*a* Matt. 26:68.
66*a* IE the Sanhedrin.
67*a* TG Jesus Christ, Trials of.
69*a* GR From now on.
b TG Jesus Christ, Son of Man.
71*a* TG Jesus Christ, Trials of.

saying, We found this *fellow* pervert-
ing the nation, and forbidding to
give tribute to [a]Cæsar, saying that
he himself is Christ a [b]King.
3 And Pilate asked him, saying, Art
thou the King of the Jews? And he
answered him and said, Thou sayest *it*.
4 Then said Pilate to the chief
priests and *to* the people, I find no
[a]fault in this man.
5 And they were the more fierce,
saying, He stirreth up the people,
teaching throughout all Jewry, beginning from Galilee to this place.
6 When Pilate heard of Galilee,
he asked whether the man were a
Galilæan.
7 And as soon as he knew that he
belonged unto Herod's jurisdiction,
he sent him to Herod, who himself
also was at Jerusalem at that time.
8 ¶ And when Herod saw Jesus,
he was exceeding glad: for he was
desirous to see him of a long *season*,
because he had heard many things
of him; and he hoped to have seen
some [a]miracle done by him.
9 Then he questioned with him
in many words; but he [a]answered
him nothing.
10 And the chief priests and [a]scribes
stood and vehemently accused him.
11 And Herod with his men of war
set him at nought, and [a]mocked *him*,
and arrayed him in a gorgeous robe,
and sent him again to Pilate.
12 ¶ And the same day Pilate and
Herod were made friends together:
for before they were at enmity between themselves.
13 ¶ And Pilate, when he had called
together the chief priests and the
rulers and the people,
14 Said unto them, Ye have brought
this man unto me, as one that per-
verteth the people: and, behold, I,
having examined *him* before you,
have found no fault in this man
touching those things whereof ye
accuse him:
15 No, nor yet Herod: for I sent you
to him; and, lo, nothing worthy of
death is done [a]unto him.
16 I will therefore chastise him,
and release *him*.
17 (For of necessity he must [a]re-
lease one unto them at the feast.)
18 And they cried out all at once,
saying, Away with this *man*, and
release unto us Barabbas:
19 (Who for a certain sedition
made in the city, and for [a]murder,
was cast into prison.)
20 Pilate therefore, willing to release Jesus, spake again to them.
21 But they cried, saying, [a]Crucify
him, crucify him.
22 And he said unto them the third
time, Why, what evil hath he done?
I have found [a]no cause of death in
him: I will therefore chastise him,
and let *him* go.
23 And they were [a]instant with
loud voices, [b]requiring that he might
be [c]crucified. And the voices of them
and of the chief priests prevailed.
24 And Pilate gave sentence that it
should be as they [a]required.
25 And he released unto them him
that for sedition and [a]murder was
cast into prison, whom they had
desired; but he delivered Jesus to
their will.
26 And as they led him away, they
laid hold upon one Simon, a Cyrenian, coming out of the country, and
on him they laid the cross, that he
might bear *it* after Jesus.
27 ¶ And there followed him a
great company of people, and of
women, which also bewailed and
lamented him.
28 But Jesus turning unto them
said, Daughters of [a]Jerusalem, weep
not for me, but weep for yourselves,
and for your children.

---

23 2*a* D&C 63:26.
b Alma 5:50.
4*a* TG Jesus Christ, Trials of.
8*a* TG Miracle; Sign Seekers.
9*a* Mosiah 14:7; 15:6.
10*a* TG Scribe.
11*a* TG Mocking.
15*a* GR by.
17*a* Matt. 27:15 (15–26).
19*a* John 18:40.
21*a* TG Jesus Christ, Trials of.
22*a* Mark 15:9 (6–15).
23*a* GR urging.
b GR demanding.
c 2 Ne. 10:3 (3–6).
24*a* GR demanded.
25*a* Acts 3:14.
28*a* TG Jerusalem.

29 For, behold, the days are coming, in the which they shall say, Blessed *are* the [a]barren, and the wombs that never bare, and the paps which never gave suck.

30 Then shall they begin to say to the [a]mountains, Fall on us; and to the hills, Cover us.

31 For if they do these things in a [a]green tree, what shall be done in the [b]dry?

32 And there were also two other, [a]malefactors, led with him to be put to death.

33 And when they were come to the place, which is called Calvary, there they crucified him, and the malefactors, one on the right hand, and the other on the left.

34 ¶ Then [a]said Jesus, Father, [b]forgive them; for they know not what [c]they do. And they parted his [d]raiment, and cast lots.

35 And the people stood beholding. And the rulers also with them [a]derided *him*, saying, He saved others; let him save himself, if he be Christ, the [b]chosen of God.

36 And the soldiers also [a]mocked him, coming to him, and offering him [b]vinegar,

37 And saying, If thou be the king of the Jews, save thyself.

38 And a superscription also was written over him in letters of Greek, and Latin, and Hebrew, THIS IS THE [a]KING OF THE [b]JEWS.

39 ¶ And one of the malefactors which were hanged [a]railed on him, saying, If thou be Christ, save thyself and us.

40 But the other answering rebuked him, saying, Dost not thou fear God, seeing thou art in the same condemnation?

41 And we indeed justly; for we receive the due [a]reward of our deeds: but this man hath done nothing amiss.

42 And he said unto Jesus, Lord, remember me when thou comest into thy kingdom.

43 And Jesus said unto him, Verily I say unto thee, To day shalt thou be with me in [a]paradise.

44 And it was about the [a]sixth hour, and there was a [b]darkness over all the [c]earth until the ninth hour.

45 And the sun was darkened, and the veil of the temple was rent in the [a]midst.

46 ¶ And when Jesus had cried with a loud voice, he said, Father, into thy hands I [a]commend my [b]spirit: and having said thus, he [c]gave up the [d]ghost.

47 Now when the centurion saw what was done, he glorified God, saying, Certainly this was a [a]righteous man.

48 And all the people that came together to that sight, beholding the things which were done, smote their breasts, and returned.

49 And all his acquaintance, and the women that followed him from Galilee, stood afar off, beholding these things.

29*a* Matt. 24:19.
30*a* Hosea 10:8; Rev. 6:16 (14–17).
31*a* D&C 135:6.
b JST Luke 23:31–32 . . . dry *tree? This he spake, signifying the scattering of Israel, and the desolation of the heathen, or in other words, the Gentiles.*
32*a* GR criminals. Isa. 53:9.
34*a* Luke 6:28; Acts 7:60 (53–60).
b TG Benevolence; Forgive; Mercy.
c JST Luke 23:35 . . . they do *(Meaning the soldiers who crucified him,)* . . .
d Ps. 22:18.
35*a* Ps. 22:7.
b TG Jesus Christ, Relationships with the Father.
36*a* TG Mocking.
b GR sour wine. Ps. 69:21.
38*a* D&C 45:53 (51–53).
b Mosiah 15:5.
39*a* GR blasphemed, reproached.
41*a* TG Reward.
43*a* John 20:17; Alma 40:21 (11–14, 21). TG Immortality; Paradise; Spirits, Disembodied.
44*a* 3 Ne. 8:19.
b Amos 8:9; Hel. 14:20. TG Darkness, Physical.
c GR earth, region, land, or country.
45*a* GR middle.
46*a* TG Commitment.
b Ps. 31:5; John 10:18 (17–18). TG Man, a Spirit Child of Heavenly Father.
c GR expired, ceased breathing, or died.
d TG Death.
47*a* TG Righteousness.

50 ¶ And, behold, *there was* a man named Joseph, a [a]counsellor; *and he was* a good man, and a just:

51 (The same had not consented to the counsel and deed of them;) *he was* of Arimathæa, a city of the Jews: who also himself waited for the kingdom of God.

52 This *man* went unto Pilate, and [a]begged the body of Jesus.

53 And he took it down, and wrapped it in linen, and laid it in a [a]sepulchre that was hewn in stone, wherein never man before was laid.

54 And that day was the [a]preparation, and the sabbath drew on.

55 And the women also, which came with him from Galilee, followed after, and beheld the [a]sepulchre, and how his body was laid.

56 And they returned, and prepared spices and ointments; and [a]rested the sabbath day according to the commandment.

CHAPTER 24

Angels announce the resurrection of Christ—He walks on the Emmaus road—He appears with a body of flesh and bones, eats food, testifies of His divinity, and promises the Holy Ghost—He ascends into heaven.

Now upon the first *day* of the week, very early in the morning, they came unto the [a]sepulchre, bringing the spices which they had prepared, and certain *others* with them.

2 [a]And they found the stone rolled away from the sepulchre.

3 And they entered in, and found not the body of the Lord Jesus.

4 And it came to pass, as they were much perplexed thereabout, behold, two men stood by them in shining garments:

5 And as they were afraid, and bowed down *their* faces to the earth, they said unto them, Why seek ye the living among the dead?

6 He is not here, but is [a]risen: remember how he spake unto you when he was yet in Galilee,

7 Saying, The Son of man must be delivered into the hands of sinful men, and be crucified, and the third day rise again.

8 And they remembered his words,

9 And returned from the sepulchre, and told all these things unto the eleven, and to all the rest.

10 It was Mary Magdalene, and Joanna, and Mary *the mother* of James, and other *women that were* with them, which told these things unto the apostles.

11 And their words seemed to them as idle tales, and they believed them not.

12 Then arose Peter, and ran unto the sepulchre; and stooping down, he beheld the linen clothes laid by themselves, and departed, wondering in himself at that which was come to pass.

13 ¶ And, behold, two of them went that same day to a village called Emmaus, which was from Jerusalem [a]*about* threescore furlongs.

14 And they talked together of all these things which had happened.

15 And it came to pass, that, while they [a]communed *together* and reasoned, [b]Jesus himself drew near, and went with them.

16 But their eyes were [a]holden that they should not know him.

17 And he said unto them, What manner of communications *are* these that ye have one to another, as ye walk, and are sad?

18 And the one of them, whose name was [a]Cleopas, answering said unto him, Art thou only a stranger in Jerusalem, and hast not known

50*a* IE member of the Sanhedrin, senator.
52*a* GR requested.
53*a* John 19:41; 1 Ne. 19:10; 2 Ne. 25:13.
54*a* TG Passover.
55*a* Luke 24:1 (1–3).
56*a* TG Rest.

24 1*a* Luke 23:55.
2*a* JST Luke 24:2–4 (Appendix).
6*a* TG Jesus Christ, Resurrection.
13*a* The distance here indicated is about 7½ miles or 12 kilometers.

15*a* OR talked.
b TG Jesus Christ, Appearances, Postmortal.
16*a* GR restrained. Heb. 13:2; Ether 3:25; D&C 25:4.
18*a* John 19:25.

the things which are come to pass
there in these days?
19 And he said unto them, What
things? And they said unto him,
Concerning Jesus of Nazareth, which
was a prophet mighty in deed and
word before God and all the people:
20 And how the chief priests and
our rulers delivered him to be condemned to death, and have crucified him.
21 But we trusted that it had been
he which should have redeemed
Israel: and beside all this, to day
is the third day since these things
were done.
22 Yea, and certain women also of
our company made us astonished,
which were early at the sepulchre;
23 And when they found not his
body, they came, saying, that they
had also seen a vision of angels,
which said that he was alive.
24 And certain of them which were
with us went to the sepulchre, and
found *it* even so as the women had
said: but him they saw not.
25 Then he said unto them, O
[a]fools, and slow of [b]heart to [c]believe
all that the prophets have spoken:
26 Ought not Christ to have suffered these things, and to enter into
his glory?
27 And beginning at [a]Moses and
all the [b]prophets, he [c]expounded
unto them in all the [d]scriptures the
things concerning himself.
28 And they drew nigh unto the
village, whither they went: and
he made as though he would have
gone further.
29 But they constrained him, saying, Abide with us: for it is toward
evening, and the day is far spent.
And he went in to tarry with them.
30 And it came to pass, as he sat
at meat with them, he took bread,
and blessed *it*, and brake, and gave
to them.
31 And their eyes were opened,
and they knew him; and he van-
ished out of their sight.
32 And they said one to another,
Did not our [a]heart [b]burn within
us, while he [c]talked with us by the
way, and while he opened to us the
scriptures?
33 And they rose up the same hour,
and returned to Jerusalem, and
found the eleven gathered together,
and them that were with them,
34 Saying, The Lord is risen indeed,
and hath [a]appeared to [b]Simon.
35 And they told what things *were
done* in the way, and how he was
known of them in breaking of bread.
36 ¶ And as they thus spake, Jesus
himself [a]stood in the midst of them,
and saith unto them, [b]Peace *be* unto
you.
37 But they were terrified and
affrighted, and supposed that they
had seen a spirit.
38 And he said unto them, Why are
ye troubled? and why do [a]thoughts
arise in your hearts?
39 Behold my hands and my feet,
that it is I myself: [a]handle me, and
see; for a [b]spirit hath not [c]flesh and
bones, as ye [d]see me have.
40 And when he had thus spoken,
he shewed them *his* hands and *his*
feet.
41 And while they yet believed
not for joy, and [a]wondered, he said
unto them, Have ye here any meat?

25*a* GR unwise.
b Matt. 14:31; Mark 4:40; 16:14.
c Luke 1:20 (19–20); 12:29; Alma 22:7.
27*a* John 5:46.
b Acts 3:18 (18–21); 1 Pet. 1:10 (1–16).
c TG Scriptures, Study of.
d TG Jesus Christ, Prophecies about.
32*a* D&C 9:8. TG Heart.
b TG Teaching with the Spirit.
c TG Jesus Christ, Teaching Mode of.
34*a* TG Jesus Christ, Appearances, Postmortal.
b 1 Cor. 15:5 (3–8).
36*a* TG Jesus Christ, Appearances, Postmortal.
b D&C 19:23.
38*a* OR doubts, hesitations.
39*a* 3 Ne. 11:14 (12–15).
b TG Man, Potential to Become like Heavenly Father; Spirits, Disembodied.
c D&C 129:2. TG God, Body of, Corporeal Nature; Jesus Christ, Appearances, Postmortal; Resurrection.
d TG God, Knowledge about.
41*a* GR marveled.

42 And they gave him a piece of a
broiled fish, and of an honeycomb.
43 And he took *it*, and did eat before them.
44 And he said unto them, These
are the words which I spake unto
you, while I was yet with you, that
all things must be [a]fulfilled, which
were written in the law of Moses, and
in the prophets, and *in* the psalms,
concerning me.
45 Then opened he their [a]under-
standing, that they might understand the scriptures,
46 And said unto them, Thus it is
written, and thus it [a]behoved Christ
to suffer, and to [b]rise from the dead
the third day:
47 And that [a]repentance and [b]re-
mission of sins should be [c]preached
in his name among all nations, beginning at Jerusalem.
48 And ye are [a]witnesses of these
things.
49 ¶ And, behold, I send the [a]prom-
ise of my Father upon you: but tarry
ye in the city of Jerusalem, until ye
be [b]endued with power from on high.
50 ¶ And he led them out as far
as to Bethany, and he lifted up his
hands, and blessed them.
51 And it came to pass, while he
blessed them, he was parted from
them, and [a]carried up into heaven.
52 And they worshipped him, and
returned to Jerusalem with great joy:
53 And were continually in the
[a]temple, praising and blessing God.
Amen.

THE GOSPEL ACCORDING TO

ST JOHN

CHAPTER 1

Christ is the Word of God—He created all things and was made flesh—John baptizes Jesus and testifies that He is the Lamb of God—John, Andrew, Simon, Philip, and Nathanael believe in Christ and follow Him.

[a]IN the [b]beginning was the Word,
and the [c]Word was with God, and
the [d]Word was [e]God.
2 The same was in the [a]beginning
with God.
3 All things were [a]made by him;
and without him was not any thing
made that was made.

44*a* TG Jesus Christ, Prophecies about.
45*a* TG Understanding.
46*a* GR was necessary for, proper for.
b TG Resurrection.
47*a* TG Repent.
b D&C 137:6. TG Forgive; Remission of Sins.
c TG Apostles; Mission of Early Saints.
48*a* Acts 1:8; 22:15 (14–16); D&C 27:12. TG Witness.
49*a* TG Promise.
b OR clothed, invested. D&C 20:8; 38:32 (32, 38).
51*a* TG Jesus Christ, Ascension of.
53*a* Acts 2:46.

[JOHN]

Title: JST entitles this book "The Testimony of St. John."
1 1*a* JST John 1:1–34 (Appendix).
b D&C 76:39. TG Jesus Christ, Firstborn; Jesus Christ, Foreordained.
c TG Jesus Christ, Messenger of the Covenant; Jesus Christ, Relationships with the Father.
d TG Jesus Christ, Jehovah.
e TG Jesus Christ, Authority of.
2*a* 1 Jn. 1:1. TG Man, Antemortal Existence of.
3*a* TG Creation; God, Power of; Jesus Christ, Creator; Jesus Christ, Mission of; Jesus Christ, Power of.

4 In him was [a]life; and the life was
the [b]light of men.
5 And the [a]light shineth in [b]dark-
ness; and the darkness [c]compre-
hended it not.
6 ¶ There was a man sent from
God, whose name *was* [a]John.
7 The same came for a [a]witness, to
bear [b]witness of the Light, that all
men through him might [c]believe.
8 He was not that Light, but *was*
sent to bear witness of that Light.
9 *That* was the true [a]Light, which
[b]lighteth [c]every man that cometh
into the world.
10 He was in the [a]world, and the
[b]world was [c]made by him, and the
world [d]knew him not.
11 He came unto his own, and his
own [a]received him not.
12 But as many as [a]received him,
to them gave he [b]power to become
the [c]sons of God, *even* to them that
believe on his [d]name:
13 Which were [a]born, not of blood,
nor of the will of the flesh, nor of
the will of man, but of God.
14 And the Word was made [a]flesh,
and [b]dwelt among us, (and we [c]be-
held his [d]glory, the glory as of the
[e]only [f]begotten of the Father,) full
of [g]grace and truth.
15 ¶ John bare [a]witness of him,
and cried, saying, This was he of
whom I spake, He that cometh after me is preferred before me: for
he was before me.
16 And of his [a]fulness have all we
received, and [b]grace for grace.
17 [a]For the [b]law was given by
Moses, *but* [c]grace and [d]truth came
by Jesus Christ.
18 No [a]man hath [b]seen God [c]at any
time; the only begotten Son, which
is in the bosom of the Father, he
hath [d]declared *him*.
19 ¶ And this is the record of
[a]John, when the Jews sent priests
and Levites from Jerusalem to ask
him, Who art thou?
20 And he confessed, and denied
not; but confessed, I am not the
Christ.
21 And they asked him, What then?
Art thou [a]Elias? And he saith, I am
not. Art thou that prophet? And he
answered, No.
22 Then said they unto him, Who
art thou? that we may give an answer to them that sent us. What
sayest thou of thyself?
23 He said, I *am* the [a]voice of one
crying in the wilderness, Make
[b]straight the [c]way of the Lord, as
said the prophet Esaias.
24 And they which were sent were
of the Pharisees.
25 And they asked him, and said

4*a* 1 Jn. 5:11 (10–21).
b TG Jesus Christ, Light of the World; Light [noun].
5*a* D&C 6:21; 34:2; 45:7.
b TG Darkness, Spiritual.
c 1 Cor. 2:11 (10–14); D&C 45:29.
6*a* 1 Ne. 11:27.
7*a* John 19:35 (35–37).
b D&C 66:7.
c John 20:31 (30–31).
9*a* John 12:46. TG Intelligence; Jesus Christ, Light of the World; Light of Christ.
b TG Discernment, Spiritual.
c D&C 84:46.
10*a* TG World.
b TG Creation.
c TG Jesus Christ, Creator.
d Isa. 53:3.
11*a* 3 Ne. 9:16; D&C 6:21.
12*a* D&C 25:1. TG Teachable.
b GR authority, right, privilege. D&C 11:30. TG Jesus Christ, Power of.
c D&C 39:4 (3–6). TG Sons and Daughters of God.
d TG Name.
13*a* TG Holy Ghost, Baptism of.
14*a* TG Flesh and Blood; God, Manifestations of; Jesus Christ, Birth of; Jesus Christ, Condescension of.
b TG God, Presence of.
c Matt. 17:2 (1–9); Luke 1:2; John 19:35; 21:24; Acts 5:32; 26:16; 2 Pet. 1:16 (16–19); D&C 93:11.
d Heb. 1:3. TG Glory; Jesus Christ, Glory of.
e TG Jesus Christ, Divine Sonship.
f D&C 76:23.
g D&C 66:12.
15*a* John 5:33.
16*a* Col. 2:10.
b D&C 93:12.
17*a* JST John 1:17–18 (Appendix).
b TG Law of Moses.
c TG Grace.
d TG Truth.
18*a* D&C 67:11; 84:22.
b TG God, Privilege of Seeing.
c JST John 1:19 . . . at any time, *except he hath borne record of the Son; for except it is through him no man can be saved.*
d Luke 10:22.
19*a* Luke 3:15 (15–16).
21*a* Mal. 4:5 (5–6).
23*a* Matt. 3:3; Mark 1:3; Luke 3:4.
b D&C 84:28.
c D&C 65:1.

COME AND SEE
John 1:39

unto him, Why baptizest thou then, if thou be not that Christ, nor Elias, neither that prophet?

26 John answered them, saying, I baptize with [a]water: but there standeth one among you, whom ye know not;

27 [a]He it is, who coming after me is preferred before me, whose [b]shoe's latchet I am not worthy to unloose.

28 These things were done in [a]Bethabara beyond Jordan, where John was baptizing.

29 ¶ The next day John seeth Jesus coming unto him, and saith, Behold the [a]Lamb of God, which taketh away the [b]sin of the world.

30 This is he of whom I said, After me cometh a man which is preferred before me: for he was before me.

31 And I knew him not: but that he should be made manifest to Israel, therefore am I come baptizing with water.

32 And John [a]bare record, saying, I saw the [b]Spirit descending from heaven like a [c]dove, and it abode upon him.

33 [a]And I knew him not: but he that sent me to baptize with water, the same said unto me, Upon whom thou shalt see the Spirit descending, and remaining on him, the same is he which baptizeth with the [b]Holy Ghost.

34 And I saw, and bare [a]record that this is the Son of God.

35 ¶ Again the next day after John stood, and two of his disciples;

36 And looking upon Jesus as he walked, he saith, Behold the [a]Lamb of God!

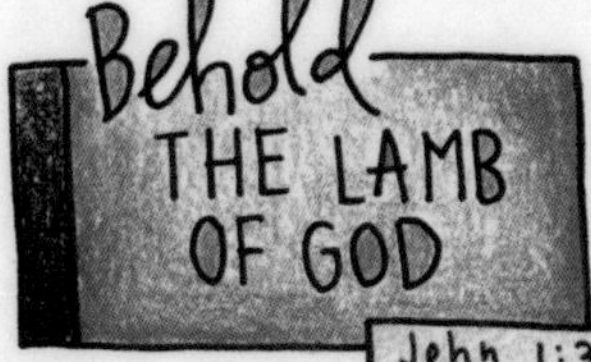

37 And the two disciples heard him speak, and they followed Jesus.

38 Then Jesus turned, and saw them following, and saith unto them, What seek ye? They said unto him, Rabbi, (which is to say, being interpreted, Master,) where dwellest thou?

39 He saith unto them, Come and see. They came and saw where he dwelt, and abode with him that day: for it was about the tenth hour.

40 One of the two which heard John *speak*, and [a]followed him, was Andrew, Simon Peter's brother.

41 He first findeth his own brother Simon, and saith unto him, We have found the [a]Messias, which is, being interpreted, the Christ.

42 And he brought him to Jesus. And when Jesus beheld him, he said, Thou art Simon the son of Jona: thou shalt be called [a]Cephas, which is by interpretation, A stone.

43 ¶ The day following Jesus would go forth into Galilee, and findeth Philip, and saith unto him, Follow me.

44 Now Philip was of Bethsaida, the city of Andrew and Peter.

45 Philip findeth Nathanael, and saith unto him, We have found him, of whom [a]Moses in the law, and the prophets, did [b]write, Jesus of Nazareth, the son of Joseph.

46 And Nathanael said unto him, Can there any good thing come out of Nazareth? Philip saith unto him, Come and see.

47 Jesus saw [a]Nathanael coming to him, and saith of him, Behold an Israelite indeed, in whom is no [b]guile!

48 Nathanael saith unto him, Whence knowest thou me? Jesus

26*a* D&C 52:10.
27*a* JST John 1:28 (Appendix).
b GR sandal strap.
28*a* 1 Ne. 10:9.
29*a* TG Jesus Christ, Lamb of God; Jesus Christ, Redeemer; Jesus Christ, Types of, in Anticipation; Passover.
b TG Jesus Christ, Atonement through; Redemption; Sin.
32*a* D&C 93:11.
b TG Jesus Christ, Baptism of.
c TG Holy Ghost, Dove, Sign of.
33*a* JST John 1:32 And I knew him; *for* he who sent me . . .
b TG Holy Ghost, Baptism of.
34*a* TG Testimony.
36*a* TG Passover.
40*a* TG Apostles.
41*a* TG Jesus Christ, Messiah.
42*a* GR Stone, Pebble. JST John 1:42 . . . Cephas, which is, by interpretation, *a seer, or* a stone. *And they were fishermen. And they straightway left all, and followed Jesus.* Matt. 16:18; Luke 6:14; Gal. 2:9.
45*a* TG Jesus Christ, Prophecies about.
b TG Record Keeping.
47*a* D&C 41:11.
b GR deceit, fraud. TG Guile.

WHAT WERE THEY LOOKING FOR?

answered and said unto him, Before
that Philip called thee, when thou
wast under the fig tree, I saw thee.
49 Nathanael answered and saith
unto him, Rabbi, thou art the [a]Son
of God; thou art the [b]King of Israel.
50 Jesus answered and said unto
him, Because I said unto thee, I saw
thee under the fig tree, believest
thou? thou shalt see greater things
than these.
51 And he saith unto him, Verily,
verily, I say unto you, Hereafter ye
shall see heaven open, and the angels
of God ascending and descending
upon the Son of man.

CHAPTER 2

Jesus turns water into wine in Cana—He attends the Passover, cleanses the temple, foretells His death and resurrection, and performs miracles.

AND the [a]third day there was a marriage in Cana of Galilee; and the
mother of Jesus was there:
2 And both Jesus was called, and
his disciples, to the marriage.
3 And when they wanted wine,
the mother of Jesus saith unto him,
They have no wine.
4 Jesus saith unto her, [a]Woman,
what have I to do with thee? mine
hour is not yet come.
5 His mother saith unto the servants, Whatsoever he saith unto
you, do *it*.
6 And there were set there six waterpots of stone, after the manner
of the [a]purifying of the Jews, con-
taining two or three firkins apiece.
7 Jesus saith unto them, Fill the
waterpots with water. And they
filled them up to the brim.
8 And he saith unto them, Draw
out now, and bear unto the governor of the feast. And they bare *it*.
9 When the ruler of the feast had
tasted the water that was made wine,
and knew not whence it was: (but
the servants which drew the water
knew;) the governor of the feast
called the bridegroom,
10 And saith unto him, Every man
at the beginning doth set forth good
wine; and when men have well
drunk, then that which is worse:
but thou hast kept the good wine
until now.
11 This [a]beginning of [b]miracles
did Jesus in Cana of Galilee, and
manifested forth his glory; and his
disciples believed on him.
12 ¶ After this he went down to
Capernaum, he, and his mother, and
his [a]brethren, and his disciples: and
they continued there not many days.
13 ¶ And the Jews' passover was
at hand, and Jesus went up to
Jerusalem,
14 And found in the temple those
that sold oxen and sheep and
doves, and the changers of [a]money
sitting:
15 And when he had made a
[a]scourge of small cords, he drove
them all out of the temple, and the
sheep, and the oxen; and poured out
the changers' money, and overthrew
the tables;
16 And said unto them that sold
doves, Take these things hence; make
not my Father's house an house of
merchandise.
17 And his disciples remembered
that it was written, The [a]zeal of thine
house hath [b]eaten me up.
18 ¶ Then answered the Jews and
said unto him, What [a]sign shewest
thou unto us, seeing that thou doest
these things?
19 Jesus answered and said unto
them, Destroy this [a]temple, and in
three days I will [b]raise it up.

49*a* TG God, Body of, Corporeal Nature.
b TG Jesus Christ, Messiah.
2 1*a* JST John 2:1 . . . third day *of the week* . . .
4*a* JST John 2:4 . . . Woman, what *wilt thou have me to do for* thee? *that will I do; for* mine hour is not yet come.
TG Woman.
6*a* TG Purification.
11*a* John 4:54.
b TG Miracle.
12*a* TG Jesus Christ, Family of.
14*a* Ps. 69:9.
15*a* GR whip.
Matt. 21:12–16.
17*a* TG Zeal.
b GR consumed me.
18*a* TG Sign Seekers.
19*a* Matt. 26:61; 27:40, 63 (62–66); Mark 14:58.
b TG Jesus Christ, Resurrection; Resurrection.

20 Then said the Jews, Forty and six years was this [a]temple in building, and wilt thou rear it up in three days?

21 But he spake of the temple of his body.

22 When therefore he was risen from the dead, his disciples remembered that he had said this unto them; and they believed the scripture, and the word which Jesus had said.

23 ¶ Now when he was in Jerusalem at the [a]passover, in the feast *day*, many believed in his [b]name, when they saw the [c]miracles which he did.

24 But Jesus did not [a]commit himself unto them, because he [b]knew all [c]*men*,

25 And needed not that any should testify of man: for he [a]knew what was in [b]man.

CHAPTER 3

Jesus tells Nicodemus that men must be born again—God so loved the world that He sent His Only Begotten Son to save men—John the Baptist testifies that he that believes on the Son has everlasting life.

THERE was a man of the Pharisees, named [a]Nicodemus, a [b]ruler of the Jews:

2 The same came to Jesus by night, and said unto him, Rabbi, we know that thou art a teacher come from God: for no man can do these [a]miracles that thou doest, except [b]God be with him.

3 Jesus answered and said unto him, Verily, verily, I say unto thee, Except a man be [a]born [b]again, he cannot [c]see the kingdom of God.

4 Nicodemus saith unto him, How can a man be born when he is old? can he enter the second time into his mother's womb, and be born?

5 Jesus answered, Verily, verily, I say unto thee, Except a man be [a]born of [b]water and *of* the [c]Spirit, he cannot [d]enter into the kingdom of God.

6 That which is born of the flesh is flesh; and that which is born of the Spirit is spirit.

7 Marvel not that I said unto thee, Ye must be [a]born again.

8 The [a]wind bloweth where it listeth, and thou hearest the sound thereof, but canst not tell whence it cometh, and whither it goeth: so is every one that is born of the [b]Spirit.

9 Nicodemus answered and said unto him, How can these things be?

10 Jesus answered and said unto him, Art thou a master of Israel, and knowest not these things?

11 [a]Verily, verily, I say unto thee, We speak that we do know, and [b]testify that we have seen; and ye receive not our witness.

12 If I have told you earthly things, and ye [a]believe not, how shall ye believe, if I tell you *of* heavenly things?

13 And no man hath [a]ascended up to heaven, but he that [b]came down from heaven, *even* the [c]Son of man which is in heaven.

14 ¶ And as Moses lifted up the

20*a* TG Temple.
23*a* TG Passover.
b TG Name.
c TG Miracle; Signs.
24*a* GR entrust.
b Luke 6:8.
c JST John 2:24 . . . *things,*
25*a* Matt. 12:25; Luke 11:17; John 6:61.
b D&C 62:1.
3 1*a* John 7:50; 19:39.
b John 7:26.
2*a* TG Miracle.
b Ex. 8:19; Luke 11:20; Acts 2:22; 10:38.
3*a* TG Man, New, Spiritually Reborn.
b GR from above, anew.
c D&C 56:18.
5*a* TG Holy Ghost, Baptism of.
b TG Baptism; Baptism, Essential.
c TG Holy Ghost, Mission of.
d 1 Cor. 6:9; 15:50.
7*a* TG Man, Natural, Not Spiritually Reborn.
8*a* GR wind, spirit.
b Eccl. 11:5.
11*a* The Greek construction suggests that verses 11–21 contain a direct quotation. This testimony of Jesus was given to a member of the Sanhedrin.
b TG Testimony.
12*a* TG Faith.
13*a* TG Jesus Christ, Ascension of.
b John 6:62. TG Jesus Christ, Condescension of.
c Moses 6:57.

[a]serpent in the wilderness, even so
must the [b]Son of man be lifted up:
15 That whosoever believeth in
him should not perish, but have
eternal life.
16 ¶ For [a]God so [b]loved the [c]world,
that he [d]gave his [e]only begotten
[f]Son, that whosoever [g]believeth in
him should not perish, but have
[h]everlasting [i]life.
17 For God [a]sent not his Son into
the world to [b]condemn the world;
but that the world through him
might be [c]saved.
18 ¶ He that believeth on him is
not condemned: but he that [a]be-
lieveth not is condemned already,
because he hath not believed in the
[b]name of the only begotten [c]Son
of God.
19 And this is the condemnation,
that [a]light is come into the world,
and men loved [b]darkness rather than
light, because their [c]deeds were evil.
20 For every one that doeth [a]evil
[b]hateth the light, neither cometh
to the light, lest his deeds should
be reproved.
21 But he that [a]doeth [b]truth cometh
to the [c]light, that his deeds may
be made manifest, that they are
wrought in God.
22 ¶ After these things came Jesus
and his disciples into the land of
Judæa; and there he tarried with
them, and [a]baptized.
23 ¶ And John also was baptizing
in Ænon near to Salim, because
there was much [a]water there: and
they came, and were [b]baptized.
24 For John was not yet cast into
prison.
25 ¶ Then there arose a question
between *some* of John's disciples and
the Jews about purifying.
26 And they came unto John, and
said unto him, Rabbi, he that was
with thee beyond Jordan, to whom
thou barest witness, behold, the
same baptizeth, [a]and all *men* come
to him.
27 John answered and said, A man
can [a]receive nothing, except it be
given him from heaven.
28 Ye yourselves bear me witness,
that I said, I am not the Christ,
but that I am sent before him.
29 He that hath the bride is the
bridegroom: but the friend of the
bridegroom, which standeth and
heareth him, rejoiceth greatly because of the bridegroom's voice: this
my joy therefore is fulfilled.
30 He must increase, but I *must*
decrease.
31 He that cometh from [a]above is
above all: he that is of the earth is
earthly, and speaketh of the earth:
he that cometh from heaven is
above all.
32 And what he hath seen and
heard, that he [a]testifieth; and no
man receiveth his testimony.
33 He that hath received his

14*a* 2 Ne. 25:20.
TG Jesus Christ, Prophecies about; Jesus Christ, Types of, in Anticipation; Symbolism.
b TG Jesus Christ, Son of Man.
16*a* TG God the Father, Elohim.
b TG God, Love of; Love; Mercy; Worth of Souls.
c TG World.
d TG God, Gifts of; Jesus Christ, Redeemer.
e Gen. 22:2 (1–14); Jacob 4:5.
f TG Jesus Christ, Divine Sonship.
g TG Faith.
h D&C 45:5.
i 1 Jn. 4:9.
17*a* D&C 49:5; 132:24 (24, 59).
TG Jesus Christ, Messenger of the Covenant.
b Luke 9:56 (54–56).
c TG Jesus Christ, Atonement through.
18*a* TG Unbelief.
b TG Name.
c JST John 3:18 . . . Son of God, *which before was preached by the mouth of the holy prophets; for they testified of me.*
19*a* TG Light [noun]; Light of Christ.
b TG Darkness, Spiritual; Secret Combinations.
c D&C 10:21; 29:45.
20*a* TG Evil.
b TG Hate.
21*a* TG Good Works.
b TG Truth.
c TG Discernment, Spiritual.
22*a* John 4:2 (1–2); JST John 4:1–4 (Appendix).
23*a* TG Baptism, Immersion.
b TG Baptism.
26*a* JST John 3:27 . . . and *he receiveth of* all *people who* come unto him.
27*a* James 1:17 (17–18).
31*a* John 8:23.
32*a* TG Testimony.

testimony hath [a]set to his [b]seal that God is true.

34 For he whom God hath sent [a]speaketh the words of God: [b]for God giveth not the Spirit by measure *unto him.*

35 The Father loveth the [a]Son, and hath [b]given all [c]things into his hand.

36 [a]He that believeth on the Son hath [b]everlasting life: and he that [c]believeth not the Son shall not see life; but the [d]wrath of God abideth on him.

CHAPTER 4

Jesus teaches a woman of Samaria—All must worship the Father in spirit and truth—Those who harvest souls gain eternal life—Many Samaritans believe—Jesus heals a nobleman's son.

[a]WHEN therefore the Lord knew how the Pharisees had heard that Jesus made and baptized more disciples than John,

2 (Though Jesus himself [a]baptized not, but his disciples,)

3 He left Judæa, and departed again into Galilee.

4 And he must needs go through Samaria.

5 Then cometh he to a city of Samaria, which is called Sychar, near to the parcel of ground that Jacob gave to his son [a]Joseph.

6 Now Jacob's well was there. Jesus therefore, being wearied with *his* journey, sat thus on the well: *and* it was about the sixth hour.

7 There cometh a woman of Samaria to draw water: Jesus saith unto her, Give me to drink.

8 (For his disciples were gone away unto the city to buy meat.)

9 Then saith the woman of Samaria unto him, How is it that thou, being a Jew, askest drink of me, which am a woman of Samaria? for the Jews have no dealings with the [a]Samaritans.

10 Jesus answered and said unto her, If thou knewest the [a]gift of God, and who it is that saith to thee, Give me to drink; thou wouldest have asked of him, and he would have given thee [b]living water.

11 The woman saith unto him, Sir, thou hast nothing to draw with, and the well is deep: from whence then hast thou that living water?

12 Art thou greater than our father Jacob, which gave us the well, and drank thereof himself, and his children, and his cattle?

13 Jesus answered and said unto her, Whosoever drinketh of this water shall thirst again:

14 But whosoever drinketh of the water that I shall give him shall never [a]thirst; but the water that I shall give him shall be in him a well of water [b]springing up into [c]everlasting life.

15 The woman saith unto him, Sir, give me this water, that I thirst not, neither come hither to draw.

16 Jesus saith unto her, Go, call thy husband, and come hither.

17 The woman answered and said, I have no husband. Jesus said unto her, Thou hast well said, I have no husband:

18 For thou hast had five husbands; and he whom thou now hast

---

33*a* OR declared that, certified that.
b TG Seal.
34*a* Isa. 61:1. TG Jesus Christ, Teaching Mode of.
b JST John 3:34 . . . for God giveth *him* not the Spirit by measure, *for he dwelleth in him, even the fullness.*
35*a* TG Jesus Christ, Divine Sonship.
b TG Jesus Christ, Authority of.
c TG Jesus Christ, Power of.
36*a* JST John 3:36 *And* he *who* believeth on the Son hath everlasting life; *and shall receive of his fullness. But* he *who* believeth not the Son, shall not *receive of his fullness; for* the wrath of God *is upon* him.
b TG Eternal Life.
c GR disbelieves, disobeys, is uncompliant to.
d TG God, Indignation of.
4 1*a* JST John 4:1–4 (Appendix).
2*a* John 3:22 (22, 26).
5*a* TG Israel, Joseph, People of.
9*a* 2 Kgs. 17:29; Luke 10:33.
10*a* TG God, Gifts of.
b TG Living Water.
14*a* Ps. 42:2 (1–3); 143:6 (5–12); Isa. 55:1 (1–3); John 6:35; 7:37 (37–39).
b D&C 63:23.
c TG Immortality.

is not thy husband: in that saidst
thou truly.
19 The woman saith unto him, Sir,
I perceive that thou art a [a]prophet.
20 Our fathers worshipped in [a]this
mountain; and ye say, that in Jerusalem is the place where men ought
to worship.
21 Jesus saith unto her, Woman,
believe me, the hour cometh, when
ye shall neither in this mountain,
nor yet at Jerusalem, worship the
Father.
22 Ye worship ye [a]know not what:
we know what we worship: for salvation is of the Jews.
23 But the hour cometh, and now
is, when the true worshippers shall
[a]worship the Father in spirit and in
[b]truth: for the Father seeketh such
to worship him.
24 [a]God *is* a [b]Spirit: and they that
worship him must worship *him* in
spirit and in [c]truth.
25 The woman saith unto him, I
know that [a]Messias cometh, which
is called Christ: when he is come,
he will [b]tell us all things.
26 Jesus saith unto her, [a]I that speak
unto thee am *he*.
27 ¶ And upon this came his disciples, and marvelled that he talked
with the woman: yet no man said,
What seekest thou? or, Why talkest
thou with her?
28 The woman then left her wa-
terpot, and went her way into the
city, and saith to the men,
29 Come, see a man, which told
me all things that ever I did: is not
this the Christ?
30 Then they went out of the city,
and came unto him.
31 ¶ In the mean while his disciples prayed him, saying, Master, eat.
32 But he said unto them, I have
meat to eat that ye know not of.
33 Therefore said the disciples one
to another, Hath any man brought
him *ought* to eat?
34 Jesus saith unto them, My meat
is to do the [a]will of him that sent
me, and to finish his [b]work.
35 Say not ye, There are yet four
months, and *then* cometh harvest?
behold, I say unto you, Lift up your
eyes, and look on the [a]fields; for
they are white already to [b]harvest.
36 And he that reapeth receiveth
[a]wages, and gathereth fruit unto life
eternal: that both he that soweth
and he that reapeth may [b]rejoice
together.
37 And herein is that saying true,
One [a]soweth, and another reapeth.
38 I sent you to [a]reap that whereon
ye bestowed no labour: [b]other men
laboured, and ye are entered into
their labours.
39 ¶ And many of the Samaritans
of that city believed on him for
the saying of the woman, which
testified, He told me all that ever
I did.
40 So when the Samaritans were
come unto him, they besought him
that he would tarry with them: and
he abode there two days.
41 And many more believed because of his own word;
42 And said unto the woman,
Now we believe, not because of
thy saying: for we have heard *him*
ourselves, and know that this is indeed the [a]Christ, the [b]Saviour of the
world.

19*a* 1 Ne. 22:20.
20*a* Deut. 11:29.
22*a* D&C 93:19 (1–20). TG Ignorance.
23*a* TG Worship.
b Ps. 145:18 (1–21).
24*a* JST John 4:26 *For unto such hath* God *promised his* Spirit. And they *who* worship him, must worship in spirit and in truth.
b D&C 93:33; 130:22.
c TG Truth.
25*a* TG Jesus Christ, Messiah.
b Deut. 18:18.
26*a* The term I AM used here in the Greek is identical with the Septuagint usage in Ex. 3:14 which identifies Jehovah. John 8:58. TG Jesus Christ, Jehovah.
34*a* Luke 2:49; John 6:38–39; 8:29; see JST Matt. 27:54 . . . *Father, it is finished, thy will is done* . . . TG God, Will of.
b John 9:4 (1–4).
35*a* Alma 26:5; D&C 4:4; 33:3.
b TG Missionary Work.
36*a* TG Wages.
b D&C 18:16 (13–16); 50:22 (17–22).
37*a* 1 Cor. 3:6 (5–8).
38*a* TG Harvest.
b JST John 4:40 . . . *the prophets have* labored . . .
42*a* TG Jesus Christ, Messiah.
b D&C 66:1.

43 ¶ Now after two days he departed thence, and went into Galilee.
44 For Jesus himself testified, that
a prophet hath no honour in his
own country.
45 Then when he was come into
Galilee, the Galilæans received him,
having seen all the things that he
did at Jerusalem at the feast: for
they also went unto the feast.
46 So Jesus came again into Cana
of Galilee, where he made the water wine. And there was a certain
nobleman, whose son was sick at
[a]Capernaum.
47 When he heard that Jesus was
come out of Judæa into Galilee, he
went unto him, and besought him
that he would come down, and heal
his son: for he was at the point of
death.
48 Then said Jesus unto him, Except ye see [a]signs and wonders, ye
will not believe.
49 The nobleman saith unto him,
Sir, come down ere my child die.
50 Jesus saith unto him, Go thy
way; thy son [a]liveth. And the man
believed the word that Jesus had
spoken unto him, and he went his
way.
51 And as he was now going down,
his servants met him, and told *him*,
saying, Thy son liveth.
52 Then inquired he of them the
hour when he began to amend.
And they said unto him, Yesterday at the seventh hour the fever
left him.
53 So the father knew that *it was*
at the same hour, in the which Jesus
said unto him, Thy son liveth: and
[a]himself believed, and his whole
house.
54 This *is* again the [a]second miracle
that Jesus did, when he was come
out of Judæa into Galilee.

CHAPTER 5

Jesus heals an invalid on the Sabbath—He explains why men must honor the Son—Jesus promises to take the gospel to the dead—Man is resurrected, judged, and assigned his glory by the Son—Jesus obeys the divine law of witnesses.

AFTER this there was [a]a feast of the
Jews; and Jesus went up to Jerusalem.
2 Now there is at Jerusalem by the
sheep *market* a pool, which is called
in the Hebrew tongue Bethesda,
having five porches.
3 In these lay a great multitude
of impotent folk, of blind, halt,
withered, waiting for the moving
of the water.
4 For an angel went down at a
certain season into the pool, and
troubled the water: whosoever then
first after the troubling of the water stepped in was made whole of
whatsoever disease he had.
5 And a certain man was there,
which had an infirmity thirty and
eight years.
6 When Jesus saw him lie, and
knew that he had been now a long
time *in that case*, he saith unto him,
Wilt thou be made whole?
7 The impotent man answered
him, Sir, I have no man, when the
water is troubled, to put me into
the pool: but while I am coming,
another steppeth down before me.
8 Jesus saith unto him, [a]Rise, take
up thy bed, and walk.
9 And immediately the man was
made [a]whole, and took up his bed,
and walked: and on the same day
was the [b]sabbath.
10 ¶ The Jews therefore said unto
him that was cured, It is the [a]sab-
bath day: it is not lawful for thee
to carry *thy* bed.
11 He answered them, He that
made me whole, the same said unto
me, Take up thy bed, and walk.

46*a* Luke 4:23 (23–24).
48*a* TG Sign Seekers.
50*a* TG Heal.
53*a* GR he himself.
54*a* John 2:11.
5 1*a* The *Koine* Greek manuscripts of the Gospels (Byzantine) read "the feast," implicitly the Passover. See also Matt. 26:5. Some earlier manuscripts do not make this identification. TG Passover.
8*a* John 7:23.
9*a* TG Heal.
b Matt. 12:1 (1–14).
10*a* Luke 6:2. TG Sabbath.

12 Then asked they him, What man
is that which said unto thee, Take
up thy bed, and walk?
13 And he that was healed [a]wist
not who it was: for Jesus had con-
veyed himself away, a multitude
being in *that* place.
14 Afterward Jesus findeth him
in the temple, and said unto him,
Behold, thou art made whole: sin
no more, lest a worse thing come
unto thee.
15 The man departed, and told the
Jews that it was Jesus, which had
made him whole.
16 And therefore did the Jews [a]per-
secute Jesus, and [b]sought to slay him,
because he had done these things
on the sabbath day.
17 ¶ But Jesus answered them,
My Father [a]worketh hitherto, and
I [b]work.
18 Therefore the Jews sought the
more to kill him, because he not
only had broken the sabbath, but
said also that God was his [a]Father,
making himself [b]equal with God.
19 Then answered Jesus and said
unto them, Verily, verily, I say unto
you, The Son can do nothing of himself, but what he [a]seeth the [b]Father
do: for what things soever he doeth,
these also doeth the Son likewise.
20 For the Father loveth the Son,
and sheweth him all things that
himself doeth: and he will shew
him greater works than these, that
ye may marvel.
21 For as the Father [a]raiseth up the
dead, and [b]quickeneth *them;* even so
the Son quickeneth whom he will.
22 For the Father judgeth no man,
but hath [a]committed all [b]judgment
unto the Son:
23 That all *men* should [a]honour
the Son, even as they honour the
Father. He that [b]honoureth not the
Son honoureth not the Father which
hath sent him.
24 Verily, verily, I say unto you,
He that heareth my word, and [a]be-
lieveth on him that sent me, hath
everlasting [b]life, and shall not come
into [c]condemnation; but is passed
from [d]death unto [e]life.
25 Verily, verily, I say unto you, The
hour is coming, and now is, when
the [a]dead shall [b]hear the voice of
the Son of God: and they that hear
shall [c]live.
26 For as the Father hath life in
himself; so hath he given to the [a]Son
to have [b]life in himself;
27 And hath given him [a]authority
to execute [b]judgment also, because
he is the [c]Son of man.
28 Marvel not at this: for the hour
is coming, in the which all that
are in the [a]graves shall [b]hear his
voice,
29 And shall [a]come forth; [b]they
that have done good, unto the [c]res-
urrection of life; and they that have
done [d]evil, unto the resurrection of
[e]damnation.
30 I can of mine own self do

13 *a* GR knew.
16 *a* TG Persecution.
b John 7:1.
17 *a* TG God, Works of.
b John 9:4.
18 *a* TG God, Body of, Corporeal Nature.
b John 10:33; 19:7; D&C 88:107. TG Jesus Christ, Relationships with the Father.
19 *a* John 8:28.
b TG Godhead.
21 *a* TG Resurrection.
b GR causes to become alive. 1 Cor. 15:45. TG God, Power of.
22 *a* TG Jesus Christ, Authority of.
b TG Judgment; Judgment, the Last.
23 *a* TG Honor; Respect.
b Luke 10:16.
24 *a* TG Faith.
b John 20:31.
c D&C 20:15.
d John 8:51; 11:26; D&C 63:49.
e 1 Jn. 3:14.
25 *a* TG Death; Genealogy and Temple Work; Salvation for the Dead; Spirits, Disembodied.
b Isa. 24:22; 61:1.
c TG Immortality.
26 *a* TG Jesus Christ, Divine Sonship.
b John 6:57.
27 *a* TG Authority; Delegation of Responsibility; Jesus Christ, Authority of.
b TG Jesus Christ, Judge.
c TG Jesus Christ, Son of Man.
28 *a* Dan. 12:2.
b D&C 76:16 (16–17).
29 *a* D&C 29:26.
b JST John 5:29 . . . they *who* have done good, *in* the resurrection of *the just;* and they *who* have done evil, *in* the resurrection of *the unjust.*
c TG Resurrection.
d TG Sin.
e TG Damnation; Hell.

nothing: as I hear, I judge: and my
judgment is [a]just; because I seek
not mine own [b]will, but the [c]will
of the Father which hath sent me.
31 If I bear witness of myself, my
witness is not true.
32 ¶ There is another that beareth
[a]witness of me; and I know that the
[b]witness which he witnesseth of
me is true.
33 Ye sent unto [a]John, and he bare
[b]witness unto the truth.
34 [a]But I receive not testimony
from man: but these things I say,
that ye might be saved.
35 He was a burning and a shining [a]light: and ye were willing for a
season to rejoice in his [b]light.
36 ¶ [a]But I have [b]greater witness
than *that* of John: for the [c]works
which the Father hath given me to
finish, the same [d]works that I do,
bear witness of me, that the Father
hath [e]sent me.
37 And the Father himself, which
hath sent me, hath borne [a]witness
of me. Ye have neither heard his
voice at any time, nor [b]seen his
shape.
38 And ye have not his word abiding in you: for whom he hath sent,
him ye [a]believe not.
39 ¶ [a]Search the scriptures; for
in them ye think ye have eternal
life: and they are they which [b]tes-
tify of me.
40 And ye will not come to me,
that ye might have [a]life.

41 I receive not [a]honour from men.
42 But I know you, that ye have
not the [a]love of God in you.
43 I am come in my [a]Father's
[b]name, and ye [c]receive me not: if
another shall come in his own name,
him ye will receive.
44 How can ye believe, which receive [a]honour one of another, and
seek not the [b]honour that *cometh*
from God only?
45 Do not think that I will accuse
you to the Father: there is *one* that
accuseth you, *even* Moses, in whom
ye trust.
46 For had ye believed [a]Moses,
ye would have believed me: for he
[b]wrote of me.
47 But if ye believe not his [a]writ-
ings, how shall ye believe my words?

CHAPTER 6

Jesus feeds the five thousand—He walks on the sea—He is the living manna sent from God—Salvation is gained by eating living bread—Jesus explains how men eat His flesh and drink His blood—Peter testifies that Jesus is the Messiah.

AFTER these things Jesus went over
the sea of Galilee, which is *the sea*
of Tiberias.
2 And a great multitude followed
him, because they saw his miracles
which he did on them that were
diseased.
3 And Jesus went up into a

30*a* TG God, Justice of.
b 2 Ne. 31:7 (7–10). TG Agency.
c TG God, Will of.
32*a* TG Holy Ghost, Source of Testimony.
b TG Witness.
33*a* D&C 35:4; 84:27 (27–28).
b John 1:15 (7, 15, 19).
34*a* JST John 5:35 *And he received* not *his* testimony *of* man, but *of God, and ye yourselves say that he is a prophet, therefore ye ought to receive his testimony.* These things I say . . .
35*a* Matt. 11:11 (7–15).
b TG Light [noun].
36*a* JST John 5:37 But I have *a* greater witness than *the testimony* of John . . .
b GR the greater witness than John's.
c TG God, Works of.
d Matt. 11:4; John 10:25.
e TG Jesus Christ, Messenger of the Covenant.
37*a* TG Witness of the Father.
b TG God, Privilege of Seeing.
38*a* TG Unbelief.
39*a* TG Education; Learn; Scriptures, Study of; Study.
b TG Scriptures, Value of; Testimony.
40*a* D&C 66:2.
41*a* John 7:18. TG Honor.
42*a* TG God, Love of; Love.
43*a* TG Jesus Christ, Authority of.
b TG Authority; Name.
c D&C 132:25.
44*a* Luke 18:9; 1 Thes. 2:6; D&C 76:61.
b TG God, the Standard of Righteousness.
46*a* Luke 24:27.
b TG Jesus Christ, Prophecies about.
47*a* TG Scriptures, Study of.

mountain, and there he sat with
his disciples.
4 And the [a]passover, a feast of the
Jews, was nigh.
5 ¶ When Jesus then lifted up
his eyes, and saw a great company
come unto him, he saith unto Philip, Whence shall we buy bread,
that these may eat?
6 And this he said to prove him: for
he himself knew what he would do.
7 Philip answered him, Two hundred pennyworth of bread is not
sufficient for them, that every one
of them may take a little.
8 One of his disciples, Andrew, Simon Peter's brother, saith unto him,
9 There is a lad here, which hath
five barley loaves, and two small
fishes: but what are they among
so many?
10 And Jesus said, Make the men
sit down. Now there was much grass
in the place. So the men sat down,
in number about [a]five thousand.
11 And Jesus took the loaves; and
when he had given [a]thanks, he distributed to the disciples, and the disciples to them that were set down;
and likewise of the fishes as much
as they would.
12 When they were filled, he said
unto his disciples, Gather up the
fragments that remain, that nothing be [a]lost.
13 Therefore they gathered *them*
together, and filled twelve baskets
with the fragments of the five barley loaves, which remained over
and above unto them that had
eaten.
14 Then those men, when they had
seen the [a]miracle that Jesus did, said,
This is of a truth that [b]prophet that
should come into the world.
15 ¶ When Jesus therefore perceived that they would come and
take him by force, to make him
a [a]king, he departed again into a
mountain himself alone.
16 And when even was *now* come,
his disciples went down unto the sea,
17 And entered into a ship, and
went over the sea toward Capernaum. And it was now dark, and
Jesus was not come to them.
18 And the sea arose by reason of
a great wind that blew.
19 So when they had rowed about
five and twenty or thirty furlongs,
they see Jesus walking on the sea,
and drawing nigh unto the ship:
and they were [a]afraid.
20 But he saith unto them, It is I;
be not afraid.
21 Then they willingly received
him into the ship: and immediately
the ship was at the land whither
they went.
22 ¶ The day following, when the
people which stood on the other
side of the sea saw that there was
none other boat there, save that one
whereinto his disciples were entered, and that Jesus went not with
his disciples into the boat, but *that*
his disciples were gone away alone;
23 (Howbeit there came other boats
from Tiberias nigh unto the place
where they did eat bread, after that
the Lord had given thanks:)
24 When the people therefore saw
that Jesus was not there, neither his
disciples, they also took shipping,
and came to Capernaum, seeking
for Jesus.
25 And when they had found him
on the other side of the sea, they
said unto him, Rabbi, when camest
thou hither?
26 Jesus answered them and said,
Verily, verily, I say unto you, Ye seek
me, [a]not because ye saw the miracles, but because ye did eat of the
loaves, and were filled.
27 [a]Labour not for the meat which

---

6 4*a* TG Passover.
10*a* Matt. 14:21 (13–21); Mark 6:44 (32–44); Luke 9:14 (10–17).
11*a* D&C 46:32; 59:7.
12*a* TG Waste.
14*a* 3 Ne. 8:1; 20:7 (1–9); Morm. 9:18 (18–19).
b TG Jesus Christ, Prophecies about.
15*a* John 18:36 (33, 36–37).
19*a* D&C 67:3.
26*a* JST John 6:26 . . . not because ye *desire to keep my sayings, neither because ye* saw the miracles . . .
27*a* TG Labor; Objectives.

perisheth, but for that meat which
endureth unto everlasting life, which
the [b]Son of man shall give unto you:
for him hath God the Father [c]sealed.
28 Then said they unto him, What
shall we do, that we might work the
works of God?
29 Jesus answered and said unto
them, This is the work of God, that ye
[a]believe on him whom he hath sent.
30 They said therefore unto him,
What [a]sign shewest thou then, that
we may see, and believe thee? what
dost thou work?
31 Our fathers did eat manna in
the desert; as it is written, He gave
them [a]bread from heaven to eat.
32 Then Jesus said unto them, Verily, verily, I say unto you, Moses gave
you not that bread from heaven;
but my Father giveth you the true
bread from heaven.
33 For the bread of God is he which
cometh down from heaven, and giveth life unto the world.
34 Then said they unto him, Lord,
evermore give us this bread.
35 And Jesus said unto them, I am
the [a]bread of life: he that cometh to
me shall never hunger; and he that
believeth on me shall never [b]thirst.
36 But I said unto you, That ye
also have seen me, and believe not.
37 All that the Father [a]giveth me
shall come to me; and him that
cometh to me I will in no wise
[b]cast out.
38 For I [a]came down from heaven,
not to do mine own [b]will, but the
[c]will of him that sent me.
39 And this is the [a]Father's [b]will
which hath sent me, that of all
which he hath given me I should
lose [c]nothing, but should [d]raise it
up again at the last day.
40 And this is the will of him that
sent me, that every one which seeth
the Son, and [a]believeth on him, may
have [b]everlasting life: and I will raise
him up [c]at the last day.
41 The Jews then murmured at
him, because he said, I am the bread
which came down from heaven.
42 And they said, Is not this Jesus,
the son of [a]Joseph, whose father
and mother we know? how is it then
that he saith, I came down from
heaven?
43 Jesus therefore answered and
said unto them, [a]Murmur not among
yourselves.
44 [a]No man can [b]come to me, except the Father which hath sent me
[c]draw him: and I will raise him up
at the last day.
45 It is written in the prophets, And
they shall be all [a]taught of God. Every man therefore that hath heard,
and hath learned of the [b]Father,
cometh unto me.
46 Not that any man hath seen the
Father, save he which is of God, he
hath [a]seen the Father.
47 Verily, verily, I say unto you,
He that [a]believeth on me hath
[b]everlasting life.
48 I am that bread of life.
49 Your fathers did eat [a]manna in
the wilderness, and are dead.
50 This is the bread which cometh

27*b* TG Jesus Christ, Son of Man.
c TG Sealing.
29*a* TG Faith.
30*a* Matt. 12:38; Jacob 7:13 (13–21); Alma 30:43 (43–60); D&C 46:9 (8–9).
31*a* Ps. 78:24.
35*a* TG Bread of Life.
b John 4:14; 7:37 (37–39).
37*a* 3 Ne. 15:24; D&C 27:14; 50:41 (41–42); 84:63.
b John 17:2.
38*a* TG Jesus Christ, Condescension of.
b TG Jesus Christ, Mission of.
c TG God, Will of.
39*a* Luke 2:49.
b 3 Ne. 27:13 (13–16).
c John 17:12; 18:9.
d 3 Ne. 15:1; D&C 5:35.
40*a* TG Faith.
b TG Eternal Life.
c JST John 6:40 . . . *in the resurrection of the just* at the last day.
42*a* Luke 4:22.
43*a* TG Murmuring.
44*a* JST John 6:44 (Appendix).
b Isa. 55:3.
c 1 Cor. 12:3; 1 Pet. 1:2; 3 Ne. 27:14; D&C 29:7.
45*a* 1 Thes. 4:9; 1 Jn. 2:27 (20, 27).
b TG Witness of the Father.
46*a* TG God, Manifestations of; God, Privilege of Seeing; Revelation.
47*a* TG Faith.
b TG Eternal Life; Exaltation.
49*a* 1 Ne. 17:28; Mosiah 7:19.

down from heaven, that a man may
eat thereof, and not die.
51 I am the living [a]bread which
came down from heaven: if any
man eat of this bread, he shall live
for ever: and the [b]bread that I will
give is my [c]flesh, which I will [d]give
for the [e]life of the world.
52 The Jews therefore strove among
themselves, saying, How can this
man give us *his* flesh to eat?
53 Then Jesus said unto them, Verily, verily, I say unto you, Except ye
[a]eat the flesh of the [b]Son of man,
and drink his blood, ye have no life
in you.
54 Whoso eateth my [a]flesh, and
drinketh my [b]blood, hath eternal
life; [c]and I will [d]raise him up at
the last day.
55 For my flesh is meat indeed,
and my blood is drink indeed.
56 He that eateth my flesh, and
drinketh my blood, [a]dwelleth in
me, and I in him.
57 As the living Father hath [a]sent
me, and I live by the Father: so he
that eateth me, even he shall [b]live
by me.
58 This is that bread which came
down from heaven: not as your
fathers did eat manna, and are dead:
he that eateth of this bread shall
live for ever.
59 These things said he in the synagogue, as he taught in Capernaum.
60 Many therefore of his disciples,
when they had heard *this*, said, This
is an hard saying; who can hear it?
61 When Jesus [a]knew in himself
that his disciples murmured at it,
he said unto them, Doth this [b]of-
fend you?
62 *What* and if ye shall see the
[a]Son of man [b]ascend up where he
was before?
63 It is the [a]spirit that quickeneth;
the flesh profiteth nothing: the
words that I speak unto you, *they*
are spirit, and *they* are life.
64 But there are some of you that
believe not. For Jesus knew from
the beginning who they were that
believed not, and who should [a]be-
tray him.
65 And he said, Therefore said I
unto you, that no man can come
unto me, [a]except it were given unto
him of my Father.
66 ¶ From that *time* many of his
[a]disciples went back, and [b]walked
no more with him.
67 Then said Jesus unto the twelve,
Will ye also go away?
68 Then Simon Peter answered
him, Lord, to whom shall we go?
thou hast the [a]words of eternal life.
69 And [a]we believe and are sure
that thou art that Christ, the [b]Son
of the living God.
70 Jesus answered them, Have not
I [a]chosen you twelve, and one of
you is a devil?
71 He spake of Judas Iscariot *the son*
of Simon: for he it was that should
betray him, being one of the twelve.

To whom shall we go? John 6:68

CHAPTER 7

Jesus' kinsmen do not believe—He teaches His Father's doctrine and proclaims His divine sonship—Truth may be known through obedience—

51*a* TG Jesus Christ, Types of, in Anticipation.
b TG Bread of Life; Jesus Christ, Types of, in Memory.
c Heb. 10:10.
d TG God, Gifts of.
e TG Jesus Christ, Atonement through.
53*a* Mark 14:22; Luke 22:19.
b TG Jesus Christ, Son of Man.
54*a* TG Sacrament.
b TG Blood, Symbolism of.
c JST John 6:54 . . . and I will raise him up *in the resurrection of the just* at the last day.
d TG Resurrection.
56*a* 1 Jn. 3:24.
57*a* TG Jesus Christ, Messenger of the Covenant.
b John 5:26.
61*a* John 2:25.
b TG Offense.
62*a* TG Jesus Christ, Son of Man.
b John 3:13. TG Jesus Christ, Ascension of.
63*a* 2 Cor. 3:6.
64*a* John 13:11.
65*a* JST John 6:65 . . . except *he doeth the will* of my Father *who hath sent me.*
66*a* TG Apostasy of Individuals.
b TG Apostasy of the Early Christian Church.
68*a* John 17:8; Acts 5:20; Moses 6:59.
69*a* GR we have had faith and have known that.
b TG God, Body of, Corporeal Nature.
70*a* 1 Ne. 12:7 (6–7).

*Jesus offers living water to all people—
The people have various opinions concerning Him.*

AFTER these things Jesus walked
in Galilee: for he would not walk
in Jewry, because the Jews [a]sought
to [b]kill him.
2 Now the Jews' [a]feast of tabernacles was at hand.
3 His [a]brethren therefore said
unto him, Depart hence, and go
into Judæa, that thy disciples also
may see the works that thou doest.
4 For *there is* no man *that* doeth
any thing in secret, and he himself seeketh to be known openly. If
thou do these things, shew thyself
to the world.
5 For neither did his brethren believe in him.
6 Then Jesus said unto them, My
[a]time is not yet come: but your time
is alway ready.
7 The world cannot hate you; but
me it [a]hateth, because I testify of
it, that the works thereof are [b]evil.
8 Go ye up unto this feast: I go not
up yet unto this feast; for my time
is not yet full come.
9 When he had said these words
unto them, he abode *still* in Galilee.
10 ¶ But when his brethren were
gone up, then went he also up unto
the feast, not openly, but as it were
in secret.
11 Then the Jews sought him at the
feast, and said, Where is he?
12 And there was much murmuring among the people concerning
him: for some said, He is a good man:
others said, Nay; but he deceiveth
the people.
13 Howbeit no man spake openly
of him for [a]fear of the Jews.
14 ¶ Now about the midst of the
feast Jesus went up into the temple,
and taught.
15 And the Jews [a]marvelled, saying, How knoweth this man letters,
having never learned?
16 Jesus answered them, and said,
My [a]doctrine is not mine, but his
that [b]sent me.
17 If any man will [a]do his [b]will, he
shall [c]know of the doctrine, whether
it be of God, or *whether* I speak of
myself.
18 He that speaketh of himself
seeketh his own [a]glory: but he
that seeketh his [b]glory that sent
him, the same is true, and no unrighteousness is in him.
19 Did not Moses give you the law,
and *yet* none of you keepeth the law?
Why go ye about to kill me?
20 The people answered and said,
Thou hast a devil: who goeth about
to kill thee?
21 Jesus answered and said unto
them, I have done one work, and
ye all marvel.
22 Moses therefore gave unto you
[a]circumcision; (not because it is
of Moses, but of the fathers;) and
ye on the sabbath day circumcise
a man.
23 If a man on the [a]sabbath day
receive circumcision, that the law
of Moses should not be broken;
are ye angry at me, because I have
made a man every whit [b]whole on
the sabbath day?
24 [a]Judge not according to [b]the
[c]appearance, but judge righteous
judgment.
25 Then said some of them of
Jerusalem, Is not this he, whom they
seek to kill?
26 But, lo, he speaketh boldly, and

7 1*a* John 5:16 (16, 18).
b John 11:53 (53–54).
2*a* Lev. 23:34 (34–43).
3*a* Matt. 12:46; 1 Cor. 9:5.
6*a* Matt. 26:18.
7*a* 1 Ne. 16:2 (1–3).
b TG Evil.
13*a* John 19:38.
15*a* Luke 2:46 (46–47).
16*a* Matt. 7:28; John 8:28; 2 Ne. 31:21. TG Gospel; Jesus Christ, Teaching Mode of.
b TG Jesus Christ, Authority of; Jesus Christ, Messenger of the Covenant.
17*a* TG Good Works; Obedience.
b TG God, Will of.
c TG Discernment, Spiritual; Testimony; Truth.
18*a* John 5:41 (41–43).
b John 8:50; D&C 88:67; Moses 4:2 (1–3).
22*a* TG Circumcision.
23*a* TG Sabbath.
b John 5:8 (8–9).
24*a* TG Judgment.
b JST John 7:24 . . . *your traditions,* but judge . . .
c Isa. 11:3.

they say nothing unto him. Do the
[a]rulers know indeed that this is the
very Christ?
27 Howbeit we know this man
whence he is: but when Christ
cometh, no man knoweth whence
he is.
28 Then cried Jesus in the temple
as he taught, saying, Ye both know
me, and ye know whence I am: and
I am not come of myself, but he that
sent me is [a]true, whom ye know not.
29 But I know him: for I am from
him, and he hath [a]sent me.
30 Then they [a]sought to take him:
but no man laid hands on him, because his [b]hour was not yet come.
31 And many of the people believed on him, and said, When Christ
cometh, will he do more miracles
than these which this *man* hath done?
32 ¶ The Pharisees heard that
the people murmured such things
concerning him; and the Pharisees
and the chief priests sent officers
to take him.
33 Then said Jesus unto them, Yet a
little while am I with you, and *then*
I go unto him that sent me.
34 Ye shall [a]seek me, and shall not
find *me:* and [b]where I am, [c]*thither* ye
[d]cannot come.
35 Then said the Jews among themselves, Whither will he go, that we
shall not find him? will he go unto
the dispersed among the [a]Gentiles,
and teach the Gentiles?
36 What *manner of* saying is this
that he said, Ye shall seek me, and
shall not find *me:* and where I am,
thither ye cannot come?
37 In the last day, that great *day*
of the feast, Jesus stood and cried,
saying, If any man [a]thirst, let him
come unto me, and [b]drink.
38 He that believeth on me, as the
scripture hath said, out of his belly
shall flow rivers of living water.
39 (But this spake he of the [a]Spirit,
which they that believe on him
should receive: [b]for the Holy Ghost
was not yet *given;* because that
Jesus was not yet glorified.)
40 ¶ Many of the people therefore,
when they heard this saying, said,
Of a truth this is the [a]Prophet.
41 Others said, This is the Christ.
But some said, Shall Christ come
out of Galilee?
42 Hath not the scripture said, That
[a]Christ cometh of the seed of [b]David,
and out of the town of [c]Bethlehem,
where David was?
43 So there was a [a]division among
the people because of him.
44 And some of them would have
taken him; but no man laid hands
on him.
45 ¶ Then came the officers to the
chief priests and Pharisees; and they
said unto them, Why have ye not
brought him?
46 The officers answered, Never
man [a]spake like this man.
47 Then answered them the Pharisees, Are ye also [a]deceived?
48 Have any of the rulers or of the
Pharisees believed on him?
49 But this people who knoweth
not the law are [a]cursed.
50 [a]Nicodemus saith unto them, (he
that came to Jesus by night, being
one of them,)
51 Doth our law judge *any* man,

26*a* John 3:1 (1–2).
28*a* TG Truth.
29*a* John 13:3.
TG Jesus Christ, Authority of; Jesus Christ, Messenger of the Covenant.
30*a* John 10:39.
b John 12:23 (23–27).
34*a* John 13:33 (33, 36).
b D&C 29:29; 76:112 (51–112).
c 1 Pet. 3:22.
d D&C 25:15.
35*a* GR Greeks.
37*a* Ps. 42:2 (1–3); 143:6 (5–12); Isa. 55:1 (1–3); John 4:14 (13–15); 6:35.
b TG Living Water.
39*a* TG Holy Ghost, Gift of.
b JST John 7:39 . . . for the Holy Ghost was *promised unto them who believe, after that* Jesus was glorified.)
40*a* John 9:17; 1 Ne. 22:20 (20–21).
42*a* 1 Chr. 5:2; Matt. 2:6.
b TG Jesus Christ, Davidic Descent of.
c 1 Sam. 16:1; Micah 5:2; Luke 2:4. TG Jesus Christ, Prophecies about.
43*a* Matt. 10:34.
46*a* TG Teaching with the Spirit.
47*a* Jacob 4:14 (13–14).
49*a* TG Curse.
50*a* John 3:1.

before it hear him, and know what
he doeth?
52 They answered and said unto
him, Art thou also of Galilee? Search,
and look: for out of Galilee ariseth
no prophet.
53 And every man went unto his
own house.

CHAPTER 8

The woman taken in adultery is brought before Christ—Christ is the Light of the world—He again proclaims that He is the Messiah—The true children of Abraham believe in Christ—Jesus says, Before Abraham was I, Jehovah.

JESUS went unto the mount of Olives.
2 And early in the morning he came
again into the [a]temple, and all the
people came unto him; and he sat
down, and taught them.
3 And the scribes and Pharisees
brought unto him a [a]woman taken
in [b]adultery; and when they had set
her in the midst,
4 They say unto him, Master, this
woman was taken in adultery, in
the very act.
5 Now Moses in the [a]law commanded us, that such should be
stoned: but what sayest thou?
6 This they said, tempting him,
that they might have to accuse him.
But Jesus stooped down, and with
his finger [a]wrote on the ground, *as
though he heard them not.*
7 So when they continued asking
him, he lifted up himself, and said
unto them, He that is without [a]sin
among you, let him [b]first cast a
[c]stone at her.
8 And again he stooped down, and
wrote on the ground.
9 And they which heard *it,* being
convicted by *their own* [a]conscience,
went out one by one, beginning at
the eldest, *even* unto the last: and
Jesus was left alone, and the woman
standing in the midst.
10 When Jesus had lifted up himself, and saw none but the woman,
he said unto her, Woman, where are
those thine accusers? hath no man
condemned thee?
11 She said, No man, Lord. And
Jesus said unto her, Neither do I [a]con-
demn thee: go, and [b]sin no [c]more.
12 ¶ Then spake Jesus again unto
them, saying, I am the [a]light of the
world: he that followeth me shall
not [b]walk in [c]darkness, but shall
have the light of life.
13 The Pharisees therefore said
unto him, Thou bearest record of
thyself; thy record is not true.
14 Jesus answered and said unto
them, Though I bear record of myself, *yet* my record is true: for I know
[a]whence I came, and whither I go;
but ye cannot tell [b]whence I come,
and whither I go.
15 Ye judge after the flesh; I [a]judge
no man.
16 And yet if I [a]judge, my [b]judg-
ment is true: for I am not [c]alone,
but I and the Father that sent me.
17 It is also written in your law, that
the [a]testimony of two men is true.
18 I am one that bear witness of
myself, and the [a]Father that sent
me beareth [b]witness of me.
19 Then said they unto him, Where
is thy Father? Jesus answered, Ye
neither know me, nor my Father: if
ye had [a]known me, ye should have
known my Father also.
20 These words spake Jesus in the

8 2*a* Matt. 26:55; Luke 21:37.
3*a* TG Woman.
b TG Adulterer.
5*a* Lev. 20:10.
6*a* TG Jesus Christ, Teaching Mode of.
7*a* 3 Ne. 14:5 (1–5).
b Deut. 17:7.
c TG Gossip.
9*a* TG Conscience.
11*a* TG Benevolence; Mercy.
b D&C 42:25.
c JST John 8:11 . . . more. *And the woman glorified God from that hour, and believed on his name.*
12*a* 1 Jn. 1:5. TG Jesus Christ, Light of the World; Light [noun]; Light of Christ.
b TG Walking in Darkness.
c TG Darkness, Spiritual.
14*a* John 16:28.
b John 9:29.
15*a* John 12:47.
16*a* TG Jesus Christ, Judge.
b TG Judgment.
c John 8:29; 16:32.
17*a* TG Witness.
18*a* TG Godhead; God the Father, Elohim.
b TG Witness of the Father.
19*a* John 14:7.

treasury, as he taught in the temple:
and no man laid hands on him; for
his hour was not yet come.
21 Then said Jesus again unto them,
I go my way, and ye shall seek me,
and shall die in your [a]sins: whither
I go, ye cannot come.
22 Then said the Jews, Will he kill
himself? because he saith, Whither
I go, ye cannot come.
23 And he said unto them, Ye are
from [a]beneath; I am from above:
ye are of this [b]world; I am not of
this world.
24 I said therefore unto you, that
ye shall [a]die in your sins: for if ye
[b]believe not that I am *he*, ye shall
die in your sins.
25 Then said they unto him, Who
art thou? And Jesus saith unto them,
Even *the same* that I said unto you
from the beginning.
26 I have many things to say and to
judge of you: but he that sent me is
true; and I speak to the world those
things which I have [a]heard of him.
27 They understood not that he
spake to them of the Father.
28 Then said Jesus unto them,
When ye have lifted up the Son of
man, then shall ye know that I am
he, and *that* I do [a]nothing of myself;
but as my [b]Father hath [c]taught me,
I [d]speak these things.
29 And he that [a]sent me is with me:
the Father hath not left me [b]alone;
for I [c]do always those things that
[d]please him.
30 As he spake these words, many
[a]believed on him.
31 Then said Jesus to those Jews
which believed on him, If ye [a]con-
tinue in my word, *then* are ye my
[b]disciples indeed;
32 And ye shall [a]know the [b]truth,
and the [c]truth shall make you [d]free.
33 ¶ They answered him, We be
[a]Abraham's seed, and were never
in bondage to any man: how sayest
thou, Ye shall be made free?
34 Jesus answered them, Verily, verily, I say unto you, Whosoever [a]com-
mitteth [b]sin is the [c]servant of sin.
35 And the servant abideth not
in the house for ever: *but* the Son
abideth ever.
36 If the Son therefore shall make
you [a]free, ye shall be free indeed.
37 I know that ye are Abraham's
seed; but ye seek to kill me, because
my word hath no place in you.
38 I speak that which I have seen
with my Father: and ye do that
which ye have seen with your father.
39 They answered and said
unto him, Abraham is our father.
Jesus saith unto them, If ye were
[a]Abraham's [b]children, ye would do
the [c]works of Abraham.
40 But now ye seek to kill me, a
man that hath told you the truth,
which I have heard of God: this did
not Abraham.
41 Ye do the deeds of your father.
Then said they to him, We be not
born of fornication; we have one
Father, *even* God.
42 Jesus said unto them, If God
were your Father, ye would love
me: for I proceeded forth and [a]came

21*a* Moro. 10:26 (24–26). TG Sin.
23*a* John 3:31 (13, 31).
b TG World.
24*a* D&C 138:32 (31–34).
b TG Faith.
26*a* TG Revelation.
28*a* John 5:19.
b John 7:16 (16–18). TG Authority.
c TG Delegation of Responsibility.
d Deut. 18:18.
29*a* TG Jesus Christ, Authority of.
b John 8:16; 16:32. TG Jesus Christ, Relationships with the Father.
c TG Obedience.
d John 4:34.
30*a* John 12:42 (11, 42).
31*a* TG Commitment; Perseverance; Steadfastness.
b Matt. 27:57.
32*a* TG Conversion; Testimony.
b D&C 50:25. TG Education; Gospel; Truth.
c Moro. 10:5.
d 3 Ne. 21:4. TG Bondage, Spiritual; Liberty.
33*a* TG Abrahamic Covenant.
34*a* D&C 29:40.
b TG Sin.
c Rom. 6:16; Alma 12:11 (9–11, 17). TG Servant.
36*a* TG Bondage, Spiritual; Liberty.
39*a* TG Abrahamic Covenant.
b TG Seed of Abraham.
c TG Good Works.
42*a* John 16:28 (27–28, 30); 17:8; Gal. 4:4.

from God; neither came I of myself,
but he [b]sent me.
43 Why do ye not understand my
speech? *even* because ye cannot
[a]hear my word.
44 Ye are of *your* father the [a]devil,
and the [b]lusts of your father ye will
do. He was a [c]murderer from the
beginning, and abode not in the
[d]truth, because there is no truth in
him. When he speaketh a [e]lie, he
speaketh of his own: for he is a [f]liar,
and the father of it.
45 And because I tell *you* the truth,
ye believe me not.
46 Which of you [a]convinceth me
of [b]sin? And if I say the truth, why
do ye not believe me?
47 [a]He that is of God [b]heareth God's
words: ye therefore hear *them* not,
because ye are not of God.
48 Then answered the Jews, and
said unto him, Say we not well that
thou art a Samaritan, and hast a
[a]devil?
49 Jesus answered, I have not a
devil; but I [a]honour my Father, and
ye do dishonour me.
50 And I seek not mine own
[a]glory: there is one that seeketh and
judgeth.
51 Verily, verily, I say unto you,
If a man keep my saying, he shall
never see [a]death.
52 Then said the Jews unto him,
Now we know that thou hast a devil.
Abraham is dead, and the prophets; and thou sayest, If a man keep
my saying, he shall never [a]taste of
death.
53 Art thou greater than our father
Abraham, which is dead? and the
prophets are dead: whom makest
thou thyself?
54 Jesus answered, If I honour
myself, my honour is nothing: it is
my [a]Father that [b]honoureth me; of
whom ye say, that he is your God:
55 Yet ye have not known him; but
I know him: and if I should say, I
know him not, I shall be a liar like
unto you: but I know him, and keep
his saying.
56 Your father [a]Abraham [b]rejoiced
to [c]see my day: and he saw *it*, and
was glad.
57 Then said the Jews unto him,
Thou art not yet fifty years old, and
hast thou seen Abraham?
58 Jesus said unto them, Verily,
verily, I say unto you, [a]Before Abraham was, [b]I am.
59 Then took they up [a]stones to
cast at him: but Jesus hid himself,
and went out of the temple, going
through the midst of them, and so
[b]passed by.

CHAPTER 9

Jesus, on the Sabbath, heals a man born blind—The Jews accuse Him of Sabbath violation—He lectures them on spiritual blindness.

AND as *Jesus* passed by, he saw a man
which was [a]blind from *his* birth.

42*b* TG Jesus Christ, Messenger of the Covenant.
43*a* JST John 8:43 . . . *bear* . . .
44*a* 1 Jn. 3:10 (10–18). TG Devil; Devil, Church of.
b TG Lust.
c TG Murder.
d TG Truth.
e TG Lying.
f TG Honesty.
46*a* GR convicts, reproves.
b Heb. 4:15.
47*a* JST John 8:47 He that is of God *receiveth* God's words; ye therefore *receive* them not, because ye are not of God.
b Dan. 12:10; 1 Jn. 4:6 (5–6); 2 Ne. 33:10 (10–11).
48*a* Mosiah 3:9.
49*a* TG God, the Standard of Righteousness; Honoring Father and Mother; Respect.
50*a* John 7:18.
51*a* John 5:24; 11:26; D&C 63:49. TG Death, Spiritual, First; Death, Spiritual, Second.
52*a* D&C 42:46 (46–47).
54*a* TG God, Body of, Corporeal Nature.
b TG Honor.
56*a* Gen. 22:8 (8–14); Hel. 8:17 (16–19).
b TG Joy.
c TG Jesus Christ, Appearances, Antemortal.
58*a* TG Man, Antemortal Existence of.
b The term I AM used here in the Greek is identical with the Septuagint usage in Ex. 3:14 which identifies Jehovah. (See also John 4:26.) TG Jesus Christ, Jehovah.
59*a* John 10:31.
b Luke 4:30.
9 1*a* Matt. 9:28 (28–31); 20:30 (30–34); Mosiah 3:5; 3 Ne. 17:9 (7–10); D&C 84:69.

2 And his disciples asked him, saying, Master, who did sin, this [a]man, or his parents, that he was born blind?
3 Jesus answered, Neither hath this man sinned, nor his parents: but that the [a]works of God should be made [b]manifest in him.
4 I must [a]work the [b]works of him that sent me, [c]while it is [d]day: the [e]night cometh, when no man can work.
5 As long as I am in the world, I am the [a]light of the world.
6 When he had thus spoken, he spat on the ground, and made clay of the spittle, and he anointed the eyes of the blind man with the clay,
7 And said unto him, Go, wash in the pool of [a]Siloam, (which is by interpretation, Sent.) He went his way therefore, and washed, and came seeing.
8 ¶ The neighbours therefore, and they which before had seen him that he was blind, said, Is not this he that sat and begged?
9 Some said, This is he: others *said,* He is like him: *but* he said, I am *he.*
10 Therefore said they unto him, How were thine eyes opened?
11 He answered and said, A man that is called Jesus made clay, and anointed mine eyes, and said unto me, Go to the pool of Siloam, and [a]wash: and I went and washed, and I received [b]sight.
12 Then said they unto him, Where is he? He said, I know not.
13 ¶ They brought to the Pharisees him that aforetime was blind.
14 And it was the [a]sabbath day when Jesus made the clay, and [b]opened his eyes.
15 Then again the Pharisees also asked him how he had received his sight. He said unto them, He put clay upon mine eyes, and I washed, and do see.
16 Therefore said some of the Pharisees, This man is not of God, because he keepeth not the sabbath day. Others said, How can a man that is a sinner do such miracles? And there was a division among them.
17 They say unto the blind man again, What sayest thou of him, that he hath opened thine eyes? He said, He is a [a]prophet.
18 But the Jews did not believe concerning him, that he had been blind, and received his sight, until they called the parents of him that had received his sight.
19 And they asked them, saying, Is this your son, who ye say was born blind? how then doth he now see?
20 His parents answered them and said, We know that this is our son, and that he was born blind:
21 But by what means he now seeth, we know not; or who hath opened his eyes, we know not: he is of age; ask him: he shall speak for himself.
22 These *words* spake his parents, because they feared the Jews: for the Jews had agreed already, that if any man did confess that he was Christ, he should be put out of the synagogue.
23 Therefore said his parents, He is of age; ask him.
24 Then again called they the man that was blind, and said unto him, Give God the praise: we know that this man is a sinner.
25 He answered and said, Whether he be a sinner *or no,* I know not: one thing I know, that, whereas I was blind, now I see.
26 Then said they to him again,

2*a* TG Man, Antemortal Existence of.
3*a* TG God, Works of.
b John 11:4.
4*a* John 5:17.
b John 4:34. TG Good Works.
c JST John 9:4 . . . while *I am with you;* the *time* cometh when *I shall have finished my work, then I go unto the Father.*
d Rom. 13:12 (11–12); Alma 34:33.
e TG Darkness, Spiritual.
5*a* TG Jesus Christ, Light of the World; Light of Christ.
7*a* Neh. 3:15; Isa. 8:6.
11*a* 2 Kgs. 5:10.
b TG Sight.
14*a* TG Sabbath.
b TG Heal.
17*a* John 7:40 (40–44).

What did he to thee? how opened
he thine eyes?
27 He answered them, I have told
you already, and ye did not hear:
wherefore would ye hear *it* again?
will ye also be his disciples?
28 Then they [a]reviled him, and
said, Thou art his disciple; but we
are Moses' disciples.
29 We know that God spake unto
Moses: *as for* this *fellow*, we know
not from [a]whence he is.
30 The man answered and said
unto them, Why herein is a marvellous thing, that ye know not
from whence he is, and *yet* he hath
opened mine eyes.
31 Now we know that God heareth
not sinners: but if any man be a
worshipper of God, and doeth his
will, him he heareth.
32 Since the world began was it
not heard that any man opened the
eyes of one that was born [a]blind.
33 If this man were not of [a]God,
he could do nothing.
34 They answered and said unto
him, Thou wast altogether born in
sins, and dost thou teach us? And
they cast him out.
35 Jesus heard that they had cast
him out; and when he had found
him, he said unto him, Dost thou
believe on the Son of God?
36 He answered and said, Who is he,
Lord, that I might believe on him?
37 And Jesus said unto him, Thou
hast both seen him, and it is he that
talketh with thee.
38 And he said, Lord, I believe.
And he worshipped him.
39 ¶ And Jesus said, For [a]judgment
I am come into this world, that
they which [b]see not might see; and
that they which see might be made
blind.
40 And *some* of the Pharisees which
were with him heard these words,
and said unto him, Are we blind
also?
41 Jesus said unto them, If ye were
[a]blind, ye should have no [b]sin: but
now ye say, We [c]see; therefore your
[d]sin remaineth.

CHAPTER 10

Jesus is the Good Shepherd—He gained power over death from His Father—He promises to visit His other sheep—He proclaims, I am the Son of God.

VERILY, verily, I say unto you, He
that entereth not by the door into
the sheepfold, but climbeth up some
other way, the same is a thief and
a robber.
2 But he that entereth in by the
door is the shepherd of the [a]sheep.
3 To him the porter openeth; and
the sheep hear his [a]voice: and he
calleth his own sheep by name, and
[b]leadeth them out.
4 And when he putteth forth his
own sheep, he goeth before them,
and the sheep follow him: for they
[a]know his [b]voice.
5 And a stranger will they not follow, but will flee from him: for they
know not the voice of [a]strangers.
6 This parable spake Jesus unto
them: but they understood not what
things they were which he spake
unto them.
7 Then said Jesus unto them again,
Verily, verily, I say unto you, I am
the [a]door of the sheep.
8 All that ever came before me [a]are
thieves and robbers: but the sheep
did not hear them.
9 I am the door: by me if any man
enter in, he shall be saved, and shall
go in and out, and find pasture.
10 The thief cometh not, but for to
[a]steal, and to kill, and to destroy: I

28*a* TG Reviling.
29*a* John 8:14.
32*a* JST John 9:32 . . . blind, *except he be of God.*
33*a* Acts 2:22.
39*a* TG Jesus Christ, Judge.
b Luke 5:32; 1 Tim. 1:13, 15.
41*a* TG Spiritual Blindness.
b John 15:22 (19–27).
c TG Accountability.
d TG Sin.
10 2*a* TG Sheep.
3*a* D&C 35:21.
b Isa. 55:4.
4*a* TG Discernment, Spiritual.
b TG Revelation.
5*a* TG Stranger.
7*a* John 14:6 (4–7).
8*a* JST John 10:8 . . . *who testified not of me* are thieves . . .
10*a* TG Stealing.

am come that they might have [b]life,
and that they might have *it* more
[c]abundantly.
11 I am the good [a]shepherd: the
good [b]shepherd giveth his life for
the sheep.
12 But he that is an hireling, and
not the shepherd, whose own the
sheep are not, seeth the wolf coming, and [a]leaveth the sheep, and
fleeth: and the wolf catcheth them,
and scattereth the sheep.
13 The [a]hireling fleeth, because
he is an hireling, and careth not
for the sheep.
14 I am the good [a]shepherd, and
[b]know my [c]*sheep*, and am known
of mine.
15 As the Father knoweth me, even
so [a]know I the Father: and I lay down
my [b]life for the sheep.
16 And [a]other [b]sheep I have, which
are not of this fold: them also I must
bring, and they shall hear my voice;
and there shall be [c]one fold, *and*
one shepherd.
17 Therefore doth my Father [a]love
me, because I [b]lay down my life,
that I might [c]take it again.
18 No man [a]taketh it from me,
but I lay it down of myself. I have
[b]power to lay it down, and I have
[c]power to take it again. This commandment have I [d]received of my
Father.
19 ¶ There was a division therefore again among the Jews for these
sayings.
20 And many of them said, He
hath a devil, and is mad; why hear
ye him?
21 Others said, These are not the
words of him that hath a devil. Can
a devil open the eyes of the blind?
22 ¶ And it was at Jerusalem the
feast of the dedication, and it was
winter.
23 And Jesus walked in the temple
in Solomon's [a]porch.
24 Then came the Jews round about
him, and said unto him, How long
dost thou make us to [a]doubt? If thou
be the Christ, tell us plainly.
25 Jesus answered them, I told you,
and ye [a]believed not: the [b]works that
I do in my Father's [c]name, they bear
witness of me.
26 But ye believe not, because ye
are not of my sheep, as I said unto
you.
27 My [a]sheep hear my voice, and
I know them, and they [b]follow me:
28 And I give unto them eternal
life; and they shall never perish,
neither shall any *man* pluck them
out of my hand.
29 My Father, which [a]gave *them*
me, is greater than all; and no *man*
is able to pluck *them* out of my
Father's hand.
30 I and *my* Father are [a]one.
31 Then the Jews took up [a]stones
again to stone him.
32 Jesus answered them, Many good
works have I shewed you from my
Father; for which of those works do
ye stone me?
33 The Jews answered him, saying,

10*b* D&C 66:2.
c TG Abundant Life; Happiness.
11*a* TG Shepherd.
b Ezek. 34:2.
12*a* TG Leadership.
13*a* TG Wages.
14*a* TG Jesus Christ, Good Shepherd.
b Ex. 33:12 (12, 17); 1 Cor. 8:3.
c 3 Ne. 18:31.
15*a* TG Jesus Christ, Relationships with the Father.
b 1 Jn. 3:16 (10–18). TG Jesus Christ, Atonement through; Martyrdom.
16*a* 3 Ne. 15:21 (11–24); 16:1 (1–3); D&C 10:59. TG Israel, Scattering of.
b TG Book of Mormon; Israel, Joseph, People of; Israel, Ten Lost Tribes of; Sheep.
c Ezek. 37:22.
17*a* TG God, Love of.
b TG Self-Sacrifice.
c TG Jesus Christ, Resurrection.
18*a* Luke 23:46.
b TG Death, Power over; God, Power of.
c GR authority, full power.
d TG Jesus Christ, Authority of.
23*a* 1 Kgs. 6:3; Acts 3:11.
24*a* TG Doubt.
25*a* TG Faith; Unbelief.
b John 5:36. TG Miracle.
c TG Name.
27*a* TG Sheep.
b D&C 38:22.
29*a* John 17:2 (2–12); D&C 50:41.
30*a* D&C 93:3 (1–6). TG Godhead; Unity.
31*a* John 8:59.

For a good work we stone thee not;
but for [a]blasphemy; and because
that thou, being a man, makest
thyself [b]God.
34 Jesus answered them, Is it not
written in your law, I said, Ye are
[a]gods?
35 If he called them gods, unto
whom the word of God came, and
the scripture cannot be broken;
36 Say ye of him, whom the Father
hath [a]sanctified, and [b]sent into the
world, Thou blasphemest; because
I said, I am the [c]Son of God?
37 If I do not the works of my
Father, believe me not.
38 But if I do, though ye believe not
me, [a]believe the works: that ye may
know, and believe, that the [b]Father
is in me, and I in him.
39 Therefore they [a]sought again
to take him: but he escaped out of
their hand,
40 And went away again beyond
Jordan into the place where John at
first baptized; and there he abode.
41 And many resorted unto him,
and said, John did no miracle: but
all things that John spake of this
man were true.
42 And many believed on him
there.

CHAPTER 11

Jesus testifies that He is the Resurrection and the Life—Mary and Martha testify of Him—He raises Lazarus from the dead—Caiaphas speaks prophetically of the death of Jesus.

NOW a certain *man* was sick, *named*
Lazarus, of Bethany, the town of
Mary and her sister [a]Martha.
2 [a](It was *that* Mary which anointed
the [b]Lord with [c]ointment, and wiped
his feet with her hair, whose brother
Lazarus was sick.)
3 Therefore his sisters sent unto
him, saying, Lord, behold, he whom
thou lovest is sick.
4 When Jesus heard *that*, he said,
This sickness is not unto death, but
for the [a]glory of God, that the Son
of God might be [b]glorified thereby.
5 Now Jesus loved Martha, and her
sister, and Lazarus.
6 When he had heard therefore
that he was sick, he abode two days
still in the same place where he was.
7 Then after that saith he to *his* disciples, Let us go into Judæa again.
8 *His* disciples say unto him,
Master, the Jews of late sought to
stone thee; and goest thou thither
again?
9 Jesus answered, Are there not
twelve hours in the day? If any man
[a]walk in the day, he stumbleth not,
because he seeth the light of this
world.
10 But if a man walk in the night,
he stumbleth, because there is no
light in him.
11 These things said he: and after
that he saith unto them, Our friend
Lazarus sleepeth; but I go, that I may
[a]awake him out of sleep.
12 Then said his disciples, Lord, if
he sleep, he shall [a]do well.
13 Howbeit Jesus spake of his
death: but they thought that he had
spoken of taking of rest in sleep.
14 Then said Jesus unto them
plainly, Lazarus is dead.
15 And I am glad for your sakes
that I was not there, to the intent
ye may [a]believe; nevertheless let us
go unto him.
16 Then said Thomas, which is
called Didymus, unto his fellow-

33*a* TG Blaspheme.
b John 5:18 (17–18); 19:7; 1 Tim. 3:16.
34*a* TG Man, Potential to Become like Heavenly Father; Sons and Daughters of God.
36*a* TG Sanctification.
b TG Jesus Christ, Messenger of the Covenant.
c TG Jesus Christ, Divine Sonship.
38*a* TG Faith.
b TG Godhead.
39*a* John 7:30.
11 1*a* Luke 10:38; John 12:2.
2*a* JST John 11:2 *And Mary, his sister, who* anointed the Lord with ointment and wiped his feet with her hair, *lived with her sister Martha, in whose house her* brother Lazarus was sick.
b TG Jesus Christ, Lord.
c Matt. 26:7 (6–13).
4*a* 3 Ne. 12:16; Ether 12:4.
b John 9:3.
9*a* TG Walking with God.
11*a* 2 Kgs. 4:31.
12*a* GR be cured, saved.
15*a* TG Faith.

disciples, Let us also go, that we
may die with [a]him.
17 Then when Jesus came, [a]he
found that he had *lain* in the grave
four days already.
18 Now Bethany was nigh unto
Jerusalem, about fifteen [a]furlongs
off:
19 And many of the Jews came to
Martha and Mary, to comfort them
concerning their brother.
20 Then Martha, as soon as she
heard that Jesus was coming, went
and met him: but Mary sat *still* in
the house.
21 Then said Martha unto Jesus,
Lord, if thou hadst been here, my
brother had not died.
22 But I know, that even now,
whatsoever thou wilt ask of God,
God will [a]give *it* thee.
23 Jesus saith unto her, Thy brother
shall rise again.
24 Martha saith unto him, I know
that he shall rise again in the resurrection at the last day.
25 Jesus said unto her, I am the
[a]resurrection, and the [b]life: he that
[c]believeth in me, though he were
[d]dead, yet shall he [e]live:
26 And whosoever liveth and believeth in me shall never [a]die.
Believest thou this?
27 She saith unto him, Yea, Lord:
I believe that thou art the Christ,
the [a]Son of God, which should come
into the world.
28 And when she had so said, she
went her way, and called Mary her
sister secretly, saying, The Master is
come, and calleth for thee.
29 As soon as she heard *that,*
she arose quickly, and came unto
him.
30 Now Jesus was not yet come
into the town, but was in that place
where Martha met him.
31 The Jews then which were with
her in the house, and comforted her,
when they saw Mary, that she rose
up hastily and went out, followed
her, saying, She goeth unto the grave
to weep there.
32 Then when Mary was come
where Jesus was, and saw him, she
fell down at his feet, saying unto
him, Lord, if thou hadst been here,
my brother had not died.
33 When Jesus therefore saw her
weeping, and the Jews also weeping
which came with her, he groaned in
the spirit, and was troubled,
34 And said, Where have ye laid
him? They said unto him, Lord,
come and see.
35 Jesus wept.
36 Then said the Jews, Behold how
he [a]loved him!
37 And some of them said, Could
not this man, which opened the eyes
of the blind, have caused that even
this man should not have died?
38 Jesus therefore again groaning
in himself cometh to the grave. It
was a cave, and a [a]stone lay upon it.
39 Jesus said, Take ye away the
stone. Martha, the sister of him that
was dead, saith unto him, Lord, by
this time he stinketh: for he hath
been *dead* four days.
40 Jesus saith unto her, Said I not
unto thee, that, if thou wouldest believe, thou shouldest see the [a]glory
of God?
41 Then they took away the stone
from the place where the dead was
laid. And Jesus lifted up *his* eyes,
and said, Father, I [a]thank thee that
thou hast heard me.
42 And I knew that thou hearest

16*a* JST John 11:16 . . . him; *for they feared lest the Jews should take Jesus and put him to death, for as yet they did not understand the power of God.*
17*a* JST John 11:17 . . . *to Bethany, to Martha's house, Lazarus had already been* in the grave four days.
18*a* GR *stadium*—607 English feet, about 185 meters.
22*a* TG God, Gifts of.
25*a* TG Jesus Christ, Resurrection; Resurrection.
b TG Jesus Christ, Atonement through.
c TG Faith.
d TG Death.
e Alma 37:46 (46–47); Hel. 8:15; 3 Ne. 15:9.
26*a* John 5:24; 8:51; D&C 42:46 (44, 46); 63:49.
27*a* TG God, Body of, Corporeal Nature.
36*a* D&C 42:45.
38*a* Matt. 27:60.
40*a* Ex. 16:7.
41*a* TG Thanksgiving.

me always: but because of the people which stand by I said *it*, that they may believe that thou hast [a]sent me.

43 And when he thus had spoken, he cried with a loud voice, [a]Lazarus, come forth.

44 And he that was [a]dead came forth, bound hand and foot with graveclothes: and his face was bound about with a [b]napkin. Jesus saith unto them, Loose him, and let him go.

45 Then many of the Jews which came to Mary, and had seen the things which Jesus did, believed on him.

46 But some of them went their ways to the Pharisees, and told them what things Jesus had done.

47 ¶ Then gathered the chief [a]priests and the Pharisees a council, and said, What do we? for this man doeth many [b]miracles.

48 If we let him thus alone, all *men* will believe on him: and the Romans shall come and take away both our place and nation.

49 And one of them, *named* [a]Caiaphas, being the [b]high priest that same year, said unto them, Ye know nothing at all,

50 Nor consider that it is expedient for us, that one man should [a]die for the people, and that the whole nation perish not.

51 And this spake he not of himself: but being high priest that year, he prophesied that Jesus should die for that nation;

52 And not for that nation only, but that also he should [a]gather together in one the [b]children of God that were scattered abroad.

53 Then from that day forth they took [a]counsel together for to put him to [b]death.

54 Jesus therefore walked no more openly among the Jews; but went thence unto a country near to the wilderness, into a city called Ephraim, and there continued with his disciples.

55 ¶ And the Jews' passover was nigh at hand: and many went out of the country up to Jerusalem before the passover, to [a]purify themselves.

56 Then sought they for Jesus, and spake among themselves, as they stood in the temple, What think ye, that he will not come to the feast?

57 Now both the chief priests and the Pharisees had given a commandment, that, if any man knew where he were, he should shew *it*, that they might take him.

CHAPTER 12

Mary anoints Jesus' feet—His triumphal entry into Jerusalem is recounted—He foretells His death—To receive Christ is to receive the Father.

THEN Jesus six days before the passover came to Bethany, where Lazarus was which had been dead, whom he raised from the dead.

2 There they made him a supper; and [a]Martha served: but Lazarus was one of them that sat at the table with him.

3 Then took Mary a pound of ointment of spikenard, very costly, and anointed the feet of Jesus, and wiped his feet with her hair: and the house was filled with the odour of the ointment.

4 Then saith one of his disciples, Judas Iscariot, Simon's *son*, which should betray him,

5 Why was not this ointment sold for three hundred pence, and given to the poor?

6 This he said, not that he cared for the poor; but because he was a

---

42*a* TG Jesus Christ, Messenger of the Covenant.
43*a* TG God, Power of.
44*a* 2 Kgs. 8:1. TG Death, Power over.
b John 20:7.
47*a* 2 Ne. 10:5.
b 3 Ne. 19:35.
49*a* Matt. 26:3 (3–5).
b TG Priesthood, Aaronic.
50*a* TG Jesus Christ, Trials of.
52*a* TG Israel, Gathering of.
b TG Sons and Daughters of God.
53*a* Matt. 21:38 (33–46). TG Counsel.
b John 7:1.
55*a* TG Purification.
12 2*a* Luke 10:38; John 11:1 (1, 5).

[a]thief, and had the [b]bag, and bare
what was put therein.
7 Then said Jesus, Let her alone:
[a]against the day of my burying hath
[b]she kept this.
8 For the poor always ye have with
you; but me ye have not always.
9 Much people of the Jews therefore knew that he was there: and
they came not for Jesus' sake only,
but that they might see Lazarus also,
whom he had raised from the dead.
10 ¶ But the chief priests consulted
that they might put Lazarus also
to death;
11 Because that by reason of him
many of the Jews went away, and
believed on Jesus.
12 ¶ On the next day much people
that were come to the feast, when
they heard that Jesus was coming
to Jerusalem,
13 Took branches of palm trees,
and went forth to meet him, and
cried, Hosanna: Blessed *is* the King
of Israel that cometh in the name
of the Lord.
14 And Jesus, when he had found a
young ass, sat thereon; as it is written,
15 Fear not, daughter of Sion: behold, thy [a]King cometh, sitting on
an ass's colt.
16 These things [a]understood not
his disciples at the first: but when
Jesus was glorified, then remembered they that these things were
written of him, and *that* they had
done these things unto him.
17 The people therefore that was
with him when he called Lazarus
out of his grave, and raised him
from the dead, bare record.
18 For this cause the people also
[a]met him, for that they heard that
he had done this [b]miracle.
19 The Pharisees therefore said
among themselves, Perceive ye how
ye prevail nothing? behold, the
[a]world is gone after him.
20 ¶ And there were certain [a]Greeks
among them that came up to [b]wor-
ship at the feast:
21 The same came therefore to
Philip, which was of Bethsaida of
Galilee, and desired him, saying,
Sir, we would see Jesus.
22 Philip cometh and telleth Andrew: and again Andrew and Philip tell Jesus.
23 ¶ And Jesus answered them,
saying, The [a]hour is come, that the
Son of man should be [b]glorified.
24 Verily, verily, I say unto you,
Except a [a]corn of wheat fall into
the ground and [b]die, it abideth
alone: but if it [c]die, it bringeth forth
much fruit.
25 He that loveth his [a]life shall lose
it; and he that [b]hateth his life in this
world shall keep it unto life eternal.
26 If any man serve me, let him
[a]follow me; and where I am, there
shall also my servant be: if any man
serve me, him will *my* Father honour.
27 Now is my soul troubled; and
what shall I say? Father, save me
from this hour: but for this cause
came I unto this hour.
28 Father, glorify thy name. Then
came there a [a]voice from heaven,
saying, I have both [b]glorified *it*, and
will glorify *it* again.
29 The people therefore, that stood
by, and heard *it*, said that it thun-
dered: others said, An [a]angel spake
to him.
30 Jesus answered and said, This
voice came not because of me, but
for your sakes.
31 Now is the judgment of this

6*a* Mosiah 2:36 (36–39).
b GR purse, money bag. John 13:29.
7*a* JST John 12:7 . . . *for she hath preserved this ointment until now, that she might anoint me in token of my burial.*
b Mark 14:9.
15*a* Zech. 9:9.
16*a* Luke 9:45; 18:34 (31–34).
18*a* Matt. 8:34.
b D&C 63:10 (7–12).
19*a* Matt. 9:31 (27–31).
20*a* Acts 17:4 (1–9).
b Acts 8:27.
23*a* John 7:30.
b TG Jesus Christ, Mission of.
24*a* GR grain, seed.
b 1 Cor. 15:36 (35–38).
c TG Death.
25*a* See JST Luke 9:24–25 (Appendix).
b TG Hate.
26*a* 2 Ne. 31:12 (12–13).
28*a* TG Godhead; Witness of the Father.
b D&C 45:4.
29*a* TG Angels.

world: now shall the [a]prince of this
world be cast out.
32 And I, if I be [a]lifted up from the
earth, will [b]draw all *men* unto me.
33 This he said, signifying what
[a]death he should die.
34 The people answered him,
We have heard out of the law that
[a]Christ abideth for ever: and how
sayest thou, The Son of man must be
lifted up? who is this Son of man?
35 Then Jesus said unto them, Yet
a little while is the [a]light with you.
Walk while ye have the [b]light, lest
darkness come upon you: for he that
walketh in [c]darkness knoweth not
whither he goeth.
36 While ye have light, [a]believe in
the light, that ye may be the [b]chil-
dren of light. These things spake
Jesus, and departed, and did hide
himself from them.
37 ¶ But though he had done so
many [a]miracles before them, yet
they [b]believed not on him:
38 That the saying of Esaias the
prophet might be fulfilled, which
he spake, Lord, who hath [a]believed
our report? and to whom hath the
arm of the Lord been revealed?
39 Therefore they could not believe, because that Esaias said again,
40 He hath [a]blinded their eyes,
and [b]hardened their heart; that they
should not see with *their* eyes, nor
understand with *their* heart, and be
converted, and I should heal them.
41 These things said Esaias, when
he [a]saw his [b]glory, and spake of him.
42 ¶ Nevertheless among the chief
[a]rulers also many [b]believed on him;
but because of the Pharisees they
did not [c]confess *him*, lest they should
be put out of the synagogue:
43 For they loved the [a]praise of
men more than the praise of God.
44 ¶ Jesus cried and said, He that
[a]believeth on me, believeth not on
me, but on him that sent me.
45 And he that seeth me seeth him
that sent me.
46 I am come a [a]light into the
world, that whosoever believeth on
me should not abide in darkness.
47 And if any man hear my words,
and believe not, I judge him not: for
I came not to [a]judge the world, but
to save the world.
48 He that [a]rejecteth me, and receiveth not my words, hath one that
[b]judgeth him: the [c]word that I have
spoken, the same shall [d]judge him
in the last day.
49 For I have not spoken of myself;
but the Father which [a]sent me, he
gave me a commandment, what I
should say, and what I should speak.
50 And I know that his commandment is life everlasting: whatsoever I
[a]speak therefore, even as the [b]Father
said unto me, so I [c]speak.

CHAPTER 13

Jesus washes the feet of the Twelve—He identifies Judas as His betrayer—He commands them to love one another.

Now before the feast of the [a]pass-
over, when Jesus knew that his hour
was come that he should depart out

31*a* TG Devil.
32*a* TG Jesus Christ, Atonement through; Jesus Christ, Crucifixion of.
b D&C 18:11.
33*a* TG Jesus Christ, Death of.
34*a* 2 Sam. 7:16.
35*a* TG Light of Christ.
b TG Light [noun].
c TG Darkness, Spiritual; Walking in Darkness.
36*a* TG Faith.
b TG Children of Light.
37*a* TG Miracle; Signs.
b Mosiah 3:9 (9–11).
38*a* Isa. 53:1; Rom. 10:16.
40*a* TG Spiritual Blindness.
b TG Hardheartedness.
41*a* TG Jesus Christ, Appearances, Antemortal.
b TG Glory.
42*a* Acts 6:7.
b John 8:30 (30–31).
c Prov. 29:25; John 19:38.
43*a* Mark 12:38 (38–40); 1 Cor. 1:26 (26–31); 1 Ne. 8:28 (26–28); Alma 11:24; D&C 3:7 (5–8).
44*a* TG Faith.
46*a* John 1:9 (4, 9).
47*a* Luke 4:19; John 8:15.
48*a* D&C 39:9.
b TG Judgment.
c TG Gospel.
d TG Judgment, the Last.
49*a* TG Jesus Christ, Authority of.
50*a* Deut. 18:18.
b 3 Ne. 15:18.
c TG Jesus Christ, Teaching Mode of.
13 1*a* Deut. 16:1.

of this world unto the Father, having loved his own which were in the
world, he [b]loved them unto the end.
2 And supper being ended, the
devil having now put into the [a]heart
of Judas Iscariot, Simon's *son*, to betray him;
3 Jesus [a]knowing that the Father
had given all [b]things into his hands,
and that he was [c]come from God,
and went to God;
4 He riseth from supper, and laid
aside his garments; and took a towel,
and girded himself.
5 After that he poureth water into
a basin, and began to [a]wash the disciples' feet, and to wipe *them* with
the towel wherewith he was girded.
6 Then cometh he to Simon Peter:
and Peter saith unto him, Lord, dost
thou wash my feet?
7 Jesus answered and said unto
him, What I do thou knowest not
now; but thou shalt know hereafter.
8 [a]Peter saith unto him, Thou shalt
never wash my feet. Jesus answered
him, If I [b]wash thee not, thou hast
no part with me.
9 Simon Peter saith unto him, Lord,
not my feet only, but also *my* hands
and *my* head.
10 Jesus saith to him, He that is
washed needeth not save to wash
his feet, but is [a]clean every whit:
and ye are [b]clean, but not all.
11 For he knew who should [a]be-
tray him; therefore said he, Ye are
not [b]all clean.
12 So after he had washed their
feet, and had taken his garments,
and was set down again, he said
unto them, Know ye what I have
done to you?
13 Ye call me [a]Master and Lord:
and ye say well; for *so* I am.
14 If I then, *your* Lord and [a]Mas-
ter, have [b]washed your feet; ye also
ought to [c]wash one another's [d]feet.
15 For I have given you an [a]ex-
ample, that ye should do as I have
done to you.
16 Verily, verily, I say unto you,
The servant is not greater than his
lord; neither he that is sent greater
than he that sent him.
17 If ye know these things, [a]happy
are ye if ye do them.
18 ¶ I speak not of you all: I know
whom I have chosen: but that the
scripture may be fulfilled, He that
eateth bread with me hath lifted
up his heel against me.
19 Now I tell you before it come,
that, when it is come to pass, ye may
believe that I am [a]*he*.
20 Verily, verily, I say unto you,
He that receiveth whomsoever I
send [a]receiveth me; and he that
[b]receiveth me receiveth him that
sent me.
21 When Jesus had thus said, he
was troubled in spirit, and testified,
and said, Verily, verily, I say unto
you, that one of you shall [a]betray
me.
22 Then the disciples looked one
on another, doubting of whom he
spake.
23 Now there was leaning on Jesus'
bosom one of his [a]disciples, whom
Jesus loved.
24 Simon Peter therefore beckoned
to him, that he should ask who it
should be of whom he spake.
25 He then lying on Jesus' breast
saith unto him, Lord, who is it?

1*b* TG God, Love of.
2*a* D&C 10:15 (13, 15); 63:28.
3*a* TG God, Omniscience of.
b TG Jesus Christ, Power of.
c John 7:29.
5*a* TG Wash.
8*a* JST John 13:8–10 (Appendix).
b TG Purification.
10*a* TG Purity.
b D&C 38:10.
11*a* John 6:64.
b D&C 66:3.
13*a* GR Teacher.
14*a* GR Teacher.
b TG Courtesy.
c TG Humility.
d TG Jesus Christ, Teaching Mode of.
15*a* TG Example; God, the Standard of Righteousness; Jesus Christ, Exemplar; Leadership.
17*a* TG Happiness.
19*a* JST John 13:19 . . . *the Christ.*
20*a* D&C 39:5; 84:37.
b 1 Jn. 4:6 (1–6).
21*a* TG Jesus Christ, Betrayal of.
23*a* John 20:2; 21:24 (20–24).

26 Jesus answered, He it is, to whom I shall give a [a]sop, when I have dipped *it*. And when he had dipped the sop, he gave *it* to Judas Iscariot, *the son* of Simon.

27 And after the sop [a]Satan entered into him. Then said Jesus unto him, That thou doest, do quickly.

28 Now no man at the table knew for what intent he spake this unto him.

29 For some *of them* thought, because Judas had the [a]bag, that Jesus had said unto him, Buy *those things* that we have need of against the feast; or, that he should give something to the poor.

30 He then having received the sop went immediately out: and it was night.

31 ¶ Therefore, when he was gone out, Jesus said, Now is the [a]Son of man glorified, and God is glorified in him.

32 If God be glorified in him, God shall also glorify him in himself, and shall straightway glorify him.

33 Little children, yet a little while I am with you. Ye shall [a]seek me: and as I said unto the Jews, Whither I go, ye cannot come; so now I say to you.

34 A new commandment I give unto you, That ye [a]love one another; as I have loved you, that ye also [b]love one another.

35 By this shall all *men* know that ye are my disciples, if ye have [a]love one to another.

36 ¶ Simon Peter said unto him, Lord, whither goest thou? Jesus answered him, Whither I go, thou canst not follow me now; but thou shalt follow me afterwards.

37 Peter said unto him, Lord, why cannot I [a]follow thee now? I will lay down my life for thy sake.

38 Jesus answered him, Wilt thou lay down thy life for my sake? Verily, verily, I say unto thee, The cock shall not crow, till thou hast denied me thrice.

CHAPTER 14

Jesus speaks of many mansions—He says that He is the way, the truth, and the life and that to see Him is to see the Father—He promises the first and second Comforters.

LET not your heart be [a]troubled: ye believe in God, believe also in me.

2 In my Father's [a]house are many [b]mansions: if *it were* not *so*, I would have told you. I go to prepare a place for you.

3 And if I go and prepare a place for you, I will [a]come again, and receive you unto myself; that [b]where [c]I am, *there* ye may be also.

4 And whither I go ye know, and the way ye know.

5 Thomas saith unto him, Lord, we know not whither thou goest; and how can we know the way?

6 Jesus saith unto him, I am the [a]way, the [b]truth, and the life: no man [c]cometh unto the Father, but by me.

7 If ye had [a]known me, ye should have known my Father also: and from henceforth ye know him, and have seen him.

8 Philip saith unto him, Lord, shew us the Father, and it sufficeth us.

9 Jesus saith unto him, Have I been so long time with you, and yet hast thou not known me, Philip? he that hath seen me hath seen the [a]Father;

26*a* GR morsel, mouthful.
27*a* TG Devil.
29*a* John 12:6.
31*a* TG Jesus Christ, Son of Man.
33*a* John 7:34 (33–36).
34*a* TG Love.
b TG Family, Love within.
35*a* TG Fellowshipping; God, Love of.
37*a* TG Commitment.

14 1*a* D&C 50:41 (41–42).
2*a* TG Heaven.
b D&C 59:2; 98:18. TG Eternal Life; Telestial Glory.
3*a* Acts 1:11 (9–11).
b D&C 27:18; 132:23.
c 1 Thes. 4:17; Rev. 22:4 (3–5).
6*a* Ex. 18:20; 33:13; 1 Sam. 12:23 (16–23); Ps. 25:4; John 10:7 (1–15). TG Example.
b TG Truth.
c Matt. 11:27; Luke 10:22. TG God, Access to.
7*a* John 8:19; 1 Jn. 2:23; D&C 88:50.
9*a* TG God, Body of, Corporeal Nature.

and how sayest thou *then,* Shew us
the Father?
10 Believest thou not that I am in
the [a]Father, and the Father in me?
the words that I speak unto you I
speak not of myself: but the Father
that dwelleth in me, he doeth the
works.
11 Believe me that I *am* [a]in the
[b]Father, and the Father in me: or
else believe me for the very works'
sake.
12 Verily, verily, I say unto you, He
that [a]believeth on me, the works that
I do shall he do also; and greater
works than these shall he do; because I [b]go unto my [c]Father.
13 And whatsoever ye shall [a]ask in
my [b]name, that will I do, that the
Father may be glorified in the Son.
14 If ye shall ask any thing in my
name, I will do *it.*
15 ¶ If ye [a]love me, [b]keep my [c]com-
mandments.
16 And I will pray the Father, and
he shall give you another [a]Com-
forter, that he may [b]abide with you
for ever;
17 *Even* the Spirit of truth; whom
the world cannot receive, because
it seeth him not, neither knoweth
him: but ye know him; for he dwelleth with you, and shall be in you.
18 I will not leave you [a]comfort-
less: I will [b]come to you.
19 Yet a little while, and the world
seeth me no more; but ye see me:
because I live, ye shall live also.
20 At that day ye shall know that
I *am* in my Father, and ye in me,
and I in you.
21 He that hath my commandments, and [a]keepeth them, he it is
that loveth me: and he that loveth
me shall be [b]loved of my Father, and
I will love him, and will [c]manifest
myself to him.
22 Judas saith unto him, not
Iscariot, Lord, how is it that thou
wilt manifest thyself unto us, and
not unto the world?
23 Jesus answered and said unto
him, If a man love me, he will keep
my words: and my Father will
[a]love him, and we will come unto
him, and make our [b]abode with
him.
24 He that loveth me not keepeth
not my sayings: and the word which
ye hear is not mine, but the Father's
which sent me.
25 These things have I spoken unto
you, being *yet* present with you.
26 But the [a]Comforter, *which is* the
[b]Holy Ghost, whom the Father will
send in my [c]name, he shall [d]teach
you all things, and bring all things
to your remembrance, whatsoever
I have said unto you.
27 [a]Peace I leave with you, my
[b]peace I give unto you: not as the
world giveth, give I unto you. Let
not your heart be [c]troubled, neither
let it be afraid.
28 Ye have heard how I said unto
you, I go away, and come *again*
unto you. If ye loved me, ye would
rejoice, because I said, I [a]go unto

10*a* D&C 93:3.
11*a* D&C 50:43.
b TG Jesus Christ, Relationships with the Father.
12*a* Acts 9:41 (36–43); 4 Ne. 1:5 (5, 32–33). TG Faith.
b TG Jesus Christ, Ascension of.
c TG God the Father, Elohim.
13*a* D&C 6:14; 29:6. TG Prayer.
b TG Name.
15*a* TG God, Love of; God, the Standard of Righteousness; Love.
b TG Duty; Obedience.
c TG Commandments of God; Commitment; Good Works.
16*a* TG Holy Ghost, Comforter.
b D&C 20:77.
18*a* GR orphans. TG Comfort.
b John 16:32; 2 Tim. 4:17 (16–17). TG God, Privilege of Seeing.
21*a* TG Obedience.
b TG God, Love of.
c TG God, Privilege of Seeing; Revelation.
23*a* TG God, Love of.
b 1 Jn. 3:24; Rev. 3:20; D&C 130:3.
26*a* TG Holy Ghost, Comforter.
b TG Guidance, Divine.
c TG Name.
d TG God, Omniscience of; Holy Ghost, Gifts of; Holy Ghost, Mission of; Inspiration; Learn; Teaching.
27*a* TG Peace of God.
b TG Contentment; Peace.
c TG Sorrow.
28*a* TG Jesus Christ, Ascension of.

the Father: for my [b]Father is greater
than I.
29 And now I have told you before
it come to pass, that, when it is come
to pass, ye might [a]believe.
30 Hereafter I will not talk much
with you: [a]for the [b]prince of this
[c]world cometh, and hath nothing
in me.
31 But that the world may know
that I love the Father; and as the
Father gave me [a]commandment,
even so I do. Arise, let us go hence.

CHAPTER 15

Jesus is the vine; His disciples are the branches—He discourses on the perfect law of love—His servants have been chosen and ordained by Him—The world hates and fights true religion—He promises the Comforter, the Spirit of Truth.

I AM the true [a]vine, and my Father
is the husbandman.
2 Every [a]branch in me that beareth
not [b]fruit he taketh away: and every *branch* that beareth fruit, he
[c]purgeth it, that it may bring forth
more fruit.
3 Now ye are clean through the
word which I have spoken unto you.
4 [a]Abide in me, and I in you. As
the branch cannot bear fruit of itself, except it abide in the vine; no
more can ye, except ye abide in me.
5 I am the [a]vine, ye *are* the branches:
He that abideth in me, and I in him,
the same bringeth forth much
fruit: for without [b]me ye can do
nothing.
6 If a man [a]abide not in me, he
is cast forth as a branch, and is
withered; and men gather them,
and cast *them* into the fire, and they
are burned.
7 If ye [a]abide in me, and my words
abide in you, ye shall [b]ask what ye
will, and it shall be done unto you.
8 Herein is my Father [a]glorified,
that ye bear much fruit; so shall ye
be my disciples.
9 As the Father hath [a]loved me,
so have I loved you: continue ye in
my love.
10 If ye [a]keep my commandments,
ye shall abide in my [b]love; even as
I have kept my Father's commandments, and abide in his love.
11 These things have I spoken unto
you, that my joy might remain in
you, and *that* your [a]joy might be full.
12 This is my commandment,
That ye [a]love one another, as I have
[b]loved you.
13 Greater [a]love hath no man than
this, that a man lay down his [b]life
for his [c]friends.
14 Ye are my [a]friends, if ye do
whatsoever I [b]command you.
15 Henceforth I call you not servants; for the servant knoweth not
what his lord doeth: but I have
called you [a]friends; for all things
that I have [b]heard of my Father I
have made [c]known unto you.
16 Ye have not chosen me, but I
have [a]chosen you, and [b]ordained

28*b* TG Godhead.
29*a* TG Faith.
30*a* JST John 14:30 . . . for the prince *of darkness, who is* of this world, cometh, *but* hath *no power over me, but he hath power over you.*
b TG Devil.
c TG Worldliness.
31*a* TG Jesus Christ, Authority of.
15 1*a* Gen. 49:11; 1 Ne. 15:15.
2*a* Matt. 15:13 (13–14).
b Matt. 7:19 (15–20); Luke 3:9.
c GR purifies. TG Test.
4*a* 1 Jn. 2:6; D&C 35:18; 43:3; 50:24.
5*a* TG Vineyard of the Lord.
b Philip. 4:13.
6*a* Col. 1:23.
7*a* TG Problem-Solving.
b TG Prayer.
8*a* Isa. 49:3; Matt. 5:16.
9*a* TG God, Love of.
10*a* 1 Ne. 17:35; Mosiah 2:4; D&C 95:12. TG Obedience.
b TG Love.
11*a* TG Joy.
12*a* TG Love.
b D&C 6:20.
13*a* 1 Jn. 3:16 (10–18). TG Love.
b TG Life, Sanctity of; Martyrdom.
c TG Brotherhood and Sisterhood; Friendship.
14*a* D&C 84:63.
b TG Commandments of God.
15*a* Luke 12:4.
b John 16:12; 3 Ne. 15:16 (13–18).
c TG Revelation.
16*a* TG Apostles; Called of God; Election; Priesthood, Qualifying for.
b TG Authority; Church Organization; Priesthood, Authority; Priesthood, History of; Priesthood, Melchizedek.

you, that ye should go and bring
forth [c]fruit, and *that* your fruit
should remain: that whatsoever ye
shall ask of the Father in my [d]name,
he may give it you.
17 These things I command you,
that ye love one another.
18 If the world [a]hate you, ye know
that it hated me before *it hated* you.
19 If ye were of the [a]world, the
world would [b]love his own: but because ye are not of the world, but I
have chosen you out of the world,
therefore the world hateth you.
20 Remember the word that I said
unto you, The [a]servant is not greater
than his lord. If they have [b]perse-
cuted me, they will also persecute
you; if they have kept my saying,
they will keep yours also.
21 But all these things will they
do unto you for my name's sake,
because they know not him that
sent me.
22 If I had not come and spoken
unto them, they had not had [a]sin:
but now they have no [b]cloak for
their sin.
23 He that hateth me hateth my
Father also.
24 If I had not done among them
the works which none other man
did, they had not had [a]sin: but now
have they both seen and hated both
me and my Father.
25 But *this cometh to pass,* that the
word might be fulfilled that is written in their law, They [a]hated me
without a cause.
26 But when the [a]Comforter is
come, whom I will send unto you
from the Father, *even* the Spirit of
truth, which proceedeth from the
Father, he shall [b]testify of me:
27 And ye also shall bear [a]witness,
because ye have been with me from
the beginning.

CHAPTER 16

Jesus discourses on the mission of the Holy Ghost—He tells of His death and resurrection, announces that He is the Son of God, and says that He has overcome the world.

THESE things have I spoken unto
you, that ye should not be [a]offended.
2 They shall put you out of the
synagogues: yea, the time cometh,
that whosoever [a]killeth you will
think that he doeth God service.
3 And these things will they do
unto you, because they have not
[a]known the Father, nor me.
4 But these things have I told you,
that when the time shall come, ye
may remember that I told you of
them. And these things I said not
unto you at the beginning, because
I was with you.
5 But now I [a]go my way to him
that sent me; and none of you asketh me, Whither goest thou?
6 But because I have said these
things unto you, sorrow hath filled
your heart.
7 Nevertheless I tell you the truth;
It is [a]expedient for you that I go
away: for if I go not away, the [b]Com-
forter will not come unto you; but if
I depart, I will send him unto you.
8 And when he is come, he will
[a]reprove the world of sin, and of
[b]righteousness, and of judgment:
9 Of [a]sin, because they believe
not on me;
10 Of righteousness, because I go to
my Father, and ye see me no more;

16*c* TG Missionary Work; Mission of Early Saints.
d D&C 18:18.
18*a* TG Hate.
19*a* TG World; Worldliness.
b Luke 6:26.
20*a* Matt. 10:24 (24–25).
b D&C 6:29. TG Persecution.
22*a* John 9:41 (39–41); 2 Ne. 9:25 (25–27); D&C 82:3 (3–4).
b IE pretext, excuse.
24*a* Alma 32:19 (17–19).
25*a* TG Hate.
26*a* TG Comfort; Holy Ghost, Comforter.
b TG Holy Ghost, Mission of; Holy Ghost, Source of Testimony.
27*a* TG Witness.
16 1*a* TG Offense.
2*a* TG Persecution.
3*a* Moses 4:6.
5*a* Luke 5:35.
7*a* GR beneficial, profitable, advantageous.
b TG Holy Ghost, Comforter.
8*a* TG Holy Ghost, Mission of; Reproof.
b TG Righteousness.
9*a* TG Sin.

11 Of judgment, because the prince
of this world is judged.
12 I have yet many things to [a]say
unto you, but ye cannot [b]bear them
now.
13 Howbeit when he, the [a]Spirit of
truth, is come, he will [b]guide you
into all [c]truth: for he shall not speak
of himself; but whatsoever he shall
hear, *that* shall he speak: and he will
[d]shew you things to come.
14 He shall [a]glorify me: for he shall
receive of mine, and shall shew *it*
unto you.
15 All [a]things that the [b]Father hath
are mine: therefore said I, that he
shall take of mine, and shall shew
it unto you.
16 A little while, and ye shall not
see me: and again, a little while,
and ye shall [a]see me, because I go
to the Father.
17 Then said *some* of his disciples
among themselves, What is this that
he saith unto us, A little while, and
ye shall not see me: and again, a little while, and ye shall see me: and,
Because I go to the Father?
18 They said therefore, What is
this that he saith, A little while? we
cannot tell what he saith.
19 Now Jesus knew that they were
desirous to ask him, and said unto
them, Do ye inquire among yourselves of that I said, A little while,
and ye shall not see me: and again,
a little while, and ye shall see me?
20 Verily, verily, I say unto you,
That ye shall weep and lament,
but the world shall rejoice: and
ye shall be sorrowful, but your [a]sor-
row shall be turned into [b]joy.
21 A [a]woman when she is in travail hath sorrow, because her hour
is come: but as soon as she is delivered of the child, she remembereth
no more the anguish, for joy that a
man is born into the world.
22 And ye now therefore have [a]sor-
row: but I will see you again, and
your heart shall rejoice, and your
[b]joy no man taketh from you.
23 And in that day ye shall ask me
[a]nothing. Verily, verily, I say unto
you, Whatsoever ye shall [b]ask the
Father in my name, he will give *it*
you.
24 Hitherto have ye asked nothing in my name: [a]ask, and ye shall
receive, that your joy may be full.
25 These things have I spoken
unto you in [a]proverbs: but the time
cometh, when I shall no more speak
unto you in proverbs, but I shall
shew you plainly of the Father.
26 At that day ye shall ask in my
name: and I say not unto you, that
I will pray the Father for you:
27 For the Father himself [a]loveth
you, because ye have loved me,
and have [b]believed that I came out
from God.
28 I [a]came [b]forth from the [c]Father,
and am come into the world: again,
I leave the world, and go to the
Father.
29 His disciples said unto him,
Lo, now speakest thou plainly, and
speakest no proverb.
30 Now are we sure that thou
[a]knowest all things, and needest
not that any man should ask thee:
by this we believe that thou camest
forth from God.

12*a* John 15:15; 3 Ne. 15:16 (13–18).
b Heb. 5:11 (11–12); 3 Ne. 17:2 (2–4); D&C 50:40; 78:18 (17–18).
13*a* TG Conscience.
b TG God, Omniscience of; Holy Ghost, Gifts of; Holy Ghost, Mission of; Inspiration; Learn.
c TG God, Intelligence of; Truth.
d TG Revelation.
14*a* Acts 3:13.
TG Holy Ghost, Mission of.
15*a* 3 Ne. 28:10; D&C 76:59; 84:38 (37–38).
b TG Jesus Christ, Divine Sonship.
16*a* D&C 35:21; 38:8.
20*a* TG Pain; Patience.
b TG Joy.
21*a* TG Marriage, Motherhood.
22*a* TG Sorrow.
b TG Joy.
23*a* JST John 16:23 . . . *nothing but it shall be done unto you.* Verily, verily, I say . . .
b TG Prayer.
24*a* D&C 66:9.
25*a* GR figurative discourse, similitudes.
27*a* TG God, Love of.
b TG Faith.
28*a* John 8:42; 17:8; Gal. 4:4.
b John 8:14.
c TG Man, Antemortal Existence of.
30*a* TG God, Omniscience of; God, Perfection of.

31 Jesus answered them, Do ye now believe?

32 Behold, the hour cometh, yea, is now come, that ye shall be scattered, every man to his own, and shall leave me alone: and yet I am not [a]alone, because the Father is with me.

33 These things I have spoken unto you, that in me ye might have [a]peace. In the [b]world ye shall have [c]tribulation: but be of good [d]cheer; I have [e]overcome the world.

CHAPTER 17

Jesus offers the great Intercessory Prayer—He is glorified by gaining eternal life—He prays for His Apostles and all the Saints—He explains how the Father and Son are one.

THESE words spake Jesus, and lifted up his eyes to heaven, and said, Father, the hour is come; glorify thy [a]Son, that thy Son also may [b]glorify thee:

2 As thou hast given him [a]power over all flesh, that he should give [b]eternal life to as many as thou hast [c]given him.

3 And this is [a]life [b]eternal, that they might [c]know thee the only true [d]God, and Jesus Christ, whom thou hast [e]sent.

4 I have [a]glorified thee on the earth: I have [b]finished the work which thou gavest me to do.

5 And now, O Father, glorify thou me with thine own self with the [a]glory which I had with thee [b]before the world was.

6 I have manifested thy name unto the men which thou gavest me [a]out of the world: thine they were, and thou gavest them me; and they have kept thy word.

7 Now they have known that all things whatsoever thou hast [a]given me are of thee.

8 For I have given unto them the [a]words which thou gavest me; and they have received *them*, and have known surely that I [b]came out from thee, and they have [c]believed that thou didst send me.

9 I [a]pray for them: I pray not for the world, but for them which [b]thou hast given me; for they are thine.

10 And all mine are thine, and thine are mine; and I am glorified in them.

11 And now I am no more in the world, but these are in the [a]world, and I come to thee. Holy Father, keep through thine own name those whom thou hast given me, that they may be [b]one, as we *are*.

12 While I was with them in the world, I kept them in thy name: those that thou gavest me I have kept, and [a]none of them is [b]lost, but the son of [c]perdition; that the scripture might be fulfilled.

13 And now come I to thee; and

32*a* John 8:16, 29; 14:18.
33*a* TG Peace of God.
b TG Earth, Purpose of; World; Worldliness.
c TG Affliction; Test; Tribulation.
d TG Happiness.
e Rev. 12:11 (10–12); D&C 50:41; 76:107.
17 1*a* TG Jesus Christ, Divine Sonship.
b TG Jesus Christ, Mission of.
2*a* TG Jesus Christ, Authority of; Jesus Christ, Power of.
b John 6:37.
c John 10:29 (27–29); D&C 50:41.
3*a* TG Eternal Life.
b 1 Jn. 1:2; 2:25; D&C 132:24.
c Jer. 9:3; Hosea 2:20; 1 Jn. 4:8 (7–8); D&C 101:16. TG God, Knowledge about; Objectives; Testimony.
d TG Godhead.
e TG Jesus Christ, Messenger of the Covenant.
4*a* D&C 65:6; 76:43 (40–43).
b D&C 19:2. TG Jesus Christ, Atonement through.
5*a* TG Celestial Glory; Jesus Christ, Glory of.
b TG Jesus Christ, Foreordained; Man, Antemortal Existence of.
6*a* 1 Kgs. 8:53; 3 Ne. 15:19 (19–20).
7*a* TG Jesus Christ, Relationships with the Father.
8*a* Deut. 18:18; John 6:68. TG Revelation.
b John 8:42; 16:28 (27–28, 30); Gal. 4:4.
c TG Faith.
9*a* TG Prayer.
b D&C 27:14; 84:63.
11*a* TG Earth, Purpose of.
b TG Unity.
12*a* John 6:39; 18:9.
b D&C 50:42.
c 3 Ne. 27:32. TG Damnation; Death, Spiritual, Second; Hell.

these things I speak in the world, that they might have my [a]joy fulfilled in themselves.
14 I have given them thy word; and the world hath hated them, because they are not of the world, even as I am not of the world.
15 I pray not that thou shouldest take them out of the [a]world, but that thou shouldest [b]keep them from the [c]evil.
16 They are not of the [a]world, even as I am not of the world.
17 [a]Sanctify them through thy [b]truth: thy word is [c]truth.
18 As thou hast [a]sent me into the world, even so have I also sent them into the world.
19 And for their sakes I [a]sanctify myself, that they also might be sanctified through the truth.
20 Neither [a]pray I for these alone, but for them also which shall [b]believe on me through their word;
21 That they all may be [a]one; as thou, [b]Father, *art* in me, and I in thee, that they also may be [c]one in us: that the world may believe that thou hast sent me.
22 And the glory which thou gavest me I have given them; that they may be [a]one, even as we are [b]one:
23 I in them, and thou in me, that they may be made [a]perfect in one; and that the world may know that thou hast sent me, and hast [b]loved them, as thou hast loved me.
24 Father, I will that they also, whom thou hast given me, be with me where I am; that they may behold my glory, which thou hast given me: for thou lovedst me before the foundation of the world.
25 O righteous Father, the world hath not [a]known thee: but I have known thee, and these have known that thou hast sent me.
26 And I have [a]declared unto them thy [b]name, and will declare *it:* that the [c]love wherewith thou hast [d]loved me may be in them, and I in them.

CHAPTER 18

Jesus is betrayed and arrested—He is examined and maltreated first before Annas, then before Caiaphas—Peter denies knowing Jesus—Jesus is arraigned before Pilate.

WHEN Jesus had spoken these words, he went forth with his disciples over the brook Cedron, where was a garden, into the which he entered, and his disciples.
2 And Judas also, which betrayed him, knew the place: for Jesus ofttimes resorted thither with his disciples.
3 Judas then, having received a band *of men* and officers from the chief priests and Pharisees, cometh thither with lanterns and torches and weapons.
4 Jesus therefore, knowing all things that should come upon him, went forth, and said unto them, Whom seek ye?
5 They answered him, Jesus of Nazareth. Jesus saith unto them, I am *he.* And Judas also, which betrayed him, stood with them.
6 As soon then as he had said unto them, I am *he,* they went backward, and fell to the ground.
7 Then asked he them again, Whom seek ye? And they said, Jesus of Nazareth.
8 Jesus answered, I have told you that I am *he:* if therefore ye seek me, let these go their way:

13*a* TG Joy.
15*a* TG World.
b TG Refuge.
c TG Evil.
16*a* TG Worldliness.
17*a* TG Sanctification.
b Jacob 4:13.
c 2 Sam. 7:28; Ps. 119:142. TG Truth.
18*a* TG Jesus Christ, Authority of.
19*a* TG Jesus Christ, Atonement through.
20*a* TG Prayer.
b D&C 45:5.
21*a* 4 Ne. 1:17 (15–17); D&C 38:27.
b TG Godhead; God the Father, Elohim.
c D&C 35:2; Moses 6:68.
22*a* Gal. 2:20.
b D&C 93:3.
23*a* TG Perfection.
b TG God, Love of.
25*a* TG God, Knowledge about.
26*a* TG Preaching.
b TG Name.
c TG God, Love of.
d TG Jesus Christ, Relationships with the Father.

9 That the saying might be fulfilled,
which he spake, Of them which thou
gavest me have I lost [a]none.
10 Then Simon Peter having a
sword drew it, and smote the high
priest's servant, and [a]cut off his
right ear. The servant's name was
[b]Malchus.
11 Then said Jesus unto Peter, Put
up thy sword into the sheath: the
[a]cup which my Father hath given
me, shall I not drink it?
12 Then the band and the captain
and officers of the Jews took Jesus,
and bound him,
13 And led him away to [a]Annas
first; for he was father in law to
Caiaphas, which was the high priest
that same year.
14 Now [a]Caiaphas was he, which
gave counsel to the Jews, that it was
expedient that one man should die
for the people.
15 ¶ And Simon Peter followed
Jesus, and *so did* another disciple:
that disciple was known unto the
high priest, and went in with Jesus
into the palace of the high priest.
16 But Peter stood at the door
without. Then went out that other
disciple, which was known unto
the high priest, and spake unto her
that kept the door, and brought in
Peter.
17 Then saith the damsel that kept
the door unto Peter, Art not thou
also *one* of this man's disciples? He
saith, I am not.
18 And the servants and officers
stood there, who had made a fire
of coals; for it was cold: and they
warmed themselves: and Peter
stood with them, and warmed
himself.
19 ¶ The high [a]priest then asked
Jesus of his disciples, and of his
doctrine.
20 Jesus answered him, I spake
openly to the world; I ever taught in
the synagogue, and in the temple,
whither the Jews always resort; and
in secret have I said nothing.
21 Why askest thou me? ask them
which heard me, what I have said
unto them: behold, they know what
I said.
22 And when he had thus spoken,
one of the officers which stood by
[a]struck Jesus with the palm of his
hand, saying, Answerest thou the
high priest so?
23 Jesus answered him, If I have
spoken evil, bear witness of the evil:
but if well, why smitest thou me?
24 Now Annas had sent him bound
unto Caiaphas the high priest.
25 And Simon Peter stood and
warmed himself. They said therefore unto him, Art not thou also *one*
of his disciples? He denied *it*, and
said, I am not.
26 One of the servants of the high
priest, being *his* kinsman whose ear
Peter cut off, saith, Did not I see thee
in the garden with him?
27 Peter then denied again: and
immediately the cock crew.
28 ¶ Then led they Jesus from Caiaphas unto the hall of judgment: and
it was early; and they themselves
went not into the judgment hall,
lest they should be defiled; but that
they might eat the [a]passover.
29 [a]Pilate then went out unto them,
and said, What accusation bring ye
against this man?
30 They answered and said unto
him, If he were not a malefactor,
we would not have delivered him
up unto thee.
31 Then said Pilate unto them, Take
ye him, and judge him according to
your law. The Jews therefore said
unto him, It is not lawful for us to
put any man to death:
32 That the saying of Jesus might
be fulfilled, which he spake, signifying what death he should die.
33 Then Pilate entered into the
judgment hall again, and called

18 9*a* John 6:39; 17:12.
10*a* TG Rashness.
b Matt. 26:51.
11*a* 3 Ne. 11:11.
13*a* Matt. 26:57; Luke 3:2. TG Jesus Christ, Trials of.
14*a* John 19:11.
19*a* TG Jesus Christ, Trials of.
22*a* Acts 23:2.
28*a* John 19:14.
29*a* TG Jesus Christ, Trials of.

Jesus, and said unto him, Art thou
the King of the Jews?
34 Jesus answered him, Sayest thou
this thing of thyself, or did others
tell it thee of me?
35 Pilate answered, Am I a Jew?
Thine own nation and the chief
priests have delivered thee unto
me: what hast thou done?
36 Jesus answered, My [a]kingdom is
not of this [b]world: if my kingdom
were of this world, then would my
servants fight, that I should not be
delivered to the Jews: but now is my
kingdom not from hence.
37 [a]Pilate therefore said unto
him, Art thou a [b]king then? Jesus
answered, Thou sayest that I am a
[c]king. To this end was I born, and
for this cause came I into the world,
that I should bear witness unto the
[d]truth. Every one that is of the truth
heareth my voice.
38 Pilate saith unto him, What is
truth? And when he had [a]said this,
he went out again unto the Jews,
and saith unto them, I find in him
no [b]fault *at all.*
39 But ye have a custom, that I
should release unto you one at the
passover: will ye therefore that I release unto you the King of the Jews?
40 Then cried they all again, saying, Not this man, but Barabbas.
Now [a]Barabbas was a robber.

CHAPTER 19

Jesus is scourged and crucified—He places His mother in John's care—He dies and His side is pierced with a spear—He is buried in the tomb of Joseph of Arimathæa.

THEN Pilate therefore took Jesus,
and [a]scourged *him.*
2 And the soldiers plaited a crown
of thorns, and put *it* on his head,
and they put on him a purple robe,
3 And said, Hail, [a]King of the
Jews! and they smote him with
their hands.
4 Pilate therefore went forth again,
and saith unto them, Behold, I bring
him forth to you, that ye may know
that I find no [a]fault in him.
5 Then came Jesus forth, wearing
the crown of thorns, and the purple
robe. And *Pilate* saith unto them,
Behold the man!
6 When the chief priests therefore
and officers saw him, they [a]cried
out, saying, Crucify *him,* crucify
him. Pilate saith unto them, Take
ye him, and crucify *him:* for I find
no [b]fault in him.
7 The Jews answered him, We have
a [a]law, and by our law he ought to
die, because he made himself the
[b]Son of God.
8 ¶ When Pilate therefore heard
that saying, he was the more afraid;
9 And went again into the judgment hall, and saith unto Jesus,
Whence art thou? But Jesus gave
him no [a]answer.
10 Then saith Pilate unto him,
Speakest thou not unto me? knowest thou not that I have power to
crucify thee, and have power to
release thee?
11 Jesus answered, Thou couldest
have no [a]power *at all* against me, except it were given thee from above:
therefore he that delivered me unto
thee hath the greater [b]sin.
12 And from thenceforth Pilate
sought to release him: but the Jews
cried out, saying, If thou let this
man go, thou art not Cæsar's friend:
whosoever maketh himself a [a]king
speaketh against Cæsar.
13 ¶ When Pilate therefore heard

36*a* John 6:15.
b TG World.
37*a* 1 Tim. 6:13.
b Isa. 55:4.
c John 19:12 (11–13).
d 3 Ne. 11:31 (31–41). TG Truth.
38*a* GR said this again.
b Matt. 27:24 (11–26); John 19:4.
40*a* Luke 23:19.
19 1*a* Mosiah 15:5.
3*a* D&C 45:53.
4*a* GR cause, crime, case. John 18:38; Mosiah 14:9.
6*a* Acts 3:13.
b GR cause, crime, motive.
7*a* Lev. 24:16.
b John 5:18 (17–18); 10:33; Mosiah 15:2.
9*a* Mosiah 14:7; 15:6.
11*a* Rom. 13:1; D&C 134:1.
b John 18:14.
12*a* John 18:37 (33, 36–37).

that saying, he brought Jesus forth,
and sat down in the judgment seat
in a place that is called the Pavement, but in the Hebrew, Gabbatha.
14 And it was the preparation of
the [a]passover, and about the sixth
hour: and he saith unto the Jews,
Behold your [b]King!
15 But they cried out, Away with
him, away with *him*, [a]crucify him.
Pilate saith unto them, Shall I crucify your King? The chief priests
answered, We have no [b]king but
Cæsar.
16 Then delivered he him therefore unto them to be crucified. And
they took Jesus, and led *him* away.
17 And he [a]bearing his [b]cross went
forth into a place called *the place* of
a [c]skull, which is called in the Hebrew Golgotha:
18 Where they crucified him, and
two other with him, on either side
one, and Jesus in the midst.
19 ¶ And Pilate wrote a title, and
put *it* on the cross. And the writing
was, JESUS OF NAZARETH THE
KING OF THE JEWS.
20 This title then read many of
the Jews: for the place where Jesus
was crucified was nigh to the city:
and it was written in Hebrew, *and*
Greek, *and* Latin.
21 Then said the chief priests of
the Jews to Pilate, Write not, The
King of the Jews; but that he said,
I am King of the Jews.
22 Pilate answered, What I have
written I have written.
23 ¶ Then the soldiers, when they
had crucified Jesus, took his garments, and made four parts, to every
soldier a part; and also *his* coat: now
the coat was without seam, woven
from the top throughout.
24 They said therefore among
themselves, Let us not rend it, but
cast lots for it, whose it shall be:
that the scripture might be fulfilled,
which saith, They parted my [a]raiment among them, and for my vesture they did cast lots. These things
therefore the soldiers did.
25 ¶ Now there stood by the cross
of Jesus his [a]mother, and his mother's
sister, Mary the *wife* of [b]Cleophas,
and Mary Magdalene.
26 When Jesus therefore saw his
mother, and the [a]disciple standing by, whom he loved, he saith
unto his mother, [b]Woman, behold
thy son!
27 Then saith he to the disciple,
Behold thy [a]mother! And from that
hour that disciple took her unto his
own *home*.
28 ¶ After this, Jesus knowing that
all things were now accomplished,
that the scripture might be fulfilled,
saith, I thirst.
29 Now there was set a vessel full
of vinegar: and they filled a sponge
with [a]vinegar, and put *it* upon hyssop, and put *it* to his mouth.
30 When Jesus therefore had received the vinegar, he said, It is
[a]finished: and he bowed his head,
and gave up the ghost.
31 The Jews therefore, because it
was the preparation, that the bodies
should not remain upon the [a]cross
on the sabbath day, (for that [b]sabbath day was an [c]high [d]day,) besought Pilate that their legs might be

---

14*a* John 18:28. TG Passover.
b D&C 45:53.
15*a* TG Jesus Christ, Trials of.
b 2 Ne. 10:14.
17*a* Gen. 22:6.
b Luke 14:27.
c JST John 19:17 . . . *burial* . . . Heb. 13:12 (11–16).
24*a* Ps. 22:18.
25*a* Luke 2:35 (34–35). TG Marriage, Motherhood.
b Luke 24:18.
26*a* John 20:2 (2–9); D&C 7:1.
b TG Woman.
27*a* TG Family, Love within; Honoring Father and Mother; Jesus Christ, Family of.
29*a* Ps. 69:21.
30*a* TG Jesus Christ, Atonement through.
31*a* TG Jesus Christ, Crucifixion of.
b Ex. 12:16 (15–17).
c Jesus arose on the first day of the week. The previous day was the weekly Sabbath. The day before the Sabbath, being also the day after the Passover meal, could be the "high" day. Ex. 12:16; Lev. 23:7; Mark 15:42.
d Ex. 12:14 (12–16).

[e]broken, and *that* they might be taken away.

32 Then came the soldiers, and brake the legs of the first, and of the other which was crucified with him.

33 But when they came to Jesus, and saw that he was dead already, they [a]brake not his legs:

34 But one of the soldiers with a spear pierced his side, and forthwith came there out blood and water.

35 And he that [a]saw *it* bare [b]record, and his record is true: and he knoweth that he saith true, that ye might believe.

36 For these things were done, that the scripture should be fulfilled, A [a]bone of him shall not be broken.

37 And again another scripture saith, They shall look on him whom they [a]pierced.

38 ¶ And after this [a]Joseph of Arimathæa, being a disciple of Jesus, but secretly for [b]fear of the Jews, besought Pilate that he might take away the body of Jesus: and Pilate gave *him* leave. He came therefore, and took the body of Jesus.

39 And there came also [a]Nicodemus, which at the first came to Jesus by night, and brought a mixture of [b]myrrh and aloes, about an hundred pound *weight*.

40 Then took they the body of Jesus, and wound it in linen clothes with the spices, as the manner of the Jews is to bury.

41 Now in the place where he was crucified there was a garden; and in the garden a new [a]sepulchre, wherein was never man yet laid.

42 There laid they Jesus therefore because of the Jews' [a]preparation *day*; for the sepulchre was nigh at hand.

CHAPTER 20

Mary Magdalene, Peter, and John find the empty tomb—The risen Christ appears to Mary Magdalene in the garden—He appears to the disciples and shows His resurrected body—Thomas feels the wounds in Jesus' hands, feet, and side—Jesus is the Christ, the Son of God.

THE [a]first *day* of the week cometh Mary Magdalene early, when it was yet [b]dark, unto the sepulchre, and seeth the [c]stone taken away from the [d]sepulchre.

2 Then she runneth, and cometh to Simon Peter, and to the other [a]disciple, whom Jesus loved, and saith unto them, They have taken away the [b]Lord out of the sepulchre, and we know not where they have laid him.

3 Peter therefore went forth, and that other disciple, and came to the sepulchre.

4 So they ran both together: and the other disciple did outrun Peter, and came first to the sepulchre.

5 And he stooping down, *and looking in,* saw the linen clothes lying; yet went he not in.

6 Then cometh Simon Peter following him, and went into the sepulchre, and seeth the linen clothes lie,

7 And the [a]napkin, that was about his head, not lying with the linen clothes, but wrapped together in a place by itself.

8 Then went in also that other disciple, which came first to the sepulchre, and he saw, and believed.

9 For as yet they knew not the scripture, that he must [a]rise again from the [b]dead.

10 Then the disciples went away again unto their own home.

31*e* Deut. 21:23 (22–23).
33*a* TG Jesus Christ, Types of, in Anticipation; Passover.
35*a* John 1:14; 21:24.
b John 1:7 (6–8).
36*a* Ex. 12:46; Num. 9:12.
37*a* TG Jesus Christ, Crucifixion of.
38*a* Matt. 27:57 (57–61).
b Prov. 29:25; John 7:13; 12:42 (42–43).
39*a* John 3:1 (1–10).
b Ps. 45:8.
41*a* Luke 23:53; 2 Ne. 25:13.
42*a* TG Passover.
20 1*a* TG Sabbath.
b Mark 16:2.
c Matt. 27:60.
d JST John 20:1 . . . sepulcher, *and two angels sitting thereon.*
2*a* John 13:23; 19:26 (26–27); 21:24 (20–24); 1 Ne. 14:27 (18–27); D&C 7:1.
b TG Jesus Christ, Lord.
7*a* John 11:44.
9*a* Mark 9:10 (9–10); Hel. 14:16 (15–17); D&C 18:12 (11–12).
b Isa. 25:8.

11 ¶ But Mary stood without at
the sepulchre weeping: and as she
wept, she stooped down, *and looked*
into the sepulchre,
12 And seeth two [a]angels in white
sitting, the one at the head, and the
other at the feet, where the body of
Jesus had lain.
13 And they say unto her, Woman,
why weepest thou? She saith unto
them, Because they have taken away
my Lord, and I know not where they
have laid him.
14 And when she had thus said,
she turned herself back, and [a]saw
Jesus standing, and knew not that
it was Jesus.
15 Jesus saith unto her, Woman,
why weepest thou? whom seekest
thou? She, supposing him to be
the gardener, saith unto him, Sir,
if thou have borne him hence, tell
me where thou hast laid him, and
I will take him away.
16 Jesus saith unto her, Mary. She
turned herself, and saith unto him,
Rabboni; which is to say, [a]Master.
17 Jesus saith unto her, [a]Touch me
not; for I am not yet [b]ascended to
my [c]Father: but go to my brethren,
and say unto them, I ascend unto
my [d]Father, and your Father; and
to my God, and your God.
18 Mary Magdalene came and told
the disciples that she had seen the
Lord, and *that* he had spoken these
things unto her.
19 ¶ Then the same day at evening, being the first *day* of the week,
when the doors were shut where the
disciples were [a]assembled for fear
of the Jews, came Jesus and [b]stood
in the midst, and saith unto them,
[c]Peace *be* unto you.
20 And when he had so said, he
shewed unto them *his* [a]hands and
his side. Then were the disciples
glad, when they [b]saw the Lord.
21 Then said Jesus to them again,
Peace *be* unto you: as *my* [a]Father
hath [b]sent me, even so [c]send I you.
22 And when he had said this, he
breathed on *them*, and saith unto
them, Receive ye the Holy Ghost:
23 Whose soever sins ye [a]remit,
they are remitted unto them; *and*
whose soever *sins* ye retain, they
are retained.
24 ¶ But Thomas, one of the twelve,
called Didymus, was not with them
when Jesus came.
25 The other disciples therefore
said unto him, We have seen the
Lord. But he said unto them, Except
I shall see in his hands the [a]print
of the nails, and put my finger into
the print of the nails, and thrust my
hand into his side, I will not believe.
26 ¶ And after eight days again his
disciples were within, and Thomas
with them: *then* came Jesus, the doors
being shut, and stood in the midst,
and said, Peace *be* unto you.
27 Then saith he to Thomas, Reach
hither thy finger, and behold my
hands; and reach hither thy hand,
and [a]thrust *it* into my side: and be
not [b]faithless, but [c]believing.
28 And Thomas answered and said
unto him, My Lord and my God.
29 Jesus saith unto him, Thomas,
because thou hast [a]seen me, thou
hast believed: [b]blessed *are* they that
have not seen, and *yet* have [c]believed.

12*a* TG Angels.
14*a* TG Jesus Christ, Appearances, Postmortal.
16*a* GR Teacher.
17*a* JST John 20:17 . . . *Hold me not . . .*
b Luke 23:43 (39–43); Alma 40:11 (6–15). TG Jesus Christ, Ascension of.
c TG God the Father, Elohim.
d TG Godhead.
19*a* TG Assembly for Worship; Meetings.
b TG Jesus Christ, Appearances, Postmortal.
c TG Peace of God.
20*a* TG Jesus Christ, Resurrection.
b TG Jesus Christ, Appearances, Postmortal.
21*a* TG Jesus Christ, Divine Sonship.
b TG Jesus Christ, Authority of.
c Mark 16:15 (14–18). TG Authority.
23*a* TG Priesthood, Keys of; Remission of Sins.
25*a* TG Jesus Christ, Crucifixion of.
27*a* 3 Ne. 11:14.
b TG Doubt.
c TG Unbelief.
29*a* TG Jesus Christ, Appearances, Postmortal.
b D&C 34:4.
c 1 Pet. 1:8; Alma 32:21 (17–21). TG Faith.

30 ¶ And many other [a]signs truly
did Jesus in the presence of his
disciples, which are not [b]written
in this book:
31 But these are [a]written, that
ye might [b]believe that Jesus is the
[c]Christ, the Son of God; and that believing ye might have [d]life through
his [e]name.

CHAPTER 21

Jesus appears to the disciples at the sea of Tiberias—He says, Feed my sheep—He foretells Peter's martyrdom and that John will not die.

AFTER these things Jesus [a]shewed
himself again to the disciples at the
sea of Tiberias; and on this wise
shewed he *himself.*
2 There were together Simon Peter,
and Thomas called Didymus, and
Nathanael of Cana in Galilee, and
the *sons* of [a]Zebedee, and two other
of his disciples.
3 Simon Peter saith unto them, I
go a fishing. They say unto him, We
also go with thee. They went forth,
and entered into a ship immediately; and that night they caught
nothing.
4 But when the morning was now
come, Jesus [a]stood on the shore:
but the disciples knew not that it
was Jesus.
5 Then Jesus saith unto them,
Children, have ye any meat? They
answered him, No.
6 And he said unto them, Cast the
net on the right side of the ship, and
ye shall find. They cast therefore,
and now they were not able to draw
it for the multitude of fishes.
7 Therefore that disciple whom
Jesus loved saith unto Peter, It is
the Lord. Now when Simon Peter
heard that it was the Lord, he girt
his fisher's coat *unto him,* (for he
was naked,) and did cast himself
into the sea.
8 And the other disciples came
in a little ship; (for they were not
far from land, but as it were two
hundred cubits,) dragging the net
with fishes.
9 As soon then as they were come to
land, they saw a fire of coals there,
and fish laid thereon, and bread.
10 Jesus saith unto them, Bring of
the fish which ye have now caught.
11 Simon Peter went up, and drew
the net to land full of great fishes,
an hundred and fifty and three: and
for all there were so many, yet was
not the net broken.
12 Jesus saith unto them, Come
and dine. And none of the disciples
durst ask him, Who art thou? knowing that it was the Lord.
13 Jesus then cometh, and taketh
bread, and giveth them, and fish
likewise.
14 This is now the [a]third time that
Jesus [b]shewed himself to his disciples, after that he was risen from
the dead.
15 ¶ So when they had dined,
Jesus saith to Simon Peter, Simon,
son of Jonas, lovest thou me more
than these? He saith unto him,
Yea, Lord; thou knowest that I love
thee. He saith unto him, Feed my
lambs.
16 He saith to him again the second time, Simon, *son* of Jonas, lovest thou me? He saith unto him,
Yea, Lord; thou knowest that I love
thee. He saith unto him, [a]Feed my
sheep.
17 He saith unto him the third
time, Simon, *son* of Jonas, lovest
thou me? Peter was grieved because he said unto him the third
time, Lovest thou me? And he said

30*a* TG Signs.
b John 21:25; 1 Ne. 14:25 (18–30); D&C 93:6 (6, 18).
31*a* 1 Jn. 5:13 (10–21).
b Luke 1:4 (3–4); John 1:7 (6–8); 1 Ne. 6:4; Morm. 5:14. TG Faith.
c TG Jesus Christ, Messiah.
d John 5:24.
e TG Jesus Christ, Taking the Name of; Name.
21 1*a* TG Jesus Christ, Resurrection.
2*a* Matt. 4:21.
4*a* TG Jesus Christ, Appearances, Postmortal.
14*a* 3 Ne. 26:13; 27:2.
b TG Jesus Christ, Appearances, Postmortal.
16*a* 1 Pet. 5:2; D&C 112:14.

unto him, Lord, thou knowest all things; thou knowest that I love thee. Jesus saith unto him, [a]Feed my [b]sheep.

18 Verily, verily, I say unto thee, When thou wast young, thou girdedst thyself, and walkedst whither thou wouldest: but when thou shalt be [a]old, thou shalt stretch forth thy hands, and another shall gird thee, and carry *thee* whither thou wouldest not.

19 This spake he, signifying by what [a]death he should glorify God. And when he had spoken this, he saith unto him, Follow me.

20 Then Peter, turning about, seeth the disciple whom Jesus loved following; which also leaned on his breast at supper, and said, Lord, which is he that betrayeth thee?

21 Peter seeing him saith to Jesus, Lord, and what *shall* this man *do?*

22 Jesus saith unto him, If I will that he [a]tarry till I come, what *is that* to thee? [b]follow thou me.

23 Then went this saying abroad among the brethren, that that disciple should not [a]die: yet Jesus said not unto him, He shall not die; but, If I will that he tarry till I come, what *is that* to thee?

24 This is the [a]disciple which testifieth of these things, and [b]wrote these things: and we know that his testimony is [c]true.

25 And there are also many other things which Jesus did, the which, if they should be [a]written every one, I suppose that even the world itself could not contain the [b]books that should be written. Amen.

THE ACTS OF THE APOSTLES

CHAPTER 1

Jesus ministers for forty days after His resurrection—The kingdom is to be restored to Israel at a later time—The Twelve are to bear witness in Jerusalem, Judæa, Samaria, and the uttermost parts of the earth—Jesus ascends into heaven—Matthias is chosen to fill the vacancy in the Twelve.

THE former treatise have [a]I made, O [b]Theophilus, of all that Jesus began both to do and teach,

2 Until the day in which he was taken up, after that he through the Holy Ghost had given [a]commandments unto the apostles whom he had chosen:

3 To whom also he [a]shewed himself

17*a* TG Fellowshipping; Jesus Christ, Teaching Mode of; Missionary Work.
b TG Sheep.
18*a* TG Old Age.
19*a* 2 Pet. 1:14.
22*a* Rev. 10:11; D&C 7:3 (3–4). TG Translated Beings.
b TG Jesus Christ, Exemplar.
23*a* Luke 9:27.
24*a* John 1:14; 13:23; 19:35; 20:2.
b TG Scriptures, Writing of.
c 3 Ne. 8:1.
25*a* John 20:30 (30–31); 1 Ne. 14:25 (18–30).
b 3 Ne. 26:6.

[ACTS]

1 1*a* 2 Tim. 4:11 (10–11).
b Luke 1:3.
2*a* TG Holy Ghost, Mission of.
3*a* TG Jesus Christ, Appearances, Postmortal; Jesus Christ, Resurrection.

alive after his [b]passion by many in-
fallible proofs, being seen of them
forty days, and speaking of the things
[c]pertaining to the kingdom of God:
4 And, being assembled together
with *them*, commanded them that
they should not depart from Jerusalem, but wait for the [a]promise of
the Father, which, *saith he,* ye have
heard of me.
5 For John truly baptized with water; but ye shall be [a]baptized with
the Holy Ghost not many days hence.
6 When they therefore were come
together, they asked of him, saying,
Lord, wilt thou at this time [a]restore
again the kingdom to Israel?
7 And he said unto them, It is not
for you to know the times or the
[a]seasons, which the Father hath put
in his own power.
8 But ye shall receive [a]power, after
that the Holy Ghost is come upon
you: and ye shall be [b]witnesses unto
me both in Jerusalem, and in all
Judæa, and in [c]Samaria, and unto
the uttermost part of the earth.
9 And when he had spoken these
things, while they beheld, he was
[a]taken [b]up; and a cloud received
him out of their sight.
10 And while they looked steadfastly toward heaven as he went up,
behold, two men stood by them in
white apparel;
11 Which also said, Ye men of Galilee, why stand ye gazing up into
[a]heaven? this same Jesus, which is
[b]taken up from you into heaven,
shall so [c]come in like [d]manner as
ye have seen him go into heaven.
12 Then returned they unto Jerusalem from the mount called Olivet,
which is from Jerusalem a sabbath
day's journey.
13 And when they were come in,
they went up into an upper room,
where abode both Peter, and James,
and John, and Andrew, Philip, and
Thomas, Bartholomew, and Matthew, James *the son* of Alphæus, and
Simon Zelotes, and Judas *the brother*
of James.
14 These all continued with [a]one
accord in prayer and [b]supplication,
with the women, and Mary the mother of Jesus, and with his [c]brethren.
15 ¶ And in those days Peter stood
up in the midst of the disciples, and
said, (the number of names together
were about an hundred and twenty,)
16 Men *and* brethren, this scripture must needs have been fulfilled,
which the Holy Ghost by the mouth
of David [a]spake before concerning
[b]Judas, which was guide to them
that took Jesus.
17 For he was numbered with
us, and had obtained part of this
ministry.
18 Now this man purchased a field
with the reward of iniquity; and
falling headlong, he [a]burst asunder in the midst, and all his bowels
gushed out.
19 And it was known unto all the
dwellers at Jerusalem; insomuch as
that field is called in their [a]proper
tongue, Aceldama, that is to say,
The field of blood.
20 For it is written in the book of
Psalms, Let his habitation be [a]deso-
late, and let no man dwell therein:
and his [b]bishoprick let another take.

3*b* GR suffering. JST Acts 1:3 . . . *sufferings* . . .
c D&C 100:11.
4*a* D&C 95:9 (8–10). TG Promise.
5*a* TG Holy Ghost, Baptism of; Holy Ghost, Gift of.
6*a* TG Dispensations.
7*a* Dan. 2:21 (19–22, 28); D&C 68:11 (7–12); 121:12 (12, 27, 31).
8*a* 2 Tim. 1:7. TG Holy Ghost, Gifts of.
b Luke 24:48; D&C 27:12.
c Acts 8:5 (5, 14).
9*a* 3 Ne. 10:18 (18–19); 11:8 (8–10). TG Jesus Christ, Resurrection.
b Ps. 68:18; Eph. 4:8.
11*a* 1 Thes. 1:10.
b TG Jesus Christ, Ascension of.
c John 14:3 (1–4).
d TG Jesus Christ, Second Coming.
14*a* TG Unity.
b Moro. 6:5 (1–5).
c TG Jesus Christ, Family of.
16*a* TG Holy Ghost, Mission of.
b Ps. 41:9; Luke 22:48 (47–48).
18*a* Matt. 27:5 (3–10).
19*a* GR own.
20*a* Ps. 69:25.
b GR overseership, office. Ps. 109:8; D&C 114:2.

21 Wherefore of these men which have companied with us all the time that the Lord Jesus went in and out among us,

22 Beginning from the baptism of John, unto that same day that he was taken up from us, must one [a]be ordained to be a [b]witness with us of his [c]resurrection.

23 And they appointed two, Joseph called Barsabas, who was surnamed Justus, and Matthias.

24 And they [a]prayed, and said, Thou, Lord, which [b]knowest the hearts of all *men*, shew [c]whether of these two thou hast [d]chosen,

25 That he may take part of this ministry and [a]apostleship, from which Judas by transgression [b]fell, that he might go to his own place.

26 And they gave forth their lots; and the lot fell upon [a]Matthias; and he was numbered with the eleven apostles.

CHAPTER 2

The Spirit is poured out on the day of Pentecost—Peter testifies of Jesus' resurrection—He tells how to gain salvation and speaks of the gift of the Holy Ghost—Many believe and are baptized.

AND when the day of [a]Pentecost was fully come, they were all with one accord in one place.

2 And suddenly there came a sound from heaven as of a rushing mighty [a]wind, and it filled all the house where they were sitting.

3 And there appeared unto them [a]cloven tongues like as of fire, and it sat upon each of them.

4 And they were all filled with the [a]Holy Ghost, and began to speak with other [b]tongues, as the [c]Spirit gave them utterance.

5 And there were dwelling at Jerusalem Jews, devout men, out of every nation under heaven.

6 Now when this was noised abroad, the multitude came together, and were confounded, because that every man heard them speak in his own [a]language.

7 And they were all amazed and marvelled, saying one to another, Behold, are not all these which speak Galilæans?

8 And how hear we every man in our own tongue, wherein we were born?

9 Parthians, and Medes, and Elamites, and the dwellers in Mesopotamia, and in Judæa, and Cappadocia, in Pontus, and Asia,

10 Phrygia, and Pamphylia, in Egypt, and in the parts of Libya about Cyrene, and strangers of Rome, Jews and [a]proselytes,

11 Cretes and Arabians, we do hear them speak in our [a]tongues the wonderful works of God.

12 And they were all amazed, and were in doubt, saying one to another, What meaneth this?

13 Others [a]mocking said, These men are full of new wine.

14 ¶ But Peter, standing up with the eleven, lifted up his voice, and said unto them, Ye men of Judæa, and all *ye* that dwell at Jerusalem, be this known unto you, and hearken to my words:

15 For these are not drunken, as ye suppose, seeing it is *but* the third hour of the day.

16 But this is that which was spoken by the prophet [a]Joel;

17 And it shall come to pass in the [a]last days, saith God, I will [b]pour out of my [c]Spirit upon all flesh: and your

---

22*a* GR become a witness.
b TG Witness.
c TG Resurrection.
24*a* D&C 9:8 (7–9).
b TG God, Omniscience of.
c GR which one.
d TG Called of God.
25*a* TG Church Organization.
b 1 Cor. 10:12; D&C 3:9.
26*a* TG Apostles.

2 1*a* Ex. 23:17; 34:22 (16, 22); Lev. 23:16 (15–16); Acts 20:16.
2*a* D&C 109:37.
3*a* D&C 109:36.
4*a* Acts 4:31. TG Holy Ghost, Baptism of.
b TG Holy Ghost, Gifts of; Holy Ghost, Mission of.
c D&C 14:8.
6*a* TG Language.
10*a* Acts 13:43.
11*a* 1 Cor. 14:22.
13*a* 1 Cor. 14:23.
16*a* JS—H 1:41.
17*a* TG Last Days.
b Joel 2:28.
c Isa. 44:3; Ezek. 36:27 (26–27); D&C 19:38; 44:2; 95:4.

sons and your daughters shall
[d]prophesy, and your young men
shall see visions, and your old men
shall [e]dream dreams:
18 And on my servants and on
my handmaidens I will pour out in
those days of my Spirit; and they
shall [a]prophesy:
19 And I will shew [a]wonders in
heaven above, and [b]signs in the
earth beneath; blood, and fire, and
vapour of smoke:
20 The sun shall be turned into
[a]darkness, and the moon into blood,
before that great and [b]notable [c]day
of the Lord come:
21 And it shall come to pass, *that*
whosoever shall call on the name
of the Lord shall be [a]saved.
22 Ye men of Israel, hear these
words; Jesus of Nazareth, a man
[a]approved of God among you by
[b]miracles and wonders and signs,
which [c]God did by him in the
midst of you, as ye yourselves also
know:
23 Him, being delivered by the
[a]determinate counsel and [b]fore-
knowledge of God, ye have taken,
and by wicked hands have [c]cruci-
fied and slain:
24 Whom God hath [a]raised up,
having loosed the [b]pains of [c]death:
because it was not possible that he
should be holden of it.
25 For David speaketh concerning him, I foresaw the [a]Lord always before my face, for he is on
my right hand, that I should not be
moved:
26 Therefore did my heart rejoice,
and my tongue was glad; moreover
also my flesh shall rest in hope:
27 Because thou wilt not leave
my soul in [a]hell, neither wilt
thou suffer thine Holy One to see
[b]corruption.
28 Thou hast made known to me
the ways of life; thou shalt make me
full of joy with thy countenance.
29 Men *and* brethren, let me freely
speak unto you of the [a]patriarch
David, that he is both dead and
[b]buried, and his sepulchre is with
us unto this day.
30 Therefore being a prophet, and
knowing that God had sworn with
an [a]oath to him, that of the fruit
of his loins, according to the flesh,
he would raise up [b]Christ to sit on
his throne;
31 He seeing this before spake of
the resurrection of Christ, that his
soul was not left in hell, neither his
flesh did see corruption.
32 This Jesus hath God [a]raised up,
whereof we all are [b]witnesses.
33 Therefore being [a]by the [b]right
hand of God [c]exalted, and having
received of the Father the promise
of the Holy Ghost, he hath [d]shed
forth this, which ye now see and
hear.
34 For [a]David is not [b]ascended into
the heavens: but he saith himself,
The LORD said unto my [c]Lord, Sit
thou on my right hand,
35 Until I make thy foes thy footstool.
36 Therefore let all the house of Israel know assuredly, that God hath
made that same Jesus, whom ye

17*d* Acts 21:9.
TG Holy Ghost, Gifts of.
e TG Dream.
18*a* Acts 11:28 (27–28);
21:11 (4, 10–11).
19*a* TG Last Days.
b TG Signs.
20*a* TG Darkness, Physical.
b GR glorious.
c TG Day of the Lord.
21*a* TG Jesus Christ, Savior;
Salvation.
22*a* John 9:33 (31–33).
b Mosiah 3:5 (5–6).
c Ex. 8:19;
Luke 11:20;
John 3:2;
Acts 10:38.
23*a* GR appointed plan,
purpose.
b TG Foreordination;
God, Foreknowledge of.
c Matt. 26:24;
Luke 22:22.
TG Jesus Christ,
Crucifixion of.
24*a* TG Resurrection.
b TG Pain.
c TG Jesus Christ, Death of.
25*a* Ps. 16:8 (8–11).
27*a* JST Acts 2:27 . . . *prison* . . .
b Acts 13:37 (34–37).
29*a* TG Patriarch.
b 1 Kgs. 2:10.
30*a* TG Oath.
b TG Jesus Christ, Davidic
Descent of.
32*a* Eph. 1:20.
TG Jesus Christ,
Resurrection.
b TG Witness.
33*a* GR to, at.
b TG Godhead.
c Heb. 2:9.
d D&C 53:2.
34*a* D&C 132:39.
b Ps. 30:3; 86:13.
c Ps. 110:1.

have [a]crucified, both [b]Lord and Christ.

37 ¶ Now when they heard *this*, they were [a]pricked in their [b]heart, and said unto Peter and to the rest of the apostles, Men *and* brethren, [c]what shall we do?

38 Then Peter [a]said unto them, [b]Repent, and be [c]baptized every one of you in the [d]name of Jesus Christ for the [e]remission of sins, and ye shall receive the [f]gift of the [g]Holy Ghost.

39 For the [a]promise is unto you, and to your children, and to all that are [b]afar off, *even* as many as the Lord our God shall call.

40 And with many other words did he testify and exhort, saying, [a]Save yourselves from this [b]untoward generation.

41 ¶ Then they that gladly [a]received his [b]word were baptized: and the same day there were added *unto them* about [c]three thousand souls.

42 And they continued [a]steadfastly in the apostles' doctrine and [b]fellowship, and in breaking of [c]bread, and in prayers.

43 And [a]fear came upon every soul: and many wonders and [b]signs were done by the apostles.

44 And all that believed were together, and had all things [a]common;

45 And sold their possessions and goods, and parted them to all *men*, as every man had [a]need.

46 And they, continuing daily with one accord in the [a]temple, and breaking bread from house to house, did eat their meat with gladness and [b]singleness of heart,

47 Praising God, and having favour with all the people. And the Lord [a]added to the [b]church daily such as should be saved.

CHAPTER 3

Peter and John heal a man lame since birth—Peter preaches repentance—He also speaks of the age of restoration preceding the Second Coming—He identifies Christ as the prophet of whom Moses spoke.

Now Peter and John went up together into the temple at the hour of prayer, *being* the ninth *hour*.

2 And a certain man [a]lame from his mother's womb was carried, whom they laid daily at the gate of the temple which is called Beautiful, to ask alms of them that entered into the temple;

3 Who seeing Peter and John about to go into the temple asked an [a]alms.

4 And Peter, fastening his eyes upon him with John, said, Look on us.

5 And he gave heed unto them, expecting to receive something of them.

6 Then Peter said, Silver and gold have I none; but such as I have [a]give I thee: In the [b]name of Jesus Christ of Nazareth rise up and walk.

7 And he took him by the right hand, and [a]lifted *him* up: and immediately his feet and ankle bones received strength.

36*a* TG Jesus Christ, Crucifixion of.
b TG Jesus Christ, Lord; Jesus Christ, Power of.
37*a* Alma 22:3 (3–11). TG Conscience; Holy Ghost, Mission of; Holy Ghost, Source of Testimony.
b TG Conversion.
c Alma 22:15.
38*a* D&C 49:11 (11–14).
b TG Baptism, Qualifications for; Repent; Salvation.
c TG Baptism; Baptism, Essential.
d TG Name.
e TG Remission of Sins.
f TG Holy Ghost, Gift of.
g Acts 8:17 (14–17). TG Holy Ghost, Baptism of.
39*a* TG Promise.
b Isa. 57:19.
40*a* D&C 36:6.
b GR crooked.
41*a* TG Teachable.
b TG Baptism, Qualifications for.
c Acts 4:4.
42*a* TG Commitment; Steadfastness; Sustaining Church Leaders.
b TG Fellowshipping.
c TG Bread; Sacrament.
43*a* TG Courage; Fearful.
b TG Signs.
44*a* TG Consecration.
45*a* Acts 4:35 (32–35); D&C 51:3.
46*a* Luke 24:53.
b D&C 36:7.
47*a* Acts 5:14.
b TG Church.
3 2*a* Acts 14:8 (8–10).
3*a* TG Almsgiving.
6*a* TG Benevolence; Generosity.
b Acts 4:10; Jacob 4:6; 3 Ne. 8:1.
7*a* Mark 9:27. TG Heal.

8 And he leaping up stood, and
walked, and entered with them into
the temple, walking, and leaping,
and praising God.
9 And all the people [a]saw him
walking and praising God:
10 And they knew that it was he
which sat for alms at the Beautiful
gate of the temple: and they were
filled with wonder and amazement
at that which had happened unto
him.
11 And as the lame man which was
healed held Peter and John, all the
people ran together unto them in
the [a]porch that is called Solomon's,
greatly wondering.
12 ¶ And when Peter saw *it*, he
answered unto the people, Ye men
of Israel, why marvel ye at this? or
why look ye so earnestly on us, as
though by our [a]own power or holiness
we had made this man to walk?
13 The God of Abraham, and of
Isaac, and of Jacob, the God of our
fathers, hath [a]glorified his Son
Jesus; whom ye [b]delivered up, and
[c]denied him in the presence of
Pilate, when he was determined to let
him go.
14 But ye denied the Holy One and
the Just, and desired a [a]murderer
to be granted unto you;
15 And killed the [a]Prince of life,
whom God hath [b]raised from the
dead; whereof we are [c]witnesses.
16 And his [a]name through faith
in his name hath made this man
strong, whom ye see and know: yea,
the [b]faith which is by him hath given
him this perfect soundness in the
presence of you all.
17 And now, brethren, [a]I [b]wot that
through [c]ignorance ye did *it*, as *did*
also your rulers.
18 But those things, which God before
had [a]shewed by the mouth of
all his [b]prophets, that Christ should
[c]suffer, he hath so fulfilled.
19 ¶ [a]Repent ye therefore, and be
[b]converted, that your sins may be
[c]blotted out, when the times of refreshing
shall come from the [d]presence
of the Lord;
20 And he shall send [a]Jesus Christ,
which before was preached unto
[b]you:
21 Whom the heaven must receive
until the times of [a]restitution of all
things, which God hath [b]spoken by
the mouth of all his holy prophets
since the world began.
22 For Moses truly said unto the
fathers, A [a]prophet shall the Lord
your God raise up unto you of your
brethren, like unto me; him shall
ye hear in all things whatsoever he
shall say unto you.
23 And it shall come to pass, *that*
every soul, which will not hear that
prophet, shall be [a]destroyed from
among the people.
24 Yea, and all the prophets from
Samuel and those that follow after,
as many as have spoken, have likewise
[a]foretold of these days.
25 Ye are the [a]children of the
prophets, and of the [b]covenant which

9*a* Acts 4:16.
11*a* 1 Kgs. 6:3; John 10:23.
12*a* Gen. 41:16; Dan. 2:30.
13*a* John 16:14; 1 Pet. 1:21 (17–21).
b Matt. 27:20; Acts 13:28.
c John 19:6.
14*a* Luke 23:25 (17–19, 25).
15*a* TG Jesus Christ, Messiah.
b Acts 10:40.
c TG Witness.
16*a* TG Name.
b TG Faith.
17*a* JST Acts 3:17 . . . I *know* that through ignorance *ye have done this,* as also your rulers.
b OR know.
c D&C 6:21.
18*a* TG Foreordination.
b Luke 24:27; Acts 28:23; Alma 18:36.
c 1 Cor. 15:3.
19*a* TG Repent.
b TG Conversion.
c Ps. 51:1; Mosiah 26:30; Alma 5:14 (11–15, 21).
d TG God, Presence of.
20*a* TG Jesus Christ, Second Coming.
b JST Acts 3:20 . . . you, *whom ye have crucified;*
21*a* TG Dispensations; Restoration of the Gospel.
b TG Prophets, Mission of.
22*a* Deut. 18:15 (15–19); Acts 7:37; 1 Ne. 22:20 (20–22); JS—H 1:40.
23*a* D&C 1:14 (14–16); 133:63.
24*a* TG Jesus Christ, Prophecies about.
25*a* TG Seed of Abraham.
b TG Abrahamic Covenant; Mission of Early Saints.

God made with our fathers, saying unto Abraham, And in thy seed shall all the kindreds of the earth be [c]blessed.
26 Unto you first God, having raised up his [a]Son Jesus, sent him to bless you, in turning away every one of you from his iniquities.

CHAPTER 4

Peter and John are arrested and brought before the council—Peter testifies that salvation comes because of Christ—The Sadducees strive to silence Peter and John—The Saints glory in the testimony of Jesus—They have all things in common.

AND as they spake unto the people, the priests, and the captain of the temple, and the Sadducees, came upon them,
2 Being grieved that they taught the people, and preached through Jesus the [a]resurrection from the dead.
3 And they laid hands on them, and put *them* in hold unto the next day: for it was now eventide.
4 Howbeit many of them which heard the word believed; and the number of the men was about [a]five thousand.
5 ¶ And it came to pass on the morrow, that their rulers, and elders, and [a]scribes,
6 And Annas the high priest, and Caiaphas, and John, and Alexander, and as many as were of the kindred of the high [a]priest, were gathered together at Jerusalem.
7 And when they had set them in the midst, they asked, By what [a]power, or by what [b]name, have ye done this?
8 Then Peter, filled with the [a]Holy Ghost, said unto them, Ye rulers of the people, and elders of Israel,
9 If we this day be examined of the good deed done to the impotent man, by what means he is made whole;
10 Be it known unto you all, and to all the people of Israel, that by the [a]name of Jesus Christ of Nazareth, whom ye crucified, whom God raised from the dead, *even* by him doth this man stand here before you whole.
11 This is the [a]stone which was set at nought of you builders, which is become the head of the corner.
12 Neither is there [a]salvation in any other: for there is none other [b]name under heaven given among men, whereby we must be [c]saved.
13 ¶ Now when they saw the boldness of Peter and John, and perceived that they were [a]unlearned and [b]ignorant men, they marvelled; and they took knowledge of them, that they had been with Jesus.
14 And beholding the man which was healed standing with them, they could say nothing against it.
15 But when they had commanded them to go aside out of the council, they conferred among themselves,
16 Saying, What shall we do to these men? for that indeed a notable [a]miracle hath been done by them *is* manifest to all them that dwell in Jerusalem; and we cannot deny *it*.
17 But that it spread no further among the people, let us straitly threaten them, that they speak henceforth to no man in this name.
18 And they called them, and [a]commanded them not to speak at all nor teach in the name of Jesus.
19 But Peter and John answered and said unto them, Whether it be

25*c* TG Israel, Mission of.
26*a* TG God, Body of, Corporeal Nature.
4 2*a* Acts 23:8.
4*a* Acts 2:41.
5*a* TG Scribe.
6*a* TG Priestcraft.
7*a* TG Priesthood, Power of.
b TG Name.
8*a* TG Teaching with the Spirit.
10*a* Acts 3:6.
11*a* TG Cornerstone; Rock.
12*a* TG Gospel.
b Ps. 9:10; Hosea 13:4; 1 Jn. 2:12; 2 Ne. 25:20; Mosiah 4:8. TG Jesus Christ, Taking the Name of.
c TG Jesus Christ, Atonement through; Jesus Christ, Savior; Salvation; Salvation, Plan of.
13*a* D&C 1:19; 35:13.
b GR ordinary, plain.
16*a* Acts 3:9 (6–9).
18*a* Acts 5:28 (27–28).

right in the sight of God to [a]hearken
unto you more than unto God,
judge ye.
20 For we cannot but [a]speak the
things which we have [b]seen and
heard.
21 So when they had further threatened them, they let them go, finding nothing how they might punish
them, because of the people: for all
men glorified God for that which
was done.
22 For the man was above forty
years old, on whom this miracle of
healing was shewed.
23 ¶ And being let go, they went
to their own company, and reported
all that the chief priests and elders
had said unto them.
24 And when they heard that, they
lifted up their voice to God with one
accord, and said, Lord, thou *art* God,
which hast made heaven, and [a]earth,
and the sea, and all that in them is:
25 Who by the mouth of thy servant David hast said, Why did the
heathen rage, and the people imag-
ine vain things?
26 The [a]kings of the earth stood
up, and the rulers were gathered together against the Lord, and against
his Christ.
27 For of a truth against thy holy
child Jesus, whom thou hast [a]anoint-
ed, both Herod, and Pontius Pilate,
with the Gentiles, and the people
of Israel, were gathered together,
28 For to do whatsoever thy hand
and thy counsel determined before
to be done.
29 And now, Lord, behold their
threatenings: and grant unto thy
servants, that with all boldness they
may speak thy word,
30 By stretching forth thine hand
to heal; and that signs and wonders
may be done by the name of thy
holy child Jesus.
31 ¶ And when they had prayed,
the place was shaken where they
were [a]assembled together; and
they were all filled with the [b]Holy
Ghost, and they spake the word of
God with boldness.
32 And the multitude of them that
believed were of [a]one heart and of
one soul: neither said any *of them*
that [b]ought of the things which he
[c]possessed was his own; but they
had all things [d]common.
33 And with great power gave the
apostles [a]witness of the resurrection
of the Lord Jesus: and great [b]grace
was upon them all.
34 Neither was there any among
them that lacked: for as many as
were possessors of lands or houses
[a]sold them, and brought the prices
of the things that were sold,
35 And laid *them* down at the
apostles' feet: and [a]distribution was
made unto every man according as
he had [b]need.
36 And Joses, who by the apostles
was surnamed [a]Barnabas, (which
is, being interpreted, The son of
consolation,) a Levite, *and* of the
country of Cyprus,
37 Having land, sold *it*, and brought
the [a]money, and laid *it* at the apostles' feet.

CHAPTER 5

Ananias and Sapphira lie to the Lord and lose their lives—The Apostles continue the miracles of Jesus—Peter and John are arrested, an angel delivers them from prison, and they testify of Christ—Gamaliel counsels moderation.

19*a* D&C 3:7.
20*a* Jer. 20:9; Amos 3:8.
b TG Witness.
24*a* D&C 14:9.
26*a* Ps. 2:2 (1–2).
27*a* TG Anointing; Jesus Christ, Authority of; Jesus Christ, Messiah.
31*a* TG Assembly for Worship; Meetings.
b Acts 2:4 (2–4); D&C 68:4 (3–4).
32*a* 1 Cor. 1:10 (10–13); 3 Ne. 11:28 (28–30); Moses 7:18. TG Unity.
b GR any.
c D&C 49:20.
d TG Consecration.
33*a* 1 Cor. 15:15. TG Witness.
b TG Grace.
34*a* Acts 5:1 (1–11).
35*a* Acts 6:1; D&C 83:6 (1–6).
b Acts 2:45. TG Welfare.
36*a* Acts 11:22 (22–24); Gal. 2:1.
37*a* D&C 19:34.

BUT a certain man named Ananias, with Sapphira his wife, [a]sold a possession,
2 And [a]kept back [b]*part* of the price, his wife also being privy *to it*, and brought a certain [c]part, and laid *it* at the apostles' feet.
3 But Peter said, Ananias, why hath Satan filled thine heart to [a]lie to the Holy Ghost, and to [b]keep back *part* of the price of the land?
4 Whiles it remained, was it not thine own? and after it was sold, was it not in thine own power? why hast thou conceived this thing in thine heart? thou hast not [a]lied unto men, but unto [b]God.
5 And Ananias hearing these words fell down, and [a]gave up the ghost: and great fear came on all them that heard these things.
6 And the young men arose, wound him up, and carried *him* out, and buried *him*.
7 And it was about the space of three hours after, when his wife, not knowing what was done, came in.
8 And Peter answered unto her, Tell me whether ye sold the land for so much? And she said, Yea, for so much.
9 Then Peter said unto her, How is it that ye have agreed together to [a]tempt the Spirit of the Lord? behold, the feet of them which have buried thy husband *are* at the door, and shall carry thee out.
10 Then fell she down [a]straightway at his feet, and yielded up the ghost: and the young men came in, and found her dead, and, carrying *her* forth, buried *her* by her husband.
11 And great fear came upon all the church, and upon as many as heard these things.
12 ¶ And by the hands of the apostles were many [a]signs and wonders wrought among the people; (and they were all with one accord in Solomon's porch.
13 And of the [a]rest durst no man join himself to them: but the people magnified them.
14 And believers were the more [a]added to the Lord, multitudes both of men and women.)
15 Insomuch that they brought forth the sick into the streets, and laid *them* on beds and couches, that at the least the [a]shadow of Peter passing by might overshadow some of them.
16 There came also a multitude *out* of the cities round about unto Jerusalem, bringing sick folks, and them which were vexed with unclean spirits: and they were [a]healed every one.
17 ¶ Then the high priest rose up, and all they that were with him, (which is the sect of the Sadducees,) and were filled with [a]indignation,
18 And laid their hands on the apostles, and put them in the common prison.
19 But the [a]angel of the Lord by night opened the [b]prison doors, and brought them forth, and said,
20 Go, stand and speak in the temple to the people all the [a]words of this life.
21 And when they heard *that*, they entered into the temple early in the morning, and taught. But the high priest came, and they that were with him, and called the council together, and all the senate of the children of Israel, and sent to the prison to have them brought.
22 But when the officers came, and found them not in the prison, they returned, and told,
23 Saying, The prison truly found we shut with all safety, and the keepers standing without before the

5 1*a* Acts 4:34 (32, 34–35); D&C 19:26 (25–26).
2*a* TG Selfishness.
b Josh. 7:21 (1–26); D&C 105:3 (2–10). TG Consecration.
c TG Welfare.
3*a* TG Honesty.
b TG Selfishness.
4*a* TG Lying.
b Josh. 7:20.
5*a* Lev. 10:2.
9*a* TG Test.
10*a* OR immediately.
12*a* Heb. 2:4. TG Signs.
13*a* JST Acts 5:13 . . . *rulers* . . .
14*a* Acts 2:47.
15*a* Luke 8:44 (43–48); Acts 19:12 (11–12).
16*a* TG Heal.
17*a* GR envy, malice.
19*a* Acts 12:7; Moro. 7:29 (29–33). TG Angels.
b Acts 16:26.
20*a* John 6:68 (63, 68).

doors: but when we had opened, we
found no man within.
24 Now when the high priest and
the captain of the temple and the
chief priests heard these things,
they doubted of them whereunto
this would grow.
25 Then came one and told them,
saying, Behold, the men whom ye
put in prison are standing in the
temple, and teaching the people.
26 Then went the captain with the
officers, and brought them without violence: for they feared the
people, lest they should have been
stoned.
27 And when they had brought
them, they set *them* before the council: and the high priest asked them,
28 Saying, Did not we straitly
[a]command you that ye should not
teach in this [b]name? and, behold,
ye have filled Jerusalem with your
doctrine, and intend to bring this
man's [c]blood upon us.
29 ¶ Then Peter and the *other* apostles answered and said, We ought to
[a]obey God rather than men.
30 The God of our fathers raised
up Jesus, whom ye slew and [a]hanged
on a tree.
31 Him hath God exalted [a]with
his right hand *to be* a [b]Prince and a
[c]Saviour, for to give repentance to
Israel, and [d]forgiveness of sins.
32 And we are his [a]witnesses of
these things; and *so is* also the [b]Holy
Ghost, whom God hath [c]given to
them that obey him.
33 ¶ When they heard *that,* they
were [a]cut *to the heart,* and took counsel to slay them.
34 Then stood there up one in the
council, a Pharisee, named [a]Gamaliel, a doctor of the law, had in
reputation among all the people,
and commanded to put the apostles
forth a little space;
35 And said unto them, Ye men
of Israel, take heed to yourselves
what ye intend to do as touching
these men.
36 For before these days rose up
Theudas, boasting himself to be
somebody; to whom a number of
men, about four hundred, joined
themselves: who was slain; and all,
as many as [a]obeyed him, were scattered, and brought to nought.
37 After this man rose up Judas
of Galilee in the days of the taxing, and drew away much people
after him: he also perished; and all,
even as many as obeyed him, were
dispersed.
38 And now I say unto you, [a]Refrain from these men, and let them
alone: for if this counsel or this work
be of [b]men, it will come to nought:
39 But if it be of God, ye cannot
overthrow it; [a]lest haply ye be found
even to [b]fight against God.
40 And to him they agreed: and
when they had called the apostles,
and beaten *them,* they commanded
that they should not speak in the
name of Jesus, and let them go.
41 ¶ And they departed from the
presence of the council, [a]rejoicing
that they were counted worthy to
[b]suffer [c]shame for his [d]name.
42 And daily in the temple, and
in every house, they ceased not to
teach and [a]preach Jesus Christ.

28*a* Acts 4:18 (15–18).
b TG Name.
c Matt. 27:25.
29*a* Ex. 1:17 (16–17); D&C 30:1. TG Courage; Duty.
30*a* TG Jesus Christ, Crucifixion of.
31*a* GR at.
b TG Jesus Christ, Messiah.
c TG Jesus Christ, Atonement through.
d TG Forgive.
32*a* Luke 1:2; John 1:14; Acts 26:16. TG Holy Ghost, Mission of; Witness.
b TG Holy Ghost, Source of Testimony.
c TG Holy Ghost, Gift of.
33*a* 1 Ne. 16:2.
34*a* Acts 22:3.
36*a* GR were persuaded by, believed him.
38*a* Acts 19:35 (35–41).
b D&C 3:3; JS—H 1:23 (22–23).
39*a* JST Acts 5:39 . . . *be careful, therefore,* lest ye be . . .
b Acts 23:9.
41*a* Luke 6:23 (22–23); Col. 1:11; 1 Thes. 1:6; 1 Pet. 4:13.
b TG Persecution; Self-Sacrifice; Suffering.
c TG Shame.
d TG Jesus Christ, Taking the Name of.
42*a* TG Missionary Work.

CHAPTER 6

The Apostles choose seven to assist them—Stephen is tried before the council.

AND in those days, when the number of the disciples was multiplied, there arose a murmuring of the Grecians against the Hebrews, because their [a]widows were [b]neglected in the daily [c]ministration.
2 Then the twelve called the multitude of the disciples *unto them,* and said, It is not reason that we should leave the word of God, and serve tables.
3 Wherefore, brethren, look ye out among you seven men of [a]honest [b]report, full of the Holy Ghost and [c]wisdom, whom we may appoint over this [d]business.
4 But we will give ourselves continually to prayer, and to the [a]ministry of the word.
5 ¶ And the saying pleased the whole multitude: and they [a]chose Stephen, a man full of faith and of the [b]Holy Ghost, and [c]Philip, and Prochorus, and Nicanor, and Timon, and Parmenas, and Nicolas a proselyte of Antioch:
6 Whom they set before the apostles: and when they had prayed, they [a]laid *their* [b]hands on them.
7 And the word of God increased; and the number of the disciples multiplied in Jerusalem greatly; and a great company of the [a]priests were obedient to the faith.
8 And Stephen, full of faith and [a]power, did great wonders and [b]miracles among the people.
9 ¶ Then there arose certain of the synagogue, which is called *the synagogue* of the [a]Libertines, and Cyrenians, and Alexandrians, and of them of Cilicia and of Asia, [b]disputing with Stephen.
10 And they were not able to resist the [a]wisdom and the spirit by which he spake.
11 Then they suborned men, which said, We have heard him speak [a]blasphemous words against Moses, and *against* God.
12 And they stirred up the people, and the elders, and the scribes, and came upon *him,* and caught him, and brought *him* to the council,
13 And set up [a]false witnesses, which said, This man ceaseth not to speak blasphemous words against this holy place, and the law:
14 For we have heard him say, that this Jesus of Nazareth shall destroy this place, and shall change the [a]customs which Moses delivered us.
15 And all that sat in the council, looking steadfastly on him, saw his face as it had been the [a]face of an [b]angel.

CHAPTER 7

Stephen recounts the history of Israel and names Moses as a prototype of Christ—He testifies of the apostasy in Israel—He sees Jesus on the right hand of God—Stephen's testimony is rejected, and he is stoned to death.

THEN said the high priest, Are these things so?
2 And he said, Men, brethren, and fathers, hearken; The God of glory appeared unto our father [a]Abraham, when he was in Mesopotamia, before he dwelt in [b]Charran,
3 And said unto him, Get thee out of thy [a]country, and from thy kindred,

---

6 1*a* TG Widows.
b TG Apathy; Welfare.
c Acts 4:35.
3*a* TG Honesty; Priesthood, Qualifying for.
b 1 Tim. 3:7.
c TG Holy Ghost, Gifts of.
d D&C 107:68 (14, 68).
4*a* Mark 16:15 (15–19); D&C 107:8.
5*a* TG Called of God.
b TG Holy Ghost, Gifts of.
c Acts 21:8.
6*a* TG Church Organization; Hands, Laying on of; Priesthood; Priesthood, Authority.
b TG Setting Apart.
7*a* John 12:42. TG Priest, Aaronic Priesthood. BD Priests.
8*a* TG Priesthood, Power of.
b TG Miracle.
9*a* GR Freed-men.
b TG Disputations.
10*a* Isa. 54:17; Luke 21:15; D&C 100:5 (5–6).
11*a* TG Blaspheme.
13*a* TG Slander.
14*a* Acts 21:21.
15*a* Hel. 5:36.
b TG Angels.
7 2*a* Gen. 12:1; Abr. 2:3 (3–4).
b Gen. 11:31 (31–32).
3*a* Abr. 1:1 (1, 5).

and come into the land which I
shall shew thee.
4 Then came he out of the land
of the [a]Chaldæans, and dwelt in
Charran: and from thence, when his
father was dead, he removed him
into this land, wherein ye now dwell.
5 And he gave him none inheritance in it, no, not *so much as* to set
his foot on: yet he [a]promised that
he would give it to him for a possession, and to his seed after him,
when *as yet* he had no child.
6 And God spake on this wise,
That his seed should [a]sojourn in a
strange land; and that they should
bring them into [b]bondage, and entreat *them* evil four hundred years.
7 And the nation to whom they
shall be in bondage will I judge,
said God: and after that shall they
come forth, and serve me in this
place.
8 And he gave him the covenant of
[a]circumcision: and so *Abraham* begat Isaac, and circumcised him the
eighth day; and Isaac *begat* Jacob; and
Jacob *begat* the twelve [b]patriarchs.
9 And the patriarchs, moved with
[a]envy, sold [b]Joseph into Egypt: but
God was with him,
10 And [a]delivered him out of all
his [b]afflictions, and gave him favour
and wisdom in the sight of Pharaoh
king of Egypt; and he made him governor over Egypt and all his house.
11 Now there came a [a]dearth over
all the land of Egypt and Chanaan,
and great affliction: and our fathers
found no sustenance.
12 But when Jacob heard that there
was [a]corn in Egypt, he sent out our
fathers first.
13 And at the second *time* [a]Joseph
was made known to his brethren;
and Joseph's kindred was made
known unto [b]Pharaoh.
14 Then sent [a]Joseph, and called
his [b]father [c]Jacob to *him*, and all his
kindred, threescore and fifteen souls.
15 So Jacob went down into Egypt,
and died, he, and our fathers,
16 And were carried over into
Sychem, and laid in the sepulchre
that Abraham [a]bought for a sum
of money of the sons of Emmor *the
father* of Sychem.
17 But when the time of the promise drew nigh, which God had sworn
to Abraham, the people grew and
multiplied in Egypt,
18 Till another [a]king arose, which
knew not Joseph.
19 The same dealt subtilly with
our kindred, and evil entreated our
fathers, so that they cast out their
young children, to the end they
might not live.
20 In which time Moses was born,
and was [a]exceeding fair, and nourished up in his father's house [b]three
months:
21 And when he was cast out, Pharaoh's daughter took him up, and
nourished him for her own [a]son.
22 And Moses was [a]learned in all
the wisdom of the Egyptians, and
was mighty in words and in deeds.
23 And when he was full [a]forty
years old, it came into his heart to
visit his [b]brethren the children of
Israel.
24 And seeing one *of them* suffer wrong, he defended *him*, and
avenged him that was [a]oppressed,
and [b]smote the Egyptian:
25 For he supposed his brethren
would have [a]understood how that

4*a* Gen. 11:31.
5*a* TG Promised Lands.
6*a* Gen. 26:3.
b TG Israel, Bondage of, in Egypt.
8*a* TG Circumcision.
b TG Patriarch.
9*a* TG Envy.
b Alma 46:24.
10*a* D&C 24:1.
b TG Affliction.
11*a* OR famine. TG Drought; Famine.
12*a* Gen. 42:1.
13*a* Gen. 45:3.
b Gen. 47:2.
14*a* TG Israel, Joseph, People of.
b Gen. 45:13.
c TG Israel, Origins of.
16*a* Gen. 23:17.
18*a* Ex. 1:8.
20*a* GR comely, beautiful to God.
b Ex. 2:2.
21*a* Ex. 2:10.
22*a* TG Education.
23*a* Ex. 7:7; Deut. 31:2 (1–2); 34:7.
b Ex. 2:11 (11–15); Heb. 11:25 (24–27).
24*a* TG Oppression.
b Ex. 2:12 (11–12).
25*a* Ex. 2:14; 3:13 (13–15); 4:1.

God by his hand would [b]deliver
them: but they understood not.
26 And the next day he shewed
himself unto them as they strove,
and would have set them at one
again, saying, Sirs, ye are brethren;
why do ye [a]wrong one to another?
27 But he that did his neighbour
wrong thrust him away, saying,
Who made thee a [a]ruler and a judge
over us?
28 Wilt thou kill me, as thou did-
dest the Egyptian yesterday?
29 Then [a]fled Moses at this saying,
and was a stranger in the land of
Madian, where he begat two [b]sons.
30 And when forty years were expired, there appeared to him in the
wilderness of mount Sina an [a]angel
of the Lord in a flame of fire in a
bush.
31 When Moses saw *it*, he wondered
at the [a]sight: and as he drew near
to behold *it*, the [b]voice of the Lord
came unto him,
32 *Saying*, I *am* the [a]God of thy
fathers, the God of Abraham, and
the God of Isaac, and the God of
Jacob. Then Moses trembled, and
durst not behold.
33 Then said the Lord to him, Put
off thy shoes from thy feet: for the
place where thou standest is holy
ground.
34 I have seen, I have seen the affliction of my people which is in
Egypt, and I have heard their groaning, and am come down to deliver
them. And now come, I will send
thee into Egypt.
35 This Moses whom they refused,
saying, Who made thee a ruler and
a judge? the same did God send *to*
be a ruler and a [a]deliverer by the
hand of the angel which appeared
to him in the bush.
36 He [a]brought them out, after that
he had shewed wonders and signs
in the land of Egypt, and in the
Red sea, and in the wilderness forty
years.
37 ¶ This is that Moses, which
said unto the children of Israel, A
[a]prophet shall the Lord your God
raise up unto you of your brethren,
like unto me; him shall ye hear.
38 This is he, that was in the
church in the wilderness with the
angel which spake to him in the
mount Sina, and *with* our fathers:
who received the lively [a]oracles to
give unto us:
39 To whom our fathers would not
[a]obey, but thrust *him* from them, and
in their hearts turned back again
into Egypt,
40 Saying unto Aaron, Make us
[a]gods to go before us: for *as for* this
Moses, which brought us out of the
land of Egypt, we wot not what is
become of him.
41 And they made a [a]calf in those
days, and offered sacrifice unto the
idol, and rejoiced in the works of
their own hands.
42 Then God turned, and [a]gave
them up to worship the host of
heaven; as it is written in the book
of the prophets, O ye house of Israel,
have ye offered to me slain beasts
and sacrifices *by the space of* forty
years in the wilderness?
43 Yea, ye took up the tabernacle
of Moloch, and the star of your god
Remphan, figures which ye made
to worship them: and I will carry
you away beyond Babylon.
44 Our fathers had the tabernacle
of witness in the wilderness, as he
had appointed, speaking unto Moses,
that he should make it according to
the [a]fashion that he had seen.
45 Which also our fathers that
came after brought in with [a]Jesus

25*b* TG Deliver.
26*a* Ex. 2:13.
TG Injustice.
27*a* 1 Ne. 17:26 (23–37).
29*a* Ex. 2:15.
b Ex. 2:22; 18:3.
30*a* Ex. 3:2.
31*a* OR vision.
b Ex. 3:4 (3–6).
32*a* Ex. 3:15.
35*a* TG Deliver; Jesus Christ, Savior; Salvation.
36*a* Ex. 12:51.
37*a* Deut. 18:15 (15–19); Acts 3:22 (22–23); JS—H 1:40. TG Jesus Christ, Prophecies about.
38*a* Rom. 3:2; D&C 90:5.
39*a* TG Disobedience.
40*a* Ex. 32:1, 23.
41*a* Ex. 32:4; Hosea 8:5 (5–7).
42*a* Ps. 81:12; Rom. 1:24.
44*a* 1 Chr. 28:19 (11, 19); Heb. 8:5.
45*a* IE Joshua. Heb. 4:8.

into the possession of the Gentiles,
whom God drave out before the
face of our fathers, unto the days
of David;
46 Who found favour before God,
and desired to find a tabernacle for
the God of Jacob.
47 But Solomon built him an house.
48 Howbeit the most High [a]dwell-
eth not in temples made with hands;
as saith the prophet,
49 Heaven *is* my [a]throne, and earth
is my footstool: what house will ye
build me? saith the Lord: or what
is the place of my rest?
50 Hath not my hand [a]made all
these things?
51 ¶ Ye [a]stiffnecked and [b]uncir-
cumcised in heart and ears, ye do
always [c]resist the [d]Holy Ghost: as
your [e]fathers *did,* so *do* ye.
52 Which of the prophets have not
your fathers [a]persecuted? and they
have slain them which shewed before of the coming of the Just One;
of whom ye have been now the be-
trayers and murderers:
53 Who have received the law by
the disposition of [a]angels, and have
not [b]kept *it.*
54 ¶ When they heard these things,
they were [a]cut to the heart, and they
gnashed on him with *their* teeth.
55 But he, being full of the [a]Holy
Ghost, looked up steadfastly into
heaven, and saw the [b]glory of [c]God,
and [d]Jesus [e]standing on the [f]right
hand of God,
56 And said, Behold, I [a]see the heavens [b]opened, and the [c]Son of man
standing on the right [d]hand of [e]God.
57 Then they cried out with a loud
voice, and stopped their ears, and
ran upon him with one accord,
58 And cast *him* out of the city,
and stoned *him:* and the witnesses
laid down their [a]clothes at a [b]young
man's feet, whose name was Saul.
59 And they [a]stoned [b]Stephen,
[c]calling upon [d]God, and saying, Lord
Jesus, receive my [e]spirit.
60 And he kneeled down, and
[a]cried with a loud voice, [b]Lord, lay
not this sin to their [c]charge. And
when he had said this, he fell asleep.

CHAPTER 8

Saul persecutes the Church—Philip's ministry in Samaria is described—Philip performs miracles and baptizes men and women—Peter and John come to Samaria and confer the gift of the Holy Ghost by the laying on of hands—Simon seeks to buy this gift and is rebuked by Peter—Philip preaches about Christ and baptizes an Ethiopian eunuch.

AND Saul was consenting unto his
death. And at that time there was
a great [a]persecution against the
[b]church which was at Jerusalem;
and they were all scattered abroad

48*a* Acts 17:24.
49*a* TG Kingdom of God, in Heaven.
50*a* TG Jesus Christ, Creator.
51*a* TG Stiffnecked.
b Jer. 6:10; Rom. 2:29 (28–29).
c TG Rebellion.
d Neh. 9:30.
e Mal. 3:7; Matt. 23:32; Hel. 13:25 (25–29).
52*a* TG Apostasy of Israel; Prophets, Rejection of.
53*a* Moses 5:58.
b TG Disobedience.
54*a* 1 Ne. 16:2 (1–4).
55*a* TG Holy Ghost, Comforter; Holy Ghost, Gifts of.
b TG Jesus Christ, Glory of.
c TG Godhead.
d D&C 137:3.
e TG Jesus Christ, Appearances, Postmortal.
f Heb. 1:3. TG Jesus Christ, Relationships with the Father.
56*a* TG God, Presence of; God, Privilege of Seeing.
b Ezek. 1:1; D&C 50:45.
c TG Jesus Christ, Son of Man.
d TG God, Body of, Corporeal Nature.
e TG God, Manifestations of; God the Father, Elohim.
58*a* Acts 22:20.
b The Greek word used identifies a man who is younger than forty years of age.
59*a* TG Persecution.
b TG Martyrdom.
c JST Acts 7:59 . . . *and he,* calling upon God, *said* . . .
d 3 Ne. 19:22 (18–36).
e TG Man, a Spirit Child of Heavenly Father; Spirits, Disembodied.
60*a* Luke 6:28; 23:34 (33–34).
b Matt. 5:44 (44–47).
c 2 Tim. 4:16; 3 Ne. 12:44.
8 1*a* TG Persecution.
b TG Church.

throughout the regions of Judæa
and Samaria, except the apostles.
2 And devout men carried Stephen
to his burial, and made great [a]lam-
entation over him.
3 As for Saul, he made [a]havoc of
the church, entering into every
house, and haling men and women
committed *them* to [b]prison.
4 Therefore they that were scattered abroad went every where
preaching the word.
5 Then Philip went down to the
city of [a]Samaria, and preached
Christ unto them.
6 And the people with one accord
gave heed unto those things which
Philip [a]spake, hearing and seeing
the miracles which he did.
7 For [a]unclean spirits, crying with
loud voice, came out of many that
were possessed *with them:* and many
[b]taken with palsies, and that were
lame, were [c]healed.
8 And there was great joy in that
city.
9 But there was a certain man,
called Simon, which beforetime in
the same city used [a]sorcery, and
[b]bewitched the people of Samaria,
giving out that himself was some
[c]great one:
10 To whom they all gave heed,
from the least to the greatest, saying, This man is the great power
of God.
11 And to him they had regard,
because that of long time he had
bewitched them with sorceries.
12 But when they believed Philip
[a]preaching the things concerning
the kingdom of God, and the [b]name
of Jesus Christ, they were [c]baptized,
both men and women.
13 Then Simon himself believed
also: and when he was baptized, he
continued with Philip, and [a]won-
dered, beholding the miracles and
signs which were done.
14 Now when the apostles which
were at Jerusalem heard that Samaria had received the [a]word of
God, they sent unto them Peter and
John:
15 Who, when they were come
down, prayed for them, that they
might receive the Holy Ghost:
16 (For as yet he was fallen upon
none of them: only they were baptized in the name of the Lord Jesus.)
17 Then [a]laid they *their* hands on
them, and they received the [b]Holy
Ghost.
18 And when Simon saw that
through [a]laying on of the apostles'
hands the Holy Ghost was given, he
offered them money,
19 Saying, Give me also this [a]power,
that on whomsoever I lay hands, he
may receive the Holy Ghost.
20 But Peter said unto him, Thy
money perish with thee, because
thou hast thought that the [a]gift of
God may be [b]purchased with money.
21 Thou hast neither part nor lot
in this matter: for thy heart is not
[a]right in the sight of God.
22 Repent therefore of this thy
[a]wickedness, and pray God, if perhaps the [b]thought of thine [c]heart
may be forgiven thee.
23 For I perceive that thou art in
the [a]gall of bitterness, and *in* the
[b]bond of iniquity.

2*a* TG Mourning.
3*a* Acts 22:4; 1 Cor. 15:9; 1 Tim. 1:13; Mosiah 27:10 (9–11).
b Acts 22:19; 4 Ne. 1:30.
5*a* Acts 1:8.
6*a* TG Counsel.
7*a* TG Spirits, Evil or Unclean.
b GR paralytic and lame.
c 3 Ne. 7:22.
9*a* TG Sorcery.
b TG Superstitions.
c 2 Ne. 26:29.
12*a* TG Missionary Work; Preaching.
b TG Name.
c TG Baptism, Essential.
13*a* OR was amazed, astonished.
14*a* Acts 11:1 (1–18).
17*a* TG Hands, Laying on of.
b Acts 2:38.
18*a* TG Priesthood, Authority.
19*a* TG Priesthood, Power of; Selfishness; Unrighteous Dominion.
20*a* TG God, Gifts of.
b TG Bribe.
21*a* D&C 49:2.
22*a* TG Wickedness.
b TG Motivations.
c 3 Ne. 12:29.
23*a* Alma 41:11; Morm. 8:31.
b TG Bondage, Spiritual.

24 Then answered Simon, and
said, Pray ye to the Lord for me,
that none of these things which ye
have spoken come upon me.
25 And they, when they had testified and preached the word of the
Lord, returned to Jerusalem, and
preached the gospel in many villages of the Samaritans.
26 And the [a]angel of the Lord spake
unto Philip, saying, Arise, and go
toward the south unto the way that
goeth down from Jerusalem unto
Gaza, which is desert.
27 And he arose and went: and,
behold, a man of Ethiopia, an eunuch of great authority under Can-
dace queen of the Ethiopians, who
had the charge of all her treasure,
and had come to Jerusalem for to
[a]worship,
28 Was returning, and sitting in
his chariot read Esaias the prophet.
29 Then the [a]Spirit said unto Philip, Go near, and join thyself to this
chariot.
30 And Philip ran thither to *him*,
and heard him read the prophet Esaias, and said, Understandest thou
what thou readest?
31 And he said, How can I, except
some man should guide me? And he
desired Philip that he would come
up and sit with him.
32 The place of the scripture which
he read was this, He was led as a
sheep to the slaughter; and like a
[a]lamb dumb before his shearer, so
opened he not his mouth:
33 In his humiliation his judgment
was taken away: and who shall declare his generation? for his life is
taken from the earth.
34 And the eunuch answered Philip, and said, I pray thee, of whom
speaketh the prophet this? of himself, or of some other man?
35 Then Philip opened his mouth,
and began at the same scripture, and
preached unto him [a]Jesus.
36 And as they went on *their* way,
they came unto a certain water: and
the eunuch said, See, *here is* water;
what doth hinder me to be baptized?
37 And Philip said, If thou [a]be-
lievest with all thine heart, thou
mayest. And he answered and said,
I believe that Jesus Christ is the Son
of God.
38 And he commanded the chariot
to stand still: and they went down
both into the water, both Philip and
the eunuch; and he [a]baptized him.
39 And when they were come up
out of the water, the [a]Spirit of the
Lord caught away Philip, that the
eunuch saw him no more: and he
went on his way rejoicing.
40 But Philip was found at Azotus:
and passing through he preached
in all the cities, till he came to
[a]Cæsarea.

CHAPTER 9

Jesus appears to Saul—Saul is a chosen vessel—Ananias restores Saul's sight—Saul is baptized and begins his ministry—Peter heals Æneas and raises Dorcas from death.

AND Saul, yet breathing out [a]threat-
enings and slaughter against the
disciples of the Lord, went unto the
high priest,
2 And desired of him [a]letters to
Damascus to the synagogues, that if
he found any of this way, whether
they were men or women, he might
bring them bound unto Jerusalem.
3 And as he journeyed, he came
near Damascus: and suddenly there
shined round about him a [a]light
from heaven:
4 And he [a]fell to the earth, and
heard a voice saying unto him, [b]Saul,
Saul, why persecutest thou me?

26*a* TG Angels.
27*a* John 12:20.
29*a* TG Holy Ghost, Gifts of.
32*a* TG Jesus Christ, Lamb of God; Jesus Christ, Trials of.
35*a* Gal. 3:14 (13–14).
37*a* TG Baptism, Qualifications for.
38*a* TG Baptism; Baptism, Immersion.
39*a* TG God, Spirit of.
40*a* Acts 21:8.
9 1*a* Acts 26:10.
2*a* Acts 22:5.
3*a* TG Light [noun].
4*a* Ezek. 1:28; Ether 3:6 (6–8); Moses 1:9.
b Acts 22:7 (6–16); 26:14 (9–17).

5 And he said, Who art thou, Lord?
And the Lord said, I am [a]Jesus whom
thou persecutest: *it is* hard for thee
to [b]kick against the pricks.
6 And he trembling and astonished
said, Lord, [a]what wilt thou have me
to do? And the Lord *said* unto him,
Arise, and go into the city, and it
shall be told thee what thou must do.
7 [a]And the men which journeyed
with him stood speechless, hearing
a [b]voice, but seeing [c]no man.
8 And Saul arose from the earth;
and when his eyes were opened,
he saw no man: but they led him
by the hand, and brought *him* into
Damascus.
9 And he was three days without
sight, and neither did eat nor drink.
10 ¶ And there was a certain disciple at Damascus, named [a]Ananias;
and to him said the Lord in a [b]vi-
sion, Ananias. And he said, Behold,
I *am here*, Lord.
11 And the Lord *said* unto him,
Arise, and go into the street which
is called Straight, and inquire in the
house of Judas for *one* called Saul,
of Tarsus: for, behold, he prayeth,
12 And hath seen in a vision a man
named Ananias coming in, and putting *his* hand on him, that he might
receive his sight.
13 Then Ananias answered, Lord,
I have heard by many of this man,
how much [a]evil he hath done to thy
saints at Jerusalem:
14 And here he hath authority
from the chief priests to bind all
that call on thy name.
15 But the Lord said unto him, Go
thy way: for he is a [a]chosen vessel
unto me, to [b]bear my [c]name before
the [d]Gentiles, and [e]kings, and the
children of Israel:
16 For I will shew him how great
things he must [a]suffer for my name's
sake.
17 And Ananias went his way, and
entered into the house; and putting
his [a]hands on him said, Brother Saul,
the Lord, *even* Jesus, that [b]appeared
unto thee in the way as thou camest,
hath [c]sent me, that thou mightest
receive thy sight, and be filled with
the [d]Holy Ghost.
18 And immediately there fell from
his eyes as it had been scales: and
he received [a]sight forthwith, and
arose, and was [b]baptized.
19 And when he had received meat,
he was strengthened. Then was Saul
certain days with the disciples which
were at Damascus.
20 And straightway he preached
Christ in the synagogues, that he
is the Son of God.
21 But all that heard *him* were
amazed, and said; Is not this he that
[a]destroyed them which called on
this name in Jerusalem, and came
hither for that intent, that he might
bring them [b]bound unto the chief
priests?
22 But Saul increased the more in
strength, and confounded the Jews
which dwelt at Damascus, proving
that this is very Christ.
23 ¶ And after that many days
were fulfilled, the Jews took counsel to [a]kill him:
24 But their [a]laying await was

5*a* TG Jesus Christ, Appearances, Postmortal.
b D&C 121:38.
6*a* TG Conversion.
7*a* JST Acts 9:7 And *they who were journeying* with him *saw indeed the light, and were afraid; but they heard not the voice of him who spake to him.*
b Acts 22:9.
c Dan. 10:7; Alma 36:11 (6–11).
10*a* Acts 22:12.
b TG Jesus Christ, Appearances, Postmortal.
13*a* Acts 26:10.
15*a* 1 Thes. 3:3.
b Acts 22:15; 26:16.
c TG Name.
d Rom. 15:10 (8–21); 1 Tim. 2:7.
e Ps. 119:46; Matt. 10:18; D&C 1:23; 124:3 (3, 16, 107). TG Kings, Earthly.
16*a* TG Self-Sacrifice.
17*a* TG Administrations to the Sick; Hands, Laying on of.
b 1 Cor. 9:1.
c TG Called of God; Delegation of Responsibility.
d TG Holy Ghost, Gift of.
18*a* TG Sight.
b TG Baptism, Essential.
21*a* Gal. 1:13.
b Acts 26:10.
23*a* 2 Cor. 11:32.
24*a* GR plot, conspiracy was known.

known of Saul. And they watched the gates day and night to kill him.
25 Then the disciples took him by night, and let *him* down by the wall in a [a]basket.
26 And when Saul was come to [a]Jerusalem, he assayed to join himself to the disciples: but they were all afraid of him, and believed not that he was a disciple.
27 But Barnabas took him, and brought *him* to the apostles, and declared unto them how he had [a]seen the Lord in the way, and that he had spoken to him, and how he had preached boldly at Damascus in the name of Jesus.
28 And he was with them coming in and going out at Jerusalem.
29 And he spake boldly in the name of the Lord Jesus, and [a]disputed against the Grecians: but they went about to slay him.
30 *Which* when the brethren knew, they brought him down to Cæsarea, and sent him forth to Tarsus.
31 Then had the churches rest throughout all Judæa and Galilee and Samaria, and were [a]edified; and walking in the fear of the Lord, and in the [b]comfort of the Holy Ghost, were multiplied.
32 ¶ And it came to pass, as Peter passed throughout all *quarters,* he came down also to the [a]saints which dwelt at Lydda.
33 And there he found a certain man named Æneas, which had kept his bed eight years, and was [a]sick of the palsy.
34 And Peter said unto him, Æneas, Jesus Christ maketh thee whole: arise, and make thy bed. And he arose immediately.
35 And all that dwelt at Lydda and Saron saw him, and turned to the Lord.
36 ¶ Now there was at Joppa a certain disciple named Tabitha, which by interpretation is called Dorcas: this [a]woman was full of good works and almsdeeds which she did.
37 And it came to pass in those days, that she was sick, and died: whom when they had washed, they laid *her* in an upper chamber.
38 And forasmuch as Lydda was nigh to Joppa, and the disciples had heard that Peter was there, they sent unto him two men, desiring *him* that he would not delay to come to them.
39 Then Peter arose and went with them. When he was come, they brought him into the upper chamber: and all the widows stood by him weeping, and shewing the coats and garments which Dorcas made, while she was with them.
40 But Peter put them all forth, and kneeled down, and prayed; and turning *him* to the body said, Tabitha, [a]arise. And she opened her eyes: and when she saw Peter, she sat up.
41 And he gave her *his* hand, and lifted her up, and when he had called the [a]saints and widows, presented her [b]alive.
42 And it was known throughout all Joppa; and many believed in the Lord.
43 And it came to pass, that he tarried many days in Joppa with one Simon a tanner.

CHAPTER 10

An angel ministers to Cornelius—Peter, in a vision, is commanded to take the gospel to the Gentiles—The gospel is taught by witnesses—The Holy Ghost falls upon the Gentiles.

THERE was a certain man in Cæsarea called Cornelius, a centurion of the band called the Italian *band,*
2 A devout *man,* and one that feared God with all his house, which

25*a* Josh. 2:15.
26*a* Gal. 1:18 (15–18).
27*a* TG Jesus Christ, Appearances, Postmortal.
29*a* TG Disputations.
31*a* TG Edification.
b TG Comfort; Holy Ghost, Comforter; Holy Ghost, Gifts of.
32*a* TG Saints.
33*a* GR paralyzed.
36*a* TG Woman.
40*a* TG Death, Power over.
41*a* TG Saints.
b John 14:12 (12–14).

gave much [a]alms to the people, and
prayed to God alway.
3 He saw in a [a]vision [b]evidently
about the ninth hour of the day an
[c]angel of God coming in to him, and
saying unto him, Cornelius.
4 And when he looked on him,
he was afraid, and said, What is it,
Lord? And he said unto him, Thy
prayers and thine alms are come up
for a memorial before God.
5 And now send men to Joppa, and
call for *one* Simon, whose surname
is Peter:
6 He lodgeth with one Simon a
tanner, whose house is by the sea
side: he shall tell thee what thou
oughtest to do.
7 And when the angel which spake
unto Cornelius was departed, he
called two of his household servants,
and a devout soldier of them that
waited on him continually;
8 And when he had declared all
these things unto them, he sent them
to Joppa.
9 ¶ On the morrow, as they went
on their journey, and drew nigh
unto the city, Peter went up upon
the [a]housetop to pray about the
sixth hour:
10 And he became very hungry, and
would have eaten: but while they
made ready, he fell into a [a]trance,
11 And saw [a]heaven opened, and a
certain vessel descending unto him,
as it had been a great sheet [b]knit
at the four corners, and let down
to the earth:
12 Wherein were all manner of
fourfooted beasts of the earth, and
wild beasts, and creeping things,
and fowls of the air.
13 And there came a voice to him,
Rise, Peter; kill, and eat.
14 But Peter said, Not so, Lord; for
I have never eaten any thing that is
common or [a]unclean.
15 And the voice *spake* unto him
again the second time, What God
hath [a]cleansed, *that* call not thou
[b]common.
16 This was done thrice: and the
vessel was received up again into
heaven.
17 Now while Peter doubted in
himself what this vision which he
had seen should mean, behold, the
men which were sent from Cornelius had made inquiry for Simon's
house, and stood before the gate,
18 And called, and asked whether
Simon, which was surnamed Peter,
were lodged there.
19 ¶ While Peter thought on the
vision, the [a]Spirit said unto him,
Behold, three men seek thee.
20 Arise therefore, and get thee
down, and [a]go with them, doubting
nothing: for I have sent them.
21 Then Peter went down to the
men which were sent unto him
from Cornelius; and said, Behold,
I am he whom ye seek: what *is* the
cause wherefore ye are come?
22 And they said, Cornelius the
centurion, a just man, and one that
feareth God, and of good report
among all the nation of the Jews,
was [a]warned from God by an holy
angel to send for thee into his house,
and to hear words of thee.
23 Then called he them in, and
lodged *them*. And on the morrow
Peter went away with them, and
certain brethren from Joppa accompanied him.
24 And the morrow after they entered into Cæsarea. And Cornelius
waited for them, and had called together his kinsmen and near friends.
25 And as Peter was coming in,
Cornelius met him, and fell down
at his feet, and worshipped *him*.
26 But Peter took him up, saying,
Stand up; I myself also am a [a]man.

10 2*a* TG Almsgiving.
3*a* TG Vision.
b GR clearly, distinctly.
c 2 Ne. 32:3; Moro. 7:22 (22–38).
9*a* 1 Sam. 9:25 (25–27).
10*a* Acts 22:17.
11*a* D&C 107:19.
b GR bound.
14*a* Lev. 11:2 (2–47).
15*a* Lev. 20:25. TG Cleanliness; Purification.
b Acts 11:9; 1 Ne. 17:35 (32–41).
19*a* TG Holy Ghost, Gifts of.
20*a* Acts 15:7.
22*a* TG Warn.
26*a* Rev. 19:10; D&C 20:19.

27 And as he talked with him, he
went in, and found many that were
come together.
28 And he said unto them, Ye know
how that it is an unlawful thing for
a man that is a Jew to keep company, or come unto one of another
nation; but God hath shewed me that
I should not call any man [a]common
or [b]unclean.
29 Therefore came I *unto you* without gainsaying, as soon as I was sent
for: I ask therefore for what intent
ye have sent for me?
30 And Cornelius said, Four days
ago I was [a]fasting until this hour;
and at the ninth hour I prayed in
my house, and, behold, a [b]man stood
before me in bright clothing,
31 And said, Cornelius, thy prayer
is heard, and thine alms are had
in remembrance in the sight of
God.
32 Send therefore to Joppa, and
call hither Simon, whose surname
is Peter; he is lodged in the house
of *one* Simon a tanner by the sea
side: who, when he cometh, shall
speak unto thee.
33 Immediately therefore I sent to
thee; and thou hast well done that
thou art come. Now therefore are
we all here present before God, to
hear all things that are commanded
thee of God.
34 ¶ Then Peter opened *his* mouth,
and said, Of a truth I perceive that
God is no [a]respecter of persons:
35 But in every [a]nation he that
[b]feareth him, and [c]worketh [d]righ-
teousness, is [e]accepted with him.
36 The [a]word which *God* sent unto
the children of Israel, preaching
peace by Jesus Christ: (he is Lord
of all:)
37 That word, *I say*, ye know, which
was published throughout all Judæa,
and began from Galilee, after the
baptism which John preached;
38 How God [a]anointed Jesus of
Nazareth with the [b]Holy Ghost and
with power: who went about doing
good, and healing all that were [c]op-
pressed of the devil; for [d]God was
with him.
39 And we are [a]witnesses of all
things which he did both in the
land of the Jews, and in Jerusalem;
whom they slew and hanged on
a tree:
40 Him God [a]raised up the third
day, and [b]shewed him openly;
41 [a]Not to all the people, but unto
witnesses chosen before of God,
even to us, who did eat and drink
with him after he rose from the
dead.
42 And he commanded us to
[a]preach unto the people, and to
testify that it is he which was [b]or-
dained of God *to be* the [c]Judge of
quick and dead.
43 To him give all the prophets
[a]witness, that through his [b]name
whosoever [c]believeth in him shall
receive [d]remission of sins.
44 ¶ While Peter yet spake these
words, the Holy Ghost fell on all
them which heard the word.
45 And they of the circumcision
which believed were astonished, as
many as came with Peter, because

28*a* 2 Ne. 26:33; Hel. 3:28 (27–30).
b TG Uncleanness.
30*a* TG Fast, Fasting.
b TG Angels.
34*a* Acts 15:9; 17:26 (25–26); Rom. 2:11; 1 Ne. 17:35; D&C 1:35; 38:16. TG Judgment.
35*a* Rom. 10:12 (12–13); Alma 26:37 (36–37). TG Nations.
b TG Reverence.
c TG Good Works.
d TG Righteousness.
e 1 Sam. 2:30.
36*a* 3 Ne. 27:13 (13–22).
38*a* TG Anointing; Jesus Christ, Messiah.
b TG Holy Ghost, Gifts of.
c TG Oppression.
d Ex. 8:19; Luke 11:20; John 3:2; Acts 2:22.
39*a* Acts 13:31 (29–33). TG Witness.
40*a* Acts 3:15 (15, 26); 17:31. TG Jesus Christ, Resurrection; Resurrection.
b TG Jesus Christ, Appearances, Postmortal.
41*a* Ether 12:7.
42*a* TG Missionary Work.
b TG Jesus Christ, Authority of; Priesthood, Authority.
c TG Jesus Christ, Judge.
43*a* TG Prophets, Mission of.
b TG Name.
c TG Faith.
d TG Remission of Sins.

that on the [a]Gentiles also was poured
out the [b]gift of the Holy Ghost.
46 For they heard them speak with
[a]tongues, and magnify God. Then
answered Peter,
47 Can any man forbid water, that
these should not be baptized, which
have received the [a]Holy Ghost as
well as we?
48 And he commanded them to be
[a]baptized in the name of the Lord.
Then prayed they him to tarry certain days.

CHAPTER 11

God grants the gift of repentance to the Gentiles—The disciples are first called Christians at Antioch—The Church is guided by revelation.

AND the apostles and brethren that
were in Judæa heard that the [a]Gentiles
had also received the [b]word
of God.
2 And when Peter was come up
to Jerusalem, they that were of the
[a]circumcision [b]contended with him,
3 Saying, Thou wentest in to men
uncircumcised, and didst eat with
them.
4 But Peter rehearsed *the matter*
from the beginning, and expounded
it by order unto them, saying,
5 I was in the city of Joppa praying:
and in a [a]trance I saw a vision,
A certain vessel descend, as it had
been a great sheet, let down from
heaven by four corners; and it came
even to me:
6 Upon the which when I had fastened
mine eyes, I considered, and
saw fourfooted beasts of the earth,
and wild beasts, and creeping things,
and fowls of the air.
7 And I heard a voice saying unto
me, Arise, Peter; slay and eat.
8 But I said, Not so, Lord: for nothing
common or unclean hath at any
time entered into my mouth.
9 But the voice answered me
again from heaven, What God hath
[a]cleansed, *that* call not thou [b]common.
10 And this was done three times:
and all were drawn up again into
heaven.
11 And, behold, immediately there
were three men already come unto
the house where I was, sent from
Cæsarea unto me.
12 And the Spirit bade me go with
them, nothing doubting. Moreover
these six brethren accompanied
me, and we entered into the man's
house:
13 And he shewed us how he had
seen an angel in his house, which
stood and said unto him, Send men
to Joppa, and call for Simon, whose
surname is Peter;
14 Who shall tell thee words,
whereby thou and all thy house
shall be saved.
15 And as I began to speak, the
Holy Ghost fell on them, as on us
at the beginning.
16 Then remembered I the word
of the Lord, how that he said, John
indeed baptized with water; but
ye shall be baptized with the Holy
Ghost.
17 Forasmuch then as God gave
them the like [a]gift as *he did* unto
us, who believed on the Lord Jesus
Christ; what was I, that I could withstand
God?
18 When they heard these things,
they held their peace, and glorified
God, saying, Then hath God also to
the [a]Gentiles granted [b]repentance
unto life.
19 ¶ Now they which were scattered
abroad upon the [a]persecution
that arose about Stephen travelled

45*a* Matt. 8:11 (11–12); Luke 13:29 (28–30); 2 Ne. 10:18 (9–18); D&C 45:9 (7–30). TG Gentiles.
b TG Holy Ghost, Gift of.
46*a* TG Holy Ghost, Gifts of.
47*a* TG Holy Ghost, Baptism of.
48*a* TG Baptism, Essential.
11 1*a* D&C 109:60.
b Acts 8:14 (14–20).
2*a* TG Circumcision.
b TG Contention.
5*a* Acts 22:17.
9*a* TG Purification; Uncleanness.
b Acts 10:15 (3, 15).
17*a* TG Holy Ghost, Gift of; Holy Ghost, Gifts of.
18*a* Mark 16:15 (15–16); Acts 21:19; D&C 84:62 (62–64).
b TG Repent.
19*a* TG Persecution.

as far as Phenice, and Cyprus, and
Antioch, preaching the word to none
but unto the Jews only.
20 And some of them were men of
Cyprus and Cyrene, which, when
they were come to Antioch, spake
unto the Grecians, preaching the
Lord Jesus.
21 And the hand of the Lord was
with them: and a great number believed, and turned unto the Lord.
22 ¶ Then tidings of these things
came unto the ears of the church
which was in Jerusalem: and they
sent forth [a]Barnabas, that he should
go as far as Antioch.
23 Who, when he came, and had
seen the grace of God, was glad,
and exhorted them all, that with
purpose of heart they would cleave
unto the Lord.
24 For he was a good man, and
full of the Holy Ghost and of faith:
and much people was added unto
the Lord.
25 Then departed Barnabas to Tarsus, for to seek Saul:
26 And when he had found him,
he brought him unto Antioch. And
it came to pass, that a whole year
they [a]assembled themselves with
the church, and taught much people. And the disciples were called
[b]Christians first in [c]Antioch.
27 ¶ And in these days came
[a]prophets from Jerusalem unto
Antioch.
28 And there stood up one of them
named Agabus, and signified by the
[a]Spirit that there should be great
[b]dearth throughout all the world:
which came to pass in the days of
Claudius Cæsar.
29 Then the disciples, every man
according to his ability, determined
to send [a]relief unto the brethren
which dwelt in Judæa:
30 Which also they did, and sent
it to the [a]elders by the hands of
Barnabas and Saul.

CHAPTER 12

The martyrdom of James is described—An angel frees Peter from prison—The Lord slays Herod by disease—The Church grows.

Now about that time Herod the
king stretched forth *his* hands to
vex certain of the church.
2 And he [a]killed [b]James the brother
of John with the sword.
3 And because he saw it pleased
the Jews, he proceeded further to
take Peter also. (Then were the days
of [a]unleavened bread.)
4 And when he had apprehended
him, he put *him* in [a]prison, and delivered *him* to four [b]quaternions
of soldiers to keep him; intending
after [c]Easter to bring him forth to
the people.
5 Peter therefore was kept in
prison: but prayer was made without ceasing of the church unto God
for him.
6 And when Herod would have
brought him forth, the same night
Peter was sleeping between two soldiers, bound with two chains: and
the keepers before the door kept
the prison.
7 And, behold, the [a]angel of the
Lord came upon *him*, and a light
shined in the prison: and he smote
Peter on the side, and raised him
up, saying, Arise up quickly. And
his chains fell off from *his* hands.
8 And the angel said unto him,
Gird thyself, and bind on thy sandals. And so he did. And he saith
unto him, Cast thy garment about
thee, and follow me.
9 And he went out, and followed

22*a* Acts 4:36.
26*a* TG Assembly for Worship; Meetings.
b Acts 26:28; 1 Pet. 4:16; Mosiah 5:8 (8–11); Alma 46:15 (13–15). TG Jesus Christ, Taking the Name of.
c Acts 14:26.
27*a* Acts 13:1 (1–13).
28*a* Acts 2:18; 21:11 (4, 10–11).
b OR famine. TG Drought.
29*a* TG Almsgiving; Welfare.
30*a* TG Elder, Melchizedek Priesthood.
12 2*a* TG Tyranny.
b TG Martyrdom.
3*a* TG Bread, Unleavened.
4*a* Alma 14:27 (22–29); Hel. 5:21 (21–50).
b GR squads; i.e., detachments of four men each.
c IE Passover.
7*a* Acts 5:19.

him; and [a]wist not that it was true
which was done by the angel; but
thought he saw a vision.
10 When they were past the first
and the second ward, they came
unto the iron gate that leadeth unto
the city; which opened to them of
his own accord: and they went out,
and passed on through one street;
and forthwith the angel departed
from him.
11 And when Peter was come to
himself, he said, Now I know of a
surety, that the Lord hath sent his
angel, and hath delivered me out of
the hand of Herod, and *from* all the
expectation of the people of the Jews.
12 And when he had considered *the*
thing, he came to the house of Mary
the mother of John, whose surname
was Mark; where many were gathered together praying.
13 And as Peter knocked at the
door of the gate, a damsel came to
hearken, named Rhoda.
14 And when she knew Peter's
voice, she opened not the gate for
gladness, but ran in, and told how
Peter stood before the gate.
15 And they said unto her, Thou
art mad. But she constantly affirmed
that it was even so. Then said they,
It is his angel.
16 But Peter continued knocking:
and when they had opened *the door,*
and saw him, they were astonished.
17 But he, [a]beckoning unto them
with the hand to hold their peace,
declared unto them how the Lord
had brought him out of the prison.
And he said, Go shew these things
unto James, and to the brethren.
And he departed, and went into
another place.
18 Now as soon as it was day, there
was no small stir among the soldiers,
what was become of Peter.
19 And when Herod had sought for
him, and found him not, he examined the keepers, and commanded
that *they* should be put to [a]death.
And he went down from Judæa to
Cæsarea, and *there* abode.
20 ¶ And Herod was highly displeased with them of Tyre and Sidon: but they came with one accord
to him, and, having made Blastus
the king's chamberlain their friend,
desired peace; because their country was nourished by the king's
country.
21 And upon a set day Herod, arrayed in royal apparel, sat upon
his throne, and made an oration
unto them.
22 And the people gave a shout,
saying, It is the voice of a god, and
not of a man.
23 And immediately the [a]angel of
the Lord smote him, because he gave
not God the glory: and he was eaten
of worms, and gave up the ghost.
24 ¶ But the word of God grew
and multiplied.
25 And Barnabas and Saul returned
from Jerusalem, when they had
fulfilled *their* [a]ministry, and took
with them John, whose surname
was Mark.

CHAPTER 13

Saul and Barnabas are called to missionary service—Saul, now called Paul, curses a sorcerer—Christ is a descendant of David—Paul offers the gospel to Israel, then to the Gentiles.

Now there were in the church that
was at Antioch certain [a]prophets and
teachers; as Barnabas, and Simeon
that was called Niger, and Lucius
of Cyrene, and Manaen, which had
been brought up with Herod the
tetrarch, and Saul.
2 As they ministered to the Lord,
and [a]fasted, the [b]Holy Ghost said,
[c]Separate me Barnabas and Saul for
the work whereunto I have [d]called
them.
3 And when they had fasted and

9*a* OR knew.
17*a* Acts 21:40.
19*a* TG Persecution.
23*a* TG Angels.
25*a* Acts 15:36 (36–37).

13 1*a* Acts 11:27. TG Church Organization.
2*a* Luke 5:35. TG Fast, Fasting.
b TG Holy Ghost, Gifts of.
c TG Setting Apart.
d TG Called of God.

prayed, and [a]laid *their* [b]hands on them, they sent *them* away.
4 ¶ So they, being sent forth by the Holy Ghost, departed unto Seleucia; and from thence they sailed to Cyprus.
5 And when they were at Salamis, they preached the word of God in the synagogues of the Jews: and they had also John to *their* minister.
6 And when they had gone through the isle unto Paphos, they found a certain [a]sorcerer, a false prophet, a Jew, whose name *was* Bar-jesus:
7 Which was with the deputy of the country, Sergius Paulus, a [a]prudent man; who called for Barnabas and Saul, and desired to hear the word of God.
8 But Elymas the sorcerer (for so is his name by interpretation) withstood them, seeking to turn away the deputy from the faith.
9 Then Saul, (who also *is called* Paul,) filled with the [a]Holy Ghost, set his eyes on him,
10 And said, O full of all subtilty and all mischief, *thou* [a]child of the devil, *thou* [b]enemy of all [c]righteousness, wilt thou not cease to pervert the right ways of the Lord?
11 And now, behold, the hand of the Lord *is* upon thee, and thou [a]shalt be [b]blind, not seeing the sun for a season. And immediately there fell on him a mist and a darkness; and he went about seeking some to lead him by the hand.
12 Then the deputy, when he saw what was done, believed, being astonished at the doctrine of the Lord.
13 Now when Paul and his company loosed from Paphos, they came to Perga in Pamphylia: and [a]John departing from them returned to Jerusalem.
14 ¶ But when they departed from Perga, they came to Antioch in Pisidia, and went into the synagogue on the sabbath day, and sat down.
15 And after the reading of the law and the prophets the rulers of the synagogue sent unto them, saying, *Ye* men *and* brethren, if ye have any word of exhortation for the people, say on.
16 Then Paul stood up, and beckoning with *his* hand said, Men of Israel, and ye that [a]fear God, give audience.
17 The God of this people of Israel chose our fathers, and exalted the people when they dwelt as [a]strangers in the land of Egypt, and with an high arm brought he them out of it.
18 And about the time of forty years suffered he their manners in the wilderness.
19 And when he had [a]destroyed seven nations in the [b]land of Chanaan, he divided their land to them by lot.
20 And after that he gave *unto them* judges about the space of four hundred and fifty years, until Samuel the prophet.
21 And afterward they desired a king: and God gave unto them Saul the son of Cis, a man of the tribe of Benjamin, by the space of forty years.
22 And when he had removed him, he raised up unto them David to be their king; to whom also he gave testimony, and said, I have found David the *son* of Jesse, a man after mine own [a]heart, which shall fulfil all my will.
23 Of this man's [a]seed hath God according to *his* [b]promise raised unto Israel a [c]Saviour, Jesus:

3*a* TG Authority; Priesthood, Authority.
b TG Hands, Laying on of; Priesthood, Ordination.
6*a* TG Sorcery.
7*a* TG Prudence.
9*a* TG Holy Ghost, Gifts of.
10*a* 1 Jn. 3:10 (10–18); Alma 11:23.
b TG Enemies.
c TG Righteousness.
11*a* Gen. 19:11.
b Alma 30:49 (48–60).
13*a* Acts 15:37 (36–40).
16*a* Moro. 7:3 (3–4).
17*a* TG Stranger.
19*a* Num. 21:3 (1–3); Ps. 80:8 (8–10).
b TG Israel, Land of.
22*a* TG Heart.
23*a* TG Jesus Christ, Davidic Descent of.
b TG Promise.
c TG Jesus Christ, Savior.

24 When John had first preached
before his coming the baptism of repentance to all the people of Israel.
25 And as John fulfilled his course,
he said, Whom think ye that I am? I
am not *he*. But, behold, there cometh
one after me, whose shoes of *his* feet
I am not worthy to loose.
26 Men *and* brethren, children of
the stock of [a]Abraham, and whosoever among you feareth God, to you
is the word of this salvation sent.
27 For they that dwell at Jerusalem, and their rulers, because they
knew him not, nor yet the voices of
the prophets which are read every
sabbath day, they have fulfilled *them*
in condemning *him*.
28 And though they found no cause
of death *in him*, yet desired they Pilate that he should be [a]slain.
29 And when they had fulfilled all
that was written of him, they took
him down from the tree, and laid
him in a sepulchre.
30 But God raised him from the
dead:
31 And he was [a]seen many days
of them which came up with him
from Galilee to Jerusalem, who are
his [b]witnesses unto the people.
32 And we declare unto you glad
tidings, how that the promise which
was made unto the [a]fathers,
33 God hath fulfilled the same
unto us their children, in that he
hath raised up Jesus again; as it is
also written in the second psalm,
Thou art my [a]Son, this day have I
begotten thee.
34 And as concerning that he raised
him up from the dead, *now* no more
to return to corruption, he said on
this wise, I will give you the [a]sure
mercies of David.
35 Wherefore he saith also in another *psalm*, Thou shalt not suffer
thine Holy One to see corruption.
36 For David, after he had served
his own generation by the will of
God, fell on sleep, and was laid unto
his fathers, and saw corruption:
37 But he, whom God [a]raised again,
saw no [b]corruption.
38 ¶ Be it known unto you therefore, men *and* brethren, that through
this man is preached unto you the
[a]forgiveness of sins:
39 And by him all that believe
are [a]justified from all things, from
which ye could not be [b]justified by
the [c]law of Moses.
40 Beware therefore, lest that come
upon you, which is spoken of in the
prophets;
41 Behold, ye despisers, and wonder, and perish: for I work a work in
your days, a [a]work which ye shall
in no wise believe, though a man
declare it unto you.
42 And when the Jews were gone
out of the synagogue, the Gentiles
besought that these words might be
preached to them the next [a]sabbath.
43 Now when the congregation
was broken up, many of the Jews
and religious [a]proselytes followed
Paul and Barnabas: who, speaking to
them, persuaded them to continue
in the grace of God.
44 ¶ And the next sabbath day
came almost the whole city together
to hear the word of God.
45 But when the Jews saw the
multitudes, they were filled with
[a]envy, and spake [b]against those
things which were spoken by Paul,
contradicting and [c]blaspheming.
46 Then Paul and Barnabas waxed
bold, and said, It was necessary that

26*a* Abr. 2:9 (9–10).
28*a* Matt. 27:20; Acts 3:13.
31*a* TG Jesus Christ, Appearances, Postmortal.
b Acts 10:39 (39–43); 22:15 (14–16).
32*a* TG Family, Patriarchal.
33*a* TG Jesus Christ, Divine Sonship.
34*a* Isa. 55:3.
37*a* TG Jesus Christ, Resurrection.
b Acts 2:27 (27, 31).
38*a* TG Forgive; Jesus Christ, Atonement through; Jesus Christ, Redeemer; Remission of Sins.
39*a* TG Justification.
b Rom. 2:13.
c TG Law of Moses.
41*a* Hab. 1:5; 3 Ne. 21:9 (9–11).
42*a* TG Sabbath.
43*a* Acts 2:10.
45*a* TG Envy.
b Luke 11:52; 1 Thes. 2:16.
c TG Blaspheme.

the word of God should first have
been spoken to you: but seeing ye
put it from you, and judge yourselves unworthy of everlasting life,
lo, we turn to the [a]Gentiles.
47 For so hath the Lord commanded us, *saying,* I have set thee to
be a [a]light of the Gentiles, that thou
shouldest be for [b]salvation unto the
ends of the earth.
48 And when the Gentiles heard
this, they were glad, and glorified
the word of the Lord: [a]and as many
as were ordained to eternal life believed.
49 And the word of the Lord was
[a]published throughout all the region.
50 But the Jews [a]stirred up the
devout and honourable [b]women,
and the chief men of the city, and
raised [c]persecution against Paul
and Barnabas, and expelled them
out of their coasts.
51 But they shook off the [a]dust of
their feet against them, and came
unto Iconium.
52 And the disciples were filled
with joy, and with the Holy Ghost.

CHAPTER 14

Persecution attends the spread of the gospel—Paul heals a crippled man; Paul and Barnabas are hailed as gods—Paul is stoned and revived; he preaches—Elders are ordained.

AND it came to pass in Iconium,
that they went both together into
the synagogue of the Jews, and so
spake, that a great multitude both
of the Jews and also of the Greeks
believed.
2 But the unbelieving Jews stirred
up the Gentiles, and made their
minds evil affected against the
brethren.
3 Long time therefore abode they
speaking boldly in the Lord, which
gave [a]testimony unto the word of
his [b]grace, and granted signs and
wonders to be done by their hands.
4 But the multitude of the city was
divided: and part held with the Jews,
and part with the apostles.
5 And when there was an assault
made both of the Gentiles, and also
of the [a]Jews with their rulers, to use
them despitefully, and to stone them,
6 They were ware of *it,* and fled
unto Lystra and Derbe, cities of
Lycaonia, and unto the region that
lieth round about:
7 And there they preached the
gospel.
8 ¶ And there sat a certain man at
Lystra, impotent in his feet, being
a [a]cripple from his mother's womb,
who never had walked:
9 The same heard Paul speak: who
steadfastly beholding him, and
perceiving that he had [a]faith to be
[b]healed,
10 Said with a loud voice, Stand
upright on thy feet. And he leaped
and walked.
11 And when the people saw what
Paul had done, they lifted up their
voices, saying in the speech of Lycaonia, The [a]gods are come down
to us in the likeness of men.
12 And they called Barnabas, [a]Ju-
piter; and Paul, [b]Mercurius, because
he was the chief speaker.
13 Then the priest of Jupiter, which
was before their city, brought oxen
and garlands unto the gates, and
would have done sacrifice with the
people.
14 *Which* when the [a]apostles,
Barnabas and Paul, heard *of,* they
rent their clothes, and ran in among
the people, crying out,

46*a* Matt. 21:43; Luke 14:24 (21–24); Acts 28:28 (27–28).
47*a* TG Example.
b TG Jesus Christ, Savior; Salvation.
48*a* JST Acts 13:48 . . . and as many as *believed* were ordained unto eternal life.
49*a* D&C 1:6.
50*a* Alma 27:2 (2, 12).
b Acts 17:4 (4, 12).
c TG Persecution.
51*a* Matt. 10:14 (14–15); Luke 10:11; Acts 18:6 (5–6); D&C 24:15; 60:15 (13–15).
14 3*a* TG Testimony.
b TG Grace.
5*a* 2 Cor. 11:26.
8*a* Acts 3:2 (1–10).
9*a* TG Faith.
b TG Heal.
11*a* Acts 28:6 (3–6).
12*a* GR Zeus.
b GR Hermes.
14*a* TG Apostles.

15 And saying, Sirs, why do ye
these things? We also are [a]men of
like [b]passions with you, and preach
unto you that ye should turn from
these [c]vanities unto the living God,
which [d]made heaven, and earth,
and the sea, and all things that are
therein:
16 Who in times past suffered all
nations to [a]walk in their own [b]ways.
17 Nevertheless he left not himself
without [a]witness, in that he did good,
and gave us [b]rain from heaven, and
fruitful seasons, filling our hearts
with [c]food and gladness.
18 And with these sayings scarce
restrained they the people, that they
had not done sacrifice unto them.
19 ¶ And there came thither *certain*
Jews from Antioch and Iconium, who
persuaded the people, and, having
[a]stoned Paul, drew *him* out of the
city, supposing he had been dead.
20 Howbeit, as the disciples stood
round about him, he rose up, and
came into the city: and the next
day he departed with Barnabas
to Derbe.
21 And when they had preached
the gospel to that city, and had
taught many, they returned again to
Lystra, and *to* Iconium, and Antioch,
22 Confirming the souls of the disciples, *and* exhorting them to continue in the faith, and that we must
through much [a]tribulation enter
into the kingdom of God.
23 And when they had [a]ordained
them [b]elders in every church, and
had prayed with [c]fasting, they commended them to the Lord, on whom
they believed.
24 And after they had passed
throughout Pisidia, they came to
Pamphylia.
25 And when they had preached
the word in Perga, they went down
into Attalia:
26 And thence sailed to [a]Antioch,
from whence they had been recommended to the grace of God for the
work which they fulfilled.
27 And when they were come, and
had gathered the church together,
they rehearsed all that God had done
with them, and how he had opened
the [a]door of faith unto the Gentiles.
28 And there they abode long time
with the disciples.

CHAPTER 15

Great dissension arises at Antioch concerning circumcision—The Apostles at Jerusalem decide the issue—Paul chooses Silas as his companion.

AND certain men which came down
from Judæa taught the brethren,
and said, Except ye be [a]circumcised
after the manner of Moses, ye cannot be saved.
2 When therefore Paul and Barnabas had no small dissension and
[a]disputation with them, they determined that Paul and Barnabas, and
certain other of them, should go up
to Jerusalem unto the [b]apostles and
elders about this question.
3 And being brought on their way
by the church, they passed through
Phenice and Samaria, declaring the
[a]conversion of the Gentiles: and
they caused great joy unto all the
brethren.
4 And when they were come to
Jerusalem, they were received of
the church, and *of* the apostles and
elders, and they declared all things
that God had done with them.
5 But there rose up certain of the

15*a* Dan. 2:46; James 5:17 (17–18); 1 Ne. 17:55.
b TG Lust.
c TG Vanity.
d TG Jesus Christ, Creator.
16*a* TG Walking in Darkness.
b Acts 17:30 (27–30).
17*a* Rom. 1:20.
b Lev. 26:4 (3–4).
c TG Food.
19*a* TG Persecution.
22*a* TG Adversity; Test; Tribulation.
23*a* TG Authority; Priesthood, History of; Priesthood, Ordination.
b TG Church Organization; Elder, Melchizedek Priesthood.
c TG Fast, Fasting.
26*a* Acts 11:26 (25–26).
27*a* 2 Cor. 2:12.
15 1*a* TG Circumcision.
2*a* TG Disputations.
b Gal. 2:1.
3*a* TG Conversion.

sect of the Pharisees which believed,
saying, That it was needful to circumcise them, and to command *them*
to keep the [a]law of Moses.
6 ¶ And the [a]apostles and [b]elders
came together for to consider of
this matter.
7 And when there had been much
[a]disputing, [b]Peter rose up, and said
unto them, Men *and* brethren, ye
know how that a good while ago
God made choice among us, that
the [c]Gentiles by my mouth should
hear the word of the [d]gospel, and
believe.
8 And God, which [a]knoweth the
hearts, bare them witness, giving
them the Holy Ghost, even as *he*
did unto us;
9 And put no [a]difference between
us and them, [b]purifying their hearts
by faith.
10 Now therefore why [a]tempt ye
God, to put a yoke upon the neck
of the disciples, which neither our
fathers nor we were able to bear?
11 But we believe that through the
[a]grace of the Lord Jesus Christ we
shall be saved, even as they.
12 ¶ Then all the multitude kept
silence, and gave audience to Barnabas and Paul, declaring what miracles and wonders God had wrought
among the Gentiles by them.
13 ¶ And after they had held their
peace, James answered, saying, Men
and brethren, hearken unto me:
14 Simeon hath declared how God
at the first did visit the [a]Gentiles,
to take out of them a people for
his [b]name.
15 And to this agree the words of
the prophets; as it is written,
16 After this I will return, and
will build again the [a]tabernacle of
David, which is fallen down; and I
will build again the ruins thereof,
and I will set it up:
17 That the [a]residue of men might
seek after the Lord, and all the
Gentiles, upon whom my name is
called, saith the Lord, who doeth
all these things.
18 [a]Known unto God are all his
works from the beginning of the
world.
19 Wherefore my sentence is, that
we trouble not them, which from
among the Gentiles are turned to
God:
20 But that we write unto them,
that they [a]abstain from [b]pollutions
of idols, and *from* [c]fornication, and
from things strangled, and *from*
[d]blood.
21 For Moses of old time hath in
every city them that preach him,
being [a]read in the synagogues every sabbath day.
22 Then pleased it the apostles
and elders, with the whole church,
to send chosen men of their own
company to Antioch with Paul and
Barnabas; *namely,* Judas surnamed
Barsabas, and Silas, chief men among
the brethren:
23 And they [a]wrote [b]*letters* by them
after this manner; The apostles and
elders and brethren *send* greeting
unto the brethren which are of the
Gentiles in Antioch and Syria and
Cilicia:
24 Forasmuch as we have heard,
that certain which went out from
us have troubled you with words,
subverting your souls, saying, *Ye*
must be [a]circumcised, and keep the
law: to whom we gave no *such* commandment:
25 It seemed good unto us, being

5*a* Gal. 5:18 (16–18).
6*a* TG Church Organization.
b TG Elder, Melchizedek Priesthood.
7*a* TG Disputations.
b D&C 7:7 (5–7); JS—H 1:72.
c Acts 10:20 (9–48).
d TG Gospel.
8*a* TG God, Omniscience of.
9*a* Acts 10:34 (34–35); 17:26 (25–26).
b TG Purification; Purity.
10*a* TG Test.
11*a* TG Grace.
14*a* Abr. 2:10 (9–10).
b TG Name.
16*a* Amos 9:11 (11–12).
17*a* Moro. 7:32.
18*a* TG God, Omniscience of.
20*a* Acts 21:25. TG Abstain.
b TG Pollution.
c TG Fornication; Sexual Immorality.
d TG Blood, Eating of.
21*a* 2 Cor. 3:14 (14–15).
23*a* TG Scriptures, Writing of.
b Acts 16:4.
24*a* Gen. 17:11 (10–27); Moro. 8:8.

assembled with [a]one accord, to send
chosen men unto you with our beloved Barnabas and Paul,
26 Men that have [a]hazarded their
lives for the name of our Lord Jesus
Christ.
27 We have sent therefore Judas
and Silas, who shall also tell *you* the
same things by mouth.
28 For it seemed good to the Holy
Ghost, and to us, to lay upon you
no greater burden than these necessary things;
29 That ye abstain from meats offered to [a]idols, and from blood, and
from things strangled, and from
fornication: from which if ye keep
yourselves, ye shall do well. Fare
ye well.
30 So when they were dismissed,
they came to Antioch: and when
they had gathered the multitude
together, they delivered the epistle:
31 *Which* when they had read, they
rejoiced for the [a]consolation.
32 And Judas and Silas, being
prophets also themselves, exhorted
the brethren with many words, and
confirmed *them*.
33 And after they had tarried *there*
a space, they were let go in peace
from the brethren unto the apostles.
34 Notwithstanding it pleased [a]Si-
las to abide there still.
35 Paul also and Barnabas continued in Antioch, teaching and
preaching the word of the Lord,
with many others also.
36 ¶ And some days after Paul said
unto Barnabas, Let us go again and
[a]visit our [b]brethren in every city
where we have preached the word
of the Lord, *and see* how they do.
37 And Barnabas determined to
take with them [a]John, whose surname was [b]Mark.
38 But Paul thought not good to
take him with them, who departed
from them from Pamphylia, and
went not with them to the work.
39 And the [a]contention was so
sharp between them, that they departed asunder one from the other:
and so Barnabas took Mark, and
sailed unto Cyprus;
40 And Paul chose Silas, and departed, being recommended by the
brethren unto the grace of God.
41 And he went through Syria and
Cilicia, [a]confirming the churches.

CHAPTER 16

Paul is directed in a vision to preach in Macedonia—He casts an evil spirit out of a woman—He and Silas are imprisoned, and they convert the jailor—They admonish all to believe on the Lord Jesus and be saved.

THEN came he to Derbe and Lystra:
and, behold, a certain disciple was
there, named [a]Timotheus, the son
of a certain woman, which was a
[b]Jewess, and believed; but his father
was a Greek:
2 Which was well reported of by
the brethren that were at Lystra
and Iconium.
3 Him would Paul have to go forth
with him; and took and [a]circumcised
him because of the Jews which were
in those quarters: for they knew all
that his father was a Greek.
4 And as they went through the cities, they delivered them the [a]decrees
for to keep, that were ordained of
the apostles and elders which were
at Jerusalem.
5 And so were the churches [a]estab-
lished in the faith, and increased in
number daily.
6 Now when they had gone throughout Phrygia and the region of
Galatia, and were forbidden of the

25*a* TG Common Consent.
26*a* 2 Tim. 3:11.
29*a* 1 Cor. 8:1.
31*a* GR consolation, exhortation, solace, persuasion.
34*a* 2 Cor. 1:19; 1 Thes. 1:1; 1 Pet. 5:12.
36*a* Acts 12:25 (20–25).
b TG Brotherhood and Sisterhood.
37*a* Acts 13:13.
b Col. 4:10; 2 Tim. 4:11.
39*a* TG Contention.
41*a* D&C 24:9.
16 1*a* Acts 17:14 (14–15); 20:4; 1 Cor. 4:17; 1 Thes. 1:1; 3:2 (2, 6); 1 Tim. 1:2.
b 2 Tim. 1:5.
3*a* TG Circumcision.
4*a* Acts 15:23 (23–29).
5*a* Moro. 7:32 (31–32).

[a]Holy Ghost to preach the word in
Asia,
7 After they were come to Mysia,
they assayed to go into Bithynia:
but the Spirit suffered them not.
8 And they passing by Mysia came
down to Troas.
9 And a [a]vision appeared to Paul
in the night; There stood a man of
Macedonia, and prayed him, saying, Come over into Macedonia,
and help us.
10 And after he had seen the vision,
immediately we endeavoured to go
into Macedonia, assuredly gathering
that the Lord had called us for to
preach the gospel unto them.
11 Therefore loosing from Troas,
we came with a straight course to
Samothracia, and the next *day* to
Neapolis;
12 And from thence to Philippi,
which is the chief city of that part
of Macedonia, *and* a colony: and we
were in that city abiding certain days.
13 And on the sabbath we went
out of the city by a river side, where
prayer was wont to be made; and
we sat down, and spake unto the
women which resorted *thither*.
14 ¶ And a certain woman named
[a]Lydia, a seller of purple, of the city
of Thyatira, which worshipped God,
heard *us:* whose [b]heart the Lord
opened, that she attended unto the
things which were spoken of Paul.
15 And when she was baptized,
and her household, she besought
us, saying, If ye have judged me to
be faithful to the Lord, come into
my house, and [a]abide *there*. And she
constrained us.
16 ¶ And it came to pass, as we
went to prayer, a certain damsel
possessed with a spirit of divination
met us, which brought her masters
much gain by [a]soothsaying:
17 The same followed Paul and us,
and cried, saying, [a]These men are
the servants of the most high God,
which shew unto us the way of
salvation.
18 And this did she many days.
But Paul, being grieved, turned
and said to the [a]spirit, I command
thee in the name of Jesus Christ to
come out of her. And he came out
the same hour.
19 ¶ And when her masters saw
that the hope of their gains was
gone, they caught Paul and Silas,
and drew *them* into the marketplace
unto the rulers,
20 And brought them to the magistrates, saying, These men, being
Jews, do exceedingly trouble our city,
21 And teach customs, which are
not lawful for us to receive, neither
to observe, being Romans.
22 And the multitude rose up together against them: and the magistrates rent off their clothes, and
commanded to [a]beat *them*.
23 And when they had laid many
[a]stripes upon them, they cast *them*
into prison, charging the jailor to
keep them safely:
24 Who, having received such a
charge, thrust them into the inner
prison, and made their feet fast in
the stocks.
25 ¶ And at [a]midnight Paul and
Silas prayed, and [b]sang praises unto
God: and the prisoners heard them.
26 And suddenly there was a great
earthquake, so that the foundations
of the prison were shaken: and immediately all the [a]doors were opened,
and every one's bands were loosed.
27 And the keeper of the prison
awaking out of his sleep, and seeing
the prison doors open, he drew out
his sword, and would have killed
himself, supposing that the prisoners had been fled.
28 But Paul cried with a loud voice,

6*a* Alma 21:16 (16–17); 22:1 (1–4).
9*a* 2 Cor. 2:12. TG Vision.
14*a* Acts 16:40.
b Alma 16:16.
15*a* 1 Tim. 5:10.
16*a* TG Sorcery.
17*a* James 2:19.
18*a* TG Spirits, Evil or Unclean.
22*a* 2 Cor. 11:25; 1 Thes. 2:2.
23*a* 2 Cor. 11:23. TG Cruelty.
25*a* Ps. 119:62.
b TG Singing.
26*a* Acts 5:19 (15–20); Alma 14:27 (27–28); 3 Ne. 28:19 (19–20); 4 Ne. 1:30.

saying, Do thyself no harm: for we
are all here.
29 Then he called for a light, and
sprang in, and came trembling, and
fell down before Paul and Silas,
30 And brought them out, and said,
Sirs, what must I do to be saved?
31 And they said, [a]Believe on the
Lord Jesus Christ, and thou shalt be
saved, and thy house.
32 And they spake unto him the
word of the Lord, and to all that
were in his house.
33 And he took them the same
hour of the night, and washed *their*
stripes; and was baptized, he and
all his, straightway.
34 And when he had brought them
into his house, he set meat before
them, and rejoiced, believing in God
with all his house.
35 And when it was day, the magistrates sent the serjeants, saying,
Let those men go.
36 And the keeper of the prison
told this saying to Paul, The magistrates have sent to let you go:
now therefore depart, and go in
peace.
37 But Paul said unto them, They
have beaten us openly uncondemned, being [a]Romans, and have
cast *us* into prison; and now do they
thrust us out [b]privily? nay verily;
but let them come themselves and
fetch us out.
38 And the serjeants told these
words unto the magistrates: and
they feared, when they heard that
they were Romans.
39 And they came and besought
them, and brought *them* out, and
desired *them* to depart out of the
city.
40 And they went out of the prison,
and entered into *the house of* [a]Ly-
dia: and when they had seen the
brethren, they comforted them,
and departed.

CHAPTER 17

Paul and Silas preach and are persecuted in Thessalonica and in Berea—Paul, in Athens, preaches from Mars' Hill about the unknown god—He says, We are the offspring of God.

Now when they had passed through
Amphipolis and Apollonia, they
came to [a]Thessalonica, where was
a synagogue of the Jews:
2 And Paul, as his manner was,
went in unto them, and three sabbath days [a]reasoned with them out
of the [b]scriptures,
3 Opening and alleging, that Christ
must needs have suffered, and risen
again from the dead; and that this
Jesus, whom I preach unto you, is
Christ.
4 And some of them believed, and
consorted with Paul and Silas; and
of the devout [a]Greeks a great multitude, and of the chief [b]women
not a few.
5 ¶ But the [a]Jews which believed
not, moved with envy, took unto
them certain [b]lewd fellows of
the baser sort, and gathered a company, and set all the city on an
[c]uproar, and [d]assaulted the house
of Jason, and sought to bring them
out to the people.
6 And when they found them
not, they drew Jason and certain
brethren unto the rulers of the
city, crying, These that have turned
the world upside down are come
hither also;
7 Whom Jason hath received: and
these all do contrary to the decrees
of Cæsar, saying that there is another
king, *one* Jesus.
8 And they troubled the people
and the rulers of the city, when
they heard these things.
9 And when they had taken secu-
rity of Jason, and of the other, they
let them go.

31*a* Mosiah 4:10 (9–10); Hel. 14:13. TG Baptism, Qualifications for.
37*a* Acts 22:25.
b OR secretly.
40*a* Acts 16:14 (14–15).
17 1*a* 1 Thes. 1:1.
2*a* Acts 18:19; 1 Thes. 2:2. TG Missionary Work.
b Alma 14:1.
4*a* John 12:20.
b Acts 13:50.
5*a* 2 Cor. 11:26.
b GR wicked, evil.
c TG Rioting and Reveling.
d 1 Thes. 1:6; 2:14.

10 ¶ And the brethren immediately sent away Paul and Silas by night unto Berea: who coming *thither* went into the synagogue of the Jews.

11 These were more noble than those in Thessalonica, in that they received the word with all readiness of mind, and [a]searched the scriptures daily, whether those things were so.

12 Therefore many of them believed; also of honourable women which were Greeks, and of men, not a few.

13 But when the Jews of Thessalonica had knowledge that the word of God was preached of Paul at Berea, they came thither also, and stirred up the people.

14 And then immediately the brethren sent away Paul to go as it were to the sea: but Silas and [a]Timotheus abode there still.

15 And they that conducted Paul brought him unto [a]Athens: and receiving a commandment unto Silas and Timotheus for to come to him with all speed, they departed.

16 ¶ Now while Paul waited for them at Athens, his spirit was stirred in him, when he saw the city [a]wholly given to [b]idolatry.

17 Therefore [a]disputed he in the [b]synagogue with the Jews, and with the devout persons, and in the market daily with them that met with him.

18 Then certain philosophers of the Epicureans, and of the Stoicks, encountered him. And some said, What will this babbler say? other some, He seemeth to be a setter forth of strange gods: because he preached unto them Jesus, and the resurrection.

19 And they took him, and brought him unto [a]Areopagus, saying, May we know what this new doctrine, whereof thou speakest, *is*?

20 For thou bringest certain strange things to our ears: we would know therefore what these things mean.

21 (For all the Athenians and strangers which were there [a]spent their time in nothing else, but either to tell, or to hear some new thing.)

22 ¶ Then Paul stood in the midst of Mars' hill, and said, *Ye* men of Athens, I perceive that in all things ye are [a]too superstitious.

23 For as I passed by, and beheld your [a]devotions, I found an altar with this inscription, TO THE [b]UNKNOWN GOD. Whom therefore ye [c]ignorantly worship, him [d]declare I unto you.

24 God that [a]made the world and all things therein, seeing that he is Lord of heaven and earth, [b]dwelleth not in temples made with hands;

25 Neither is [a]worshipped with men's hands, as though he needed any thing, seeing he giveth to all life, and [b]breath, and all things;

26 And hath [a]made of [b]one [c]blood [d]all [e]nations of men for to dwell on all the face of the earth, and hath [f]determined the [g]times before [h]appointed, and the [i]bounds of their habitation;

27 That they should [a]seek the

11*a* TG Scriptures, Study of.
14*a* Acts 16:1 (1–4).
15*a* 1 Thes. 3:1.
16*a* GR full of idols; i.e., grossly idolatrous.
b TG Idolatry.
17*a* TG Disputations.
b Acts 18:4 (4, 19); 19:8.
19*a* GR Hill of Ares (Mars); probably meaning the civil council which met there. Acts 17:34.
21*a* TG Waste.
22*a* GR most religious; i.e., careful in divine things.
23*a* GR sacred, venerated objects.
b D&C 93:19. TG God, Knowledge about.
c TG Ignorance.
d TG Preaching.
24*a* TG Creation.
b Acts 7:48.
25*a* TG Worship.
b TG Breath of Life.
26*a* Job 31:15; Mal. 2:10.
b Acts 10:34 (34–35); 15:9.
c D&C 38:25 (24–27).
d TG Gentiles.
e TG Nations.
f TG God, Foreknowledge of; God, Omniscience of.
g Eccl. 3:2; Alma 40:10. TG Time.
h TG Foreordination.
i Deut. 32:8 (8–9); Job 14:5. TG Order; Separation.
27*a* TG God, Access to.

Lord, [b]if haply they might [c]feel after him, and find him, though he be
not far from every one of us:
28 For in him we [a]live, and move,
and have our being; as certain also
of your own poets have said, For we
are also his [b]offspring.
29 Forasmuch then as we are the
[a]offspring of God, we ought not to
think that the Godhead is like unto
[b]gold, or silver, or stone, graven by
art and man's [c]device.
30 And the times of this [a]ignorance
God [b]winked at; but now [c]com-
mandeth all men every where to
[d]repent:
31 Because he hath appointed a
day, in the which he will [a]judge the
world in righteousness by *that* man
whom he hath [b]ordained; *whereof* he
hath given assurance unto all *men,*
in that he hath [c]raised him from
the dead.
32 ¶ And when they heard of the
[a]resurrection of the dead, some
[b]mocked: and others said, We will
hear thee again of this *matter.*
33 So Paul departed from among
them.
34 Howbeit certain men clave unto
him, and believed: among the which
was Dionysius the [a]Areopagite, and
a woman named Damaris, and others with them.

CHAPTER 18

Being rejected by the Jews, Paul turns to the Gentiles—He preaches, ministers, and travels—Apollos also preaches with power.

AFTER these things Paul departed
from Athens, and came to Corinth;
2 And found a certain Jew named
[a]Aquila, born in Pontus, lately come
from Italy, with his wife Priscilla;
(because that Claudius had commanded all Jews to depart from
Rome:) and came unto them.
3 And because he was of the same
craft, he abode with them, and
[a]wrought: for by their occupation
they were [b]tentmakers.
4 And he reasoned in the [a]syna-
gogue every [b]sabbath, and persuaded
the Jews and the Greeks.
5 And when Silas and [a]Timo-
theus were come from Macedonia,
Paul was pressed in the spirit, and
[b]testified to the Jews *that* Jesus *was*
[c]Christ.
6 And when they opposed themselves, and blasphemed, he [a]shook
his raiment, and said unto them,
Your [b]blood *be* upon your own heads;
I *am* clean: from henceforth I will
go unto the Gentiles.
7 ¶ And he departed thence, and
entered into a certain *man's* house,
named Justus, *one* that worshipped
God, whose house joined hard to
the synagogue.
8 And [a]Crispus, the chief ruler of
the synagogue, believed on the Lord
with all his house; and many of the
Corinthians hearing [b]believed, and
were baptized.

27*b* JST Acts 17:27 . . . if they *are willing to* find him, *for* he *is* not far from every one of us;
c D&C 101:8.
28*a* Deut. 30:20; D&C 45:1.
b TG Man, Antemortal Existence of.
29*a* TG Man, a Spirit Child of Heavenly Father; Man, Physical Creation of; Man, Potential to Become like Heavenly Father; Sons and Daughters of God; Spirit Creation.
b TG Idolatry.
c Jer. 44:8.
30*a* Acts 14:16 (16–17); 1 Pet. 1:14 (1–16); 2 Ne. 9:25 (25–27); D&C 76:72.
b OR overlooked, disregarded. Moro. 8:22 (9–26).
c D&C 18:9.
d TG Repent.
31*a* TG Jesus Christ, Judge; Judgment, the Last.
b TG Jesus Christ, Authority of.
c Acts 10:40.
32*a* Alma 12:15 (12–18).
b TG Mocking.
34*a* Acts 17:19 (19, 22).
18 2*a* 1 Cor. 16:19.
3*a* Acts 20:34; 1 Thes. 2:9.
b TG Skill.
4*a* Acts 17:17; 19:8.
b TG Sabbath.
5*a* 1 Thes. 1:1.
b Alma 7:26 (16, 26).
c TG Jesus Christ, Messiah.
6*a* Matt. 10:14; Acts 13:51 (44–51); D&C 24:15; 60:15.
b Ezek. 33:4 (3–5).
8*a* 1 Cor. 1:14.
b TG Baptism, Qualifications for.

9 Then spake the Lord to Paul in
the night by a [a]vision, Be not afraid,
but speak, and hold not thy peace:
10 For I am with thee, and no man
shall set on thee to hurt thee: for I
have much [a]people in this city.
11 And he continued *there* a year
and six months, teaching the word
of God among them.
12 ¶ And when Gallio was the
deputy of Achaia, the Jews made insurrection with one accord against
Paul, and brought him to the judgment seat,
13 Saying, This *fellow* persuadeth
men to [a]worship God contrary to
the law.
14 And when Paul was now about to
open *his* mouth, Gallio said unto the
Jews, If it were a matter of wrong or
[a]wicked [b]lewdness, O *ye* Jews, reason
would that I should bear with you:
15 But if it be a [a]question of words
and names, and *of* your law, look ye
to it; for I will be no judge of such
matters.
16 And he drave them from the
judgment seat.
17 Then all the Greeks took Sosthenes, the chief ruler of the synagogue, and beat *him* before the
judgment seat. And Gallio cared
for none of those things.
18 ¶ And Paul *after this* tarried
there yet a good while, and then
took his leave of the brethren, and
sailed thence into Syria, and with
him Priscilla and Aquila; having
shorn *his* head in Cenchrea: for he
had a [a]vow.
19 And he came to Ephesus, and
left them there: but he himself entered into the synagogue, and [a]reasoned with the Jews.
20 When they desired *him* to tarry
longer time with them, he consented not;
21 But bade them farewell, saying,
I must by all means keep this feast
that cometh in Jerusalem: but I will
return again unto you, if God will.
And he sailed from Ephesus.
22 And when he had landed at
Cæsarea, and gone up, and saluted
the church, he went down to Antioch.
23 And after he had spent some
time *there,* he departed, and went
over *all* the country of Galatia and
Phrygia in order, strengthening all
the disciples.
24 ¶ And a certain Jew named
[a]Apollos, born at Alexandria, an
eloquent man, *and* [b]mighty in the
scriptures, came to Ephesus.
25 This man was [a]instructed in
the way of the Lord; and being
[b]fervent in the spirit, he spake and
taught [c]diligently the things of the
Lord, knowing only the baptism
of [d]John.
26 And he began to speak boldly in
the synagogue: whom when Aquila
and Priscilla had heard, they took
him unto *them,* and expounded unto
him the way of God more perfectly.
27 And when he was disposed
to pass into Achaia, the brethren
[a]wrote, exhorting the disciples to
receive him: who, when he was
come, helped them much which
had believed through grace:
28 For he mightily convinced the
Jews, *and that* publickly, [a]shewing
by the scriptures that [b]Jesus was
Christ.

CHAPTER 19

Paul confers the gift of the Holy Ghost by the laying on of hands—He preaches and works many miracles—The sons of Sceva fail to cast out devils by exorcism—The worshippers of Diana (Artemis) raise a tumult against Paul.

AND it came to pass, that, while
Apollos was at Corinth, Paul having

9*a* TG Jesus Christ, Appearances, Postmortal; Vision.
10*a* D&C 111:2 (2–11).
13*a* Alma 30:7 (7–11).
14*a* Acts 25:5.
b GR crime.
15*a* Acts 23:29.
18*a* TG Vow.
19*a* Acts 17:2.
24*a* 1 Cor. 16:12.
b D&C 100:11.
25*a* TG Education.
b TG Zeal.
c GR accurately, precisely, diligently.
d Acts 19:3 (3–6).
27*a* D&C 42:11.
28*a* TG Scriptures, Study of.
b OR Jesus is the Christ.

passed through the upper [a]coasts
came to Ephesus: and finding certain disciples,
2 He said unto them, Have ye received the Holy Ghost since ye believed? And they said unto him, We
have not so much as heard whether
there be any Holy Ghost.
3 And he said unto them, Unto
what then were ye baptized? And
they said, Unto [a]John's baptism.
4 Then said Paul, John verily baptized with the baptism of [a]repen-
tance, saying unto the people, that
they should believe on him which
should come after him, that is, on
Christ Jesus.
5 When they heard *this,* they were
[a]baptized in the name of the Lord
Jesus.
6 And when Paul had laid *his* hands
upon them, the Holy Ghost came on
them; and they spake with [a]tongues,
and prophesied.
7 And all the men were about
twelve.
8 And he went into the [a]synagogue,
and spake boldly for the space of
three months, [b]disputing and persuading the things concerning the
kingdom of God.
9 But when divers were hardened,
and believed not, but spake evil of
that way before the multitude, he
departed from them, and separated
the disciples, disputing daily in the
school of one Tyrannus.
10 And this continued by the space
of two years; so that all they which
dwelt in Asia heard the word of the
Lord Jesus, both Jews and Greeks.
11 And God wrought special
[a]miracles by the hands of Paul:
12 So that from his body were
brought unto the sick [a]handker-
chiefs or aprons, and the diseases
departed from them, and the evil
spirits went out of them.
13 ¶ Then certain of the vagabond
Jews, [a]exorcists, took upon them to
call over them which had evil spirits
the [b]name of the Lord Jesus, saying,
We [c]adjure you by Jesus whom Paul
preacheth.
14 And there were seven sons of
one Sceva, a Jew, *and* chief of the
priests, which did so.
15 And the [a]evil spirit answered
and said, Jesus I know, and Paul I
know; but who are ye?
16 And the man in whom the evil
spirit was leaped on them, and overcame them, and prevailed against
them, so that they fled out of that
house naked and wounded.
17 And this was known to all the
Jews and Greeks also dwelling at
Ephesus; and fear fell on them all,
and the name of the Lord Jesus was
magnified.
18 And many that believed came,
and [a]confessed, and shewed their
deeds.
19 Many of them also which used
curious [a]arts brought their books
together, and burned them before
all *men:* and they counted the price
of them, and found *it* fifty thousand
pieces of silver.
20 So mightily grew the word of
God and prevailed.
21 ¶ After these things were ended,
Paul purposed in the [a]spirit, when
he had passed through Macedonia
and Achaia, to go to Jerusalem, saying, After I have been there, I must
also see [b]Rome.
22 So he sent into Macedonia
two of them that ministered unto
him, Timotheus and Erastus; but
he himself stayed in Asia for a
season.

---

19 1*a* OR parts, region.
3*a* Matt. 3:11; Acts 18:25.
4*a* TG Baptism, Qualifications for.
5*a* TG Baptism, Essential.
6*a* TG Holy Ghost, Mission of; Language.
8*a* Acts 17:17; 18:4 (4, 19).
b TG Disputations.
11*a* TG Priesthood, Authority; Priesthood, Power of.
12*a* 2 Kgs. 4:29; Luke 8:44 (43–48); Acts 5:15.
13*a* Mark 9:38 (38–49); Luke 11:19. TG Sorcery.
b TG Profanity.
c TG Unrighteous Dominion.
15*a* TG Spirits, Evil or Unclean.
18*a* TG Confession.
19*a* TG Sorcery.
21*a* Acts 20:22.
b Acts 23:11.

23 And the same time there arose
no small stir about that way.
24 For a certain *man* named Demetrius, a silversmith, which made
silver shrines for [a]Diana, brought
no small gain unto the craftsmen;
25 Whom he called together with
the workmen of like occupation,
and said, Sirs, ye know that by this
craft we have our wealth.
26 Moreover ye see and hear, that
not alone at Ephesus, but almost
throughout all Asia, this Paul hath
persuaded and turned away much
people, saying that they be no gods,
which are made with hands:
27 So that not only this our [a]craft
is in danger to be set at nought; but
also that the temple of the great
goddess Diana should be despised,
and her magnificence should be
destroyed, whom all Asia and the
world worshippeth.
28 And when they heard *these sayings*, they were full of wrath, and
cried out, saying, Great *is* Diana of
the Ephesians.
29 And the whole city was filled
with confusion: and having caught
Gaius and [a]Aristarchus, men of
Macedonia, Paul's companions in
travel, they rushed with one accord
into the theatre.
30 And when Paul would have entered in unto the people, the disciples suffered him not.
31 And certain of the chief of Asia,
which were his friends, sent unto
him, desiring *him* that he would not
adventure himself into the theatre.
32 Some therefore cried one thing,
and some another: for the assembly
was confused; and the more part
knew not wherefore they were come
together.
33 And they drew Alexander out of
the multitude, the Jews putting him
forward. And [a]Alexander beckoned
with the hand, and would have
made his defence unto the people.
34 But when they knew that he was
a Jew, all with one voice about the
space of two hours cried out, Great
is Diana of the Ephesians.
35 And when the townclerk had
[a]appeased the people, he said, Ye
men of Ephesus, what man is there
that knoweth not how that the city
of the Ephesians is a [b]worshipper of
the great goddess Diana, and of the
image which fell down from [c]Jupiter?
36 Seeing then that these things
cannot be spoken against, ye ought to
be quiet, and to do nothing [a]rashly.
37 For ye have brought hither these
men, which are neither robbers of
churches, nor yet blasphemers of
your goddess.
38 Wherefore if Demetrius, and the
craftsmen which are with him, have
a matter against any man, [a]the law
is open, and there are deputies: let
them implead one another.
39 But if ye inquire any thing concerning other matters, it shall be
determined in a lawful assembly.
40 For we are in danger to be called
in question for this day's [a]uproar,
there being no cause whereby we
may give an account of this concourse.
41 And when he had thus spoken,
he dismissed the assembly.

CHAPTER 20

Paul raises Eutychus from death—Paul is free from the blood of all men—He predicts apostasy from within the Church—He reveals a teaching from Jesus, It is more blessed to give than to receive.

AND after the [a]uproar was ceased, Paul called unto *him* the disciples, and [b]embraced *them*, and departed for to go into Macedonia.

24*a* GR Artemis.
27*a* Alma 11:24 (23–24).
29*a* Acts 20:4; 27:2; Col. 4:10.
33*a* 1 Tim. 1:20.
35*a* Acts 5:38 (34–42).
b GR temple keeper, guardian.
c GR Zeus.
36*a* TG Rashness.
38*a* GR court days are conducted.
40*a* TG Rioting and Reveling.
20 1*a* TG Rioting and Reveling.
b OR greeted, bade farewell, expressed good wishes.

2 And when he had gone over those
parts, and had given them much
exhortation, he came into Greece,
3 And *there* abode three months.
And when the Jews laid wait for
him, as he was about to sail into
Syria, he purposed to return through
Macedonia.
4 And there accompanied him
into Asia Sopater of Berea; and of
the Thessalonians, [a]Aristarchus and
Secundus; and Gaius of Derbe, and
[b]Timotheus; and of Asia, [c]Tychicus
and [d]Trophimus.
5 These going before tarried for
us at Troas.
6 And we sailed away from Philippi after the days of [a]unleavened
bread, and came unto them to Troas
in five days; where we abode seven
days.
7 And upon the [a]first [b]*day* of the
week, when the disciples came
[c]together to [d]break [e]bread, Paul
preached unto them, ready to depart on the morrow; and continued
his speech until midnight.
8 And there were many lights in
the upper chamber, where they were
gathered together.
9 And there sat in a window a certain young man named Eutychus,
being fallen into a deep sleep: and
as Paul was long preaching, he sunk
down with sleep, and fell down
from the third loft, and was taken
up dead.
10 And Paul went down, and fell
on him, and [a]embracing *him* said,
Trouble not yourselves; for his life
is in him.
11 When he therefore was come up
again, and had broken bread, and
eaten, and talked a long while, even
till break of day, so he departed.
12 And they brought the young
man [a]alive, and were not a little
comforted.
13 ¶ And we went before to ship,
and sailed unto Assos, there intending to take in Paul: for so had
he appointed, minding himself to
[a]go afoot.
14 And when he met with us at
Assos, we took him in, and came
to Mitylene.
15 And we sailed thence, and came
the next *day* over against Chios;
and the next *day* we arrived at
Samos, and tarried at Trogyllium;
and the next *day* we came to Miletus.
16 For Paul had determined to
sail by Ephesus, because he would
not spend the time in Asia: for
he [a]hasted, if it were possible for
him, to be at Jerusalem the day of
[b]Pentecost.
17 ¶ And from Miletus he sent to
Ephesus, and called the [a]elders of
the church.
18 And when they were come to
him, he said unto them, Ye know,
from the first day that I came into
Asia, after what manner I have been
with you at all seasons,
19 [a]Serving the Lord with all [b]hu-
mility of mind, and with many [c]tears,
and [d]temptations, which befell me
by the lying in wait of the Jews:
20 *And* how I kept back nothing
that was profitable *unto you*, but
have shewed you, and have taught
you publickly, and from house
to house,
21 Testifying both to the Jews,
and also to the Greeks, repentance
toward God, [a]and faith toward our
Lord [b]Jesus Christ.
22 And now, behold, I go bound
in the [a]spirit unto Jerusalem, not
knowing the things that shall be-
fall me there:

4*a* Acts 19:29; 27:2; Col. 4:10.
b Acts 16:1.
c Eph. 6:21.
d Acts 21:29.
6*a* Ex. 12:15 (14–15).
7*a* TG Sabbath.
b TG Jesus Christ, Types of, in Memory.
c TG Assembly for Worship; Meetings.
d D&C 20:75. TG Sacrament.
e TG Bread.
10*a* 1 Kgs. 17:21.
12*a* TG Death, Power over.
13*a* GR travel by land, on foot.
16*a* TG Haste.
b Acts 2:1.
17*a* D&C 67:1.
19*a* D&C 4:2 (2, 6).
b TG Humility.
c 2 Ne. 33:3.
d TG Test.
21*a* JST Acts 20:21 . . . and faith *on the name of* our Lord Jesus Christ.
b D&C 68:25.
22*a* Acts 19:21; 1 Ne. 4:6.

23 Save that the Holy Ghost witnesseth in every city, saying that bonds and [a]afflictions [b]abide me.

24 But none of these things [a]move me, neither count I my [b]life dear unto myself, so that I might finish my course with joy, and the ministry, which I have received of the Lord Jesus, to testify the [c]gospel of the [d]grace of God.

25 And now, behold, I know that ye all, among whom I have gone preaching the kingdom of God, shall see my face no more.

26 Wherefore I take you to record this day, that I *am* pure from the [a]blood of all *men.*

27 For I have not shunned to declare unto you all the [a]counsel of God.

28 ¶ Take heed therefore unto yourselves, and to all the [a]flock, over the which the Holy Ghost hath made you [b]overseers, to feed the [c]church of God, which he hath purchased with his own [d]blood.

29 For I know this, that after my departing shall [a]grievous wolves enter in among you, not sparing the flock.

30 Also of your own selves shall men arise, speaking [a]perverse things, to [b]draw away disciples after them.

31 Therefore watch, and remember, that by the space of three years I ceased not to [a]warn every one night and day with tears.

32 And now, brethren, I commend you to God, and to the word of his grace, which is able to build you up, and to give you an [a]inheritance among all them which are sanctified.

33 I have [a]coveted no man's silver, or [b]gold, or apparel.

34 Yea, ye yourselves know, that these [a]hands have [b]ministered unto my necessities, and to them that were with me.

35 I have shewed you all things, how that so labouring ye ought to support the weak, and to remember the words of the Lord Jesus, how he said, It is more blessed to [a]give than to receive.

36 ¶ And when he had thus spoken, he kneeled down, and prayed with them all.

37 And they all wept sore, and fell on Paul's neck, and kissed him,

38 [a]Sorrowing most of all for the words which he spake, that they should see his face no more. And they accompanied him unto the ship.

CHAPTER 21

Paul journeys to Jerusalem—He is persecuted, arrested, and bound.

AND it came to pass, that after we were gotten from them, and had launched, we came with a straight course unto Coos, and the *day* following unto Rhodes, and from thence unto Patara:

2 And finding a ship sailing over unto Phenicia, we went aboard, and set forth.

3 Now when we had discovered Cyprus, we left it on the left hand, and sailed into Syria, and landed at Tyre: for there the ship was to unlade her burden.

4 And finding disciples, we tarried there seven days: who said to Paul through the [a]Spirit, that he should not go up to Jerusalem.

5 And when we had accomplished those days, we departed and went

---

23*a* 1 Thes. 3:3.
b GR wait for me.
24*a* Dan. 3:16; Matt. 10:19.
b Acts 21:13. TG Martyrdom.
c TG Gospel.
d TG Grace.
26*a* Jacob 1:19.
27*a* D&C 100:5 (5–8). TG Counsel.
28*a* TG Church.
b OR bishops. TG Bishop.
c TG Church.
d Heb. 9:12; 1 Jn. 1:7.
29*a* TG Apostasy of the Early Christian Church.
30*a* TG False Doctrine.
b Rom. 16:17 (17–19). TG Apostasy of Individuals.
31*a* Hel. 10:4. TG Warn.
32*a* TG Inheritance.
33*a* TG Covet.
b Mosiah 2:12 (12–18).
34*a* Acts 18:3; 1 Cor. 9:18 (4–18); 1 Thes. 2:9.
b TG Labor.
35*a* TG Almsgiving; Generosity.
38*a* TG Mourning.
21 4*a* D&C 38:33.

our way; and they all brought us on
our way, with wives and children,
till *we were* out of the city: and we
kneeled down on the shore, and
prayed.
6 And when we had taken our leave
one of another, we took ship; and
they returned home again.
7 And when we had finished *our*
course from Tyre, we came to Ptolemais,
and saluted the brethren, and
abode with them one day.
8 And the next *day* we that were of
Paul's company departed, and came
unto [a]Cæsarea: and we entered into
the house of [b]Philip the [c]evangelist,
which was *one* of the seven; and
abode with him.
9 And the same man had four
daughters, virgins, which did
[a]prophesy.
10 And as we tarried *there* many
days, there came down from Judæa
a certain prophet, named Agabus.
11 And when he was come unto
us, he took Paul's girdle, and bound
his own hands and feet, and said,
Thus saith the [a]Holy Ghost, So shall
the Jews at Jerusalem bind the man
that owneth this girdle, and shall
deliver *him* into the hands of the
Gentiles.
12 And when we heard these
things, both we, and they of that
place, besought him not to go up to
Jerusalem.
13 Then Paul answered, What mean
ye to weep and to break mine heart?
for I am ready not to be bound only,
but also to [a]die at Jerusalem for the
name of the Lord Jesus.
14 And when he would not be persuaded,
we ceased, saying, The [a]will
of the Lord be done.
15 And after those days we [a]took
up our carriages, and went up to
Jerusalem.
16 There went with us also *certain*
of the disciples of Cæsarea, and
brought with them one Mnason of
Cyprus, an [a]old disciple, with whom
we should lodge.
17 And when we were come to
Jerusalem, the brethren received
us gladly.
18 And the *day* following Paul went
in with us unto [a]James; and all the
elders were present.
19 And when he had saluted them,
he declared particularly what things
God had wrought among the [a]Gentiles
by his ministry.
20 And when they heard *it*, they
glorified the Lord, and said unto
him, Thou seest, brother, how many
thousands of Jews there are which
believe; and they are all [a]zealous
of the law:
21 And they are informed of
thee, that thou teachest all the
Jews which are among the Gentiles
to forsake Moses, saying that
they ought not to [a]circumcise *their*
children, neither to walk after the
[b]customs.
22 What is it therefore? the multitude
must needs come together: for
they will hear that thou art come.
23 Do therefore this that we say to
thee: We have four men which have
a [a]vow on them;
24 Them take, and purify thyself
with them, and [a]be at charges with
them, that they may [b]shave *their*
heads: and all may know that those
things, whereof they were informed
concerning thee, are nothing; but
that thou thyself also walkest orderly,
and keepest the law.
25 As touching the Gentiles which
believe, we have written *and* concluded
that they observe no such
thing, save only that they keep
themselves from *things* offered to

8*a* Acts 8:40.
b Acts 6:5; Eph. 4:11.
c 2 Tim. 4:5.
9*a* Judg. 4:4 (4–5); Acts 2:17.
11*a* Acts 2:18; 11:28 (27–28).
13*a* Acts 20:24; D&C 103:28 (27–28).
14*a* Matt. 26:42.
15*a* GR made preparation, packed baggage.
16*a* TG Old Age.
18*a* Gal. 1:19.
19*a* Acts 11:18; Alma 26:31 (11–36).
20*a* TG Zeal.
21*a* TG Circumcision.
b Acts 6:14.
23*a* TG Vow.
24*a* GR pay expenses for them.
b Lev. 14:8; Num. 6:18 (2–18).

[a]idols, and from blood, and from
strangled, and from [b]fornication.
26 Then Paul took the men, and
the next day purifying himself
with them entered into the temple,
to signify the [a]accomplishment of
the days of [b]purification, until that
an [c]offering should be offered for
every one of them.
27 And when the [a]seven days were
almost ended, the Jews which were
of Asia, when they saw him in the
temple, stirred up all the people,
and laid hands on him,
28 Crying out, Men of Israel, help:
This is the man, that teacheth all
men every where against the people, and the law, and this place: and
further brought Greeks also into the
[a]temple, and hath [b]polluted this holy
place.
29 (For they had seen before with
him in the city [a]Trophimus an Ephe-
sian, whom they supposed that Paul
had brought into the temple.)
30 And all the city was moved,
and the people ran together: and
they took Paul, and drew him out
of the temple: and forthwith the
doors were shut.
31 And as they went about to [a]kill
him, tidings came unto the chief
captain of the band, that all Jerusalem was in an [b]uproar.
32 Who immediately took soldiers
and centurions, and ran down unto
them: and when they saw the chief
[a]captain and the soldiers, they left
beating of Paul.
33 Then the chief [a]captain came
near, and took him, and commanded
him to be bound with two chains;
and demanded who he was, and
what he had done.
34 And some cried one thing,
some another, among the multitude:
and when he could not know the
certainty for the tumult, he commanded him to be carried into the
[a]castle.
35 And when he came upon the
stairs, so it was, that he was borne
of the soldiers for the violence of
the people.
36 For the multitude of the people followed after, crying, Away
with him.
37 And as Paul was to be led into
the castle, he said unto the chief
captain, May I speak unto thee?
Who said, Canst thou speak Greek?
38 Art not thou that Egyptian,
which before these days madest
an uproar, and leddest out into the
wilderness four thousand men that
were murderers?
39 But Paul said, I am a man *which
am* a Jew of [a]Tarsus, *a city* in Cilicia, a citizen of no mean city: and,
I beseech thee, suffer me to speak
unto the people.
40 And when he had given him licence, Paul stood on the stairs, and
[a]beckoned with the hand unto the
people. And when there was made
a great [b]silence, he spake unto *them*
in the Hebrew tongue, saying,

CHAPTER 22

Paul recounts the story of his conversion and also tells of seeing Jesus in a vision—He is accorded some privileges as a Roman citizen.

MEN, brethren, and fathers, hear
ye my defence *which I make* now
unto you.
2 (And when they heard that he
spake in the Hebrew tongue to
them, they kept the more silence:
and he saith,)
3 I am verily a man *which am* a [a]Jew,
born in Tarsus, *a city* in Cilicia, yet
brought up in this city at the [b]feet
of [c]Gamaliel, *and* taught according to the perfect manner of the

25*a* Acts 15:20 (19–20).
b TG Fornication.
26*a* Num. 6:13.
b TG Purification.
c Num. 6:11 (9–12).
27*a* Num. 6:9.
28*a* Acts 24:6.
b TG Pollution.
29*a* Acts 20:4.
31*a* Acts 26:21; 2 Cor. 11:26.
b TG Rioting and Reveling.
32*a* Acts 23:27.
33*a* Acts 24:7.
34*a* Acts 22:24.
39*a* Acts 23:34.
40*a* Acts 12:17.
b TG Silence.
22 3*a* Rom. 11:1.
b Deut. 33:3.
c Acts 5:34.

[d]law of the fathers, and was [e]zealous
toward God, as ye all are this day.
4 And I [a]persecuted this way unto
the death, binding and delivering
into prisons both men and women.
5 As also the high priest doth bear
me witness, and all the estate of the
elders: from whom also I received
[a]letters unto the brethren, and went
to Damascus, to bring them which
were there bound unto Jerusalem,
for to be punished.
6 And it came to pass, that, as I
made my journey, and was come
nigh unto Damascus about noon,
suddenly there shone from heaven
a great [a]light round about me.
7 And I fell unto the ground, and
heard a voice saying unto me, [a]Saul,
Saul, why persecutest thou me?
8 And I answered, Who art thou,
Lord? And he said unto me, I am
[a]Jesus of Nazareth, whom thou persecutest.
9 And they that were with me saw
indeed the light, and were afraid;
but they heard not the [a]voice of him
that spake to me.
10 And I said, What shall I do, Lord?
And the Lord said unto me, Arise,
and go into Damascus; and there it
shall be told thee of all things which
are appointed for thee to do.
11 And when I could not see for
the glory of that light, being led by
the hand of them that were with
me, I came into Damascus.
12 And one [a]Ananias, a devout
man according to the law, having a
good [b]report of all the Jews which
dwelt *there*,
13 Came unto me, and stood, and
said unto me, Brother Saul, receive
thy [a]sight. And the same hour I
looked up upon him.
14 And he said, The God of our
fathers hath chosen thee, that thou
shouldest know his [a]will, and see
that Just One, and shouldest hear
the voice of his mouth.
15 For thou shalt be his [a]witness
unto all men of what thou hast seen
and heard.
16 And now why tarriest thou?
arise, and be [a]baptized, and [b]wash
away thy sins, calling on the name
of the Lord.
17 And it came to pass, that, when
I was come again to Jerusalem, even
while I prayed in the temple, I was
in a [a]trance;
18 And [a]saw him saying unto me,
Make haste, and get thee quickly out
of Jerusalem: for they will not receive thy testimony concerning me.
19 And I said, Lord, they know that
I [a]imprisoned and beat in every synagogue them that believed on thee:
20 And when the blood of thy
[a]martyr Stephen was shed, I also was
standing by, and [b]consenting unto
his death, and kept the [c]raiment of
them that slew him.
21 And he said unto me, Depart:
for I will send thee far hence unto
the [a]Gentiles.
22 And they gave him [a]audience
unto this word, and *then* lifted up
their voices, and said, Away with
such a *fellow* from the earth: for it
is not fit that he should live.
23 And as they cried out, and cast
off *their* clothes, and threw dust
into the air,
24 The chief captain commanded
him to be brought into the [a]castle,
and bade that he should be examined by [b]scourging; that he might
know wherefore they cried so
against him.

3*d* Acts 26:5.
e TG Zeal.
4*a* Acts 8:3; 26:10; 1 Tim. 1:13.
5*a* Acts 9:2.
6*a* TG Vision.
7*a* Acts 9:4 (1–9); 26:14 (9–17).
8*a* Acts 23:9.
9*a* Acts 9:7.
12*a* Acts 9:10.
b 1 Tim. 3:7.
13*a* TG Sight.
14*a* TG God, Will of.
15*a* Luke 24:48 (45–49); Acts 9:15; 13:31 (29–33); 26:16.
16*a* TG Baptism; Baptism, Essential; Conversion.
b TG Wash.
17*a* Acts 10:10 (9–18); 11:5 (1–18).
18*a* TG Jesus Christ, Appearances, Postmortal.
19*a* Acts 8:3 (3–4).
20*a* TG Martyrdom.
b Luke 11:48 (47–49).
c Acts 7:58.
21*a* Acts 26:17 (17–18); Rom. 11:13.
22*a* 2 Ne. 27:32.
24*a* Acts 21:34.
b TG Cruelty.

25 And as they bound him with thongs, Paul said unto the centurion that stood by, Is it lawful for you to scourge a man that is a [a]Roman, and uncondemned?

26 When the centurion heard *that*, he went and told the chief captain, saying, Take heed what thou doest: for this man is a Roman.

27 Then the chief captain came, and said unto him, Tell me, art thou a Roman? He said, Yea.

28 And the [a]chief captain answered, With a great sum obtained I this freedom. And Paul said, But I was *free* born.

29 [a]Then straightway they departed from him which should have examined him: and the chief captain also was afraid, after he knew that he was a Roman, and because he had bound him.

30 On the morrow, because he would have known the certainty wherefore he was [a]accused of the Jews, he loosed him from *his* bands, and commanded the chief priests and all their council to appear, and brought Paul down, and set him before them.

CHAPTER 23

Paul is smitten at Ananias's order—The Lord again appears to Paul—Forty Jews plot his death—He is delivered over to Felix.

AND Paul, earnestly beholding the council, said, Men *and* brethren, I have lived in all good [a]conscience before God until this day.

2 And the high priest [a]Ananias commanded them that stood by him to [b]smite him on the mouth.

3 Then said Paul unto him, God shall smite thee, *thou* [a]whited wall: for sittest thou to judge me after the law, and commandest me to be smitten contrary to the law?

4 And they that stood by said, [a]Revilest thou God's high priest?

5 Then said Paul, I [a]wist not, brethren, that he was the high priest: for it is written, Thou shalt not speak evil of the [b]ruler of thy people.

6 But when Paul perceived that the one part were Sadducees, and the other Pharisees, he cried out in the council, Men *and* brethren, I am a [a]Pharisee, the son of a Pharisee: of the [b]hope and [c]resurrection of the dead I am called in question.

7 And when he had so said, there arose a dissension between the Pharisees and the Sadducees: and the multitude was divided.

8 For the [a]Sadducees say that there is no [b]resurrection, neither angel, nor spirit: but the Pharisees confess both.

9 And there arose a great cry: and the [a]scribes *that were* of the Pharisees' part arose, and strove, saying, We find no evil in this man: but if a spirit or an [b]angel hath spoken to him, let us not [c]fight against God.

10 And when there arose a great dissension, the chief captain, fearing lest Paul should have been pulled in pieces of them, commanded the soldiers to go down, and to take him by force from among them, and to bring *him* into the castle.

11 And the night following the [a]Lord [b]stood by him, and said, Be of good [c]cheer, Paul: for as thou hast testified of me in Jerusalem, so must thou bear witness also at [d]Rome.

12 And when it was day, certain of the Jews banded together, and

---

25*a* Acts 16:37; 23:27.
28*a* Acts 23:26.
29*a* JST Acts 22:29–30 (Appendix).
30*a* Acts 23:28.
23 1*a* TG Conscience.
2*a* Acts 24:1.
b John 18:22 (20–23).
3*a* Ps. 5:9 (9–10); Matt. 23:27; Luke 11:44.
4*a* TG Reviling.
5*a* OR knew.
b TG Citizenship.
6*a* Acts 26:5; Philip. 3:5.
b Acts 28:20.
c Acts 24:21.
8*a* Matt. 22:23.
b Acts 4:2.
9*a* TG Scribe.
b Acts 22:8 (6–10).
c Acts 5:39 (34–40).
11*a* TG Vision.
b TG Jesus Christ, Appearances, Postmortal.
c Hel. 10:4 (2–5); D&C 121:7 (1–7).
d Acts 19:21.

bound themselves under a [a]curse,
saying that they would neither eat
nor drink till they had [b]killed Paul.
13 And they were more than forty
which had made this [a]conspiracy.
14 And they came to the chief
priests and elders, and said, We
have bound ourselves under a great
curse, that we will eat nothing until
we have slain Paul.
15 Now therefore ye with the council signify to the chief captain that
he bring him down unto you to
morrow, as though ye would inquire
something more perfectly concerning him: and we, [a]or ever he come
near, are ready to kill him.
16 And when Paul's sister's son
heard of their lying in wait, he
went and entered into the castle,
and told Paul.
17 Then Paul called one of the
centurions unto *him,* and said, Bring
this young man unto the chief captain: for he hath a certain thing to
tell him.
18 So he took him, and brought
him to the chief captain, and said,
Paul the prisoner called me unto
him, and prayed me to bring this
young man unto thee, who hath
something to say unto thee.
19 Then the chief captain took
him by the hand, and went *with*
him aside privately, and asked *him,*
What is that thou hast to tell me?
20 And he said, The Jews have
agreed to desire thee that thou
wouldest bring down Paul to morrow into the council, as though they
would inquire somewhat of him
more perfectly.
21 But do not thou yield unto them:
for there lie in wait for him of them
more than forty men, which have
bound themselves with an [a]oath,
that they will neither eat nor drink
till they have killed him: and now
are they ready, looking for a promise from thee.
22 So the chief captain *then* let the
young man depart, and charged
him, See thou tell no man that
thou hast shewed these things
to me.
23 And he called unto *him* two
centurions, saying, Make ready two
hundred soldiers to go to Cæsarea,
and horsemen threescore and ten,
and spearmen two hundred, at the
third hour of the night;
24 And provide *them* beasts, that
they may set Paul on, and bring *him*
safe unto Felix the governor.
25 And he wrote a letter after this
manner:
26 Claudius [a]Lysias unto the most
excellent governor Felix *sendeth*
greeting.
27 This man was taken of the Jews,
and [a]should have been killed of
them: then came I with an [b]army,
and rescued him, having understood
that he was a [c]Roman.
28 And when I would have known
the cause wherefore they [a]accused
him, I brought him forth into their
council:
29 Whom I perceived to be accused
of [a]questions of their law, but to have
nothing laid to his charge worthy
of [b]death or of bonds.
30 And when it was told me how
that the Jews laid wait for the man,
I sent [a]straightway to thee, and gave
commandment to his accusers also
to say before thee what *they had*
against him. Farewell.
31 Then the soldiers, as it was
commanded them, took Paul, and
brought *him* by night to Antipatris.
32 On the morrow they left the
horsemen to go with him, and returned to the castle:
33 Who, when they came to
Cæsarea, and delivered the epistle
to the governor, presented Paul also
before him.
34 And when the governor had
read *the letter,* he asked of what

12*a* TG Curse.
b Acts 25:3 (2–3); Alma 49:27 (26–27); 51:9.
13*a* TG Conspiracy.
15*a* OR before he gets here.
21*a* TG Vow.
26*a* Acts 22:28; 24:22.
27*a* JST Acts 23:27 . . . *would* . . .
b Acts 21:32.
c Acts 22:25.
28*a* Acts 22:30.
29*a* Acts 18:15 (12–17).
b Acts 25:25.
30*a* GR immediately.

province he was. And when he understood that *he was* of [a]Cilicia;
35 I will hear thee, said he, when
thine accusers are also come. And
he commanded him to be kept in
Herod's [a]judgment hall.

CHAPTER 24

Paul is accused of sedition—He answers in defense of his life and doctrine—He teaches Felix of righteousness, temperance, and the judgment to come.

AND after five days [a]Ananias the
high priest descended with the elders, and *with* a certain orator *named*
Tertullus, who informed the governor against Paul.
2 And when he was called forth,
Tertullus began to accuse *him,* saying, Seeing that by thee we enjoy
great quietness, and that very worthy deeds are done unto this nation
by thy providence,
3 We accept *it* always, and in all
places, most noble Felix, with all
thankfulness.
4 Notwithstanding, that I be not
further tedious unto thee, I pray
thee that thou wouldest hear us of
thy clemency a few words.
5 For we have found this man *a*
pestilent *fellow,* and a mover of sedition among all the Jews throughout
the world, and a ringleader of the
sect of the Nazarenes:
6 Who also hath gone about to profane the [a]temple: whom we took,
and would have judged according
to our law.
7 But the chief [a]captain Lysias
came *upon us,* and with great violence took *him* away out of our
hands,
8 Commanding his accusers to
come unto thee: by examining of
whom thyself mayest take knowledge of all these things, whereof we
accuse him.
9 And the Jews also assented, saying that these things were so.
10 Then Paul, after that the governor had beckoned unto him to
speak, answered, Forasmuch as I
know that thou hast been of many
years a judge unto this nation, I
do the more cheerfully answer for
myself:
11 Because that thou mayest understand, that there are yet but twelve
days since I went up to Jerusalem
for to worship.
12 And they neither found me
in the temple [a]disputing with any
man, neither raising up the people, neither in the synagogues, nor
in the city:
13 Neither can they prove the
things whereof they now accuse me.
14 But this I confess unto thee,
that after the way which they call
heresy, so worship I the God of my
fathers, believing all things which
are written in the law and in the
[a]prophets:
15 And have hope toward God,
which they themselves also allow,
that there shall be a [a]resurrection of
the dead, both of the just and unjust.
16 And herein do I exercise myself,
to have always a [a]conscience void of
offence toward God, and *toward* men.
17 Now after many years I came
to bring [a]alms to my nation, and
offerings.
18 Whereupon certain Jews from
Asia found me [a]purified in the
temple, neither with multitude, nor
with tumult.
19 Who ought to have been here
before thee, and object, if they had
ought against me.
20 Or else let these same *here* say,
if they have found any evil doing in
me, while I stood before the council,
21 Except it be for this one voice,
that I cried standing among them,
Touching the [a]resurrection of the

34*a* Acts 21:39.
35*a* GR *praetorium* (the governor's headquarters).
24 1*a* Acts 23:2 (1–5).
6*a* Acts 21:28.
7*a* Acts 21:33.
12*a* TG Disputations.
14*a* Acts 28:23.
15*a* TG Resurrection.
16*a* TG Conscience.
17*a* 1 Cor. 16:1. TG Almsgiving.
18*a* TG Purification.
21*a* Acts 23:6 (6–8).

dead I am called in question by you this day.

22 And when Felix heard these things, having more perfect knowledge of *that* way, he deferred them, and said, When [a]Lysias the chief captain shall come down, I will know the uttermost of your matter.

23 And he commanded a centurion to keep Paul, and to let *him* have liberty, and that he should forbid none of his acquaintance to minister or come unto him.

24 And after certain days, when Felix came with his wife Drusilla, which was a Jewess, he sent for Paul, and heard him concerning the faith in Christ.

25 And as he reasoned of righteousness, [a]temperance, and judgment to come, Felix [b]trembled, and answered, Go thy way for this time; when I have a convenient season, I will call for thee.

26 He hoped also that [a]money should have been given him of Paul, that he might loose him: wherefore he sent for him the oftener, and communed with him.

27 But after two years Porcius Festus came into Felix' room: and Felix, willing to shew the Jews a pleasure, left Paul bound.

CHAPTER 25

Paul, before Festus, appeals unto Cæsar—Agrippa desires to hear Paul.

NOW when Festus was come into the province, after three days he ascended from Cæsarea to Jerusalem.

2 Then the high priest and the chief of the Jews informed him against Paul, and besought him,

3 And desired favour against him, that he would send for him to Jerusalem, laying wait in the way to [a]kill him.

4 But Festus answered, that Paul should be kept at Cæsarea, and that he himself would depart shortly *thither.*

5 Let them therefore, said he, which among you are able, go down with *me,* and accuse this man, if there be any [a]wickedness in him.

6 And when he had tarried among them more than ten days, he went down unto Cæsarea; and the next day sitting on the judgment seat commanded Paul to be brought.

7 And when he was come, the Jews which came down from Jerusalem stood round about, and laid many and grievous complaints against Paul, which they could not prove.

8 While he answered for himself, Neither against the law of the Jews, neither against the temple, nor yet against Cæsar, have I offended any thing at all.

9 But Festus, willing to do the Jews a pleasure, answered Paul, and said, Wilt thou go up to Jerusalem, and there be judged of these things before me?

10 Then said Paul, I stand at Cæsar's judgment seat, where I ought to be judged: to the Jews have I done no wrong, as thou very well knowest.

11 For if I be an offender, or have committed any thing worthy of death, I refuse not to die: but if there be none of these things whereof these accuse me, no man may deliver me unto them. I appeal unto [a]Cæsar.

12 Then Festus, when he had conferred with the council, answered, Hast thou appealed unto Cæsar? unto Cæsar shalt thou go.

13 And after certain days king Agrippa and Bernice came unto Cæsarea to salute Festus.

14 And when they had been there many days, Festus declared Paul's cause unto the king, saying, There is a certain man left in bonds by Felix:

15 About whom, when I was at Jerusalem, the chief priests and the elders of the Jews informed *me,* desiring *to have* judgment against him.

22*a* Acts 23:26 (17–30).
25*a* GR self-control.
b GR feared.
26*a* TG Bribe; Selfishness.
25 3*a* Acts 23:12.
5*a* Acts 18:14. TG Wickedness.
11*a* Acts 26:32.

16 To whom I answered, It is not the manner of the Romans to deliver any man to die, before that he which is accused have the accusers face to face, and have licence to answer for himself concerning the crime laid against him.
17 Therefore, when they were come hither, without any delay on the morrow I sat on the judgment seat, and commanded the man to be brought forth.
18 Against whom when the accusers stood up, they brought none accusation of such things as I supposed:
19 But had certain questions against him of their own [a]superstition, and of one Jesus, which was dead, whom Paul affirmed to be alive.
20 And because I [a]doubted of such manner of questions, I asked *him* whether he would go to Jerusalem, and there be judged of these matters.
21 But when Paul had appealed to be reserved unto the hearing of Augustus, I commanded him to be kept till I might send him to Cæsar.
22 Then Agrippa said unto Festus, I would also hear the man myself. To morrow, said he, thou shalt hear him.
23 And on the morrow, when Agrippa was come, and Bernice, with great pomp, and was entered into the place of hearing, with the chief captains, and principal men of the city, at Festus' commandment Paul was brought forth.
24 And Festus said, King Agrippa, and all men which are here present with us, ye see this man, about whom all the multitude of the Jews have dealt with me, both at Jerusalem, and *also* here, crying that he ought not to live any longer.
25 But when I found that he had committed nothing worthy of [a]death, and that he himself hath appealed to Augustus, I have determined to send him.
26 Of whom I have no certain thing to write unto my lord. Wherefore I have brought him forth before you, and specially before thee, O king Agrippa, that, after examination had, I might have somewhat to write.
27 For it seemeth to me unreasonable to send a prisoner, and not withal to signify the crimes *laid* against him.

CHAPTER 26

Paul recounts his former persecution of the Saints as a Pharisee—He testifies of the appearance of Jesus on the Damascus road—Paul bears his testimony to King Agrippa.

THEN Agrippa said unto Paul, Thou art permitted to speak for thyself. Then Paul stretched forth the hand, and answered for himself:
2 I think myself happy, king Agrippa, because I shall answer for myself this day before thee touching all the things whereof I am accused of the Jews:
3 Especially *because I know* thee to be expert in all customs and questions which are among the Jews: wherefore I beseech thee to hear me patiently.
4 My manner of life from my youth, which was at the first among mine own nation at Jerusalem, know all the Jews;
5 Which knew me from the beginning, if they would testify, that after the most straitest sect of our religion I lived a [a]Pharisee.
6 And now I stand and am judged for the hope of the promise made of God unto our fathers:
7 Unto which *promise* our [a]twelve tribes, [b]instantly serving *God* day and night, hope to come. For which hope's sake, king Agrippa, I am accused of the Jews.

19*a* GR religion.
20*a* GR was perplexed concerning this inquiry or dispute.
25*a* Acts 23:29.
26 5*a* Acts 22:3; 23:6 (6–9).
7*a* TG Israel, Twelve Tribes of.
b GR earnestly, intently.

8 Why should it be thought a thing
incredible with you, that God should
[a]raise the dead?
9 I verily thought with myself, that
I ought to do many things [a]contrary
to the [b]name of Jesus of Nazareth.
10 Which thing I also did in Jerusalem: and many of the [a]saints did
I shut up in prison, having received
authority from the chief priests;
and when they were put to [b]death,
I gave my [c]voice against *them*.
11 And I punished them oft in every synagogue, and compelled *them*
to blaspheme; and being exceedingly
mad against them, I persecuted *them*
even unto [a]strange cities.
12 Whereupon as I went to Damascus with authority and commission
from the chief priests,
13 At midday, O king, I saw in the
way a [a]light from heaven, above
the brightness of the sun, shining
round about me and them which
journeyed with me.
14 And when we were all fallen to
the earth, I heard a voice speaking
unto me, and saying in the Hebrew
tongue, [a]Saul, Saul, why persecutest
thou me? *it is* hard for thee to kick
[b]against the pricks.
15 And I said, Who art thou, Lord?
And he said, I am Jesus whom thou
persecutest.
16 But rise, and stand upon thy
feet: for I have [a]appeared unto
thee for this purpose, to make thee
a minister and a [b]witness both of
these things which thou hast seen,
and of those things in the which I
will appear unto thee;
17 Delivering thee from the people,
and *from* the Gentiles, unto whom
now I [a]send thee,
18 To open their eyes, *and* to turn
them from [a]darkness to [b]light, and
from the power of Satan unto God,
that they may receive forgiveness of
sins, and inheritance among them
which are sanctified by faith that
is in me.
19 Whereupon, O king Agrippa, I
was not [a]disobedient unto the heavenly [b]vision:
20 But shewed first unto them of
Damascus, and at Jerusalem, and
throughout all the coasts of Judæa,
and *then* to the Gentiles, that they
should repent and turn to God, and
do works meet for repentance.
21 For these causes the Jews caught
me in the temple, and went about
to [a]kill *me*.
22 Having therefore obtained help
of God, I continue unto this day,
witnessing both to small and great,
saying none other things than those
which the [a]prophets and Moses did
say should come:
23 That Christ should [a]suffer, *and*
that he should be the first that
should [b]rise from the dead, and
should shew light unto the people,
and to the Gentiles.
24 And as he thus spake for himself, Festus said with a loud voice,
Paul, thou art beside thyself; much
learning doth make thee [a]mad.
25 But he said, I am not mad, most
noble Festus; but speak forth the
words of truth and soberness.
26 For the king knoweth of these
things, before whom also I speak
freely: for I am persuaded that none
of these things are hidden from
him; for this thing was not done in
a corner.
27 King Agrippa, believest thou
the prophets? I know that thou
[a]believest.

8*a* TG Resurrection.
9*a* 1 Tim. 1:13.
b TG Name.
10*a* Acts 9:1, 13 (13–14), 21; 22:4 (4–5).
b TG Martyrdom.
c GR vote.
11*a* GR foreign.
13*a* JS—H 1:16.
14*a* Acts 9:4 (1–9); 22:7 (6–16).
b TG Opposition.
16*a* TG Jesus Christ, Appearances, Postmortal.
b Luke 1:2; John 1:14; Acts 5:32; 9:15; 22:15; D&C 14:8. TG Conversion.
17*a* Acts 22:21.
18*a* TG Walking in Darkness.
b TG Light [noun].
19*a* TG Disobedience.
b TG Vision.
21*a* Acts 21:31 (30–31).
22*a* Acts 28:23.
23*a* TG Martyrdom.
b TG Jesus Christ, Resurrection.
24*a* JS—H 1:24 (24–25).
27*a* Alma 30:42 (41–42).

28 Then Agrippa said unto Paul,
Almost thou [a]persuadest me to be
a [b]Christian.
29 And Paul said, I would to God,
that not only thou, but also all that
hear me this day, were both almost,
and altogether such as I am, except
these bonds.
30 And when he had thus spoken,
the king rose up, and the governor,
and Bernice, and they that sat with
them:
31 And when they were gone aside,
they talked between themselves,
saying, This man doeth nothing
worthy of [a]death or of bonds.
32 Then said Agrippa unto Festus,
This man might have been set
at liberty, if he had not appealed
unto [a]Cæsar.

CHAPTER 27

Paul, in a perilous voyage, travels toward Rome—An angel comforts him—He uses the gift of seership—He is shipwrecked.

AND when it was determined that we
should sail into Italy, they delivered
Paul and certain other prisoners
unto *one* named Julius, a centurion
of Augustus' band.
2 And entering into a ship of
Adramyttium, we launched, meaning
to sail by the coasts of Asia; *one*
[a]Aristarchus, a Macedonian of Thessalonica,
being with us.
3 And the next *day* we touched at
Sidon. And Julius courteously entreated
Paul, and gave *him* liberty
to go unto his friends to refresh
himself.
4 And when we had launched from
thence, we sailed under Cyprus,
because the winds were contrary.
5 And when we had sailed over
the sea of Cilicia and Pamphylia,
we came to Myra, *a city* of Lycia.
6 And there the centurion found
a ship of Alexandria sailing into
Italy; and he put us therein.
7 And when we had sailed slowly
many days, and scarce were come
over against Cnidus, the wind not
suffering us, we sailed under Crete,
over against Salmone;
8 And, hardly passing it, came
unto a place which is called The
fair havens; nigh whereunto was
the city *of* Lasea.
9 Now when much time was spent,
and when sailing was now dangerous,
because the [a]fast was now already
past, Paul admonished *them*,
10 And said unto them, Sirs, I perceive
that this voyage will be with
hurt and much damage, not only
of the lading and ship, but also of
our lives.
11 Nevertheless the centurion believed
the master and the [a]owner
of the ship, more than those things
which were spoken by Paul.
12 And because the haven was
not commodious to winter in, the
more part advised to depart thence
also, if by any means they might attain
to Phenice, *and there* to winter;
which is an haven of Crete, and lieth
toward the south west and north
west.
13 And when the south wind blew
softly, supposing that they had obtained
their purpose, loosing *thence*,
they sailed close by Crete.
14 But not long after there arose
against it a tempestuous wind, called
Euroclydon.
15 And when the ship was caught,
and could not bear up into the wind,
we let *her* drive.
16 And running under a certain
island which is called Clauda, we
had much work to come by the
boat:
17 Which when they had taken up,
they used helps, undergirding the
ship; and, fearing lest they should
fall into the quicksands, strake sail,
and so were driven.
18 And we being exceedingly
tossed with a temptest, the next *day*
they lightened the ship;

28*a* TG Missionary Work.
b Acts 11:26.
31*a* TG Capital Punishment.
32*a* Acts 25:11.
27 2*a* Acts 19:29; 20:4; Col. 4:10.
9*a* Lev. 23:27 (27, 29). TG Fast, Fasting.
11*a* GR ship master, captain.

19 And the third *day* we cast out
with our own hands the tackling
of the ship.
20 And when neither sun nor stars
in many days appeared, and no
small tempest lay on *us*, all hope
that we should be saved was then
taken away.
21 But after long abstinence Paul
stood forth in the midst of them,
and said, Sirs, ye should have heark-
ened unto me, and not have loosed
from Crete, and to have gained this
harm and loss.
22 And now I exhort you to be of
good cheer: for there shall be no
loss of *any man's* [a]life among you,
but of the ship.
23 For there stood by me this night
the [a]angel of God, whose I am, and
whom I serve,
24 Saying, Fear not, Paul; thou must
be brought before Cæsar: and, lo,
God hath given thee all them that
sail with thee.
25 Wherefore, sirs, be of good
cheer: for I believe God, that it shall
be even as it was told me.
26 Howbeit we must be cast upon
a certain island.
27 But when the fourteenth night
was come, as we were driven up and
down in [a]Adria, about midnight the
shipmen deemed that they drew
near to some country;
28 And sounded, and found *it*
twenty fathoms: and when they had
gone a little further, they sounded
again, and found *it* fifteen fathoms.
29 Then fearing lest we should
have fallen upon rocks, they cast
four anchors out of the stern, and
wished for the day.
30 And as the shipmen were about
to flee out of the ship, when they
had let down the boat into the sea,
under colour as though they would
have cast anchors out of the foreship,
31 Paul said to the centurion and
to the soldiers, Except these abide
in the ship, ye cannot be saved.
32 Then the soldiers cut off the
ropes of the boat, and let her fall off.
33 And while the day was coming
on, Paul besought *them* all to take
meat, saying, This day is the fourteenth day that ye have tarried and
continued [a]fasting, having taken
nothing.
34 Wherefore I pray you to take
some meat: for this is for your [a]health:
for there shall not an hair fall from
the head of any of you.
35 And when he had thus spoken,
he took bread, and gave thanks to
God in presence of them all: and
when he had broken *it*, he began
to eat.
36 Then were they all of good cheer,
and they also took *some* meat.
37 And we were in all in the ship
two hundred threescore and six-
teen souls.
38 And when they had eaten
enough, they lightened the ship,
and cast out the wheat into the sea.
39 And when it was day, they knew
not the land: but they discovered
a certain [a]creek with a shore, into
the which they were minded, if it
were possible, to thrust in the ship.
40 And when they had [a]taken up
the anchors, they committed *themselves* unto the sea, and loosed the
rudder bands, and hoised up the
mainsail to the wind, and made
toward shore.
41 And falling into a place where
two seas met, they ran the ship
aground; and the forepart stuck fast,
and remained unmoveable, but the
hinder part was broken with the
violence of the waves.
42 And the soldiers' counsel was to
kill the prisoners, lest any of them
should swim out, and escape.
43 But the centurion, willing to
save Paul, kept them from *their*
purpose; and commanded that they
which could swim should cast *themselves* first *into the sea*, and get to land:
44 And the rest, some on boards,

22*a* Acts 27:44.
23*a* TG Angels; Vision.
27*a* IE the Adriatic Sea.
33*a* TG Fast, Fasting.
34*a* TG Health.
39*a* GR bay.
40*a* GR cut off anchors (they left them in the sea).

and some on *broken pieces* of the
ship. And so it came to pass, that
they escaped all [a]safe to land.

CHAPTER 28

Paul is unharmed by a viper's bite—He heals the sick in Melita—He preaches in Rome, first to the Jews and then to the Gentiles.

AND when they were escaped, then
they knew that the island was called
Melita.
2 And the [a]barbarous people
shewed us no little [b]kindness: for
they kindled a fire, and received us
every one, because of the present
rain, and because of the cold.
3 And when Paul had gathered a
bundle of sticks, and laid *them* on
the fire, there came a [a]viper out of
the heat, and fastened on his hand.
4 And when the barbarians saw the
venomous beast hang on his hand,
they said among themselves, No
doubt this man is a murderer, whom,
though he hath escaped the sea, yet
vengeance suffereth not to live.
5 And he shook off the beast into
the fire, and felt no [a]harm.
6 Howbeit they looked when he
should have swollen, or fallen down
dead suddenly: but after they had
looked a great while, and saw no
harm come to him, they changed
their minds, and said that he was
a [a]god.
7 In the same quarters were possessions of the chief man of the island,
whose name was Publius; who received us, and lodged us three days
[a]courteously.
8 And it came to pass, that the
father of Publius lay [a]sick of a fever
and of a [b]bloody flux: to whom Paul
entered in, and prayed, and laid
his [c]hands on him, and healed him.
9 So when this was done, others
also, which had diseases in the island, came, and were healed:
10 Who also honoured us with
many honours; and when we departed, they laded *us* with such
things as were necessary.
11 And after three months we departed in a ship of Alexandria, which
had wintered in the isle, whose sign
was Castor and Pollux.
12 And landing at Syracuse, we
tarried *there* three days.
13 And from thence we [a]fetched
a compass, and came to Rhegium:
and after one day the south wind
blew, and we came the next day to
Puteoli:
14 Where we found brethren, and
were desired to tarry with them
seven days: and so we went toward
Rome.
15 And from thence, when the
brethren heard of us, they came to
meet us as far as Appii forum, and
The three taverns: whom when Paul
saw, he [a]thanked God, and took
[b]courage.
16 And when we came to Rome, the
centurion delivered the prisoners to
the captain of the guard: but Paul
was suffered to dwell by himself
with a soldier that kept him.
17 And it came to pass, that after
three days Paul called the chief of
the Jews together: and when they
were come together, he said unto
them, Men *and* brethren, though I
have committed nothing against the
people, or customs of our fathers, yet
was I delivered prisoner from Jerusalem into the hands of the Romans.
18 Who, when they had examined
me, would have let *me* go, because
there was no cause of death in me.
19 But when the Jews spake against
it, I was constrained to appeal unto
Cæsar; not that I had ought to accuse my nation of.

44*a* Acts 27:22.
28 2*a* Rom. 1:14.
b TG Hospitality.
3*a* Mark 16:18; D&C 24:13; 84:72 (71–72); 124:99 (98–100).
5*a* Luke 10:19.
6*a* Acts 14:11 (8–11).
7*a* TG Courtesy.
8*a* TG Sickness.
b GR dysentery.
c TG Administrations to the Sick; Hands, Laying on of.
13*a* GR went around, took a circuitous course.
15*a* TG Thanksgiving.
b TG Courage.

20 For this cause therefore have
I called for you, to see *you*, and to
speak with *you*: because that for
the [a]hope of Israel I am bound with
this chain.
21 And they said unto him, We neither received letters out of Judæa
concerning thee, neither any of the
brethren that came shewed or spake
any harm of thee.
22 But we desire to hear of thee
what thou thinkest: for as concerning this sect, we know that every
where it is spoken against.
23 And when they had appointed
him a day, there came many to
him into *his* lodging; to whom he
[a]expounded and testified the kingdom of God, persuading them concerning Jesus, both out of the law
of Moses, and *out of* the [b]prophets,
from morning till evening.
24 And some believed the things
which were spoken, and some [a]believed not.
25 And when they agreed not
among themselves, they departed,
after that Paul had spoken one
word, Well [a]spake the Holy Ghost
by Esaias the prophet unto our
fathers,
26 Saying, Go unto this people, and
say, Hearing ye shall hear, and shall
not understand; and seeing ye shall
see, and not [a]perceive:
27 For the [a]heart of this people is
waxed gross, and their ears are dull
of hearing, and their [b]eyes have they
closed; lest they should see with *their*
eyes, and hear with *their* ears, and
understand with *their* heart, and
should be converted, and I should
heal them.
28 Be it known therefore unto you,
that the salvation of God is sent
unto the [a]Gentiles, and *that* they
will hear it.
29 And when he had said these
words, the Jews departed, and had
great reasoning among themselves.
30 And Paul dwelt two whole years
in his own hired house, and received
all that came in unto him,
31 Preaching the kingdom of
God, and teaching those things
which concern the Lord Jesus Christ,
with all confidence, no man forbidding him.

THE EPISTLE OF PAUL THE APOSTLE TO THE ROMANS

CHAPTER 1

The gospel is the power of God unto salvation through Jesus Christ—The wrath of God rests on those guilty of murder, homosexual practices, fornication, and other sins if the guilty do not repent.

PAUL, a [a]servant of Jesus Christ,
called *to be* an [b]apostle, [c]separated unto the gospel of God,

20*a* Acts 23:6.
TG Hope.
23*a* D&C 68:1.
b Acts 3:18 (18–21); 24:14; 26:22; Alma 18:36.
24*a* TG Unbelief.
25*a* TG Holy Ghost, Mission of.
26*a* Isa. 6:9.
27*a* TG Hardheartedness.
b TG Spiritual Blindness.
28*a* Acts 13:46.

[ROMANS]

1 1*a* TG Servant.
b 1 Cor. 4:9 (1–21); D&C 18:9.
c GR set apart.
TG Setting Apart.

2 (Which he had promised afore by
his prophets in the holy scriptures,)
3 Concerning his Son [a]Jesus Christ
our Lord, which was made of the
[b]seed of [c]David according to the
flesh;
4 And [a]declared *to be* the [b]Son of
God with [c]power, according to the
spirit of holiness, by the resurrection [d]from the dead:
5 By whom we have received [a]grace
and apostleship, [b]for [c]obedience to
the faith among all nations, for his
name:
6 Among whom are ye also the
called of Jesus Christ:
7 To all that be in Rome, beloved
of God, called *to be* [a]saints: Grace to
you and peace from God our Father,
and the Lord Jesus Christ.
8 First, I thank my God through
Jesus Christ for you all, that your
[a]faith is [b]spoken of throughout the
whole world.
9 For God is my witness, whom I
serve with my spirit in the gospel
of his Son, that without ceasing
I make mention of you always in
my prayers;
10 Making request, if by any means
now at length I might have a pros-
perous journey by the will of God
to come unto you.
11 For I long to see you, that I may
impart unto you some spiritual [a]gift,
to the end ye may be established;
12 That is, that I may be [a]comforted
together with you by the mutual
faith both of you and me.
13 Now I would not have you ignorant, brethren, that oftentimes
I purposed to come unto you, (but
was [a]let hitherto,) that I might have
some [b]fruit among you also, even as
among other Gentiles.
14 I am debtor both to the Greeks,
and to the [a]Barbarians; both to the
wise, and to the unwise.
15 So, as much as in me is, I am
[a]ready to preach the gospel to you
that are at Rome also.
16 For I am not [a]ashamed of the
[b]gospel of Christ: for it is the [c]power
of God unto [d]salvation to every one
that believeth; to the Jew first, and
also to the Greek.
17 For therein is the [a]righteous-
ness of God revealed [b]from faith to
faith: as it is written, The just shall
live by [c]faith.
18 For the [a]wrath of God is revealed
from heaven against all ungodliness
and unrighteousness of men, [b]who
[c]hold the truth in [d]unrighteousness;
19 Because that which may be
known of God is manifest [a]in them;
for God hath shewed *it* unto them.
20 For the [a]invisible things of him

3*a* The Greek text omits the name and title at this point.
b TG Jesus Christ, Birth of.
c TG Jesus Christ, Davidic Descent of.
4*a* GR appointed, decreed, set forth.
b D&C 10:57; 11:28; 14:9; 45:52.
c TG Jesus Christ, Power of.
d GR from the dead of Jesus Christ our Lord.
5*a* TG Grace.
b JST Rom. 1:5–6 . . . *through* obedience, *and* faith *in his name, to preach the gospel* among all nations; among whom ye also *are* called of Jesus Christ;
c TG Obedience.
7*a* TG Saints.
8*a* Rom. 16:19.
b GR proclaimed.
11*a* D&C 46:11 (8–32).
12*a* TG Sustaining Church Leaders.
13*a* GR hindered, restrained, prevented. Rom. 15:22.
b D&C 111:2 (2–11).
14*a* Acts 28:2.
15*a* TG Commitment.
16*a* Ps. 119:46; Matt. 10:33 (32–33); 2 Tim. 1:12; 2:12 (10–15); 2 Ne. 31:14 (12–21); D&C 101:5 (1–5). TG Loyalty; Shame.
b TG Gospel.
c 1 Cor. 1:18; 1 Pet. 1:5; D&C 68:4. TG Jesus Christ, Power of.
d 1 Cor. 15:2. TG Salvation.
17*a* Ps. 4:1; 2 Cor. 5:21. TG God, the Standard of Righteousness.
b JST Rom. 1:17 . . . *through* faith *on his name;* as it is written . . .
c TG Faith.
18*a* TG God, Indignation of.
b JST Rom. 1:18 . . . who *love not* the truth, *but remain* in unrighteousness,
c IE restrain the truth by unrighteousness.
d TG Unrighteous Dominion.
19*a* GR among, within.
20*a* Acts 14:17.

from the creation of the world are clearly seen, being understood by the things that are made, *even* his [b]eternal [c]power and Godhead; so that they are without excuse:
21 Because that, when they knew God, they glorified *him* not as God, neither were [a]thankful; but became [b]vain in their imaginations, and their [c]foolish heart was [d]darkened.
22 Professing themselves to be [a]wise, they became fools,
23 And changed the glory of the [a]uncorruptible God into an [b]image made like to [c]corruptible man, and to birds, and fourfooted beasts, and creeping things.
24 Wherefore God also [a]gave them up to [b]uncleanness through the lusts of their own hearts, to dishonour their own bodies between themselves:
25 Who changed the truth of God into a lie, and worshipped and served the creature more than the Creator, who is blessed for ever. Amen.
26 For this cause God [a]gave them up unto [b]vile [c]affections: for even their [d]women did change the natural use into that which is against nature:
27 And likewise also the men, leaving the natural use of the woman, burned in their [a]lust one toward another; men with men working that which is unseemly, and receiving in themselves that recompence of their error which was meet.
28 And even as they did not like to [a]retain God in *their* knowledge, God [b]gave them over to a [c]reprobate mind, to do those things which are not convenient;
29 Being filled with all unrighteousness, fornication, [a]wickedness, covetousness, [b]maliciousness; full of envy, murder, [c]debate, [d]deceit, malignity; whisperers,
30 [a]Backbiters, haters of God, [b]despiteful, [c]proud, [d]boasters, inventors of evil things, [e]disobedient to parents,
31 Without [a]understanding, covenantbreakers, without natural affection, implacable, unmerciful:
32 Who knowing the judgment of God, that they which commit such things are worthy of [a]death, not only do the same, but [b]have [c]pleasure in them that do them.

CHAPTER 2

God will render to every person according to his or her deeds—Both Jews and Gentiles will be judged by gospel laws.

THEREFORE thou art inexcusable, O man, whosoever thou art that judgest: for wherein thou [a]judgest another, thou condemnest thyself; for thou that judgest doest the same things.
2 But we [a]are sure that the [b]judgment of God is according to truth against them which commit such things.

20*b* TG God, Eternal Nature of.
c TG Jesus Christ, Power of.
21*a* TG Ingratitude.
b GR corrupt in their reasonings, deliberations. 2 Kgs. 17:15.
c Isa. 44:20; Hosea 4:12.
d TG Darkness, Spiritual.
22*a* 2 Ne. 9:28. TG Learn.
23*a* GR incorruptible, immortal.
b Ex. 32:4.
c GR (also) perishable.
24*a* Acts 7:42.
b TG Uncleanness.
26*a* GR abandoned, delivered.
b GR sufferings, passions of dishonor. 2 Tim. 3:3.
c Judg. 19:22.
d TG Woman.
27*a* TG Homosexual Behavior; Lust.
28*a* GR discern, choose.
b Ps. 81:12.
c GR worthless, unable to stand test.
29*a* TG Wickedness.
b TG Malice.
c GR strife, discord.
d TG Deceit.
30*a* GR Slanderers. TG Backbiting.
b GR violent, overbearing.
c TG Pride.
d TG Boast; Haughtiness.
e TG Disobedience; Family, Children, Duties of.
31*a* TG Understanding.
32*a* TG Capital Punishment.
b GR approve of them, sympathize with them.
c Jer. 5:31.
2 1*a* TG Judgment.
2*a* GR know.
b TG Judgment, the Last.

3 And thinkest thou this, O man,
that [a]judgest them which do such
things, and doest the same, that
thou shalt escape the [b]judgment
of God?
4 Or despisest thou the [a]riches of
his [b]goodness and [c]forbearance and
longsuffering; not knowing that the
goodness of God leadeth thee to repentance?
5 But [a]after thy [b]hardness and im-
penitent heart treasurest up unto
thyself wrath against the day of
wrath and revelation of the righteous judgment of God;
6 Who will [a]render to every man
[b]according to his [c]deeds:
7 To them who by [a]patient [b]continu-
ance in well doing seek for glory
and honour and [c]immortality, eternal life:
8 But unto them that are [a]conten-
tious, and do not [b]obey the truth,
but obey unrighteousness, [c]indig-
nation and wrath,
9 [a]Tribulation and [b]anguish, upon
every soul of man that doeth evil,
of the Jew first, and also of the
[c]Gentile;
10 But glory, honour, and [a]peace,
to every man that [b]worketh good,
to the Jew first, and also to the
[c]Gentile:
11 For there is no [a]respect of [b]per-
sons with God.
12 For as many as have sinned
without [a]law shall also perish
without law: and as many as have
sinned in the law shall be judged by
the law;
13 (For not the hearers of the law
are just before God, but the [a]doers
of the law shall be [b]justified.
14 For when the Gentiles, which
have not the law, do by nature the
things contained in the law, these,
having not the law, are a law unto
themselves:
15 [a]Which shew the work of the
[b]law written in their hearts, their
[c]conscience also bearing [d]witness,
and *their* thoughts the mean while
accusing or else excusing one another;)
16 In the day when God shall [a]judge
the secrets of men by Jesus Christ
according to my [b]gospel.
17 Behold, thou art called a Jew,
and restest in the law, and makest
thy boast of God,
18 And knowest *his* will, and ap-
provest the things that are more
excellent, being instructed out of
the law;
19 And art confident that thou
thyself art a guide of the blind, a
light of them which are in darkness,
20 An instructor of the foolish, a
teacher of babes, which hast the
[a]form of knowledge and of the truth
in the law.
21 Thou therefore which teachest
another, [a]teachest thou not thyself?
thou that [b]preachest a man should
not [c]steal, dost thou steal?
22 Thou that sayest a man should

3*a* Ezek. 16:52.
b D&C 10:28.
TG Judgment, the Last.
4*a* TG Treasure.
b Mosiah 4:20 (19–20).
c TG Forbear.
5*a* GR in accordance with.
b TG Hardheartedness; Stiffnecked.
6*a* GR give back, recompense, restore.
b TG Accountability.
c Rom. 11:6 (5–6).
TG Good Works.
7*a* TG Patience.
b D&C 67:13.
TG Perseverance.
c TG Immortality.
8*a* TG Contention.
b TG Disobedience.
c TG God, Indignation of.
9*a* Ps. 32:10.
b TG Sorrow.
c GR Greek.
10*a* TG Peace of God.
b TG Work, Value of.
c GR Greek.
11*a* GR partiality.
Deut. 10:17;
Acts 10:34;
Rom. 10:12 (12–13);
Hel. 3:28 (27–30).
TG God, Access to.
b 1 Ne. 17:35 (35–40);
2 Ne. 26:33 (23–33).
12*a* Luke 12:48.
TG Accountability; Law of Moses.
13*a* TG Good Works.
b Acts 13:39 (26–41).
15*a* GR Who.
b Jer. 31:33 (31–34);
D&C 84:46 (44–47).
c 2 Ne. 32:5.
TG Conscience.
d D&C 6:23 (22–23).
16*a* 1 Cor. 4:5.
TG Jesus Christ, Judge.
b TG Gospel.
20*a* GR system, appearance.
2 Tim. 3:5.
21*a* TG Hypocrisy.
b 1 Cor. 9:14 (13–14);
Alma 39:11 (11–12).
c TG Stealing.

not commit [a]adultery, dost thou
commit adultery? thou that ab-
horrest idols, dost thou [b]commit
[c]sacrilege?
23 Thou that makest thy boast of
the law, through breaking the law
dishonourest thou God?
24 For the name of God is [a]blas-
phemed among the Gentiles through
you, as it is written.
25 For [a]circumcision verily profiteth, if thou keep the law: but if
thou be a breaker of the law, thy circumcision is made uncircumcision.
26 Therefore if the uncircumcision keep the righteousness of the
law, shall not his uncircumcision be
counted for circumcision?
27 And shall not uncircumcision
which is by nature, if it fulfil the
law, judge thee, who by the letter
and circumcision dost transgress
the law?
28 For he is not a Jew, which is one
outwardly; neither *is that* circumcision, which is outward in the flesh:
29 But he *is* a Jew, which is one
inwardly; and [a]circumcision *is that*
of the heart, in the [b]spirit, *and* not
in the letter; whose praise *is* not of
men, but of God.

CHAPTER 3

Man is not justified by the law of Moses—He is justified through righteousness, which comes through faith in Christ, made possible through Christ's atoning sacrifice.

[a]WHAT [b]advantage then hath the
Jew? or what profit *is there* of [c]cir-
cumcision?
2 Much every way: chiefly, because
that unto them were committed the
[a]oracles of God.
3 For what if some did not believe?
shall their [a]unbelief make the faith
of God without effect?
4 [a]God forbid: yea, let God be true,
but every man a [b]liar; as it is written,
That thou mightest be [c]justified in
thy sayings, and mightest overcome
when thou art judged.
5 [a]But if our unrighteousness [b]com-
mend the righteousness of God, what
shall we say? *Is* God [c]unrighteous
who taketh vengeance? (I speak as
a man)
6 [a]God forbid: for then how shall
God [b]judge the world?
7 For if the truth of God hath more
abounded [a]through my lie unto his
glory; why yet am I also judged as
a sinner?
8 And not *rather*, (as we be slanderously reported, and as some affirm
that we say,) Let us do evil, that
good may come? whose [a]damnation
is just.
9 What then? are we better *than
they?* No, in no wise: for we have before proved both Jews and Gentiles,
that they are all under sin;
10 As it is written, There is [a]none
[b]righteous, no, not one:
11 There is none that understandeth, there is none that seeketh
after God.
12 They are all gone out of the
[a]way, they are together become [b]un-
profitable; there is none that doeth
[c]good, no, not one.
13 Their [a]throat *is* an open sepulchre; with their tongues they have

---

22*a* TG Adulterer.
b GR rob shrines, temples.
c TG Sacrilege.
24*a* TG Blaspheme.
25*a* Gal. 5:3.
TG Circumcision.
29*a* Acts 7:51; 2 Ne. 9:33.
TG Circumcision.
b Rom. 7:6.
3 1*a* JST Rom. 3:1–2 What advantage then hath the Jew *over the Gentile?* or what profit of circumcision, *who is not a Jew from the heart? But he who is a Jew from the heart, I say hath* much every way . . .
b GR preeminence.
c TG Circumcision.
2*a* Acts 7:38;
2 Ne. 29:4 (4–6).
3*a* 1 Ne. 8:28 (26–28).
4*a* GR May it not be!
b Alma 30:42 (37–42).
c Ps. 51:4.
5*a* JST Rom. 3:5–8 (Appendix).
b GR recommend.
c 2 Ne. 26:7;
Alma 42:1 (1, 13–25).
6*a* GR May it not be!
b TG Jesus Christ, Judge.
7*a* GR in, by, because of.
8*a* TG Damnation.
10*a* Ps. 14:2–3; 53:1 (1–3).
b TG Man, Natural, Not Spiritually Reborn.
12*a* D&C 82:6.
b Luke 17:10 (7–10);
Mosiah 2:21 (20–21).
c D&C 33:4; 35:12.
13*a* Ps. 5:9.

used deceit; the [b]poison of asps *is*
under their lips:
14 Whose mouth *is* full of cursing
and [a]bitterness:
15 Their feet *are* swift to [a]shed
blood:
16 Destruction and [a]misery *are* in
their ways:
17 And the way of [a]peace have
they not known:
18 There is no [a]fear of God before
their eyes.
19 Now we know that what things
soever the law saith, it saith to them
who are under the law: that every
[a]mouth may be stopped, and all
the world may become [b]guilty before God.
20 Therefore by the [a]deeds of the
[b]law there shall no flesh be [c]justi-
fied in his sight: for [d]by the law *is*
the knowledge of sin.
21 But now the [a]righteousness of
God [b]without the law is manifested,
being witnessed by the law and the
prophets;
22 Even the righteousness of God
which is by faith of Jesus Christ unto
all and upon all them that believe:
for there is no difference:
23 For all have [a]sinned, and come
short of the glory of God;
24 [a]Being [b]justified freely by his
[c]grace through the [d]redemption that
is in Christ Jesus:
25 Whom God hath [a]set forth *to
be* a [b]propitiation through faith in
his [c]blood, to declare his righteousness for the [d]remission of sins that
are past, through the [e]forbearance
of God;
26 To declare, *I say,* at this time
his righteousness: that he might be
[a]just, and the justifier of him which
believeth in Jesus.
27 Where *is* [a]boasting then? It is
excluded. By what law? of works?
Nay: but by the law of faith.
28 Therefore we conclude that a
man is [a]justified by [b]faith [c]without
the deeds of the law.
29 *Is he* the [a]God of the Jews only?
is he not also of the Gentiles? Yes,
of the [b]Gentiles also:
30 Seeing *it is* [a]one God, which
shall justify the [b]circumcision by
faith, and uncircumcision through
faith.
31 Do we then make void the law
through faith? [a]God forbid: [b]yea,
we establish the law.

CHAPTER 4

Abraham's faith was accounted to him for righteousness—Man is justified by faith, righteous works, and grace.

WHAT shall we say then that Abraham our father, as pertaining to the
flesh, hath found?
2 [a]For if Abraham were justified
by works, he hath [b]*whereof* to glory;
but not before God.
3 For what saith the scripture?

13*b* Ps. 140:3 (1–13).
14*a* Alma 41:11; Morm. 8:31.
15*a* Isa. 59:7 (7–8).
16*a* Mosiah 3:25; Morm. 8:38.
17*a* 1 Ne. 20:22 (18–22).
18*a* D&C 10:56 (55–56).
19*a* Ezek. 16:63.
b TG Guilt.
20*a* 2 Ne. 25:23.
b TG Law of Moses.
c 2 Ne. 2:5 (5–8).
d GR through.
21*a* TG God, the Standard of Righteousness.
b GR apart from, without intervention of.
23*a* Prov. 20:9; 1 Ne. 10:6. TG Man, Natural, Not Spiritually Reborn; Sin.
24*a* JST Rom. 3:24 *Therefore being justified only by his grace . . .*
b D&C 20:30.
c TG Grace.
d TG Jesus Christ, Redeemer.
25*a* GR purposed, designed beforehand.
b GR mercy seat. TG Jesus Christ, Atonement through; Redemption.
c TG Blood, Symbolism of.
d TG Remission of Sins.
e TG Forbear.
26*a* TG God, Justice of.
27*a* Alma 26:36 (10–12, 36); D&C 3:4; 84:73.
28*a* TG Justification.
b TG Faith.
c GR apart from, without intervention of.
29*a* 2 Ne. 30:2 (1–2).
b TG Gentiles.
30*a* 1 Tim. 2:5; D&C 121:28.
b TG Circumcision.
31*a* GR May it not be!
b GR but.
4 2*a* JST Rom. 4:2–5 (Appendix).
b GR ground, reason for boasting.

Abraham [a]believed God, and it was counted unto him for [b]righteousness.

4 Now to him that worketh is the [a]reward not [b]reckoned of grace, but of debt.

5 But to him that worketh not, but believeth on him that justifieth the ungodly, his faith is counted for righteousness.

6 Even as David also describeth the blessedness of the man, unto whom God imputeth righteousness without works,

7 *Saying,* [a]Blessed *are* they whose iniquities are forgiven, and whose sins are covered.

8 Blessed *is* the man to whom the Lord will not impute sin.

9 *Cometh* this blessedness then upon the circumcision *only,* or upon the uncircumcision also? for we say that faith was reckoned to Abraham for righteousness.

10 How was it then reckoned? when he was in circumcision, or in uncircumcision? Not in circumcision, but in uncircumcision.

11 And he received the [a]sign of [b]circumcision, a seal of the righteousness of the faith which *he had yet* being uncircumcised: that he might be the [c]father of all them that believe, though they be not circumcised; that righteousness might be imputed unto them also:

12 And the father of circumcision to them who are not of the circumcision only, but who also [a]walk in the steps of that faith of our father Abraham, which *he had* being *yet* uncircumcised.

13 For the promise, that he should be the [a]heir of the world, *was* not to Abraham, or to his [b]seed, through the law, but through the righteousness of faith.

14 For if they which are of the law *be* heirs, faith is made void, and the promise made of none effect:

15 Because the law worketh wrath: for where no [a]law is, *there is* no [b]transgression.

16 [a]Therefore *it is* of faith, that *it might be* by [b]grace; to the end the promise might be sure to all the seed; not to that only which is of the law, but to that also which is of the [c]faith of Abraham; who is the [d]father of us all,

17 (As it is written, I have made thee a father of many nations,) before him whom he believed, *even* God, who [a]quickeneth the dead, and calleth those things which be not as though they were.

18 Who against hope believed in [a]hope, that he might become the father of many [b]nations, according to that which was spoken, So shall thy [c]seed be.

19 And being not weak in faith, he considered not his own body now dead, when he was about an hundred years [a]old, neither yet the deadness of Sara's womb:

20 He [a]staggered not at the promise of God through unbelief; but was strong in faith, giving glory to God;

21 And being fully persuaded that, what he had [a]promised, he was able also to perform.

22 And therefore it was imputed to him for righteousness.

3*a* See JST Gen. 15:9–12 (Appendix). TG Faith.
b TG Righteousness.
4*a* GR wage, hire.
b GR considered a favor but as his due.
7*a* Ps. 32:1.
11*a* TG Signs.
b TG Circumcision.
c Abr. 2:10.
12*a* TG Walking with God.
13*a* TG Birthright.
b TG Seed of Abraham.
15*a* Rom. 5:13; 2 Ne. 9:25; Alma 42:17 (12–24).
b TG Transgress.
16*a* JST Rom. 4:16 Therefore *ye are justified* of faith *and works, through* grace, to the end the promise might be sure to all the seed; not to *them* only *who are* of the law, but to *them* also *who are* of the faith of Abraham; who is the father of us all,
b TG Grace.
c TG Faith.
d TG Family, Patriarchal.
17*a* TG God, Power of; Resurrection.
18*a* TG Hope.
b TG Nations.
c TG Seed of Abraham.
19*a* TG Old Age.
20*a* GR doubted, hesitated.
21*a* Gen. 18:14; Luke 1:37. TG Promise.

23 Now it was not written for his sake alone, that it was imputed to him;

24 But for [a]us also, to whom it shall be imputed, if we believe on him that raised up Jesus our Lord from the dead;

25 Who was delivered for our [a]offences, and was raised again for our [b]justification.

CHAPTER 5

Man is justified through the blood of Christ—Adam fell, and Christ atoned that man might be saved.

THEREFORE being [a]justified by [b]faith, we have [c]peace with God through our Lord Jesus Christ:

2 By whom also we have access by [a]faith into this grace wherein we stand, and rejoice in hope of the glory of God.

3 And not only *so,* but we glory in [a]tribulations also: knowing that [b]tribulation worketh [c]patience;

4 And patience, experience; and experience, hope:

5 And [a]hope maketh not ashamed; because the [b]love of God is shed abroad in our hearts by the Holy Ghost which is given unto us.

6 For when we were yet without [a]strength, in due time Christ died for the ungodly.

7 For scarcely for a righteous man will one die: yet peradventure for a good man some would even dare to die.

8 But God commendeth his love toward us, in that, while we were yet [a]sinners, [b]Christ died for us.

9 Much more then, being now [a]justified by his [b]blood, we shall be saved from wrath through him.

10 For if, when we were enemies, we were [a]reconciled to God by the [b]death of his Son, much more, being reconciled, we shall be saved by his life.

11 And not only *so,* but we also joy in God through our Lord Jesus Christ, by whom we have now received the [a]atonement.

12 Wherefore, as by one man [a]sin entered into the world, and [b]death by sin; and so [c]death passed upon all men, for that all have [d]sinned:

13 (For until the law sin was in the world: but [a]sin is not imputed when there is no [b]law.

14 Nevertheless death reigned from Adam to Moses, even over them that had not sinned after the similitude of Adam's [a]transgression, who is the [b]figure of him that was to come.

15 But not as the offence, so also *is* the free gift. For if through the offence of one many be dead, much more the grace of God, and the gift by grace, *which is* by [a]one man, Jesus Christ, hath abounded unto many.

16 And not as *it was* by one that sinned, *so is* the gift: for the judgment *was* by one to condemnation, but the free gift *is* of many offences unto justification.

17 For if by one man's offence death reigned by one; much more they which receive abundance of [a]grace and of the gift of righteousness shall reign in life by one, Jesus Christ.)

18 Therefore as by the offence of

24*a* 3 Ne. 20:25 (24–27).
25*a* Isa. 53:5; Mark 10:45.
b TG Justification.
5 1*a* TG Justification.
b TG Faith.
c TG Peace of God.
2*a* Gal. 5:5 (5–6).
3*a* 2 Cor. 4:17.
b TG Tribulation.
c TG Patience.
5*a* Ps. 119:116. TG Hope.
b TG Love.
6*a* TG Strength.
8*a* Mosiah 4:11.
b TG Salvation, Plan of.
9*a* TG Jesus Christ, Atonement through.
b TG Blood, Symbolism of.
10*a* TG Jesus Christ, Redeemer; Reconciliation.
b TG Jesus Christ, Death of.
11*a* GR reconciliation, restoration to favor. TG Jesus Christ, Atonement through; Redemption.
12*a* Gen. 3:6. TG Fall of Man; Sin.
b 1 Cor. 15:21.
c TG Death.
d TG Man, Natural, Not Spiritually Reborn.
13*a* TG Sin.
b Rom. 4:15; 2 Ne. 9:25; Alma 42:17 (12–24).
14*a* TG Transgress.
b GR type, pattern. 1 Cor. 15:45.
15*a* 2 Cor. 5:14.
17*a* TG Grace.

one *judgment came* upon all men to
condemnation; even so by the [a]righ-
teousness of one *the free gift came*
upon all men unto [b]justification
of life.
19 For as by one man's [a]disobedi-
ence many were made sinners, so
by the [b]obedience of one shall many
be made righteous.
20 Moreover the law entered, that
the offence might abound. But
where sin abounded, grace did much
more abound:
21 That as sin hath reigned unto
death, even so might grace reign
through [a]righteousness unto [b]eter-
nal life by Jesus Christ our Lord.

CHAPTER 6

Baptism is in similitude of the death, burial, and resurrection of Christ—The wages of sin is death—Christ brings eternal life.

WHAT shall we say then? Shall we
continue in sin, that [a]grace may
abound?
2 [a]God forbid. How shall we, that
are dead to [b]sin, live any longer
therein?
3 Know ye not, that so many of us
as were [a]baptized into Jesus Christ
were baptized into his death?
4 Therefore we are [a]buried with
him by [b]baptism into death: that
like as Christ was raised up from
the [c]dead by the glory of the Father,
even so we also should [d]walk in
[e]newness of life.
5 For if we have been planted together in the [a]likeness of his [b]death,
we shall be also *in the likeness* of *his*
[c]resurrection:
6 Knowing this, that our [a]old man
is crucified with *him*, that the [b]body
of sin might be [c]destroyed, that
henceforth we should not serve
[d]sin.
7 For he that is [a]dead is [b]freed
from sin.
8 Now if we be [a]dead with Christ,
we believe that we shall also live
with him:
9 Knowing that Christ being [a]raised
from the dead dieth no more;
death hath no more dominion over
him.
10 For in that he died, he died unto
[a]sin [b]once: but in that he liveth, he
liveth unto God.
11 Likewise reckon ye also yourselves to be dead indeed unto sin,
but [a]alive unto God through Jesus
Christ our Lord.
12 Let not sin therefore reign in
your [a]mortal body, that ye should
obey it in the [b]lusts thereof.
13 Neither [a]yield ye your [b]members
as [c]instruments of unrighteousness
unto sin: but [d]yield yourselves unto
God, as those that are alive from
the dead, and your members *as* in-
struments of [e]righteousness unto
God.
14 [a]For sin shall not have [b]domin-
ion over you: for ye are not under
the law, but under grace.
15 What then? shall we sin, because

18*a* TG Righteousness.
b TG Justification.
19*a* TG Disobedience.
b TG Obedience.
21*a* TG Righteousness.
b TG Eternal Life.
6 1*a* D&C 20:32 (29–34).
2*a* GR May it not be!
b Mosiah 2:41.
3*a* Mosiah 27:25.
4*a* TG Baptism, Immersion.
b TG Baptism.
c TG Jesus Christ, Death of.
d TG Walking with God.
e TG Baptism, Qualifications for; Man, New, Spiritually Reborn.
5*a* TG Jesus Christ, Types of, in Memory.
b Col. 2:20; 3:3; 2 Tim. 2:11.
c TG Resurrection.
6*a* Eph. 4:22 (22–24); Col. 3:9.
b Col. 2:11.
c GR brought to an end, freed.
d Moro. 10:32 (32–33).
7*a* JST Rom. 6:7 . . . dead *to sin* . . .
b GR acquitted, cleared.
8*a* TG Jesus Christ, Death of.
9*a* TG Jesus Christ, Resurrection.
10*a* Heb. 9:28.
b Heb. 7:27; 10:10.
11*a* Gal. 2:19.
12*a* TG Mortality.
b TG Lust.
13*a* 2 Ne. 4:27 (27–28).
b Col. 3:5.
c GR weapons.
d Mosiah 3:19; Hel. 3:35.
e TG Righteousness.
14*a* JST Rom. 6:14 For *in so doing* sin . . .
b 2 Ne. 2:29 (26–29).

we are not under the law, but under
[a]grace? [b]God forbid.
16 Know ye not, that to whom ye
yield yourselves [a]servants to obey,
his servants ye are to whom ye
[b]obey; whether of sin unto death,
or of obedience unto righteousness?
17 But God be thanked, that ye
were the servants of sin, but ye have
[a]obeyed from the heart that form of
doctrine which was delivered you.
18 Being then made [a]free from
[b]sin, ye became the servants of
righteousness.
19 I speak after the manner of men
because of the infirmity of your
flesh: for as ye have yielded your
members servants to uncleanness
and to iniquity unto iniquity; even
so now yield your members servants
to righteousness unto holiness.
20 For when ye were the servants of
sin, ye were [a]free from righteousness.
21 What [a]fruit had ye then in those
things whereof ye are now ashamed?
for the end of those things *is* death.
22 But now being made [a]free from
sin, and become servants to God, ye
have your [b]fruit unto [c]holiness, and
the end everlasting life.
23 For the [a]wages of [b]sin *is* [c]death;
but the [d]gift of God *is* [e]eternal life
through Jesus Christ our Lord.

CHAPTER 7

The law of Moses is fulfilled in Christ—Paul delights in the law of God after the inward man.

KNOW ye not, brethren, (for I speak
to them that know the law,) how
that the [a]law hath dominion over
a man as long as he liveth?
2 For the [a]woman which hath an
[b]husband is bound by the law to *her*
husband so long as he liveth; but if
the husband be dead, she is loosed
from the law of *her* husband.
3 So then if, while *her* husband liveth, she be married to another man,
she shall be called an adulteress:
but if her husband be dead, she is
free from that law; so that she is no
adulteress, though she be married
to another man.
4 Wherefore, my brethren, ye also
are become [a]dead to the [b]law by
the body of Christ; that ye should
be married to another, *even* to him
who is raised from the dead, that
we should bring forth fruit unto
God.
5 [a]For when we were in the flesh,
the [b]motions of sins, which were by
the law, did work in our members
to bring forth fruit unto [c]death.
6 But now we are [a]delivered from
the law, that being [b]dead wherein
we were held; that we should serve
in newness of [c]spirit, and not *in* the
oldness of the letter.
7 What shall we say then? *Is* the
law sin? [a]God forbid. Nay, I had not
known sin, but by the [b]law: for I had
not known [c]lust, except the law had
said, Thou shalt not [d]covet.
8 But sin, taking occasion by the
commandment, wrought in me all
manner of concupiscence. For without the [a]law sin *was* dead.

15*a* TG Grace.
b GR May it not be!
16*a* John 8:34.
b Alma 3:27 (26–27); 34:34 (33–36); Hel. 14:31 (29–31). TG Obedience.
17*a* TG Commitment.
18*a* Mosiah 5:8 (7–8). TG Remission of Sins.
b TG Bondage, Spiritual; Sin.
20*a* GR unrestricted by.
21*a* GR benefit, reward.
22*a* Rom. 8:2 (1–4); Rev. 2:17 (17, 26).
b GR benefit, reward.
c TG Sanctification.
23*a* TG Wages.
b TG Sin.
c TG Death; Death, Spiritual, First.
d TG God, Gifts of.
e TG Eternal Life.
7 1*a* Mosiah 13:30 (29–32).
2*a* TG Marriage, Wives.
b TG Marriage, Marry.
4*a* Gal. 2:19; 2 Ne. 25:25 (24–27); D&C 74:5 (2–6).
b Mosiah 13:28 (27–29).
5*a* JST Rom. 7:5–27 (Appendix).
b GR sufferings, afflictions.
c 2 Ne. 2:5 (4–10); 25:23; Alma 42:14 (12–16).
6*a* GR released, freed from.
b 2 Cor. 5:17.
c Rom. 2:29 (28–29).
7*a* GR May it not be!
b D&C 82:3 (3–4). TG Law of Moses.
c TG Lust.
d GR lust for, set the heart upon. TG Covet.
8*a* Alma 42:17 (14–24).

9 For I was alive without the law
once: but when the commandment
came, sin revived, and I died.
10 And the commandment, which
was ordained to life, I found *to be*
unto [a]death.
11 For sin, [a]taking occasion by the
commandment, deceived me, and
by it slew *me*.
12 Wherefore the law *is* holy, and
the commandment holy, and just,
and good.
13 Was then that which is good
made death unto me? [a]God forbid.
But sin, that it might appear sin,
working death in me by that which is
good; that sin by the commandment
might become exceeding sinful.
14 For we know that the [a]law is
spiritual: but I am [b]carnal, [c]sold
under sin.
15 [a]For [b]that which I do I [c]allow
not: for what I [d]would, that do I not;
but what I hate, that do I.
16 If then I do that which I [a]would
not, I consent unto the law that *it*
is good.
17 Now then it is no more I that
[a]do it, but sin that dwelleth in me.
18 For I know that in me (that is,
in my [a]flesh,) [b]dwelleth no good
thing: for to will is present with me;
but *how* to [c]perform that which is
good I find not.
19 For the [a]good that I [b]would I
do not: but the evil which I would
not, that I do.
20 Now if I do [a]that I would not, it
is no more I that do it, but sin that
dwelleth in me.
21 I find then a law, that, when
I would do good, evil is [a]present
with me.
22 For I [a]delight in the law of God
after the inward man:
23 But I see another law in my
members, [a]warring against the law
of my mind, and bringing me into
[b]captivity to the law of sin which
is in my members.
24 O [a]wretched man that I am! who
shall deliver me from the body of
this death?
25 I thank God through Jesus Christ
our Lord. So then with the mind I
myself serve the law of God; but
with the flesh the law of sin.

CHAPTER 8

The law of Christ brings life and peace—Those adopted as children of God become joint heirs with Christ—God's elect are foreordained to eternal life—Christ makes intercession for man.

THERE *is* therefore now no condemnation to them which are in Christ
Jesus, who [a]walk not after the [b]flesh,
but after the [c]Spirit.
2 For the law of the Spirit of life
in Christ Jesus hath made me [a]free
from the law of sin and death.
3 For what the law could not do,
in that it was [a]weak through the
flesh, God sending his own Son
in the likeness of sinful [b]flesh,
and for sin, condemned sin in the
flesh:
4 That the righteousness of the
law might be fulfilled in us, who
walk not after the flesh, but after
the [a]Spirit.

10*a* 2 Cor. 3:7.
11*a* GR having taken opportunity.
13*a* GR May it not be!
14*a* D&C 29:34.
b TG Carnal Mind.
c GR devoted to, a slave to.
15*a* JST Rom. 7:15–17 (Appendix).
b GR what I produce, achieve.
c GR know, understand.
d GR choose, intend, design.
16*a* GR choose, intend, design.
17*a* GR produce, work.
18*a* TG Man, Natural, Not Spiritually Reborn.
b Alma 22:15.
c 2 Ne. 4:19 (17–20, 26).
19*a* TG Opposition.
b GR intend, choose.
20*a* GR what I do not intend, choose.
21*a* Heb. 12:1; 2 Ne. 4:18 (17–19).
22*a* TG Spirituality.
23*a* Alma 13:28.
b TG Bondage, Spiritual.
24*a* 2 Ne. 4:17. TG Sorrow.
8 1*a* TG Walking with God.
b TG Trust Not in the Arm of Flesh.
c Alma 13:12 (12, 28); D&C 11:12 (12–13).
2*a* Rom. 6:22 (11–22); 2 Cor. 3:17; Mosiah 5:2 (2–9). TG Bondage, Spiritual.
3*a* Heb. 7:18.
b TG Jesus Christ, Condescension of.
4*a* Mosiah 3:19.

5 For they that are after the flesh
do [a]mind the things of the flesh; but
they that are after the Spirit the
things of the Spirit.
6 For to be [a]carnally minded *is*
[b]death; but to be [c]spiritually minded
is life and [d]peace.
7 Because the [a]carnal mind *is*
[b]enmity against God: for it is not
subject to the law of God, neither
indeed can be.
8 So then they that are [a]in the flesh
cannot please God.
9 [a]But ye are not in the flesh, but
in the Spirit, if so be that the [b]Spirit
of God [c]dwell in you. Now if any
man have not the [d]Spirit of Christ,
he is none of his.
10 And if [a]Christ *be* in you, [b]the
body *is* dead because of sin; but
the Spirit *is* life because of [c]righ-
teousness.
11 But if the Spirit of him that
raised up Jesus from the dead dwell
in you, he that raised up Christ from
the dead shall also [a]quicken your
[b]mortal bodies by his Spirit that
dwelleth in you.
12 Therefore, brethren, we are
debtors, not to the flesh, to live after the flesh.
13 For if ye live after the flesh,
ye [a]shall die: but if ye through the
Spirit do [b]mortify the deeds of the
body, ye shall live.
14 For as many as are [a]led by the
[b]Spirit of God, they are the [c]sons
of God.
15 For ye have not received the
spirit of [a]bondage again to fear; but
ye have received the Spirit of [b]adop-
tion, whereby we cry, Abba, Father.
16 The Spirit itself beareth [a]wit-
ness with our [b]spirit, that we are
the [c]children of God:
17 And if children, then heirs;
[a]heirs of God, and joint-heirs with
Christ; if so be that we [b]suffer with
him, that we may be also glorified
together.
18 For I reckon that the [a]sufferings
of this present time *are* not worthy
to be compared with the [b]glory which
shall be revealed [c]in us.
19 For the [a]earnest expectation of
the [b]creature waiteth for the [c]mani-
festation of the sons of God.
20 For the creature was made subject to [a]vanity, not willingly, but by
reason of him who hath subjected
the same in hope,
21 Because the [a]creature itself also
shall be [b]delivered from the bondage of [c]corruption into the glorious
[d]liberty of the children of God.
22 For we know that the whole
creation [a]groaneth and travaileth
in pain together until now.
23 And not only *they,* but ourselves
also, [a]which have the [b]firstfruits of

5*a* GR watch, guard.
6*a* TG Carnal Mind; Chastity; Man, Natural, Not Spiritually Reborn.
b TG Death; Death, Spiritual, First.
c TG Spirituality.
d TG Peace of God.
7*a* TG Fall of Man.
b TG Opposition.
8*a* JST Rom. 8:8 . . . *after* the flesh . . .
9*a* JST Rom. 8:9 But ye are not *after* the flesh, but *after* the Spirit . . .
b D&C 8:2.
c 1 Jn. 3:24 (19–24).
d TG Holy Ghost, Loss of.
10*a* 2 Cor. 13:5.
b JST Rom. 8:10 . . . *though* the body *shall die* because of sin, *yet* the Spirit is life, because of righteousness.
c TG Righteousness.
11*a* GR make alive. D&C 84:33. TG God, Power of; Resurrection.
b TG Mortality.
13*a* GR are at the point of withering, dying.
b GR put to death, subdue. Col. 3:5.
14*a* TG Leadership.
b TG God, Spirit of.
c TG Sons and Daughters of God.
15*a* TG Bondage, Spiritual.
b Isa. 56:3 (3–8).
16*a* TG Witness.
b TG Spirit Creation.
c TG Man, a Spirit Child of Heavenly Father.
17*a* Luke 12:44 (42–44). TG Birthright; Election; Eternal Life; Exaltation; Man, Potential to Become like Heavenly Father.
b TG Persecution; Suffering.
18*a* TG Adversity; Pain; Self-Sacrifice.
b D&C 58:4; 63:66; 136:31.
c GR to us.
19*a* GR eager hope.
b GR creation, material universe.
c GR revelation.
20*a* JST Rom. 8:20 . . . *tribulation* . . . TG Vanity.
21*a* GR creation, material universe.
b TG Deliver.
c 1 Cor. 15:42.
d TG Liberty.
22*a* TG Earth, Curse of.
23*a* GR who.
b Gal. 5:22 (16–26).

the Spirit, even we ourselves groan
within ourselves, waiting for the
[c]adoption, *to wit,* the redemption
of our body.
24 For we are saved by [a]hope: but
hope that is [b]seen is not hope: for
what a man seeth, why doth he yet
hope for?
25 But if we hope for that we see
not, *then* do we with patience wait
for *it.*
26 Likewise the Spirit also [a]help-
eth our infirmities: for we know
not what we should [b]pray for as we
ought: but the Spirit itself maketh
[c]intercession for us with [d]groanings
which cannot be uttered.
27 And he that [a]searcheth the
hearts knoweth what *is* the mind of
the Spirit, because he maketh [b]in-
tercession for the saints according
to *the will of* God.
28 And we know that all things
work together for [a]good to them
that love God, to them who are the
called according to *his* purpose.
29 [a]For whom he did [b]foreknow,
he also [c]did predestinate [d]*to be* conformed to the [e]image of his Son, that
he might be the [f]firstborn among
many brethren.
30 Moreover whom he [a]did predestinate, them he also called: and
whom he called, them he also justified: and whom he justified, them
he also glorified.
31 What shall we then say to these
things? If God *be* for us, who *can* [a]*be*
against us?
32 He that spared not his own
[a]Son, but [b]delivered him up for us
all, how shall he not with him also
freely give us [c]all things?
33 Who shall [a]lay any thing to the
charge of God's elect? *It is* God that
justifieth.
34 Who *is* he that condemneth? *It
is* Christ that died, yea rather, that
is risen again, who is even at the
right hand of God, who also maketh
[a]intercession for us.
35 Who shall separate us from
the [a]love of Christ? *shall* [b]tribula-
tion, or distress, or [c]persecution, or
famine, or nakedness, or peril, or
sword?
36 As it is written, For thy sake
we are [a]killed all the day long; we
are accounted as [b]sheep for the
slaughter.
37 Nay, in all these things we are
[a]more than [b]conquerors through
him that loved us.
38 For I am persuaded, that neither death, nor life, nor angels, nor
principalities, nor powers, nor things
present, nor things to come,
39 Nor height, nor depth, nor any
other creature, shall be able to
[a]separate us from the [b]love of God,
which is in Christ Jesus our Lord.

CHAPTER 9

Paul explains how the law of election (foreordination) operates—The people of Israel are chosen (foreordained) to receive the adoption, covenants,

23*c* 2 Cor. 5:2.
24*a* TG Hope.
b 2 Cor. 4:18.
26*a* TG Holy Ghost, Gifts of.
b James 4:3; D&C 46:28 (28–30); 88:65 (64–65).
c TG Communication.
d GR sighings.
27*a* TG Judgment.
b TG Holy Ghost, Mission of.
28*a* Ezra 8:22; Alma 36:3; D&C 90:24; 100:15.
29*a* JST Rom. 8:29–30 (Appendix).
b TG God, Foreknowledge of; Man, Antemortal Existence of.
c GR appointed beforehand, foreordained. TG Foreordination.
d GR to have the same form as.
e 2 Cor. 3:18; Col. 3:10. TG God, Body of, Corporeal Nature.
f TG Jesus Christ, Firstborn.
30*a* GR appointed beforehand, foreordained.
31*a* JST Rom. 8:31 . . . *prevail* against us?
32*a* TG Jesus Christ, Atonement through.
b Isa. 50:8.
c D&C 84:38 (33–41).
33*a* GR accuse God's elect.
34*a* Isa. 53:12; Heb. 7:25.
35*a* D&C 29:5.
b TG Tribulation.
c TG Persecution.
36*a* Ps. 44:22; 2 Cor. 4:11.
b TG Sheep.
37*a* GR abundantly victorious.
b 2 Cor. 2:14.
39*a* Matt. 10:31 (29–31); D&C 121:33.
b 2 Ne. 1:15.

*promises, and blessings of the gospel;
yet they are not all Israel who are of
Israel—They must seek their blessings
by faith—The Gentiles also attain to
righteousness and salvation by faith.*

I SAY the truth in Christ, I [a]lie not,
my [b]conscience also bearing me
witness in the Holy Ghost,
2 That I have great heaviness and
continual sorrow in my heart.
3 [a]For I could wish that myself
were [b]accursed from Christ for my
brethren, my kinsmen according
to the flesh:
4 Who are Israelites; to whom *pertaineth* the [a]adoption, and the glory,
and the [b]covenants, and the giving
of the law, and the service *of God,*
and the promises;
5 Whose *are* the fathers, and of
whom as concerning the [a]flesh
Christ *came,* who is over all, God
blessed for ever. Amen.
6 Not as though the word of God
[a]hath taken none effect. For they
are not all Israel, which are of
[b]Israel:
7 [a]Neither, because they are the
seed of Abraham, *are they* all children: but, In [b]Isaac shall thy seed
be called.
8 That is, They which are the children of the flesh, these *are* not the
[a]children of God: but the children
of the promise are counted for
the seed.
9 For this *is* the word of promise,
At this time will I come, and Sara
shall have a [a]son.
10 And not only *this;* but when
[a]Rebecca also had conceived by one,
even by our father Isaac;
11 (For *the children* being not yet
born, neither having done any good
or evil, that the purpose of God according to [a]election might stand, not
of works, but of him that calleth;)
12 It was said unto her, The [a]elder
shall serve the younger.
13 As it is written, Jacob have I
[a]loved, but Esau have I hated.
14 What shall we say then? *Is there*
[a]unrighteousness with God? [b]God
forbid.
15 For he saith to Moses, I will have
mercy on whom I will have mercy,
and I will have [a]compassion on
whom I will have compassion.
16 So then *it is* not of him that will-
eth, nor of him that runneth, but of
God that sheweth [a]mercy.
17 For the scripture saith unto
Pharaoh, Even for this same [a]pur-
pose have I raised thee up, that I
might shew my power in thee, and
that my name might be declared
throughout all the earth.
18 Therefore hath he [a]mercy on
whom he will *have mercy,* and whom
he will he [b]hardeneth.
19 Thou wilt say then unto me,
Why doth he yet find fault? For
who hath resisted his will?
20 Nay but, O man, who art thou
that [a]repliest against God? Shall the
thing formed say to him that formed
it, Why hast thou [b]made me thus?
21 Hath not the [a]potter power over
the clay, of the same lump to make
one vessel unto honour, and another
unto dishonour?

9 1*a* 1 Tim. 2:7.
b TG Conscience.
3*a* JST Rom. 9:3 (For *once* I could *have wished* that myself were accursed from Christ,) . . .
b Ex. 32:32.
4*a* TG Election; Sons and Daughters of God.
b TG Abrahamic Covenant.
5*a* TG Jesus Christ, Condescension of.
6*a* GR has been fruitless, ineffectual.
b 2 Ne. 30:2.
7*a* JST Rom. 9:7 Neither, because they are *all children* of Abraham, are they *the seed;* but, In Isaac . . .
b TG Seed of Abraham.
8*a* TG Sons and Daughters of God.
9*a* TG Seed of Abraham.
10*a* Gen. 22:23.
11*a* TG Foreordination; God, Foreknowledge of.
12*a* Gen. 25:23.
13*a* Mal. 1:2 (2–3).
14*a* Ps. 92:15. TG God, Perfection of.
b GR May it not be!
15*a* TG Compassion.
16*a* TG God, Mercy of.
17*a* Ex. 9:16 (15–17).
18*a* TG Forgive.
b GR leaves to stubbornness, hardness. Deut. 2:30.
20*a* GR contradictest, disputest.
b Job 9:12.
21*a* Isa. 45:9; Jer. 18:6.

22 *What* if God, willing to shew
his wrath, and to make his power
known, endured with much long-
suffering the vessels of wrath fitted
to [a]destruction:
23 And that he might make known
the [a]riches of his [b]glory on the vessels of mercy, which he had afore
prepared unto glory,
24 Even us, whom he hath called,
not of the Jews only, but also of the
Gentiles?
25 As he saith also in [a]Osee, I will
call them my people, which were
not my [b]people; and her beloved,
which was not beloved.
26 And it shall come to pass, *that*
in the place where it was said unto
them, Ye *are* not my people; there
shall they be called the [a]children
of the living God.
27 [a]Esaias also crieth concerning
Israel, Though the [b]number of the
children of [c]Israel be as the sand of
the sea, a [d]remnant shall be saved:
28 For he will finish the work,
and cut *it* short in [a]righteousness:
because a short work will the Lord
make upon the earth.
29 And as Esaias said before, Except the Lord of [a]Sabaoth had left
us a [b]seed, we had been as Sodoma,
and been made like unto Gomorrha.
30 What shall we say then? That
the Gentiles, which followed not after righteousness, have attained to
righteousness, even the [a]righteous-
ness which is of faith.
31 But [a]Israel, which followed after
the law of righteousness, hath not
attained to the law of righteousness.
32 [a]Wherefore? Because *they sought*
it not by faith, but as it were by the
works of the law. For they [b]stumbled
at that stumblingstone;
33 As it is written, Behold, I lay in
Sion a [a]stumblingstone and [b]rock of
[c]offence: and whosoever believeth
on him shall not be ashamed.

CHAPTER 10

Salvation comes through righteousness to those who believe in Christ—Faith comes by hearing the gospel taught by legal administrators sent of God.

BRETHREN, my heart's desire and
prayer to God for Israel is, that they
might be [a]saved.
2 For I bear them record that they
have a [a]zeal of God, but not according to knowledge.
3 For they being ignorant of God's
[a]righteousness, and [b]going about to
establish their own righteousness,
have not [c]submitted themselves
unto the righteousness of God.
4 For Christ *is* the [a]end of the law
for righteousness to every one that
believeth.
5 For Moses describeth the righteousness which is of the law, That
the man which doeth those things
shall live by them.
6 But the [a]righteousness which is
of faith speaketh on this wise, Say
not in thine heart, Who shall ascend
into heaven? (that is, to bring Christ
down *from above:*)
7 Or, Who shall descend into the
deep? (that is, to bring up Christ
again from the dead.)
8 But what saith it? The word is
nigh thee, *even* in thy mouth, and in

22*a* 1 Pet. 2:8 (4–8).
23*a* TG Treasure.
b TG Celestial Glory; God, Glory of.
25*a* IE Hosea.
b Hosea 2:23; Zech. 13:9.
26*a* GR sons. TG Sons and Daughters of God.
27*a* IE Isaiah.
b Isa. 10:22.
c TG Israel, Blessings of.
d TG Israel, Remnant of.
28*a* D&C 52:11.
29*a* HEB hosts.
b GR posterity.
30*a* TG Righteousness.
31*a* TG Apostasy of Israel.
32*a* GR Why?
b Isa. 8:14 (13–15); Matt. 21:44 (43–45); Luke 2:34.
33*a* TG Cornerstone; Jesus Christ, Prophecies about.
b TG Rock.
c TG Offense.
10 1*a* TG Reconciliation.
2*a* TG Zeal.
3*a* TG God, the Standard of Righteousness.
b GR desiring, endeavoring.
c TG Apostasy of Israel; Submissiveness.
4*a* 2 Ne. 2:7 (7–10).
6*a* TG Righteousness.

thy heart: that is, the word of faith, which we preach;

9 That if thou shalt confess with thy mouth the Lord Jesus, and shalt believe in thine heart that God hath raised him from the dead, thou shalt be saved.

10 For with the [a]heart man [b]believeth unto righteousness; and with the mouth confession is made unto [c]salvation.

11 For the scripture saith, Whosoever believeth on him shall not be ashamed.

12 For there is no [a]difference between the Jew and the Greek: for the same Lord over all is [b]rich unto all that [c]call upon him.

13 For whosoever shall [a]call upon the name of the Lord shall be saved.

14 How then shall they call on him in whom they have not [a]believed? and how shall they believe in him of whom they have not heard? and how shall they hear without a [b]preacher?

15 And how shall they [a]preach, except they be [b]sent? as it is written, How beautiful are the [c]feet of them that preach the [d]gospel of [e]peace, and bring glad tidings of good things!

16 But they have not all [a]obeyed the gospel. For Esaias saith, Lord, who hath [b]believed our report?

17 So then [a]faith *cometh* by [b]hearing, and hearing by the word of God.

18 But I say, Have they not heard? Yes verily, their sound went into all the earth, and their [a]words unto the ends of the [b]world.

19 But I say, Did not Israel know? First Moses saith, I will provoke you to [a]jealousy by *them that are* no people, *and* by a foolish nation I will anger you.

20 But [a]Esaias is very bold, and saith, I was found of them that [b]sought me not; I was made manifest unto them that asked not after me.

21 But to Israel he saith, All day long I have stretched forth my hands unto a [a]disobedient and [b]gainsaying people.

CHAPTER 11

Israel was chosen (foreordained) according to the election of grace—But some harden their hearts against it—The Gentiles are adopted into the house of Israel—The gospel goes preferentially to the Gentiles until the fulness of the Gentiles.

I SAY then, Hath God cast away his people? [a]God forbid. For I also am an [b]Israelite, of the seed of Abraham, *of* the tribe of Benjamin.

2 God hath not cast away his [a]people which he [b]foreknew. [c]Wot ye not what the scripture saith of [d]Elias? how he maketh intercession to God against Israel, saying,

3 Lord, they have [a]killed thy prophets, and digged down thine altars; and I am [b]left alone, and they seek my life.

4 But what saith the answer of God unto him? I have [a]reserved to myself seven thousand men, who have not bowed the knee to *the image of* Baal.

10*a* TG Heart.
b D&C 46:14 (11–14).
c TG Salvation.
12*a* Acts 10:35 (34–35); Rom. 2:11; Gal. 3:28 (26–29).
b TG Treasure.
c TG God, Access to.
13*a* TG Prayer.
14*a* TG Apostasy of Israel; Hypocrisy.
b D&C 42:6.
15*a* TG Missionary Work; Preaching.
b TG Called of God.
c Nahum 1:15.
d TG Gospel.
e TG Peacemakers; Peace of God.
16*a* TG Apostasy of Israel.
b Isa. 53:1; John 12:38.
17*a* TG Faith.
b Gal. 3:2; 2 Ne. 33:1 (1–4); Alma 31:5 (5, 8–11); D&C 100:8 (7–8).
18*a* Ps. 19:4.
b D&C 23:2; 24:10.
19*a* Deut. 32:21. TG Jealous.
20*a* IE Isaiah.
b Isa. 65:1.
21*a* Isa. 65:2. TG Apostasy of Israel; Disobedience.
b GR contradicting, opposing.
11 1*a* GR May it not be!
b Acts 22:3; 2 Cor. 11:22.
2*a* TG Israel, Blessings of.
b TG Foreordination; God, Foreknowledge of.
c GR Know.
d IE Elijah.
3*a* TG Apostasy of Israel; Martyrdom.
b 1 Kgs. 19:14 (10–18).
4*a* D&C 49:8.

5 Even so then at this present time
also there is a remnant according
to the [a]election of grace.
6 And if by [a]grace, then *is it* no
more of [b]works: otherwise grace is
no more grace. But if *it be* of works,
then is it no more grace: otherwise
work is no more work.
7 What then? Israel hath not obtained that which he seeketh for;
but the election hath obtained it,
and the rest [a]were blinded
8 (According as it is written, God
hath given them the spirit of [a]slumber, eyes that they should not see,
and ears that they should not [b]hear;)
unto this day.
9 And David saith, Let their table
be made a [a]snare, and a trap, and a
stumblingblock, and a [b]recompence
unto them:
10 Let their eyes be darkened, that
they may not see, and bow down
their back alway.
11 I say then, Have they stumbled
that they should fall? [a]God forbid:
but *rather* through their fall salvation *is come* unto the Gentiles, for
to provoke them to [b]jealousy.
12 Now if the fall of them *be* the
riches of the world, and the [a]diminishing of them the riches of
the Gentiles; how much more their
fulness?
13 For I speak to you [a]Gentiles, inasmuch as I am the apostle of the
Gentiles, I [b]magnify mine office:
14 If by any means I may provoke
to emulation *them which are* my flesh,
and might save some of them.
15 For if the casting away of them
be the [a]reconciling of the world,
what *shall* the receiving *of them be*,
but life from the dead?
16 For if the firstfruit *be* holy, the
lump *is* also *holy:* and if the [a]root *be*
holy, so *are* the branches.
17 And if some of the branches be
broken off, and thou, being a wild
olive [a]tree, wert grafted in among
them, and with them partakest of
the root and fatness of the olive tree;
18 [a]Boast not against the branches.
But if thou boast, thou bearest not
the root, but the root thee.
19 Thou wilt say then, The branches
were broken off, that I might be
grafted in.
20 Well; because of [a]unbelief they
were [b]broken off, and thou standest by [c]faith. Be not highminded,
but [d]fear:
21 For if God spared not the [a]natural branches, *take heed* lest he also
[b]spare not thee.
22 Behold therefore the goodness
and severity of God: on them which
fell, severity; but toward thee, goodness, if thou continue in *his* goodness: otherwise thou also shalt be
cut off.
23 And they also, if they abide not
still in unbelief, shall be grafted in:
for God is able to graft them in again.
24 For if thou wert cut out of the
olive tree which is wild by nature,
and wert grafted contrary to nature
into a good olive tree: how much
more shall these, which be the natural *branches*, be grafted into their
own olive tree?
25 For I would not, brethren, that
ye should be ignorant of this mystery, lest ye should be wise in your
own [a]conceits; that [b]blindness in
part is happened to Israel, until
the [c]fulness of the [d]Gentiles be
come in.

5*a* TG Election.
6*a* TG Grace.
b Rom. 2:6 (5–10).
7*a* GR became callous.
8*a* GR deep sleep, stupor. Isa. 29:10.
b Matt. 13:14; 2 Ne. 16:10.
9*a* Ps. 69:22.
b GR retribution, requital.
11*a* GR May it not be!
b TG Jealous.
12*a* GR default, failure.
13*a* Acts 22:21.
b Jacob 2:2 (2–3); D&C 24:3; 66:11.
15*a* TG Reconciliation.
16*a* TG Israel, Mission of.
17*a* TG Vineyard of the Lord.
18*a* TG Boast.
20*a* TG Apostasy of Israel; Unbelief.
b Ps. 80:12 (12–16). TG Israel, Scattering of.
c 2 Cor. 1:24.
d TG Reverence.
21*a* Jacob 5:3 (1–77); 6:1 (1–13).
b TG Apostasy of the Early Christian Church.
25*a* Prov. 26:12.
b GR callousness. Jacob 4:14.
c TG Restoration of the Gospel.
d TG Gentiles.

26 And so all [a]Israel shall be saved:
as it is written, There shall come
out of [b]Sion the [c]Deliverer, and
shall turn away ungodliness from
Jacob:
27 For this *is* my [a]covenant unto
them, when I shall take away their
sins.
28 As concerning the gospel, *they
are* enemies for your sakes: but as
touching the election, *they are* beloved for the fathers' sakes.
29 For the gifts and calling of God
are without repentance.
30 For as ye in times past [a]have
not believed God, yet have now
obtained mercy through their
[b]unbelief:
31 Even so have these also now not
[a]believed, that through your mercy
they also may obtain mercy.
32 For God hath [a]concluded them
all in unbelief, that he might have
mercy upon all.
33 O the depth of the [a]riches both
of the [b]wisdom and [c]knowledge
of God! how [d]unsearchable *are* his
judgments, and his ways past [e]find-
ing out!
34 For who hath known the [a]mind
of the Lord? or who hath been his
[b]counsellor?
35 Or who hath first given to him,
and it shall be recompensed unto
him again?
36 For of him, and [a]through him,
and to him, *are* all things: to whom
be glory for ever. Amen.

CHAPTER 12

Paul counsels the Saints to present their bodies as a living sacrifice, to use their own grace-given gifts, and to live as Saints should live.

I BESEECH you therefore, brethren,
by the mercies of God, that ye present your [a]bodies a living [b]sacrifice,
holy, [c]acceptable unto God, *which is*
your reasonable [d]service.
2 And be not conformed to this
[a]world: but be ye [b]transformed by
the [c]renewing of your [d]mind, that
ye may [e]prove what *is* that good,
and acceptable, and perfect, [f]will
of God.
3 For I say, through the grace given
unto me, to every man that is among
you, not to [a]think *of himself* more
highly than he ought to think; but
to think [b]soberly, according as [c]God
hath dealt to every man the measure of faith.
4 For as we have many members
in one body, and all members have
not the same [a]office:
5 So we, *being* many, are [a]one [b]body
in Christ, and every one members
one of another.
6 Having then gifts differing according to the [a]grace that is given to
us, whether prophecy, *let us prophesy*
according to the proportion of [b]faith;
7 Or ministry, *let us wait* on *our*
ministering: or he that teacheth,
on teaching;
8 Or he that exhorteth, on

26*a* TG Israel, Restoration of.
b TG Zion.
c Isa. 59:20; Alma 11:40 (37–41).
27*a* Isa. 59:21 (20–21); Heb. 10:16 (16–17); D&C 49:9 (5–9). TG Abrahamic Covenant.
30*a* GR were disbelieving, disobedient to.
b GR disobedience, disbelief.
31*a* GR obeyed.
32*a* GR closed up together.
33*a* TG Treasure.
b TG God, Intelligence of.
c TG God, Omniscience of.
d Isa. 40:28.
e Prov. 25:2.
34*a* Jacob 4:8 (8–13); Mosiah 4:9.
b 1 Cor. 2:16; D&C 22:4. TG Counselor.
36*a* D&C 76:24 (22–24); 93:10.
12 1*a* TG Body, Sanctity of.
b Mosiah 2:34; Moro. 10:32 (30–33); D&C 93:1. TG Self-Sacrifice.
c Lev. 1:4.
d TG Service.
2*a* TG World; Worldliness.
b Eph. 5:8; 1 Jn. 5:4 (1–5). TG Self-Mastery.
c TG Man, New, Spiritually Reborn.
d TG Mind.
e GR test, try, prove.
f TG God, Will of.
3*a* TG Humility.
b D&C 18:21; 43:35.
c 1 Cor. 7:17.
4*a* GR function, operation.
5*a* TG Unity.
b TG Church.
6*a* TG Grace.
b TG Faith.

exhortation: he that giveth, *let him*
do it with simplicity; he that ruleth,
with diligence; he that sheweth
mercy, with [a]cheerfulness.
9 *Let* love be [a]without dissimu-
lation. Abhor that which is [b]evil;
cleave to that which is good.
10 *Be* kindly [a]affectioned one to
another with [b]brotherly [c]love; in
honour preferring one another;
11 Not slothful in [a]business; [b]fer-
vent in spirit; serving the Lord;
12 Rejoicing in hope; [a]patient in
[b]tribulation; [c]continuing instant
in prayer;
13 Distributing to the necessity of
saints; given to [a]hospitality.
14 Bless them which [a]persecute
you: bless, and [b]curse not.
15 Rejoice with them that do rejoice, and [a]weep with them that
weep.
16 *Be* of the same mind one toward
another. Mind not high things, but
[a]condescend to men of low estate.
Be not wise in your own [b]conceits.
17 [a]Recompense to no man [b]evil
for evil. Provide things [c]honest in
the [d]sight of all men.
18 If it be possible, as much as lieth
in you, live [a]peaceably with all men.
19 Dearly beloved, [a]avenge not
yourselves, but *rather* give place
unto wrath: for it is written, Vengeance *is* mine; I will repay, saith
the Lord.
20 Therefore if thine [a]enemy hunger, feed him; if he thirst, give him
drink: for in so doing thou shalt
heap coals of fire on his head.
21 Be not overcome of evil, but
[a]overcome evil with good.

CHAPTER 13

Paul counsels, Be subject unto God's ministers; keep the commandments; love one another; righteousness leads to salvation.

LET every soul [a]be subject unto
the higher [b]powers. For there is no
[c]power [d]but of God: the [e]powers that
be are ordained of God.
2 Whosoever therefore resisteth
the power, resisteth the ordinance
of God: and they that [a]resist shall
receive to themselves [b]damnation.
3 For rulers are not a terror to good
works, but to the evil. Wilt thou then
not be afraid of the [a]power? do that
which is [b]good, and thou shalt have
praise of the same:
4 For he is [a]the minister of God
to thee for good. But if thou do
that which is evil, be afraid; for
he beareth not the sword in vain:
for he is the minister of God, a re-
venger to *execute* wrath upon him
that doeth evil.
5 Wherefore *ye* must needs be subject, not only for wrath, but also for
[a]conscience sake.
6 [a]For for this cause pay ye tribute
also: for they are God's ministers,
attending continually upon this
very thing.

8*a* TG Cheerful.
9*a* GR sincere, unfeigned, real.
b Ps. 26:4; 2 Ne. 4:31; Alma 13:12; D&C 38:42. TG Evil.
10*a* Philip. 2:2 (1–4).
b TG Brotherhood and Sisterhood.
c TG Love.
11*a* GR haste, diligence.
b TG Zeal.
12*a* D&C 24:8; 31:9.
b TG Adversity.
c GR constantly persisting in.
13*a* TG Hospitality.
14*a* TG Enemies; Persecution.
b TG Curse.
15*a* TG Compassion.
16*a* GR conforming willingly with the humble. 3 Ne. 12:5.
b Prov. 26:12. TG Pride.
17*a* TG Forgive; Retribution.
b TG Evil.
c TG Honesty.
d 2 Cor. 8:21.
18*a* Prov. 3:30. TG Peace; Peacemakers.
19*a* TG Forbear; Retribution.
20*a* 2 Kgs. 6:22. TG Enemies.
21*a* Rev. 2:17.
13 1*a* GR be submissive, render obedience. D&C 58:22 (21–22). TG Citizenship; Governments.
b GR authorities.
c John 19:11 (10–12).
d JST Rom. 13:1 . . . *in the church* but of God . . .
e TG Governments.
2*a* TG Rebellion.
b TG Damnation.
3*a* GR authority.
b TG Retribution.
4*a* GR a servant.
5*a* TG Conscience.
6*a* JST Rom. 13:6–7 (Appendix).

7 Render therefore to all their dues:
tribute to whom tribute *is due;* custom to whom custom; fear to whom
fear; [a]honour to whom honour.
8 [a]Owe no man any thing, but to
love one another: for he that [b]loveth
another hath fulfilled the law.
9 For this, Thou shalt not commit
[a]adultery, Thou shalt not kill, Thou
shalt not [b]steal, Thou shalt not bear
false witness, Thou shalt not [c]covet;
and if *there be* any other commandment, it is briefly comprehended in
this saying, namely, Thou shalt love
thy [d]neighbour as thyself.
10 [a]Love worketh no ill to his neighbour: therefore love *is* the fulfilling
of the [b]law.
11 And that, knowing the time,
that now *it is* high [a]time to awake
out of [b]sleep: for now *is* our salvation nearer than when we believed.
12 The night is far spent, the [a]day
is at hand: let us therefore cast off
the works of [b]darkness, and let us
put on the [c]armour of [d]light.
13 Let us walk [a]honestly, as in the
day; not in [b]rioting and [c]drunk-
enness, not in [d]chambering and
wantonness, not in strife and
[e]envying.
14 But [a]put ye on the Lord Jesus
Christ, and make not provision for
the flesh, to *fulfil* the [b]lusts *thereof.*

CHAPTER 14

Avoid quarreling about opinions and making unrighteous judgment of each other—Every knee will bow to Christ—The kingdom of God embraces righteousness, peace, and joy in the Holy Ghost.

HIM that is [a]weak in the faith receive
ye, *but* not to [b]doubtful [c]disputations.
2 For one believeth that he may
eat all things: another, who is weak,
eateth [a]herbs.
3 Let not him that eateth despise
him that eateth not; and let not him
which eateth not [a]judge him that
eateth: for God hath received him.
4 Who art thou that [a]judgest another man's servant? to his own
master he standeth or falleth. Yea,
he shall be holden up: for God is
able to make him stand.
5 One man esteemeth one [a]day
above another: another esteemeth
every day *alike.* Let every man be
fully persuaded in his own mind.
6 He that regardeth the day, regardeth *it* unto the Lord; and he
that regardeth not the day, to the
Lord he doth not regard *it.* He that
eateth, eateth to the Lord, for he giveth God thanks; and he that eateth
not, to the Lord he eateth not, and
giveth God thanks.
7 For none of us [a]liveth to himself,
and no man dieth to himself.
8 For whether we live, we live unto
the Lord; and whether we die, we
[a]die unto the Lord: whether we live
therefore, or die, we are the Lord's.
9 For to this end Christ both died,
and rose, and revived, that he might

7*a* D&C 134:6.
TG Honor.
8*a* TG Debt.
b TG Love.
9*a* TG Adulterer.
b TG Stealing.
c TG Covet.
d TG Neighbor.
10*a* Moro. 7:47 (1, 44–47).
TG Motivations.
b Matt. 22:40 (36–40);
Gal. 5:14 (13–14).
11*a* TG Time.
b TG Apathy;
Sleep.
12*a* John 9:4;
Alma 34:31 (31–34).
b 2 Cor. 5:17;
1 Thes. 5:4.
TG Darkness,
Spiritual.
c Isa. 59:17 (16–17);
2 Cor. 6:7;
Eph. 6:11 (10–24);
1 Thes. 5:8;
D&C 27:15 (15–18).
d TG Children of Light;
Light [noun].
13*a* GR with propriety,
decently, gracefully.
TG Honesty.
b TG Rioting and
Reveling.
c TG Drunkenness.
d GR lewdness,
whoredoms.
e TG Envy.
14*a* Gal. 3:27 (24–29).
b TG Lust.
14 1*a* Isa. 35:3;
Rom. 15:1 (1–3);
1 Cor. 8:9;
Gal. 6:1;
D&C 81:5; 84:106.
b TG Doubt.
c TG Disputations.
2*a* GR vegetables.
3*a* Col. 2:16.
4*a* D&C 11:12.
5*a* Gal. 4:10 (9–10).
7*a* 2 Cor. 5:15 (14–16);
Gal. 2:20.
8*a* D&C 42:44 (44–47);
63:49.

be [a]Lord both of the [b]dead and
living.
10 But why dost thou [a]judge thy
brother? or why dost thou set at
nought thy brother? for we shall
all stand before the [b]judgment seat
of Christ.
11 For it is written, *As* I live, saith
the Lord, every [a]knee shall bow to
me, and every tongue shall [b]con-
fess to God.
12 So then every one of us shall
give account of himself to God.
13 Let us not therefore judge one
another any more: but judge this
rather, that no man put a [a]stum-
blingblock or an occasion to fall in
his brother's way.
14 I know, and am persuaded by
the Lord Jesus, that *there is* nothing
[a]unclean of itself: but to him that
[b]esteemeth any thing to be unclean,
to him *it is* unclean.
15 But if thy brother be grieved
with *thy* meat, [a]now walkest thou not
[b]charitably. Destroy not him [c]with
thy meat, for whom Christ died.
16 Let not then your good be evil
spoken of:
17 For the kingdom of God is not
[a]meat and drink; but [b]righteous-
ness, and [c]peace, and [d]joy in the
Holy Ghost.
18 For he that in these things
serveth Christ *is* acceptable to God,
and approved of men.
19 Let us therefore follow after the
things which make for [a]peace, and
things wherewith one may [b]edify
another.
20 [a]For meat destroy not the [b]work
of God. All things indeed *are* pure;
but *it is* evil for that man who eateth with offence.
21 *It is* good neither to eat flesh,
nor to drink wine, nor *any thing*
whereby thy brother stumbleth, or
is [a]offended, or is made weak.
22 Hast thou faith? have *it* to thyself before God. Happy *is* he that
condemneth not himself [a]in that
thing which he alloweth.
23 And he that [a]doubteth is
damned if he eat, because *he eateth*
not of faith: for whatsoever *is* not
of [b]faith is [c]sin.

CHAPTER 15

True Saints fellowship one another—Paul recounts his diligence in preaching the gospel—The gifts of the Spirit are poured out upon the Gentiles.

WE then that are strong ought to
[a]bear the infirmities of the [b]weak,
and not to please ourselves.
2 Let every one of us please *his*
[a]neighbour for *his* good to [b]edifi-
cation.
3 For even Christ pleased not himself; but, as it is written, The [a]re-
proaches of them that reproached
thee fell on me.
4 For whatsoever things were
[a]written aforetime were [b]written
for our [c]learning, that we through

9*a* TG Jesus Christ, Authority of; Jesus Christ, Power of.
b Luke 20:38. TG Genealogy and Temple Work; Salvation for the Dead.
10*a* TG Judgment.
b TG Judgment, the Last.
11*a* Isa. 45:23; Philip. 2:10.
b GR praise, profess openly.
13*a* Lev. 19:14; 1 Cor. 8:9 (9–13); 10:32 (24–33); 2 Cor. 6:3; Alma 39:11.
14*a* GR ceremonially unclean. TG Uncleanness.
b TG Motivations.
15*a* JST Rom. 14:15 . . . *thou* walkest not charitably *if thou eatest. Therefore* destroy not him with thy meat . . .
b GR according to love.
c GR on account of food.
17*a* GR food. TG Food.
b TG Righteousness.
c TG Contentment; Peace of God.
d TG Joy.
19*a* TG Peace; Peacemakers.
b TG Edification.
20*a* GR Because of food.
b TG God, Works of.
21*a* 1 Cor. 8:13.
22*a* GR by what he tries, approves.
23*a* TG Doubt.
b TG Faith.
c TG Sin.
15 1*a* GR remove, endure, bear with. Alma 31:33.
b Rom. 14:1 (1–3).
2*a* TG Neighbor.
b TG Edification.
3*a* GR revilings, insults. TG Reproach.
4*a* 1 Cor. 10:11. TG Scriptures, Writing of.
b 1 Cor. 9:10.
c TG Scriptures, Value of; Understanding.

[d]patience and comfort of the [e]scrip-
tures might have [f]hope.
5 Now the God of patience and
[a]consolation grant you to be [b]like-
minded one toward another according to Christ Jesus:
6 That ye may with one mind *and*
one mouth glorify God, even the
[a]Father of our Lord Jesus Christ.
7 Wherefore receive ye one another, as Christ also received us to
the glory of God.
8 Now I say that Jesus Christ was
a minister of the [a]circumcision for
the truth of God, to [b]confirm the
[c]promises *made* unto the fathers:
9 And that the Gentiles might glorify God for *his* [a]mercy; as it is written, For this cause I will [b]confess to
thee among the [c]Gentiles, and sing
unto thy name.
10 And again he saith, Rejoice, ye
[a]Gentiles, with his people.
11 And again, Praise the Lord, all
ye Gentiles; and laud him, all ye
people.
12 And again, [a]Esaias saith, There
shall be a root of [b]Jesse, and he that
shall rise to reign over the Gentiles;
in him shall the Gentiles trust.
13 Now the God of hope fill you
with all joy and [a]peace in believing, that ye may abound in [b]hope,
through the power of the Holy
Ghost.
14 And I myself also am persuaded
of you, my brethren, that ye also
are full of goodness, filled with all
[a]knowledge, able also to [b]admonish
one another.
15 Nevertheless, brethren, I have
written the more boldly unto you in
[a]some sort, as putting you in mind,
because of the [b]grace that is given
to me of God,
16 That I should be the [a]minister
of Jesus Christ to the Gentiles, ministering the gospel of God, that the
[b]offering up of the Gentiles might
be acceptable, being [c]sanctified by
the Holy Ghost.
17 I have therefore whereof I may
[a]glory through Jesus Christ in those
things which pertain to God.
18 For I will not dare to speak of
any of those things which Christ
hath not wrought by me, to make
the Gentiles obedient, by word and
deed,
19 Through mighty [a]signs and wonders, by the power of the [b]Spirit of
God; so that from Jerusalem, and
round about unto Illyricum, I have
fully preached the gospel of Christ.
20 Yea, so have I strived to preach
the gospel, not where Christ was
named, lest I should build upon
another man's [a]foundation:
21 But as it is written, To whom he
was not [a]spoken of, they shall see:
and they that have not heard shall
understand.
22 For which cause also I have been
much [a]hindered from coming to you.
23 But now having no more [a]place
in these parts, and having a great
desire these many years to come
unto you;
24 Whensoever I take my journey
into Spain, I will come to you: for I
trust to see you in my journey, and
to be brought on my way thither-
ward by you, if first I be somewhat
filled with your *company*.

4*d* TG Patience.
e TG Scriptures, Study of.
f TG Hope.
5*a* GR comfort.
b 1 Cor. 1:10 (9–16); 1 Thes. 5:13 (13–15); Mosiah 18:21.
6*a* TG Jesus Christ, Divine Sonship.
8*a* TG Circumcision.
b GR establish, make constant.
c 2 Cor. 1:20.
9*a* TG God, Mercy of.
b GR profess openly, praise.
c Ps. 18:49.
10*a* Acts 9:15 (1–19); 3 Ne. 30:2 (1–2).
12*a* IE Isaiah.
b TG Jesus Christ, Davidic Descent of.
13*a* TG Peace of God.
b TG Hope.
14*a* TG Knowledge.
b TG Warn.
15*a* GR part.
b TG Grace.
16*a* GR servant at one's own expense.
b GR sacrifice, offering.
c TG Holy Ghost, Gifts of.
17*a* Alma 26:16 (16, 35).
19*a* Morm. 9:19 (19–21); D&C 63:10 (7–10).
b TG God, Spirit of.
20*a* 2 Cor. 10:15; D&C 52:33.
21*a* Isa. 52:15.
22*a* Rom. 1:13.
23*a* GR opportunity.

25 But now I go unto Jerusalem to minister unto the saints.
26 For it hath pleased them of Macedonia and Achaia to make a certain [a]contribution for the poor saints which are at Jerusalem.
27 It hath pleased them verily; and their debtors they are. For if the Gentiles have been made partakers of their [a]spiritual things, their [b]duty is also to minister unto them in [c]carnal things.
28 When therefore I have performed this, and have sealed to them this [a]fruit, I will come by you into Spain.
29 And I am sure that, when I come unto you, I shall come in the [a]fulness of the blessing of the gospel of Christ.
30 Now I beseech you, brethren, for the Lord Jesus Christ's sake, and for the love of the Spirit, that ye strive together with me in *your* prayers to God for me;
31 That I may be delivered from them that [a]do not believe in Judæa; and that my service which *I have* for Jerusalem may be accepted of the saints;
32 That I may come unto you with joy by the will of God, and may with you be [a]refreshed.
33 Now the God of peace *be* with you all. Amen.

CHAPTER 16

Paul sends greetings to various Saints—He counsels the Saints to avoid those who cause divisions—The Saints should be wise concerning good and innocent concerning evil.

I COMMEND unto you Phebe our sister, which is a servant of the church which is at Cenchrea:
2 That ye receive her in the Lord, as becometh saints, and that ye assist her in whatsoever business she hath need of you: for she hath been a succourer of many, and of myself also.
3 Greet Priscilla and Aquila my helpers in Christ Jesus:
4 Who have for my life laid down their own necks: unto whom not only I give thanks, but also all the churches of the Gentiles.
5 Likewise *greet* the church that is in their house. Salute my wellbeloved Epænetus, who is the firstfruits of Achaia unto Christ.
6 Greet Mary, who bestowed much labour on us.
7 Salute Andronicus and Junia, my kinsmen, and my fellowprisoners, who are of note among the apostles, who also were in Christ before me.
8 Greet Amplias my beloved in the Lord.
9 Salute Urbane, our helper in Christ, and Stachys my beloved.
10 Salute Apelles approved in Christ. Salute them which are of Aristobulus' [a]*household.*
11 Salute Herodion my kinsman. Greet them that be of the [a]*household* of Narcissus, which are in the Lord.
12 Salute Tryphena and Tryphosa, who labour in the Lord. Salute the beloved Persis, which laboured much in the Lord.
13 Salute Rufus chosen in the Lord, and his mother and mine.
14 Salute Asyncritus, Phlegon, Hermas, Patrobas, Hermes, and the brethren which are with them.
15 Salute Philologus, and Julia, Nereus, and his sister, and Olympas, and all the saints which are with them.
16 Salute one another with an holy [a]kiss. The [b]churches of Christ salute you.
17 Now I beseech you, brethren, [a]mark them which cause [b]divisions

26*a* TG Almsgiving; Welfare.
27*a* 1 Cor. 9:11.
b TG Duty.
c GR material, temporal.
28*a* Philip. 4:17; Titus 3:14.
29*a* D&C 1:23; 14:10; 35:17; 39:11 (11–18); 42:12; JS—H 1:34.
31*a* GR refuse belief or obedience.
32*a* 2 Cor. 7:13.
16 10*a* JST Rom. 16:10 . . . *church.*
11*a* JST Rom. 16:11 . . . *church . . .*
16*a* JST Rom. 16:16 . . . *salutation . . .*
b TG Jesus Christ, Head of the Church.
17*a* GR watch, beware of.
b Acts 20:30 (28–30); 1 Cor. 1:10 (10–13); 2 Thes. 3:6 (2–6); 2 Ne. 26:21 (20–21).

and [c]offences contrary to the [d]doc-
trine which ye have learned; and
[e]avoid them.
18 For they that are such serve
not our Lord Jesus Christ, but their
own belly; and by good words and
[a]fair speeches deceive the hearts of
the [b]simple.
19 For your [a]obedience is come
abroad unto all *men*. I am glad therefore on your behalf: but yet I would
have you [b]wise unto that which is
good, and [c]simple concerning evil.
20 And the God of [a]peace shall
[b]bruise [c]Satan under your feet
shortly. The grace of our Lord Jesus
Christ *be* with you. Amen.
21 Timotheus my workfellow, and
Lucius, and Jason, and Sosipater, my
kinsmen, salute you.
22 I Tertius, who wrote *this* epistle,
salute you in the Lord.
23 Gaius mine host, and of the
whole church, saluteth you. Erastus
the chamberlain of the city saluteth
you, and Quartus a brother.
24 The [a]grace of our Lord Jesus
Christ *be* with you all. Amen.
25 Now to him that is of power
to [a]stablish you according to my
gospel, and the preaching of Jesus
Christ, according to the revelation
of the [b]mystery, which was kept secret since the world began,
26 But now is made manifest, and
by the scriptures of the prophets, according to the commandment of the
[a]everlasting God, made known to all
nations for the [b]obedience of faith:
27 To God only wise, *be* glory
through Jesus Christ for ever. Amen.

¶ Written to the Romans from Corinthus, *and sent* by Phebe servant of the church at Cenchrea.

THE FIRST EPISTLE OF PAUL THE APOSTLE TO THE CORINTHIANS

CHAPTER 1

True Saints are perfectly united in the same mind and in the same judgment—Preach the gospel and save souls—The gospel is preached by the weak and the simple.

PAUL, called *to be* an apostle of
Jesus Christ through the will of
God, and Sosthenes *our* brother,
2 Unto the church of God which is
at Corinth, to them that are [a]sanc-
tified in Christ Jesus, called *to be*
[b]saints, with all that in every place

17*c* GR stumbling blocks, scandals.
d 3 Ne. 11:40 (31–41).
e 1 Cor. 5:11.
18*a* 2 Pet. 2:3.
b GR innocent, guileless.
19*a* Rom. 1:8.
b TG Wisdom.
c GR blameless, innocent.
20*a* Moro. 7:3 (3–4).
b GR break the power of, crush. Gen. 3:15. TG Jesus Christ, Prophecies about; Redemption.
c TG Devil.
24*a* Rev. 22:21 (17–21).
25*a* 1 Thes. 3:2.
b Eph. 3:4; Col. 1:26 (25–26); D&C 6:7 (7–11); 42:65 (61–65); 121:27 (25–27).
26*a* Gen. 21:33.
b TG Obedience.

[1 CORINTHIANS]

1 2*a* TG Sanctification.
b TG Mission of Early Saints; Saints.

call upon the name of Jesus Christ
our Lord, both theirs and ours:
3 Grace *be* unto you, and [a]peace,
from God our Father, and *from* the
Lord Jesus Christ.
4 I thank my God always on your
behalf, for the grace of God which
is given you by Jesus Christ;
5 That in every thing ye are enriched by him, in all utterance, and
in all knowledge;
6 Even as the [a]testimony of Christ
was [b]confirmed in you:
7 So that ye [a]come behind in no
gift; waiting for the [b]coming of our
Lord Jesus Christ:
8 Who shall also [a]confirm you unto
the end, *that ye may be* [b]blameless
in the day of our Lord Jesus Christ.
9 God *is* faithful, by whom ye were
called unto the [a]fellowship of his
Son Jesus Christ our Lord.
10 Now I beseech you, brethren, by
the name of our Lord Jesus Christ,
that ye all speak the same thing, and
that there be no [a]divisions among
you; but *that* ye be perfectly joined
together in the same [b]mind and in
the same judgment.
11 For it hath been declared unto
me [a]of you, my brethren, by them
which are of the house of Chloe, that
there are [b]contentions among you.
12 Now this I say, that every one
of you saith, I am of Paul; and I of
Apollos; and I of Cephas; and I
of [a]Christ.
13 Is Christ [a]divided? was Paul
crucified for you? or were ye baptized in the name of Paul?
14 I thank God that I baptized none
of you, [a]but [b]Crispus and Gaius;
15 Lest any should say that I had
baptized in mine own name.
16 And I baptized also the household of [a]Stephanas: besides, I
know not whether I baptized any
other.
17 For Christ sent me not to baptize, but to preach the gospel: not
with [a]wisdom of words, lest the
cross of Christ should be made of
none effect.
18 For the [a]preaching of the cross
is to them that perish foolishness;
but unto us which are saved it is
the [b]power of God.
19 For it is written, I will destroy
the wisdom of the wise, and will
bring to nothing the [a]understand-
ing of the [b]prudent.
20 Where *is* the wise? where *is*
the [a]scribe? where *is* the [b]disputer
of this [c]world? hath not God made
foolish the [d]wisdom of this [e]world?
21 For after that in the wisdom of
God the world [a]by wisdom knew
not God, it pleased God by the foolishness of [b]preaching to save them
that believe.
22 For the Jews require a [a]sign,
and the Greeks seek after wisdom:
23 But we [a]preach Christ [b]crucified,
unto the Jews a [c]stumblingblock,
and unto the Greeks foolishness;
24 But unto them [a]which are

3*a* TG Peace of God.
6*a* TG Testimony.
b GR established, strengthened.
7*a* GR come short, miss, need.
b GR revelation. 1 Thes. 3:13; D&C 45:44 (25–44).
8*a* GR secure, establish, strengthen.
b 3 Ne. 27:20; D&C 4:2.
9*a* TG Fellowshipping.
10*a* GR factions, schisms. Acts 4:32; Rom. 15:5 (1–7); 16:17 (17–18); Eph. 4:13 (11–14); 3 Ne. 11:28 (28–30). TG Church.
b 1 Cor. 12:25; 2 Cor. 13:11; D&C 38:27. TG Mind.
11*a* GR about, concerning.
b TG Apostasy of the Early Christian Church; Contention.
12*a* 3 Ne. 27:8 (4–9).
13*a* 2 Ne. 28:3 (3–5, 12–13).
14*a* GR except.
b Acts 18:8.
16*a* 1 Cor. 16:15.
17*a* TG Wisdom.
18*a* 1 Pet. 2:8 (4–8).
b Rom. 1:16; 1 Cor. 4:20.
19*a* TG Understanding.
b TG Prudence.
20*a* TG Scribe.
b TG Disputations.
c GR age.
d Isa. 44:25; Jer. 8:8 (8–9); D&C 133:58.
e TG Worldliness.
21*a* GR by means of, through.
b TG Gospel.
22*a* TG Sign Seekers.
23*a* TG Missionary Work.
b TG Jesus Christ, Crucifixion of.
c Jacob 4:15.
24*a* JST 1 Cor. 1:24 . . . *who believe,* both Jews and Greeks . . .

called, both Jews and Greeks, Christ
the [b]power of God, and the [c]wisdom
of God.
25 Because the [a]foolishness of God
is wiser than men; and the weakness
of God is stronger than men.
26 For ye see your calling, brethren, how that not many wise men
after the [a]flesh, not many mighty,
not many noble, *are* [b]*called:*
27 But God hath chosen the [a]fool-
ish things of the world to [b]confound
the wise; and God hath chosen the
[c]weak things of the world to con-
found the things which are mighty;
28 And base things of the world,
and things which are despised, hath
God chosen, *yea,* and things which
are not, to bring to nought things
that are:
29 That no flesh should glory in
his presence.
30 But of him are ye in Christ Jesus,
who of God is made unto us wisdom,
and righteousness, and [a]sanctifica-
tion, and redemption:
31 That, according as it is written,
He that glorieth, let him [a]glory in
the Lord.

CHAPTER 2

The gospel is preached by the power of the Spirit—The Spirit reveals all things to the Saints—The unrepentant natural man cannot receive the things of the Spirit of God.

AND I, brethren, when I came to you,
came not with excellency of speech
or of wisdom, declaring unto you
the [a]testimony of God.
2 For I determined not to know
any thing among you, [a]save Jesus
Christ, and him [b]crucified.
3 And I was with you in [a]weakness,
and in fear, and in much trembling.
4 And my [a]speech and my preaching *was* not with [b]enticing words of
man's wisdom, but in demonstration
of the [c]Spirit and of [d]power:
5 That your faith should not stand
in the wisdom of men, but in the
[a]power of God.
6 Howbeit we speak wisdom
among them that are [a]perfect: yet
not the wisdom of this world, nor
of the princes of this world, that
come to nought:
7 But we speak the [a]wisdom of God
in a [b]mystery, *even* the hidden [c]*wis-*
dom, which God [d]ordained before
the world unto our glory:
8 Which none of the princes of this
world knew: for had they known *it,*
they would not have [a]crucified the
Lord of glory.
9 But as it is written, [a]Eye hath not
seen, nor ear heard, neither have
entered into the heart of man, the
things which God hath [b]prepared
for them that love him.
10 But God hath [a]revealed *them*
unto us by his [b]Spirit: for the [c]Spirit
[d]searcheth all things, yea, the deep
things of God.
11 For what man [a]knoweth the
things of a man, save the spirit of
man which is in him? even so the

24*b* TG God, Power of.
c TG Jesus Christ, Relationships with the Father.
25*a* TG Foolishness.
26*a* TG Man, Natural, Not Spiritually Reborn.
b JST 1 Cor. 1:26 . . . *chosen* . . . John 12:43 (42–43). TG Called of God.
27*a* James 2:5 (1–9); D&C 1:23 (18–20, 23).
b GR shame, frustrate. Alma 37:7 (6–7); D&C 133:58 (58–59).
c Ether 12:27 (23–29); D&C 35:13; 124:1.
30*a* TG Sanctification.
31*a* Jer. 9:24 (23–24); 1 Cor. 5:6; Alma 26:16 (16, 35).
2 1*a* TG Testimony.
2*a* GR except.
b TG Jesus Christ, Crucifixion of.
3*a* Gal. 4:13; Ether 12:23 (23–29).
4*a* 1 Thes. 1:5.
b GR persuasive.
c TG Teaching with the Spirit.
d 2 Ne. 28:4 (3–5). TG Priesthood, Power of.
5*a* 2 Cor. 4:7.
6*a* TG Perfection.
7*a* TG Wisdom.
b TG Mysteries of Godliness.
c Col. 2:3.
d GR foreordained.
8*a* TG Jesus Christ, Crucifixion of.
9*a* Isa. 64:4; D&C 76:10.
b TG Blessing; Reward.
10*a* Alma 5:46 (45–48). TG Revelation.
b 1 Thes. 4:8; 1 Jn. 3:24; D&C 42:17.
c D&C 35:19.
d GR explores, investigates. D&C 63:59.
11*a* TG Education.

things of God [b]knoweth no man, [c]but the [d]Spirit of God.
12 Now we have received, not the [a]spirit of the world, but the spirit which is of God; that we might know the things that are freely given to us of God.
13 Which things also we speak, not in the words which man's [a]wisdom teacheth, but which the Holy Ghost [b]teacheth; comparing spiritual things with spiritual.
14 But the [a]natural man [b]receiveth not the things of the [c]Spirit of God: for they are [d]foolishness unto him: neither can he [e]know *them*, because they are [f]spiritually [g]discerned.
15 But he that is spiritual [a]judgeth all things, yet he himself is judged of no man.
16 For who hath known the mind of the Lord, that he may [a]instruct him? But we have the [b]mind of Christ.

CHAPTER 3

Milk comes before meat in the Church—Men's works will be tried by fire—The Saints are the temple of God, and if they are faithful, they will inherit all things.

AND I, brethren, could not speak unto you as unto spiritual, but as unto carnal, *even* as unto babes in Christ.
2 I have fed you with [a]milk, and not with meat: for hitherto ye were not able *to bear it*, neither yet now are ye able.
3 For ye are yet [a]carnal: for whereas *there is* among you [b]envying, and [c]strife, and [d]divisions, are ye not carnal, and walk as men?
4 For while one saith, I am of Paul; and another, I *am* of Apollos; are ye not carnal?
5 Who then is Paul, and who *is* Apollos, but [a]ministers by whom ye believed, even as the Lord gave to every man?
6 I have [a]planted, Apollos watered; but God [b]gave the [c]increase.
7 So then neither is he that planteth any thing, neither he that watereth; but God that giveth the increase.
8 Now he that planteth and he that watereth are one: and every man shall receive his own [a]reward according to his own labour.
9 For we are [a]labourers together with God: ye are God's [b]husbandry, *ye are* God's building.
10 According to the [a]grace of God which is given unto me, as a wise masterbuilder, I have laid the foundation, and another buildeth thereon. But let every man take heed how he buildeth thereupon.
11 For other [a]foundation can no man lay than that is laid, which is Jesus Christ.
12 Now if any man build upon this foundation gold, silver, precious stones, wood, hay, stubble;
13 Every man's work shall be made manifest: for the day shall

11*b* Mark 6:52; John 1:5; Jacob 4:8 (8–10, 13); Alma 26:21 (21–22).
c JST 1 Cor. 2:11 . . . *except he has* the Spirit of God.
d TG Holy Ghost, Source of Testimony.
12*a* D&C 50:15.
13*a* 2 Cor. 1:12.
b TG Holy Ghost, Mission of.
14*a* 2 Ne. 9:43 (42–43). TG Learn; Man, Natural, Not Spiritually Reborn.
b TG Teachable.
c TG God, Spirit of.
d Ether 12:25 (23–28, 38). TG Foolishness.
e TG God, Knowledge about; Knowledge.
f TG Spirituality.
g GR examined, tried, judged. TG Discernment, Spiritual.
15*a* GR examines, tries, judges.
16*a* Rom. 11:34; D&C 22:4. TG Counsel.
b 1 Jn. 3:24 (19–24); 4:12 (7–21); Moses 4:6.
3 2*a* Heb. 5:12 (11–14); 1 Pet. 2:2 (1–3); D&C 19:22; 50:40.
3*a* TG Carnal Mind; Man, Natural, Not Spiritually Reborn.
b TG Envy.
c TG Strife.
d TG Apostasy of the Early Christian Church.
5*a* GR servants. 2 Cor. 3:6.
6*a* John 4:37 (36–38); 1 Cor. 9:1.
b GR caused, gave growth.
c Mark 4:27 (26–29).
8*a* TG Reward; Wages.
9*a* 2 Cor. 6:1.
b GR cultivated field, farm.
10*a* TG Grace.
11*a* Matt. 16:18; 2 Ne. 4:30. TG Cornerstone.

declare it, because it shall be revealed by fire; and the [a]fire shall [b]try
every man's work of what sort it is.
14 If any man's work abide which
he hath built thereupon, he shall
receive a reward.
15 If any man's work shall be
burned, he shall suffer loss: but
he himself [a]shall be saved; yet so
as by fire.
16 Know ye not that ye are the
[a]temple of God, and *that* the [b]Spirit
of God dwelleth [c]in you?
17 If any man [a]defile the temple
of God, him shall God destroy; for
the temple of God is [b]holy, which
temple ye are.
18 Let no man deceive himself. If
any man among you [a]seemeth to be
wise in this world, let him become
a [b]fool, that he may be [c]wise.
19 For the [a]wisdom of this [b]world
is [c]foolishness with God. For it is
written, He taketh the wise in their
own [d]craftiness.
20 And again, The Lord [a]knoweth
the thoughts of the wise, that they
are [b]vain.
21 Therefore let no man [a]glory in
men. For all things are yours;
22 Whether [a]Paul, or Apollos, or
Cephas, or the world, or life, or
death, or things present, or things
to come; [b]all are yours;
23 And ye are [a]Christ's; and Christ
is God's.

CHAPTER 4

Christ's ministers must be faithful—The Apostles suffer, minister, and keep the faith—The kingdom of God is not in word but in power.

LET a man so account of us, as of the
ministers of Christ, and stewards of
the [a]mysteries of God.
2 Moreover it is required in [a]stew-
ards, that a man be found [b]faithful.
3 But with me it is a very small
thing that I should be judged of
you, or of man's judgment: yea, I
judge not mine own self.
4 For I know nothing [a]by myself;
yet am I not hereby justified: but he
that [b]judgeth me is the Lord.
5 Therefore judge nothing before
the time, until the Lord come, who
both will bring to light the [a]hidden
things of darkness, and will make
[b]manifest the counsels of the hearts:
and then shall every man have
praise of God.
6 And these things, brethren, I have
in a figure transferred to myself
and *to* Apollos for your sakes; that
ye might learn in us not to think
of men above that which is written,
that no one of you be [a]puffed up
for one against another.
7 For who maketh thee [a]to differ
from another? and what hast thou
that thou didst not [b]receive? now
if thou didst receive *it*, why dost
thou glory, as if thou hadst not received *it*?
8 Now ye are full, now ye are rich,
ye have reigned as kings without
us: and I would to God ye did reign,
that we also might reign with you.

13*a* Mal. 3:2 (2–3).
b GR test, put to proof. TG Test.
15*a* JST 1 Cor. 3:15 . . . *may* . . .
16*a* TG Body, Sanctity of; Life, Sanctity of; Temple.
b TG God, Spirit of.
c GR in, within, among.
17*a* GR spoil, corrupt, deprave. TG Cleanliness; Filthiness; Holy Ghost, Loss of; Pollution; Sacrilege; Uncleanness; Word of Wisdom.
b TG Holiness; Sacred.
18*a* TG Boast.
b 2 Ne. 9:42 (42–43).
c TG Learn.
19*a* TG God, Wisdom of; Knowledge; Wisdom.
b TG World; Worldliness.
c TG Foolishness.
d GR cunning, villainy.
20*a* TG God, Omniscience of.
b GR deceptive, fruitless.
21*a* 1 Cor. 5:6; D&C 76:61 (58–62).
22*a* D&C 76:99.
b Luke 12:44.
23*a* 2 Cor. 10:7.
4 1*a* TG God, Knowledge about; Mysteries of Godliness.
2*a* TG Delegation of Responsibility; Stewardship.
b TG Trustworthiness.
4*a* JST 1 Cor. 4:4 . . . *against myself* . . .
b TG Jesus Christ, Judge.
5*a* D&C 123:13.
b Rom. 2:16.
6*a* GR proud, arrogant. D&C 38:24.
7*a* GR different from, superior to.
b Mosiah 4:19.

9 For I think that God hath set forth
us the [a]apostles last, as it were [b]ap-
pointed to death: for we are made
a spectacle unto the world, and to
angels, and to men.
10 We *are* fools for Christ's sake, but
ye *are* wise in Christ; we *are* weak,
but ye *are* strong; ye *are* honourable,
but we *are* despised.
11 Even unto this present hour
we both hunger, and thirst, and are
naked, and are [a]buffeted, and have
no certain dwellingplace;
12 And [a]labour, working with our
[b]own [c]hands: being [d]reviled, we
bless; being [e]persecuted, we [f]suffer
it:
13 Being defamed, we entreat: we
are made as the filth of the world,
and are the offscouring of all things
unto this day.
14 I write not these things to
[a]shame you, but as my beloved [b]sons
I [c]warn *you.*
15 For though ye have ten thousand instructors in Christ, yet *have
ye* not many fathers: for in Christ
Jesus I have begotten you through
the [a]gospel.
16 Wherefore I beseech you, be ye
[a]followers of me.
17 For this cause have I sent unto
you [a]Timotheus, who is my beloved
son, and faithful in the Lord, who
shall bring you into remembrance
of my ways which be in Christ, as I
teach every where in every church.
18 Now some are [a]puffed up, as
though I would not come to you.
19 But I will come to you shortly,
if the Lord will, and will know, not
the speech of them which are puffed
up, but the power.
20 For the kingdom of God *is* not
in word, but in [a]power.
21 [a]What will ye? shall I come unto
you with a rod, or in love, and *in*
the spirit of [b]meekness?

CHAPTER 5

The Church cannot fellowship sinners —Christ, our passover, was sacrificed for us.

IT is reported commonly *that there
is* [a]fornication among you, and
such fornication as is not so much
as named among the Gentiles, that
one should have his father's wife.
2 And ye are [a]puffed up, and have
not rather mourned, that he that
hath done this deed might be taken
away from among you.
3 For I verily, [a]as absent in body,
but present in spirit, have judged
already, as though I were present,
concerning him that hath so done
this deed,
4 In the name of our Lord Jesus
Christ, when ye are gathered together, [a]and my spirit, with the
power of our Lord Jesus Christ,
5 To [a]deliver such an one unto Satan for the [b]destruction of the flesh,
that the spirit may be saved in the
[c]day of the Lord Jesus.
6 Your [a]glorying *is* not good. Know
ye not that a little leaven leaveneth
the whole lump?
7 [a]Purge out therefore the old
leaven, that ye may be a new lump,
as ye are [b]unleavened. For even

9*a* GR last apostles. Rom. 1:1; 1 Ne. 11:34 (33–34).
b D&C 42:48.
11*a* GR roughly treated, afflicted.
12*a* TG Labor.
b TG Self-Sacrifice.
c D&C 38:40.
d TG Malice; Reviling.
e TG Persecution.
f GR endure patiently.
14*a* TG Shame.
b 1 Thes. 2:11.
c TG Warn.
15*a* TG Gospel.
16*a* GR imitators. 1 Cor. 11:1.
17*a* Acts 16:1; 1 Tim. 1:2.
18*a* TG Apostasy of the Early Christian Church.
20*a* 1 Cor. 1:18 (17–18); D&C 18:47; 42:14. TG Priesthood, Power of.
21*a* IE Which do you choose?
b GR gentleness, kindness.
5 1*a* GR sexual immorality. TG Sexual Immorality.
2*a* Alma 5:53 (53–56); 6:3.
3*a* GR as it were.
4*a* JST 1 Cor. 5:4 . . . and *have the Spirit,* with . . .
5*a* 1 Tim. 1:20; D&C 78:12 (11–12).
b TG Punish.
c D&C 2:1; 19:3; 39:21; 45:12 (12–34); Moses 7:65 (59–67).
6*a* GR boasting. 1 Cor. 1:31; 3:21 (18–21).
7*a* D&C 43:11.
b TG Bread, Unleavened.

Christ our [c]passover is sacrificed
for us:
8 Therefore let us keep the [a]feast,
not with old [b]leaven, neither with
the leaven of malice and wickedness; but with the unleavened *bread*
of [c]sincerity and truth.
9 I wrote unto you in an [a]epistle
not to [b]company with [c]fornicators:
10 Yet not altogether with the for-
nicators of this world, or with the
[a]covetous, or [b]extortioners, or with
idolaters; for then must ye needs go
out of the world.
11 But now I have written unto you
not to keep [a]company, if any man
that is called a brother be a fornicator,
or covetous, or an idolater, or a railer,
or a [b]drunkard, or an extortioner; with
such an one [c]no not to [d]eat.
12 For what have I to do to judge
them also that are [a]without? do not
ye [b]judge them that are within?
13 But them that are without God
judgeth. Therefore put away from
among yourselves that wicked person.

CHAPTER 6

Church members should not fight one another in the courts—The unrighteous will not be saved—True Saints are the temple of the Holy Ghost.

DARE any of you, having a [a]matter
against another, go to [b]law before
the unjust, and not before the saints?
2 Do ye not know that the saints
shall [a]judge the [b]world? and if the
world shall be judged by you, are
ye unworthy to judge the smallest
matters?
3 Know ye not that we shall judge
angels? how much more things that
pertain to this life?
4 If then ye have judgments of
things pertaining to this life, set
them to judge who are least esteemed in the church.
5 I speak to your [a]shame. Is it so,
that there is not a wise man among
you? no, not one that shall be able
to judge between his brethren?
6 But brother goeth to law with
brother, and that before the unbelievers.
7 Now therefore there is utterly
a fault among you, because ye go
to law one with another. Why do
ye not rather take [a]wrong? why
do ye not rather [b]*suffer yourselves to*
be [c]defrauded?
8 Nay, ye do wrong, and [a]defraud,
and that *your* brethren.
9 Know ye not that the [a]unrigh-
teous shall not [b]inherit the kingdom
of God? Be not deceived: neither
[c]fornicators, nor idolaters, nor [d]adul-
terers, nor [e]effeminate, nor [f]abusers
of themselves with mankind,
10 Nor [a]thieves, nor covetous, nor
[b]drunkards, nor [c]revilers, nor [d]ex-
tortioners, shall inherit the kingdom of God.
11 And such were some of you: but
ye are [a]washed, but ye are [b]sancti-
fied, but ye are justified in the [c]name

7*c* TG Jesus Christ, Types of, in Anticipation; Passover.
8*a* Ex. 12:14 (14–17).
b TG Leaven.
c TG Sincere.
9*a* TG Scriptures, Lost.
b 2 Thes. 3:6 (6, 11–15).
c GR sexually immoral persons, male prostitutes. TG Fornication.
10*a* TG Covet.
b GR swindlers, robbers.
11*a* Rom. 16:17.
b TG Drunkenness.
c GR not even.
d 2 Jn. 1:10.
12*a* GR outside, foreign, not belonging.
b 1 Cor. 6:1.
6 1*a* Ex. 18:16.
b Matt. 18:17; 1 Cor. 5:12; D&C 64:12 (9–12).
2*a* See JST Matt. 7:1–2 (Matt. 7:1 note *a*). Dan. 7:22; Rev. 20:4. TG Judgment, the Last.
b TG World.
5*a* TG Shame.
7*a* TG Retribution.
b TG Forbear.
c Luke 6:29 (29–30).
8*a* TG Fraud; Injustice; Selfishness.
9*a* 1 Ne. 10:21; Alma 11:37; 40:26; Moses 6:57. TG Worthiness.
b John 3:5; 1 Cor. 15:50.
c GR sexually immoral persons, male prostitutes. TG Fornication.
d TG Adulterer; Sexual Immorality.
e GR catamites.
f GR male homosexuals. TG Homosexual Behavior.
10*a* TG Stealing.
b TG Drunkenness; Word of Wisdom.
c TG Reviling.
d GR robbers.
11*a* TG Baptism; Wash.
b TG Sanctification.
c TG Jesus Christ, Taking the Name of; Name.

of the Lord Jesus, and by the [d]Spirit
of our God.
12 [a]All things are lawful unto me,
but all things are not [b]expedient:
all things are lawful for me, but
I will not be brought under the
power of any.
13 Meats for the belly, and the belly
for meats: but God shall destroy both
it and them. Now the body *is* not for
[a]fornication, but for the Lord; and
the Lord for the body.
14 And God hath both raised up
the Lord, and will also [a]raise up us
by his own power.
15 Know ye not that your bodies
are the [a]members of Christ? shall
I then take the members of Christ,
and make *them* the members of an
harlot? God forbid.
16 What? know ye not that he
which is joined to an harlot is one
body? for two, saith he, shall be
[a]one flesh.
17 But he that is joined unto the
Lord is [a]one spirit.
18 Flee fornication. Every sin that
a man doeth is without the body;
but he that committeth fornication
sinneth against his own body.
19 What? know ye not that your
[a]body is the [b]temple of the Holy
Ghost *which is* in you, which ye
have of God, and ye are not your
[c]own?
20 For ye are [a]bought with a price:
therefore glorify God in your body,
and in your spirit, which are God's.

CHAPTER 7

Paul answers special questions about marriage among those called on missions—Paul praises self-discipline.

NOW concerning the things whereof
ye wrote unto me: [a]*It is* good for a
man not to touch a woman.
2 Nevertheless, [a]*to avoid* [b]fornica-
tion, let every man have his own
[c]wife, and let every woman have
her own husband.
3 Let the [a]husband render unto the
[b]wife due [c]benevolence: and likewise
also the wife unto the husband.
4 The wife hath not power of her
own body, but the husband: and
likewise also the husband hath
not power of his own body, but the
wife.
5 [a]Defraud ye not one the other,
except *it be* with consent for a time,
that ye may give yourselves to fasting and prayer; and come together
again, that [b]Satan [c]tempt you not
for your incontinency.
6 But I speak this by permission,
and not of commandment.
7 For I would that all men were
even as I myself. But every man hath
his [a]proper [b]gift of God, one after
this manner, and another after that.
8 I say therefore to the unmarried
and [a]widows, It is good for them if
they abide even as I.
9 [a]But if they cannot [b]contain, let
them marry: for it is better to marry
than to [c]burn.

11*d* TG God, Spirit of.
12*a* JST 1 Cor. 6:12 All *these* things are *not* lawful unto me, *and* all *these* things are not expedient. All things are *not* lawful for me, *therefore* I will not . . .
b GR beneficial, advantageous.
13*a* GR sexual immorality. TG Chastity; Fornication.
14*a* TG Resurrection.
15*a* Eph. 5:30.
16*a* TG Marriage, Marry.
17*a* 3 Ne. 19:23 (23, 29).
19*a* TG Body, Sanctity of; Chastity.
b TG Temple.
c 1 Cor. 7:23.
20*a* Ex. 15:16; 1 Pet. 1:18 (17–21); 2 Pet. 2:1.
7 1*a* JST 1 Cor. 7:1 . . . *saying,* It is good . . .
2*a* JST 1 Cor. 7:2 . . . *I say,* to avoid . . .
b TG Fornication.
c TG Marriage, Marry; Marriage, Wives.
3*a* TG Marriage, Husbands.
b TG Marriage, Wives.
c TG Benevolence; Family, Love within; Marriage, Continuing Courtship in.
5*a* JST 1 Cor. 7:5 *Depart* ye not one *from* the other . . . TG Family, Love within; Fraud.
b TG Devil.
c TG Test.
7*a* GR own.
b TG God, Gifts of; Holy Ghost, Gifts of.
8*a* TG Widows.
9*a* JST 1 Cor. 7:9 But if they cannot *abide,* let them marry; for it is better to marry than *that any should commit sin.*
b GR use self-control.
c GR burn with lust.

10 And unto the married I command, *yet* not I, but the Lord, Let not the [a]wife [b]depart from *her* husband:
11 But and if she depart, let her remain unmarried, or be [a]reconciled to *her* husband: and let not the husband [b]put away *his* wife.
12 But to the rest speak I, not the Lord: If any brother hath a wife that believeth not, and she be pleased to dwell with him, let him not put her away.
13 And the woman which hath an [a]husband that believeth not, and if he be pleased to dwell with her, let her not leave him.
14 [a]For the unbelieving [b]husband is [c]sanctified by the wife, and the unbelieving wife is [d]sanctified by the husband: else were your children unclean; but now are they holy.
15 But if the unbelieving depart, let him depart. A brother or a sister is not under bondage in such *cases:* but God hath called us [a]to peace.
16 For what knowest thou, O wife, whether thou shalt [a]save *thy* husband? or how knowest thou, O man, whether thou shalt save *thy* wife?
17 But as [a]God hath distributed to every man, as the Lord hath called every one, so let him walk. And so [b]ordain I in all churches.
18 Is any man called being circumcised? let him not [a]become uncircumcised. Is any called in uncircumcision? let him not be circumcised.
19 [a]Circumcision is nothing, and uncircumcision is nothing, but the keeping of the commandments of God.
20 Let every man abide in the same calling wherein he was called.
21 Art thou called *being* a servant? care not for it: but if thou mayest be made free, use *it* rather.
22 For he that is called in the Lord, *being* a servant, is the Lord's [a]freeman: likewise also he that is called, *being* free, is Christ's [b]servant.
23 Ye are [a]bought with a price; be not ye the [b]servants of men.
24 Brethren, let every man, wherein he is called, therein abide with God.
25 Now concerning virgins I have no commandment of the Lord: yet I give my judgment, as one that hath obtained [a]mercy of the Lord to be faithful.
26 I suppose therefore that this is good for the present [a]distress, *I say,* that *it is* good for a man so to be.
27 Art thou bound unto a wife? seek not to be loosed. Art thou loosed from a wife? seek not a wife.
28 But and if thou marry, thou hast not sinned; and if a virgin marry, she hath not sinned. Nevertheless such shall have trouble in the flesh: but I spare you.
29 [a]But this I say, brethren, the time *is* short: it remaineth, that both they that have wives be as though they had none;
30 And they that weep, as though they wept not; and they that rejoice, as though they rejoiced not; and they that buy, as though they possessed not;
31 And they that use this world, as not abusing *it:* for the [a]fashion of this [b]world passeth away.

10*a* Matt. 5:32. TG Chastity; Family, Patriarchal.
b TG Divorce.
11*a* TG Peacemakers; Reconciliation.
b TG Divorce.
13*a* TG Marriage, Husbands.
14*a* D&C 74.
b TG Marriage, Interfaith.
c TG Sanctification.
d GR cleansed.
15*a* GR in.
16*a* TG Family, Love within.
17*a* Rom. 12:3.
b GR order, prescribe.
18*a* GR conceal, obliterate circumcision.
19*a* TG Circumcision.
22*a* Mosiah 5:8; D&C 88:86.
b Eph. 6:6; Col. 3:24.
23*a* 1 Cor. 6:19 (19–20).
b GR slaves.
25*a* 1 Tim. 1:13.
26*a* GR trial, affliction. JST 1 Cor. 7:26 . . . distress, for a man so to *remain that he may do greater good.*
29*a* JST 1 Cor. 7:29–33, 38 (Appendix).
31*a* James 4:14; 1 Jn. 2:17.
b TG Worldliness.

32 But I would have you without
[a]carefulness. He that is unmarried
careth for the things that belong
to the Lord, how he may please
the Lord:
33 But he that is married careth
for the things that are of the world,
how he may please *his* wife.
34 There is difference *also* between
a wife and a virgin. The unmarried
woman careth for the things of the
Lord, that she may be holy both
in body and in spirit: but she that
is married careth for the things of
the world, how she may please *her*
husband.
35 And this I speak for your own
profit; not that I may cast a snare
upon you, but for that which is
comely, and that ye may attend
upon the Lord without distraction.
36 But if any man think that he
behaveth himself uncomely toward
his virgin, if she pass the flower of
her age, and need so require, let him
do what he will, he sinneth not: let
them marry.
37 Nevertheless he that standeth
steadfast in his heart, having no
necessity, but hath power over his
own will, and hath so decreed in his
heart that he will keep his virgin,
doeth well.
38 [a]So then he that giveth *her* in
marriage doeth well; but he that
giveth *her* not in marriage doeth
better.
39 The [a]wife is bound by the [b]law
as long as her husband liveth; but
if her husband be dead, she is at
liberty to be married to whom she
will; only in the Lord.
40 But she is happier if she so abide,
after my judgment: and I think also
that I have the Spirit of God.

CHAPTER 8

There are many gods and many lords—To us there is one God (the Father) and one Lord, who is Christ.

Now [a]as touching things offered
unto [b]idols, we know that we all
have knowledge. Knowledge puffeth
up, but [c]charity [d]edifieth.
2 And if any man think that he
knoweth any thing, he knoweth
nothing yet as he ought to [a]know.
3 But if any man love God, the
same is [a]known of him.
4 As concerning therefore the eating of those things [a]that are offered
in sacrifice unto [b]idols, we know that
an [c]idol *is* nothing in the world, and
that *there is* none other God but one.
5 For though there be that are
called gods, whether in heaven or
in earth, (as there be gods many,
and lords many,)
6 But to us *there is but* one [a]God,
the [b]Father, of whom *are* all things,
and we in him; and one [c]Lord Jesus
Christ, by whom *are* [d]all things, and
we by him.
7 Howbeit *there is* not in every man
that knowledge: for some with conscience of the idol unto this hour
eat *it* as a thing offered unto an idol;
and their [a]conscience being weak
is defiled.
8 But [a]meat commendeth us not to
God: for neither, if we eat, are we
the better; neither, if we eat not, are
we the worse.
9 But take heed lest by any means
this [a]liberty of yours become a

32*a* GR cares.
38*a* JST 1 Cor. 7:38 So then he that giveth *himself* in marriage doeth well; but he that giveth *himself* not in marriage doeth better.
39*a* TG Marriage, Wives.
b TG Marriage, Temporal.
8 1*a* GR concerning.
b Acts 15:29.
c GR love. TG Charity.
d GR builds up, strengthens, establishes, repairs. TG Edification.
2*a* TG Education; Study.
3*a* John 10:14.
4*a* JST 1 Cor. 8:4 . . . *which* are *in the world* offered in sacrifice unto idols, we know that an idol is nothing, and . . .
b Gal. 4:8. TG Idolatry.
c 1 Cor. 10:19 (19–20).
6*a* TG Godhead.
b Dan. 2:47; Eph. 4:6.
c TG Jesus Christ, Lord.
d TG Jesus Christ, Power of.
7*a* TG Conscience.
8*a* TG Food.
9*a* TG Liberty; Motivations.

[b]stumblingblock to them that are [c]weak.

10 For if any man see thee which hast knowledge sit at meat in the idol's temple, shall not the conscience of him which is weak be emboldened to eat those things which are offered to idols;

11 And through thy knowledge shall the weak brother perish, for whom Christ died?

12 But when ye sin so against the [a]brethren, and wound their weak conscience, ye sin against Christ.

13 Wherefore, if meat [a]make my brother to [b]offend, I will [c]eat no flesh while the world standeth, lest I make my brother to offend.

CHAPTER 9

Paul rejoices in his Christian liberty—He preaches the gospel to all without charge—He is all things to all men to gain converts.

AM I not an [a]apostle? am I not free? have I not [b]seen Jesus Christ our Lord? are not ye my [c]work in the Lord?

2 If I be not an apostle unto others, yet doubtless I am to you: for the [a]seal of mine apostleship are ye in the Lord.

3 Mine [a]answer to them that do [b]examine me is this,

4 Have we not power to eat and to drink?

5 Have we not power to lead about a sister, a [a]wife, as well as other apostles, and *as* the [b]brethren of the Lord, and Cephas?

6 Or I only and Barnabas, have not we power to forbear working?

7 Who goeth a [a]warfare any time at his own charges? who planteth a [b]vineyard, and [c]eateth not of the fruit thereof? or who feedeth a flock, and eateth not of the milk of the flock?

8 Say I these things as a man? or saith not the law the same also?

9 For it is written in the law of Moses, Thou shalt not [a]muzzle the mouth of the ox that treadeth out the corn. Doth God take care for oxen?

10 Or saith he *it* altogether for our sakes? For our sakes, no doubt, *this* is [a]written: that he that ploweth should plow in hope; and that he that thresheth in hope should be [b]partaker of his hope.

11 If we have sown unto you [a]spiritual things, *is it* a great thing if we shall reap your carnal things?

12 If others be partakers of *this* power over you, *are* not we rather? Nevertheless we have not used this [a]power; but suffer all things, lest we should hinder the gospel of Christ.

13 Do ye not know that they which [a]minister about holy things [b]live *of the things* of the temple? and they which wait at the altar are partakers with the altar?

14 Even so hath the Lord ordained that they which [a]preach the [b]gospel should [c]live of the gospel.

15 But I have used none of these things: neither have I written these things, that it should be so done unto me: for *it were* better for me to die, than that any man should make my glorying void.

16 For though I preach the [a]gospel, I have nothing to glory of: for

---

9*b* Rom. 14:13; 1 Cor. 10:32 (24–33).
c Rom. 14:1.
12*a* 1 Jn. 3:14 (10–18).
13*a* GR cause my brother to stumble, falter.
b Rom. 14:21 (20–21).
c TG Abstain.
9 1*a* 2 Cor. 12:11 (11–12); Gal. 2:7 (7–8); 1 Tim. 2:7.
b Acts 9:17 (3, 17); 2 Cor. 12:1 (1, 7); Gal. 1:12.
c 1 Cor. 3:6.
2*a* GR certification, proof, token. 2 Cor. 3:2.
3*a* GR defense.
b GR question, call into account, judge.
5*a* Matt. 8:14.
b Matt. 12:46; John 7:3 (3, 5, 10).
7*a* 2 Cor. 10:4.
b Deut. 20:6.
c Prov. 27:18.
9*a* Deut. 25:4.
10*a* Rom. 15:4.
b 2 Tim. 2:6 (5–6).
11*a* Rom. 15:27.
12*a* GR authority.
13*a* Deut. 18:1 (1–2).
b GR eat.
14*a* Rom. 2:21 (21–23); Alma 39:11 (11–12).
b TG Gospel.
c Matt. 10:10.
16*a* TG Gospel.

[b]necessity is laid upon me; yea, woe is
unto me, if I [c]preach not the gospel!
17 For if I do this thing [a]willingly,
I have a [b]reward: but if against my
will, a [c]dispensation *of the gospel* is
committed unto me.
18 What is my reward then? *Verily*
that, when I preach the gospel, I may
make the gospel of Christ without
[a]charge, that I abuse not my power
in the gospel.
19 For though I be free from all
men, yet have I made myself [a]servant unto all, that I might gain the
more.
20 And unto the Jews I became as
a Jew, that I might gain the Jews; to
them that are under the law, as under the law, that I might gain them
that are under the law;
21 To them that are without law,
as without law, (being not without
law to God, but under the law to
Christ,) that I might gain them that
are without law.
22 To the weak became I as [a]weak,
that I might gain the weak: I am
made [b]all things to all *men,* that I
might by all means save some.
23 And this I do for the gospel's
sake, that I might be partaker thereof
with *you.*
24 Know ye not that they which
run in a race run all, but one receiveth the prize? So run, that ye
may obtain.
25 And every man that striveth
for the [a]mastery is [b]temperate in
all things. Now they *do it* to obtain
a corruptible [c]crown; but we an [d]incorruptible.
26 I therefore so run, not as uncertainly; so fight I, not as one that
beateth the air:
27 But I [a]keep under my [b]body,
and bring *it* into subjection: lest
that by any means, when I have
preached to others, I myself should
be a castaway.

CHAPTER 10

Christ is the God of Israel and the spiritual Rock that guided them—Ancient Israel rebelled against Christ—Paul contrasts true and false sacraments.

MOREOVER, brethren, I would not
that ye should be ignorant, how that
all our fathers were under the [a]cloud,
and all passed through the [b]sea;
2 And were all [a]baptized unto Moses in the cloud and in the sea;
3 And did all eat the same spiritual [a]meat;
4 And did all drink the same spiritual drink: for they drank of that
spiritual Rock that followed them:
and that [a]Rock was Christ.
5 But with many of them [a]God
was not well [b]pleased: for they were
[c]overthrown in the [d]wilderness.
6 Now these things were our [a]examples, to the intent we should not
[b]lust after evil things, as they also
lusted.
7 Neither be ye idolaters, as *were*
some of them; as it is written, The
[a]people sat down to eat and drink,
and rose up to play.
8 Neither let us commit [a]fornication, as some of them committed,

16*b* TG Duty.
c TG Missionary Work; Preaching.
17*a* TG Initiative.
b TG Reward.
c Gal. 2:7. TG Dispensations.
18*a* Acts 20:34 (33–34); 2 Cor. 11:7; 1 Thes. 2:9; Mosiah 2:14 (12, 14–18).
19*a* 2 Cor. 4:5. TG Servant.
22*a* 2 Cor. 11:29.
b 1 Cor. 10:33 (32–33).
25*a* 2 Tim. 2:5. TG Self-Mastery.
b TG Temperance.
c TG Reward.
d 1 Pet. 1:4 (1–16).
27*a* GR rigorously discipline.
b TG Chastity.
10 1*a* Ps. 99:7; D&C 103:20 (19–20).
b TG Israel, Deliverance of.
2*a* TG Baptism; Baptism, Essential.
3*a* Ex. 16:15.
4*a* 3 Ne. 15:5. TG Cornerstone; Jesus Christ, Jehovah; Jesus Christ, Types of, in Anticipation; Rock.
5*a* Num. 21:5; Ezek. 20:13 (10–26).
b D&C 68:31.
c GR strewn, buried. Heb. 3:17.
d Num. 26:65 (64–65); Jude 1:5.
6*a* GR types.
b GR desire, long for. TG Lust.
7*a* Ex. 32:6.
8*a* TG Fornication.

and fell in one day three and twenty thousand.

9 Neither let us [a]tempt Christ, as some of them also tempted, and were destroyed of serpents.

10 Neither [a]murmur ye, as some of them also murmured, and were [b]destroyed of the destroyer.

11 Now all these things happened unto them for [a]ensamples: [b]and they are [c]written for our [d]admonition, upon whom the ends of the world are come.

12 Wherefore let him that thinketh he [a]standeth take heed lest he [b]fall.

13 There hath no temptation [a]taken you but such as is common to man: but God *is* faithful, who will not suffer you to be [b]tempted above that ye are able; but will with the [c]temptation also make a way to [d]escape, that ye may be able to [e]bear *it*.

14 Wherefore, my dearly beloved, flee from [a]idolatry.

15 I speak as to wise men; judge ye what I say.

16 The [a]cup of [b]blessing which we bless, is it not the [c]communion of the blood of Christ? The bread which we break, is it not the communion of the body of Christ?

17 For we *being* many are one bread, *and* one body: for we are all partakers of that one bread.

18 Behold Israel after the flesh: are not they which eat of the sacrifices [a]partakers of the altar?

19 What say I then? that the idol is any thing, or that which is offered in sacrifice to [a]idols is any thing?

20 But I *say,* that the things which the Gentiles sacrifice, they [a]sacrifice to devils, and not to God: and I would not that ye should have fellowship with devils.

21 Ye cannot drink the [a]cup of the Lord, and the cup of devils: ye cannot be partakers of the Lord's table, and of the table of devils.

22 Do we provoke the Lord to [a]jealousy? are we stronger than he?

23 [a]All things are lawful for me, but all things are not [b]expedient: all things are lawful for me, but all things [c]edify not.

24 Let no man seek his [a]own, but every man another's [b]*wealth.*

25 Whatsoever is sold in the [a]shambles, *that* eat, asking no question for conscience sake:

26 For the [a]earth *is* the Lord's, and the fulness thereof.

27 If any of them that believe not bid you *to a* [a]*feast,* and ye be disposed to go; whatsoever is set before you, eat, asking no question for conscience sake.

28 But if any man say unto you, This is offered in sacrifice unto idols, eat not for his sake that shewed it, and for conscience sake: for the earth *is* the Lord's, and the fulness thereof:

29 Conscience, I say, not thine own, but of the other: for why is my

---

9*a* TG Test.
10*a* TG Murmuring.
b Num. 14:37.
11*a* GR types. TG Example.
b JST 1 Cor. 10:11 . . . and they *were* written for our admonition *also, and for an admonition for those* upon whom the *end* of the world *shall* come.
c Rom. 15:4.
d TG Warn.
12*a* Philip. 4:1 (1–7).
b Acts 1:25; D&C 3:9; 58:15.
13*a* GR seized upon.
b Job 4:7 (1, 2, 7); 37:23; Ps. 34:17 (17, 19); 1 Ne. 22:19; Alma 14:11. TG Test.
c TG Temptation.
d D&C 95:1.
e TG Strength.
14*a* TG Idolatry.
16*a* Matt. 26:27 (26–29).
b TG Blessing.
c GR aid, fellowship, partnership.
18*a* GR sharers, partners.
19*a* 1 Cor. 8:4.
20*a* Deut. 32:17. TG Sacrifice; Superstitions.
21*a* 2 Cor. 6:16 (14–17).
22*a* TG Jealous.
23*a* JST 1 Cor. 10:23 All things are *not* lawful for me, *for* all things are not expedient; all things are *not* lawful, *for* all things edify not.
b GR advantageous, appropriate, beneficial.
c TG Edification.
24*a* Philip. 2:21 (17–30).
b JST 1 Cor. 10:24 . . . *good.*
25*a* GR market.
26*a* Ps. 24:1. TG God, Works of.
27*a* Ex. 34:15.

liberty judged of another *man's*
[a]conscience?
30 For if I [a]by grace be a partaker,
why am I evil spoken of for that for
which I give thanks?
31 Whether therefore ye eat, or
drink, or whatsoever ye do, [a]do all
to the glory of God.
32 Give none [a]offence, neither to
the Jews, nor to the Gentiles, nor
to the church of God:
33 Even as I please all *men* in all
things, not [a]seeking mine own profit,
but the [b]*profit* of many, that they
may be [c]saved.

CHAPTER 11

Paul speaks of certain customs of hair and grooming—Heresies will arise that test and prove the faithful—The sacramental emblems are partaken in remembrance of the flesh and blood of Christ—Beware of partaking unworthily.

BE ye [a]followers of me, even as I
also *am* of Christ.
2 Now I praise you, brethren, [a]that
ye remember me in all things, and
keep the [b]ordinances, as I delivered
them to you.
3 But I would have you know, that
the head of every man is Christ;
and the [a]head of the [b]woman *is*
the man; and the [c]head of Christ *is*
God.
4 Every man praying or prophesying, having *his* head covered, dishonoureth his head.
5 But every woman that prayeth
or prophesieth with *her* head uncovered dishonoureth her head: for
that is [a]even all one as if she were
shaven.
6 For if the woman be not covered,
let her also be shorn: but if it be a
[a]shame for a woman to be shorn or
shaven, let her be covered.
7 For a man indeed ought not to
cover *his* head, forasmuch as he is
the image and glory of God: but
the woman is the glory of the man.
8 For the man is not of the woman;
but the woman of the man.
9 Neither was the man created
for the woman; but the woman for
the man.
10 For this cause ought the woman
to have power on *her* head because
of the angels.
11 Nevertheless neither is the
[a]man without the woman, neither
the [b]woman without the man, in
the Lord.
12 For as the woman *is* of the
man, even so *is* the man also by the
woman; but all things of God.
13 Judge in yourselves: is it [a]comely
that a woman pray unto God uncovered?
14 Doth not even nature itself teach
you, that, if a man have long [a]hair,
it is a shame unto him?
15 But if a woman have long hair,
it is a glory to her: for *her* hair is
given her for a covering.
16 But if any man seem to be [a]con-
tentious, we have no such custom,
neither the churches of God.
17 Now in this that I declare *unto
you* I praise *you* not, that ye come
together not for the better, but for
the worse.
18 For first of all, when ye come

29*a* TG Conscience.
30*a* GR with gratitude, graciousness.
31*a* Col. 3:17 (17–23).
32*a* Rom. 14:13 (11–21); 1 Cor. 8:9 (7–13). TG Offense.
33*a* 2 Cor. 12:14.
b GR benefit, advantage.
c 1 Cor. 9:22 (19–23).
11 1*a* GR imitators. 1 Cor. 4:16; Eph. 5:1 (1–5).
2*a* GR because.
b GR precepts, doctrines, traditions. TG Ordinance.
3*a* TG Marriage, Husbands.
b TG Marriage, Wives; Woman.
c TG Jesus Christ, Relationships with the Father.
5*a* GR one and the same as.
6*a* TG Shame.
11*a* TG Family, Eternal; Marriage, Celestial; Marriage, Continuing Courtship in; Marriage, Husbands.
b TG Marriage, Wives.
13*a* GR proper, fitting, becoming.
14*a* Ezek. 44:20.
16*a* 1 Cor. 14:33 (33, 40); 3 Ne. 11:22. TG Contention.

together in the [a]church, I hear that
there be [b]divisions among you; and
I partly believe it.
19 For there must be also [a]here-
sies among you, that they which are
approved may be made manifest
among you.
20 When ye come together therefore into one place, [a]*this* is not to
eat the Lord's supper.
21 For in eating every one taketh
before *other* his own supper: and one
is hungry, and another is drunken.
22 What? have ye not houses to eat
and to drink in? or despise ye the
[a]church of God, and [b]shame them
that have not? What shall I say to
you? shall I praise you in this? I
praise *you* not.
23 For I have received of the Lord
that which also I delivered unto you,
That the Lord Jesus the *same* night in
which he was betrayed took [a]bread:
24 And when he had given thanks,
he brake *it*, and said, Take, eat: this
is my body, which is broken for you:
this do in [a]remembrance of me.
25 After the same manner also *he
took* the cup, when he had supped,
saying, This cup is the new testament in my blood: this do ye, as
oft as ye drink *it*, in remembrance
of me.
26 For as often as ye eat this [a]bread,
and drink this cup, ye do [b]shew the
Lord's [c]death till he come.
27 Wherefore whosoever shall eat
this [a]bread, and drink *this* cup of the
Lord, [b]unworthily, shall [c]be [d]guilty
of the body and blood of the Lord.
28 But let a man [a]examine himself,
and so let him eat of *that* bread, and
drink of *that* cup.
29 For he that eateth and drinketh
[a]unworthily, eateth and drinketh
[b]damnation to himself, not discern-
ing the Lord's body.
30 For this cause many *are* weak
and [a]sickly among you, and many
sleep.
31 For if we would [a]judge ourselves,
we should not be judged.
32 But when we are judged, we
are [a]chastened of the Lord, that
we should not be condemned with
the world.
33 Wherefore, my brethren, when
ye come together to eat, tarry one
for another.
34 And if any man hunger, let him
eat at home; that ye come not together unto condemnation. And the
rest will I set in order when I come.

CHAPTER 12

The Holy Ghost reveals that Jesus is the Christ—Spiritual gifts are present among the Saints—Apostles, prophets, and miracles are found in the true Church.

NOW concerning spiritual *gifts*, brethren, I would not have you ignorant.
2 Ye know that ye were Gentiles,
[a]carried away unto these dumb
[b]idols, even as ye were led.
3 Wherefore I give you to understand, that no man speaking by the
Spirit of God calleth Jesus accursed:
and *that* no man can [a]say that Jesus
is the [b]Lord, but by the [c]Holy Ghost.
4 Now there are diversities of [a]gifts,
but the same Spirit.

18*a* TG Assembly for Worship; Meetings.
b GR dissensions, schisms. TG Apostasy of the Early Christian Church; Church.
19*a* GR sects, factions.
20*a* JST 1 Cor. 11:20 . . . *is it* not to eat the Lord's supper?
22*a* TG Church.
b TG Shame.
23*a* 3 Ne. 20:8 (3–9).
24*a* TG Jesus Christ, Types of, in Memory.
26*a* TG Sacrament.
b GR proclaim, announce.
c TG Jesus Christ, Death of.
27*a* TG Bread of Life.
b 3 Ne. 18:29 (28–32); Morm. 9:29.
c GR offend against.
d TG Guilt.
28*a* 2 Cor. 13:5 (5–7).
29*a* TG Sacrament.
b GR condemnation, judgment. TG Damnation.
30*a* TG Sickness.
31*a* GR scrutinize, examine.
32*a* TG Chastening.
12 2*a* GR led astray.
b TG Idolatry.
3*a* TG Revelation; Testimony.
b TG Jesus Christ, Lord.
c John 6:44 (44, 63–65). TG Holy Ghost, Mission of; Holy Ghost, Source of Testimony; Inspiration.
4*a* TG God, Gifts of; Holy Ghost, Gifts of; Holy Ghost, Mission of.

5 And there are differences of administrations, but the same Lord.
6 And there are diversities of opera-
tions, but it is the same God which
worketh all in all.
7 But the manifestation of the
[a]Spirit is given to every man to
profit withal.
8 For to one is [a]given by the [b]Spirit
the [c]word of [d]wisdom; to another
the word of [e]knowledge by the
same Spirit;
9 To another [a]faith by the same
Spirit; to another the gifts of [b]heal-
ing by the same Spirit;
10 To another the working of [a]mira-
cles; to another [b]prophecy; to another
[c]discerning of spirits; to another
divers kinds of tongues; to another
the interpretation of [d]tongues:
11 But all these worketh that one
and the selfsame Spirit, dividing
to every man severally as he will.
12 For as the body is one, and hath
many members, and all the members of that one body, being many,
are one body: so also *is* Christ.
13 For by one Spirit are we all
baptized into one [a]body, whether
we be Jews or [b]Gentiles, whether *we*
be [c]bond or free; and have been all
made to drink into one Spirit.
14 For the body is not one member, but many.
15 If the foot shall say, Because
I am not the hand, I am not of
the body; is it therefore not of the
body?
16 And if the ear shall say, Because I am not the eye, I am not of
the body; is it therefore not of the
body?
17 If the whole body *were* an eye,
where *were* the hearing? If the
whole *were* hearing, where *were* the
smelling?
18 But now hath God set the members every one of them in the body,
as it hath pleased him.
19 And if they were all one member, where *were* the body?
20 But now *are they* many members,
yet but one body.
21 And the eye cannot say unto the
hand, I have no need of thee: nor
again the [a]head to the feet, I have
no need of you.
22 Nay, much more those members of the body, which seem to be
[a]more feeble, are necessary:
23 And those *members* of the body,
which we think to be less honourable, upon these we bestow more
abundant honour; and our uncomely *parts* have more abundant
comeliness.
24 For our comely *parts* have no
need: but God hath tempered the
body together, having given more
abundant honour to that *part* which
lacked:
25 That there should be no schism
in the body; but *that* the members
should have the same [a]care one for
another.
26 And whether one member [a]suf-
fer, all the members [b]suffer with it;
or one member be honoured, all the
members rejoice with it.
27 Now ye are the body of [a]Christ,
and [b]members in particular.
28 And God hath set some in the
church, first [a]apostles, secondarily
[b]prophets, thirdly [c]teachers, after
that miracles, then gifts of healings,
helps, [d]governments, diversities of
tongues.
29 *Are* all apostles? *are* all prophets?

7*a* D&C 46:16 (8–18).
TG God, Spirit of.
8*a* D&C 35:23.
b D&C 25:7; 35:19.
c D&C 89:2.
d TG Wisdom.
e Moro. 10:10.
TG Holy Ghost, Gifts of; Knowledge.
9*a* TG Faith.
b TG Heal.
10*a* TG Miracle.
b TG Prophecy.
c TG Discernment, Spiritual.
d TG Language.
13*a* TG Church.
b GR Greeks.
Col. 3:11.
c GR slaves.
D&C 24:11; 43:20.
21*a* D&C 84:109.
TG Leadership.
22*a* GR weaker.
25*a* 1 Cor. 1:10 (10–15).
26*a* TG Suffering.
b TG Compassion.
27*a* TG Jesus Christ, Head of the Church.
b TG Church Organization.
28*a* TG Apostles.
b TG Prophets, Mission of.
c TG Teacher.
d TG Governments.

are all teachers? *are* all workers of
[a]miracles?
30 Have all the gifts of healing?
do all speak with tongues? do all
interpret?
31 But [a]covet earnestly the best
[b]gifts: and yet shew I unto you a
more [c]excellent way.

CHAPTER 13

Paul discusses the high status of charity—Charity, a pure love, excels and exceeds almost all else.

THOUGH I speak with the tongues
of men and of angels, and have not
[a]charity, I am become *as* sounding
brass, or a tinkling cymbal.
2 And though I have *the gift of*
[a]prophecy, and understand all
[b]mysteries, and all knowledge; and
though I have all faith, so that I
could remove mountains, and have
not charity, I am nothing.
3 And though I bestow all my goods
to feed *the* [a]*poor*, and though I give
my body to be burned, and have
not charity, it profiteth me nothing.
4 [a]Charity [b]suffereth long, *and* is
[c]kind; charity [d]envieth not; charity
vaunteth not itself, is not puffed up,
5 Doth not behave itself [a]unseemly,
[b]seeketh not her own, is not easily
[c]provoked, thinketh no evil;
6 Rejoiceth not in [a]iniquity, but
rejoiceth in the [b]truth;
7 Beareth all things, believeth all
things, hopeth all things, endureth
all things.
8 Charity never [a]faileth: but
whether *there be* prophecies, they
shall fail; whether *there be* tongues,
they shall cease; whether *there be*
knowledge, it shall vanish away.
9 For we know in part, and we
prophesy in part.
10 But when that which is perfect
is come, then that which is in part
shall be done away.
11 When I was a child, I spake as
a child, I understood as a child, I
thought as a child: but when I became a man, I put away childish
things.
12 For now we see through a [a]glass,
[b]darkly; but then face to face: now I
know in part; but then shall I know
even as also I am known.
13 And now abideth [a]faith, [b]hope,
[c]charity, these three; but the greatest of these *is* charity.

CHAPTER 14

People should desire spiritual gifts—Tongues and prophecy are compared—Prophecy is the greater gift—Paul says, You may all prophesy; covet to prophesy.

[a]FOLLOW after charity, and desire
spiritual [b]*gifts*, but rather that ye
may prophesy.
2 For he that speaketh in [a]an *unknown* tongue speaketh not unto
men, but unto God: for no man
understandeth *him;* howbeit in the
spirit he speaketh mysteries.
3 But he that [a]prophesieth speaketh unto men *to* [b]edification, and
exhortation, and comfort.
4 He that speaketh in an *unknown*
tongue edifieth himself; but he that
prophesieth edifieth the church.

29*a* TG Miracle.
31*a* GR seek earnestly, be zealous for. D&C 46:8 (8–9). TG Covet.
b TG Holy Ghost, Gifts of.
c Ether 12:11 (11–12, 32).
13 1*a* GR love.
2*a* TG Prophecy.
b TG Mysteries of Godliness.
3*a* TG Welfare.
4*a* TG Charity; Courtesy.
b TG Forbear; Suffering.
c TG Benevolence.
d TG Envy.
5*a* GR indecently, unbecomingly.
b TG Selfishness.
c TG Anger; Provoking; Self-Mastery.
6*a* GR injustice, unrighteousness.
b TG Truth.
8*a* TG Dependability.
12*a* 2 Cor. 3:18; James 1:23 (22–27). TG Veil.
b GR obscurely, enigmatically.
13*a* TG Faith.
b TG Hope.
c TG Love.
14 1*a* GR Pursue, follow eagerly, earnestly.
b TG Holy Ghost, Gifts of.
2*a* JST 1 Cor. 14:2 . . . *another* tongue . . . (Note: JST uses "another" in place of "an unknown" in every instance in vv. 4, 13, 14, 19, 27.)
3*a* TG Prophecy.
b TG Edification.

5 I [a]would that ye all spake with tongues, but rather that ye [b]prophesied: for greater *is* he that prophesieth than he that speaketh with tongues, except he interpret, that the church may receive edifying.

6 Now, brethren, if I come unto you speaking with tongues, what shall I profit you, [a]except I shall speak to you either by [b]revelation, or by knowledge, or by prophesying, or by doctrine?

7 And even things without life giving sound, whether pipe or harp, except they give a distinction in the sounds, how shall it be known what is piped or harped?

8 For if the trumpet give an uncertain sound, who shall prepare himself to the battle?

9 So likewise ye, except ye utter by the tongue words easy to be understood, how shall it be known what is spoken? for ye shall speak into the air.

10 There are, it may be, so many kinds of [a]voices in the world, and none of them *is* without signification.

11 Therefore if I know not the meaning of the voice, I shall be unto him that speaketh a barbarian, and he that speaketh *shall be* a barbarian unto me.

12 Even so ye, [a]forasmuch as ye are zealous of spiritual [b]*gifts*, seek that ye may excel to the [c]edifying of the church.

13 Wherefore let him that speaketh in an *unknown* tongue pray that he may interpret.

14 For if I pray in an *unknown* tongue, my spirit prayeth, but my [a]understanding is unfruitful.

15 What is it then? I will pray with the spirit, and I will pray with the understanding also: I will sing with the spirit, and I will sing with the understanding also.

16 Else when thou shalt bless with the spirit, how shall he that occupieth the room of the unlearned say Amen at thy giving of thanks, seeing he understandeth not what thou sayest?

17 For thou verily givest thanks well, but the other is not edified.

18 I thank my God, I speak with tongues more than ye all:

19 Yet in the church I had rather [a]speak five words with my understanding, that *by my voice* I might teach others also, than ten thousand words in an *unknown* tongue.

20 Brethren, be not [a]children in [b]understanding: howbeit in [c]malice be ye children, but in [d]understanding be men.

21 In the law it is written, With *men of* other tongues and other lips will I speak unto this people; and yet for all that will they not [a]hear me, saith the Lord.

22 Wherefore [a]tongues are for a [b]sign, not to them that believe, but to them that believe not: but [c]prophesying *serveth* not for them that believe not, but for them which believe.

23 If therefore the whole church be come together into one place, and all speak with tongues, and there come in *those that are* unlearned, or [a]unbelievers, will they not say that ye are mad?

24 But if all prophesy, and there come in one that believeth not, or *one* unlearned, he is convinced of all, he is judged of all:

25 And thus are the [a]secrets of his heart made manifest; and so falling down on *his* face he will worship God, and report that God is in you of a truth.

26 How is it then, brethren? when ye come together, every one of you hath a psalm, hath a doctrine, hath a tongue, hath a revelation, hath an

5*a* GR wish.
b TG Prophecy.
6*a* GR unless.
b TG Revelation.
10*a* TG Revelation.
12*a* GR since.
b D&C 46:10.
c TG Edification.
14*a* GR mind.
19*a* TG Language.
20*a* Matt. 18:3 (1–6); Eph. 4:14.
b TG Understanding.
c GR wickedness, depravity. TG Malice.
d TG Education.
21*a* GR listen to, heed.
22*a* Acts 2:11.
b TG Signs.
c TG Prophecy.
23*a* Acts 2:13 (12–13).
25*a* Heb. 4:12 (12–13).

interpretation. Let all things be
done unto [a]edifying.
27 If any man speak in an *unknown*
tongue, *let it be* by two, or at the most
by three, and *that* by course; and let
one interpret.
28 But if there be no interpreter,
let him keep [a]silence in the church;
and let him speak to himself, and
to God.
29 Let the prophets speak two or
three, and let the other judge.
30 If *any thing* be revealed to another that sitteth by, let the first
hold his peace.
31 For ye may all prophesy one
by one, that all may learn, and all
may be comforted.
32 And the spirits of the prophets
are subject to the prophets.
33 For God is not *the* [a]*author* of
[b]confusion, but of [c]peace, as in all
[d]churches of the [e]saints.
34 Let your [a]women keep silence
in the churches: for it is not permitted unto them to [b]speak; but *they are*
commanded [c]to be under [d]obedience,
as also saith the law.
35 And if they will learn any thing,
let them ask their husbands at home:
for it is a shame for women to [a]speak
in the church.
36 What? came the word of God
out from you? or came it unto
you only?
37 If any man think himself to
be a prophet, or spiritual, let him
acknowledge that the things that I
write unto you are the commandments of the Lord.
38 But if any man be ignorant, let
him be ignorant.
39 Wherefore, brethren, [a]covet to
prophesy, and forbid not to speak
with tongues.
40 Let all things be done decently
and in [a]order.

CHAPTER 15

Christ died for our sins—He rose from the dead and was seen by many—All men will be resurrected—Paul speaks of baptism for the dead—The three degrees of glory are described—Victory over death comes through Christ.

MOREOVER, brethren, I [a]declare unto
you the [b]gospel which I preached
unto you, which also ye have received, and wherein ye stand;
2 By which also ye are [a]saved, if ye
[b]keep in memory what I preached
unto you, unless ye have believed
in vain.
3 For I delivered unto you first of
all that which I also received, how
that Christ [a]died for our [b]sins according to the scriptures;
4 And that he was buried, and that
he [a]rose again the third day according to the scriptures:
5 And that he was [a]seen of [b]Cephas,
then of the twelve:
6 After that, he was [a]seen of [b]above
five hundred brethren at once; of
whom the greater part remain unto
this present, but some are fallen
asleep.
7 After that, he was seen of James;
then of all the apostles.
8 And last of all he was [a]seen of me
also, as of one born out of due time.
9 For I am the least of the apostles,
that am not [a]meet to be called an

26*a* 2 Cor. 12:19; D&C 50:23.
28*a* TG Silence.
33*a* 1 Cor. 11:16 (16–19).
b Eph. 4:5 (3–6), 13; D&C 1:30.
c TG Peace; Peace of God.
d TG Church.
e TG Saints.
34*a* TG Woman.
b JST 1 Cor. 14:34 . . . *rule* . . .
c GR to be submissive.
d TG Obedience.
35*a* JST 1 Cor. 14:35 . . . *rule* . . .
39*a* IE be eager, zealous. TG Covet.
40*a* TG Order.
15 1*a* TG Missionary Work.
b TG Gospel.
2*a* Rom. 1:16.
b GR hold fast to, retain.
3*a* D&C 54:1. TG Jesus Christ, Death of; Jesus Christ, Redeemer.
b Acts 3:18; Alma 5:27.
4*a* TG Jesus Christ, Resurrection.
5*a* TG Jesus Christ, Appearances, Postmortal.
b Luke 24:34 (33–36).
6*a* TG Jesus Christ, Appearances, Postmortal.
b GR more than, over.
8*a* TG Jesus Christ, Appearances, Postmortal.
9*a* GR adequate, sufficient, competent.

apostle, because I [b]persecuted the
church of God.
10 But by the [a]grace of God I am
what I am: and his grace which *was*
bestowed upon me was not in vain;
but I [b]laboured more abundantly
than they all: yet not I, but the grace
of God which was with me.
11 Therefore whether *it were* I or
they, so we preach, and so ye believed.
12 Now if Christ be preached that
he rose from the dead, how say some
among you that there is no resurrection of the dead?
13 But if there be no resurrection of the dead, then is Christ not
risen:
14 And if Christ be not risen, then
is our preaching vain, and your faith
is also vain.
15 Yea, and we are found false
witnesses of God; because we have
[a]testified of God that he raised up
Christ: whom he raised not up, if
so be that the dead rise not.
16 For if the dead rise not, then is
not Christ raised:
17 And if Christ be not raised, your
faith *is* [a]vain; ye are yet in your sins.
18 Then they also which are fallen
asleep in Christ are [a]perished.
19 If in this [a]life only we have
[b]hope in Christ, we are of all men
most miserable.
20 But now is [a]Christ [b]risen from
the dead, *and* become the [c]firstfruits
of them that slept.
21 For since by man *came* [a]death,
by man *came* also the [b]resurrection
of the dead.
22 For as in [a]Adam all [b]die, even so
in [c]Christ shall all be made [d]alive.
23 But every man in his own [a]or-
der: Christ the [b]firstfruits; afterward they that are Christ's at his
[c]coming.
24 Then *cometh* the end, when he
shall have delivered up the kingdom
to God, even the Father; when he
shall have [a]put down all [b]rule and
all [c]authority and [d]power.
25 For he must [a]reign, till he hath
put all [b]enemies under his [c]feet.
26 The last [a]enemy *that* shall be
[b]destroyed *is* [c]death.
27 For he hath put all things under his feet. But when he saith all
things are put under *him, it is* [a]mani-
fest that he is excepted, which did
put all things under him.
28 And when all things shall be
[a]subdued unto him, then shall the
Son also himself be [b]subject unto
him that put all things under him,
that God may be all in all.
29 Else what shall they do which
are [a]baptized [b]for the dead, if the
dead [c]rise not at all? why are they
then baptized for the [d]dead?
30 And why stand we in [a]jeopardy
every hour?

9*b* Acts 8:3.
10*a* TG Grace.
b 2 Cor. 11:23.
15*a* Acts 4:33.
17*a* GR useless, empty, ineffective.
18*a* GR lost, destroyed.
19*a* TG Salvation for the Dead.
b TG Hope.
20*a* 1 Pet. 1:3.
b Eph. 1:20.
c GR firstling.
21*a* Rom. 5:12. TG Death.
b TG Resurrection.
22*a* TG Adam; Fall of Man.
b Ps. 82:7.
c TG Salvation, Plan of.
d TG Immortality; Jesus Christ, Atonement through; Jesus Christ, Mission of; Jesus Christ, Resurrection; Salvation.
23*a* GR rank. TG Order.
b GR firstling. TG Resurrection.
c TG Jesus Christ, Second Coming.
24*a* GR brought to an end, abolished.
b Isa. 60:12; Dan. 2:44; 7:9.
c TG Authority.
d TG Jesus Christ, Power of.
25*a* TG Jesus Christ, Millennial Reign.
b D&C 88:106.
c Heb. 2:8.
26*a* TG Enemies.
b TG Death, Power over.
c 2 Tim. 1:10; Rev. 20:14 (11–15).
27*a* GR clear, plain, evident.
28*a* Philip. 3:21; D&C 76:106.
b TG Jesus Christ, Relationships with the Father.
29*a* TG Baptism, Essential; Baptism for the Dead; Genealogy and Temple Work.
b GR in behalf of, for the sake of.
c TG Immortality.
d TG Salvation for the Dead.
30*a* GR danger, peril.

31 [a]I protest by your rejoicing
which I have in Christ Jesus our
Lord, I die daily.
32 If after the manner of men I
have fought with beasts at Ephesus,
what advantageth it me, if the dead
rise not? let us [a]eat and drink; for
[b]to morrow we die.
33 Be not deceived: evil [a]commu-
nications corrupt good manners.
34 Awake to righteousness, and sin
not; for some have not the knowledge
of God: I speak *this* to your [a]shame.
35 But some *man* will say, How are
the dead raised up? and with what
body do they come?
36 *Thou* fool, that which thou sowest is not quickened, except it [a]die:
37 And that which thou sowest,
thou sowest not that body that shall
be, but bare grain, [a]it may chance
of wheat, or of some other *grain:*
38 But God giveth it a body as it
hath pleased him, and to every seed
his own body.
39 All flesh *is* not the same flesh:
but *there is* one *kind of* flesh of men,
another flesh of beasts, another of
fishes, *and* another of birds.
40 [a]*There are* also celestial bodies,
and bodies terrestrial: but the glory
of the [b]celestial *is* one, and the
glory of the [c]terrestrial *is* another.
41 *There is* one glory of the [a]sun,
and another glory of the moon, and
another glory of the [b]stars: for *one*
star [c]differeth from *another* star in
[d]glory.
42 So also *is* the resurrection of the
dead. It is sown in [a]corruption; it is
raised in incorruption:
43 It is sown in dishonour; it is
raised in [a]glory: it is sown in weakness; it is raised in power:
44 It is sown a [a]natural body; it is
raised a [b]spiritual body. There is a
natural body, and there is a spiritual body.
45 And so it is written, The [a]first
man [b]Adam was made a living soul;
the last [c]Adam *was made* a [d]quick-
ening spirit.
46 Howbeit that *was* not [a]first
which is spiritual, but that which is
natural; and afterward that which
is spiritual.
47 The first man *is* of the earth,
earthy: the second man *is* the Lord
from heaven.
48 As *is* the earthy, such *are* they
also that are earthy: and as *is* the
heavenly, such *are* they also that
are heavenly.
49 And as we have borne the image of the earthy, we shall also bear
the image of the heavenly.
50 Now this I say, brethren, that
[a]flesh and [b]blood cannot [c]inherit
the kingdom of God; neither doth
[d]corruption inherit incorruption.
51 Behold, I shew you a mystery;
We shall not all [a]sleep, but we shall
all be [b]changed,
52 In a moment, in the [a]twinkling
of an eye, at the last trump: for the
[b]trumpet shall sound, and the [c]dead
shall be raised incorruptible, and
we shall be [d]changed.

31*a* JST 1 Cor. 15:31 I protest *unto you the resurrection of the dead; and this is my* rejoicing which I have in Christ Jesus our Lord *daily, though I die.*
32*a* Isa. 22:13; Luke 12:19; 2 Ne. 28:7.
b TG Procrastination.
33*a* GR conversations, associations.
34*a* TG Shame.
36*a* John 12:24 (24–29).
37*a* IE whether it be.
40*a* JST 1 Cor. 15:40 Also celestial bodies, and bodies terrestrial, *and bodies telestial;* but the glory of the celestial, one; and the terrestrial, another; *and the telestial, another.*
b TG Celestial Glory.
c TG Terrestrial Glory.
41*a* TG Astronomy.
b TG Telestial Glory.
c D&C 76:98.
d TG Glory.
42*a* Rom. 8:21; Mosiah 16:10.
43*a* Col. 3:4.
44*a* D&C 29:43.
b Alma 11:45; D&C 88:27.
45*a* D&C 84:16.
b TG Adam.
c Rom. 5:14.
d John 5:21.
46*a* D&C 29:32; 128:14 (13–14).
50*a* TG Flesh and Blood.
b Lev. 17:14 (11, 14).
c John 3:5; 1 Cor. 6:9.
d Alma 41:4.
51*a* GR die, sleep in death. 1 Thes. 4:17.
b Philip. 3:21; D&C 43:32.
52*a* D&C 63:51 (50–51).
b D&C 29:26.
c TG Death.
d D&C 101:31.

53 For this [a]corruptible must put
on incorruption, and this [b]mortal
must put on immortality.
54 So when this corruptible shall
have put on incorruption, and this
mortal shall have put on [a]immor-
tality, then shall be brought to pass
the saying that is written, [b]Death is
swallowed up in victory.
55 O [a]death, where *is* thy sting? O
[b]grave, where *is* thy victory?
56 The sting of [a]death *is* sin; and
the [b]strength of sin *is* the law.
57 But [a]thanks *be* to God, which
giveth us the [b]victory through our
Lord Jesus Christ.
58 Therefore, my beloved brethren,
be ye [a]steadfast, unmoveable, always
abounding in the work of the Lord,
forasmuch as ye know that your
labour is not in vain in the Lord.

CHAPTER 16

Paul counsels, Stand fast in the faith; let all things be done with charity.

Now concerning the [a]collection for
the saints, as I have [b]given order
to the churches of Galatia, even so
do ye.
2 Upon the [a]first *day* of the week let
every one of you lay by him in store,
as *God* hath [b]prospered him, that
there be no gatherings when I come.
3 And when I come, whomsoever ye
shall approve by *your* letters, them
will I send to bring your [a]liberality
unto Jerusalem.
4 And if it be [a]meet that I go also,
they shall go with me.
5 Now I will come unto you, when
I shall pass through Macedonia: for
I do pass through Macedonia.
6 And it may be that I will abide,
yea, and winter with you, that ye
may bring me on my journey whithersoever I go.
7 For I will not see you now [a]by the
way; but I [b]trust to [c]tarry a while
with you, if the Lord permit.
8 But I will tarry at Ephesus until
Pentecost.
9 For a great [a]door and [b]effectual
is opened unto me, and *there are*
many adversaries.
10 Now if [a]Timotheus come, see
that he may be with you without
fear: for he worketh the work of the
Lord, as I also *do*.
11 Let no man therefore [a]despise
him: but conduct him forth in peace,
that he may come unto me: for I look
for him with the brethren.
12 As touching *our* brother [a]Apol-
los, I greatly desired him to come
unto you with the brethren: but his
will was not at all to come at this
time; but he will come when he
shall have convenient time.
13 [a]Watch ye, [b]stand fast in the
[c]faith, [d]quit you like [e]men, be strong.
14 Let all your things be done with
[a]charity.
15 I beseech you, brethren, (ye
know the house of [a]Stephanas, that it
is the firstfruits of Achaia, and *that*
they have [b]addicted themselves to
the ministry of the saints,)
16 That ye submit yourselves unto
such, and to every one that helpeth
with *us*, and laboureth.
17 I am glad of the coming of
Stephanas and Fortunatus and
Achaicus: for that which was [a]lack-
ing on your part they have supplied.
18 For they have refreshed my

53*a* Alma 41:4.
b TG Mortality.
54*a* TG Immortality.
b Isa. 25:8.
55*a* Mosiah 16:8 (7–8).
b GR Hades, hell.
56*a* D&C 42:45–46.
b GR power.
57*a* TG Thanksgiving.
b 1 Jn. 5:4 (4–5).
58*a* TG Perseverance; Steadfastness.
16 1*a* Acts 24:17 (17, 26).
b GR directed, arranged.
2*a* TG Sabbath.
b Deut. 16:10.
3*a* GR gift. TG Generosity.
4*a* GR suitable, worthwhile.
7*a* GR in passing.
b GR hope.
c 2 Cor. 1:15 (15–16).
9*a* Col. 4:3.
b GR energetic, efficient.
10*a* 2 Cor. 1:19; 1 Thes. 3:2.
11*a* 1 Tim. 4:12.
12*a* Acts 18:24.
13*a* TG Watch.
b Philip. 4:1 (1–7).
c D&C 9:14.
d GR behave like men.
e 1 Sam. 4:9; Isa. 46:8.
14*a* TG Charity.
15*a* 1 Cor. 1:16.
b GR devoted, appointed.
17*a* 2 Cor. 11:9.

spirit and yours: therefore acknowledge ye them that are such.
19 The churches of Asia salute
you. [a]Aquila and Priscilla salute you much in the Lord, with the church that is in their house.
20 All the brethren greet you.
Greet ye one another with an holy [a]kiss.
21 The salutation of *me* Paul with
mine own hand.
22 If any man love not the Lord
Jesus Christ, let him be Anathema [a]Maran-atha.
23 The grace of our Lord Jesus
Christ *be* with you.
24 My love *be* with you all in Christ
Jesus. Amen.

¶ The first *epistle* to the Corinthians was written from Philippi by Stephanas, and Fortunatus, and Achaicus, and Timotheus.

THE SECOND EPISTLE OF PAUL THE APOSTLE TO THE CORINTHIANS

CHAPTER 1

God comforts and cares for His Saints—The Saints are sealed and given assurance by the Spirit in their hearts.

PAUL, an [a]apostle of Jesus Christ by the will of God, and Timothy *our* brother, unto the church of God which is at Corinth, with all the saints which are in all Achaia:
2 Grace *be* to you and peace from
God our Father, and *from* the Lord Jesus Christ.
3 Blessed *be* God, even the Father
of our Lord Jesus Christ, the Father of [a]mercies, and the God of all [b]comfort;
4 Who comforteth us in all our
[a]tribulation, that we may be able to comfort them which are in any trouble, by the [b]comfort wherewith we ourselves are comforted of God.
5 For as the [a]sufferings of Christ
abound in us, so our consolation also aboundeth by Christ.
6 And whether we be afflicted, *it is*
for your consolation and salvation, which is [a]effectual in the [b]enduring of the same sufferings which we also suffer: or whether we be comforted, *it is* for your consolation and salvation.
7 And our hope of you *is* steadfast,
knowing, that as ye are partakers of the [a]sufferings, so *shall ye be* also of the consolation.
8 For we would not, brethren,
have you ignorant of our trouble which came to us in Asia, that we were pressed out of measure, above strength, insomuch that we [a]despaired even of life:

19*a* Acts 18:2.
20*a* JST 1 Cor. 16:20 . . . *salutation.*
22*a* Aramaic, meaning "The Lord will come!" or "Come, O Lord!"

[2 CORINTHIANS]
1 1*a* D&C 21:1.
3*a* TG God, Mercy of.
b TG Comfort.
4*a* TG Tribulation.
b Philip. 3:10; 2 Thes. 2:16.
5*a* Col. 1:24. TG Suffering.
6*a* GR active, operative.
b D&C 63:20; 101:35.
7*a* TG Persecution; Suffering.
8*a* TG Despair.

9 But we had the sentence of death in ourselves, that we should not trust in ourselves, but in God which [a]raiseth the dead:

10 Who [a]delivered us from so great a death, and doth deliver: in whom we trust that he will yet deliver *us;*

11 Ye also helping together by [a]prayer for us, that for the gift *bestowed* upon us by the means of many persons thanks may be given by many on our behalf.

12 For our rejoicing is this, the [a]testimony of our conscience, that in [b]simplicity and godly sincerity, not with fleshly [c]wisdom, but by the grace of God, we have had our conversation in the world, and more abundantly to you-ward.

13 For we [a]write none other things unto you, than what ye read or acknowledge; and I trust ye shall acknowledge even to the end;

14 As also ye have acknowledged us in part, that we are your rejoicing, even as ye also *are* ours in the [a]day of the Lord Jesus.

15 And in this confidence I was minded to [a]come unto you before, that ye might have a second benefit;

16 And to pass by you into Macedonia, and to come again out of Macedonia unto you, and of you to be brought on my way toward Judæa.

17 When I therefore was thus minded, did I use [a]lightness? or the things that I purpose, do I purpose according to the flesh, that with me there should be yea yea, and nay nay?

18 But *as* God *is* true, our word toward you was not yea and nay.

19 For the [a]Son of God, Jesus Christ, who was preached among you by us, *even* by me and [b]Silvanus and [c]Timotheus, was not yea and nay, but in him was yea.

20 For all the [a]promises of God in him *are* yea, and in him Amen, unto the glory of God by us.

21 Now he which stablisheth us with you in Christ, and hath [a]anointed us, *is* God;

22 Who hath also [a]sealed us, and given the earnest of the Spirit in our hearts.

23 Moreover I call God for a record upon my soul, that to spare you I came not as yet unto Corinth.

24 Not for that we have dominion over your faith, but are helpers of your joy: for by [a]faith ye stand.

CHAPTER 2

Saints should love and forgive one another—They always triumph in Christ.

BUT I determined this with myself, that I would not come again to you in heaviness.

2 For if I make you sorry, who is he then that maketh me glad, but the same which is made sorry by me?

3 And I wrote this same unto you, lest, when I came, I should have sorrow from them of whom I ought to rejoice; having [a]confidence in you all, that my joy is *the joy* of you all.

4 For out of much affliction and anguish of heart I wrote unto you with many tears; not that ye should be grieved, but that ye might know the love which I have more abundantly unto you.

5 But if any have caused grief, he hath not grieved me, but in part: that I may not overcharge you all.

6 Sufficient to such a man *is* this punishment, which *was inflicted* of many.

7 So that contrariwise ye *ought* rather to [a]forgive *him,* and comfort *him,* lest perhaps such a one should

9*a* TG Resurrection.
10*a* TG Deliver.
11*a* Philip. 1:19; Philem. 1:22.
12*a* TG Testimony.
b GR plainness, singleness of heart.
c 1 Cor. 2:13.
13*a* TG Scriptures, Writing of.
14*a* D&C 1:9 (8–10).
15*a* 1 Cor. 16:7 (5–7).
17*a* GR light-mindedness, levity.
19*a* Luke 1:35.
b Acts 15:34 (32–34); 1 Thes. 1:1; 1 Pet. 5:12.
c 1 Cor. 16:10 (10–11); 1 Thes. 3:2.
20*a* Rom. 15:8.
21*a* TG Anointing.
22*a* TG Sealing.
24*a* Rom. 11:20.
2 3*a* 2 Cor. 8:22.
7*a* TG Forgive.

be swallowed up with overmuch
sorrow.
8 Wherefore I beseech you that ye
would confirm *your* love toward him.
9 For to this end also did I [a]write,
that I might know the proof of
you, whether ye be [b]obedient in all
things.
10 To whom ye forgive any thing, I
forgive also: for if I forgave any thing,
to whom I forgave *it*, for your sakes
forgave I it in the [a]person of Christ;
11 Lest [a]Satan should get an advantage of us: for we are not ignorant
of his devices.
12 Furthermore, when I came to
Troas to *preach* Christ's gospel, and
a [a]door was opened unto me of the
Lord,
13 I had no rest in my spirit, because I found not Titus my brother:
but taking my leave of them, I went
from thence into Macedonia.
14 Now thanks *be* unto God, which
always causeth us to [a]triumph in
Christ, and maketh manifest the
savour of his knowledge by us in
every place.
15 For we are unto God a sweet
savour of Christ, in them that are
saved, and in them that perish:
16 To the one *we are* the savour of
death unto death; and to the other
the savour of life unto life. And
who *is* [a]sufficient for these things?
17 For we are not as many, which
[a]corrupt the [b]word of God: but as of
[c]sincerity, but as of God, in the sight
of God speak we in Christ.

CHAPTER 3

The gospel surpasses the law of Moses—Where the Spirit of the Lord is, there is liberty.

Do we begin again to commend ourselves? or need we, as some *others*,
epistles of commendation to you, or
letters of commendation from you?
2 Ye are our [a]epistle written in our
hearts, known and read of all men:
3 *Forasmuch as ye are* manifestly
declared to be the epistle of Christ
ministered by us, [a]written not with
ink, but with the Spirit of the living
God; not in [b]tables of stone, but in
[c]fleshy tables of the [d]heart.
4 And such trust have we through
Christ to God-ward:
5 Not that we are sufficient of
ourselves to think any thing as of
ourselves; but our [a]sufficiency *is*
of God;
6 Who also hath made us able
[a]ministers of the new testament;
not of the letter, but of the spirit:
for the letter killeth, but the [b]spirit
giveth life.
7 But if the ministration of [a]death,
written *and* engraven in stones, was
glorious, so that the children of Israel could not steadfastly behold
the face of Moses for the [b]glory of
his countenance; which *glory* was to
be done away:
8 How shall not the ministration
of the spirit be rather glorious?
9 For if the ministration of condemnation *be* glory, much more doth
the ministration of righteousness
exceed in glory.
10 For even that which was made
glorious had no glory in this respect,
by reason of the glory that excelleth.
11 For if that which is done away
was glorious, much more that which
remaineth *is* glorious.
12 Seeing then that we have such
hope, we use great [a]plainness of
speech:
13 And not as Moses, *which* put a
veil over his face, that the children

9*a* TG Scriptures, Writing of.
b 2 Cor. 7:15.
10*a* GR presence.
11*a* 2 Pet. 2:20 (20–22).
12*a* Acts 14:27;
1 Cor. 16:9.
14*a* Rom. 8:37.
16*a* 2 Cor. 3:5 (5–6).
17*a* 2 Cor. 4:2.
TG Apostasy of the
Early Christian Church.
b TG Scriptures,
Preservation of.
c TG Sincere.
3 2*a* 1 Cor. 9:2.
3*a* Deut. 9:10 (10–11).
b Ex. 24:12; 31:18; 34:1;
Deut. 4:13;
Prov. 3:3.
c Ezek. 11:19 (19–20).
d Jer. 31:33;
Heb. 8:10.
5*a* 2 Cor. 2:16;
Alma 26:12.
6*a* 1 Cor. 3:5.
b John 6:63.
7*a* Rom. 7:10.
b TG Transfiguration.
12*a* GR boldness, frankness.

of Israel could not steadfastly look to
the end of that which is abolished:
14 But their [a]minds were [b]blinded:
for until this day remaineth the same
veil untaken away in the [c]reading
of the old testament; which [d]*veil* is
done away in Christ.
15 But even unto this day, when
Moses is read, the veil is upon their
[a]heart.
16 Nevertheless when it shall turn
to the Lord, the veil shall be taken
away.
17 Now the Lord is [a]that Spirit:
and where the [b]Spirit of the Lord
is, there *is* [c]liberty.
18 But we all, with open face beholding as in a [a]glass the [b]glory of
the Lord, are changed into the same
[c]image from [d]glory to glory, *even* as
by the Spirit of the Lord.

CHAPTER 4

Gospel light shines on the Saints—Mortal trials are nothing as contrasted with eternal glory.

THEREFORE seeing we have this ministry, as we have received [a]mercy,
we faint not;
2 But have [a]renounced the hidden
things of [b]dishonesty, not walking
in craftiness, nor handling the word
of God [c]deceitfully; but by manifestation of the [d]truth commending
ourselves to every man's [e]conscience
in the sight of God.
3 But if our gospel be hid, it is hid
to them that are lost:
4 In whom the [a]god of this [b]world
hath [c]blinded the [d]minds of them
which [e]believe not, lest the [f]light of
the glorious gospel of Christ, who
is the [g]image of [h]God, should shine
unto them.
5 For we [a]preach not ourselves, but
Christ Jesus the Lord; and ourselves
your [b]servants for Jesus' sake.
6 For God, who [a]commanded the
light to shine out of darkness, hath
[b]shined in our hearts, to *give* the
[c]light of the knowledge of the [d]glory
of God in the face of Jesus Christ.
7 But we have this treasure in
earthen vessels, that the excellency
of the [a]power may be of God, and
not of us.
8 *We are* [a]troubled on every side,
yet not distressed; *we are* perplexed,
but not in [b]despair;
9 [a]Persecuted, but not forsaken;
cast down, but not [b]destroyed;
10 Always bearing about in the
body the dying of the Lord Jesus,
that the life also of Jesus might be
made manifest in our body.
11 For we which live are alway delivered unto [a]death for Jesus' sake,
that the life also of Jesus might
be made manifest in our [b]mortal
flesh.
12 So then death worketh in us,
but life in you.
13 We having the same spirit of

14*a* TG Mind.
b TG Spiritual Blindness.
c Acts 15:21.
d TG Jesus Christ, Types of, in Anticipation; Veil.
15*a* TG Hardheartedness.
17*a* GR the Spirit.
b Alma 61:15. TG God, Spirit of.
c Rom. 8:2. TG Governments; Liberty.
18*a* 1 Cor. 13:12.
b TG Celestial Glory.
c Rom. 8:29.
d TG Man, Potential to Become like Heavenly Father.
4 1*a* Alma 12:34.
2*a* TG Priesthood, Qualifying for.
b GR shame, disgrace. TG Honesty.
c 2 Cor. 2:17; 1 Thes. 2:3 (3, 5).
d D&C 19:37; 75:4.
e TG Conscience.
4*a* Eph. 6:12. TG Devil.
b TG Worldliness.
c Alma 19:6; Moro. 7:12; D&C 93:39 (38–39). TG Spiritual Blindness.
d TG Mind.
e TG Unbelief.
f TG Light [noun].
g TG God, Body of, Corporeal Nature.
h TG Godhead.
5*a* Gal. 1:11 (11–12). TG Missionary Work.
b 1 Cor. 9:19; Alma 26:3.
6*a* Ps. 33:9; Moses 2:5 (4–5).
b D&C 45:9.
c TG Intelligence; Light of Christ.
d TG God, Glory of; Jesus Christ, Relationships with the Father.
7*a* 1 Cor. 2:5; D&C 19:3; 88:13 (7–13).
8*a* 2 Cor. 7:5. TG Adversity.
b TG Despair.
9*a* 2 Cor. 11:23 (23–27); D&C 101:35.
b Ps. 129:2.
11*a* Rom. 8:36. TG Martyrdom.
b TG Mortality.

faith, according as it is written, I
[a]believed, and therefore have I spoken; we also believe, and therefore
[b]speak;
14 Knowing that he which raised
up the Lord Jesus shall raise up us
also by Jesus, and shall present *us*
with you.
15 For all things *are* for your sakes,
that the abundant grace might
through the [a]thanksgiving of many
redound to the glory of God.
16 For which cause we faint not;
but though our outward man perish, yet the [a]inward *man* is renewed
day by day.
17 For our light [a]affliction, which
is but for a moment, worketh for us
a far more exceeding *and* [b]eternal
[c]weight of glory;
18 While we look not at the
things which are [a]seen, but at
the things which are not seen: for
the things which are seen *are* temporal; but the things which are
not [b]seen *are* [c]eternal.

CHAPTER 5

Saints walk by faith and seek tabernacles of immortal glory—The gospel reconciles man to God—God's ministers carry the word of reconciliation to the world.

FOR we know that if our earthly
house of *this* tabernacle were dissolved, we have a building of God,
an house not made with hands,
eternal in the heavens.
2 For in this we groan, earnestly
desiring to be [a]clothed upon with
our house which is from heaven:
3 If so be that being clothed we
shall not be found naked.
4 For we that are in *this* tabernacle
do [a]groan, being burdened: not for
that we would be unclothed, but
clothed upon, that [b]mortality might
be swallowed up of life.
5 Now he that hath wrought us
for the selfsame thing *is* God, who
also hath given unto us the earnest
of the Spirit.
6 Therefore *we are* always [a]confi-
dent, knowing that, whilst we are
at home in the body, we are absent
from the Lord:
7 (For we walk by [a]faith, not by
[b]sight:)
8 We are confident, *I say,* and willing rather to be absent from the body,
and to be present with the Lord.
9 Wherefore we [a]labour, that,
whether present or absent, we may
be accepted of him.
10 For we must all appear before
the [a]judgment seat of Christ; that
every one may receive the things
done in *his* body, [b]according to that
he hath [c]done, whether *it be* good
or bad.
11 Knowing therefore the terror
of the Lord, we persuade men; but
we are made manifest unto God;
and I trust also are made manifest
in your [a]consciences.
12 For we commend not ourselves
again unto you, but give you occasion to glory on our behalf, that ye
may have somewhat to *answer* them
which glory in appearance, and not
in heart.
13 [a]For whether we be beside ourselves, *it is* to God: or whether we
be sober, *it is* for your cause.
14 For the love of Christ con-
straineth us; because we thus judge,
that if [a]one [b]died for all, then were
all dead:
15 And *that* he died for all, that

13*a* D&C 14:8.
b D&C 18:21.
15*a* TG Thanksgiving.
16*a* 2 Ne. 4:20; Mosiah 24:15.
17*a* Rom. 5:3. TG Persecution; Suffering.
b TG Eternal Life.
c D&C 63:66.
18*a* Rom. 8:24.
b Ether 12:6.
c TG Eternity.
5 2*a* Rom. 8:23.
4*a* TG Mourning.
b TG Mortality.
6*a* GR of good courage, of good cheer.
7*a* TG Faith.
b TG Sight.
9*a* Moro. 9:6.
10*a* TG Jesus Christ, Judge.
b TG Accountability.
c TG Good Works.
11*a* TG Conscience.
13*a* JST 2 Cor. 5:13 For *we bear record that we are not* beside ourselves; *for whether we glory,* it is to God, or whether we be sober, it is for your *sakes.*
14*a* Rom. 5:15.
b D&C 19:16.

they which live should not henceforth [a]live unto themselves, but
unto him which died for them, and
rose again.
16 [a]Wherefore henceforth know
we no man after the flesh: yea,
though we have known Christ after
the flesh, yet now henceforth know
we *him* no more.
17 Therefore if any man *be* [a]in
Christ, *he is* a [b]new creature: [c]old
things are [d]passed away; behold,
all things are become [e]new.
18 And all things *are* of God, who
hath [a]reconciled us to himself by
Jesus Christ, and hath given to us
the ministry of reconciliation;
19 To wit, that God was in Christ,
[a]reconciling the world unto himself,
not imputing their trespasses unto
them; and hath committed unto us
the word of reconciliation.
20 Now then we are [a]ambassadors
for Christ, as though God did beseech
you by us: we pray *you* in Christ's
stead, be ye reconciled to God.
21 For he hath made him *to be* [a]sin
for us, who knew no [b]sin; that we
might be made the [c]righteousness
of God in him.

CHAPTER 6

Now is the day of salvation—God's ministers must walk uprightly and bear all things—Saints should not be unequally yoked with unbelievers.

WE then, *as* [a]workers together *with*
[b]*him*, beseech *you* also that ye
receive not the [c]grace of God in vain.
2 (For he saith, I have heard thee
in a [a]time accepted, and in the
[b]day of [c]salvation have I succoured
thee: behold, now *is* the accepted
time; behold, now *is* the day of
salvation.)
3 Giving no [a]offence in any thing,
that the ministry be not blamed:
4 But in all *things* approving ourselves as the [a]ministers of God, in
much [b]patience, in [c]afflictions, in
necessities, in distresses,
5 In stripes, in imprisonments, in
[a]tumults, in labours, in watchings,
in fastings;
6 By [a]pureness, by knowledge, by
[b]longsuffering, by [c]kindness, by the
Holy Ghost, by [d]love unfeigned,
7 By the word of truth, by the
power of God, by the [a]armour of
[b]righteousness on the right hand
and on the left,
8 By honour and dishonour, by evil
report and good report: as deceivers,
and *yet* true;
9 As unknown, and *yet* well known;
as dying, and, behold, we live; as
chastened, and not killed;
10 As [a]sorrowful, yet alway rejoicing; as [b]poor, yet making many [c]rich;
as having nothing, and *yet* possess-
ing all things.
11 O *ye* Corinthians, our mouth is
open unto you, our heart is [a]enlarged.
12 Ye are not straitened in us,
but ye are straitened in your own
[a]bowels.
13 Now for a recompence in the
same, (I speak as unto *my* children,)
be ye also enlarged.

15*a* Rom. 14:7 (7–9).
16*a* JST 2 Cor. 5:16 Wherefore, henceforth *live* we no *more* after the flesh; *yea, though we once lived after the flesh, yet since* we have known Christ, now henceforth *live* we no more *after the flesh.*
17*a* 1 Jn. 2:5 (2–5).
b TG Man, New, Spiritually Reborn.
c Rom. 7:6; 13:12 (12–14); Heb. 8:13.
d D&C 29:24; 63:49.
e Rev. 21:5.
18*a* TG Reconciliation.
19*a* TG Reconciliation.
20*a* Luke 14:23.
21*a* Isa. 53:6.
b 1 Jn. 3:3.
c Rom. 1:17.
6 1*a* 1 Cor. 3:9.
b JST 2 Cor. 6:1 . . . *Christ* . . .
c TG Grace.
2*a* Isa. 49:8.
b Alma 34:32 (31–34).
c TG Salvation.
3*a* Rom. 14:13. TG Offense.
4*a* 2 Cor. 11:23. TG Priesthood, Magnifying Callings within.
b TG Patience.
c D&C 127:2 (2–3).
5*a* TG Rioting and Reveling.
6*a* TG Purity.
b TG Forbear.
c TG Kindness.
d D&C 121:41 (41–42).
7*a* Rom. 13:12.
b TG Righteousness.
10*a* TG Mourning.
b 2 Cor. 8:9.
c TG Treasure.
11*a* Ps. 119:32 (25–32).
12*a* D&C 121:45.

14 Be ye not unequally [a]yoked together with unbelievers: for what
[b]fellowship hath righteousness with
[c]unrighteousness? and what communion hath [d]light with darkness?
15 And what concord hath Christ
with Belial? or what part hath he
that believeth with an infidel?
16 And what [a]agreement hath the
temple of God with idols? for ye are
the [b]temple of the living God; as
God hath said, I will [c]dwell in them,
and walk in *them;* and I will be their
God, and they shall be my people.
17 Wherefore [a]come out from
among them, and be ye [b]sepa-
rate, saith the Lord, and touch not
the [c]unclean *thing;* and I will receive you,
18 And will be a [a]Father unto you,
and ye shall be my [b]sons and daughters, saith the Lord [c]Almighty.

CHAPTER 7

*Godly sorrow for sin leads to repen-
tance—The sorrow of the world leads
to death.*

HAVING therefore these promises,
dearly beloved, let us [a]cleanse ourselves from all [b]filthiness of the flesh
and spirit, perfecting [c]holiness in
the fear of God.
2 Receive us; we have [a]wronged no
man, we have corrupted no man, we
have [b]defrauded no man.
3 I speak not *this* to condemn
you: for I have said before, that ye
are in our hearts to die and live
with *you.*
4 Great *is* my boldness of speech
toward you, great *is* my glorying
of you: I am filled with [a]comfort,
I am exceeding [b]joyful in all our
[c]tribulation.
5 For, when we were come into
Macedonia, our flesh had no rest,
but we were [a]troubled on every
side; without *were* fightings, within
were [b]fears.
6 Nevertheless God, that comforteth those that are cast down, comforted us by the coming of Titus;
7 And not by his coming only, but
by the consolation wherewith he was
[a]comforted in you, when he told us
your earnest desire, your mourning,
your fervent mind toward me; so
that I rejoiced the more.
8 For though I made you sorry with
a letter, I do not repent, though I did
repent: for I perceive that the same
epistle hath made you sorry, though
it were but for a season.
9 Now I rejoice, not that ye were
made sorry, but that ye sorrowed to
repentance: for ye were made [a]sorry
after a godly manner, that ye might
receive damage by us in nothing.
10 For [a]godly [b]sorrow worketh
[c]repentance to [d]salvation not to be
repented of: but the [e]sorrow of the
world worketh death.
11 For behold this selfsame thing,
that ye sorrowed after a godly sort,
what carefulness it wrought in
you, yea, *what* clearing of yourselves,
yea, *what* indignation, yea, *what*
fear, yea, *what* vehement desire, yea,
what zeal, yea, *what* revenge! In all
things ye have approved yourselves
to be clear in this matter.

14*a* TG Marriage, Interfaith; Marriage, Temporal.
b TG Fellowshipping.
c 2 Kgs. 3:13; Ezek. 14:3.
d TG Light [noun].
16*a* 1 Cor. 10:21 (19–22).
b TG Body, Sanctity of; Temple.
c Lev. 26:12. TG God, Presence of.
17*a* D&C 25:10; 53:2; 84:50 (49–53).
b TG Separation.
c Isa. 52:11. TG Uncleanness.
18*a* Jer. 31:9 (1, 9).
b TG Sons and Daughters of God.
c TG God, Power of.
7 1*a* TG Chastity; Cleanliness; Purification.
b GR pollution, stain, defilement. TG Filthiness.
c TG Holiness.
2*a* 1 Thes. 2:3 (3–10).
b TG Fraud.
4*a* TG Comfort.
b TG Joy.
c 3 Ne. 12:12 (11–12).
5*a* 2 Cor. 4:8.
b D&C 10:55.
7*a* TG Comfort.
9*a* TG Poor in Spirit.
10*a* TG Godliness.
b Eccl. 7:3; Isa. 22:12; Joel 2:17; James 4:9 (8–10); Alma 36:17 (5–28); 42:29. TG Mourning; Sorrow.
c TG Repent.
d TG Salvation.
e Morm. 2:13.

12 Wherefore, though I wrote unto
you, *I did it* not for his cause that
had done the wrong, nor for his
cause that suffered wrong, but that
our care for you in the sight of God
might appear unto you.
13 Therefore we were comforted
in your comfort: yea, and exceedingly the more joyed we for the joy
of Titus, because his spirit was [a]re-
freshed by you all.
14 For if I have [a]boasted any thing
to him of you, I am not ashamed;
but as we spake all things to you
in truth, even so our [b]boasting,
which I *made* before Titus, is found
a truth.
15 And his [a]inward affection is
more abundant toward you, whilst
he remembereth the [b]obedience of
you all, how with fear and trembling
ye received him.
16 I rejoice therefore that I have
confidence in you in all *things.*

CHAPTER 8

True Saints impart of their substance to the poor—Christ, out of His poverty, brought eternal riches.

MOREOVER, brethren, [a]we do you to
wit of the grace of God bestowed on
the churches of Macedonia;
2 How that in a great [a]trial of [b]af-
fliction the abundance of their joy
and their deep [c]poverty abounded
unto the riches of their [d]liberality.
3 For to *their* power, I bear record,
yea, and beyond *their* power *they
were* willing of themselves;
4 Praying us with much entreaty
that we would receive the gift, and
take upon us the [a]fellowship of the
ministering to the saints.
5 And *this they did,* not as we hoped,
but first [a]gave their own selves to
the Lord, and unto us by the will
of God.
6 Insomuch that we desired Titus,
that as he had begun, so he would
also finish in you the same grace also.
7 Therefore, as ye abound in every
thing, in faith, and utterance, and
knowledge, and *in* all [a]diligence,
and *in* your love to us, *see* that ye
abound in this grace also.
8 I speak [a]not by commandment,
but by occasion of the forwardness
of others, and to prove the [b]sincer-
ity of your love.
9 For ye know the [a]grace of our
Lord Jesus Christ, that, though he
was [b]rich, yet for your sakes he
became [c]poor, that ye through his
[d]poverty might be rich.
10 And herein I give *my* advice:
for this is expedient for you, who
have begun before, not only to do,
but also to be forward a year ago.
11 Now therefore perform the do-
ing *of it;* that as *there was* a readiness
to will, so *there may be* a performance
also out of that which ye have.
12 For if there be first a [a]willing
[b]mind, *it is* accepted according to
that a man hath, *and* not according
to that he hath not.
13 For *I mean* not that other men
be eased, and ye burdened:
14 But by an equality, *that* now at
this time your abundance *may be
a supply* for their want, that their
[a]abundance also may be *a supply*
for your want: that there may be
[b]equality:
15 As it is written, He that *had*
[a]*gathered* much had nothing over;
and he that *had gathered* little had
no lack.
16 But thanks *be* to God, which
put the same earnest care into the
heart of Titus for you.

13*a* Rom. 15:32.
14*a* 2 Cor. 9:2.
b TG Boast.
15*a* GR heart, tender affections, compassion.
b 2 Cor. 2:9; 10:6.
TG Obedience.
8 1*a* GR we make known (or declare) to you the grace.
2*a* TG Probation; Test.
b TG Affliction.
c Mark 12:44 (43–44).
d GR sincerity, purity of mind.
TG Generosity.
4*a* D&C 88:133.
5*a* TG Self-Sacrifice.
7*a* TG Diligence.
8*a* D&C 63:22.
b TG Sincere.
9*a* TG Grace.
b TG Treasure.
c Philip. 2:7 (5–8).
d 2 Cor. 6:10.
12*a* Ex. 25:2 (1–7).
b D&C 64:34.
14*a* Alma 1:30 (29–30).
b TG Consecration.
15*a* Ex. 16:18.

17 For indeed he accepted the exhortation; but being more forward,
of his own accord he went unto you.
18 And we have sent with him
the brother, whose praise *is* in the
gospel throughout all the churches;
19 And not *that* only, but who was
also chosen of the churches to travel
with us with this grace, which is administered by us to the glory of the
same Lord, and *declaration of* your
ready mind:
20 Avoiding this, that no man
should blame us in this abundance
which is administered by us:
21 Providing for [a]honest things,
not only in the sight of the Lord,
but also in the [b]sight of men.
22 And we have sent with them our
brother, whom we have oftentimes
proved diligent in many things, but
now much more diligent, upon the
great [a]confidence which *I have* in
you.
23 Whether *any do inquire* of Titus,
he is my partner and fellowhelper
concerning you: or our brethren
be inquired of, they are the messengers of the churches, *and* the glory
of Christ.
24 Wherefore shew ye to them,
and before the churches, the proof
of your love, and of our boasting on
your behalf.

CHAPTER 9

God loves and rewards a cheerful giver—Thanks be to God for His unspeakable gift.

FOR as touching the ministering to
the saints, it is superfluous for me
to write to you:
2 For I know the forwardness of
your mind, for which I [a]boast of you
to them of Macedonia, that Achaia
was ready a year ago; and your zeal
hath [b]provoked very many.
3 Yet have I sent the brethren, lest
our boasting of you should be in
vain in this behalf; that, as I said,
ye may be ready:
4 Lest haply if they of Macedonia
come with me, and find you un-
prepared, we (that we say not, ye)
should be ashamed in this same
confident boasting.
5 Therefore I thought it necessary
to exhort the brethren, that they
would go before unto you, and
make up beforehand your [a]bounty,
whereof ye had notice before, that
the same might be ready, as *a matter*
of bounty, and not as *of* covetousness.
6 But this *I say*, He which soweth
sparingly shall [a]reap also sparingly;
and he which [b]soweth bountifully
shall reap also bountifully.
7 Every man according as he [a]pur-
poseth in his heart, *so let him give*;
not [b]grudgingly, or of necessity: for
God loveth a [c]cheerful [d]giver.
8 And God *is* able to make all [a]grace
abound toward you; that ye, always
having all sufficiency in all *things*,
may abound to every good work:
9 (As it is written, He hath dispersed abroad; he hath given to the
poor: his righteousness remaineth
for ever.
10 Now he that ministereth seed
to the sower both minister bread
for *your* food, and multiply your
seed sown, and increase the fruits
of your [a]righteousness;)
11 Being enriched in every thing
to all bountifulness, which causeth
through us [a]thanksgiving to God.
12 For the [a]administration of this
service not only supplieth the want
of the saints, but is abundant also
by many thanksgivings unto God;
13 Whiles by the experiment of
this ministration they glorify God
for your professed subjection unto
the gospel of Christ, and for *your*
liberal distribution unto them, and
unto all *men*;

21*a* TG Honesty.
b Rom. 12:17.
22*a* 2 Cor. 2:3.
9 2*a* 2 Cor. 7:14.
b TG Provoking.
5*a* GR gift, blessing, benevolence.
6*a* TG Harvest.
b TG Accountability.
7*a* D&C 6:33 (33–34).
b TG Hypocrisy.
c TG Cheerful.
d TG Generosity.
8*a* Philip. 4:18 (15–23); Jacob 2:19 (17–19). TG Grace.
10*a* TG Righteousness.
11*a* TG Thanksgiving.
12*a* Heb. 13:16.

14 And by their prayer for you,
which long after you for the exceeding grace of God in you.
15 [a]Thanks *be* unto God for his
unspeakable [b]gift.

CHAPTER 10

*Bring every thought into obedience—
Paul glories in the Lord.*

NOW I Paul myself beseech you by
the [a]meekness and gentleness of
Christ, who in presence *am* base
among you, but being absent am
bold toward you:
2 But I beseech *you*, that I may not
be bold when I am present with that
confidence, wherewith I think to
be bold against some, which think
of us as if we walked according to
the flesh.
3 For though we walk in the flesh,
we do not [a]war after the flesh:
4 (For the [a]weapons of our [b]warfare
are not carnal, but mighty through
God to the pulling down of strong
holds;)
5 Casting down imaginations, and
every high thing that exalteth itself against the knowledge of God,
and bringing into captivity every
[a]thought to the [b]obedience of Christ;
6 And having in a readiness to revenge all [a]disobedience, when your
[b]obedience is fulfilled.
7 Do ye look on things after the
outward [a]appearance? If any man
trust to himself that he is Christ's,
let him of himself think this again,
that, as he *is* Christ's, even so *are* we
[b]Christ's.
8 For though I should boast somewhat more of our [a]authority, which
the Lord hath given us for [b]edifica-
tion, and not for your destruction,
I should not be ashamed:
9 That I may not seem as if I would
terrify you by letters.
10 For *his* letters, say they, *are*
weighty and powerful; but *his* [a]bod-
ily presence *is* weak, and *his* speech
[b]contemptible.
11 Let such an one think this,
that, such as we are in word by
letters when we are absent, such
will we be also in deed when we are
present.
12 For we dare not make ourselves
of the number, or compare ourselves
with some that commend themselves: but they measuring themselves by themselves, and comparing themselves among themselves,
are not wise.
13 But we will not [a]boast of things
without *our* measure, but according
to the measure of the rule which
God hath distributed to us, a measure to reach even unto you.
14 For we stretch not ourselves
beyond *our measure*, as though we
reached not unto you: for we are
come as far as to you also in *preaching* the gospel of Christ:
15 Not boasting of things without
our measure, *that is*, of other men's
[a]labours; but having hope, when
your faith is increased, that we shall
be enlarged by you according to our
rule abundantly,
16 To preach the gospel in the *regions* beyond you, *and* not to boast in
another man's line of things made
ready to our hand.
17 But he that glorieth, let him
[a]glory in the Lord.
18 For not he that [a]commendeth
himself is approved, but whom the
Lord commendeth.

CHAPTER 11

*Maintain the simplicity that is in
Christ—Satan sends forth false apos-
tles—Paul glories in his sufferings for
Christ.*

15*a* TG Thanksgiving.
b James 1:17.
10 1*a* D&C 19:23; 25:5 (5, 14).
3*a* TG War.
4*a* Eph. 6:11 (10–24).
b 1 Cor. 9:7.
5*a* TG Motivations.
b TG Obedience.
6*a* TG Disobedience.
b 2 Cor. 7:15.
7*a* 1 Sam. 16:7.
b 1 Cor. 3:23.
8*a* 2 Cor. 13:10.
TG Called of God.
b TG Edification.
10*a* Gal. 4:13.
b 2 Cor. 11:6.
13*a* TG Boast.
15*a* Rom. 15:20.
17*a* Jer. 9:24 (23–24);
Alma 26:16 (11–16).
18*a* Luke 18:14.
TG Boast.

WOULD to God ye could bear with
me a little in *my* folly: and indeed
bear with me.
2 For I am [a]jealous over you with
godly jealousy: for I have [b]espoused you to one husband, that I
may present *you as* a chaste virgin
to Christ.
3 But I fear, lest by any means, as
the [a]serpent [b]beguiled Eve through
his [c]subtilty, so your minds should
be [d]corrupted from the [e]simplicity
that is in Christ.
4 For if he that cometh preacheth
another [a]Jesus, whom we have not
preached, or *if* ye receive another
spirit, which ye have not received,
or another [b]gospel, which ye have
not accepted, ye might well bear
with *him.*
5 For I suppose I was not a whit
behind the very chiefest apostles.
6 But though *I be* [a]rude in speech,
yet not in knowledge; but we have
been throughly made manifest
among you in all things.
7 Have I committed an offence in
abasing myself that ye might be
exalted, because I have preached
to you the gospel of God [a]freely?
8 I [a]robbed other churches, taking
[b]wages *of them,* to do you service.
9 And when I was present with
you, and wanted, I was [a]chargeable
to no man: for that which was [b]lacking to me the brethren which came
from Macedonia [c]supplied: and in
all *things* I have kept myself from
being burdensome unto you, and
so will I keep *myself.*
10 As the truth of Christ is in me,
no man shall stop me of this boasting in the regions of Achaia.
11 Wherefore? because I love you
not? God knoweth.
12 But what I do, that I will do,
that I may cut off occasion from
them which desire occasion; that
wherein they [a]glory, they may be
found even as we.
13 For such *are* [a]false apostles,
deceitful workers, transforming
themselves into the apostles of
Christ.
14 And no marvel; for [a]Satan himself is transformed into an [b]angel
of light.
15 Therefore *it is* no great thing if
his ministers also be transformed
as the ministers of righteousness;
whose [a]end shall be according to
their works.
16 I say again, Let no man think
me a fool; if otherwise, yet as a fool
[a]receive me, that I may [b]boast myself a little.
17 That which I speak, I speak *it* not
after the Lord, but as it were foolishly, in this confidence of boasting.
18 Seeing that many glory after
the flesh, I will glory also.
19 For ye suffer fools gladly, seeing ye *yourselves* are wise.
20 For ye suffer, if a man bring
you into [a]bondage, if a man devour
you, if a man take *of you,* if a man
exalt himself, if a man smite you
on the face.
21 I speak as concerning [a]reproach,
as though we had been weak. Howbeit whereinsoever any is bold, (I
speak foolishly,) I am bold also.
22 Are they [a]Hebrews? so *am* I. Are
they [b]Israelites? so *am* I. Are they
the seed of Abraham? so *am* I.
23 Are they [a]ministers of Christ?

---

11 2*a* TG Jealous.
b D&C 20:77.
3*a* TG Devil.
b TG Fall of Man; Temptation.
c Gen. 3:1.
d Heb. 13:9.
e Jacob 4:14.
4*a* Gal. 1:6.
b TG Gospel.
6*a* 2 Cor. 10:10.
7*a* 1 Cor. 9:18.
8*a* GR despoiled other churches, having taken provisions for you.
b TG Wages.
9*a* 2 Cor. 12:13 (13, 16); 1 Thes. 2:9.
b 1 Cor. 16:17.
c Philip. 4:10.
12*a* GR boast; so in chapters 11–12.
13*a* TG False Priesthoods; False Prophets.
14*a* 2 Ne. 9:9; D&C 129:8. TG Devil.
b TG Angels.
15*a* Philip. 3:19.
16*a* GR listen to, bear with, follow.
b TG Boast.
20*a* TG Bondage, Physical.
21*a* TG Reproach.
22*a* Philip. 3:5.
b Rom. 11:1.
23*a* 2 Cor. 6:4 (4–10).

(I speak as a fool) [b]I *am* more; in [c]labours more abundant, in [d]stripes above measure, in [e]prisons more frequent, in deaths oft.

24 Of the Jews five times received I [a]forty *stripes* save one.

25 Thrice was I [a]beaten with rods, once was I stoned, thrice I suffered shipwreck, a night and a day I have been in the deep;

26 *In* journeyings often, *in* perils of waters, *in* perils of robbers, *in* perils by *mine own* [a]countrymen, *in* perils by the [b]heathen, *in* [c]perils in the city, *in* perils in the wilderness, *in* perils in the sea, *in* perils among false brethren;

27 In [a]weariness and [b]painfulness, in watchings often, in hunger and thirst, in fastings often, in cold and nakedness.

28 Beside those things that are without, that which cometh upon me daily, the care of all the churches.

29 Who is weak, and I am not [a]weak? who is offended, and I [b]burn not?

30 If I must needs glory, I will glory of the things which concern mine infirmities.

31 The God and Father of our Lord Jesus Christ, which is blessed for evermore, knoweth that I lie not.

32 In Damascus the governor under Aretas the king kept the city of the Damascenes with a garrison, desirous to [a]apprehend me:

33 And through a window in a basket was I let down by the wall, and escaped his hands.

CHAPTER 12

Paul is caught up to the third heaven—The Lord gives men weaknesses that they may triumph over them—Paul manifests the signs of an Apostle.

IT is not expedient for me doubtless to [a]glory. I will come to [b]visions and [c]revelations of the Lord.

2 [a]I knew a man in Christ above fourteen years ago, (whether in the [b]body, I cannot tell; or whether out of the body, I cannot tell: God knoweth;) such an one caught up to the [c]third [d]heaven.

3 And I knew such a man, (whether in the body, or out of the body, I cannot tell: God knoweth;)

4 How that he was caught up into [a]paradise, and heard [b]unspeakable words, which it is [c]not [d]lawful for a man to utter.

5 Of such an one will I glory: yet of myself I will not [a]glory, but in mine infirmities.

6 For though I would desire to glory, I shall not be a fool; for I will say the truth: but *now* I forbear, lest any man should think of me above that which he seeth me *to be*, or *that* he heareth of me.

7 And lest I should be [a]exalted above measure through the abundance of the revelations, there was given to me a [b]thorn in the flesh, the messenger of Satan to buffet me, lest I should be exalted above measure.

8 For this thing I besought the Lord thrice, that it might depart from me.

9 And he said unto me, My [a]grace is sufficient for thee: for my [b]strength

---

23*b* JST 2 Cor. 11:23 . . . *so am I*; in labors . . .
c 1 Cor. 15:10.
d Acts 16:23; James 5:10 (10–11); Alma 26:29 (29–31).
e 2 Cor. 4:9.
24*a* Deut. 25:3.
25*a* Acts 16:22. TG Persecution.
26*a* Acts 14:5; 17:5.
b TG Heathen.
c Acts 21:31.
27*a* GR toil, trouble.
b TG Pain.
29*a* 1 Cor. 9:22.
b JST 2 Cor. 11:29 . . . *anger* not?
32*a* Acts 9:23 (23–25).
12 1*a* TG Boast.
b 1 Cor. 9:1.
c TG Revelation.
2*a* GR I know a man in Christ who fourteen years ago.
b D&C 137:1.
c TG Celestial Glory.
d TG Heaven.
4*a* TG Paradise.
b GR ineffable.
c 3 Ne. 17:17; 19:34 (32–34).
d GR possible, permitted.
5*a* TG Boast.
7*a* D&C 3:4.
b TG Pain.
9*a* TG Grace.
b TG Strength.

is made perfect in [c]weakness. Most gladly therefore will I rather glory in my infirmities, that the power of Christ may [d]rest upon me.

10 Therefore I take pleasure in [a]infirmities, in reproaches, in necessities, in [b]persecutions, in distresses for Christ's sake: for when I am [c]weak, then am I [d]strong.

11 I am become a fool in glorying; ye have compelled me: for I ought to have been commended of you: for in nothing am I behind the very [a]chiefest apostles, though I be nothing.

12 Truly the [a]signs of an apostle were wrought among you in all patience, in signs, and wonders, and mighty deeds.

13 For what is it wherein ye were inferior to other churches, except *it be* that I myself was not [a]burdensome to you? forgive me this wrong.

14 Behold, the third time I am ready to come to you; and I will not be burdensome to you: for I [a]seek not yours, but you: for the children ought not to lay up for the parents, but the parents for the children.

15 And I will very gladly spend and be spent for you; though the more abundantly I love you, the less I be loved.

16 But be it so, I did not burden you: nevertheless, being crafty, I caught you with guile.

17 Did I make a gain of you by any of them whom I sent unto you?

18 I desired Titus, and with *him* I sent a brother. Did Titus make a gain of you? walked we not in the same spirit? *walked we* not in the same steps?

19 Again, think ye that we excuse ourselves unto you? we speak before God in Christ: but *we do* all things, dearly beloved, for your [a]edifying.

20 For I fear, lest, when I come, I shall not find you such as I would, and *that* I shall be found unto you such as ye would not: lest *there be* debates, envyings, wraths, [a]strifes, [b]backbitings, whisperings, swellings, [c]tumults:

21 *And* lest, when I come again, my God will humble me among you, and *that* I shall bewail many which have sinned already, and have not repented of the uncleanness and fornication and lasciviousness which they have committed.

CHAPTER 13

Saints should test themselves as to righteousness—Be perfect and of one mind; live in peace.

THIS *is* the third *time* I am coming to you. In the mouth of two or three [a]witnesses shall every word be established.

2 I told you before, and foretell you, as if I were present, the second time; and being absent now I write to them which heretofore have sinned, and to all other, that, if I come again, I will not spare:

3 Since ye seek a proof of Christ speaking in me, which to you-ward is not weak, but is mighty in you.

4 For though he was [a]crucified through weakness, yet he liveth by the power of God. For we also are weak in him, but we shall live with him by the power of God toward you.

5 [a]Examine yourselves, whether ye be in the faith; prove your own selves. Know ye not your own selves, how that [b]Jesus [c]Christ is in you, except ye be reprobates?

6 But I trust that ye shall know that we are not reprobates.

7 Now I pray to God that ye do no evil; not that we should appear approved, but that ye should do that

---

9*c* 2 Cor. 13:9; Ether 12:27 (26–28).
d D&C 39:12.
10*a* TG Adversity.
b TG Persecution.
c TG Humility.
d Joel 3:10; D&C 50:16.
11*a* 1 Cor. 9:1.
12*a* TG Signs.
13*a* 2 Cor. 11:9 (8–9).
14*a* 1 Cor. 10:33.
19*a* 1 Cor. 14:26. TG Edification.
20*a* TG Strife.
b TG Backbiting.
c TG Rioting and Reveling.
13 1*a* Deut. 19:15; D&C 6:28. TG Book of Mormon; Witness.
4*a* TG Jesus Christ, Crucifixion of.
5*a* 1 Cor. 11:28 (27–31).
b 1 Jn. 3:24 (19–24); 4:12 (7–21).
c Rom. 8:10.

which is [a]honest, though we be as
reprobates.
8 For we can do nothing against
the truth, but for the truth.
9 For we are glad, when we are
[a]weak, and ye are strong: and this
also we wish, *even* your perfection.
10 Therefore I write these things
being absent, lest being present I
should use sharpness, according
to the [a]power which the Lord hath
given me to edification, and not to
destruction.
11 Finally, brethren, farewell. Be
[a]perfect, be of good comfort, be of
[b]one [c]mind, live in [d]peace; and the
God of [e]love and peace shall be
with you.
12 Greet one another with an holy
[a]kiss.
13 All the saints salute you.
14 The grace of the Lord Jesus
Christ, and the love of God, and the
communion of the Holy Ghost, *be*
with you all. Amen.

¶ The second *epistle* to the Corinthians was written from Philippi, *a city* of Macedonia, by Titus and Lucas.

THE EPISTLE OF PAUL THE APOSTLE TO THE GALATIANS

CHAPTER 1

Preachers of false gospels are accursed—Paul received the gospel by revelation—He believed, was taught, and preached to the Gentiles.

PAUL, an [a]apostle, (not of men,
neither by man, but by Jesus
Christ, and God the Father, who
raised him from the dead;)
2 And all the brethren which are
with me, unto the churches of Galatia:
3 Grace *be* to you and peace from
God the Father, and *from* our Lord
Jesus Christ,
4 Who [a]gave himself for our sins,
that he might [b]deliver us from this
present evil world, according to the
[c]will of God and our Father:
5 To whom *be* glory for ever and
ever. Amen.
6 I marvel that ye are so soon [a]re-
moved from him that called you
into the grace of Christ unto another [b]gospel:
7 Which is not another; but there be
some that [a]trouble you, and would
[b]pervert the [c]gospel of Christ.
8 But though we, or an [a]angel from
heaven, preach any [b]other [c]gospel
unto you than that which we have
preached unto you, let him be
[d]accursed.
9 As we said before, so say I now
again, If any *man* preach any other

7*a* TG Honesty.
9*a* 2 Cor. 12:9.
10*a* 2 Cor. 10:8.
11*a* TG Perfection.
b TG Unity.
c 1 Cor. 1:10 (10–13).
d TG Peace.
e TG God, Love of.
12*a* JST 2 Cor. 13:12 . . . *salutation.*

[GALATIANS]
1 1*a* TG Apostles; Priesthood, Authority.
4*a* TG Jesus Christ, Redeemer.
b TG Redemption.
c TG God, Will of.
6*a* TG Apostasy of Individuals; Apostasy of the Early Christian Church.
b 2 Cor. 11:4.
7*a* GR agitate, raise doubts, perplex.
b Gal. 5:10.
c TG Gospel.
8*a* TG Angels.
b 1 Tim. 1:3.
c TG Gospel.
d Gal. 5:12.

[a]gospel unto you than that ye have received, let him be [b]accursed.

10 For do I now [a]persuade men, or God? or do I seek to [b]please men? for if I yet [c]pleased men, I should not be the servant of Christ.

11 But I [a]certify you, brethren, that the gospel which was [b]preached of me is not after man.

12 For I neither received it [a]of man, neither was I taught *it*, but [b]by the [c]revelation of Jesus Christ.

13 For ye have heard of my [a]conversation in time past in the Jews' religion, how that beyond measure I [b]persecuted the church of God, and [c]wasted it:

14 And [a]profited in the Jews' religion above many [b]my equals in mine own nation, being more exceedingly [c]zealous of the [d]traditions of my fathers.

15 But when it pleased God, who separated me from my mother's womb, and called *me* by his [a]grace,

16 To reveal his Son in me, that I might preach him among the [a]heathen; immediately I conferred not with [b]flesh and blood:

17 Neither went I up to Jerusalem to them which were apostles before me; but I went into Arabia, and returned again unto Damascus.

18 Then after three years I went up to [a]Jerusalem to see Peter, and abode with him fifteen days.

19 But other of the [a]apostles saw I none, save [b]James the Lord's [c]brother.

20 Now the things which I [a]write unto you, behold, before God, I lie not.

21 Afterwards I came into the regions of Syria and Cilicia;

22 And was unknown by face unto the churches of Judæa which were in Christ:

23 But they had heard only, That he which persecuted us in times past now preacheth the faith which once he destroyed.

24 And they glorified God in me.

CHAPTER 2

Paul goes to Jerusalem—He contends for the true gospel—Salvation comes through Christ.

THEN fourteen years after I went up again to [a]Jerusalem with [b]Barnabas, and took Titus with *me* also.

2 And I went up by [a]revelation, and [b]communicated unto them that gospel which I preach among the Gentiles, but privately to them which were of reputation, lest by any means I should run, or had run, in vain.

3 But neither Titus, who was with me, being a Greek, was compelled to be [a]circumcised:

4 [a]And that because of false brethren unawares brought in, who came in privily to spy out our [b]liberty which we have in Christ Jesus, that they might bring us into [c]bondage:

5 To whom we gave place by subjection, no, not for an hour; that the truth of the gospel might continue with you.

6 But of these who seemed to be somewhat, (whatsoever they were, it maketh no matter to me: God accepteth no man's person:) for they

---

9*a* TG False Doctrine.
b 2 Ne. 28:15.
10*a* GR appease, aspire to the favor of. JST Gal. 1:10 . . . *please* . . .
b TG Peer Influence.
c TG Courage.
11*a* GR declare, make known to.
b 2 Cor. 4:5.
12*a* GR from a man.
b GR through a revelation.
c 1 Cor. 9:1; D&C 84:1. TG Testimony.
13*a* GR conduct.
b Acts 9:21 (10–22).
c GR was ravaging, destroying.
14*a* GR was advancing.
b GR men of my age.
c TG Zeal.
d TG Traditions of Men.
15*a* TG Grace.
16*a* GR nations, Gentiles. TG Heathen.
b TG Flesh and Blood.
18*a* Acts 9:26.
19*a* TG Apostles.
b Acts 21:18.
c TG Jesus Christ, Family of.
20*a* TG Scriptures, Writing of.
2 1*a* Acts 15:2.
b Acts 4:36 (36–37).
2*a* Alma 8:16; Hel. 13:3.
b GR reported.
3*a* TG Circumcision.
4*a* JST Gal. 2:4 *Notwithstanding, there were some brought in by* false brethren unawares, who . . .
b TG Liberty.
c TG Bondage, Spiritual.

who seemed *to be somewhat* in conference added nothing to me:
7 But contrariwise, when they saw
that the [a]gospel of the uncircumcision was committed unto me, as *the gospel* of the [b]circumcision *was* unto [c]Peter;
8 (For he that wrought effectually
in Peter to the apostleship of the circumcision, the same was mighty in me toward the Gentiles:)
9 And when James, [a]Cephas, and
John, who seemed to be pillars, perceived the [b]grace that was given unto me, they gave to me and Barnabas the right hands of [c]fellowship; that we *should go* unto the [d]heathen, and they unto the circumcision.
10 Only *they would* that we should
remember the poor; the same which I also was forward to do.
11 But when Peter was come to
Antioch, I withstood him to the face, because he was to be blamed.
12 For before that certain came
from James, he did eat with the Gentiles: but when they were come, he withdrew and separated himself, fearing them which were of the circumcision.
13 And the other Jews dissembled
likewise with him; insomuch that Barnabas also was carried away with their [a]dissimulation.
14 But when I saw that they walked
not uprightly according to the truth of the gospel, I said unto Peter before *them* all, If thou, being a Jew, livest after the manner of Gentiles, and not as do the Jews, why compellest thou the Gentiles to live as do the Jews?
15 We *who are* Jews by nature, and
not sinners of the Gentiles,
16 Knowing that a man is not [a]jus-
tified by the works of the [b]law, but by the faith of Jesus Christ, even we have believed in Jesus Christ, that we might be justified by the [c]faith of Christ, and not by the [d]works of the [e]law: for by the works of the law shall no flesh be [f]justified.
17 But if, while we seek to be jus-
tified by Christ, we ourselves also are found sinners, *is* therefore Christ the minister of sin? God forbid.
18 For if I build again the things
which I destroyed, I make myself a transgressor.
19 For I through the law am [a]dead
to the law, that I might [b]live unto God.
20 I am crucified with Christ: nev-
ertheless I live; yet not I, but [a]Christ [b]liveth in me: and the life which I now live in the flesh I live by the [c]faith of the Son of God, who loved me, and gave himself for me.
21 I do not frustrate the [a]grace of
God: for if righteousness *come* by the [b]law, then Christ is dead in vain.

CHAPTER 3

God gave the gospel to Abraham—The Mosaic law was added because of transgressions—The law was a schoolmaster until Christ—The Saints are children of God by faith—All who are of the faith and baptized into Christ become Abraham's seed.

O FOOLISH Galatians, who hath [a]bewitched you, that ye should not obey the truth, before whose eyes Jesus Christ hath been evidently set forth, crucified among you?
2 This only would I learn of you,
Received ye the Spirit by the works of the [a]law, or by the [b]hearing of faith?
3 Are ye so foolish? having begun

7*a* 1 Cor. 9:17.
b TG Circumcision.
c 1 Cor. 9:1.
9*a* John 1:42.
b TG Grace.
c TG Fellowshipping.
d GR nations, Gentiles.
13*a* GR hypocrisy.
16*a* TG Justification.
b D&C 22:2.
c Moro. 7:33 (7–33).
d Mosiah 13:28 (27–32).
e 2 Ne. 2:5 (5–8).
f GR vindicated, approved, guiltless.
19*a* Rom. 7:4 (1–7).
b Rom. 6:11 (9–11).
20*a* John 17:22 (20–23).
b Rom. 14:7 (7–9).
c TG Faith.
21*a* TG Grace.
b Mosiah 13:28 (27–31).
3 1*a* Jacob 7:18 (16–18). TG Apostasy of the Early Christian Church.
2*a* 2 Ne. 2:5; Mosiah 13:28 (27–28).
b Rom. 10:17.

in the Spirit, are ye now made perfect by the flesh?

4 Have ye suffered so many things in vain? if *it be* yet in vain.

5 He therefore that [a]ministereth to you the Spirit, and worketh miracles among you, *doeth he it* by the works of the law, or by the hearing of faith?

6 Even as Abraham believed God, and it was accounted to him for [a]righteousness.

7 Know ye therefore that they which are of faith, the same are the [a]children of Abraham.

8 And the scripture, foreseeing that God would justify the [a]heathen through faith, preached before the [b]gospel unto Abraham, *saying,* In thee shall all [c]nations be [d]blessed.

9 So then they which be of faith are [a]blessed with faithful Abraham.

10 For as many as are of the works of the law are under the curse: for it is written, [a]Cursed *is* every one that continueth not in all things which are written in the book of the law to do them.

11 But that no man is justified by the law in the sight of God, *it is* evident: for, The just shall live by [a]faith.

12 And the law is not of faith: but, The man that doeth them shall live in them.

13 Christ hath [a]redeemed us from the [b]curse of the [c]law, being made a curse for us: for it is written, [d]Cursed *is* every one that hangeth on a tree:

14 That the [a]blessing of Abraham might come on the Gentiles through [b]Jesus Christ; that we might receive the [c]promise of the Spirit through faith.

15 Brethren, I speak after the manner of men; Though *it be* but a man's covenant, yet *if it be* confirmed, no man disannulleth, or addeth thereto.

16 Now to [a]Abraham and his seed were the [b]promises made. He saith not, And to seeds, as of many; but as of one, And to thy seed, which is Christ.

17 And this I say, *that* the covenant, that was confirmed before of God in Christ, the law, which was [a]four hundred and thirty years after, cannot disannul, that it should make the promise of none effect.

18 For if the [a]inheritance *be* of the law, *it is* no more of promise: but God gave *it* to Abraham by promise.

19 [a]Wherefore then *serveth* the law? It was [b]added because of transgressions, till the seed should come to whom the promise was made; *and it was* ordained by angels in the hand of a mediator.

20 Now a mediator is not *a mediator* of one, but God is one.

21 *Is* the law then against the promises of God? God forbid: for if there had been a law given which could have given life, verily righteousness should have been by the law.

22 But the scripture hath concluded all under [a]sin, that the promise by faith of Jesus Christ might be given to them that believe.

23 But before faith came, we were kept under the law, shut up unto the faith which should afterwards be revealed.

24 Wherefore the [a]law was our [b]schoolmaster *to bring us* unto Christ,

---

5*a* GR grants, furnishes.
6*a* TG Righteousness.
7*a* TG Abrahamic Covenant.
8*a* TG Heathen.
b TG Gospel.
c TG Israel, Mission of.
d TG Mission of Latter-day Saints.
9*a* TG Israel, Blessings of.
10*a* TG Curse.
11*a* TG Faith.
13*a* Gal. 4:5.
b TG Bondage, Spiritual; Curse.
c Alma 42:22 (1–28).
d Deut. 21:23.
14*a* TG Blessing; Israel, Mission of.
b Acts 8:35 (29–35).
c TG Promise.
16*a* Ps. 132:11; Luke 1:55 (54–55).
b D&C 107:40.
17*a* TG Israel, Bondage of, in Egypt.
18*a* TG Inheritance.
19*a* JST Gal. 3:19–20 (Appendix).
b 1 Tim. 1:9.
22*a* D&C 49:8.
24*a* TG Law of Moses.
b GR pedagogue, director, supervisor of children. JST Gal. 3:24 . . . schoolmaster *until* Christ . . . TG Jesus Christ, Types of, in Anticipation.

that we might be [c]justified by
faith.
25 But after that faith is come, we
are no longer under a schoolmaster.
26 For ye are all the [a]children of
God by [b]faith in Christ Jesus.
27 For as many of you as have been
[a]baptized into Christ have put on
Christ.
28 There is neither Jew nor [a]Greek,
there is neither bond nor free, there
is neither male nor female: for ye
are all [b]one in Christ Jesus.
29 And if ye *be* Christ's, then are
ye [a]Abraham's [b]seed, and [c]heirs according to the promise.

CHAPTER 4

The Saints are children of God by adoption—Paul calls the Galatians back to Christ—He compares the two covenants.

Now I say, *That* the heir, as long as
he is a child, differeth nothing from
a servant, though he be lord of all;
2 But is under tutors and governors until the time appointed of
the father.
3 Even so we, when we were children, were in [a]bondage under the
elements of the world:
4 But when the fulness of the time
was come, God [a]sent forth his [b]Son,
[c]made of a [d]woman, made under
the law,
5 To [a]redeem them that were under the law, that we might receive
the [b]adoption of sons.
6 And because ye are sons, God
hath sent forth the Spirit of his
Son into your hearts, crying, Abba,
Father.
7 Wherefore thou art no more a
[a]servant, but a [b]son; and if a son,
then an [c]heir of God through Christ.
8 Howbeit then, when ye knew
not God, ye [a]did [b]service unto them
which by nature are no [c]gods.
9 But now, after that ye have known
God, or rather are known of God,
how turn ye again to the weak and
beggarly elements, whereunto ye
desire again to be in [a]bondage?
10 Ye observe [a]days, and months,
and times, and years.
11 I am afraid [a]of you, lest I have
bestowed upon you labour in vain.
12 Brethren, I beseech you, be as
I *am*; for I *am* as ye *are*: ye have not
injured me at all.
13 Ye know how through [a]infirmity
of the [b]flesh I preached the gospel
unto you at the first.
14 And my [a]temptation which was
in my flesh ye despised not, nor rejected; but received me as an angel
of God, *even* as Christ Jesus.
15 Where is then the blessedness
ye spake of? for I bear you record,
that, if *it had been* possible, ye would
have plucked out your own eyes,
and have given them to me.
16 Am I therefore become your enemy, because I tell you the [a]truth?
17 They zealously affect you, *but*
not well; yea, they would exclude
you, that ye might affect them.
18 But *it is* good to be [a]zealously
affected always in *a* good *thing*, and
not only when I am present with
you.

24*c* See JST Rom. 4:16 (Rom. 4:16 note *a*). Moro. 10:32 (32–33).
26*a* TG Sons and Daughters of God.
b TG Baptism, Qualifications for.
27*a* Rom. 13:14; 2 Ne. 31:13 (12–13); Mosiah 5:8 (2–14). TG Baptism.
28*a* TG Gentiles.
b Rom. 10:12 (12–13). TG Unity.
29*a* TG Conversion.
b TG Seed of Abraham.
c Gal. 4:28.
4 3*a* TG Bondage, Spiritual.
4*a* John 8:42; 16:28 (27–28, 30); 17:8. TG Jesus Christ, Condescension of.
b TG Jesus Christ, Birth of.
c GR born.
d TG Woman.
5*a* Gal. 3:13.
b TG Election.
7*a* GR slave.
b TG Sons and Daughters of God.
c TG Eternal Life; Man, Potential to Become like Heavenly Father.
8*a* GR were slaves, were in bondage.
b 1 Cor. 8:4.
c Jer. 44:3.
9*a* D&C 84:51 (50–51).
10*a* Rom. 14:5 (5–6).
11*a* GR concerning.
13*a* GR weakness, feebleness. 1 Cor. 2:3 (2–4).
b 2 Cor. 10:10.
14*a* GR trial, test.
16*a* Hel. 13:26. TG Truth.
18*a* TG Zeal.

19 My little children, of whom I
travail in birth again until Christ
be formed in you,
20 I desire to be present with you
now, and to change my voice; for I
[a]stand in doubt of you.
21 Tell me, ye that desire to be
under the law, do ye not hear
the law?
22 For it is written, that Abraham
had two sons, the one by a [a]bond-
maid, the other by a freewoman.
23 But he *who was* of the bondwoman was born after the flesh; but
he of the freewoman *was* by promise.
24 Which things are an allegory: for
these are the two covenants; the one
from the mount Sinai, which gen-
dereth to [a]bondage, which is [b]Agar.
25 For this Agar is mount Sinai in
Arabia, and answereth to Jerusalem
which now is, and is in bondage
with her children.
26 But [a]Jerusalem which is above is
free, which is the mother of us all.
27 For it is written, [a]Rejoice, *thou*
[b]barren that bearest not; break forth
and cry, thou that travailest not:
for the desolate hath many more
children than she which hath an
husband.
28 Now we, brethren, as Isaac was,
are the [a]children of promise.
29 But as then he that was born
after the [a]flesh [b]persecuted him
that was born after the Spirit, even
so *it is* now.
30 Nevertheless what saith the
scripture? [a]Cast out the bondwoman
and her son: for the son of the bondwoman shall not be heir with the
son of the freewoman.
31 So then, brethren, we are not
children of the bondwoman, but
of the free.

CHAPTER 5

Stand fast in gospel liberty—Seek faith, love, Christ, and the Spirit—The works of the flesh and the fruits of the Spirit are named.

[a]STAND fast therefore in the [b]liberty
wherewith Christ hath made us
[c]free, and be not [d]entangled again
with the yoke of [e]bondage.
2 Behold, I Paul say unto you, that
if ye be circumcised, Christ shall
profit you nothing.
3 For I testify again to every man
that is [a]circumcised, that he is a
debtor to do the whole law.
4 Christ is become of no effect
unto you, whosoever of you are justified by the [a]law; ye are fallen from
[b]grace.
5 For we through the Spirit wait for
the hope of righteousness by [a]faith.
6 For in Jesus Christ neither [a]cir-
cumcision [b]availeth any thing, nor
uncircumcision; but [c]faith which
worketh by [d]love.
7 Ye did run well; who did hinder you that ye should not [a]obey
the truth?
8 This persuasion *cometh* not of
him that calleth you.
9 A little leaven leaveneth the
whole lump.
10 I have [a]confidence in you
through the Lord, that ye [b]will be
none otherwise minded: but he that
[c]troubleth you shall bear his judgment, whosoever he be.

20*a* GR am perplexed about.
22*a* Gen. 16:2 (1–3); D&C 132:30 (30–34), 65; Abr. 2:9 (9–11).
24*a* TG Law of Moses.
b Gen. 16:1.
26*a* TG Jerusalem, New.
27*a* Gen. 21:6.
b TG Barren.
28*a* Gal. 3:29. TG Mission of Early Saints; Seed of Abraham.
29*a* TG Man, Natural, Not Spiritually Reborn.
b Gen. 21:9.
30*a* Gen. 21:10.
5 1*a* Philip. 4:1 (1–7).
b TG Liberty.
c 2 Ne. 2:26 (26–27); Mosiah 5:8; Alma 61:9 (9, 21).
d D&C 88:86.
e TG Bondage, Spiritual; Law of Moses.
3*a* Rom. 2:25.
4*a* TG Law of Moses.
b TG Grace.
5*a* Rom. 5:2 (1–5); 1 Pet. 1:21 (21–22).
6*a* TG Circumcision.
b GR has any power, validity, service.
c TG Faith.
d TG Love.
7*a* TG Disobedience.
10*a* TG Dependability.
b GR will take no other view, will not have a different opinion.
c Gal. 1:7.

11 And I, brethren, if I yet preach circumcision, why do I yet suffer persecution? then is the [a]offence of the cross ceased.
12 I would they were even [a]cut off which [b]trouble you.
13 For, brethren, ye have been called unto [a]liberty; only *use* not liberty for an occasion to the flesh, but by love [b]serve one another.
14 For all the [a]law is fulfilled in one word, *even* in this; Thou shalt [b]love thy neighbour as thyself.
15 But if ye bite and devour one another, take heed that ye be not consumed one of another.
16 *This* I say then, [a]Walk in the [b]Spirit, and ye shall not fulfil the [c]lust of the flesh.
17 For the flesh lusteth against the [a]Spirit, and the Spirit against the flesh: and these are contrary the one to the other: so that ye cannot do the things that ye would.
18 But if ye be [a]led of the Spirit, ye are not under the [b]law.
19 Now the works of the [a]flesh are manifest, which are *these;* Adultery, [b]fornication, [c]uncleanness, lasciviousness,
20 Idolatry, witchcraft, hatred, variance, emulations, wrath, [a]strife, seditions, heresies,
21 [a]Envyings, murders, [b]drunkenness, [c]revellings, and such like: of the which I tell you before, as I have also told *you* in time past, that they which do such things shall not inherit the kingdom of God.
22 But the [a]fruit of the [b]Spirit is [c]love, [d]joy, [e]peace, [f]longsuffering, [g]gentleness, goodness, [h]faith,
23 [a]Meekness, [b]temperance: against such there is no law.
24 And they that are Christ's have crucified the flesh with the [a]affections and lusts.
25 If we live in the Spirit, let us also walk in the Spirit.
26 Let us not be desirous of vain glory, [a]provoking one another, envying one another.

CHAPTER 6

Bear one another's burdens—As you sow, so shall you reap—Be not weary in well-doing.

BRETHREN, if a man be [a]overtaken in a [b]fault, ye which are spiritual, [c]restore such an one in the spirit of meekness; [d]considering thyself, lest thou also be tempted.
2 Bear ye one another's [a]burdens, and so fulfil the law of Christ.
3 For if a man think himself to be something, when he is nothing, he deceiveth himself.
4 But let every man [a]prove his own [b]work, and then shall he have rejoicing in himself alone, and not in another.
5 For every man shall [a]bear his own burden.

11*a* GR stumbling block, cause of misery.
12*a* TG Excommunication.
b Gal. 1:8 (8–9).
13*a* TG Abundant Life; Liberty.
b TG Self-Sacrifice.
14*a* Rom. 13:10 (8–10); 1 Tim. 1:5. TG God, Law of.
b TG Love.
16*a* TG Walking with God.
b TG Guidance, Divine.
c TG Chastity; Lust.
17*a* TG Holy Ghost, Loss of.
18*a* D&C 20:45; 28:4; 42:13.
b Acts 15:5 (1–11); Mosiah 13:29 (29–31).
19*a* Mosiah 16:3 (3–5); D&C 67:12 (10–12).
b TG Fornication.
c TG Uncleanness.
20*a* TG Strife.
21*a* TG Envy.
b TG Drunkenness; Word of Wisdom.
c TG Rioting and Reveling.
22*a* Rom. 8:23. TG Holy Ghost, Mission of.
b TG Inspiration; Spirituality.
c Col. 3:12.
d TG Joy.
e TG Contentment; Peace of God.
f TG Forbear.
g TG Benevolence; Kindness.
h TG Faith.
23*a* TG Meek.
b GR self-control. TG Temperance.
24*a* GR sufferings, afflictions, passions.
26*a* TG Provoking.
6 1*a* Rom. 14:1; D&C 20:80.
b GR transgression, trespass.
c Heb. 12:13.
d GR watching.
2*a* TG Compassion.
4*a* TG Test.
b TG Good Works.
5*a* Prov. 9:12.

6 Let him that is taught in the
word [a]communicate unto him that
teacheth in all good things.
7 Be not [a]deceived; God is not
[b]mocked: for whatsoever a man
[c]soweth, that shall he also [d]reap.
8 For he that soweth to his flesh
shall of the flesh reap corruption;
but he that soweth to the Spirit
shall of the Spirit reap life everlasting.
9 And let us not be [a]weary in well
doing: for in due season we shall
[b]reap, if we faint not.
10 As we have therefore opportunity, let us do [a]good unto all *men*,
especially unto them who are of the
household of faith.
11 Ye see how large a letter I have
written unto you with mine own
hand.
12 As many as desire to make a
fair shew in the flesh, they con-
strain you to be circumcised; only
lest they should suffer [a]persecution
for the cross of Christ.
13 For neither they themselves
who are circumcised keep the law;
but desire to have you circumcised,
that they may glory in your flesh.
14 But God forbid that I should
glory, save in the cross of our Lord
Jesus Christ, by whom the world is
crucified unto me, and I unto the
world.
15 For in Christ Jesus neither [a]cir-
cumcision availeth any thing, nor
uncircumcision, but a new creature.
16 And as many as walk according
to this rule, [a]peace *be* on them, and
mercy, and upon the Israel of God.
17 From henceforth let no man
trouble me: for I bear in my body
the marks of the Lord Jesus.
18 Brethren, the grace of our Lord
Jesus Christ *be* with your spirit.
Amen.

¶ Unto the Galatians written from Rome.

THE EPISTLE OF PAUL THE APOSTLE
TO THE
EPHESIANS

CHAPTER 1

The Saints are foreordained to receive the gospel—The gospel is to be restored in the latter days—The Saints are sealed by the Holy Spirit of Promise—They know God and Christ by revelation.

PAUL, an apostle of Jesus Christ
by the will of God, to the [a]saints
which are at Ephesus, and to
the faithful in Christ Jesus:
2 Grace *be* to you, and peace, from
God our Father, and *from* the Lord
Jesus Christ.
3 Blessed *be* the God and Father
of our Lord Jesus Christ, who hath
blessed us with all [a]spiritual blessings in heavenly *places* in Christ:
4 According as he hath [a]chosen us
in him [b]before the foundation of the
world, that we should be [c]holy and
without blame before him in love:

6*a* TG Communication.
7*a* TG Deceit.
b TG Mocking.
c Ezek. 32:27. TG Accountability; Agency; Good Works.
d Ps. 7:16. TG Harvest.
9*a* Luke 8:14 (14–15); 2 Thes. 3:13; D&C 64:33. TG Steadfastness.
b TG Abundant Life.
10*a* Prov. 3:27.
12*a* TG Persecution.
15*a* TG Circumcision.
16*a* Ps. 125:5.

[EPHESIANS]

1 1*a* TG Saints.
3*a* TG Spirituality.
4*a* TG Election; Foreordination.
b TG Man, Antemortal Existence of.
c TG Holiness.

5 Having [a]predestinated us unto
the [b]adoption of children by Jesus
Christ to himself, according to the
good pleasure of his will,
6 To the praise of the glory of his
grace, wherein he hath made us
accepted in the beloved.
7 In whom we have [a]redemption
through his blood, the [b]forgiveness
of sins, according to the [c]riches of
his [d]grace;
8 Wherein he hath abounded toward us in all [a]wisdom and [b]pru-
dence;
9 Having made known unto us the
[a]mystery of his [b]will, according to
his good pleasure which he hath
purposed in himself:
10 That in the [a]dispensation of the
fulness of times he might [b]gather
together in one [c]all things in Christ,
both which are in heaven, and which
are on earth; *even* in him:
11 In whom also we have obtained
an inheritance, being [a]predestinated
according to the purpose of him who
worketh all things after the counsel
of his own will:
12 That we should be to the praise
of his glory, who [a]first trusted in
Christ.
13 In whom ye also *trusted,* after
that ye heard the word of truth,
the [a]gospel of your salvation: in
whom also after that ye believed, ye
were [b]sealed with that holy Spirit
of [c]promise,
14 Which is the earnest of our inheritance until the redemption of
the purchased possession, unto the
praise of his glory.
15 Wherefore I also, after I heard
of your [a]faith in the Lord Jesus, and
love unto all the saints,
16 Cease not to give thanks for
you, making mention of you in my
prayers;
17 That the God of our Lord Jesus
Christ, the Father of glory, may
give unto you the spirit of [a]wisdom
and [b]revelation in the knowledge
of him:
18 The eyes of your [a]understand-
ing being [b]enlightened; that ye may
know what is the hope of his calling,
and what the [c]riches of the glory of
his [d]inheritance in the saints,
19 And what *is* the exceeding great-
ness of his [a]power to us-ward who
believe, according to the working
of his mighty power,
20 Which he wrought in Christ,
when he [a]raised him from the dead,
and set *him* at his own right hand
in the [b]heavenly *places,*
21 Far above all principality, and
power, and might, and dominion,
and every [a]name that is named, not
only in this world, but also in that
which is to come:
22 And hath put [a]all *things* under
his [b]feet, and gave him *to be* the
[c]head over all *things* to the [d]church,
23 Which is his body, the fulness
of him that filleth all in all.

CHAPTER 2

We are saved by grace through faith—The blood of Christ saves Jew and Gentile alike—The Church is built upon the foundation of apostles and prophets.

5*a* GR foreordained. Eph. 1:11. TG Foreordination.
b TG Sons and Daughters of God.
7*a* TG Jesus Christ, Atonement through; Jesus Christ, Redeemer; Redemption.
b TG Forgive.
c TG Treasure.
d TG Grace.
8*a* TG God, Omniscience of.
b TG Prudence.
9*a* Eph. 3:4; D&C 107:19.
b TG God, Will of.
10*a* TG Dispensations; Last Days; Restoration of the Gospel.
b TG Israel, Gathering of.
c TG Jesus Christ, Power of.
11*a* Eph. 1:5.
12*a* GR trusted, hoped beforehand.
13*a* D&C 93:51. TG Gospel.
b TG Sealing.
c TG Promise.
15*a* Col. 1:4 (4–5).
17*a* TG Wisdom.
b TG Revelation.
18*a* TG Understanding.
b D&C 6:15; 11:13. TG Education.
c TG Treasure.
d TG Inheritance.
19*a* Col. 2:12.
20*a* Acts 2:32; 1 Cor. 15:20 (14–20).
b Heb. 7:26.
21*a* Heb. 1:4. TG Name.
22*a* TG Jesus Christ, Power of.
b Heb. 2:8.
c TG Jesus Christ, Head of the Church; Jesus Christ, Messiah.
d TG Church.

AND you *hath he quickened*, who were
[a]dead in trespasses and sins;
2 Wherein in time past ye walked
according to the course of this
[a]world, according to the prince of
the power of the air, the spirit that
now worketh in the children of
[b]disobedience:
3 Among whom also we all had
our conversation in times past in
the [a]lusts of our flesh, fulfilling the
desires of the flesh and of the mind;
and were by [b]nature the children
of wrath, even as others.
4 But God, who is rich in [a]mercy,
for his great love wherewith he
loved us,
5 Even when we were dead in sins,
hath [a]quickened us together with
Christ, (by grace ye are saved;)
6 And hath raised *us* up together,
and made *us* sit together in heavenly *places* in Christ Jesus:
7 That in the ages to come he
might shew the exceeding [a]riches
of his grace in *his* kindness toward
us through Christ Jesus.
8 For by [a]grace are ye [b]saved
through [c]faith; and that not of yourselves: *it is* the [d]gift of God:
9 Not of works, lest any man should
[a]boast.
10 For we are his [a]workmanship,
created in Christ Jesus unto good
[b]works, which God hath before ordained that we should [c]walk in them.
11 Wherefore remember, that ye *be-*
ing in time past Gentiles in the flesh,
who are called [a]Uncircumcision by
that which is called the Circumcision
in the flesh made by hands;
12 That at that time ye were
without Christ, being aliens from
the commonwealth of Israel, and
[a]strangers from the [b]covenants of
promise, having no [c]hope, and [d]with-
out God in the world:
13 But now in Christ Jesus ye who
sometimes were far off are made
nigh by the blood of Christ.
14 For he is our [a]peace, who hath
made both one, and hath broken
down the middle [b]wall of partition
between us;
15 Having [a]abolished in his flesh
the enmity, *even* the law of commandments *contained* in [b]ordinances;
for to make in himself of twain one
[c]new man, *so* making peace;
16 And that he might [a]reconcile
both unto God in one body by
the cross, having slain the enmity
thereby:
17 And came and preached peace
to you which were afar off, and to
them that were nigh.
18 For through him we both have
access by one Spirit unto the Father.
19 Now therefore ye are no more
[a]strangers and foreigners, but [b]fel-
lowcitizens with the [c]saints, and of
the [d]household of God;
20 And are built upon the foundation of the [a]apostles and [b]prophets,
Jesus Christ himself being the chief
[c]corner *stone;*
21 In whom all the building fitly
framed together groweth unto an
holy temple in the Lord:
22 In whom ye also are builded
together for an habitation of God
through the Spirit.

---

2 1*a* Col. 1:21; Rev. 3:1.
2*a* TG Worldliness.
b D&C 121:17. TG Disobedience.
3*a* TG Lust.
b TG Man, Natural, Not Spiritually Reborn.
4*a* TG God, Mercy of.
5*a* TG Resurrection.
7*a* TG Treasure.
8*a* Alma 22:14 (13–14); 42:14 (10–25); D&C 20:30 (29–34). TG Grace.
b TG Salvation; Salvation, Plan of.
c TG Faith.
d TG God, Gifts of.
9*a* TG Boast.
10*a* Ps. 100:3; Isa. 60:21; D&C 29:25.
b TG Good Works.
c TG Walking with God.
11*a* TG Circumcision.
12*a* TG Stranger.
b TG Covenants.
c 1 Thes. 4:13.
d 1 Thes. 4:5; Mosiah 27:31; Alma 41:11.
14*a* TG Peace; Peace of God.
b TG Veil.
15*a* Col. 2:14.
b TG Ordinance.
c TG Man, New, Spiritually Reborn.
16*a* TG Jesus Christ, Atonement through.
19*a* TG Gentiles; Stranger.
b TG Citizenship; Fellowshipping.
c TG Saints.
d TG Sons and Daughters of God.
20*a* TG Apostles; Church Organization.
b TG Prophets, Mission of.
c TG Cornerstone.

CHAPTER 3

The Gentiles are fellow heirs with Israel—The love of Christ surpasses all understanding.

FOR this cause I Paul, the prisoner
of Jesus Christ for you Gentiles,
2 If ye have heard of the [a]dispen-
sation of the grace of God which is
given me to you-ward:
3 How that by revelation he made
[a]known unto me the mystery; (as I
[b]wrote afore in few words,
4 Whereby, when ye read, ye may
understand my knowledge in the
[a]mystery of Christ)
5 Which in other ages was not
made known unto the sons of men,
as it is now [a]revealed unto his holy
apostles and [b]prophets by the Spirit;
6 That the [a]Gentiles should be fel-
lowheirs, and of the same body, and
partakers of his promise in Christ
by the gospel:
7 Whereof I was made a minister,
according to the gift of the grace of
God given unto me by the effectual
working of his power.
8 Unto me, who am less than the
least of all saints, is this [a]grace given,
that I should preach among the
Gentiles the unsearchable [b]riches
of Christ;
9 And to make all *men* see what
is the fellowship of the [a]mystery,
which from the beginning of the
world hath been hid in God, who
[b]created all things by [c]Jesus Christ:
10 To the intent that now unto the
principalities and powers in heavenly *places* might be known by the
church the manifold wisdom of God,
11 According to the eternal [a]pur-
pose which he purposed in Christ
Jesus our Lord:
12 In whom we have boldness and
access with confidence by the faith
of him.
13 Wherefore I desire that ye faint
not at my tribulations for you, which
is your glory.
14 For this cause I bow my knees
unto the [a]Father of our Lord Jesus
Christ,
15 Of whom the whole [a]family in
heaven and earth is named,
16 That he would grant you, according to the [a]riches of his glory,
to be [b]strengthened with might by
his Spirit in the inner man;
17 That Christ may dwell in your
hearts by faith; that ye, being [a]rooted
and [b]grounded in love,
18 May be able to comprehend
with all saints what *is* the breadth,
and length, and depth, and height;
19 And to know the [a]love of Christ,
which passeth knowledge, that ye
might be filled with all the fulness
of God.
20 Now unto him that is able to
do exceeding abundantly above all
that we ask or think, according to
the power that worketh in us,
21 Unto him *be* glory in the church
by Christ Jesus throughout all ages,
[a]world without end. Amen.

CHAPTER 4

There is one Lord, one faith, and one baptism—Apostles and prophets are essential to the Church—The Saints are exhorted to live righteously—They are sealed unto the day of redemption.

I THEREFORE, the prisoner of the
Lord, beseech you that ye walk
[a]worthy of the [b]vocation wherewith
ye are called,
2 With all lowliness and meekness,
with longsuffering, [a]forbearing one
another in love;

3 2*a* TG Dispensations.
3*a* Col. 1:27 (26–27).
b TG Scriptures, Lost.
4*a* Rom. 16:25; Eph. 1:9 (9–11).
5*a* TG Revelation.
b TG Prophets, Mission of.
6*a* TG Gentiles.
8*a* TG Grace.
b TG Treasure.
9*a* TG Mysteries of Godliness.
b TG Creation; God, Creator; Jesus Christ, Creator.
c TG Jesus Christ, Jehovah.
11*a* TG Earth, Purpose of.
14*a* TG Godhead.
15*a* TG Family.
16*a* TG Treasure.
b Col. 1:11. TG Strength.
17*a* Col. 2:7.
b Col. 1:23.
19*a* TG God, Love of.
21*a* D&C 76:112.
4 1*a* TG Worthiness.
b GR calling.
2*a* TG Forbear.

3 Endeavouring to keep the [a]unity
of the Spirit in the bond of peace.
4 *There is* one [a]body, and one Spirit,
even as ye are called in one hope of
your calling;
5 One Lord, one [a]faith, one [b]bap-
tism,
6 One God and [a]Father of all, who
is above all, and through all, and
in you all.
7 But unto every one of us is given
[a]grace according to the measure of
the gift of Christ.
8 Wherefore he saith, When he
[a]ascended up on high, he led captivity captive, and gave gifts unto
men.
9 (Now that he ascended, what is
it but that he also descended first
into the lower parts of the earth?
10 He that descended is the same
also that [a]ascended up far above
all heavens, that he might fill all
things.)
11 And he [a]gave some, [b]apostles;
and some, [c]prophets; and some,
[d]evangelists; and some, [e]pastors and
[f]teachers;
12 For the [a]perfecting of the saints,
for the work of the ministry, for
the [b]edifying of the body of Christ:
13 Till we all come in the [a]unity
of the faith, and of the [b]knowledge
of the Son of God, unto a [c]perfect
man, unto the measure of the stature of the fulness of Christ:
14 That we *henceforth* be no more
[a]children, tossed to and fro, and
carried about with every wind of
[b]doctrine, by the sleight of men,
and cunning craftiness, whereby
they lie in wait to deceive;
15 But speaking the [a]truth in love,
may grow up into him in all things,
which is the [b]head, *even* Christ:
16 From whom the whole body fitly
joined together and compacted by
that which every joint supplieth,
according to the effectual working
in the measure of every part, maketh increase of the body unto the
edifying of itself in love.
17 This I say therefore, and testify
in the Lord, that ye henceforth walk
not as other [a]Gentiles walk, in the
[b]vanity of their [c]mind,
18 Having the [a]understanding
darkened, being alienated from
the life of God through the [b]igno-
rance that is in them, because of the
[c]blindness of their [d]heart:
19 Who being [a]past [b]feeling have
given themselves over unto lasciviousness, to work all uncleanness
with greediness.
20 But ye have not so learned
Christ;
21 If so be that ye have heard him,
and have been taught by him, as the
truth is in Jesus:
22 That ye [a]put off concerning the
former conversation the [b]old man,
which is corrupt according to the
deceitful [c]lusts;
23 And be renewed in the spirit
of your mind;

3*a* TG Unity.
4*a* TG Church.
5*a* 1 Cor. 14:33; Eph. 4:13; D&C 1:30. TG Gospel.
b TG Baptism, Essential; Baptism, Immersion.
6*a* Mal. 2:10; 1 Cor. 8:6. TG God the Father, Elohim.
7*a* TG Grace.
8*a* Ps. 68:18; Acts 1:9; D&C 88:6.
10*a* TG Jesus Christ, Ascension of.
11*a* TG Authority.
b TG Apostles; Church Organization; Priesthood, History of.
c TG Prophets, Mission of.
d Acts 21:8; 2 Tim. 4:5. TG Patriarch.
e TG Bishop.
f TG Teacher.
12*a* TG Priesthood, Magnifying Callings within.
b TG Edification.
13*a* 1 Cor. 1:10; 14:33; Eph. 4:5 (3–6); 3 Ne. 11:28 (28–30); D&C 1:30; 38:27.
b TG Learn.
c TG God, Perfection of; Man, Potential to Become like Heavenly Father; Perfection.
14*a* 1 Cor. 14:20.
b Heb. 13:9.
15*a* TG Reproof.
b Col. 2:19. TG Jesus Christ, Head of the Church.
17*a* 1 Thes. 4:5.
b TG Vanity.
c TG Mind.
18*a* D&C 10:2. TG Understanding.
b TG Ignorance.
c GR hardness. TG Spiritual Blindness.
d TG Hardheartedness.
19*a* 1 Ne. 17:45.
b TG Conscience.
22*a* Col. 3:8.
b Rom. 6:6 (1–7).
c TG Lust.

24 And that ye put on the [a]new
man, which after God is created in
[b]righteousness and true holiness.
25 Wherefore putting away [a]lying,
speak every man [b]truth with
his neighbour: for we are members
one of another.
26 [a]Be ye angry, and sin not: let not
the sun go down upon your [b]wrath:
27 Neither give place to the [a]devil.
28 Let him that stole [a]steal no more:
but rather let him [b]labour, working
with *his* hands the thing which is
good, that he may have to [c]give to
him that needeth.
29 Let no corrupt [a]communication
proceed out of your mouth, but that
which is good to the use of edifying,
that it may minister grace unto
the hearers.
30 And [a]grieve not the holy [b]Spirit
of God, whereby ye are [c]sealed unto
the day of redemption.
31 Let all bitterness, and wrath,
and [a]anger, and clamour, and [b]evil
[c]speaking, be put away from you,
with all [d]malice:
32 And be ye [a]kind one to another,
tenderhearted, [b]forgiving one another,
even as God for Christ's sake
hath forgiven you.

CHAPTER 5

The Saints are exhorted to avoid uncleanness and walk uprightly—Husbands and wives should love each other.

BE ye therefore [a]followers of God,
as dear children;
2 And [a]walk in love, as Christ also
hath loved us, and hath given himself
for us an [b]offering and a [c]sacrifice
to God for a sweetsmelling
[d]savour.
3 But [a]fornication, and all uncleanness,
or covetousness, let it
not be once named among you, as
becometh [b]saints;
4 Neither [a]filthiness, nor [b]foolish
[c]talking, nor jesting, which are not
convenient: but rather giving of
thanks.
5 For this ye know, that no [a]whoremonger,
nor [b]unclean person, nor
covetous man, who is an idolater,
hath any [c]inheritance in the kingdom
of Christ and of God.
6 Let no man [a]deceive you with
vain words: for because of these
things cometh the [b]wrath of God
upon the children of [c]disobedience.
7 Be not ye therefore partakers
with them.
8 For ye were sometimes darkness,
but now *are ye* light in the Lord:
walk as [a]children of [b]light:
9 (For the fruit of the Spirit *is* in
all [a]goodness and righteousness
and truth;)
10 Proving what is acceptable unto
the Lord.
11 And have no [a]fellowship with
the unfruitful works of [b]darkness,
but rather [c]reprove *them*.

24*a* TG Man, New, Spiritually Reborn; Mission of Early Saints.
b TG Righteousness.
25*a* TG Lying.
b TG Honesty; Truth.
26*a* JST Eph. 4:26 *Can ye be* angry, and *not sin?* . . .
b TG Anger.
27*a* Mosiah 2:32 (32–33); 3 Ne. 11:29.
28*a* TG Stealing.
b TG Labor; Work, Value of.
c Prov. 21:26.
29*a* TG Communication; Gossip; Profanity.
30*a* Gen. 6:6.
b TG God, Spirit of.
c TG Sealing.
31*a* TG Anger.
b TG Backbiting.
c TG Slander.
d TG Malice.
32*a* TG Benevolence; Courtesy; Family, Love within; Kindness.
b TG Forgive.
5 1*a* GR imitators. 1 Cor. 11:1; Philip. 3:17 (13–21). TG God, the Standard of Righteousness; Jesus Christ, Exemplar.
2*a* TG Walking with God.
b Heb. 8:3.
c TG Self-Sacrifice.
d Gen. 8:21; Lev. 1:9.
3*a* TG Chastity; Fornication; Sexual Immorality.
b TG Saints.
4*a* TG Filthiness.
b TG Levity.
c Eccl. 5:2; Matt. 12:36.
5*a* TG Chastity; Whore.
b TG Uncleanness.
c TG Inheritance; Worthiness.
6*a* TG Deceit.
b TG God, Indignation of.
c TG Disobedience.
8*a* TG Children of Light.
b Rom. 12:2.
9*a* TG Good Works.
11*a* Gen. 49:6; Ps. 1:1 (1–2); Prov. 1:10 (10–19).
b TG Darkness, Spiritual.
c TG Reproof.

12 For it is a [a]shame even to speak
of those things which are done of
them in secret.
13 But all things that are reproved
are made manifest by the light: for
whatsoever doth make manifest is
light.
14 Wherefore he saith, Awake
thou that sleepest, and arise from
the dead, and Christ shall give thee
[a]light.
15 See then that ye walk circum-
spectly, not as fools, but as wise,
16 Redeeming the time, because
the days are evil.
17 Wherefore be ye not [a]unwise,
but understanding what the will of
the Lord *is*.
18 And be not [a]drunk with wine,
wherein is [b]excess; but be filled
with the Spirit;
19 Speaking to yourselves in psalms
and [a]hymns and spiritual songs,
singing and making [b]melody in your
heart to the Lord;
20 Giving [a]thanks always for all
things unto God and the Father in
the name of our Lord Jesus Christ;
21 [a]Submitting yourselves one to
another in the fear of God.
22 [a]Wives, [b]submit yourselves unto
your own husbands, as unto the Lord.
23 For the [a]husband is the head of
the wife, even as Christ is the [b]head
of the [c]church: and he is the saviour
of the body.
24 Therefore as the church is subject unto Christ, so *let* the wives *be* to
their own husbands in every thing.
25 [a]Husbands, [b]love your [c]wives,
even as Christ also loved the church,
and gave himself for it;
26 That he might [a]sanctify and
[b]cleanse it with the washing of water by the word,
27 That he might present it to himself a glorious church, not having
spot, or wrinkle, or any such thing;
but that it should be holy and without blemish.
28 So ought men to love their wives
as their own bodies. He that loveth
his [a]wife loveth himself.
29 For no man ever yet [a]hated
his own [b]flesh; but nourisheth and
cherisheth it, even as the Lord the
church:
30 For we are [a]members of his
body, of his flesh, and of his bones.
31 For this cause shall a man leave
his father and mother, and shall be
joined unto his wife, and they two
shall be [a]one flesh.
32 This is a great [a]mystery: but I
speak concerning Christ and the
church.
33 Nevertheless let every one of
you in particular so love his wife
even as himself; and the [a]wife *see*
that she [b]reverence *her* husband.

CHAPTER 6

Children should honor their parents—Servants and masters are judged by the same law—Saints should put on the whole armor of God.

[a]CHILDREN, [b]obey your parents in
the Lord: for this is right.
2 [a]Honour thy father and mother;
(which is the first commandment
with promise;)
3 That it may be well with thee, and
thou mayest live long on the earth.

12*a* TG Shame.
14*a* TG Jesus Christ, Light of the World; Light [noun].
17*a* TG Wisdom.
18*a* TG Drunkenness; Word of Wisdom.
b TG Temperance.
19*a* TG Singing.
b 2 Kgs. 3:15.
20*a* TG Thanksgiving.
21*a* TG Reconciliation.
22*a* TG Marriage, Continuing Courtship in.
b Esth. 1:20 (20–22). TG Submissiveness.
23*a* TG Marriage, Husbands.
b TG Jesus Christ, Head of the Church.
c TG Church.
25*a* TG Family, Patriarchal.
b TG Family, Love within; Love.
c TG Marriage, Continuing Courtship in.
26*a* TG Sanctification.
b TG Purification.
28*a* TG Marriage, Wives.
29*a* TG Hate.
b TG Body, Sanctity of.
30*a* 1 Cor. 6:15.
31*a* TG Marriage, Celestial; Unity.
32*a* TG Mysteries of Godliness.
33*a* TG Marriage, Wives.
b TG Courtesy; Respect.
6 1*a* TG Children.
b TG Counsel; Family, Children, Duties of; Respect.
2*a* TG Honoring Father and Mother.

4 And, ye [a]fathers, [b]provoke not
your [c]children to wrath: but bring
them up in the nurture and admonition of the Lord.
5 [a]Servants, be obedient to them
that are *your* [b]masters according to
the flesh, with fear and trembling,
in singleness of your heart, as unto
Christ;
6 Not with eyeservice, as menpleasers; but as the [a]servants of
Christ, doing the [b]will of God from
the heart;
7 With good will doing [a]service, as
to the Lord, and not to men:
8 Knowing that whatsoever good
thing any man doeth, the same shall
he [a]receive of the Lord, whether *he*
be bond or free.
9 And, ye [a]masters, do the same
things unto them, forbearing threat-
ening: knowing that your [b]Master
also is in heaven; neither is there
[c]respect of persons with him.
10 Finally, my brethren, be [a]strong
in the Lord, and in the power of
his might.
11 Put on the whole [a]armour of
God, that ye may be able to stand
against the wiles of the devil.
12 For we [a]wrestle not [b]against
[c]flesh and blood, but against principalities, against powers, against
the [d]rulers of the [e]darkness of this
world, against spiritual [f]wickedness
in high *places*.
13 Wherefore take unto you the
whole armour of God, that ye may
be able to withstand in the evil day,
and having done all, to stand.
14 Stand therefore, having your
loins [a]girt about with [b]truth, and
having on the [c]breastplate of [d]righ-
teousness;
15 And your feet shod with the
preparation of the gospel of [a]peace;
16 Above all, taking the shield of
[a]faith, wherewith ye shall be able
to quench all the fiery [b]darts of the
wicked.
17 And take the helmet of [a]salva-
tion, and the sword of the Spirit,
which is the word of God:
18 [a]Praying always with all prayer
and supplication in the Spirit, and
watching thereunto with all [b]per-
severance and supplication for all
saints;
19 And for me, that utterance may
be given unto me, that I may open
my mouth boldly, to make known
the [a]mystery of the gospel,
20 For which I am an ambassador
in bonds: that therein I may speak
[a]boldly, as I ought to speak.
21 But that ye also may know my
affairs, *and* how I do, [a]Tychicus, a
beloved brother and faithful minister in the Lord, shall make known
to you all things:
22 Whom I have sent unto you for
the same purpose, that ye might
know our affairs, and *that* he might
comfort your hearts.
23 Peace *be* to the brethren, and
love with faith, from God the Father
and the Lord Jesus Christ.
24 Grace *be* with all them that love
our Lord Jesus Christ in [a]sincerity.
Amen.

¶ Written from Rome unto the Ephesians by Tychicus.

4*a* TG Family, Love within; Family, Patriarchal; Marriage, Fatherhood.
b TG Provoking.
c TG Family, Children, Responsibilities toward.
5*a* Titus 2:9.
b 1 Pet. 2:18 (13–25).
6*a* 1 Cor. 7:22 (21–24).
b TG God, Will of.
7*a* TG Service.
8*a* Col. 3:24.
9*a* Mal. 3:5; Col. 4:1.
b TG Leadership.
c Moro. 8:12; D&C 38:16.
10*a* TG Strength.
11*a* Ps. 91:4; Rom. 13:12; 2 Cor. 10:4 (3–6); 1 Thes. 5:8; D&C 27:15 (15–18). TG Chastity; Protection, Divine; Watch.
12*a* JS—H 1:15 (15–17).
b TG Opposition.
c TG Flesh and Blood.
d 2 Cor. 4:4.
e TG Darkness, Spiritual; Secret Combinations.
f TG Governments; Wickedness.
14*a* Isa. 11:5.
b TG Truth.
c Isa. 59:17; 61:10.
d TG Righteousness.
15*a* TG Peace of God.
16*a* TG Faith.
b 1 Ne. 15:24; D&C 3:8.
17*a* TG Salvation.
18*a* TG Prayer.
b TG Perseverance.
19*a* TG Mysteries of Godliness.
20*a* D&C 60:2 (2–3).
21*a* Acts 20:4.
24*a* TG Sincere.

THE EPISTLE OF PAUL THE APOSTLE

TO THE

PHILIPPIANS

CHAPTER 1

All that happened to Paul furthered the gospel cause—Our conduct should be worthy of the gospel.

PAUL and Timotheus, the [a]ser-
vants of Jesus Christ, to all the
saints in Christ Jesus which are
at Philippi, with the [b]bishops and
[c]deacons:
2 Grace *be* unto you, and peace,
from God our Father, and *from* the
Lord Jesus Christ.
3 I thank my God upon every remembrance of you,
4 Always in every prayer of mine
for you all making request with joy,
5 For your fellowship in the gospel
from the first day until now;
6 Being confident of this very
thing, that he which hath begun a
good work in you will [a]perform *it*
until the day of Jesus Christ:
7 Even as it is [a]meet for me to think
this of you all, because I have you
in my heart; inasmuch as both in
my bonds, and in the defence and
[b]confirmation of the gospel, ye all
are partakers of my [c]grace.
8 For God is my [a]record, how
greatly I long after you all in the
[b]bowels of Jesus Christ.
9 And this I pray, that your [a]love
may abound yet more and more
in knowledge and *in* all judgment;
10 That ye may [a]approve things
that are excellent; that ye may be
[b]sincere and without offence till
the day of Christ;
11 Being filled with the fruits of
[a]righteousness, which are by Jesus
Christ, unto the glory and praise
of God.
12 But I would ye should understand, brethren, that the things
which happened unto me have [a]fallen
out rather unto the furtherance of
the gospel;
13 So that my bonds in Christ are
manifest in all the [a]palace, and in
all other *places;*
14 And many of the brethren in
the Lord, waxing confident by my
bonds, are much more bold to speak
the word without [a]fear.
15 Some indeed preach Christ even
of envy and [a]strife; and some also
of good will:
16 The one preach Christ of contention, not sincerely, supposing to
add affliction to my bonds:
17 But the other of love, knowing
that I am set for the defence of the
gospel.
18 What then? notwithstanding,
every way, whether in pretence, or
in truth, Christ is preached; and
I therein do rejoice, yea, and will
rejoice.
19 For I know that this shall turn to
my salvation through your [a]prayer,
and the supply of the [b]Spirit of
Jesus Christ,
20 According to my earnest

---

1 1*a* TG Servant.
b TG Bishop; Church Organization.
c TG Deacon.
6*a* GR complete, accomplish.
7*a* GR just, right.
b GR establishment, strengthening.
c TG Grace.
8*a* GR witness.
b GR affections, compassions.
9*a* Moses 7:18.
10*a* GR prove, put to the test.
b GR pure, spotless.
11*a* TG Righteousness.
12*a* GR come.
13*a* Philip. 4:22.
14*a* Luke 1:74 (68–75); 1 Jn. 4:18 (15–18); D&C 68:6 (5–6).
15*a* TG Strife.
19*a* 2 Cor. 1:11; Philem. 1:22.
b TG God, Spirit of.

expectation and *my* [a]hope, that in
nothing I shall be ashamed, but *that*
with all boldness, as always, *so* now
also Christ shall be [b]magnified in
my body, whether *it be* by life, or
by death.
21 For to me to live *is* Christ, and
to die *is* gain.
22 But if I live in the flesh, this *is*
the fruit of my labour: yet what I
shall choose I [a]wot not.
23 For I am [a]in a strait betwixt two,
having a desire to depart, and to
be with Christ; which is far better:
24 Nevertheless to [a]abide in the
flesh *is* more needful for you.
25 And having this confidence, I
know that I shall abide and continue
with you all for your furtherance
and joy of faith;
26 That your rejoicing may be more
abundant in Jesus Christ for me by
my coming to you again.
27 Only let your conversation be
as it becometh the gospel of Christ:
that whether I come and see you, or
else be absent, I may hear of your
affairs, that ye [a]stand fast in one
spirit, with [b]one [c]mind [d]striving
together for the faith of the gospel;
28 And in nothing terrified by your
adversaries: [a]which is to them an
evident token of perdition, but to
you of salvation, and that of God.
29 For unto you it is given in the behalf of Christ, not only to believe on
him, but also to [a]suffer for his sake;
30 Having the same conflict which
ye saw in me, and now hear *to be*
in me.

CHAPTER 2

Saints should be of one mind and one spirit—Every knee will bow to Christ—Saints must work out their salvation—Paul faces martyrdom with joy.

IF *there be* therefore any consolation
in Christ, if any comfort of love, if
any fellowship of the Spirit, if any
[a]bowels and mercies,
2 Fulfil ye my joy, that ye be likeminded, having the same [a]love, *being*
of [b]one [c]accord, of one mind.
3 *Let* nothing *be done* through [a]strife
or vainglory; but in lowliness of
mind let each [b]esteem other better
than themselves.
4 Look not every man on his own
things, but every man also on the
things of others.
5 Let this mind be in you, which
was also in Christ Jesus:
6 Who, being in the [a]form of God,
thought it not robbery to be [b]equal
with God:
7 But made himself of no reputation, and took upon him the form
of a [a]servant, and was made in the
likeness of men:
8 And being found in [a]fashion as
a man, he [b]humbled himself, and
became [c]obedient unto [d]death, even
the [e]death of the cross.
9 Wherefore God also hath highly
[a]exalted him, and given him a [b]name
which is above every name:
10 That at the [a]name of Jesus every [b]knee should bow, of *things* in
heaven, and *things* in earth, and
things under the earth;

20*a* Ps. 119:116.
b Ps. 34:3 (1–3).
22*a* GR know.
23*a* GR hard-pressed to choose.
24*a* 3 Ne. 28:9 (1–12); D&C 7:5 (1–8).
27*a* Philip. 4:1 (1–7).
b TG Unity.
c TG Mind.
d Jude 1:3.
28*a* JST Philip. 1:28 . . . *who reject the gospel, which bringeth on them destruction;* but you *who receive the gospel,* salvation; and that of God.
29*a* TG Suffering.
2 1*a* GR tender affections of the heart and compassion.
2*a* TG Benevolence.
b TG Unity.
c Rom. 12:10 (10–18); Moses 7:18 (18–21).
3*a* TG Strife.
b TG Humility; Love; Respect.
6*a* TG God, Body of, Corporeal Nature; Man, Physical Creation of.
b TG Jesus Christ, Relationships with the Father.
7*a* Isa. 53:4 (3–7); 2 Cor. 8:9 (8–15); Heb. 2:9.
8*a* GR outward appearance.
b TG Humility; Meek.
c Isa. 50:5.
d TG Jesus Christ, Death of.
e TG Jesus Christ, Atonement through.
9*a* TG Exaltation.
b Mal. 1:11; Heb. 1:4. TG Name.
10*a* Mosiah 27:31; D&C 76:110 (106–11); 88:104 (103–4).
b Isa. 45:23; Rom. 14:11.

11 And *that* every tongue should
confess that Jesus Christ *is* [a]Lord, to
the glory of God the Father.
12 Wherefore, my beloved, as ye
have always obeyed, not as in my
presence only, but now much more
in my absence, [a]work out your own
[b]salvation with fear and trembling.
13 For it is God which worketh
in you both to will and to do of *his*
good pleasure.
14 Do all things without murmur-
ings and [a]disputings:
15 That ye may be blameless and
harmless, the [a]sons of God, without
rebuke, in the midst of a crooked
and perverse [b]nation, among whom
ye [c]shine as lights in the world;
16 Holding forth the word of life;
that I may rejoice in the day of
Christ, that I have not run in vain,
neither laboured in vain.
17 Yea, and if I be [a]offered upon
the sacrifice and service of your
faith, I joy, and rejoice with you all.
18 For the same cause also do ye
joy, and rejoice with me.
19 But I trust in the Lord Jesus to
send Timotheus shortly unto you,
that I also may be of good comfort,
when I know your state.
20 For I have no man likeminded,
who will naturally care for your
state.
21 For all [a]seek their [b]own, not
the things which are Jesus Christ's.
22 But ye know the [a]proof of him,
that, as a son with the father, he
hath served with me in the gospel.
23 Him therefore I hope to send
presently, so soon as I shall see how
it will go with me.
24 But I trust in the Lord that I also
myself shall come shortly.
25 Yet I supposed it necessary
to send to you [a]Epaphroditus, my
brother, and companion in labour,
and fellowsoldier, but your messenger, and he that ministered to
my wants.
26 For he longed after you all, and
was full of heaviness, because that
ye had heard that he had been sick.
27 For indeed he was sick nigh
unto death: but God had mercy on
him; and not on him only, but on
me also, lest I should have sorrow
upon sorrow.
28 I sent him therefore the more
carefully, that, when ye see him
again, ye may rejoice, and that I
may be the less sorrowful.
29 Receive him therefore in the
Lord with all [a]gladness; and [b]hold
such in [c]reputation:
30 Because for the work of Christ
he was nigh unto death, not regard-
ing his life, to supply your [a]lack of
service toward me.

CHAPTER 3

Paul sacrifices all things for Christ—True ministers set examples of righteousness.

FINALLY, my brethren, rejoice in the
Lord. To write the same things to
you, to me indeed *is* not grievous,
but for you *it is* safe.
2 Beware of dogs, beware of evil
workers, beware of the concision.
3 For we are the [a]circumcision,
which [b]worship God in the spirit,
and rejoice in Christ Jesus, and have
no confidence in the [c]flesh.
4 Though I might also have confidence in the flesh. If any other
man thinketh that he hath whereof
he might trust in the flesh, I more:
5 Circumcised the eighth day, of
the stock of Israel, *of* the tribe of Benjamin, an [a]Hebrew of the Hebrews;
as touching the law, a [b]Pharisee;
6 Concerning zeal, persecuting the

11*a* TG Jesus Christ, Messiah.
12*a* Alma 34:37; Morm. 9:27. TG Good Works.
b TG Salvation.
14*a* TG Disputations.
15*a* TG Sons and Daughters of God.
b GR generation.
c TG Mission of Early Saints.
17*a* 1 Thes. 2:8; D&C 98:13.
21*a* TG Apathy.
b 1 Cor. 10:24.
22*a* GR trial.
25*a* Philip. 4:18.
29*a* TG Cheerful.
b 1 Thes. 5:13.
c GR honor.
30*a* Philip. 4:10.
3 3*a* TG Circumcision.
b TG Worship.
c TG Trust Not in the Arm of Flesh.
5*a* 2 Cor. 11:22.
b Acts 23:6.

church; touching the righteousness
which is in the law, blameless.
7 But what things were gain to
me, those I counted loss for Christ.
8 Yea doubtless, and I count all
things *but* loss for the excellency of
the knowledge of Christ Jesus my
Lord: for whom I have [a]suffered the
[b]loss of all things, and do count them
but [c]dung, that I may win Christ,
9 And be found in him, not having
mine own righteousness, which is of
the law, but that which is through
the faith of Christ, the [a]righteous-
ness which is of God by faith:
10 That I may know him, and the
power of his resurrection, and the
[a]fellowship of his sufferings, being
made conformable unto his death;
11 If by any means I might attain
unto the resurrection of the [a]dead.
12 Not as though I had already
attained, either were already [a]per-
fect: but I [b]follow after, if that I may
apprehend that for which also I am
apprehended of Christ Jesus.
13 Brethren, I count not myself to
have apprehended: but *this* one thing
I do, forgetting those things which
are behind, and reaching forth unto
those things which are before,
14 I [a]press toward the mark for the
[b]prize of the high calling of God in
Christ Jesus.
15 Let us therefore, as many as be
[a]perfect, be thus minded: and if in
any thing ye be otherwise minded,
God shall reveal even this unto you.
16 Nevertheless, whereto we have
already attained, let us walk by the
same rule, let us mind the same
thing.
17 Brethren, be [a]followers together
of me, and mark them which walk
so as ye have us for an [b]ensample.
18 (For many walk, of whom I
have told you often, and now tell
you even weeping, *that they are* the
enemies of the cross of Christ:
19 Whose [a]end *is* destruction,
whose God *is their* belly, [b]and *whose*
glory *is* in their [c]shame, who mind
earthly things.)
20 For our conversation is in
heaven; from whence also we look for
the [a]Saviour, the Lord Jesus Christ:
21 Who shall [a]change our [b]vile
body, [c]that it may be fashioned like
unto his glorious [d]body, according
to the working whereby he is able
even to [e]subdue all things unto
himself.

CHAPTER 4

Stand fast in the Lord—We believe in being honest, true, and chaste.

THEREFORE, my brethren dearly
beloved and longed for, my joy and
crown, so [a]stand fast in the Lord, *my*
dearly beloved.
2 I beseech Euodias, and beseech
Syntyche, that they be of the same
mind in the Lord.
3 And I entreat thee also, true
[a]yokefellow, help those women
which laboured with me in the
gospel, with Clement also, and *with*
other my fellowlabourers, whose
names *are* in the [b]book of life.
4 Rejoice in the Lord alway: *and*
again I say, Rejoice.
5 Let your [a]moderation be known
unto all men. The Lord *is* at hand.

8*a* TG Self-Sacrifice; Suffering.
b Omni 1:26; Mosiah 2:34.
c GR refuse.
9*a* TG Righteousness.
10*a* 2 Cor. 1:4; 2 Thes. 2:16.
11*a* JST Philip. 3:11 . . . *just.*
12*a* TG Perfection.
b GR press forward.
14*a* TG Steadfastness.
b TG Objectives.
15*a* Moro. 10:32 (32–33).
17*a* Matt. 16:24 (24–26); Eph. 5:1; 1 Thes. 1:6.
b TG Example.
19*a* 2 Cor. 11:15.
b JST Philip. 3:19 . . . and *who* glory in their shame . . .
c TG Shame.
20*a* TG Jesus Christ, Savior.
21*a* 1 Cor. 15:51. TG Jesus Christ, Resurrection.
b GR humble, of low estate.
c TG Resurrection.
d TG God, Body of, Corporeal Nature.
e 1 Cor. 15:28; D&C 19:2; 76:106.
4 1*a* 1 Cor. 10:12; 16:13 (13–14); Gal. 5:1; Philip. 1:27; D&C 87:8.
3*a* GR associate.
b TG Book of Life.
5*a* GR gentleness. TG Modesty; Temperance.

6 [a]Be [b]careful for nothing; but in every thing by [c]prayer and supplication with [d]thanksgiving let your requests be made known unto God.

7 And the [a]peace of God, which passeth all [b]understanding, shall [c]keep your hearts and minds through Christ Jesus.

8 Finally, brethren, whatsoever things are [a]true, whatsoever things *are* [b]honest, whatsoever things *are* [c]just, whatsoever things *are* [d]pure, whatsoever things *are* [e]lovely, [f]whatsoever things *are* of good report; if *there be* any [g]virtue, and if *there be* any praise, [h]think on these things.

9 Those things, which ye have both learned, and [a]received, and heard, and seen in me, do: and the God of peace shall be with you.

10 But I rejoiced in the Lord greatly, that now at the last your [a]care of me hath flourished again; wherein ye were also careful, but ye [b]lacked opportunity.

11 Not that I speak in respect of want: for I have learned, in whatsoever state I am, *therewith* to be [a]content.

12 I know both how to be [a]abased, and I know how to abound: every where and in all things I am instructed both to be full and to be hungry, both to abound and to suffer need.

13 I can do all things through [a]Christ which [b]strengtheneth me.

14 Notwithstanding ye have well done, that ye did [a]communicate with my affliction.

15 Now ye Philippians know also, that in the beginning of the gospel, when I departed from Macedonia, no church communicated with me as concerning giving and receiving, but ye only.

16 For even in Thessalonica ye sent once and again unto my necessity.

17 Not because I desire a gift: but I desire [a]fruit that may abound to your account.

18 But I have all, and [a]abound: I am full, having received of [b]Epaphroditus the things *which were sent* from you, an odour of a sweet smell, a sacrifice acceptable, wellpleasing to God.

19 But my God shall supply all your [a]need according to his [b]riches in glory by Christ Jesus.

20 Now unto God and our Father *be* glory for ever and ever. Amen.

21 Salute every saint in Christ Jesus. The brethren which are with me greet you.

22 All the saints salute you, chiefly they that are of [a]Cæsar's household.

23 The grace of our Lord Jesus Christ *be* with you all. Amen.

¶ It was written to the Philippians from Rome by Epaphroditus.

6*a* GR Don't be unduly concerned about anything.
b JST Philip. 4:6 . . . *afflicted* . . .
Ps. 55:22;
Prov. 16:3;
Matt. 6:25.
c TG Prayer.
d TG Thanksgiving.
7*a* TG Peace of God.
b TG Understanding.
c GR guard.
8*a* TG Truth.
b TG Honesty.
c TG Righteousness.
d TG Purity.
e TG Beauty.
f A of F 1:13.
g TG Chastity; Virtue.
h TG Motivations; Study.
9*a* 1 Thes. 4:1.
10*a* 2 Cor. 11:9.
b Philip. 2:30 (25, 30).
11*a* TG Contentment.
12*a* GR humble.
TG Self-Sacrifice.
13*a* John 15:5 (4–5).
b 1 Tim. 1:12;
Alma 26:12 (11–13).
14*a* GR participate.
17*a* Rom. 15:28 (25–28);
Titus 3:14.
18*a* 2 Cor. 9:8.
b Philip. 2:25 (25–30).
19*a* Ps. 23:1.
b TG Treasure.
22*a* Philip. 1:13.

THE EPISTLE OF PAUL THE APOSTLE TO THE
COLOSSIANS

CHAPTER 1

Redemption comes through Christ—He created all things, is in the image of God, and is the Firstborn of the Father.

PAUL, an apostle of Jesus Christ by the will of God, and Timotheus *our* brother,
2 To the saints and faithful brethren in Christ which are at Colosse: Grace *be* unto you, and peace, from God our Father and the Lord Jesus Christ.
3 We give thanks to God and the Father of our Lord Jesus Christ, praying always for you,
4 Since we heard of your [a]faith in Christ Jesus, and of the [b]love *which ye have* to all the saints,
5 For the [a]hope which is laid up for you in heaven, whereof ye heard before in the word of the truth of the [b]gospel;
6 Which is come unto you, [a]as *it is* in all the world; and bringeth forth [b]fruit, as *it doth* also in you, since the day ye heard *of it*, and knew the [c]grace of God in truth:
7 As ye also learned of [a]Epaphras our dear fellowservant, who is for you a faithful minister of Christ;
8 Who also declared unto us your love in the Spirit.
9 For this cause we also, since the day we heard *it*, do not cease to pray for you, and to desire that ye might be filled with the [a]knowledge of his [b]will in all wisdom and spiritual [c]understanding;
10 That ye might [a]walk [b]worthy of the Lord unto all [c]pleasing, being fruitful in every good work, and increasing in the [d]knowledge of God;
11 [a]Strengthened with all might, according to his [b]glorious [c]power, unto all patience and longsuffering with [d]joyfulness;
12 Giving [a]thanks unto the Father, which hath [b]made us meet to be partakers of the [c]inheritance of the saints in light:
13 Who hath delivered us from the power of [a]darkness, and hath translated *us* into the [b]kingdom of his dear [c]Son:
14 In whom we have [a]redemption through his blood, *even* the [b]forgiveness of sins:
15 Who is the [a]image of the invisible [b]God, the [c]firstborn of [d]every creature:

---

1 4*a* Eph. 1:15 (12–15); 1 Thes. 5:8.
b Heb. 6:10.
5*a* 1 Pet. 1:4.
b TG Gospel.
6*a* JST Col. 1:6 . . . as in all *generations of* the world . . .
b Alma 32:42 (28–42); 3 Ne. 14:16; D&C 52:34 (18, 34).
c TG Grace.
7*a* Col. 4:12 (12–13); Philem. 1:23.
9*a* TG Knowledge.
b TG God, Will of.
c TG Understanding.
10*a* TG Walking with God.
b TG Worthiness.
c 1 Thes. 4:1.
d TG Education.
11*a* Eph. 3:16.
b TG Glory.
c TG Jesus Christ, Power of.
d Acts 5:41 (40–41). TG Joy.
12*a* Col. 3:17.
b GR qualified us.
c 2 Ne. 9:18; D&C 45:58 (57–58); 84:38 (33–38).
13*a* D&C 21:6; 38:11.
b TG Kingdom of God, in Heaven.
c TG Jesus Christ, Divine Sonship.
14*a* TG Jesus Christ, Atonement through; Redemption.
b TG Remission of Sins.
15*a* TG God, Body of, Corporeal Nature.
b TG Godhead.
c TG Firstborn; Jesus Christ, Firstborn.
d GR all creation.

16 For by him were all [a]things [b]cre-
ated, that are in heaven, and that
are in earth, visible and invisible,
whether *they be* thrones, or domin-
ions, or [c]principalities, or powers:
all things were [d]created by him,
and for him:
17 And he is before all things, and
by him all things [a]consist.
18 And he is the [a]head of the body,
the church: who is the beginning,
the [b]firstborn from the dead; that
in all *things* he might have the preeminence.
19 For it pleased *the Father* that in
him should all [a]fulness dwell;
20 And, having made peace through
the blood of his cross, by him to
[a]reconcile all things unto himself;
by him, *I say*, whether *they be* things
in earth, or things in heaven.
21 And you, that were [a]sometime
[b]alienated and enemies in *your* mind
by wicked works, yet now hath he
reconciled
22 In the body of his flesh through
[a]death, to present you holy and
[b]unblameable and unreproveable
in his sight:
23 If ye [a]continue in the faith
[b]grounded and settled, and *be* not
[c]moved away from the [d]hope of the
gospel, which ye have heard, *and*
which was preached to every creature which is under heaven; whereof
I Paul am made a minister;
24 Who now rejoice in my sufferings for you, and fill up that
which is behind of the [a]afflictions
of Christ in my flesh for his body's
sake, which is the church:
25 Whereof I am made a minister,
according to the [a]dispensation of
God which is given to me for you,
to fulfil the word of God;
26 *Even* the [a]mystery which hath
been hid from ages and from generations, but now is made [b]manifest
to his saints:
27 To whom God would make
[a]known what *is* the [b]riches of the
glory of this mystery among the
Gentiles; which is Christ in you,
the hope of glory:
28 Whom we [a]preach, [b]warning
every man, and teaching every man
in all wisdom; that we may present
every man perfect in Christ Jesus:
29 Whereunto I also labour, striv-
ing according to his working, which
worketh in me mightily.

CHAPTER 2

The fulness of the Godhead dwells in Christ—Beware of being deceived by the traditions of men—The handwriting against us was nailed to the cross of Christ.

FOR I would that ye knew what great
[a]conflict I have for you, and *for* them
at [b]Laodicea, and *for* as many as
have not seen my face in the flesh;
2 That their hearts might be comforted, being knit together in love,
and unto all riches of the full assurance of [a]understanding, to the
acknowledgement of the mystery
of God, [b]and of the Father, and of
Christ;
3 In whom are hid all the [a]trea-
sures of [b]wisdom and [c]knowledge.

16*a* Heb. 2:10 (9–10).
b TG Creation.
c Col. 2:10; 1 Pet. 3:22.
d TG Jesus Christ, Creator.
17*a* D&C 88:13 (5–13).
18*a* TG Jesus Christ, Head of the Church.
b TG Jesus Christ, Firstborn; Jesus Christ, Resurrection.
19*a* TG Jesus Christ, Relationships with the Father.
20*a* TG Reconciliation.
21*a* GR formerly.
b Eph. 2:1.
22*a* TG Jesus Christ, Death of.
b Mosiah 3:21; D&C 4:2.
23*a* TG Perseverance.
b GR established and steadfast. Eph. 3:17 (17–19).
c John 15:6.
d TG Hope.
24*a* 2 Cor. 1:5.
25*a* TG Dispensations.
26*a* Rom. 16:25 (25–26). TG Mysteries of Godliness.
b 2 Tim. 1:10.
27*a* Eph. 3:3.
b TG Treasure.
28*a* TG Preaching.
b TG Warn.
2 1*a* GR anguish.
b Col. 4:15 (12–16); Rev. 1:11.
2*a* TG Understanding.
b JST Col. 2:2 . . . *and of Christ, who is of God, even the Father;*
3*a* TG Treasure.
b 1 Cor. 2:7 (6–7). TG God, Intelligence of; God, Omniscience of.
c TG Knowledge.

4 And this I say, lest any man
should beguile you with enticing
words.
5 For though I be absent in the
flesh, yet am I with you in the spirit,
joying and beholding your [a]order,
and the steadfastness of your faith
in Christ.
6 As ye have therefore received
Christ Jesus the Lord, *so* [a]walk ye
in him:
7 [a]Rooted and built up in him, and
stablished in the faith, as ye have
been taught, abounding therein
with [b]thanksgiving.
8 Beware lest any man [a]spoil you
through [b]philosophy and vain [c]de-
ceit, after the [d]tradition of men,
after the rudiments of the [e]world,
and not after Christ.
9 For in him dwelleth all the [a]ful-
ness of the Godhead bodily.
10 And ye are [a]complete in him,
which is the head of all [b]principal-
ity and power:
11 In whom also ye are circumcised with the [a]circumcision made
without hands, in putting off the
[b]body of the sins of the flesh by the
circumcision of Christ:
12 [a]Buried with him in [b]baptism,
wherein also ye are [c]risen with *him*
through the faith of the [d]operation
of God, who hath raised him from
the dead.
13 And you, being dead in your
sins and the uncircumcision of your
flesh, hath he [a]quickened together
with him, having forgiven you all
trespasses;
14 [a]Blotting out the handwriting
of ordinances that was against us,
which was contrary to us, and took
it out of the way, nailing it to his
cross;
15 *And* having spoiled principalities and powers, he made a shew
of them openly, triumphing over
them in it.
16 Let no man therefore [a]judge you
in [b]meat, or in drink, or in respect
of an holyday, or of the new moon,
or of the [c]sabbath *days:*
17 Which are a [a]shadow of things
to come; but the body *is* of Christ.
18 Let no man [a]beguile you of
your reward in a voluntary [b]hu-
mility and worshipping of angels,
intruding into those things which
he hath not seen, vainly puffed up
by his fleshly mind,
19 And not holding the [a]Head, from
which all the body by joints and
bands having nourishment ministered, and knit together, increaseth
with the increase of God.
20 Wherefore if ye be [a]dead with
Christ from the rudiments of the
world, why, as though living in the
world, are ye subject to [b]ordinances,
21 [a](Touch not; taste not; handle
not;
22 Which all are to perish with the
using;) after the [a]commandments
and [b]doctrines of men?
23 Which things have indeed a
shew of wisdom in will worship,
and humility, and neglecting of
the body; not in any honour to the
satisfying of the flesh.

5*a* TG Order.
6*a* TG Walking with God.
7*a* Eph. 3:17.
b TG Thanksgiving.
8*a* Heb. 13:9.
b D&C 123:12.
TG Learn.
c TG Deceit; Education; Fraud.
d TG Traditions of Men.
e TG Worldliness.
9*a* TG Jesus Christ, Relationships with the Father.
10*a* John 1:16.
b Col. 1:16; 1 Pet. 3:22.
11*a* TG Circumcision.
b Rom. 6:6.
12*a* TG Jesus Christ, Types of, in Memory.
b TG Baptism; Baptism, Immersion.
c Col. 3:1.
d Eph. 1:19 (19–20).
13*a* GR caused to become alive.
TG Resurrection.
14*a* Eph. 2:15.
16*a* Rom. 14:3 (1–3).
b TG Word of Wisdom.
c TG Sabbath.
17*a* TG Jesus Christ, Types of, in Anticipation.
18*a* Matt. 24:4 (4–5); Mosiah 26:6; D&C 123:12.
b TG Humility.
19*a* Eph. 4:15 (15–16).
20*a* Rom. 6:5 (2–5); Col. 3:3.
b TG Ordinance.
21*a* JST Col. 2:21–22 (Appendix).
22*a* Titus 1:14; D&C 46:7; JS—H 1:19.
TG Apostasy of the Early Christian Church.
b Matt. 15:9; 2 Ne. 28:9.

CHAPTER 3

Some lives are hidden with God in Christ—The Saints are told to be holy and to serve the Lord Jesus Christ.

IF ye then be [a]risen with Christ, seek those things which are above, where Christ sitteth on the right hand of God.
2 Set your [a]affection on [b]things [c]above, not on things on the [d]earth.
3 For ye are [a]dead, and your life is hid with Christ in God.
4 When Christ, *who is* our [a]life, shall [b]appear, then shall ye also appear with him in [c]glory.
5 [a]Mortify therefore your [b]members which are upon the earth; fornication, uncleanness, [c]inordinate affection, evil concupiscence, and [d]covetousness, which is [e]idolatry:
6 For which things' sake the [a]wrath of God cometh on the children of [b]disobedience:
7 In the which ye also walked [a]some time, when ye lived in them.
8 But now ye also [a]put off all these; [b]anger, wrath, [c]malice, [d]blasphemy, filthy [e]communication out of your mouth.
9 [a]Lie not one to another, seeing that ye have put off the [b]old man with his deeds;
10 And have put on the [a]new *man*, which is renewed in knowledge after the [b]image of him that [c]created him:
11 Where there is neither [a]Greek nor Jew, [b]circumcision nor uncircumcision, Barbarian, Scythian, bond *nor* free: but Christ *is* all, and in all.
12 Put on therefore, as the [a]elect of God, holy and beloved, [b]bowels of [c]mercies, [d]kindness, [e]humbleness of mind, [f]meekness, longsuffering;
13 [a]Forbearing one another, and [b]forgiving one another, if any man have a quarrel against any: even as Christ forgave you, so also *do* ye.
14 And above all these things *put on* [a]charity, which is the bond of perfectness.
15 And let the [a]peace of God rule in your hearts, to the which also ye are called in one body; and be ye [b]thankful.
16 Let the [a]word of Christ dwell in you richly in all [b]wisdom; [c]teaching and admonishing one another in psalms and [d]hymns and spiritual songs, singing with grace in your hearts to the Lord.
17 And whatsoever ye do in word or deed, [a]*do* all in the name of the Lord Jesus, giving [b]thanks to God and the Father by him.
18 [a]Wives, submit yourselves unto your own husbands, as it is fit in the Lord.
19 [a]Husbands, [b]love *your* wives, and be not bitter against them.
20 [a]Children, [b]obey *your* parents in

---

3 1*a* Col. 2:12.
2*a* GR mind.
b Matt. 6:33.
c Prov. 15:24.
d TG Worldliness.
3*a* Rom. 6:5 (2–5); Col. 2:20.
4*a* Ether 4:12.
b 1 Jn. 3:2.
c 1 Cor. 15:43 (42–44).
5*a* Rom. 8:13.
b Rom. 6:13.
c TG Sexual Immorality.
d TG Covet.
e TG Idolatry.
6*a* TG God, Indignation of.
b TG Disobedience.
7*a* GR formerly.
8*a* Eph. 4:22 (22–24).
b TG Anger.
c TG Malice.
d TG Blaspheme.
e TG Profanity.
9*a* TG Honesty; Lying.
b Rom. 6:6; Mosiah 3:19.
10*a* TG Man, New, Spiritually Reborn.
b Rom. 8:29.
c TG Jesus Christ, Creator; Man, Physical Creation of.
11*a* 1 Cor. 12:13.
b TG Circumcision.
12*a* TG Election.
b Gal. 5:22.
c TG Mercy.
d TG Benevolence.
e TG Humility.
f TG Meek.
13*a* TG Forbear.
b Mosiah 26:31 (30–31).
14*a* TG Charity.
15*a* TG Peace of God.
b TG Thanksgiving.
16*a* 2 Ne. 32:3.
b TG God, Intelligence of.
c TG Teaching.
d TG Singing.
17*a* 1 Cor. 10:31.
b Col. 1:12. TG Prayer.
18*a* TG Marriage, Wives.
19*a* TG Marriage, Husbands.
b TG Marriage, Continuing Courtship in.
20*a* TG Children; Family, Love within.
b TG Family, Children, Duties of; Honoring Father and Mother.

all things: for this is well pleasing
unto the Lord.
21 [a]Fathers, [b]provoke not your
children *to* [c]*anger,* lest they be dis-
couraged.
22 [a]Servants, obey in all things *your*
masters according to the flesh; not
with eyeservice, as menpleasers;
but in [b]singleness of heart, [c]fearing
God:
23 And whatsoever ye do, do *it*
[a]heartily, as to the Lord, and not
unto men;
24 Knowing that of the Lord ye
shall [a]receive the [b]reward of the
[c]inheritance: for ye [d]serve the Lord
Christ.
25 But he that doeth [a]wrong shall
receive for the wrong which he
hath done: and there is no [b]respect
of persons.

CHAPTER 4

The Saints are told to be wise in all things—Luke and others greet the Colossians.

[a]MASTERS, give unto *your* servants
that which is just and equal; knowing that ye also have a [b]Master in
[c]heaven.
2 Continue in prayer, and watch in
the same with thanksgiving;
3 Withal praying also for us, that
God would open unto us a [a]door of
utterance, to speak the mystery of
Christ, for which I am also in bonds:
4 That I may make it manifest, as
I ought to speak.
5 [a]Walk in [b]wisdom toward them
that are without, redeeming the
time.
6 Let your [a]speech *be* alway with
grace, seasoned with [b]salt, that ye
may know how ye ought to answer
every man.
7 All my state shall Tychicus declare unto you, *who is* a beloved
brother, and a faithful minister and
fellowservant in the Lord:
8 Whom I have sent unto you for
the same purpose, that he might
know your estate, and comfort your
hearts;
9 With [a]Onesimus, a faithful and
beloved brother, who is *one* of you.
They shall make known unto you
all things which *are done* here.
10 [a]Aristarchus my fellowprisoner
saluteth you, and [b]Marcus, [c]sister's
son to Barnabas, (touching whom
ye received commandments: if he
come unto you, receive him;)
11 And Jesus, which is called Justus, who are of the [a]circumcision.
These only *are my* fellowworkers
unto the kingdom of God, which
have been a comfort unto me.
12 [a]Epaphras, who is *one* of you,
a servant of Christ, saluteth you,
always labouring fervently for you
in prayers, that ye may stand perfect and complete in all the will
of God.
13 For I bear him record, that he
hath a great [a]zeal for you, and them
that are in Laodicea, and them in
Hierapolis.
14 Luke, the beloved physician,
and [a]Demas, greet you.
15 Salute the brethren which are
in [a]Laodicea, and Nymphas, and the
church which is in his house.
16 And when this epistle is read
among you, cause that it be read also
in the church of the Laodiceans; and

21*a* TG Family, Children, Responsibilities toward.
b TG Provoking.
c TG Anger.
22*a* 1 Tim. 6:1 (1–2); Titus 2:9 (9–10); 1 Pet. 2:18.
b TG Sincere.
c TG Reverence.
23*a* TG Commitment; Industry; Laziness.
24*a* Eph. 6:8.
b TG Reward.
c TG Inheritance.
d 1 Cor. 7:22.
25*a* TG Injustice.
b D&C 1:35; 38:16.
4 1*a* Mal. 3:5; Eph. 6:9.
b Matt. 23:8.
c TG Heaven.
3*a* 1 Cor. 16:9.
5*a* TG Walking with God.
b TG Wisdom.
6*a* TG Communication.
b TG Salt.
9*a* Philem. 1:10.
10*a* Acts 19:29; 20:4; 27:2.
b Acts 15:37 (37–39); 2 Tim. 4:11.
c GR cousin, kinsman.
11*a* TG Circumcision.
12*a* Col. 1:7 (7–8); Philem. 1:23.
13*a* TG Zeal.
14*a* 2 Tim. 4:10; Philem. 1:24.
15*a* Col. 2:1; Rev. 1:11.

that ye likewise read the [a]*epistle*
from Laodicea.
17 And say to [a]Archippus, Take
heed to the ministry which thou
hast received in the Lord, that thou
fulfil it.
18 The salutation by the [a]hand
of me Paul. Remember my [b]bonds.
Grace *be* with you. Amen.

¶ Written from Rome to the Colossians by Tychicus and Onesimus.

THE FIRST EPISTLE OF PAUL THE APOSTLE TO THE THESSALONIANS

CHAPTER 1

The gospel comes both in word and in power.

PAUL, and [a]Silvanus, and [b]Timo-
theus, [c]unto the [d]church of the
[e]Thessalonians *which is* in God
the Father and *in* the Lord Jesus
Christ: Grace *be* unto you, and peace,
from God our Father, and the Lord
Jesus Christ.
2 We give [a]thanks to God always
for you all, making mention of you
in our prayers;
3 Remembering without ceasing
your work of [a]faith, and [b]labour of
love, and [c]patience of hope in our
Lord Jesus Christ, in the sight of
God and our Father;
4 Knowing, brethren [a]beloved, your
[b]election of God.
5 For our [a]gospel [b]came not unto
you in [c]word only, but also in [d]power,
and in the [e]Holy Ghost, and in much
assurance; as ye know what [f]man-
ner of men we were among you for
your sake.
6 And ye became [a]followers of us,
and of the Lord, having received the
word in much [b]affliction, with [c]joy
of the Holy Ghost:
7 So that ye were [a]ensamples to
all that believe in Macedonia and
Achaia.
8 For from you sounded out the
word of the Lord not only in Macedonia and Achaia, but also in every
[a]place your faith to God-ward is
spread abroad; so that we need not
to speak any thing.
9 For they themselves shew of us
what manner of entering in we had

16*a* TG Scriptures, Lost.
17*a* Philem. 1:2.
18*a* 2 Thes. 3:17.
b Heb. 13:3.

[1 THESSALONIANS]

1 1*a* Acts 15:34 (32–34); 2 Cor. 1:19; 1 Pet. 5:12.
b Acts 16:1 (1–2); 18:5 (1, 5); 1 Thes. 3:2 (2, 6).
c JST 1 Thes. 1:1 . . . *servants of God the Father and the Lord Jesus Christ,* unto the church of the Thessalonians; grace unto you . . .
d TG Jesus Christ, Head of the Church.
e Acts 17:1 (1, 11).
2*a* D&C 46:32.
3*a* 1 Thes. 5:8; James 2:17.
b Heb. 6:10.
c TG Patience.
4*a* GR beloved of God, your election.
b TG Election.
5*a* TG Gospel.
b 1 Thes. 2:1.
c 1 Cor. 2:4.
d TG Holy Ghost, Gifts of.
e TG Holy Ghost, Source of Testimony.
f 1 Thes. 2:10; 2 Thes. 3:7.
6*a* GR imitators. Philip. 3:17.
b Acts 17:5 (5–10). TG Affliction.
c Acts 5:41.
7*a* TG Example.
8*a* 2 Thes. 1:4.

unto you, and how ye turned to God
from [a]idols to serve the [b]living and
true God;
10 And to wait for his Son from
[a]heaven, whom he raised from the
dead, *even* Jesus, which [b]delivered
us from the [c]wrath to come.

CHAPTER 2

True ministers preach in a godly manner—Converts are the glory and joy of missionaries.

FOR yourselves, brethren, know our
[a]entrance in unto you, that it was
not in vain:
2 But even after that we had suffered before, and were shamefully
[a]entreated, as ye know, at Philippi,
we were bold in our God to [b]speak
unto you the gospel of God with
much contention.
3 For our exhortation *was* not of
[a]deceit, nor of uncleanness, nor in
[b]guile:
4 But as we were [a]allowed of God
to be [b]put in [c]trust with the gospel,
even so we [d]speak; not as [e]pleasing
men, but God, which [f]trieth our
hearts.
5 For neither at any time used
we [a]flattering words, as ye know,
nor a cloak of [b]covetousness; God
is witness:
6 Nor of men sought we [a]glory, neither of you, nor *yet* of others, when
we might have been burdensome,
as the apostles of Christ.
7 But we were gentle among you,
even as a nurse cherisheth her
children:
8 So being affectionately desirous
of you, we were willing to have im-
parted unto you, not the gospel of
God only, but also our own [a]souls,
because ye were dear unto us.
9 For ye remember, brethren, our
labour and [a]travail: for [b]labouring
night and day, because we would
not be [c]chargeable unto any of you,
we preached unto you the gospel
of God.
10 Ye *are* [a]witnesses, and God *also*,
how holily and justly and unblame-
ably we behaved ourselves among
you that believe:
11 As ye know how we exhorted
and comforted and charged every one of you, as a father *doth* his
[a]children,
12 That ye would [a]walk [b]worthy
of God, who hath called you unto
his kingdom and glory.
13 For this cause also [a]thank we
God without ceasing, because, when
ye received the word of God which
ye heard of us, ye received *it* not *as*
the word of men, but as it is in truth,
the word of God, which effectually
worketh also in you that believe.
14 For ye, brethren, became [a]fol-
lowers of the churches of God which
in Judæa are in Christ Jesus: for ye
also have [b]suffered like things of
your own countrymen, even as they
have of the Jews:
15 Who both [a]killed the Lord Jesus,
and their own prophets, and have
persecuted us; and they please not
God, and are contrary to all men:
16 [a]Forbidding us to speak to the
Gentiles that they might be saved,

9*a* TG Idolatry.
b D&C 20:19.
10*a* Acts 1:11 (9–11).
b TG Deliver.
c 1 Thes. 5:9.
2 1*a* 1 Thes. 1:5.
2*a* Acts 16:22 (19–24).
b Acts 17:2 (2–3).
3*a* 2 Cor. 4:2; 7:2.
b TG Guile.
4*a* GR approved, found worthy, chosen. 2 Tim. 1:11.
b GR entrusted.
c D&C 12:8; 124:113.
d Titus 2:1; 1 Pet. 4:11.
e TG Peer Influence.
f GR examines, proves by trial. TG Test.
5*a* TG Flatter.
b TG Covet.
6*a* John 5:44 (41–44); D&C 76:61.
8*a* Philip. 2:17.
9*a* GR toil.
b Acts 18:3; 20:34. TG Work, Value of.
c GR burdensome. 1 Cor. 9:18 (4–18); 2 Cor. 11:9.
10*a* 1 Thes. 1:5.
11*a* 1 Cor. 4:14.
12*a* TG Walking with God.
b 1 Pet. 1:15 (15–16).
13*a* TG Thanksgiving.
14*a* GR imitators.
b Acts 17:5 (5–7); 2 Thes. 1:4 (4–5).
15*a* TG Martyrdom; Prophets, Rejection of.
16*a* Luke 11:52; Acts 13:45 (45, 50).

to fill up their sins [b]alway: for the
wrath is come upon them to the
uttermost.
17 But we, brethren, being taken
from you for a short time in presence, not in heart, endeavoured the
more abundantly to see your [a]face
with great desire.
18 Wherefore we would have come
unto you, even I Paul, once and
again; but Satan hindered us.
19 For what *is* our hope, or joy, or
crown of rejoicing? *Are* not even ye
in the presence of our Lord Jesus
Christ at his [a]coming?
20 For ye are our glory and joy.

CHAPTER 3

The Saints are told to perfect that which is lacking in their faith.

WHEREFORE when we could no longer forbear, we thought it good to
be left at [a]Athens alone;
2 And sent [a]Timotheus, our brother,
and minister of God, and our fellowlabourer in the gospel of Christ, to
[b]establish you, and to comfort you
concerning your faith:
3 That no man should be [a]moved
by these [b]afflictions: for yourselves
know that we are [c]appointed thereunto.
4 For verily, when we were with
you, we told you before that we
should suffer tribulation; even as
it came to pass, and ye know.
5 For this cause, when I could
no longer forbear, I sent to know
your faith, lest by some means the
[a]tempter have [b]tempted you, and
our labour be in vain.
6 But now when Timotheus came
from you unto us, and brought us
good tidings of your faith and charity, and that ye have good remembrance of us always, desiring greatly
to see us, as we also *to see* you:
7 Therefore, brethren, we were
[a]comforted over you in all our [b]af-
fliction and distress by your faith:
8 For now we live, if ye stand fast
in the Lord.
9 For what thanks can we render
to God again for you, for all the [a]joy
wherewith we joy for your sakes
before our God;
10 Night and day praying exceedingly that we might see your [a]face,
and might [b]perfect that which is
lacking in your faith?
11 Now God himself and our
Father, and our Lord Jesus Christ,
direct our way unto you.
12 And the Lord make you to increase and [a]abound in [b]love one toward another, and toward all *men*,
even as we *do* toward you:
13 To the end he may stablish your
hearts unblameable in holiness before God, even our Father, at the
[a]coming of our Lord Jesus Christ
with all his [b]saints.

CHAPTER 4

The Saints are told to be holy, sanctify themselves, and love one another—The Lord will come, and the dead will rise.

FURTHERMORE then we beseech you,
brethren, and exhort *you* by the Lord
Jesus, that as ye have [a]received of
us how ye ought to [b]walk and to
[c]please God, *so* ye would [d]abound
more and more.
2 For ye know what commandments [a]we gave you by the Lord
Jesus.

16*b* GR always.
17*a* 1 Thes. 3:10.
19*a* 1 Thes. 3:13; Rev. 1:7; 22:12; D&C 88:97.
3 1*a* Acts 17:15.
2*a* Acts 16:1 (1–2); 1 Cor. 16:10 (10–11); 2 Cor. 1:19; 1 Thes. 1:1.
b Rom. 16:25.
3*a* GR disturbed, perturbed.
b Acts 20:23; JS—H 1:24 (23–24).
c Acts 9:15 (15–16).
5*a* D&C 29:39 (39–40, 47); Moses 4:4 (3–4).
b GR put to trial, test.
7*a* TG Sustaining Church Leaders.
b TG Affliction.
9*a* Alma 26:11 (11–13); D&C 18:16 (14–16).
10*a* 1 Thes. 2:17.
b TG Perfection.
12*a* 1 Thes. 4:1.
b D&C 121:45.
13*a* 1 Cor. 1:7 (7–8); 1 Thes. 2:19; Rev. 1:7; 22:12.
b TG Saints.
4 1*a* Philip. 4:9.
b TG Walking with God.
c Col. 1:10.
d 1 Thes. 3:12.
2*a* D&C 1:38.

3 For this is the will of God, *even*
your [a]sanctification, that ye should
[b]abstain from [c]fornication:
4 That every one of you should
know how to possess his [a]vessel in
[b]sanctification and honour;
5 Not in the [a]lust of concupiscence,
even as the [b]Gentiles which [c]know
not God:
6 That no *man* [a]go beyond and de-
fraud his brother in [b]*any* matter: because that the Lord *is* the [c]avenger of
all such, as we also have forewarned
you and testified.
7 For God hath not called us unto
[a]uncleanness, but unto holiness.
8 He therefore that [a]despiseth, [b]de-
spiseth not man, but God, who hath
also given unto us his [c]holy Spirit.
9 But as touching [a]brotherly love
ye need not that I write unto you:
for ye yourselves are [b]taught of God
to [c]love one another.
10 And indeed ye do it toward all
the brethren which are in all Macedonia: but we beseech you, brethren,
that ye increase more and more;
11 And that ye [a]study to be quiet,
and to do your own business, and
to [b]work with your own [c]hands, as
we commanded you;
12 That ye may walk [a]honestly
toward them that are without, and
that ye may have lack of nothing.
13 But I would not have you to
be ignorant, brethren, concerning
them which are asleep, that ye [a]sor-
row not, even as others which have
no [b]hope.
14 For if we believe that Jesus
died and rose again, even so them
also which [a]sleep in Jesus will God
bring with him.
15 For this we say unto you by the
word of the Lord, [a]that [b]we which
are alive *and* remain unto the coming of the Lord shall not [c]prevent
them which are asleep.
16 For the Lord himself shall [a]de-
scend from heaven with [b]a shout,
with the voice of the [c]archan-
gel, and with the [d]trump of God:
and the dead in Christ shall [e]rise
first:
17 [a]Then we which are alive *and*
remain shall be [b]caught up together
with them in the clouds, to meet
the [c]Lord in the [d]air: and so shall
we [e]ever be with the [f]Lord.
18 Wherefore comfort one another
with these words.

CHAPTER 5

The Saints will know the season of the Second Coming of Christ—Live the way Saints should live—Rejoice evermore—Do not despise prophesyings.

3*a* Heb. 12:14.
b TG Abstain.
c GR immorality. TG Chastity; Fornication; Sexual Immorality; Whore.
4*a* TG Body, Sanctity of.
b TG Sanctification.
5*a* GR passion of lust. TG Lust; Marriage, Husbands.
b Eph. 4:17 (17, 19).
c Eph. 2:12 (11–12).
6*a* GR take advantage of, wrong.
b GR the matter.
c 2 Thes. 1:8.
7*a* TG Uncleanness.
8*a* GR rejects, sets aside, violates.
b Luke 10:16.
c 1 Cor. 2:10; 1 Jn. 3:24.
9*a* TG Brotherhood and Sisterhood.
b John 6:45; 1 Jn. 2:27 (20, 27).
c TG Love.
11*a* GR strive, endeavor earnestly.
b TG Industry; Labor; Skill; Work, Value of.
c Prov. 31:13.
12*a* TG Dependability; Honesty.
13*a* TG Despair; Mourning; Sorrow.
b Eph. 2:12.
14*a* Zech. 14:5.
15*a* JST 1 Thes. 4:15 . . . that *they who* are alive *at* the coming of the Lord, shall not prevent them *who remain unto the coming of the Lord, who* are asleep.
b 2 Thes. 2:2 (1–3).
c GR precede, make progress over.
16*a* TG Jesus Christ, Second Coming.
b GR a cry of command, a cheer.
c TG Adam.
d Matt. 24:31.
e TG Resurrection.
17*a* JST 1 Thes. 4:17 Then *they who* are alive, shall be caught up together *into* the clouds *with them who remain,* to meet the Lord in the air; and so shall we be ever with the Lord.
b 1 Cor. 15:51; D&C 88:96 (96–97); 101:31; 109:75.
c Jude 1:14 (14–16).
d Moro. 10:34.
e TG Immortality.
f John 14:3; Rev. 22:4 (3–5).

BUT of the times and the seasons,
brethren, ye have no need that I
write unto you.
2 For yourselves know perfectly
that the [a]day of the Lord so cometh
as a [b]thief in the night.
3 For when they shall say, Peace
and [a]safety; then sudden destruction
cometh upon them, as travail upon
a woman with child; and they shall
not [b]escape.
4 But ye, brethren, are not in [a]dark-
ness, that that [b]day should overtake
you as a thief.
5 Ye are all the [a]children of light,
and the children of the day: we are
not of the night, nor of darkness.
6 Therefore let us not [a]sleep, as
do others; but let us [b]watch and be
[c]sober.
7 For they that sleep sleep in the
night; and they that be drunken are
drunken in the night.
8 But let us, who are of the day, be
[a]sober, putting on the [b]breastplate
of [c]faith and love; and for an helmet, the [d]hope of salvation.
9 For God hath not appointed us
to [a]wrath, but to obtain [b]salvation
by our Lord Jesus Christ,
10 Who died for us, that, whether
we wake or sleep, we should [a]live
together with him.
11 Wherefore [a]comfort yourselves
together, and [b]edify one another,
even as also ye do.
12 And we beseech you, brethren,
to know them which [a]labour among
you, and are over you in the Lord,
and admonish you;
13 And to [a]esteem them very highly
in love for their work's sake. *And* be
at [b]peace among yourselves.
14 Now we exhort you, brethren,
[a]warn them that are [b]unruly, [c]com-
fort the [d]feebleminded, [e]support
the [f]weak, be patient toward all
men.
15 See that none [a]render [b]evil for
evil unto any [c]*man;* but ever follow
that which is good, both among
yourselves, and to all *men.*
16 [a]Rejoice evermore.
17 [a]Pray without ceasing.
18 In every thing give [a]thanks: for
this is the will of God in Christ Jesus
concerning you.
19 [a]Quench not the [b]Spirit.
20 Despise not prophesyings.
21 [a]Prove all things; hold fast that
which is good.
22 [a]Abstain from all [b]appearance
of [c]evil.
23 And the very God of peace [a]sanc-
tify you wholly; and *I pray God* your
whole spirit and soul and body be
preserved blameless unto the coming of our Lord Jesus Christ.

---

5 2*a* TG Day of the Lord; Millennium, Preparing a People for.
b D&C 106:4.
3*a* TG Refuge.
b D&C 1:2.
4*a* Rom. 13:12 (12–13).
b Luke 17:24; 21:34.
5*a* GR sons. TG Children of Light.
6*a* TG Sleep.
b TG Watch.
c GR sober, vigilant, circumspect. TG Abstain.
8*a* TG Levity.
b Rom. 13:12; Eph. 6:11 (11–18).
c Col. 1:4 (4–5); 1 Thes. 1:3.
d TG Hope.
9*a* 1 Thes. 1:10; 1 Pet. 2:8 (6–8).
b TG Salvation.
10*a* TG Immortality.
11*a* GR exhort, console, encourage.
b TG Edification.
12*a* TG Leadership.
13*a* Philip. 2:29. TG Respect.
b Mark 9:50; Rom. 15:5 (1–7); D&C 20:54 (53–55).
14*a* TG Warn.
b 2 Thes. 3:11.
c GR encourage, console.
d GR faint-hearted, despondent.
e GR care for.
f GR infirm, doubting, timid.
15*a* TG Retribution.
b TG Forbear.
c TG Enemies.
16*a* TG Joy.
17*a* TG Prayer.
18*a* TG Communication; Thanksgiving.
19*a* GR Extinguish, Hinder, Suppress.
b TG Holy Ghost, Gifts of; Holy Ghost, Loss of.
21*a* GR Examine, Put to the test. 1 Jn. 4:1 (1–6). TG Study; Test.
22*a* TG Abstain.
b GR kinds. TG Apparel.
c TG Evil.
23*a* TG Sanctification.

24 Faithful *is* he that calleth you,
who also will do *it*.
25 Brethren, pray for us.
26 Greet all the brethren with an
holy [a]kiss.
27 I charge you by the Lord that
this epistle be read unto all the holy
brethren.
28 The grace of our Lord Jesus
Christ *be* with you. Amen.

¶ The first *epistle* unto the Thessalonians was written from Athens.*

THE SECOND EPISTLE OF PAUL THE APOSTLE TO THE THESSALONIANS

CHAPTER 1

At His Second Coming, the Lord Jesus will take vengeance upon the ungodly.

PAUL, and Silvanus, and Timotheus, [a]unto the [b]church of
the Thessalonians in God our
Father and the Lord Jesus Christ:
2 Grace unto you, and peace, from
God our Father and the Lord Jesus
Christ.
3 We are bound to thank God always for you, brethren, as it is meet,
because that your faith groweth exceedingly, and the charity of every
one of you all toward each other
aboundeth;
4 So that we ourselves glory in
you in the [a]churches of God for
your [b]patience and faith in all your
[c]persecutions and tribulations that
ye endure:
5 *Which is* a manifest token of the
righteous judgment of God, that
ye may be counted worthy of the
kingdom of God, for which ye also
[a]suffer:
6 Seeing *it is* a righteous thing with
God to recompense tribulation to
them that trouble you;
7 And to you who are troubled [a]rest
with us, when the [b]Lord Jesus shall
be [c]revealed from heaven with his
mighty [d]angels,
8 In flaming [a]fire taking [b]vengeance on them that know not God,
and that [c]obey not the [d]gospel of our
Lord Jesus Christ:
9 Who shall be [a]punished with
[b]everlasting [c]destruction from the
presence of the Lord, and from the
glory of his power;
10 When he shall come to be [a]glorified in his [b]saints, and to be admired in all them that believe (because our testimony among you was
believed) in that day.
11 Wherefore also we pray always

26*a* JST 1 Thes. 5:26 . . . *salutation.*

* More recent scholarship concludes that 1 and 2 Thes. were most likely written from Corinth.

[2 THESSALONIANS]

1 1*a* JST 2 Thes. 1:1 . . . *the servants of God the Father and our Lord Jesus Christ,* unto the church of the Thessalonians;
b TG Jesus Christ, Head of the Church.
4*a* 1 Thes. 1:8.
b GR endurance. D&C 58:2.
c 1 Thes. 2:14.
5*a* TG Suffering.
7*a* TG Rest.
b TG Day of the Lord.
c TG Jesus Christ, Second Coming.
d D&C 76:21.
8*a* TG World, End of.
b 1 Thes. 4:6.
c TG Disobedience.
d TG Gospel.
9*a* TG Punish.
b TG Eternity.
c TG Damnation; Sons of Perdition.
10*a* Isa. 66:5.
b TG Saints.

for you, that our God would count you [a]worthy of *this* calling, and fulfil all the good pleasure of *his* goodness, and the work of faith with power:

12 That the name of our Lord Jesus Christ may be glorified in you, and ye in him, according to the [a]grace of our God and the Lord Jesus Christ.

CHAPTER 2

Apostasy is to precede the Second Coming—The gospel prepares men for eternal glory.

NOW we beseech you, brethren, [a]by the coming of our Lord Jesus Christ, and *by* our gathering together unto him,

2 That ye be not soon shaken in mind, [a]or be troubled, neither by spirit, nor by word, nor by [b]letter as from us, as that the [c]day of Christ is at hand.

3 Let no man deceive you by any means: [a]for *that day shall not come,* except there come a [b]falling away first, and that [c]man of [d]sin be revealed, the son of perdition;

4 Who [a]opposeth and exalteth himself above all that is called God, or that is worshipped; so that he as God sitteth in the temple of God, shewing himself that he is God.

5 Remember ye not, that, when I was yet with you, I told you these things?

6 And now ye know [a]what withholdeth that he might be [b]revealed in his time.

7 [a]For the [b]mystery of [c]iniquity doth already work: only [d]he who now letteth *will let,* until he be taken out of the way.

8 And then shall that [a]Wicked be revealed, whom the Lord shall consume with the spirit of his mouth, and shall destroy with the brightness of his [b]coming:

9 *Even him,* whose coming is after the working of Satan with all [a]power and [b]signs and lying wonders,

10 And with all deceivableness of unrighteousness in them that perish; because they received not the love of the truth, that they might be saved.

11 And for this cause God shall send them strong delusion, that they should believe a lie:

12 That they all might be [a]damned who [b]believed not the truth, but had pleasure in unrighteousness.

13 But we are bound to give thanks alway to God for you, brethren beloved of the Lord, because God hath from the beginning [a]chosen you to salvation through [b]sanctification of the Spirit and belief of the truth:

14 Whereunto he called you by our [a]gospel, to the obtaining of the glory of our Lord Jesus Christ.

15 Therefore, brethren, stand fast, and hold the traditions which ye have been taught, whether by word, or our epistle.

16 Now our Lord Jesus Christ himself, and God, even our Father, which hath [a]loved us, and hath

---

11*a* TG Worthiness.
12*a* TG Grace.
2 1*a* GR concerning.
2*a* JST 2 Thes. 2:2 . . . or be troubled *by letter, except ye receive it from us;* neither by spirit, nor by word, as that the day of Christ is at hand.
b 1 Thes. 4:15 (13–17).
c Luke 19:11.
3*a* JST 2 Thes. 2:3 . . . for there *shall* come a falling away first . . .
b GR apostasy, defection. TG Apostasy of the Early Christian Church.
c TG Antichrist; Devil.
d TG Sin.
4*a* TG Opposition.
6*a* GR the one who possesses, holds in firm grasp, restrains.
b GR disclosed, discovered, manifested.
7*a* JST 2 Thes. 2:7–9 (Appendix).
b TG Conspiracy; Secret Combinations.
c GR lawlessness.
d GR he who now possesses, holds in firm grasp, restrains.
8*a* GR Lawless one.
b TG Jesus Christ, Second Coming.
9*a* TG False Priesthoods.
b TG Signs.
12*a* GR brought to account, trial. TG Damnation.
b TG Unbelief.
13*a* TG Election; Foreordination.
b TG Sanctification.
14*a* TG Gospel.
16*a* 1 Jn. 4:10.

given *us* everlasting [b]consolation and
good hope through [c]grace,
17 Comfort your hearts, and stablish you in every good word and
work.

CHAPTER 3

Pray for the triumph of the gospel cause—Paul preaches the gospel of work—Be not weary in well-doing.

FINALLY, brethren, pray for us, that
the word of the Lord [a]may have *free*
course, and be glorified, even as *it*
is with you:
2 And that we may be delivered
from [a]unreasonable and wicked
men: for all *men* have not faith.
3 But the Lord is faithful, who shall
stablish you, and keep *you* from
[a]evil.
4 And we have [a]confidence in the
Lord touching you, that ye both do
and will do the things which we
command you.
5 And the Lord [a]direct your hearts
into the [b]love of God, and into the
patient waiting for Christ.
6 Now we command you, brethren,
in the name of our Lord Jesus Christ,
that ye [a]withdraw yourselves from
every brother that walketh [b]disor-
derly, and not after the tradition
which he received of us.
7 For yourselves know how ye
ought to [a]follow us: for we [b]behaved
not ourselves disorderly among
you;
8 Neither did we eat any man's
bread [a]for nought; but wrought with
[b]labour and travail night and day,
that we might not be chargeable to
any of you:
9 Not because we have not [a]power,
but to make ourselves an [b]ensample
unto you to follow us.
10 For even when we were with
you, this we commanded you, that
if any would not [a]work, neither
should he eat.
11 For we hear that there are some
which walk among you [a]disorderly,
working not at all, but are busy-
bodies.
12 Now them that are such we
command and exhort by our Lord
Jesus Christ, that with quietness
they work, and eat their own [a]bread.
13 But ye, brethren, be not [a]weary
in well doing.
14 And if any man obey not our
word by this epistle, note that man,
and have no company with him,
that he may be ashamed.
15 Yet count *him* not as an [a]enemy,
but [b]admonish *him* as a [c]brother.
16 Now the Lord of peace himself
give you peace always by all means.
The Lord *be* with you all.
17 The salutation of Paul with mine
own [a]hand, which is the token in
every epistle: so I write.
18 The grace of our Lord Jesus
Christ *be* with you all. Amen.

¶ The second *epistle* to the Thessalonians was written from Athens.*

16*b* 2 Cor. 1:4; Philip. 3:10.
c TG Grace.
3 1*a* GR may progress freely, rapidly.
2*a* GR unsuitable, absurd, improper.
3*a* GR the evil one, the devil.
4*a* TG Dependability.
5*a* TG Guidance, Divine.
b Deut. 11:13.
6*a* 1 Cor. 5:9 (1–13); Alma 1:24 (21–24); 5:57 (56–57). TG Excommunication.
b Rom. 16:17 (17–19).
7*a* GR imitate.
b 1 Thes. 1:5.
8*a* GR undeservedly, gratuitously.
b TG Work, Value of.
9*a* GR authority.
b TG Example.
10*a* TG Idleness; Industry; Labor; Laziness.
11*a* 1 Thes. 5:14.
12*a* TG Bread.
13*a* Gal. 6:9.
15*a* TG Enemies.
b TG Warn.
c TG Brotherhood and Sisterhood.
17*a* Col. 4:18.

* More recent scholarship concludes that 1 and 2 Thes. were most likely written from Corinth.

THE FIRST EPISTLE OF PAUL THE APOSTLE TO TIMOTHY

CHAPTER 1

Counsel is given to teach true doctrine only—Christ came to save repentant sinners.

PAUL, an apostle of Jesus Christ by the commandment of God our Saviour, and Lord Jesus Christ, *which is* our hope;

2 Unto [a]Timothy, [b]*my* [c]own son in the faith: Grace, mercy, *and* peace, from God our Father and Jesus Christ our Lord.

3 As I besought thee to abide still at Ephesus, when I went into Macedonia, that thou mightest charge some that they [a]teach no [b]other doctrine,

4 Neither give heed to [a]fables and endless genealogies, which [b]minister [c]questions, rather than godly [d]edifying which is in faith: *so do.*

5 Now the end of the [a]commandment is [b]charity out of a [c]pure heart, and *of* a good conscience, and *of* faith unfeigned:

6 From which some having [a]swerved have [b]turned aside unto [c]vain jangling;

7 Desiring to be teachers of the law; understanding neither what they say, nor whereof they [a]affirm.

8 But we know that the law *is* good, if a man use it lawfully;

9 Knowing this, that the [a]law is not made for a [b]righteous man, but for the [c]lawless and [d]disobedient, for the ungodly and for sinners, for unholy and profane, for murderers of fathers and murderers of mothers, for manslayers,

10 For [a]whoremongers, for [b]them that [c]defile themselves with mankind, for [d]menstealers, for liars, for perjured persons, and if there be any other thing that is contrary to sound [e]doctrine;

11 According to the glorious gospel of the blessed God, which was committed to my [a]trust.

12 And I thank Christ Jesus our Lord, who hath [a]enabled me, for that he counted me faithful, putting me into the ministry;

13 Who was before a [a]blasphemer, and a [b]persecutor, and [c]injurious: but I obtained [d]mercy, because I did *it* [e]ignorantly in unbelief.

14 And the [a]grace of our Lord was exceeding abundant with faith and love which is in Christ Jesus.

15 This *is* a faithful [a]saying, and worthy of all acceptation, that Christ

---

1 2*a* Acts 16:1 (1–4); 1 Cor. 4:17.
b GR a true son according to.
c GR lawful, true.
3*a* 1 Tim. 6:3 (3–5); 3 Ne. 11:40.
b Gal. 1:8 (6–8).
4*a* Titus 1:14; 2 Pet. 1:16.
b GR offer, present.
c 1 Tim. 6:4.
d TG Edification.
5*a* Gal. 5:14.
b TG Charity.
c 2 Tim. 2:22.
6*a* GR missed the mark.
b TG Apostasy of the Early Christian Church.
c GR vain, idle, fruitless discussion.
7*a* GR strongly assert.
9*a* TG Law of Moses.
b TG Godliness.
c Gal. 3:19.
d TG Disobedience.
10*a* TG Whore.
b GR homosexuals.
c TG Homosexual Behavior.
d GR kidnappers.
e 2 Tim. 4:3.
11*a* TG Trustworthiness.
12*a* Philip. 4:13.
13*a* Acts 26:9.
b Acts 8:3; 22:4.
c GR violent.
d 1 Cor. 7:25.
e John 9:39 (39–41). TG Ignorance.
14*a* TG Grace.
15*a* 1 Tim. 3:1.

Jesus came into the world to [b]save
[c]sinners; of whom I am chief.
16 Howbeit for this cause I obtained
[a]mercy, that in me first Jesus Christ
might shew forth all [b]longsuffering, for a [c]pattern to them which
should hereafter believe on him to
life everlasting.
17 Now unto the [a]King eternal,
[b]immortal, invisible, the only wise
God, *be* honour and glory for ever
and ever. Amen.
18 This charge I commit unto
thee, son Timothy, according to the
[a]prophecies which went before on
thee, that thou by them mightest
war a good warfare;
19 [a]Holding faith, and a good conscience; which some having put
away concerning faith have made
[b]shipwreck:
20 Of whom is [a]Hymenæus and
[b]Alexander; whom I have [c]delivered
unto Satan, that they may learn not
to blaspheme.

CHAPTER 2

We should pray for all people—Christ is our Mediator—Women should dress modestly—Women are blessed in childbearing and are admonished to continue in faith, charity, and holiness.

I EXHORT therefore, that, first of all,
supplications, prayers, intercessions,
and giving of thanks, be made for
all men;
2 For [a]kings, and *for* all that are in
authority; that we may lead a quiet
and [b]peaceable [c]life in all godliness
and [d]honesty.
3 For this *is* good and acceptable
in the sight of God our Saviour;
4 [a]Who [b]will have [c]all men to be
[d]saved, and to come unto the knowledge of the truth.
5 For *there is* [a]one God, and one
[b]mediator between God and men,
the man Christ Jesus;
6 Who [a]gave himself a [b]ransom
for all, to be [c]testified in due time.
7 Whereunto I am [a]ordained a
[b]preacher, and an [c]apostle, (I speak
the truth in Christ, *and* [d]lie not;)
a teacher of the [e]Gentiles in faith
and [f]verity.
8 I [a]will therefore that men [b]pray
every where, lifting up holy [c]hands,
without wrath and [d]doubting.
9 In like manner also, that [a]women
adorn themselves in [b]modest [c]apparel, with [d]shamefacedness and
sobriety; not with [e]broided hair, or
gold, or pearls, or costly array;
10 But (which becometh women
professing [a]godliness) with good
works.
11 Let the woman learn in [a]silence
with all subjection.
12 But I suffer not a woman to

15*b* Matt. 9:13 (12–13). TG Jesus Christ, Atonement through.
c Luke 5:32; John 9:39 (39–41).
16*a* TG God, Mercy of.
b TG Forbear.
c TG Example.
17*a* 1 Tim. 6:15 (15–16).
b TG God, Eternal Nature of; Immortality.
18*a* 1 Tim. 4:14 (14–16); 2 Tim. 1:6.
19*a* 1 Ne. 15:24; D&C 6:13.
b TG Apostasy of Individuals; Apostasy of the Early Christian Church.
20*a* 2 Tim. 2:17.
b Acts 19:33 (33–34).
c 1 Cor. 5:5; D&C 78:12; 104:10 (9–10); 132:26.

2 2*a* TG Governments; Kings, Earthly.
b TG Peace; Peacemakers.
c TG Citizenship.
d GR dignity, gravity. TG Honesty.
4*a* JST 1 Tim. 2:4 (Appendix).
b GR desires.
c D&C 6:11.
d Ezek. 18:23 (23–24).
5*a* Rom. 3:30 (28–31); D&C 121:28.
b Heb. 12:24. TG Jesus Christ, Authority of.
6*a* TG Self-Sacrifice.
b Job 33:24. TG Jesus Christ, Atonement through; Jesus Christ, Redeemer.
c Heb. 9:16 (16–17); D&C 135:5.
7*a* TG Called of God.
b TG Preaching.
c 1 Cor. 9:1. TG Apostles.
d Rom. 9:1.
e Acts 9:15.
f GR truth.
8*a* GR desire.
b D&C 19:28; 20:47; 23:6.
c Ps. 24:4.
d GR dispute, contention, doubt. TG Doubt.
9*a* TG Marriage, Wives; Woman.
b TG Chastity; Modesty.
c TG Apparel.
d GR modesty, reverence.
e GR plaited, braided.
10*a* TG Godliness.
11*a* TG Silence.

[a]teach, nor to [b]usurp authority over the man, but to be in [c]silence.

13 For Adam was first [a]formed, then Eve.

14 And Adam was not deceived, but the woman being [a]deceived was in the [b]transgression.

15 Notwithstanding [a]she shall be saved in [b]childbearing, if they continue in faith and charity and [c]holiness with [d]sobriety.

CHAPTER 3

Qualifications are given for bishops and deacons—Great is the mystery of godliness.

THIS *is* a true [a]saying, If a man desire the office of a [b]bishop, he desireth a good work.

2 A bishop then must be [a]blameless, the husband of one wife, vigilant, [b]sober, of good behaviour, given to [c]hospitality, apt to [d]teach;

3 Not given to [a]wine, no [b]striker, not greedy of [c]filthy lucre; but patient, not a brawler, not covetous;

4 One that [a]ruleth well his own [b]house, having his [c]children in subjection with all gravity;

5 (For if a man know not how to [a]rule his own house, how shall he take care of the church of God?)

6 Not a [a]novice, lest being lifted up with [b]pride he fall into the [c]condemnation of the devil.

7 Moreover he must have a good [a]report of them which are [b]without; lest he fall into reproach and the [c]snare of the devil.

8 Likewise *must* the [a]deacons *be* [b]grave, not [c]doubletongued, not given to much wine, not greedy of filthy lucre;

9 Holding the mystery of the faith in a pure [a]conscience.

10 And let these also first be [a]proved; then let them use the office of a deacon, being *found* blameless.

11 [a]Even so *must their* [b]wives *be* [c]grave, not [d]slanderers, [e]sober, [f]faithful in all things.

12 Let the deacons be the husbands of one wife, ruling their children and their own houses well.

13 For they that have used the office of a deacon well [a]purchase to themselves a good degree, and great boldness in the faith which is in Christ Jesus.

14 These things write I unto thee, hoping to come unto thee shortly:

15 [a]But if I tarry long, that thou mayest know how thou oughtest to behave thyself in the house of God, which is the [b]church of the living

---

12*a* TG Teaching.
b GR exercise dominion, be autocratic, domineer.
c GR quietness, tranquillity.
13*a* TG Man, Physical Creation of.
14*a* TG Fall of Man.
b TG Transgress.
15*a* JST 1 Tim. 2:15 . . . *they* . . .
b TG Birth Control; Marriage, Motherhood.
c TG Holiness.
d GR modesty.
3 1*a* 1 Tim. 1:15.
b TG Bishop.
2*a* TG Priesthood, Qualifying for.
b GR temperate, circumspect. TG Levity.
c TG Hospitality.
d 2 Tim. 2:24.
3*a* TG Drunkenness; Word of Wisdom.
b GR bully, violent person.
c TG Filthiness.
4*a* TG Marriage, Husbands.
b TG Marriage, Fatherhood.
c TG Family, Children, Responsibilities toward; Family, Patriarchal.
5*a* Esth. 1:22; D&C 93:43 (41–43, 50). TG Family, Love within.
6*a* GR recent convert.
b TG Pride.
c 2 Pet. 2:4.
7*a* Acts 6:3; 22:12.
b GR outside the faith.
c TG Bondage, Spiritual.
8*a* TG Deacon.
b GR honorable, dignified. TG Levity.
c GR deceitful.
9*a* TG Conscience.
10*a* 1 Tim. 5:22. TG Test.
11*a* GR Women in like manner.
b TG Marriage, Wives.
c GR honorable, dignified.
d TG Slander.
e GR temperate, vigilant, circumspect.
f TG Trustworthiness.
13*a* GR earn, acquire for themselves good standing rank.
15*a* JST 1 Tim. 3:15–16 (Appendix). Note the change, emphasizing that the "pillar and ground of the truth" is Jesus Christ.
b TG Church.

God, the pillar and [c]ground of the
[d]truth.
16 And without controversy great is
the [a]mystery of godliness: [b]God was
[c]manifest in the [d]flesh, [e]justified in
the Spirit, seen of angels, preached
unto the Gentiles, believed on in
the world, [f]received up into glory.

CHAPTER 4

Paul describes the latter-day apostasy—Christ is the Savior of all men, especially of those who believe.

Now the Spirit speaketh expressly,
that in the [a]latter times some shall
[b]depart from the faith, giving heed
to [c]seducing spirits, and [d]doctrines
of devils;
2 Speaking [a]lies in [b]hypocrisy; having their [c]conscience seared with a
hot iron;
3 [a]Forbidding to [b]marry, *and commanding* to [c]abstain from [d]meats,
which God hath [e]created to be received with [f]thanksgiving of them
which believe and know the truth.
4 For every [a]creature of God *is*
[b]good, and nothing to be refused,
if it be received with [c]thanksgiving:
5 For it is sanctified by the word
of God and prayer.
6 If thou put the brethren in remembrance of these things, thou
shalt be a good minister of Jesus
Christ, nourished up in the words of
faith and of good doctrine, [a]where-
unto thou hast attained.
7 But refuse profane and old wives'
fables, and exercise thyself *rather*
unto godliness.
8 For bodily exercise profiteth [a]lit-
tle: but [b]godliness is profitable unto
all things, having promise of the
life that now is, and of that which
is to come.
9 This *is* a faithful saying and worthy of all acceptation.
10 For therefore we both [a]labour
and suffer [b]reproach, because we
[c]trust in the living God, who is the
[d]Saviour of all men, specially of
those that [e]believe.
11 These things command and
teach.
12 Let no man [a]despise thy youth;
but be thou an [b]example of the believers, in word, in [c]conversation, in
charity, in spirit, in faith, in [d]purity.
13 Till I come, give attendance to
[a]reading, to exhortation, to doctrine.
14 [a]Neglect not the [b]gift that is
in thee, which was given thee by
[c]prophecy, with the [d]laying on of
the [e]hands of the [f]presbytery.
15 [a]Meditate upon these things;

15*c* GR foundation.
d TG Truth.
16*a* D&C 19:10.
TG Mysteries of Godliness.
b Ps. 1:3 (2–3);
John 10:33 (30–33);
Mosiah 3:5; 15:1 (1–5).
TG Jesus Christ, Jehovah.
c TG God, Manifestations of.
d TG Jesus Christ, Condescension of.
e GR approved by the.
f TG Jesus Christ, Ascension of.
4 1*a* TG Last Days.
b TG Holy Ghost, Loss of.
c GR deceitful.
TG Apostasy of the Early Christian Church;
Spirits, Evil or Unclean.
d TG False Doctrine.
2*a* TG Lying.
b TG Hypocrisy.
c TG Conscience;
Spiritual Blindness.
3*a* Matt. 8:14;
D&C 49:15.
TG Marriage, Temporal.
b TG Marriage, Marry.
c TG Abstain.
d TG Food;
Word of Wisdom.
e D&C 49:19.
f D&C 89:11 (11–13).
4*a* GR creation.
b Gen. 1:31.
c TG Thanksgiving.
6*a* GR which thou hast followed closely.
8*a* GR a little while.
b Luke 12:31.
TG Godliness.
10*a* TG Labor.
b TG Reproach.
c TG Trust in God.
d TG Jesus Christ, Atonement through;
Jesus Christ, Savior.
e TG Faith.
12*a* 1 Cor. 16:11 (10–11).
b TG Example;
Priesthood, Qualifying for.
c GR conduct, behavior.
d TG Chastity;
Purity;
Virtue.
13*a* TG Study.
14*a* TG Priesthood, Magnifying Callings within.
b TG God, Gifts of;
Stewardship;
Talents.
c 1 Tim. 1:18.
TG Prophecy.
d TG Priesthood, Authority;
Priesthood, Ordination.
e TG Hands, Laying on of.
f GR elders.
15*a* TG Meditation.

give thyself wholly to them; that
thy [b]profiting may [c]appear to all.
16 Take heed unto thyself, and unto
the doctrine; continue in them: for
in doing this thou shalt both [a]save
thyself, and them that hear thee.

CHAPTER 5

Saints are to care for their worthy poor—Policies concerning elders are given.

[a]REBUKE not an elder, but [b]entreat
him as a father; *and* the younger
men as brethren;
2 The elder women as mothers; the
younger as [a]sisters, with all purity.
3 Honour [a]widows that are widows indeed.
4 But if any widow have [a]children
or [b]nephews, let them learn first to
shew [c]piety at home, and to requite
their parents: for that is good and
acceptable before God.
5 Now she that is a widow indeed,
and [a]desolate, trusteth in God, and
continueth in supplications and
prayers night and day.
6 But she that liveth [a]in [b]pleasure
is dead while she liveth.
7 And these things [a]give in charge,
that they may be blameless.
8 But if any [a]provide not for his
own, and specially for those of
his own house, he hath denied the
faith, and is worse than an infidel.
9 Let not a widow be taken into
the number under threescore years
[a]old, having been the wife of one
man,
10 Well reported of for good
works; if she have brought up children, if she have [a]lodged strangers,
if she have [b]washed the saints'
[c]feet, if she have relieved the afflicted, if she have diligently followed every good work.
11 But the younger widows refuse:
for when they have begun to wax
wanton against Christ, they will
marry;
12 Having [a]damnation, because
they have cast off their first faith.
13 And withal they learn *to be*
[a]idle, wandering about from house
to house; and not only idle, but tat-
tlers also and [b]busybodies, speaking
things which they ought not.
14 I [a]will therefore that the younger
[b]women marry, bear [c]children, guide
the [d]house, give none occasion to the
adversary to speak reproachfully.
15 For some are already turned
aside after Satan.
16 If any man or woman that believeth have widows, let them [a]re-
lieve them, and let not the church be
[b]charged; that it may relieve them
that are widows indeed.
17 Let the [a]elders that rule well be
counted worthy of double honour,
especially they who labour in the
word and doctrine.
18 For the scripture saith, Thou
shalt not [a]muzzle the ox that treadeth out the corn. And, The [b]labourer
is worthy of his [c]reward.
19 Against an elder receive not an
accusation, but before two or three
[a]witnesses.
20 Them that sin [a]rebuke before
all, that others also may fear.

15*b* GR progress, advancement.
c GR be manifest in all.
16*a* James 5:20 (19–20); D&C 101:39 (39–40).
5 1*a* TG Chastening.
b TG Respect.
2*a* TG Brotherhood and Sisterhood.
3*a* TG Widows.
4*a* TG Children.
b GR grandchildren, descendants.
c TG Family, Love within; Respect.
5*a* GR left alone.
6*a* GR wantonly.
b TG Pleasure.
7*a* GR instruct, command.
8*a* TG Family, Children, Responsibilities toward; Family, Managing Finances in; Marriage, Husbands.
9*a* TG Old Age.
10*a* Acts 16:15 (14–15).
b TG Wash.
c JST 1 Tim. 5:10 . . . *clothes* . . .
12*a* GR judgment, condemnation. TG Damnation.
13*a* TG Idleness.
b TG Gossip.
14*a* GR desire.
b TG Marriage, Wives; Woman.
c TG Children.
d Titus 2:5 (4–5).
16*a* TG Welfare.
b GR burdened down, troubled.
17*a* TG Elder, Melchizedek Priesthood.
18*a* Deut. 25:4.
b TG Labor.
c GR wage. TG Wages.
19*a* Deut. 19:15.
20*a* TG Chastening.

21 I charge *thee* before God, and the Lord Jesus Christ, and the elect [a]angels, that thou observe these things [b]without preferring one before another, doing nothing by partiality.

22 [a]Lay [b]hands suddenly on no [c]man, neither be [d]partaker of other men's sins: keep thyself [e]pure.

23 Drink no longer water, but use a little wine for thy stomach's sake and thine often infirmities.

24 Some men's sins are open beforehand, going before to judgment; and some *men* they [a]follow after.

25 Likewise also the good works *of some* are manifest beforehand; and they that are otherwise cannot be hid.

CHAPTER 6

The love of money is the root of all evil—Fight the good fight of faith—Do not trust in worldly riches.

LET as many [a]servants as are under the [b]yoke count their own masters worthy of all honour, that the name of God and *his* doctrine be not blasphemed.

2 And they that have believing masters, let them not despise *them,* because they are [a]brethren; but rather do *them* [b]service, because they are faithful and beloved, partakers of the benefit. These things teach and exhort.

3 If any man [a]teach otherwise, and consent not to [b]wholesome words, *even* the words of our Lord Jesus Christ, and to the doctrine which is according to godliness;

4 He is [a]proud, knowing nothing, but [b]doting about [c]questions and [d]strifes of words, whereof cometh [e]envy, strife, railings, [f]evil surmisings,

5 Perverse [a]disputings of men of corrupt minds, and destitute of the truth, supposing that [b]gain is godliness: from such withdraw thyself.

6 But [a]godliness with [b]contentment is great gain.

7 For we brought [a]nothing into *this* world, *and it is* certain we can carry nothing out.

8 And having [a]food and raiment let us be therewith [b]content.

9 But [a]they that will be [b]rich fall into [c]temptation and a snare, and *into* many foolish and hurtful [d]lusts, which drown men in destruction and [e]perdition.

10 For the [a]love of [b]money is the root of all evil: which while some [c]coveted after, they have [d]erred from the faith, and pierced themselves through with many [e]sorrows.

11 But thou, O man of God, flee these things; and follow after [a]righteousness, godliness, faith, love, patience, meekness.

12 Fight the good fight of faith, lay hold on [a]eternal life, whereunto thou art also called, and hast [b]professed a good profession before many witnesses.

13 I give thee charge in the sight of God, who [a]quickeneth all things,

---

21*a* TG Angels.
b GR apart from prejudice.
22*a* TG Setting Apart.
b TG Hands, Laying on of.
c 1 Tim. 3:10.
d 2 Jn. 1:11.
e James 1:27 (22–27).
24*a* GR appear later.
6 1*a* GR slaves. Col. 3:22; Titus 2:9 (9–10); 1 Pet. 2:18.
b TG Bondage, Physical.
2*a* 1 Jn. 3:14 (10–18).
b TG Service.
3*a* 1 Tim. 1:3; D&C 10:68.
b Titus 2:8.
4*a* TG Pride.
b GR obsessed with questions.
c 1 Tim. 1:4.
d TG Strife.
e TG Envy.
f GR wicked suspicions.
5*a* TG Disputations.
b Titus 1:11.
6*a* TG Godliness.
b TG Contentment.
7*a* Job 1:21.
8*a* TG Food.
b TG Contentment.
9*a* GR those desiring to be rich.
b TG Treasure.
c TG Temptation.
d TG Lust.
e TG Death, Spiritual, Second.
10*a* Ps. 119:36; James 5:3 (1–6).
b TG Selfishness.
c TG Covet.
d GR wandered, apostatized.
e TG Sorrow.
11*a* TG Priesthood, Magnifying Callings within; Righteousness.
12*a* TG Eternal Life.
b Heb. 10:23.
13*a* GR brings to life. D&C 33:16; 88:17. TG God, Power of; Resurrection.

and *before* Christ Jesus, who before [b]Pontius Pilate [c]witnessed a good confession;
14 That thou keep *this* commandment without spot, unrebukeable, until the appearing of our Lord Jesus Christ:
15 [a]Which in his times he shall shew, *who is* the blessed and only [b]Potentate, the [c]King of kings, and Lord of lords;
16 Who only hath [a]immortality, dwelling in the [b]light which no man can approach unto; whom no man hath [c]seen, nor can see: to whom *be* honour and power everlasting. Amen.
17 Charge them that are [a]rich in this world, that they be not highminded, nor trust in uncertain [b]riches, but in the living God, who giveth us richly all things to enjoy;
18 That they do good, that they be rich in good works, ready to [a]distribute, willing to [b]communicate;
19 [a]Laying up in [b]store for themselves a good foundation [c]against the time to come, that they may lay hold on [d]eternal life.
20 O Timothy, keep that which is committed to thy [a]trust, avoiding profane *and* vain babblings, and [b]oppositions of science falsely so called:
21 Which some professing have erred concerning the faith. Grace *be* with thee. Amen.

¶ The first to Timothy was written from Laodicea, which is the chiefest city of Phrygia Pacatiana.

THE SECOND EPISTLE OF PAUL THE APOSTLE TO TIMOTHY

CHAPTER 1

Christ brings immortality and eternal life through the gospel—Be strong in the faith.

PAUL, an apostle of Jesus Christ by the will of God, according to the [a]promise of life which is in Christ Jesus,
2 To Timothy, *my* dearly beloved son: Grace, mercy, *and* peace, from God the Father and Christ Jesus our Lord.
3 I thank God, whom I serve from *my* forefathers with pure [a]conscience, that without ceasing I have remembrance of thee in my prayers night and day;
4 Greatly desiring to see thee, being mindful of thy tears, that I may be filled with joy;
5 When I call to remembrance the

13*b* John 18:37 (29–40).
c GR testified. TG God, the Standard of Righteousness.
15*a* JST 1 Tim. 6:15–16 (Appendix).
b D&C 41:4.
c Zech. 14:16; 1 Tim. 1:17; Rev. 17:14.
16*a* TG Immortality.
b D&C 88:12 (6–13); 130:7 (6–9).
c TG God, Privilege of Seeing.
17*a* Hel. 4:12 (11–13); 3 Ne. 6:12 (10–16).
b James 1:11 (8–16).
18*a* TG Generosity.
b TG Communication.
19*a* D&C 14:3.
b D&C 4:4.
c GR for the future.
d D&C 11:3.
20*a* TG Trustworthiness.
b GR disputations of what is falsely called knowledge. 2 Ne. 26:20; D&C 1:19.

[2 TIMOTHY]

1 1*a* Titus 1:2.
3*a* TG Conscience.

unfeigned faith that is in thee, which dwelt first in thy grandmother Lois, and thy mother [a]Eunice; and I am persuaded that in thee also.
6 Wherefore I put thee in remembrance that thou [a]stir up the [b]gift of God, which is in thee by the putting on of my [c]hands.
7 For God hath not given us the spirit of [a]fear; but of [b]power, and of [c]love, and of a sound mind.
8 Be not thou therefore [a]ashamed of the [b]testimony of our Lord, nor of me his prisoner: but be thou partaker of the afflictions of the gospel according to the power of God;
9 Who hath saved us, and called *us* with an holy [a]calling, not according to our works, but according to his own purpose and [b]grace, which was given us in Christ Jesus before the world began,
10 But is now made [a]manifest by the appearing of our Saviour Jesus Christ, who hath abolished [b]death, and hath brought [c]life and [d]immortality to light through the gospel:
11 Whereunto I am [a]appointed a preacher, and an [b]apostle, and a teacher of the Gentiles.
12 For the which cause I also suffer these things: nevertheless I am not [a]ashamed: for I know whom I have believed, and am persuaded that he is able to keep that which I have committed unto him against that day.
13 Hold fast the [a]form of [b]sound words, which thou hast heard of me, in faith and love which is in Christ Jesus.
14 That good thing which was committed unto thee keep by the Holy Ghost which [a]dwelleth in us.
15 This thou knowest, that all they which are in Asia be [a]turned away from me; of whom are Phygellus and Hermogenes.
16 The Lord give mercy unto the house of Onesiphorus; for he oft [a]refreshed me, and was not ashamed of my chain:
17 But, when he was in Rome, he sought me out very diligently, and found *me*.
18 The Lord grant unto him that he may find [a]mercy of the Lord in that day: and in how many things he ministered unto me at Ephesus, thou knowest very well.

CHAPTER 2

Christ gives eternal glory to the elect—Shun contention and seek godliness.

THOU therefore, my son, be strong in the grace that is in Christ Jesus.
2 And the things that thou hast heard of me among many witnesses, the same commit thou to faithful men, who shall be able to [a]teach others also.
3 Thou therefore endure [a]hardness, as a good soldier of Jesus Christ.
4 No man that warreth entangleth himself with the affairs of *this* life; that he may please him who hath chosen him to be a soldier.
5 And if a man also [a]strive for [b]masteries, *yet* is he not [c]crowned, except he strive lawfully.
6 The husbandman that laboureth

5*a* Acts 16:1.
6*a* GR rekindle, revive. TG Priesthood, Magnifying Callings within.
b 1 Tim. 1:18; D&C 8:4. TG Holy Ghost, Gifts of.
c TG Hands, Laying on of.
7*a* TG Courage; Fearful.
b Acts 1:8.
c TG Love.
8*a* TG Shame.
b TG Testimony.
9*a* TG Foreordination.
b TG Grace.
10*a* Col. 1:26.
b 1 Cor. 15:26; Heb. 2:14; Rev. 20:13 (11–15). TG Jesus Christ, Atonement through; Jesus Christ, Death of.
c 1 Jn. 5:11 (10–21).
d TG Immortality.
11*a* 1 Thes. 2:4.
b TG Apostles.
12*a* Rom. 1:16.
13*a* GR sketch, model, example.
b GR uncorrupted.
14*a* D&C 130:22.
15*a* TG Apostasy of the Early Christian Church.
16*a* TG Hospitality.
18*a* TG God, Mercy of.
2 2*a* D&C 38:23. TG Teaching.
3*a* GR afflictions, vexations.
5*a* GR compete in a contest.
b 1 Cor. 9:25.
c TG Reward.

must be first [a]partaker of the fruits.

7 Consider what I say; and the Lord give thee understanding in all things.

8 Remember that Jesus Christ of the seed of David was [a]raised from the dead according to my [b]gospel:

9 Wherein I suffer trouble, as an evil doer, *even* unto bonds; but the word of God is not bound.

10 Therefore I endure all things for the elect's sakes, that they may also obtain the salvation which is in Christ Jesus with eternal glory.

11 *It is* a faithful saying: For if we be [a]dead with *him,* we shall also live with *him:*

12 If we [a]suffer, we shall also [b]reign with *him:* if we [c]deny *him,* he also will deny us:

13 If we [a]believe not, *yet* he abideth faithful: he cannot [b]deny himself.

14 Of these things put *them* in remembrance, charging *them* before the Lord that they [a]strive not about words to no profit, *but* to the subverting of the hearers.

15 [a]Study to shew thyself approved unto God, a workman that needeth not to be ashamed, [b]rightly dividing the word of truth.

16 But shun profane *and* [a]vain babblings: for they will increase unto more [b]ungodliness.

17 And their [a]word will eat as doth a canker: of whom is [b]Hymenæus and Philetus;

18 Who concerning the truth have [a]erred, saying that the resurrection is past already; and overthrow the faith of some.

19 Nevertheless the foundation of God standeth sure, having this seal, The Lord knoweth them that are his. And, Let every one that nameth the name of Christ depart from iniquity.

20 But in a great house there are not only vessels of gold and of silver, but also of wood and of [a]earth; and some to honour, and some to dishonour.

21 If a man therefore purge himself from these, he shall be a [a]vessel unto honour, [b]sanctified, and [c]meet for the master's use, *and* prepared unto every good work.

22 Flee also youthful [a]lusts: but follow [b]righteousness, faith, charity, [c]peace, with them that call on the Lord out of a [d]pure heart.

23 But [a]foolish and unlearned [b]questions avoid, knowing that they do gender [c]strifes.

24 And the servant of the Lord must not [a]strive; but be gentle unto all *men,* apt to [b]teach, patient,

25 In [a]meekness [b]instructing those that oppose themselves; if God [c]peradventure will give them repentance to the acknowledging of the truth;

26 And *that* they may recover themselves out of the snare of the devil, who are taken [a]captive by him at his will.

6*a* 1 Cor. 9:10.
8*a* TG Jesus Christ, Resurrection.
b TG Gospel.
11*a* Rom. 6:5 (5, 8).
12*a* GR endure, remain constant. TG Persecution; Suffering.
b TG Millennium, Preparing a People for.
c Matt. 10:33 (32–33); Rom. 1:16 (15–18); 2 Ne. 31:14 (12–21); D&C 101:5 (1–5).
13*a* GR are unfaithful.
b D&C 39:16. TG God, Perfection of.
14*a* GR dispute not about words, or trivialities.
15*a* TG Scriptures, Study of.
b GR setting forth without perversion, distortion.
16*a* GR vain disputation.
b TG Godliness.
17*a* GR teaching will spread like gangrene.
b 1 Tim. 1:20.
18*a* TG Apostasy of the Early Christian Church.
20*a* GR clay, earthenware.
21*a* TG Body, Sanctity of.
b Isa. 52:11.
c GR useful, profitable.
22*a* GR impure, violent desires. TG Chastity; Lust.
b TG Priesthood, Magnifying Callings within.
c TG Peace.
d 1 Tim. 1:5.
23*a* Titus 3:9.
b D&C 19:31 (29–31).
c TG Strife.
24*a* 3 Ne. 11:29 (29–30); D&C 18:20; 136:23.
b 1 Tim. 3:2.
25*a* TG Meek.
b D&C 20:53.
c GR perchance.
26*a* Moses 7:26. TG Bondage, Spiritual.

CHAPTER 3

Paul describes the apostasy and perilous times of the last days—The scriptures guide man to salvation.

THIS know also, that in the [a]last days
perilous [b]times shall come.
2 For men shall be lovers of their
own selves, [a]covetous, boasters,
[b]proud, blasphemers, [c]disobedient
to parents, [d]unthankful, unholy,
3 Without [a]natural [b]affection,
[c]trucebreakers, [d]false accusers, [e]in-
continent, fierce, despisers of those
that are good,
4 [a]Traitors, [b]heady, [c]highminded,
lovers of [d]pleasures more than lovers of God;
5 Having a [a]form of godliness, but
[b]denying the power thereof: from
such turn away.
6 For of this sort are they which
creep into houses, and lead captive
silly [a]women laden with sins, led
away with divers [b]lusts,
7 Ever [a]learning, and never able
to come to the [b]knowledge of the
[c]truth.
8 Now as Jannes and Jambres
withstood Moses, so do these also
[a]resist the truth: men of [b]corrupt
minds, reprobate concerning the
faith.
9 But they shall proceed no further: for their [a]folly shall be manifest unto all *men*, as theirs also
was.
10 But thou hast [a]fully known
my doctrine, manner of life, purpose, faith, longsuffering, charity,
patience,
11 Persecutions, afflictions, which
came unto me at Antioch, at Iconium, at Lystra; what [a]persecutions
I endured: but out of *them* all the
Lord delivered me.
12 Yea, and all that will live [a]godly
in Christ Jesus shall [b]suffer [c]perse-
cution.
13 But evil men and [a]seducers shall
wax worse and worse, deceiving,
and being deceived.
14 But [a]continue thou in the things
which thou hast learned and hast
been assured of, knowing of whom
thou hast learned *them*;
15 And that from a [a]child thou hast
known the holy [b]scriptures, which
are able to make thee [c]wise unto
[d]salvation through faith which is
in Christ Jesus.
16 [a]All [b]scripture *is* given by [c]inspi-
ration of God, and *is* [d]profitable for
[e]doctrine, for [f]reproof, for correction,
for [g]instruction in [h]righteousness:
17 That the man of God may be
[a]perfect, throughly furnished unto
all [b]good works.

---

3 1*a* Morm. 1:17 (13–17); 8:28 (26–33). TG Last Days.
b 2 Tim. 4:3.
2*a* TG Covet.
b TG Pride.
c TG Contention; Disobedience; Family, Children, Duties of.
d TG Ingratitude.
3*a* Rom. 1:26 (26–28).
b TG Sexual Immorality.
c TG Honesty.
d GR slanderers.
e GR without self-control.
4*a* TG Rebellion.
b GR rash, reckless.
c GR puffed up, conceited.
d TG Pleasure.
5*a* Rom. 2:20; 2 Ne. 28:5; JS—H 1:19.
b TG Apostasy of the Early Christian Church.
6*a* TG Woman.
b TG Lust.
7*a* TG Learn.
b TG Ignorance; Knowledge.
c TG Truth.
8*a* TG Opposition.
b Ps. 14:1; D&C 10:21 (20–23); 112:23 (23–24).
9*a* D&C 35:7; 45:49; 63:15.
10*a* GR followed closely, conformed to.
11*a* Acts 15:26.
12*a* TG Godliness.
b Ps. 34:19. TG Suffering.
c TG Cruelty; Persecution.
13*a* GR diviners, imposters, cheats.
14*a* D&C 66:12.
15*a* Deut. 4:9 (6–9).
b TG Scriptures, Study of.
c TG Understanding.
d TG Salvation.
16*a* JST 2 Tim. 3:16 *And all scripture given by inspiration of God, is profitable . . .*
b TG Book of Mormon; Scriptures, Writing of; Scriptures to Come Forth.
c TG Inspiration.
d GR beneficial or useful for instruction.
e TG Scriptures, Value of.
f TG Chastening; Reproof.
g TG Education.
h TG Righteousness.
17*a* GR suited, ready, complete. TG Perfection.
b TG Good Works.

CHAPTER 4

Paul gives a solemn charge to preach the gospel in a day of apostasy—Paul and all Saints are assured of exaltation.

I CHARGE *thee* therefore before God,
and the Lord Jesus Christ, who shall
[a]judge the quick and the dead at his
appearing and his kingdom;
2 [a]Preach the word; [b]be [c]instant
in season, out of season; [d]reprove,
rebuke, exhort with all longsuffering and doctrine.
3 For the time will come when
they will not [a]endure sound [b]doc-
trine; but after their own [c]lusts shall
they heap to themselves [d]teachers,
having itching ears;
4 And they shall turn away *their*
ears from the [a]truth, and shall be
turned unto [b]fables.
5 But [a]watch thou in all things,
endure afflictions, do the work of
an [b]evangelist, [c]make full proof of
thy ministry.
6 For I am now ready to be offered,
and the time of my departure is at
hand.
7 I have fought a good [a]fight, I
have [b]finished *my* course, I have
kept the faith:
8 Henceforth there is laid up for me
a [a]crown of [b]righteousness, which
the Lord, the righteous [c]judge, shall
give me at that day: and not to me
only, but unto all them also that
love his appearing.
9 Do thy diligence to come shortly
unto me:
10 For [a]Demas hath [b]forsaken me,
having loved this present [c]world,
and is departed unto Thessalonica; Crescens to Galatia, Titus unto
Dalmatia.
11 Only [a]Luke is with me. Take
[b]Mark, and bring him with thee:
for he is profitable to me for the
ministry.
12 And Tychicus have I sent to
Ephesus.
13 The cloak that I left at Troas
with Carpus, when thou comest,
bring *with thee*, and the [a]books, *but*
especially the parchments.
14 Alexander the coppersmith did
me much evil: the Lord reward him
according to his [a]works:
15 Of whom be thou ware also;
for he hath greatly [a]withstood
our words.
16 At my first [a]answer no man
stood with me, but all *men* forsook
me: *I pray God* that it may not be
laid to their [b]charge.
17 Notwithstanding the [a]Lord
stood with me, and strengthened me;
that by me the preaching might be
fully known, and *that* all the Gentiles
might hear: and I was delivered out
of the mouth of the lion.
18 And the Lord shall deliver me
from every evil work, and will [a]pre-
serve *me* unto his heavenly kingdom: to whom *be* glory for ever and
ever. Amen.
19 Salute Prisca and Aquila, and
the household of Onesiphorus.
20 Erastus abode at Corinth: but
Trophimus have I left at Miletum
sick.

---

4 1*a* TG Jesus Christ, Judge.
2*a* TG Missionary Work; Preaching.
b JST 2 Tim. 4:2 . . . be instant in season, *those who are* out of season . . .
c GR urgent, earnest.
d TG Chastening; Reproof.
3*a* 2 Tim. 3:1; Hel. 13:28 (26–30).
b 1 Tim. 1:10.
c TG Lust.
d TG False Prophets; Teacher.
4*a* TG Truth.
b TG Apostasy of the Early Christian Church.
5*a* TG Watch.
b Acts 21:8; Eph. 4:11 (11–14).
c GR fulfill your ministry.
7*a* TG Contentment.
b TG Dedication.
8*a* TG Exaltation; Reward.
b TG God, the Standard of Righteousness.
c TG Jesus Christ, Judge.
10*a* Col. 4:14; Philem. 1:24.
b TG Apostasy of Individuals.
c TG Worldliness.
11*a* Acts 1:1.
b Acts 15:37 (37–39); Col. 4:10.
13*a* Luke 1:1 (1–4); 1 Ne. 13:26 (24–26).
14*a* D&C 64:11.
15*a* GR opposed, resisted.
16*a* GR defense.
b Acts 7:60 (59–60); 3 Ne. 12:44.
17*a* John 14:18.
18*a* GR save, rescue.

TITUS

WHO IS THE AUTHOR?
Paul

WHEN WAS IT WRITTEN?
Approximately dated between AD 63–64

WHO WAS THE INTENDED AUDIENCE?
Written to Titus, a church leader and coworker of Paul in the ministry. This letter to Titus is a pastoral letter—a letter written to encourage Titus, a leader in the church. It encourages good works among believers and the power of renewal. It is considered to be a simple blueprint of day-to-day Christian life. In the Christian life, it strongly encourages the need for mentors and godly friends.

DON'T MISS THIS IN **TITUS!**

TITUS 1:8–9 *A Lover of Hospitality*

TITUS 2:3–5 *Being a Mentor*

21 Do thy diligence to come before
winter. Eubulus greeteth thee, and
Pudens, and Linus, and Claudia, and
all the brethren.
22 The [a]Lord Jesus Christ *be* with
thy spirit. Grace *be* with you. Amen.

¶ The second *epistle* unto Timotheus, ordained the first bishop of the church of the Ephesians, was written from Rome, when Paul was brought before Nero the second time.

THE EPISTLE OF PAUL TO

TITUS

CHAPTER 1

Eternal life was promised before the world began—The qualifications of bishops are given—Unto the pure, all things are pure.

PAUL, a [a]servant of God, and an
[b]apostle of Jesus Christ, according to the faith of God's [c]elect,
and the acknowledging of the truth
which is after godliness;
2 In [a]hope of [b]eternal life, which
God, that cannot [c]lie, [d]promised before the world began;
3 But hath in due times manifested
his word through preaching, which is
committed unto me according to the
commandment of God our Saviour;
4 To Titus, [a]*mine* own son after the
common faith: Grace, mercy, *and*
peace, from God the Father and
the Lord Jesus Christ our Saviour.
5 For this cause left I thee in Crete,
that thou shouldest set in [a]order the
things that are wanting, and [b]ordain [c]elders in every city, as I had
[d]appointed thee:
6 If any be blameless, the husband
of one wife, having faithful children
not accused of [a]riot or unruly.
7 For a [a]bishop must be blameless, as the [b]steward of God; not
[c]selfwilled, not soon [d]angry, not
given to wine, no striker, not given
to filthy lucre;
8 But a lover of [a]hospitality, a
lover of [b]good men, sober, just, holy,
[c]temperate;
9 Holding fast the faithful word as
he hath been taught, that he may
be able by sound doctrine both to
exhort and to [a]convince the [b]gainsayers.
10 For there are many unruly
and [a]vain talkers and [b]deceivers,
specially they of the [c]circumcision:
11 Whose mouths must be stopped,
who subvert whole houses, teaching

22*a* TG Jesus Christ, Lord.

[TITUS]

1 1*a* TG Servant.
b TG Apostles.
c TG Election.
2*a* TG Hope.
b TG Salvation, Plan of.
c TG God, Perfection of; Lying.
d 2 Tim. 1:1; Abr. 3:26.
4*a* GR a true son according to.
5*a* TG Order.
b TG Priesthood, Authority; Priesthood, Ordination.
c TG Church Organization; Elder, Melchizedek Priesthood.
d GR directed, ordered.
6*a* GR debauchery or insubordination.
7*a* TG Bishop; Leadership.
b TG Delegation of Responsibility; Stewardship.
c GR obstinate, arrogant.
d TG Anger.
8*a* TG Hospitality.
b GR what is good.
c GR self-controlled. TG Temperance.
9*a* D&C 11:21.
b GR those who deny, contradict.
10*a* GR idle speakers, disputers.
b TG Apostasy of the Early Christian Church.
c TG Circumcision.

things which they ought not, for filthy [a]lucre's sake.

12 One of themselves, *even* a prophet of their own, said, The Cretians *are* alway liars, evil beasts, [a]slow bellies.

13 This witness is true. Wherefore [a]rebuke them sharply, that they may be sound in the faith;

14 Not giving heed to Jewish [a]fables, and [b]commandments of men, [c]that turn from the truth.

15 [a]Unto the pure all things *are* [b]pure: but unto them that are [c]defiled and unbelieving *is* nothing pure; but even their [d]mind and [e]conscience is [f]defiled.

16 They [a]profess that they [b]know God; but in [c]works they [d]deny *him*, being abominable, and [e]disobedient, and unto every good work [f]reprobate.

CHAPTER 2

Saints should live righteously, deny ungodliness, and seek the Lord.

BUT [a]speak thou the things which become sound [b]doctrine:

2 That the [a]aged men be [b]sober, grave, [c]temperate, sound in faith, in charity, in patience.

3 The aged women likewise, that *they be* in behaviour as becometh holiness, not [a]false [b]accusers, not given to much wine, teachers of good things;

4 That they may teach the young [a]women to be sober, to [b]love their husbands, to love their children,

5 *To be* discreet, [a]chaste, [b]keepers at [c]home, good, obedient to their own husbands, that the word of God be not blasphemed.

6 Young men likewise exhort to be sober minded.

7 In all things shewing thyself a pattern of good works: in doctrine *shewing* uncorruptness, [a]gravity, [b]sincerity,

8 [a]Sound speech, that cannot be [b]condemned; that he that is [c]of the contrary part may be ashamed, having no evil thing to say of you.

9 *Exhort* [a]servants to be obedient unto their own masters, *and* to please *them* well in all *things;* not [b]answering again;

10 Not [a]purloining, but shewing all good fidelity; that they may [b]adorn the doctrine of God our Saviour in all things.

11 For the [a]grace of God [b]that bringeth salvation hath appeared to all men,

12 Teaching us that, denying [a]ungodliness and [b]worldly [c]lusts, we should live [d]soberly, [e]righteously, and godly, in this present world;

11*a* 1 Tim. 6:5; Mosiah 29:40; Alma 11:24.
12*a* GR lazy gluttons.
13*a* D&C 84:117 (87, 117).
14*a* 1 Tim. 1:4.
b Matt. 15:9; Col. 2:22; D&C 3:6 (6–7); 45:29; 46:7; JS—H 1:19.
c GR who reject, repudiate the truth.
15*a* JST Titus 1:15 Unto the pure, *let* all things *be* pure . . .
b TG Purity.
c TG Pollution.
d Luke 11:39 (39–41). TG Mind.
e TG Conscience.
f Mark 7:15; 2 Ne. 19:17; D&C 93:35.
16*a* Matt. 7:21 (21–23). TG False Prophets; Hypocrisy.
b Hosea 8:2. TG Ignorance.
c Matt. 15:8 (7–9).
d TG Apostasy of the Early Christian Church.
e TG Disobedience.
f GR unfit, worthless.
2 1*a* 1 Thes. 2:4; 1 Pet. 4:11. TG Teaching.
b D&C 88:77 (77–78).
2*a* TG Old Age.
b GR circumspect.
c TG Temperance.
3*a* GR slanderers, traitors, devils.
b TG Gossip.
4*a* TG Marriage, Wives.
b TG Family, Love within.
5*a* TG Chastity; Modesty.
b GR housekeepers, guards.
c 1 Tim. 5:14.
7*a* GR dignity, respectfulness.
b TG Sincere.
8*a* 1 Tim. 6:3.
b 1 Pet. 2:12 (11–12).
c GR an opponent, enemy.
9*a* Eph. 6:5; Col. 3:22; 1 Tim. 6:1 (1–2); 1 Pet. 2:18.
b GR arguing against, opposing, contradicting.
10*a* GR misappropriating, robbing. TG Stealing.
b GR honor, put in order.
11*a* TG Grace.
b JST Titus 2:11 . . . *which* bringeth salvation *to all men,* hath appeared;
12*a* TG Godliness.
b TG Worldliness.
c TG Lust.
d TG Levity.
e TG Abundant Life; Righteousness.

13 Looking for that blessed hope, and the [a]glorious appearing of the great God and our Saviour Jesus Christ;
14 Who gave [a]himself for us, that he might [b]redeem us from all iniquity, and [c]purify unto himself a [d]peculiar people, [e]zealous of good works.
15 These things speak, and exhort, and [a]rebuke with all [b]authority. Let no man [c]despise thee.

CHAPTER 3

Saints must live righteously after baptism.

PUT them in mind to be [a]subject to [b]principalities and powers, to obey magistrates, to be ready to every good work,
2 To [a]speak evil of no man, to be [b]no brawlers, *but* gentle, shewing all [c]meekness unto all men.
3 For we ourselves also were [a]sometimes foolish, [b]disobedient, deceived, serving divers [c]lusts and pleasures, living in [d]malice and envy, hateful, *and* hating one another.
4 But after that the kindness and love of God our Saviour toward man appeared,
5 Not by works of [a]righteousness which we have done, but according to his [b]mercy he saved us, by the [c]washing of regeneration, and [d]renewing of the Holy Ghost;
6 Which he shed on us abundantly through Jesus Christ our Saviour;
7 That being [a]justified by his grace, we should be made [b]heirs according to the hope of eternal life.
8 *This is* a faithful saying, and these things I will that thou affirm constantly, that they which have believed in God might be careful to maintain good [a]works. These things are good and profitable unto men.
9 But avoid [a]foolish questions, and genealogies, and [b]contentions, and strivings about the law; for they are unprofitable and vain.
10 A man that is an [a]heretick after the first and second [b]admonition reject;
11 Knowing that he that is such is [a]subverted, and sinneth, being condemned of himself.
12 When I shall send Artemas unto thee, or Tychicus, be diligent to come unto me to Nicopolis: for I have determined there to winter.
13 Bring Zenas the lawyer and Apollos on their journey diligently, that nothing be wanting unto them.
14 And let [a]ours also learn to maintain [b]good works for necessary uses, that they be not unfruitful.
15 All that are with me salute thee. Greet them that love us in the faith. Grace *be* with you all. Amen.

¶ It was written to Titus, ordained the first bishop of the church of the Cretians, from Nicopolis of Macedonia.

13*a* TG Glory.
14*a* TG Self-Sacrifice.
b TG Jesus Christ, Atonement through; Jesus Christ, Redeemer; Redemption.
c TG Purification; Purity.
d TG Peculiar People.
e TG Zeal.
15*a* TG Chastening.
b TG Authority.
c GR disregard.

3 1*a* TG Citizenship.
b TG Governments.
2*a* TG Slander.
b GR not quarrelsome.
c D&C 38:41.
3*a* GR once, formerly.
b TG Disobedience.
c TG Lust.
d TG Malice.
5*a* TG Righteousness.
b TG God, Mercy of.
c TG Baptism, Essential.
d TG Holy Ghost, Gifts of.

7*a* TG Justification.
b D&C 70:8.
8*a* TG Good Works.
9*a* 2 Tim. 2:23 (23–26).
b TG Contention.
10*a* TG Apostasy of Individuals.
b Matt. 18:17.
11*a* GR perverted, changed.
14*a* GR our people.
b Rom. 15:28 (25–28); Philip. 4:17.

THE EPISTLE OF PAUL TO

PHILEMON

The gospel changes a servant into a brother.

PAUL, a prisoner of Jesus Christ,
and Timothy *our* brother, unto
Philemon our dearly beloved,
and fellowlabourer,
2 And to *our* beloved Apphia, and
[a]Archippus our fellowsoldier, and
to the church in thy house:
3 Grace to you, and peace, from
God our Father and the Lord Jesus
Christ.
4 I thank my God, making mention of thee always in my prayers,
5 Hearing of thy love and faith,
which thou hast toward the Lord
Jesus, and toward all saints;
6 That the [a]communication of thy
faith may become [b]effectual by the
acknowledging of every good thing
which is in you in Christ Jesus.
7 For we have great joy and consolation in thy love, because the
[a]bowels of the saints are refreshed
by thee, brother.
8 Wherefore, though I might be
much bold in Christ to enjoin thee
that which is convenient,
9 Yet for love's sake I rather beseech
thee, being such an one as Paul the
aged, and now also a prisoner of
Jesus Christ.
10 I beseech thee for my son [a]Ones-
imus, whom I have begotten in my
bonds:
11 Which in time past was to thee
unprofitable, but now profitable to
thee and to me:
12 Whom I have sent again: thou
therefore receive him, that is, mine
own bowels:
13 Whom I would have retained
with me, that in thy stead he might
have ministered unto me in the
bonds of the gospel:
14 But without thy [a]mind would I
do nothing; that thy benefit should
not be as it were of necessity, but
willingly.
15 For perhaps he therefore departed for a season, that thou shouldest receive him for ever;
16 Not now as a servant, but above
a servant, a [a]brother beloved, specially to me, but how much more
unto thee, both in the flesh, and in
the Lord?
17 If thou count me therefore a
partner, receive him as myself.
18 If he hath wronged thee, or
oweth *thee* [a]ought, put that on mine
account;
19 I Paul have written *it* with mine
own hand, I will repay *it:* albeit I
do not say to thee how thou owest
unto me even thine own self besides.
20 Yea, brother, let me have joy of
thee in the Lord: refresh my bowels
in the Lord.
21 Having confidence in thy obedience I wrote unto thee, knowing that
thou wilt also do more than I say.
22 But withal prepare me also a
lodging: for I trust that through your
[a]prayers I shall be given unto you.
23 There salute thee [a]Epaphras,
my fellowprisoner in Christ Jesus;
24 Marcus, Aristarchus, [a]Demas,
Lucas, my fellowlabourers.
25 The grace of our Lord Jesus
Christ *be* with your spirit. Amen.

¶ Written from Rome to Philemon, by Onesimus a servant.

---

1 2*a* Col. 4:17.
6*a* GR participation, fellowship.
b GR active.
7*a* GR affections, compassion.
10*a* Col. 4:9.
14*a* GR assent, suggestion. TG Mind.
16*a* TG Brotherhood and Sisterhood.
18*a* GR something, anything.
22*a* 2 Cor. 1:11; Philip. 1:19.
23*a* Col. 1:7 (7–8); 4:12 (12–13).
24*a* Col. 4:14; 2 Tim. 4:10.

THE EPISTLE OF PAUL THE APOSTLE

TO THE

HEBREWS

CHAPTER 1

The Son is in the express image of the person of the Father—Christ is the Only Begotten Son and thus above the angels.

GOD, who [a]at sundry times and
in divers manners spake in
time past unto the [b]fathers
by the [c]prophets,
2 Hath in these last days spoken
unto us by *his* [a]Son, whom he hath
[b]appointed [c]heir of all things, by
whom also he [d]made the [e]worlds;
3 Who being the brightness of *his*
[a]glory, and the express image of his
[b]person, and upholding all things
by the word of his [c]power, when
he had by himself [d]purged our sins,
sat down on the [e]right hand of the
[f]Majesty on high;
4 Being made so much better than
the angels, as he hath by inheritance
obtained a more excellent [a]name
than they.
5 For unto which of the angels said
he at any time, Thou art my [a]Son,
this day have I begotten thee? And
again, I will be to him a [b]Father,
and he shall be to me a Son?
6 And again, when he bringeth in
the [a]firstbegotten into the world, he
saith, [b]And let all the angels of God
[c]worship him.
7 And of the angels he saith, Who
maketh his angels spirits, and his
ministers a flame of fire.
8 But unto the Son *he saith*, Thy
[a]throne, O God, *is* for [b]ever and
ever: a sceptre of righteousness *is*
the sceptre of thy kingdom.
9 Thou hast loved [a]righteousness,
and hated iniquity; therefore God,
even thy God, hath anointed thee
with the oil of gladness above thy
fellows.
10 And, Thou, Lord, in the beginning hast laid the [a]foundation of
the earth; and the heavens are the
works of thine [b]hands:
11 They shall perish; but thou re-
mainest; and they all shall [a]wax old
as doth a garment;
12 And as a vesture shalt thou fold

---

1 1*a* GR in many locations and various ways.
b TG Family, Patriarchal.
c TG Prophets, Mission of.
2*a* TG Godhead; Jesus Christ, Divine Sonship; Jesus Christ, Jehovah.
b TG Jesus Christ, Authority of.
c Matt. 21:38 (33–46). TG Jesus Christ, Relationships with the Father.
d TG Jesus Christ, Creator.
e TG Astronomy; Creation; God, Creator.
3*a* John 1:14. TG Celestial Glory.
b TG God, Body of, Corporeal Nature.
c TG God, Power of.
d GR made purification, expiation for.
e Acts 7:55 (55–56); D&C 76:23.
f Heb. 12:2.
4*a* Eph. 1:21 (20–21); Philip. 2:9 (9–10). TG Name.
5*a* Heb. 5:5. TG Jesus Christ, Divine Sonship.
b 2 Sam. 7:14; 1 Chr. 17:13.
6*a* TG Jesus Christ, Firstborn.
b JST Heb. 1:6–7 . . . And let all the angels of God worship him, *who maketh his ministers as a flame of fire.* And of the angels he saith, *Angels are ministering spirits.*
c TG Worship.
8*a* TG Kingdom of God, in Heaven.
b D&C 88:104.
9*a* TG Righteousness.
10*a* TG Jesus Christ, Creator.
b D&C 67:2.
11*a* GR grow old, become worn.

them up, and they shall be changed:
but thou art the same, and thy years
shall not fail.
13 But to which of the angels said
he at any time, Sit on my [a]right
hand, until I make thine enemies
thy footstool?
14 Are they not all [a]ministering
[b]spirits, sent forth [c]to minister for
them who shall be heirs of salvation?

CHAPTER 2

Jesus came to suffer death and save men—He came to make reconciliation for the sins of the people.

THEREFORE we ought to give the
more [a]earnest [b]heed to the things
which we have heard, lest at any
time we should let *them* slip.
2 For if the word spoken by angels
was steadfast, and every transgression and [a]disobedience received a
[b]just recompence of reward;
3 How shall we [a]escape, if we neglect so great salvation; which at
the first began to be spoken by the
Lord, and was confirmed unto us
by them that heard *him;*
4 God also bearing *them* witness,
both with [a]signs and [b]wonders,
and with divers miracles, and gifts
of the Holy Ghost, according to his
own [c]will?
5 For unto the angels hath he not
put in subjection the world to come,
whereof we speak.
6 But one in a certain place testified, saying, What is [a]man, that thou
art mindful of him? or the son of
man, that thou visitest him?
7 Thou madest him a little lower
than the [a]angels; thou crownedst him
with glory and honour, and didst
set him over the works of thy hands:
8 Thou hast put all things in subjection under his [a]feet. For in that
he put all in subjection under him,
he left nothing *that is* not put under him. But now we see not yet all
things put under him.
9 But we see Jesus, who was made
a little [a]lower than the [b]angels [c]for
the suffering of [d]death, [e]crowned
with glory and honour; that he by
the [f]grace of God should taste [g]death
for every man.
10 For [a]it became him, for whom
are all things, and by whom *are*
all [b]things, in bringing many sons
unto glory, to make the [c]captain
of their salvation [d]perfect through
sufferings.
11 For both he that sanctifieth
and they who are [a]sanctified *are*
all of [b]one: for which cause he is
not ashamed to call them [c]brethren,
12 Saying, I will declare thy [a]name
unto my brethren, in the midst of
the church will I sing praise unto
thee.
13 And again, I will put my [a]trust
in him. And again, Behold I and
the children which God hath given
me.
14 [a]Forasmuch then as the children
are partakers of [b]flesh and blood,
he also himself likewise took part
of the same; that through death he
might [c]destroy him that had the
power of [d]death, that is, the [e]devil;
15 And deliver them who through

13*a* Ps. 110:1.
14*a* D&C 7:6.
TG Angels.
b Zech. 6:5 (4–8).
c GR for service.
2 1*a* TG Zeal.
b D&C 21:4.
2*a* TG Disobedience.
b TG God, Justice of.
3*a* Heb. 10:29; 12:25.
4*a* Acts 5:12 (12–23).
TG Holy Ghost, Gifts of; Symbolism.
b TG Miracle.
c TG God, Will of.
6*a* Ps. 8:4 (4–6).
7*a* HEB gods;
GR angels.
8*a* Matt. 28:18;
1 Cor. 15:25;
Eph. 1:22.
9*a* TG Jesus Christ, Condescension of.
b Philip. 2:7 (7–9).
c GR through.
d TG Jesus Christ, Death of.
e Acts 2:33.
f TG Grace.
g TG Jesus Christ, Atonement through.
10*a* GR it was fitting, suitable, proper for Him.
b Col. 1:16 (13–19).
c TG Jesus Christ, Messiah.
d TG Perfection.
11*a* TG Sanctification.
b TG Unity.
c TG Brotherhood and Sisterhood.
12*a* Ps. 22:22.
13*a* Ps. 18:2.
14*a* GR Since.
b TG Flesh and Blood.
c Gen. 3:15.
d 2 Tim. 1:10.
TG Redemption.
e TG Devil.

fear of death were all their lifetime
subject to [a]bondage.
16 For verily he took not on *him*
the nature of [a]angels; but he took on
him the [b]seed of Abraham.
17 Wherefore in all things it be-
hoved him to be made like unto *his*
brethren, that he might be a merciful and faithful high priest in things
pertaining to God, to make [a]recon-
ciliation for the sins of the people.
18 For in that he himself hath suffered being [a]tempted, he is able to
[b]succour them that are tempted.

CHAPTER 3

Christ is the Apostle and High Priest of our profession—Jesus, being the Son, is more than a servant—Now is the time and the day of our salvation.

WHEREFORE, holy brethren, partakers of the heavenly calling, [a]consider
the [b]Apostle and [c]High Priest of our
profession, Christ Jesus;
2 Who was faithful to him that
appointed him, as also Moses *was*
faithful in all his house.
3 For this *man* was counted worthy
of more glory than Moses, inasmuch
as he who hath builded the house
hath more honour than the house.
4 For every house is builded by
some *man;* but he that built all
things *is* God.
5 And Moses verily *was* faithful
in all his house, as a [a]servant, for
a testimony of those things which
were to be spoken after;
6 But Christ as a son over his own
[a]house; whose [b]house are we, if we
hold fast the confidence and the rejoicing of the hope firm unto the end.
7 Wherefore (as the [a]Holy Ghost
saith, [b]To day if ye will hear his
voice,
8 [a]Harden not your hearts, as in the
[b]provocation, in the day of temptation in the wilderness:
9 When your fathers tempted me,
[a]proved me, and saw my works
forty years.
10 Wherefore I was grieved with
that [a]generation, and said, They do
alway err in *their* heart; and they
have not known my ways.
11 So I sware in my wrath, They
shall not [a]enter into my [b]rest.)
12 Take heed, brethren, lest there
be in any of you an evil [a]heart of
[b]unbelief, in [c]departing from the
living God.
13 But [a]exhort one another daily,
while it is called [b]To day; lest any
of you be hardened through the
deceitfulness of sin.
14 For we are made partakers of
Christ, if we hold the beginning
of our confidence [a]steadfast unto
the end;
15 While it is said, To day if ye
will hear his voice, [a]harden not
your hearts, as in the [b]provocation.
16 For some, when they had heard,
did provoke: howbeit not all that
came out of Egypt by Moses.
17 But with whom was he grieved
forty years? *was it* not with them
that had sinned, whose [a]carcases
fell in the wilderness?

15*a* TG Bondage, Spiritual; Law of Moses.
16*a* TG Angels.
b TG Seed of Abraham.
17*a* TG Jesus Christ, Redeemer; Reconciliation.
18*a* GR tried, subjected to trial. TG Jesus Christ, Temptation of; Test.
b Alma 7:12; D&C 62:1.
3 1*a* TG Meditation.
b TG Jesus Christ, Messenger of the Covenant.
c TG High Priest, Melchizedek Priesthood.
5*a* TG Servant.
6*a* TG Church.
b 1 Pet. 2:5 (4–8).
7*a* Heb. 10:15.
b Ps. 95:7 (7–11).
8*a* TG Hardheartedness.
b Num. 14:23 (2–23); Jacob 1:7 (7–8); Alma 12:36.
9*a* TG Test.
10*a* Prov. 30:12 (11–14).
11*a* Ps. 95:11.
b D&C 84:24. TG God, Presence of; God, Privilege of Seeing; Rest.
12*a* Gen. 6:5; Matt. 15:19; Hel. 12:4.
b TG Stiffnecked.
c GR apostatizing, withdrawing from. TG Apostasy of Individuals.
13*a* Alma 34:39; D&C 38:23. TG Chastening.
b D&C 45:6.
14*a* TG Perseverance; Steadfastness.
15*a* TG Contrite Heart.
b TG Provoking.
17*a* Num. 14:29 (29, 37); 1 Cor. 10:5 (2–7).

18 And to whom sware he that they
should not enter into his rest, but
to them that believed not?
19 So we see that they could not
enter in because of [a]unbelief.

CHAPTER 4

The gospel was offered to ancient Israel—Saints enter into the rest of the Lord—Though tempted in all points, Jesus was without sin.

LET us therefore fear, lest, a promise being left *us* of entering into
his [a]rest, any of you should seem
to come short of it.
2 For unto us was the [a]gospel
preached, as well as unto them: but
the word preached did not profit
them, not being mixed with [b]faith
in them that heard *it*.
3 [a]For we which have believed do
enter into rest, as he said, As I have
sworn in my wrath, if they shall enter into my [b]rest: although the works
were finished from the foundation
of the world.
4 For he spake in a certain place of
the [a]seventh *day* on this wise, And
God did rest the seventh day from
all his works.
5 [a]And in this *place* again, If they
shall enter into my rest.
6 Seeing therefore it remaineth
that some must enter therein, and
[a]they to whom it was first preached
entered not in because of [b]unbelief:
7 Again, he [a]limiteth a certain day,
saying in David, To day, after so
long a time; as it is said, To day if
ye will [b]hear his voice, [c]harden not
your hearts.
8 For if [a]Jesus had given them rest,
then would he not afterward have
spoken of another day.
9 There remaineth therefore a rest
to the people of God.
10 For he that is entered into his
rest, he also hath ceased from his
own works, as God *did* from his.
11 Let us [a]labour therefore to enter into that rest, lest any man fall
after the same example of [b]unbelief.
12 For the [a]word of God *is* [b]quick,
and powerful, and sharper than any
twoedged [c]sword, [d]piercing even to
the dividing asunder of [e]soul and
spirit, and of the joints and marrow,
and *is* a [f]discerner of the [g]thoughts
and [h]intents of the heart.
13 Neither is there any creature
that is not manifest in his sight:
but all things *are* naked and opened
unto the [a]eyes of him with whom
we have to do.
14 Seeing then that we have a great
high priest, that is passed into the
[a]heavens, Jesus the Son of God, let
us hold fast *our* profession.
15 For we have not an high priest
[a]which cannot be touched with the
feeling of our infirmities; but was
in all points [b]tempted like as *we are*,
yet without [c]sin.
16 Let us therefore come boldly
unto the throne of [a]grace, that we
may obtain mercy, and find grace
to help in time of need.

19*a* TG Unbelief.
4 1*a* TG God, Glory of; Rest.
2*a* TG Gospel.
b TG Faith.
3*a* JST Heb. 4:3 (Appendix).
b D&C 19:9.
4*a* TG Sabbath.
5*a* JST Heb. 4:5 And in this place again, If they *harden not their hearts they* shall enter into my rest.
6*a* GR those who formerly were taught the gospel.
b GR disobedience, unbelief, obstinacy.
7*a* GR appoints, decrees, constitutes.
b Ps. 95:7.
c TG Hardheartedness.
8*a* Ex. 17:9; Acts 7:45.
11*a* GR hasten, be eager.
b GR obstinacy, disobedience. TG Unbelief.
12*a* Alma 31:5; D&C 6:2; 11:2; 12:2; 14:2; 33:1.
b GR living.
c Isa. 49:2; Rev. 2:12 (12–17).
d Hosea 6:5; D&C 85:6.
e JST Heb. 4:12 . . . *body* . . .
f 1 Cor. 14:25 (24–25). TG God, Omniscience of.
g D&C 6:16.
h TG Motivations.
13*a* Prov. 5:21.
14*a* Heb. 9:24.
15*a* GR unable to sympathize with our frailties, imperfections.
b TG Jesus Christ, Exemplar; Jesus Christ, Temptation of; Temptation; Test.
c John 8:46; Heb. 7:26; D&C 45:4. TG Sin.
16*a* TG Grace.

CHAPTER 5

For a man to hold the priesthood, he must be called of God as was Aaron—Christ was a priest forever after the order of Melchizedek—Jesus Christ is the Author of eternal salvation.

FOR every high priest taken from
among men is [a]ordained for men
in things *pertaining* to God, that he
may offer both gifts and [b]sacrifices
for sins:
2 Who can have [a]compassion on
the ignorant, and on them that are
[b]out of the way; for that he himself
also is compassed with infirmity.
3 And by reason hereof he ought,
as for the people, so also for himself, to offer for [a]sins.
4 And no man taketh this [a]honour
unto himself, but he that is [b]called
of God, as *was* [c]Aaron.
5 So also Christ glorified not himself to be made an high priest; but
he that said unto him, Thou art my
[a]Son, to day have I begotten thee.
6 As he saith also in another *place*,
Thou *art* a [a]priest [b]for ever after the
order of [c]Melchisedec.
7 Who in the days of his flesh, when
he had offered up [a]prayers and supplications with [b]strong crying and
tears unto him that was able to save
him from death, and was heard [c]in
that he feared;
8 Though he were a Son, yet
[a]learned he [b]obedience by the things
which he [c]suffered;
9 And being made [a]perfect, he became the [b]author of eternal [c]salva-
tion unto all them that obey him;
10 [a]Called of God an [b]high priest
after the order of Melchisedec.
11 Of whom we have many things
to say, and [a]hard to be [b]uttered, seeing ye are dull of [c]hearing.
12 For when for the time ye ought
to be teachers, ye have need that
one teach you again which *be* the
first principles of the oracles of God;
and are become such as have need
of [a]milk, and not of strong meat.
13 For every one that useth [a]milk *is*
unskilful in the word of righteousness: for he is a babe.
14 But strong meat belongeth to
them that are of full age, *even* those
who by reason of use have their
senses exercised to discern both
good and evil.

CHAPTER 6

Let us go on to perfection—The sons of perdition crucify Christ anew—God swears with an oath that the faithful will be saved.

THEREFORE [a]leaving the principles
of the doctrine of Christ, let us go on
unto [b]perfection; not laying again

5 1*a* TG Priesthood; Priesthood, Ordination.
b TG Sacrifice.
2*a* TG Compassion.
b GR straying, wandering.
3*a* Lev. 4:3.
4*a* TG Leadership.
b TG Called of God; Priesthood, Authority; Priesthood, Qualifying for.
c Ex. 28:1. TG Priesthood, Aaronic.
5*a* Heb. 1:5.
6*a* TG Priesthood, Melchizedek.
b D&C 124:130.
c TG Priesthood, History of.
7*a* Matt. 26:39 (39, 42, 44).
b GR mighty, powerful supplication.
c GR because of his piety, reverence.
8*a* TG Jesus Christ, Exemplar.
b TG Agency; Obedience.
c TG Jesus Christ, Temptation of; Pain; Suffering.
9*a* TG God, Perfection of; Perfection.
b TG Jesus Christ, Authority of.
c TG Gospel; Jesus Christ, Atonement through; Jesus Christ, Mission of; Salvation; Salvation, Plan of.
10*a* TG Jesus Christ, Authority of.
b TG High Priest, Melchizedek Priesthood; Jesus Christ, Types of, in Anticipation.
11*a* GR difficult to be explained.
b John 16:12 (12–13).
c Ezek. 33:31 (30–33); Matt. 11:15; 2 Ne. 9:31; D&C 1:14.
12*a* 1 Cor. 3:2 (2–3); D&C 19:22 (21–22); 50:40.
13*a* 1 Pet. 2:2 (1–3).
6 1*a* GR having left behind the beginning of the doctrine. JST Heb. 6:1 . . . *not* leaving . . .
b TG Perfection.

the foundation of [c]repentance from
dead works, and of faith toward God,
2 Of the [a]doctrine of [b]baptisms,
and of [c]laying on of [d]hands, and
of resurrection of the dead, and of
eternal judgment.
3 [a]And this will we do, if God
permit.
4 For *it is* impossible for those who
were once [a]enlightened, and have
tasted of the heavenly gift, and were
made partakers of the Holy Ghost,
5 And have [a]tasted the good word
of God, and the powers of the [b]world
to come,
6 If they shall [a]fall away, to renew
them again unto repentance; seeing
they [b]crucify to themselves the Son
of God afresh, and put *him* to an
open [c]shame.
7 For the earth which drinketh
in the rain that cometh oft upon
it, and bringeth forth herbs [a]meet
for them by whom it is [b]dressed,
receiveth blessing from God:
8 But that which beareth thorns
and briers *is* rejected, and *is* nigh
unto [a]cursing; whose end *is* to be
burned.
9 But, beloved, we are persuaded
better things of you, and things
that accompany salvation, though
we thus speak.
10 For God *is* not [a]unrighteous to
forget your work and [b]labour of
[c]love, which ye have shewed toward
his [d]name, in that ye have ministered to the saints, and do minister.
11 And we desire that every one
of you do shew the same [a]diligence
to the full assurance of hope unto
the end:
12 That ye be not [a]slothful, but fol-
lowers of them who through [b]faith
and [c]patience inherit the [d]promises.
13 For when God made promise to
Abraham, because he could [a]swear
by no greater, he [b]sware by himself,
14 Saying, Surely blessing I will
[a]bless thee, and multiplying I
will multiply thee.
15 And so, after he had patiently
[a]endured, he obtained the promise.
16 For men verily swear by the
greater: and an [a]oath for confirma-
tion *is* to them an end of all [b]strife.
17 Wherein God, willing more
abundantly to shew unto the heirs
of promise the immutability of his
[a]counsel, [b]confirmed *it* by an [c]oath:
18 That by two immutable things,
in which *it was* impossible for
God to [a]lie, we might have a strong
consolation, who have fled for [b]ref-
uge to lay hold upon the [c]hope set
before us:
19 Which *hope* we have as an [a]an-
chor of the soul, both sure and
steadfast, and which entereth into
that within the [b]veil;
20 Whither the forerunner is for us
entered, *even* Jesus, made an [a]high
priest for ever after the order of
Melchisedec.

CHAPTER 7

*The Melchizedek Priesthood brings ex-
altation and administers the gospel—It
is received with an oath and covenant*

1*c* TG Repent.
2*a* D&C 68:25.
b TG Baptism, Essential.
c D&C 107:67.
d TG Hands, Laying on of.
3*a* JST Heb. 6:3–10 (Appendix).
4*a* 2 Pet. 2:20.
5*a* 1 Pet. 2:3 (1–3).
b TG World.
6*a* TG Apostasy of Individuals; Holy Ghost, Loss of; Sin.
b TG Holy Ghost, Unpardonable Sin against; Jesus Christ, Crucifixion of.
c TG Shame.
7*a* GR suitable, fit, proper.
b GR cultivated, tilled.
8*a* D&C 104:3.
10*a* TG God, Perfection of.
b 1 Thes. 1:3.
c Col. 1:4.
d TG Name.
11*a* TG Dependability; Diligence.
12*a* TG Idleness; Laziness.
b Heb. 10:22 (22–24).
c TG Patience.
d TG Promise.
13*a* GR promise, confirm by an oath.
b Jer. 44:26; Amos 6:8.
14*a* TG Abrahamic Covenant.
15*a* TG Perseverance.
16*a* TG Oath.
b TG Strife.
17*a* GR design, purpose. TG Counselor.
b TG Vow.
c TG Covenants.
18*a* TG God, Perfection of.
b TG Refuge.
c TG Hope.
19*a* Ether 12:4.
b TG Veil.
20*a* TG High Priest, Melchizedek Priesthood.

—The superiority of the Melchizedek Priesthood over the Aaronic Priesthood is explained—Salvation comes through the intercession of Christ.

FOR this Melchisedec, king of Salem,
[a]priest of the most high God, who
met Abraham returning from the
slaughter of the kings, and blessed
him;
2 To whom also Abraham gave a
[a]tenth part of all; first being by interpretation King of [b]righteousness,
and after that also King of [c]Salem,
which is, King of peace;
3 [a]Without father, without mother,
without descent, having neither
[b]beginning of days, nor end of life;
but made like unto the Son of God;
abideth a [c]priest continually.
4 Now consider how great this man
was, unto whom even the [a]patri-
arch Abraham gave the tenth of the
spoils.
5 And verily they that are of the
sons of [a]Levi, who receive the [b]office
of the priesthood, have a commandment to take tithes of the people according to the law, that is, of their
brethren, though they come out of
the loins of Abraham:
6 But he whose descent is not
counted from them received tithes
of Abraham, and blessed him that
had the promises.
7 And without all contradiction
the less is blessed of the better.
8 And here men that die receive
tithes; but there he *receiveth them,*
of whom it is witnessed that he
liveth.
9 And as I may so say, Levi also,
who receiveth tithes, payed tithes
in Abraham.
10 For he was yet in the loins of his
father, when Melchisedec met him.
11 If therefore [a]perfection were by
the [b]Levitical priesthood, (for under
it the people received the law,) what
further need *was there* that another
priest should rise after the order of
Melchisedec, and not be called after
the order of Aaron?
12 For the [a]priesthood being
changed, there is made of necessity a change also of the law.
13 For he of whom these things are
spoken pertaineth to another tribe,
of which no man gave attendance
at the altar.
14 For *it is* evident that our Lord
sprang out of [a]Juda; of which tribe
Moses spake nothing concerning
priesthood.
15 And it is yet far more evident:
for that after the similitude of
Melchisedec there ariseth another
priest,
16 Who is made, not after the law
of a [a]carnal commandment, but after
the power of an endless life.
17 For he testifieth, Thou *art* a
priest for ever after the order of
[a]Melchisedec.
18 For there is verily a disannulling
of the commandment going before
for the [a]weakness and unprofitable-
ness thereof.
19 [a]For the law made nothing
[b]perfect, but the bringing in of a
[c]better hope *did;* by the which we
draw nigh unto God.
20 And inasmuch as not without
an [a]oath *he was made priest:*
21 (For those [a]priests were made
without an oath; but this with an
[b]oath by him that said unto him,
The Lord sware and will not repent,

7 1*a* TG Priesthood, Melchizedek.
2*a* TG Tithing.
b TG Righteousness.
c TG Jerusalem.
3*a* JST Heb. 7:3 (Appendix).
b D&C 84:17.
c TG Jesus Christ, Authority of.
4*a* TG Family, Patriarchal; Patriarch.
5*a* TG Priest, Aaronic Priesthood.
BD Priests.
b TG Priesthood, Aaronic.
11*a* Heb. 8:7.
TG Perfection.
b TG Priesthood, Aaronic.
12*a* TG Priesthood, History of.
14*a* Isa. 11:1; Micah 5:2.
TG Israel, Judah, People of.
16*a* Heb. 9:10.
17*a* Ps. 110:4.
18*a* Rom. 8:3.
19*a* JST Heb. 7:19–21 (Appendix).
b Heb. 9:9.
c Heb. 12:24.
20*a* TG Oath; Priesthood, Oath and Covenant.
21*a* TG Priesthood, Aaronic.
b TG Priesthood, Oath and Covenant.

Thou *art* a priest for ever after the
order of Melchisedec:)
22 By so much was Jesus made a
surety of a better [a]testament.
23 And they truly were many
priests, because they were not suffered to continue by reason of death:
24 But this *man,* because he continueth ever, hath an unchangeable
[a]priesthood.
25 Wherefore he is able also to save
them [a]to the uttermost that [b]come
unto God by him, seeing he ever liveth to make [c]intercession for them.
26 [a]For such an [b]high priest became
us, *who is* holy, harmless, undefiled,
[c]separate from [d]sinners, and made
[e]higher than the [f]heavens;
27 Who needeth not [a]daily, as those
high priests, to offer up [b]sacrifice,
first for his own sins, and then for
the people's: for this he did [c]once,
when he [d]offered up himself.
28 For the law maketh men high
priests which have infirmity; but
the word of the [a]oath, which was
since the law, *maketh* the [b]Son, who
is [c]consecrated for evermore.

CHAPTER 8

Christ offered Himself as a sacrifice for sin—God promised to make a new covenant with Israel.

Now of the things which we have
spoken *this is* the sum: We have
such an [a]high priest, who is set on
the right hand of the throne of the
Majesty in the heavens;
2 A minister of the sanctuary, and
of the [a]true [b]tabernacle, which the
Lord pitched, and not man.
3 For every high priest is ordained
to offer gifts and sacrifices: wherefore *it is* of necessity that this man
have somewhat also to [a]offer.
4 [a]For if he were on earth, he
should not be a priest, seeing that
there are [b]priests that offer gifts
according to the law:
5 Who serve unto the example and
[a]shadow of heavenly things, as Moses was admonished of God when he
was about to make the [b]tabernacle:
for, See, saith he, *that* thou make
all things according to the [c]pattern
shewed to thee in the mount.
6 But now hath he obtained a more
excellent ministry, by how much
also he is the [a]mediator of a better
[b]covenant, which was established
upon better [c]promises.
7 For if that first *covenant* had been
[a]faultless, then should no place have
been sought for the second.
8 For finding fault with them, he
saith, Behold, the days come, saith
the Lord, when I will make a new
covenant with the house of Israel
and with the house of [a]Judah:
9 Not according to the [a]covenant
that I made with their fathers in
the day when I took them by the
hand to lead them out of the land

22*a* Heb. 8:6.
24*a* TG Jesus Christ, Authority of; Priesthood.
25*a* GR perfectly.
b Isa. 55:3; Heb. 11:6.
c Isa. 59:16; Rom. 8:34.
26*a* JST Heb. 7:25–26 (Appendix).
b TG High Priest, Melchizedek Priesthood.
c Lev. 3:6. TG Separation.
d Heb. 4:15; D&C 45:4.
e TG Priesthood, Magnifying Callings within.
f Eph. 1:20.
27*a* Heb. 10:11.
b TG Sacrifice.
c Rom. 6:10; Heb. 10:10.
d TG Jesus Christ, Atonement through; Jesus Christ, Redeemer.
28*a* TG Oath.
b TG Jesus Christ, Divine Sonship.
c GR perfected.
8 1*a* TG High Priest, Melchizedek Priesthood; Jesus Christ, Authority of.
2*a* Heb. 9:24.
b Ex. 40:2; Heb. 9:11 (11–24).
3*a* Eph. 5:2.
4*a* JST Heb. 8:4 *Therefore while he was on the* earth, he *offered for a sacrifice his own life for the sins of the people. Now every priest under the law, must needs* offer gifts, *or sacrifices,* according to the law.
b TG Priest, Aaronic Priesthood. BD Priests.
5*a* TG Jesus Christ, Types of, in Anticipation.
b Ex. 35:11.
c Acts 7:44.
6*a* TG Jesus Christ, Atonement through; Jesus Christ, Authority of.
b Heb. 7:22. TG Covenants; Priesthood, Melchizedek.
c TG Promise.
7*a* Heb. 7:11 (11–16).
8*a* TG Israel, Judah, People of.
9*a* TG Law of Moses.

of Egypt; because they continued
not in my covenant, and I regarded
them not, saith the Lord.
10 For this *is* the covenant that I
will make with the house of Israel
after those days, saith the Lord; I
will put my [a]laws into their [b]mind,
and write them in their [c]hearts: and
I will be to them a God, and they
shall be to me a people:
11 And they shall not teach every
man his neighbour, and every man
his brother, saying, Know the Lord:
for all shall know me, from the least
to the greatest.
12 For I will be merciful to their
[a]unrighteousness, and their sins
and their iniquities will I [b]remem-
ber no more.
13 In that he saith, A [a]new *covenant*,
he hath made the first old. Now that
which decayeth and waxeth [b]old *is*
ready to [c]vanish away.

CHAPTER 9

The Mosaic ordinances prefigured Christ's ministry—Christ is the Mediator of the new covenant.

THEN verily the first [a]*covenant* had
also [b]ordinances of divine [c]service,
and a worldly sanctuary.
2 For there was a [a]tabernacle
made; the first, wherein *was* the
[b]candlestick, and the [c]table, and
the [d]shewbread; which is called the
sanctuary.
3 And after the second [a]veil, the
tabernacle which is called the [b]Ho-
liest of all;
4 Which had the golden censer,
and the [a]ark of the covenant over-
laid round about with gold, wherein
was the golden [b]pot that had manna,
and [c]Aaron's rod that budded, and
the [d]tables of the covenant;
5 And over it the [a]cherubims of
glory shadowing the [b]mercyseat;
of which we cannot now speak particularly.
6 Now when these things were thus
[a]ordained, the [b]priests went always
into the first tabernacle, accomplishing the service *of God*.
7 But into the second *went* the [a]high
priest alone [b]once every year, not
without blood, which he offered
for himself, and *for* the errors of
the people:
8 The Holy Ghost this signifying,
that the way into the holiest of all
was not yet made manifest, while as
the first tabernacle was yet standing:
9 Which *was* a [a]figure for the time
then present, in which were offered
both gifts and sacrifices, that could
not make him that did the service
[b]perfect, as pertaining to the conscience;
10 *Which stood* only in meats and
drinks, and divers [a]washings, and
[b]carnal [c]ordinances, [d]imposed *on
them* until the time of reformation.
11 But Christ being come an [a]high
priest of good things to come, by a
greater and more perfect [b]taberna-
cle, not made with hands, that is to
say, not of this building;
12 Neither by the blood of goats
and calves, but by his own [a]blood he

10*a* TG God, Law of.
b TG Mind.
c Jer. 31:33; 2 Cor. 3:3.
12*a* D&C 38:14.
b TG Forgive.
13*a* Heb. 9:15; 3 Ne. 12:47 (46–47); 15:3 (2–10); Ether 13:9. TG New and Everlasting Covenant.
b 2 Cor. 5:17.
c 3 Ne. 12:46 (19, 46).
9 1*a* TG Law of Moses.
b TG Ordinance.
c TG Service.
2*a* Ex. 26:1 (1–37); 39:33.
b Ex. 25:31 (31–39); 26:35.
c Ex. 25:23 (23–29); Lev. 24:6.
d Ex. 25:30.
3*a* TG Jesus Christ, Types of, in Anticipation; Veil.
b GR Holy of holies.
4*a* TG Ark of the Covenant.
b Ex. 16:33 (33–34).
c Num. 17:10.
d Ex. 25:16 (16, 20, 40).
5*a* TG Cherubim.
b Ex. 25:17.
6*a* GR prepared, built.
b TG Priest, Aaronic Priesthood. BD Priests.
7*a* Heb. 9:25; 10:3.
b Ex. 30:10.
9*a* GR similitude, type, parable. TG Jesus Christ, Types of, in Anticipation.
b Heb. 7:19.
10*a* TG Wash.
b Heb. 7:16.
c TG Ordinance.
d Mosiah 13:29 (27–32).
11*a* TG High Priest, Melchizedek Priesthood.
b Mark 14:58; Heb. 8:2.
12*a* Acts 20:28; Heb. 10:10.

entered in once into the [b]holy place,
having obtained eternal [c]redemp-
tion *for us*.
13 For if the [a]blood of bulls and
of goats, and the ashes of an heifer
sprinkling the unclean, sanctifieth
to the [b]purifying of the flesh:
14 How much more shall the [a]blood
of Christ, who through the eternal
Spirit offered himself [b]without [c]spot
to God, [d]purge your [e]conscience
from dead works to serve the living
God?
15 And for this cause he is the
[a]mediator of the [b]new [c]testament,
that by means of [d]death, for the redemption of the [e]transgressions *that*
were under the first [f]testament, they
which are called might receive the
[g]promise of eternal [h]inheritance.
16 For where a [a]testament *is*, there
must also of necessity be the [b]death
of the [c]testator.
17 For a [a]testament *is* of force after men are dead: [b]otherwise it is
of no strength at all while the testator liveth.
18 Whereupon neither the first *tes-*
tament was dedicated without blood.
19 For when Moses had [a]spoken
every precept to all the people
according to the law, he took the
[b]blood of calves and of goats, with
water, and scarlet wool, and hyssop,
and [c]sprinkled both the book, and
all the people,
20 Saying, This *is* the blood of the
testament which God hath enjoined
unto you.
21 Moreover he sprinkled with
blood both the tabernacle, and all
the vessels of the ministry.
22 And almost all things are by the
law purged with blood; and without
[a]shedding of blood is no [b]remission.
23 *It was* therefore necessary that
the [a]patterns of things in the heavens should be purified with these;
but the heavenly things themselves
with better sacrifices than these.
24 For Christ is not entered into
the holy places made with hands,
which are the figures of the [a]true;
but into [b]heaven itself, now to appear in the [c]presence of God for us:
25 Nor yet that he should offer
himself often, as the [a]high priest
entereth into the holy place every
year with blood of others;
26 For then must he often have
suffered since the foundation of the
world: but now once [a]in the [b]end of
the world hath he appeared to put
away sin by the [c]sacrifice of himself.
27 And as it is appointed unto
men once to die, but after this the
judgment:
28 So Christ was once [a]offered to
[b]bear the [c]sins of many; and unto
them that look for him shall he [d]ap-
pear the second time without sin
unto salvation.

12*b* Lev. 16:2 (2–4); Heb. 10:19.
c D&C 138:23 (18–23). TG Jesus Christ, Redeemer; Redemption.
13*a* Lev. 4:5.
b TG Purification.
14*a* TG Blood, Symbolism of.
b GR blameless.
c Lev. 1:3; 22:20.
d TG Purification.
e TG Conscience.
15*a* TG Jesus Christ, Authority of; Jesus Christ, Mission of.
b Heb. 8:13.
c JST Heb. 9:15 . . . *covenant* . . . (Note: JST uses "covenant" in place of "testament" in every instance in vv. 15–18, 20.)
d TG Jesus Christ, Death of.
e TG Transgress.
f JST Heb. 9:15 . . . *covenant* . . .
g Heb. 10:36.
h D&C 137:7 (7–10). TG Inheritance.
16*a* JST Heb. 9:16 . . . *covenant* . . .
b Ex. 24:8 (3–8); Matt. 26:28 (26–28). TG Martyrdom.
c JST Heb. 9:16 . . . *victim*. (Note: JST uses "victim" in place of "testator" also in v. 17.) 1 Tim. 2:5–6; D&C 135:5.
17*a* TG Witness.
b GR since.
19*a* Ex. 24:7.
b Ex. 24:6.
c Ex. 24:8.
22*a* TG Blood, Symbolism of.
b TG Remission of Sins.
23*a* TG Symbolism.
24*a* Heb. 8:2.
b Heb. 4:14.
c TG Jesus Christ, Atonement through.
25*a* Heb. 9:7.
26*a* JST Heb. 9:26 . . . in the *meridian* of *time* hath he . . .
b GR consummation of the ages.
c TG Self-Sacrifice.
28*a* TG Jesus Christ, Atonement through; Jesus Christ, Redeemer; Remission of Sins.
b D&C 76:41.
c Rom. 6:10.
d 2 Pet. 3:12; Rev. 1:7.

CHAPTER 10

We are sanctified by the shedding of the blood of Christ—The superiority of His sacrifice is explained—Those who fall from grace through willful sin are damned—The just will live by faith.

FOR the [a]law having a [b]shadow of good things to come, *and* not the very image of the things, can never with those sacrifices which they offered [c]year by year continually make the comers thereunto perfect.

2 For then would they not have ceased to be offered? because that the worshippers once [a]purged should have had no more [b]conscience of sins.

3 But in those [a]*sacrifices there is* a [b]remembrance again *made* of sins every year.

4 For *it is* not possible that the blood of bulls and of goats should take away sins.

5 Wherefore when he cometh into the world, he saith, Sacrifice and offering thou wouldest not, but a body hast thou prepared me:

6 In burnt offerings and [a]*sacrifices* for sin thou hast had no pleasure.

7 Then said I, Lo, I come (in the volume of the book it is written of me,) to do thy will, O God.

8 Above when he said, Sacrifice and offering and burnt offerings and *offering* for sin thou wouldest not, neither hadst pleasure *therein;* which are offered by the law;

9 Then said he, Lo, I come to do thy will, O God. He taketh away the first, that he may establish the second.

10 By the which will we are [a]sanctified through the [b]offering [c]of the [d]body of Jesus Christ [e]once *for all.*

11 And every priest standeth [a]daily ministering and offering oftentimes the same sacrifices, which can never take away [b]sins:

12 But this man, after he had offered one [a]sacrifice for sins for ever, sat down on the right hand of God;

13 [a]From henceforth expecting till his enemies be made his footstool.

14 For by one offering he hath perfected for ever them that are sanctified.

15 *Whereof* the [a]Holy Ghost also is a [b]witness to us: for after that he had said before,

16 This *is* the [a]covenant that I will make with them after those days, saith the Lord, I will put my laws into their hearts, and in their [b]minds will I write them;

17 And their sins and iniquities will I remember no more.

18 Now where [a]remission of these *is, there is* no more offering for sin.

19 Having therefore, brethren, [a]boldness to enter into the [b]holiest by the blood of Jesus,

20 By a new and living way, which he hath consecrated for us, through the [a]veil, that is to say, his flesh;

21 And *having* an [a]high priest over the house of God;

22 Let us [a]draw [b]near with a true heart in full assurance of [c]faith, having our hearts [d]sprinkled from an evil [e]conscience, and our bodies washed with pure water.

---

10 1*a* Mosiah 3:15 (14–15); 13:28 (28–32).
b TG Jesus Christ, Types of, in Anticipation; Symbolism.
c JST Heb. 10:1 . . . *continually* year by year make . . .
2*a* TG Remission of Sins.
b TG Peace of God.
3*a* TG Sacrifice.
b Lev. 16:21; Heb. 9:7.
6*a* 1 Sam. 15:22; Micah 6:7.
10*a* TG Sanctification.
b TG Jesus Christ, Types of, in Anticipation.
c JST Heb. 10:10 . . . *once* of the body of Jesus Christ.
d John 6:51; Heb. 9:12.
e Rom. 6:10.
11*a* Heb. 7:27.
b Lev. 4:20 (20, 26).
12*a* TG Sacrifice; Self-Sacrifice.
13*a* JST Heb. 10:13 From henceforth *to reign until* his enemies . . .
15*a* Heb. 3:7.
b TG Holy Ghost, Mission of; Witness.
16*a* Isa. 59:21 (20–21); Rom. 11:27; D&C 49:9 (5–9).
b Jer. 31:31–33.
18*a* TG Remission of Sins.
19*a* GR license, authority.
b Lev. 16:2 (2–4); Heb. 9:12.
20*a* TG Veil.
21*a* TG High Priest, Melchizedek Priesthood.
22*a* TG God, Presence of.
b TG God, Access to.
c Heb. 6:12 (10–12); 1 Pet. 1:5 (3–8).
d GR purified.
e TG Conscience.

23 Let us hold fast the [a]profession
of *our* [b]faith without wavering; (for
he *is* faithful that promised;)
24 And let us [a]consider one another to [b]provoke unto love and to
good works:
25 Not forsaking the [a]assembling
of ourselves together, as the manner of some *is;* but exhorting *one*
another: and so much the more, as
ye see the day approaching.
26 For if we [a]sin [b]wilfully after that
we have received the knowledge of
the truth, there remaineth no more
sacrifice for sins,
27 But a certain fearful looking for
of judgment and fiery [a]indignation,
which shall devour the adversaries.
28 He that [a]despised Moses' law
died without mercy under two or
three witnesses:
29 Of how much sorer [a]punishment,
suppose ye, shall he be thought worthy, who hath trodden under foot
the Son of God, and hath counted
the blood of the covenant, wherewith he was sanctified, an unholy
thing, and hath done [b]despite unto
the Spirit of grace?
30 For we know him that hath
said, [a]Vengeance *belongeth* unto me,
I will [b]recompense, saith the Lord.
And again, The Lord shall [c]judge
his people.
31 *It is* a fearful thing to fall into
the hands of the living God.
32 But call to remembrance the
former days, in which, after ye were
illuminated, ye endured a great
[a]fight of afflictions;
33 Partly, whilst ye were made a
gazingstock both by reproaches and
afflictions; and partly, whilst ye
became companions of them that
were so used.
34 For ye had compassion of me
in my bonds, and took [a]joyfully the
spoiling of your goods, knowing in
yourselves that ye have in heaven a
better and an enduring [b]substance.
35 Cast not away therefore your
confidence, which hath great recompence of reward.
36 For ye have need of [a]patience,
that, after ye have done the [b]will of
God, ye might receive the [c]promise.
37 For yet a little while, and he
that shall come will come, and will
not tarry.
38 Now the just shall live by faith:
but if *any man* [a]draw back, my soul
shall have no pleasure in him.
39 But we are not of them who
[a]draw back unto [b]perdition; but of
them that believe to the saving of
the soul.

CHAPTER 11

By faith we understand the word and work of God—The faith of the ancients was centered in Christ—By faith, men subdued kingdoms, wrought righteousness, and worked miracles.

Now [a]faith is the [b]substance of
things [c]hoped for, the [d]evidence
of things not seen.
2 For by it the elders [a]obtained a
good [b]report.
3 Through faith we understand
that the worlds were [a]framed by the
[b]word of God, so that things which

23*a* 1 Tim. 6:12 (12–13).
b GR hope.
24*a* GR understand.
b TG Provoking.
25*a* TG Assembly for Worship; Meetings.
26*a* TG Apostasy of Individuals; Sin.
b TG Holy Ghost, Unpardonable Sin against.
27*a* TG God, Indignation of.
28*a* GR rejected, violated.
29*a* Heb. 2:3.
b GR insult.
30*a* TG Retribution.
b TG God, Justice of.
c TG Jesus Christ, Judge.
32*a* Heb. 12:4.
34*a* TG Joy.
b Matt. 6:20.
36*a* TG Patience.
b TG God, Will of.
c Heb. 9:15; 1 Pet. 1:9 (1–16).
38*a* TG Apostasy of Individuals.
39*a* 2 Pet. 2:21 (20–21).
b GR ruin, destruction. TG Death, Spiritual, Second; Sons of Perdition.
11 1*a* TG Faith.
b GR assurance, basis, foundation. JST Heb. 11:1 . . . *assurance* of things hoped for . . .
c TG Hope.
d GR proof.
2*a* GR received witness, testimony.
b Heb. 11:39.
3*a* TG Creation.
b TG Jesus Christ, Creator.

are seen were not made of things
which do appear.
4 By faith [a]Abel offered unto God a
more excellent [b]sacrifice than Cain,
by which he obtained witness that
he was righteous, God testifying of
his gifts: and by it he being dead
yet speaketh.
5 By faith [a]Enoch was [b]translated
that he should not see death; and
was not found, because God had
translated him: for before his translation he had this [c]testimony, that
he pleased God.
6 But without [a]faith *it is* impossible
to please *him:* for he that [b]cometh
to God must believe that he is, and
that he is a [c]rewarder of them that
[d]diligently [e]seek him.
7 By faith [a]Noah, being [b]warned
of God of things not seen as yet,
[c]moved with fear, prepared an ark
to the saving of his house; by the
which he condemned the world, and
became heir of the [d]righteousness
which is by faith.
8 By faith [a]Abraham, when he was
called to go out into a place which
he should after receive for an [b]in-
heritance, [c]obeyed; and he went
out, not [d]knowing whither he went.
9 By faith he [a]sojourned in the
[b]land of [c]promise, as *in* a strange
country, dwelling in [d]tabernacles
with Isaac and Jacob, the heirs with
him of the same promise:
10 For he looked for a [a]city which
hath foundations, whose builder
and maker *is* God.
11 Through faith also Sara herself
received strength to conceive seed,
and was delivered of a child when
she was past age, because she judged
him faithful who had promised.
12 Therefore sprang there even
of one, and him as good as dead, *so
many* as the stars of the sky in [a]mul-
titude, and as the sand which is by
the sea shore innumerable.
13 These all died in faith, not
having received the [a]promises, but
having seen them afar off, and were
persuaded of *them,* and embraced
them, and confessed that they were
[b]strangers and pilgrims on the earth.
14 For they that say such things
declare plainly that they seek a
[a]country.
15 And truly, if they had been
mindful of that *country* from whence
they came out, they might have had
opportunity to have returned.
16 But now they desire a better
[a]*country,* that is, an heavenly: wherefore God is not ashamed to be called
their God: for he hath prepared for
them a city.
17 By [a]faith Abraham, when he
was [b]tried, [c]offered up Isaac: and
he that had received the [d]promises
offered up his only begotten *son,*
18 Of whom it was said, That in
[a]Isaac shall thy [b]seed be called:
19 [a]Accounting that God *was* able
to raise *him* up, even from the dead;
from whence also he received him
in a figure.
20 By faith Isaac [a]blessed Jacob
and Esau concerning things to come.
21 By faith [a]Jacob, when he was

4*a* Gen. 4:4.
b TG Sacrifice.
5*a* Jude 1:14 (14–16).
b TG Translated Beings; Zion.
c TG Testimony.
6*a* TG Faith.
b Heb. 7:25.
c TG Reward.
d TG Diligence.
e Ps. 34:4 (4, 6, 10); Lam. 3:25; Alma 37:37 (36–37).
7*a* Gen. 6:22; 8:1; 1 Pet. 3:20 (20–21); 2 Pet. 2:5.
b TG Warn.
c GR being cautious, reverent.
d TG Righteousness.
8*a* Gen. 12:1.
b TG Lands of Inheritance.
c TG Obedience.
d 2 Chr. 20:12; 1 Ne. 4:6.
9*a* Gen. 26:3.
b TG Israel, Land of; Promised Lands.
c D&C 38:18.
d Gen. 25:27.
10*a* D&C 76:66.
12*a* TG Seed of Abraham.
13*a* Matt. 13:17; 1 Pet. 1:10 (10–11).
b TG Stranger.
14*a* GR homeland, native place.
16*a* D&C 45:12 (12–14).
17*a* James 2:21 (21–23).
b TG Test.
c TG Sacrifice.
d TG Promise.
18*a* TG Seed of Abraham.
b TG Abrahamic Covenant.
19*a* GR Considering.
20*a* Gen. 27:27.
21*a* Gen. 48:2 (1–2, 5, 16).

a dying, blessed both the sons of
Joseph; and worshipped, *leaning*
upon the top of his staff.
22 By faith [a]Joseph, when he died,
made mention of the departing of
the children of Israel; and gave
commandment concerning his
bones.
23 By faith [a]Moses, when he was
born, was hid three months of his
parents, because they saw *he was* a
[b]proper child; and they were not
afraid of the king's commandment.
24 By faith Moses, when he was
come to years, refused to be called
the [a]son of Pharaoh's daughter;
25 Choosing rather to [a]suffer affliction with the [b]people of God,
than to enjoy the pleasures of sin
for a season;
26 Esteeming the [a]reproach of
Christ greater [b]riches than the treasures in Egypt: for he had respect
unto the recompence of the reward.
27 By faith he forsook Egypt, not
fearing the wrath of the king: for
he endured, as seeing him who is
invisible.
28 Through faith he kept the [a]pass-
over, and the sprinkling of [b]blood,
lest he that destroyed the firstborn
should touch them.
29 By faith they passed through
the [a]Red sea as by dry *land:* which
the Egyptians assaying to do were
drowned.
30 By faith the [a]walls of Jericho fell
down, after they were compassed
about seven days.
31 By [a]faith the harlot [b]Rahab perished not with [c]them that believed
not, when she had received the spies
with peace.
32 And what shall I more say?
for the time would fail me to tell
of Gedeon, and *of* [a]Barak, and *of*
Samson, and *of* [b]Jephthae; *of* David also, and Samuel, and *of* the
prophets:
33 Who through faith subdued
kingdoms, wrought righteousness,
obtained [a]promises, stopped the
mouths of [b]lions,
34 Quenched the violence of [a]fire,
escaped the edge of the sword, out of
weakness were made [b]strong, waxed
valiant in fight, turned to flight the
armies of the aliens.
35 Women received their dead
raised to life again: and others were
tortured, not accepting [a]deliverance;
that they might obtain [b]a better
resurrection:
36 And others had trial of [a]*cruel*
[b]mockings and scourgings, yea, moreover of bonds and imprisonment:
37 They were [a]stoned, they were
sawn asunder, were tempted, were
slain with the sword: they wandered about in sheepskins and
goatskins; being destitute, afflicted,
tormented;
38 (Of whom the world was not
worthy:) they wandered in deserts,
and *in* mountains, and *in* dens and
caves of the earth.
39 And these all, having obtained
a [a]good [b]report through faith, received not the promise:
40 [a]God having [b]provided some
better thing for us, that they without us should not be made [c]perfect.

22*a* TG Israel, Joseph, People of.
23*a* Ex. 2:2.
b GR handsome.
24*a* Ex. 2:10.
25*a* TG Suffering.
b Ex. 2:11 (11–15); Acts 7:23 (22–36).
26*a* TG Reproach.
b TG Treasure.
28*a* Ex. 12:28 (21–28).
b Ex. 12:22 (21–22).
29*a* TG Israel, Deliverance of.
30*a* Josh. 6:20.
31*a* James 2:25.
b Josh. 2:1.
c GR those who were unbelieving, disobedient.
32*a* Judg. 4:6 (1–24).
b Judg. 11:6.
33*a* TG Promise.
b Dan. 6:22.
34*a* Dan. 3:27.
b Joel 3:10; Ether 12:27.
35*a* TG Deliver.
b JST Heb. 11:35 . . . *the first* resurrection;
36*a* TG Cruelty.
b TG Mocking; Persecution.
37*a* TG Martyrdom; Prophets, Rejection of.
39*a* GR testimony, witness.
b Heb. 11:2.
40*a* JST Heb. 11:40 God having provided some better *things* for *them through their sufferings, for without sufferings they could* not be made perfect.
b GR provided beforehand.
c TG Perfection.

CHAPTER 12

Whom the Lord loves He chastens—God is the Father of spirits—To see God, follow peace and holiness—Exalted Saints belong to the Church of the Firstborn.

WHEREFORE seeing we also are compassed about with so great a cloud of witnesses, let us lay aside every weight, and the [a]sin which doth so easily [b]beset *us*, and let us run with [c]patience the race that is set before us,
2 Looking unto Jesus the [a]author and [b]finisher of *our* faith; who for the joy that was set before him [c]endured the cross, despising the [d]shame, and is set down at the right hand of the [e]throne of God.
3 For consider him that endured such [a]contradiction of sinners against himself, lest ye be wearied and faint in your minds.
4 Ye have not yet resisted unto blood, [a]striving against sin.
5 And ye have forgotten the exhortation which speaketh unto you as unto children, My son, despise not thou the chastening of the Lord, nor faint when thou art rebuked of him:
6 For whom the Lord loveth he [a]chasteneth, and scourgeth every son whom he receiveth.
7 If ye [a]endure [b]chastening, God dealeth with you as with [c]sons; for what son is he whom the father chasteneth not?
8 But if ye be without chastisement, whereof all are partakers, then are ye bastards, and not sons.
9 Furthermore we have had [a]fathers of our flesh which [b]corrected *us*, and we gave *them* [c]reverence: shall we not much rather be in [d]subjection unto the [e]Father of [f]spirits, and live?
10 For they verily for a few days chastened *us* after their own pleasure; but he for *our* profit, that *we* might be partakers of his [a]holiness.
11 Now no chastening for the present seemeth to be joyous, but grievous: nevertheless afterward it yieldeth the [a]peaceable fruit of righteousness unto them which are [b]exercised thereby.
12 Wherefore lift up the hands which hang down, and the [a]feeble knees;
13 And make straight paths for your feet, lest that which is lame be turned out of the way; but let it rather be [a]healed.
14 Follow [a]peace with all *men*, and [b]holiness, without which no man shall [c]see the Lord:
15 Looking diligently lest any man [a]fail of the [b]grace of God; lest any root of bitterness springing up trouble *you*, and thereby many be defiled;
16 Lest there *be* any fornicator, or profane person, as Esau, who for one morsel of meat sold his [a]birthright.
17 For ye know how that afterward, when he would have inherited the blessing, he was rejected: for he found no place of repentance, though he sought it carefully with [a]tears.

---

12 1*a* TG Sin.
b Rom. 7:21 (15–25); 2 Ne. 4:18 (17–19).
c TG Patience; Perseverance.
2*a* TG Jesus Christ, Authority of; Jesus Christ, Messiah.
b GR one who completes, perfects.
c 1 Pet. 1:11.
d TG Shame.
e Heb. 1:3.
3*a* GR rebellion, opposition.
4*a* Heb. 10:32 (32–34).
6*a* TG Chastening; Persecution.
7*a* TG Steadfastness.
b GR correction, instruction. TG Teachable.
c TG Sons and Daughters of God.
9*a* TG Marriage, Fatherhood.
b TG Family, Love within.
c TG Reverence.
d TG Agency; Submissiveness.
e TG God the Father, Elohim; Man, Potential to Become like Heavenly Father.
f TG Man, Antemortal Existence of; Man, a Spirit Child of Heavenly Father; Spirit Body; Spirit Creation.
10*a* TG Holiness.
11*a* TG Peace.
b GR trained, disciplined.
12*a* Isa. 35:3.
13*a* Gal. 6:1.
14*a* TG Peace of God.
b 1 Thes. 4:3.
c TG God, Privilege of Seeing.
15*a* GR want, fall short of, lack.
b TG Grace.
16*a* TG Birthright.
17*a* Gen. 27:38 (34–38).

18 For ye are not come unto the
[a]mount that might be touched,
and that burned with fire, nor
unto blackness, and darkness, and
tempest,
19 And the sound of a trumpet,
and the voice of words; which [a]*voice*
they that heard entreated that the
word should not be spoken to them
any more:
20 (For they could not endure that
which was commanded, And if so
much as a beast touch the mountain,
it shall be stoned, or thrust through
with a dart:
21 And so terrible was the sight,
that Moses said, I exceedingly fear
and quake:)
22 But ye are come unto mount
[a]Sion, and unto the city of the living
God, the heavenly Jerusalem, and to
an innumerable company of [b]angels,
23 To the general assembly and
church of the [a]firstborn, which are
[b]written in heaven, and to God the
[c]Judge of all, and to the [d]spirits of
[e]just men made perfect,
24 And to Jesus the [a]mediator of the
[b]new [c]covenant, and to the [d]blood
of sprinkling, that speaketh [e]better
things than *that of* Abel.
25 See that ye refuse not him that
speaketh. For if they [a]escaped not
who refused him that spake on earth,
much more *shall not* we *escape,* if we
turn away from him that *speaketh*
from heaven:
26 Whose voice then shook the
earth: but now he hath promised,
saying, Yet once more I [a]shake not
the earth only, but also heaven.
27 And this *word,* Yet once more, sig-
nifieth the removing of those things
that are shaken, as of things that are
made, that those things which cannot be shaken may remain.
28 Wherefore we receiving a kingdom which cannot be moved, let us
have grace, whereby we may serve
God acceptably with [a]reverence and
godly [b]fear:
29 For our God *is* a consuming fire.

CHAPTER 13

Marriage is honorable—Christ is the same everlastingly—Paul explains how the Saints are to offer acceptable sacrifices.

LET [a]brotherly [b]love continue.
2 Be not forgetful to [a]entertain
[b]strangers: for thereby some have
entertained [c]angels [d]unawares.
3 Remember them that are in
[a]bonds, as bound with them; *and*
them which [b]suffer adversity, as
being yourselves also in the body.
4 [a]Marriage *is* honourable in all,
and the bed undefiled: but [b]whore-
mongers and [c]adulterers God will
[d]judge.
5 *Let your* conversation *be* without
[a]covetousness; *and be* [b]content with
such things as ye have: for he hath
said, I will never leave thee, nor
[c]forsake thee.
6 So that we may boldly say, The
Lord *is* my helper, and I will not
fear what man shall do unto me.
7 Remember them which have the
rule over you, who have spoken unto
you the word of God: whose faith
follow, considering the end of *their*
conversation.

18*a* Ex. 19:12 (12, 16, 18).
19*a* Ex. 20:19.
22*a* TG Zion.
b TG Angels.
23*a* TG Firstborn; Jesus Christ, Firstborn.
b Luke 10:20; D&C 128:6 (6–7).
c TG Jesus Christ, Judge; Judgment.
d TG Spirits, Disembodied.
e Ezek. 18:5 (5–9); D&C 76:69 (66–69).
24*a* 1 Tim. 2:5.
b TG New and Everlasting Covenant.
c TG Covenants.
d Lev. 1:5; 1 Pet. 1:2.
e Heb. 7:19.
25*a* Heb. 2:3.
26*a* TG Last Days.
28*a* TG Reverence.
b Eccl. 3:14; Mosiah 4:1.
13 1*a* TG Brotherhood and Sisterhood.
b TG Benevolence; Love.
2*a* TG Hospitality.
b TG Stranger.
c TG Angels; Translated Beings.
d Luke 24:16 (13–16, 28).
3*a* Matt. 25:36; Col. 4:18.
b TG Compassion.
4*a* TG Marriage, Marry; Marriage, Temporal.
b TG Whore.
c TG Adulterer.
d TG Jesus Christ, Judge.
5*a* TG Covet.
b TG Contentment.
c Josh. 1:5; 1 Kgs. 6:13.

8 Jesus Christ the [a]same yesterday,
and to day, and for ever.
9 Be not [a]carried about with divers
and strange [b]doctrines. For *it is* a
good thing that the heart be established with grace; not with meats,
which have not profited them that
have been occupied therein.
10 We have an altar, whereof they
have no right to eat which serve the
tabernacle.
11 For the bodies of those beasts,
whose blood is brought into the
sanctuary by the high priest for
sin, are burned without the camp.
12 Wherefore Jesus also, that he
might [a]sanctify the people with
his own [b]blood, [c]suffered [d]without
the gate.
13 Let us go forth therefore unto
him without the camp, bearing his
[a]reproach.
14 For here have we no continuing city, but we seek one to come.
15 By him therefore let us offer
the [a]sacrifice of praise to God continually, that is, the [b]fruit of *our* lips
giving thanks to his name.
16 But to do good and to [a]com-
municate forget not: for with such
[b]sacrifices God is well pleased.
17 [a]Obey them that have the rule
over you, and [b]submit yourselves: for
they watch for your souls, as they
that must give account, that they
may do it with joy, and not with
grief: for that *is* unprofitable for you.
18 Pray for us: for we trust we have
a good [a]conscience, in all things
willing to live [b]honestly.
19 But I beseech *you* the rather to
do this, that I may be restored to
you the sooner.
20 Now the God of peace, that
brought again from the dead our
Lord Jesus, that great [a]shepherd of
the sheep, through the blood of the
[b]everlasting [c]covenant,
21 Make you perfect in every good
[a]work to do his [b]will, working in you
that which is wellpleasing in his
sight, through Jesus Christ; to whom
be glory for ever and ever. Amen.
22 And I beseech you, brethren,
suffer the word of exhortation: for
I have written a letter unto you in
few words.
23 Know ye that *our* brother Timothy is set at liberty; with whom, if
he come shortly, I will see you.
24 Salute all them that have the
rule over you, and all the saints.
They of Italy salute you.
25 Grace *be* with you all. Amen.

¶ Written to the Hebrews from Italy by Timothy.

8*a* TG God, Eternal Nature of.
9*a* 2 Cor. 11:3; Col. 2:8.
b Eph. 4:14.
12*a* TG Sanctification.
b TG Blood, Symbolism of.
c John 19:17 (17–18).
d GR outside of. Lev. 4:12.
13*a* TG Reproach.
15*a* Ps. 119:108.
b Isa. 57:19.
16*a* TG Communication.
b 2 Cor. 9:12 (7–12).
17*a* TG Sustaining Church Leaders.
b TG Submissiveness.
18*a* TG Conscience.
b TG Honesty.
20*a* TG Jesus Christ, Good Shepherd; Shepherd.
b TG New and Everlasting Covenant.
c TG Covenants.
21*a* TG Good Works.
b TG God, Will of.

THE GENERAL EPISTLE OF

JAMES

CHAPTER 1

If any of you lack wisdom, let him ask of God—Resist temptation—Be doers of the word—James explains how to recognize pure religion.

JAMES, a [a]servant of God and of the Lord Jesus Christ, to the twelve tribes which are [b]scattered abroad, greeting.
2 My brethren, count it all joy when ye fall into [a]divers [b]temptations;
3 Knowing *this,* that the [a]trying of your faith worketh [b]patience.
4 But let patience have *her* perfect work, that ye may be [a]perfect and entire, wanting nothing.
5 [a]If any of you lack [b]wisdom, let him ask of God, that [c]giveth to all *men* liberally, and [d]upbraideth not; and it shall be given him.
6 But let him [a]ask in [b]faith, nothing [c]wavering. For he that wavereth is like a wave of the sea driven with the wind and tossed.
7 For let not that man think that he shall receive any thing of the Lord.
8 A [a]double minded man *is* unstable in all his ways.
9 Let the brother of [a]low degree rejoice in that he is exalted:
10 But the rich, in that he is made low: because as the flower of the [a]grass he shall pass away.
11 For the sun is no sooner risen with a burning heat, but it withereth the grass, and the flower thereof falleth, and the [a]grace of the fashion of it perisheth: so also shall the [b]rich man fade away in his ways.
12 [a]Blessed *is* the man that [b]endureth temptation: for when he is [c]tried, he shall receive the [d]crown of life, which the Lord hath promised to them that love him.
13 Let no man say when he is tempted, I am tempted of God: for God cannot be [a]tempted with [b]evil, neither tempteth he any man:
14 But every man is [a]tempted, when he is drawn away of his own [b]lust, and enticed.
15 Then when lust hath conceived, it bringeth forth [a]sin: and sin, when it is finished, bringeth forth death.
16 Do not err, my beloved brethren.
17 Every [a]good [b]gift and every perfect [c]gift is from above, and [d]cometh down from the [e]Father of lights, with whom is no [f]variableness, neither shadow of turning.

---

1 1*a* TG Servant.
b TG Israel, Twelve Tribes of.
2*a* JST James 1:2 . . . *many afflictions;*
b TG Temptation.
3*a* GR approval by trial. TG Opposition; Test.
b TG Patience.
4*a* TG Perfection.
5*a* D&C 42:68; JS—H 1:11.
b TG Guidance, Divine; Learn; Wisdom.
c TG Benevolence; Revelation.
d GR reproaches, censures.
6*a* TG Prayer.
b TG Faith.
c GR doubting, hesitating. TG Doubt.
8*a* 1 Kgs. 18:21; Ps. 12:2; Hosea 10:2. TG Integrity.
9*a* Matt. 23:12.
10*a* Isa. 40:6–8.
11*a* GR beauty of its appearance.
b 1 Tim. 6:17 (17–19).
12*a* 1 Pet. 3:14. TG Blessing.
b JST James 1:12 . . . *resisteth* temptation . . . TG Steadfastness.
c TG Test.
d TG Exaltation; Reward.
13*a* TG God, Perfection of.
b TG Evil.
14*a* TG Temptation.
b TG Chastity; Lust; Motivations; Sensuality.
15*a* TG Sin.
17*a* Ps. 85:12.
b Moro. 7:12 (12–13).
c John 3:27; 2 Cor. 9:15. TG God, Gifts of.
d D&C 67:9.
e D&C 67:4, 9.
f TG God, Perfection of.

18 Of his own will begat he us with
the word of truth, that we should be
a kind of firstfruits of his creatures.
19 Wherefore, my beloved brethren, let every man be swift to hear,
slow to [a]speak, [b]slow to [c]wrath:
20 For the wrath of man worketh
not the righteousness of God.
21 Wherefore lay apart all [a]filth-
iness and [b]superfluity of naughti-
ness, and receive with [c]meekness
the [d]engrafted word, which is able
to save your souls.
22 But be ye [a]doers of the word,
and not hearers only, deceiving your
own selves.
23 For if any be a [a]hearer of the
word, and not a doer, he is like unto
a man beholding his natural face
in a [b]glass:
24 For he beholdeth himself, and
goeth his way, and straightway for-
getteth what manner of man he was.
25 But whoso looketh into the perfect [a]law of [b]liberty, and continueth *therein,* he being not a forgetful
hearer, but a doer of the work, this
man shall be blessed in his deed.
26 If any man among you seem
to be religious, and bridleth not
his [a]tongue, but deceiveth his own
heart, this man's religion *is* [b]vain.
27 Pure [a]religion and undefiled
before God and the Father is this,
To [b]visit the [c]fatherless and [d]wid-
ows in their [e]affliction, *and* to keep
himself [f]unspotted from [g]the [h]world.

CHAPTER 2

God has chosen the poor of this world who are rich in faith—Salvation is gained by keeping the whole law—Faith without works is dead.

MY brethren, [a]have not the faith of
our [b]Lord Jesus Christ, *the Lord* of
glory, with respect of persons.
2 For if there come unto your assembly a man with a gold ring, in
goodly apparel, and there come in
also a [a]poor man in [b]vile raiment;
3 And ye have respect to him that
weareth the [a]gay clothing, and say
unto him, Sit thou here in a good
place; and say to the poor, Stand
thou there, or sit here under my
footstool:
4 [a]Are ye not then partial in yourselves, and are become judges of
evil thoughts?
5 Hearken, my beloved brethren,
Hath not God chosen the [a]poor of
this world rich in faith, and heirs of
the kingdom which he hath promised to them that love him?
6 But ye have despised the poor.
Do not rich men [a]oppress you, and
draw you before the judgment
seats?
7 Do not they blaspheme that
worthy [a]name by the which ye are
called?
8 If ye fulfil the royal law according to the scripture, Thou shalt [a]love
thy [b]neighbour as thyself, ye do well:

19*a* Prov. 17:27.
b TG Patience.
c TG Anger.
21*a* TG Filthiness.
b GR overabundance of malice, trouble, evil.
c TG Meek.
d GR implanted, ingrafted.
22*a* TG Commitment; Duty; Good Works; Hypocrisy.
23*a* Luke 6:49 (47–49).
b 1 Cor. 13:12.
25*a* TG God, Law of.
b TG Liberty.
26*a* TG Gossip; Profanity.
b GR useless, deceptive, erroneous.
27*a* TG Charity.
b D&C 44:6. TG Benevolence; Good Works; Welfare.
c Deut. 26:13; Job 22:9; 31:21 (21–22); Ps. 10:14; 146:9 (1–10); 3 Ne. 24:5; D&C 136:8 (7–9).
d TG Widows.
e TG Affliction.
f 1 Tim. 5:22; 1 Jn. 5:18; D&C 59:9. TG Chastity.
g JST James 1:27 . . . *the vices of* the world.
h TG Worldliness.

2 1*a* GR not with partiality, have the faith of our Lord. JST James 2:1 . . . *ye cannot* have the faith of our Lord Jesus Christ, the Lord of glory, *and yet have* respect *to* persons.
b TG Jesus Christ, Lord.
2*a* TG Poor.
b GR dirty.
3*a* GR splendid.
4*a* JST James 2:4 Are ye not then in yourselves *partial judges,* and become evil *in your* thoughts?
5*a* Prov. 15:16; Matt. 5:3; Luke 6:20; 1 Cor. 1:27 (27–28). TG Poor.
6*a* TG Oppression.
7*a* TG Name.
8*a* TG Love.
b TG Neighbor.

9 But if ye have [a]respect to persons, ye commit sin, and are convinced of the law as transgressors.

10 For whosoever shall keep the [a]whole law, and yet [b]offend in one *point,* he is [c]guilty of all.

11 For he that said, Do not commit [a]adultery, said also, Do not kill. Now if thou commit no adultery, yet if thou kill, thou art become a transgressor of the law.

12 So speak ye, and so do, as they that shall be judged by the law of [a]liberty.

13 For he shall have [a]judgment without [b]mercy, that hath shewed no mercy; and mercy rejoiceth against judgment.

14 [a]What *doth it* profit, my brethren, though a man say he hath [b]faith, and have not works? can faith save him?

15 If a [a]brother or sister be naked, and destitute of daily [b]food,

16 And one of you say unto them, Depart in peace, be *ye* warmed and filled; notwithstanding ye [a]give them not those things which are needful to the body; what *doth it* profit?

17 Even so [a]faith, if it hath not [b]works, is dead, being alone.

18 Yea, a man may say, Thou hast faith, and I have works: shew me thy faith without thy works, and I will shew thee my [a]faith by my [b]works.

19 Thou believest that there is one God; thou doest well: the [a]devils also [b]believe, and tremble.

20 But wilt thou know, O vain man, that [a]faith without [b]works is dead?

21 Was not Abraham our father [a]justified by works, when he had [b]offered Isaac his son upon the altar?

22 Seest thou how faith wrought with his works, and by [a]works was faith made [b]perfect?

23 And the scripture was fulfilled which saith, Abraham [a]believed God, and it was imputed unto him for [b]righteousness: and he was called the [c]Friend of God.

24 Ye see then how that by [a]works a man is [b]justified, and not by faith only.

25 Likewise also was not [a]Rahab the harlot [b]justified by works, when she had received the messengers, and had sent *them* out another way?

26 For as the body without the [a]spirit is [b]dead, so faith without [c]works is dead also.

CHAPTER 3

By governing the tongue, we gain perfection—Heavenly wisdom is pure, peaceable, and full of mercy.

MY brethren, [a]be not many [b]masters, knowing that we shall [c]receive the greater condemnation.

2 For in many things we [a]offend all. If any man [b]offend not in [c]word, the

---

9*a* Deut. 1:17; Prov. 28:21.
10*a* D&C 50:28 (28–29).
b GR stumble, err. TG Offense; Sin.
c TG Guilt.
11*a* TG Adulterer.
12*a* TG Liberty.
13*a* Ps. 109:7.
b TG Mercy.
14*a* JST James 2:14–21 (Appendix).
b D&C 20:69.
15*a* TG Brotherhood and Sisterhood.
b TG Food.
16*a* Luke 3:11 (8–14); D&C 104:18.
17*a* 1 Thes. 1:3.
b TG Obedience.
18*a* TG Faith.
b Matt. 7:20 (15–20); D&C 20:37.
19*a* JST James 2:19 . . . devils also believe, and tremble; *thou hast made thyself like unto them, not being justified.* Acts 16:17.
b Luke 8:28 (27–28).
20*a* TG Faith.
b Prov. 24:12.
21*a* Heb. 11:17.
b Gen. 22:9 (9–12).
22*a* TG Good Works.
b TG Perfection.
23*a* Gen. 22:12. TG Faith.
b TG Righteousness.
c Isa. 41:8. TG Friendship.
24*a* 2 Ne. 25:23. TG Commitment.
b TG Justification.
25*a* Josh. 2:1.
b Heb. 11:31.
26*a* TG Spirit Body; Spirits, Disembodied.
b TG Death.
c TG Good Works.
3 1*a* JST James 3:1 . . . *strive not for the mastery,* knowing that *in so doing* we shall receive the greater condemnation.
b GR (also) teachers.
c D&C 82:3.
2*a* GR stumble, err.
b TG Offense.
c Ps. 39:1; Prov. 21:23.

same *is* a [d]perfect man, *and* able also
to bridle the whole body.
3 Behold, we put bits in the horses'
mouths, that they may obey us; and
we turn about their whole body.
4 Behold also the ships, which
though *they be* so great, and *are*
driven of fierce winds, yet are they
turned about with a very small
helm, whithersoever the [a]governor
listeth.
5 Even so the tongue is a little
member, and [a]boasteth great things.
Behold, how great a [b]matter a little
fire kindleth!
6 And the [a]tongue *is* a fire, a world
of iniquity: so is the tongue among
our members, that it defileth the
whole body, and setteth on fire the
course of nature; and it is set on
fire of hell.
7 For every kind of beasts, and of
birds, and of serpents, and of things
in the sea, is tamed, and hath been
tamed of mankind:
8 But the [a]tongue can no man
tame; *it is* an [b]unruly evil, full of
deadly poison.
9 Therewith bless we God, even
the Father; and therewith [a]curse
we men, which are made after the
[b]similitude of God.
10 Out of the same [a]mouth proceedeth blessing and cursing. My
brethren, these things ought not
so to be.
11 Doth a [a]fountain send forth
at the same place sweet *water* and
bitter?
12 Can the fig tree, my brethren,
bear olive berries? either a vine,
figs? so *can* no fountain both yield
salt water and fresh.
13 Who *is* a wise man and endued
with knowledge among you? let him
shew out of a good [a]conversation his
works with [b]meekness of wisdom.
14 But if ye have bitter envying
and [a]strife in your hearts, [b]glory
not, and lie not against the truth.
15 This wisdom descendeth not
from above, but *is* earthly, sensual,
devilish.
16 For where [a]envying and [b]strife
is, there *is* confusion and every evil
work.
17 But the [a]wisdom that is from
above is first pure, then peaceable,
gentle, *and* [b]easy to be entreated, full
of [c]mercy and good fruits, without
partiality, and without [d]hypocrisy.
18 And the fruit of [a]righteousness
is sown in [b]peace of them that make
[c]peace.

CHAPTER 4

Wars are born of lusts—The friends of the world are the enemies of God—Sin is failure to walk in the light we have received.

FROM whence *come* [a]wars and [b]fight-
ings among you? *come they* not hence,
even of your [c]lusts that war in your
members?
2 Ye lust, and have not: ye kill, and
desire to have, and cannot obtain:
ye fight and war, yet ye have not,
because ye ask not.
3 Ye [a]ask, and receive not, because
ye [b]ask [c]amiss, that ye may [d]consume
it upon your [e]lusts.
4 Ye [a]adulterers and adulteresses,

2*d* TG Perfection.
4*a* GR helmsman, pilot.
5*a* TG Boast; Rashness.
b GR forest.
6*a* Prov. 16:27; Mark 7:20 (19–23); Alma 12:14; D&C 88:121.
8*a* TG Gossip; Profanity.
b GR untameable, uncontrollable.
9*a* TG Curse.
b TG God, Body of, Corporeal Nature.
10*a* Matt. 12:34; Luke 6:45. TG Hypocrisy.
11*a* GR spring, well. Moro. 7:11 (6–11).
13*a* Prov. 12:13 (13–19).
b TG Meek.
14*a* TG Strife.
b GR do not assume superiority over.
16*a* TG Envy.
b TG Contention.
17*a* TG God, Intelligence of; Wisdom.
b GR pliant, easily persuaded.
c TG God, Mercy of.
d D&C 121:42.
18*a* TG Righteousness.
b TG Peace; Peace of God.
c TG Peacemakers.
4 1*a* TG War.
b TG Apostasy of the Early Christian Church.
c GR pleasures, gratifications, passions.
3*a* TG Prayer.
b Hel. 10:5 (4–6).
c GR wickedly, wrongly. Rom. 8:26 (26–27); D&C 46:30 (28–30); 88:65 (64–65).
d GR waste, expend. D&C 46:9.
e TG Lust.
4*a* TG Whore.

know ye not that the friendship of
the [b]world is [c]enmity with God?
whosoever therefore will be a
friend of the world is the [d]enemy
of God.
5 Do ye think that the scripture
saith in vain, The spirit that dwelleth in us lusteth to [a]envy?
6 But he giveth more [a]grace.
Wherefore he saith, God resisteth
the [b]proud, but giveth grace unto
the [c]humble.
7 [a]Submit yourselves therefore to
God. [b]Resist the [c]devil, and he will
flee from you.
8 [a]Draw [b]nigh to God, and he will
draw nigh to you. [c]Cleanse *your*
hands, *ye* sinners; and [d]purify *your*
hearts, *ye* double minded.
9 [a]Be afflicted, and mourn, and
[b]weep: let your laughter be turned to
[c]mourning, and *your* joy to heaviness.
10 [a]Humble yourselves in the
sight of the Lord, and he shall lift
you up.
11 [a]Speak not evil one of another,
brethren. He that speaketh evil of
his brother, and judgeth his brother,
speaketh evil of the [b]law, and judgeth the law: but if thou judge the
law, thou art not a doer of the law,
but a judge.
12 There is one lawgiver, who is
able to save and to destroy: who art
thou that [a]judgest another?
13 Go to now, ye that say, To day
or to [a]morrow we will go into such a
city, and continue there a year, and
buy and sell, and get gain:
14 Whereas ye know not what *shall*
be on the morrow. For what *is* your
life? It is even a [a]vapour, that appeareth for a little time, and then
vanisheth away.
15 For that ye *ought* to say, If the
Lord will, we shall live, and do this,
or that.
16 But now ye rejoice in your
[a]boastings: all such rejoicing is
evil.
17 Therefore to him that [a]knoweth
to do good, and [b]doeth *it* not, to him
it is [c]sin.

CHAPTER 5

Misery awaits the wanton rich—Await the Lord's coming with patience—The elders are to anoint and heal the sick.

Go to now, *ye* rich men, [a]weep and
howl for your miseries that shall
come upon *you*.
2 Your [a]riches are corrupted, and
your garments are motheaten.
3 Your [a]gold and silver is [b]can-
kered; and the [c]rust of them shall
be a witness against you, and shall
eat your flesh as it were fire. Ye have
heaped treasure together for the last
days.
4 Behold, the [a]hire of the [b]labourers
who have reaped down your fields,
which is of you kept back by fraud,
crieth: and the cries of them which
have reaped are entered into the
ears of the Lord of sabaoth.
5 Ye have lived [a]in pleasure on the
earth, and been wanton; ye have
nourished your hearts, as in a day
of slaughter.

4*b* TG World; Worldliness.
c TG Opposition.
d TG Enemies.
5*a* TG Envy.
6*a* TG Grace.
b TG Pride.
c TG Poor in Spirit.
7*a* TG Reconciliation; Submissiveness.
b TG Abstain; Self-Mastery.
c TG Devil.
8*a* TG God, Presence of.
b Ps. 69:18; D&C 88:63.
c TG Repent.
d TG Purification; Purity.
9*a* GR Endure hardship, Suffer harassment.
b Isa. 22:12; Joel 2:17; 2 Cor. 7:10.
c TG Mourning.
10*a* TG Contrite Heart; Humility.
11*a* TG Gossip.
b TG Citizenship.
12*a* Morm. 8:20 (19–20).
13*a* Prov. 27:1.
14*a* 1 Cor. 7:31 (29–31); Jacob 7:26.
16*a* TG Boast.
17*a* Luke 12:47; 2 Ne. 9:25 (25–27).
b TG Disobedience; Good Works; Obedience.
c TG Sin.
5 1*a* TG Mourning.
2*a* TG Treasure.
3*a* 1 Tim. 6:10 (10, 17); Jacob 2:17 (17–19).
b GR rusted, tarnished. D&C 56:16.
c GR venom, poison.
4*a* TG Wages.
b Jer. 22:13.
5*a* GR luxuriously, delicately.

6 Ye have condemned *and* killed
the just; *and* he doth not resist you.
7 Be patient therefore, brethren,
unto the coming of the Lord. Behold, the husbandman waiteth for
the precious fruit of the earth, and
hath long patience for it, until he
receive the early and latter rain.
8 Be ye also [a]patient; [b]stablish your
hearts: for the [c]coming of the Lord
draweth nigh.
9 [a]Grudge not one against another,
brethren, lest ye be condemned:
behold, the judge standeth before
the door.
10 Take, my brethren, the prophets,
who have spoken in the name of the
Lord, for an [a]example of [b]suffering
affliction, and of patience.
11 Behold, we count them [a]happy
which [b]endure. Ye have heard of
the patience of [c]Job, and have seen
the end of the Lord; that the Lord is
very [d]pitiful, and of tender [e]mercy.
12 But above all things, my brethren, [a]swear not, neither by heaven,
neither by the earth, neither by any
other [b]oath: but let your yea be yea;
and *your* nay, nay; lest ye fall into
condemnation.
13 Is any among you [a]afflicted?
let him pray. Is any merry? let him
sing psalms.
14 Is any [a]sick among you? let him
call for the [b]elders of the church; and
let them [c]pray over him, [d]anointing him with oil in the name of
the Lord:
15 And the [a]prayer of [b]faith shall
save the sick, and the Lord shall raise
him up; and if he have committed
sins, they shall be [c]forgiven him.
16 [a]Confess *your* faults one to another, and [b]pray one for another,
that ye may be healed. [c]The effectual [d]fervent [e]prayer of a righteous
man availeth much.
17 Elias was a man subject to like
[a]passions as we are, and he prayed
earnestly that it might not rain: and
it [b]rained not on the earth by the
space of three years and six months.
18 And he prayed again, and the
heaven gave rain, and the earth
brought forth her fruit.
19 Brethren, if any of you do err
from the truth, and one convert him;
20 Let him know, that he which
[a]converteth the sinner from the
error of his way shall [b]save a soul
from death, and shall [c]hide a multitude of sins.

8*a* TG Patience.
b 2 Ne. 31:20 (17–21).
c D&C 106:4.
9*a* TG Backbiting; Malice.
10*a* TG Example.
b 2 Cor. 11:23 (23–33); Mosiah 17:13 (10–20); Alma 14:26 (20–27); JS—H 1:22. TG Suffering.
11*a* TG Happiness.
b TG Perseverance; Steadfastness.
c Job 1:1.
d TG Compassion.
e TG God, Mercy of; Kindness.
12*a* TG Swearing.
b TG Oath.
13*a* TG Affliction.
14*a* TG Sickness.
b TG Elder, Melchizedek Priesthood; Heal.
c TG Prayer.
d Ex. 31:11. TG Administrations to the Sick; Anointing.
15*a* D&C 104:80.
b Matt. 15:28 (25–28). TG Faith.
c Mark 2:5 (3–9). TG Forgive.
16*a* TG Confession.
b TG Benevolence.
c Ex. 33:17.
d Jer. 29:13; 1 Ne. 1:5 (5–8); 2 Ne. 4:24 (23–25); Moro. 7:9.
e TG Prayer.
17*a* Acts 14:15 (11–15).
b TG Drought.
20*a* D&C 6:11. TG Conversion.
b 1 Tim. 4:16.
c See JST 1 Pet. 4:8 (1 Pet. 4:8 note *a*).

THE FIRST EPISTLE GENERAL OF

PETER

CHAPTER 1

The trial of our faith precedes salvation—Christ was foreordained to be the Redeemer.

PETER, an apostle of Jesus
Christ, to the [a]strangers scattered throughout Pontus, Galatia, Cappadocia, Asia, and Bithynia,
2 [a]Elect according to the [b]fore-
knowledge of God the Father,
through [c]sanctification of the Spirit,
unto [d]obedience and [e]sprinkling
of the [f]blood of Jesus Christ: Grace
unto you, and peace, be multiplied.
3 Blessed *be* the God and Father
of our Lord Jesus Christ, which according to his abundant [a]mercy hath
[b]begotten us again unto a [c]lively
[d]hope by the resurrection of [e]Jesus
Christ from the dead,
4 To an [a]inheritance incorruptible,
and undefiled, and that fadeth not
away, reserved in heaven for you,
5 Who are kept by the [a]power of
God through [b]faith unto salvation
[c]ready to be revealed in the last
time.
6 Wherein ye greatly rejoice,
though now for a [a]season, if need be,
ye are in heaviness through manifold [b]temptations:
7 That the [a]trial of your faith, being much more precious than of
gold that perisheth, though it be
tried with fire, might be found unto
praise and honour and glory at the
[b]appearing of Jesus Christ:
8 Whom having not seen, ye love;
in whom, though now ye see *him*
not, yet [a]believing, ye rejoice with
joy unspeakable and full of glory:
9 Receiving the [a]end of your [b]faith,
even the [c]salvation of *your* souls.
10 Of which [a]salvation the [b]proph-
ets have inquired and searched diligently, who prophesied of the grace
that should come unto you:
11 Searching what, or what manner
of time the Spirit of Christ which
was in them did signify, when it
[a]testified beforehand the [b]suffer-
ings of Christ, and the [c]glory that
should follow.
12 Unto whom it was revealed, that
not unto themselves, but unto us
they did minister the things, which
are now reported unto you by them
that have [a]preached the gospel unto
you with the Holy Ghost sent down
from heaven; which things the [b]an-
gels desire to look into.
13 Wherefore gird up the loins of
your mind, be [a]sober, and hope [b]to

---

1 1*a* TG Stranger.
2*a* John 6:44 (44, 63–65). TG Election.
b TG Foreordination; God, Foreknowledge of.
c TG Sanctification.
d TG Obedience.
e Isa. 52:15.
f Ex. 24:8 (5–8); Heb. 12:24.
3*a* TG God, Mercy of.
b TG Holy Ghost, Baptism of; Man, New, Spiritually Reborn.
c GR living.
d TG Hope.
e 1 Cor. 15:20.
4*a* Matt. 6:20; 1 Cor. 9:25 (24–25); Col. 1:5.
5*a* Rom. 1:16.
b Heb. 10:22 (22–24); 1 Pet. 1:21 (21–22).
c GR prepared.
6*a* TG Probation.
b GR trials, afflictions. TG Temptation.
7*a* TG Opposition; Test.
b GR revelation.
8*a* John 20:29.
9*a* GR goal, purpose, consummation. JST 1 Pet. 1:9 . . . *object* of your faith . . .
b D&C 76:51 (51–70).
c Heb. 10:36.
10*a* TG Salvation.
b Matt. 13:17; Luke 24:27 (26–27); Heb. 11:13; 2 Pet. 3:2.
11*a* Jacob 4:4; 7:11 (11–12); Mosiah 13:33 (33–35); D&C 20:26.
b Heb. 12:2.
c D&C 58:3 (3–4).
12*a* TG Holy Ghost, Mission of.
b TG Angels.
13*a* TG Levity.
b GR perfectly, completely.

the end for the [c]grace that is to be
brought unto you at the revelation
of Jesus Christ;
14 As obedient children, not fash-
ioning yourselves according to the
former [a]lusts in your [b]ignorance:
15 But as he which hath called you
is holy, so be ye [a]holy in all manner
of [b]conversation;
16 Because it is written, Be ye holy;
for I am [a]holy.
17 And if ye call on the Father, who
without respect of persons judgeth
according to every man's [a]work,
pass the time of your sojourning
here in [b]fear:
18 Forasmuch as ye know that ye
were not [a]redeemed with corruptible things, *as* silver and gold, from
your [b]vain conversation *received* by
[c]tradition from your fathers;
19 But with the precious [a]blood of
Christ, as of a [b]lamb without [c]blem-
ish and without spot:
20 [a]Who verily was [b]foreordained
before the foundation of the world,
but was manifest in these last times
for you,
21 Who by him do believe in God,
that raised him up from the dead,
and gave him [a]glory; that your [b]faith
and [c]hope might be in God.
22 Seeing ye have [a]purified your
[b]souls in obeying the truth through
the Spirit unto unfeigned [c]love of
the brethren, *see that ye* [d]love one
another with a pure heart fervently:
23 Being [a]born again, not of corruptible seed, but of incorruptible,
by the word of God, which liveth
and [b]abideth for ever.
24 For all [a]flesh *is* as grass, and all
the glory of man as the flower of
grass. The grass withereth, and the
flower thereof falleth away:
25 But the [a]word of the Lord endureth for ever. And this is the word
which by the gospel is preached
unto you.

CHAPTER 2

Converts are newborn babes in Christ—He is the chief cornerstone—Saints hold a royal priesthood and are a peculiar people—Saints are in subjection to the laws of man.

WHEREFORE laying aside all [a]mal-
ice, and all [b]guile, and hypocrisies,
and envies, and all evil [c]speakings,
2 As [a]newborn babes, desire the
[b]sincere [c]milk of the word, that ye
may grow thereby:
3 If so be ye have [a]tasted that the
Lord *is* gracious.
4 To whom coming, *as unto* a living
stone, disallowed indeed of men,
but [a]chosen of God, *and* precious,
5 Ye also, as [a]lively stones, are
built up a [b]spiritual [c]house, an holy
priesthood, to offer up [d]spiritual
[e]sacrifices, acceptable to God by
Jesus Christ.
6 Wherefore also it is contained in

13*c* TG Grace.
14*a* TG Lust.
b Acts 17:30 (29–31).
15*a* 1 Thes. 2:12.
b 2 Pet. 3:11; D&C 136:24 (23–24).
16*a* 1 Jn. 3:3.
17*a* TG Good Works.
b TG Reverence.
18*a* 1 Cor. 6:20. TG Jesus Christ, Redeemer.
b GR erroneous, fruitless conduct.
c TG Traditions of Men.
19*a* TG Jesus Christ, Atonement through.
b TG Jesus Christ, Lamb of God; Jesus Christ, Types of, in Anticipation; Passover.
c Lev. 1:3; 3:6; 22:20; Deut. 15:21.
20*a* GR Having been foreknown before the foundation.
b TG Foreordination; Jesus Christ, Authority of; Jesus Christ, Foreordained; Salvation, Plan of.
21*a* Acts 3:13 (13–15).
b Gal. 5:5 (5–6); 1 Pet. 1:5 (3–8).
c TG Hope.
22*a* TG Purification; Purity.
b TG Soul.
c Moro. 8:26 (25–26).
d TG Love.
23*a* TG Holy Ghost, Baptism of.
b TG Steadfastness.
24*a* TG Mortality.
25*a* Ps. 119:89.
2 1*a* TG Malice.
b TG Guile.
c TG Backbiting; Slander.
2*a* TG Man, New, Spiritually Reborn.
b GR pure, genuine.
c 1 Cor. 3:2 (2–3); Heb. 5:13 (13–14); Mosiah 3:19.
3*a* GR experienced. Heb. 6:5 (4–6); Alma 36:26 (24–26).
4*a* D&C 50:44.
5*a* GR living.
b TG Spirituality.
c Heb. 3:6.
d TG Priesthood, Magnifying Callings within.
e TG Jesus Christ, Types of, in Memory; Sacrifice.

the scripture, Behold, I lay in Sion a
chief [a]corner [b]stone, elect, precious:
and he that [c]believeth on him shall
not be [d]confounded.
7 Unto you therefore which believe
he is precious: but unto them which
be [a]disobedient, the stone which
the builders [b]disallowed, the same
is made the head of the corner,
8 And a [a]stone of [b]stumbling, and
a [c]rock of [d]offence, *even to them*
which [e]stumble at the word, being
disobedient: whereunto also they
were [f]appointed.
9 But ye *are* a [a]chosen generation, a
[b]royal [c]priesthood, an [d]holy [e]nation,
a [f]peculiar people; that ye should
shew forth the praises of him who
hath called you out of [g]darkness
into his marvellous [h]light:
10 Which in time past *were* not a
people, but *are* now the people of
God: which had not obtained mercy,
but now have obtained mercy.
11 Dearly beloved, I beseech *you*
as [a]strangers and [b]pilgrims, [c]ab-
stain from fleshly [d]lusts, which [e]war
against the soul;
12 Having your conversation [a]hon-
est among the Gentiles: that, whereas
they speak against you as evildoers,
they may by *your* good [b]works, which
they shall behold, glorify God in the
day of visitation.
13 [a]Submit yourselves to every
[b]ordinance of man for the Lord's
sake: whether it be to the king, as
[c]supreme;
14 Or unto governors, as unto them
that are sent by him for the punishment of evildoers, and for the
praise of them that do well.
15 For so is the will of God, that
with well doing ye may put to [a]si-
lence the [b]ignorance of foolish men:
16 As free, and not using *your* [a]lib-
erty for a cloak of [b]maliciousness,
but as the [c]servants of God.
17 [a]Honour all *men*. Love the
[b]brotherhood. [c]Fear God. Honour the
[d]king.
18 [a]Servants, *be* subject to *your*
[b]masters with all fear; not only to
the good and gentle, but also to the
[c]froward.
19 For this *is* [a]thankworthy, if a
man for conscience toward God endure [b]grief, suffering wrongfully.
20 For what glory *is it*, if, when ye
be buffeted for your faults, ye shall
take it [a]patiently? but if, when ye
do well, and [b]suffer *for it*, ye take it
[c]patiently, this *is* [d]acceptable with
God.

6*a* TG Cornerstone.
b Isa. 28:16.
c 3 Ne. 11:39 (37–40).
d GR ashamed, disappointed.
7*a* TG Disobedience.
b Matt. 21:42 (42–46); Luke 9:22.
8*a* 1 Cor. 1:18 (18–24).
b Isa. 28:16; 2 Ne. 18:14 (13–15).
c TG Rock.
d TG Offense.
e Matt. 21:44 (33–46).
f Rom. 9:22 (9–23); 1 Thes. 5:9.
9*a* TG Election.
b TG Mission of Early Saints; Mission of Latter-day Saints.
c TG Priesthood; Priesthood, Melchizedek.
d Ex. 19:6. TG Israel, Blessings of.
e TG Nations.
f GR purchased, preserved; note that in Ex. 19:5 the Hebrew word is *segullah*, meaning "special possession or property." TG Israel, Mission of; Modesty; Peculiar People.
g TG Walking in Darkness.
h TG Light [noun].
11*a* TG Stranger.
b GR resident aliens, sojourners.
c TG Abstain.
d TG Lust.
e TG War.
12*a* TG Children of Light; Honesty.
b Matt. 5:16 (14–16); Titus 2:8.
13*a* TG Citizenship; Submissiveness.
b TG Governments.
c GR superior.
15*a* TG Silence.
b TG Ignorance.
16*a* TG Liberty.
b TG Malice.
c TG Servant.
17*a* TG Respect.
b TG Brotherhood and Sisterhood.
c Prov. 24:21.
d TG Citizenship; Kings, Earthly.
18*a* Col. 3:22; 1 Tim. 6:1 (1–2); Titus 2:9 (9–10).
b Eph. 6:5 (5–8).
c GR crooked, wicked.
19*a* GR pleasing, gracious.
b TG Tribulation.
20*a* D&C 122:7 (7–8).
b TG Forbear; Suffering.
c Alma 12:24. TG Patience.
d GR pleasing, gracious.

21 For even hereunto were ye called: because Christ also [a]suffered for us, leaving us an [b]example, that ye should follow his steps:

22 Who did no [a]sin, neither was [b]guile found in his mouth:

23 Who, when he was [a]reviled, reviled not again; when he suffered, he threatened not; but [b]committed *himself* to him that judgeth righteously:

24 Who his own self [a]bare our [b]sins in his own body on the tree, that we, being dead to sins, should live unto righteousness: by whose [c]stripes ye were healed.

25 For ye were as [a]sheep going astray; but are now returned unto the [b]Shepherd and [c]Bishop of your souls.

CHAPTER 3

Husbands and wives should honor each other—Saints should live by gospel standards—Christ preached to the spirits in prison.

LIKEWISE, ye [a]wives, *be* in subjection to your own husbands; that, if any [b]obey not the word, they also may without the word be won by the [c]conversation of the wives;

2 While they behold your [a]chaste [b]conversation *coupled* with fear.

3 Whose adorning let it not be that outward [a]*adorning* of plaiting the hair, and of wearing of gold, or of putting on of apparel;

4 But *let it be* the hidden man of the heart, in that which is not corruptible, *even the* [a]*ornament* of a [b]meek and quiet spirit, which is in the sight of God of great price.

5 For after this manner in the old time the holy [a]women also, who [b]trusted in God, adorned themselves, being [c]in subjection unto their own husbands:

6 Even as Sara obeyed Abraham, calling him lord: whose [a]daughters ye are, as long as ye do well, and are not afraid with any [b]amazement.

7 Likewise, ye [a]husbands, dwell with *them* according to [b]knowledge, giving [c]honour unto the [d]wife, as unto the weaker vessel, and as being [e]heirs together of the grace of life; that your [f]prayers be not hindered.

8 Finally, *be ye* all of [a]one mind, having [b]compassion one of another, love as [c]brethren, *be* [d]pitiful, *be* [e]courteous:

9 Not [a]rendering [b]evil for evil, or railing for railing: but contrariwise blessing; knowing that ye are thereunto called, that ye should inherit a [c]blessing.

10 For he that will love life, and see good days, let him [a]refrain his [b]tongue from evil, and his lips that they speak no [c]guile:

21*a* TG Jesus Christ, Atonement through; Redemption; Self-Sacrifice.
b TG Example; Jesus Christ, Exemplar.
22*a* Isa. 53:9. TG Sin.
b TG Guile; Sincere.
23*a* Isa. 53:3 (3–6). TG Jesus Christ, Trials of; Retribution; Reviling.
b TG Commitment.
24*a* TG Accountability; Self-Sacrifice.
b TG Jesus Christ, Atonement through; Jesus Christ, Redeemer.
c Isa. 53:5.
25*a* TG Sheep.
b TG Jesus Christ, Good Shepherd; Shepherd.
c TG Bishop.
3 1*a* TG Family, Love within; Marriage, Wives.
b TG Disobedience.
c JST 1 Pet. 3:1 . . . *conduct* . . .
2*a* TG Chastity.
b JST 1 Pet. 3:2 . . . *conduct* . . .
3*a* TG Apparel; Modesty.
4*a* TG Beauty.
b GR gentle, mild, forgiving.
5*a* TG Woman.
b TG Trust in God.
c GR obedient, submissive to.
6*a* TG Seed of Abraham.
b GR dismay, consternation.
7*a* TG Family; Marriage, Husbands.
b D&C 121:42.
c TG Marriage, Continuing Courtship in.
d TG Marriage, Wives; Woman.
e TG Marriage, Celestial.
f TG Prayer.
8*a* TG Unity.
b TG Compassion; Kindness; Welfare.
c TG Brotherhood and Sisterhood.
d GR tenderhearted, compassionate.
e TG Courtesy.
9*a* TG Retribution.
b TG Forbear.
c TG Blessing.
10*a* TG Self-Mastery.
b TG Gossip; Slander.
c TG Guile.

11 Let him [a]eschew evil, and do good; let him seek [b]peace, and [c]ensue it.

12 For the [a]eyes of the Lord *are* over the [b]righteous, and his ears *are open* unto their [c]prayers: but the face of the Lord *is* against them that do [d]evil.

13 And who *is* he that will harm you, if ye be [a]followers of that which is good?

14 But and if ye [a]suffer for [b]righteousness' sake, [c]happy *are ye:* and be not afraid of their terror, neither be troubled;

15 But [a]sanctify the Lord God in your hearts: and *be* ready always to *give* [b]an answer to every man that asketh you a reason of the [c]hope that is in you with [d]meekness and [e]fear:

16 Having a good [a]conscience; that, whereas they speak evil of you, as of evildoers, they may be ashamed that falsely accuse your good [b]conversation in Christ.

17 For *it is* better, if the will of God be so, that ye [a]suffer for well doing, than for evil doing.

18 For Christ also hath once [a]suffered for sins, the just for the [b]unjust, that he might bring us to God, being put to [c]death in the flesh, but quickened by the [d]Spirit:

19 By which also he went and [a]preached unto the [b]spirits in [c]prison;

20 [a]Which sometime were [b]disobedient, when once the [c]longsuffering of God waited in the days of [d]Noah, while the ark was a preparing, wherein few, that is, eight souls were [e]saved by [f]water.

21 The like figure whereunto *even* [a]baptism doth also now save us (not the putting away of the filth of the flesh, but the answer of a good conscience toward God,) by the resurrection of Jesus Christ:

22 Who is gone into [a]heaven, and is on the right hand of God; [b]angels and [c]authorities and powers being made subject unto him.

CHAPTER 4

Peter explains why the gospel is preached to the dead—Saints should speak as the oracles of God—The righteous will be tried and tested in all things.

FORASMUCH then as Christ hath suffered for us in the flesh, arm yourselves likewise with the same [a]mind: [b]for he that hath suffered in the flesh hath ceased from [c]sin;

2 That he no longer should live the rest of *his* time in the flesh to

---

11*a* GR turn away from, avoid.
b TG Peacemakers; Peace of God.
c GR pursue, follow eagerly.
12*a* Ps. 33:18. TG Abundant Life; Reward.
b TG Righteousness.
c TG Prayer.
d TG Evil.
13*a* TG Commitment.
14*a* Luke 6:22; James 1:12 (8–16). TG Suffering.
b TG Righteousness.
c TG Happiness.
15*a* GR reverence as holy.
b GR a defense.
c TG Hope.
d TG Meek.
e GR reverence, awe.
16*a* TG Conscience.
b JST 1 Pet. 3:16 . . . *conduct* . . .
17*a* TG Self-Sacrifice.
18*a* TG Jesus Christ, Atonement through; Jesus Christ, Redeemer; Pain; Redemption.
b TG Injustice.
c TG Death; Jesus Christ, Death of.
d TG God, Spirit of.
19*a* TG Genealogy and Temple Work; Preaching.
b TG Salvation for the Dead; Spirit Body; Spirits, Disembodied; Spirits in Prison.
c Luke 1:79 (77–79); D&C 138:8 (5–10, 18). TG Hell.
20*a* JST 1 Pet. 3:20 *Some of whom* were disobedient *in the days of Noah, while* the long-suffering of God waited, while the ark was preparing . . .
b TG Disobedience.
c TG Forbear.
d Gen. 7:1. TG Earth, Cleansing of.
e Gen. 8:1; Heb. 11:7; 2 Pet. 2:5.
f TG Flood.
21*a* TG Baptism; Baptism, Essential.
22*a* John 7:34.
b TG Angels.
c Col. 1:16; 2:10. TG Authority.
4 1*a* GR intent, idea, thought.
b JST 1 Pet. 4:2 For *you who have* suffered in the flesh *should cease* from sin, that *you* no longer *the rest of your time in the flesh,* should live to the lusts of men, but to the will of God.
c TG Sin.

the [a]lusts of men, but to the will
of God.
3 For the time past of *our* life may
suffice us to have wrought the will
of the Gentiles, when we walked
in lasciviousness, lusts, [a]excess of
wine, [b]revellings, banquetings, and
[c]abominable [d]idolatries:
4 Wherein they think it strange
that ye run not with *them* to the same
excess of riot, speaking evil of *you:*
5 Who shall give account to him
that is ready to [a]judge the [b]quick
and the dead.
6 [a]For for this cause was the [b]gos-
pel [c]preached also to them that are
[d]dead, that they might be [e]judged
according to men in the flesh, but
live according to God in the spirit.
7 [a]But the end of all things is at
hand: be ye therefore sober, and
[b]watch unto prayer.
8 And above all things have fervent charity among yourselves: [a]for
[b]charity shall cover the multitude
of sins.
9 Use [a]hospitality one to another
without [b]grudging.
10 As every man hath received the
gift, *even so* [a]minister the same one
to another, as good [b]stewards of the
manifold grace of God.
11 If any man [a]speak, *let him speak*
as the [b]oracles of God; if any man
minister, *let him do it* as of the ability which God giveth: that God in
all things may be glorified through
Jesus Christ, to whom be praise and
dominion for ever and ever. Amen.
12 Beloved, think it not strange
concerning the fiery [a]trial which is
to try you, as though some strange
thing happened unto you:
13 But [a]rejoice, inasmuch as ye
are [b]partakers of Christ's [c]suffer-
ings; that, when his glory shall be
[d]revealed, ye may be glad also with
exceeding joy.
14 If ye be [a]reproached for the
name of Christ, [b]happy *are ye;* for
the spirit of glory and of God rest-
eth upon you: on their part he is
evil spoken of, but on your part he
is glorified.
15 But let none of you suffer as
a murderer, or *as* a thief, or *as* an
evildoer, or as a busybody in other
men's matters.
16 Yet if *any man suffer* as a [a]Chris-
tian, let him not be ashamed; but
let him glorify God on this behalf.
17 For the time *is come* that [a]judg-
ment must begin at the house of
God: and if *it* first *begin* at us, what
shall the end *be* of them that [b]obey
not the gospel of God?
18 And if the [a]righteous scarcely
be saved, where shall the [b]ungodly
and the sinner appear?
19 Wherefore let them that suffer
according to the [a]will of God commit the [b]keeping of their souls *to*
him in well doing, as unto a faithful
Creator.

2*a* TG Lust.
3*a* TG Temperance.
b TG Rioting and Reveling.
c TG Devil, Church of.
d TG Idolatry.
5*a* TG Jesus Christ, Judge.
b OR living.
6*a* JST 1 Pet. 4:6 *Because of this, is* the gospel preached to them *who* are dead, that they might be judged according to men in the flesh, but live *in the spirit* according to *the will of* God.
b TG Gospel.
c TG Genealogy and Temple Work.
d TG Hell; Salvation, Plan of; Salvation for the Dead; Spirits, Disembodied; Spirits in Prison.
e D&C 88:99; 138:10, 34.
7*a* JST 1 Pet. 4:7 But *to you,* the end of all things is at hand . . .
b TG Watch.
8*a* JST 1 Pet. 4:8 . . . for charity *preventeth a* multitude of sins.
b TG Charity.
9*a* TG Hospitality.
b TG Motivations.
10*a* TG Priesthood, Magnifying Callings within.
b TG Stewardship.
11*a* 1 Thes. 2:4; Titus 2:1.
b TG Authority; Teaching with the Spirit.
12*a* TG Test.
13*a* Acts 5:41.
b TG Persecution.
c TG Suffering.
d D&C 66:2.
14*a* TG Reproach.
b TG Happiness.
16*a* Acts 11:26 (19–26).
17*a* TG Judgment.
b D&C 18:46. TG Disobedience.
18*a* TG Righteousness.
b TG Godliness.
19*a* TG God, Will of.
b TG Refuge.

CHAPTER 5

The elders are to feed the flock of God—Humility and godly graces lead to perfection.

THE [a]elders which are among you I
exhort, who am also an elder, and a
witness of the sufferings of Christ,
and also a [b]partaker of the glory
that shall be revealed:
2 [a]Feed the [b]flock of God which
is among you, taking the [c]oversight
thereof, not by constraint, but [d]will-
ingly; not for [e]filthy [f]lucre, but of a
ready mind;
3 Neither as being [a]lords over *God's*
heritage, but being [b]ensamples to
the flock.
4 And when the chief [a]Shepherd
shall appear, ye shall receive a
[b]crown of [c]glory that fadeth not
away.
5 Likewise, ye younger, [a]submit
yourselves unto the elder. Yea, all *of
you* be subject one to another, and
be clothed with [b]humility: for God
[c]resisteth the [d]proud, and giveth
grace to the [e]humble.
6 [a]Humble yourselves therefore
under the mighty hand of God, that
he may exalt you in due time:
7 Casting all your care upon him;
for he careth for you.
8 Be [a]sober, be [b]vigilant; because
your adversary the [c]devil, as a roaring lion, walketh about, seeking
whom he may devour:
9 Whom resist [a]steadfast in the
faith, knowing that the same afflictions are [b]accomplished in your
brethren that are in the world.
10 But the God of all [a]grace, who
hath called us unto his eternal
glory by Christ Jesus, after that ye
have suffered a while, make you
[b]perfect, stablish, strengthen, settle
you.
11 To him *be* glory and dominion
for ever and ever. Amen.
12 By [a]Silvanus, a faithful brother
unto you, as I suppose, I have written briefly, exhorting, and testifying that this is the true grace of God
wherein ye stand.
13 The *church that is* at [a]Bab-
ylon, elected together with *you,*
saluteth you; and *so doth* Marcus
my son.
14 Greet ye one another with a
kiss of charity. Peace *be* with you
all that are in Christ Jesus. Amen.

---

5 1*a* TG Elder, Melchizedek Priesthood; Leadership.
b D&C 66:2; 93:22.
2*a* GR Tend, Superintend. John 21:16 (15–16).
b TG Church.
c GR overseeing, guarding, watching.
d TG Initiative.
e TG Filthiness.
f TG Priestcraft.
3*a* D&C 121:41 (41–42).
b TG Example.
4*a* TG Jesus Christ, Good Shepherd; Shepherd.
b Luke 12:44. TG Exaltation.
c D&C 66:12.
5*a* TG Respect; Submissiveness.
b TG Humility.
c GR opposes, is adverse to.
d TG Pride.
e TG Poor in Spirit.
6*a* TG Contrite Heart.
8*a* TG Levity.
b TG Watch.
c TG Devil.
9*a* TG Perseverance; Steadfastness.
b GR laid upon, endured by.
10*a* TG Grace.
b TG Worthiness.
12*a* Acts 15:34 (32–34); 2 Cor. 1:19; 1 Thes. 1:1.
13*a* TG Babylon.

THE SECOND EPISTLE GENERAL OF

PETER

CHAPTER 1

Peter urges the Saints to make their calling and election sure—Prophecy comes by the power of the Holy Ghost.

SIMON Peter, a [a]servant and
an [b]apostle of Jesus Christ, to
them that have obtained [c]like
precious faith with us through the
[d]righteousness [e]of God and our Saviour Jesus Christ:
2 Grace and peace be multiplied
unto you through the [a]knowledge
of God, and of Jesus our Lord,
3 According as his divine power
hath given unto us [a]all things that
pertain unto [b]life and [c]godliness,
through the knowledge of him that
hath called us [d]to glory and [e]virtue:
4 Whereby are given unto us exceeding great and precious [a]promises: that by these ye might be [b]partakers of the [c]divine [d]nature, having
[e]escaped the [f]corruption that is in
the world through [g]lust.
5 And beside this, giving all [a]diligence, add to your faith [b]virtue; and
to virtue [c]knowledge;
6 And to knowledge [a]temperance;
and to temperance [b]patience; and
to patience [c]godliness;
7 And to godliness [a]brotherly
[b]kindness; and to brotherly kindness [c]charity.
8 For if these things be in you, and
[a]abound, they make *you that ye shall*
neither *be* [b]barren nor [c]unfruitful
in the knowledge of our Lord Jesus
Christ.
9 But he that lacketh these things
is blind, and cannot see afar off, and
hath forgotten that he was purged
from his old sins.
10 Wherefore the rather, brethren,
give diligence to make your calling
and [a]election sure: for if ye do these
things, ye shall never [b]fall:
11 For so an entrance shall be
ministered unto you abundantly
into the [a]everlasting [b]kingdom of
our Lord and Saviour Jesus Christ.
12 Wherefore I will not be negligent to put you always in remembrance of these things, though ye
know *them,* and be established in
the present truth.
13 Yea, I think it [a]meet, as long as
I am in this [b]tabernacle, to stir you
up by putting *you* in remembrance;
14 Knowing that shortly I must put
off *this* my tabernacle, even as our
Lord Jesus Christ hath [a]shewed me.
15 Moreover I will endeavour that
ye may be able after my decease to

---

1 1*a* TG Servant.
b D&C 107:23.
c GR equally precious.
d TG God, the Standard of Righteousness.
e GR of our God and Savior.
2*a* D&C 76:7 (5–10).
3*a* D&C 76:55 (53–60).
b D&C 45:8.
c TG Godliness.
d GR through, by.
e TG Virtue.
4*a* TG Promise.
b D&C 93:28 (27–28).
c TG Earth, Purpose of.
d 1 Sam. 10:6.
e 2 Pet. 2:18.
f TG Man, Natural, Not Spiritually Reborn.
g TG Lust.
5*a* TG Diligence.
b TG Chastity; Good Works; Virtue.
c TG Knowledge; Learn; Study.
6*a* GR self-control. TG Temperance.
b TG Patience.
c GR reverence, piety, godliness.
7*a* TG Brotherhood and Sisterhood.
b TG Benevolence; Kindness.
c TG Charity.
8*a* TG Abundant Life.
b GR idle, unprofitable, injurious. TG Barren.
c D&C 107:31 (30–31).
10*a* TG Election.
b D&C 50:44.
11*a* TG Immortality.
b TG Kingdom of God, on Earth.
13*a* GR right, just, righteous.
b D&C 93:4, 35.
14*a* John 21:19 (18–19).

have these things always in remembrance.

16 For we have not followed cunningly devised [a]fables, when we made known unto you the power and coming of our Lord Jesus Christ, but were [b]eyewitnesses of his majesty.

17 For he received from God the Father honour and glory, when there came such a voice to him from the excellent glory, This is my [a]beloved Son, in whom I am well pleased.

18 And this [a]voice which came from heaven we heard, when we were with him in the holy [b]mount.

19 [a]We have also a more [b]sure word of [c]prophecy; whereunto ye do well that ye take heed, as unto a light that shineth in a dark place, until the day dawn, and the day [d]star arise in your hearts:

20 Knowing this first, that [a]no [b]prophecy of the [c]scripture is of any private [d]interpretation.

21 For the [a]prophecy came not in old time by the will of man: but holy men of God [b]spake *as they were* [c]moved by the [d]Holy Ghost.

CHAPTER 2

False teachers among the Saints are damned—Lustful Saints will perish in their own corruption.

BUT there were [a]false prophets also among the people, even as there shall be [b]false [c]teachers among you, who privily shall bring in damnable heresies, even denying the Lord that [d]bought them, and bring upon themselves swift destruction.

2 And many shall follow their pernicious ways; by reason of whom the way of [a]truth shall be evil spoken of.

3 And through covetousness shall they with [a]feigned words make merchandise of you: whose [b]judgment now of a long time lingereth not, and their [c]damnation slumbereth not.

4 For if God spared not the [a]angels that sinned, but cast *them* down to [b]hell, and delivered *them* into chains of darkness, to be reserved unto [c]judgment;

5 And spared not the old world, but saved [a]Noah the eighth *person*, a preacher of [b]righteousness, bringing in the [c]flood upon the world of the ungodly;

6 And turning the cities of [a]Sodom and Gomorrha into ashes condemned *them* with an overthrow, making *them* an [b]ensample unto those that after should live ungodly;

7 And delivered just [a]Lot, [b]vexed with the [c]filthy conversation of the wicked:

8 (For that righteous man dwelling among them, in seeing and hearing,

16*a* 1 Tim. 1:4.
b Matt. 17:2 (1–9); John 1:14. TG Witness.
17*a* TG Witness of the Father.
18*a* TG Revelation; Witness of the Father.
b Luke 9:28 (28–36).
19*a* JST 2 Pet. 1:19 We have *therefore* a more sure *knowledge of the* word of prophecy, *to which word of prophecy* ye do well that ye take heed . . .
b D&C 68:12; 88:3 (3–4); 132:19, 49.
c D&C 131:5.
d Rev. 2:28; 22:16 (6–16).
20*a* JST 2 Pet. 1:20 . . . no prophecy of the *scriptures* is *given* of any private *will of man.*
b TG Prophecy.
c TG Scriptures, Study of.
d Gen. 40:8.
21*a* TG Prophecy; Scriptures, Value of; Scriptures, Writing of.
b TG Holy Ghost, Mission of.
c TG Inspiration.
d TG Holy Ghost, Gifts of.
2 1*a* TG Apostasy of the Early Christian Church; False Prophets.
b TG False Doctrine; False Priesthoods.
c TG Teacher.
d 1 Cor. 6:20.
2*a* TG Truth.
3*a* Rom. 16:18.
b Deut. 32:35.
c TG Damnation.
4*a* TG Angels; Death, Spiritual, First; Spirits, Evil or Unclean.
b 1 Tim. 3:6. TG Hell.
c TG Judgment, the Last.
5*a* Gen. 8:1; Heb. 11:7; 1 Pet. 3:20 (20–21).
b TG Righteousness.
c TG Earth, Cleansing of; Flood.
6*a* Gen. 19:24; Jude 1:7 (4–7).
b GR token, example.
7*a* Gen. 19:15 (12–22).
b GR oppressed by the outrageous behavior of the lawless.
c TG Filthiness.

[a]vexed *his* righteous soul from day
to day with *their* unlawful deeds;)
9 The Lord knoweth how to [a]de-
liver the [b]godly out of [c]temptations,
and to [d]reserve the unjust unto the
day of [e]judgment to be punished:
10 But chiefly them that [a]walk
after the flesh in the [b]lust of [c]un-
cleanness, and despise [d]government.
[e]Presumptuous *are they,* selfwilled,
they are not afraid to speak evil of
dignities.
11 Whereas angels, which are
greater in power and might, bring
not railing accusation against them
before the Lord.
12 But these, as [a]natural brute
beasts, made to be taken and destroyed, speak evil of the things that
they understand not; and shall utterly [b]perish in their own corruption;
13 And shall receive the [a]reward of
unrighteousness, *as* they that count
it [b]pleasure to [c]riot in the day time.
Spots *they are* and blemishes, sport-
ing themselves with their own de-
ceivings while they feast with you;
14 Having eyes full of adultery,
and that cannot cease from sin;
beguiling unstable souls: an heart
they have exercised with covetous
practices; cursed children:
15 Which have [a]forsaken the right
[b]way, and are gone [c]astray, following the way of [d]Balaam *the son* of
Bosor, who loved the [e]wages of unrighteousness;
16 But was rebuked for his iniquity: the dumb [a]ass speaking with
man's voice forbad the madness of
the prophet.
17 These are [a]wells without water,
clouds that are carried with a tempest; to whom the [b]mist of [c]darkness
is reserved for ever.
18 For when they [a]speak great
swelling *words* of [b]vanity, they [c]al-
lure through the [d]lusts of the flesh,
through much wantonness, those that
were clean [e]escaped from them who
live in error.
19 While they promise them [a]lib-
erty, they themselves are the [b]ser-
vants of [c]corruption: for of whom
a man is overcome, of the same is
he brought in [d]bondage.
20 For if after they have [a]escaped
the [b]pollutions of the world through
the knowledge of the Lord and Saviour Jesus Christ, they are [c]again
[d]entangled therein, and [e]overcome,
the latter end is [f]worse with them
than the beginning.
21 For it had been better for
them not to have [a]known the way
of [b]righteousness, than, after they
have known *it,* to [c]turn from the
holy commandment delivered unto
them.
22 But it is happened unto them
according to the true proverb, The
dog *is* turned to his own [a]vomit
again; and the sow that was [b]washed
to her wallowing in the mire.

8*a* GR oppressed, afflicted.
9*a* TG Deliver.
b TG Godliness.
c TG Temptation.
d D&C 38:5 (5–6).
e Alma 11:44 (41–44); 12:15 (14–18).
10*a* TG Walking in Darkness.
b TG Lust; Sexual Immorality.
c TG Uncleanness.
d GR constituted authority. TG Governments.
e TG Boast.
12*a* Mosiah 3:19.
b Morm. 4:5.
13*a* TG Reward.
b TG Pleasure.
c TG Rioting and Reveling.
15*a* TG Apostasy of Individuals.
b Hag. 1:7.
c Prov. 21:16; Isa. 53:6.
d Num. 22:5; Deut. 23:4; Rev. 2:14 (12–17).
e TG Selfishness; Wages.
16*a* Num. 22:30.
17*a* Jude 1:12 (7–21).
b 1 Ne. 8:23 (23–24); 12:17.
c D&C 95:12; 133:72 (71–74).
18*a* Ps. 73:8; Jude 1:16.
b TG Vanity.
c GR entice, entrap.
d Jude 1:11 (7–21).
e 2 Pet. 1:4.
19*a* TG Liberty.
b GR slaves. Jude 1:4.
c TG Sin.
d TG Bondage, Spiritual.
20*a* Heb. 6:4 (4–6); 1 Ne. 8:28 (24–28).
b TG Pollution.
c Ps. 85:8; D&C 42:26.
d 2 Cor. 2:11; D&C 20:5.
e D&C 76:35 (34–35).
f Alma 24:30.
21*a* TG God, Knowledge about.
b TG Righteousness.
c Heb. 10:39.
22*a* Prov. 26:11. TG Apostasy of Individuals; Apostasy of the Early Christian Church.
b TG Wash.

CHAPTER 3

Some in the latter days will doubt the Second Coming—The elements will melt at the coming of the Lord.

THIS second epistle, beloved, I now
[a]write unto you; in *both* which I stir
up your pure minds by way of [b]re-
membrance:
2 That ye may be mindful of the
words which were spoken before
by the holy [a]prophets, and of the
commandment of us the apostles
of the Lord and Saviour:
3 [a]Knowing this first, that there
shall come in the [b]last days scoffers, walking after their own [c]lusts,
4 And saying, [a]Where is the [b]prom-
ise of his [c]coming? for since the
fathers fell asleep, all things continue as *they were* from the beginning of the creation.
5 For this they willingly are [a]igno-
rant of, that by the [b]word of God the
heavens were of old, and the [c]earth
standing out of the water and in
the water:
6 Whereby the world that then
was, being [a]overflowed with [b]wa-
ter, perished:
7 But the heavens and the earth,
which are now, by the same word
are kept in store, reserved unto [a]fire
against the day of judgment and
[b]perdition of ungodly men.
8 But, beloved, be not ignorant of
this one thing, that one day *is* with
the Lord as a thousand [a]years, and
a thousand years as one day.
9 The Lord is not slack concerning his promise, as some men count
slackness; but is [a]longsuffering to
us-ward, not willing that any should
[b]perish, but that all should come to
[c]repentance.
10 But the [a]day of the Lord will
[b]come as a thief in the night; in
the which the heavens shall [c]pass
away with a great noise, and the
[d]elements shall melt with fervent
heat, the [e]earth also and the works
that are therein shall be burned up.
11 *Seeing* then *that* all these things
shall be dissolved, what [a]manner
of persons ought ye to be in *all* holy
[b]conversation and godliness,
12 [a]Looking for and [b]hasting unto
the [c]coming of the [d]day of God,
wherein the heavens being on fire
shall be dissolved, and the elements
shall melt with fervent heat?
13 Nevertheless we, according to
his promise, look for new [a]heavens
and a [b]new [c]earth, wherein dwelleth
[d]righteousness.
14 Wherefore, beloved, seeing that
ye look for such things, be [a]diligent
that ye may be found of him in
peace, without [b]spot, and blameless.
15 And [a]account *that* the [b]longsuf-
fering of our Lord *is* salvation; even
as our beloved brother Paul also according to the wisdom given unto
him hath written unto you;
16 As also in all *his* epistles, speaking in them of these things; in which
are some things hard to be understood, which they that are unlearned

---

3 1*a* TG Scriptures, Writing of.
b Alma 5:6 (3–13).
2*a* 1 Pet. 1:10. TG Prophets, Mission of.
3*a* JST 2 Pet. 3:3–13 (Appendix).
b TG Last Days.
c TG Lust; Selfishness.
4*a* D&C 45:26.
b Matt. 16:3 (1–5).
c Isa. 5:19 (18–19).
5*a* TG Ignorance.
b TG Jesus Christ, Creator.
c TG Creation.
6*a* TG Flood.
b Gen. 7:19.
7*a* TG Earth, Cleansing of.
b TG Death, Spiritual, Second; Sons of Perdition.
8*a* Alma 40:8; Abr. 3:4 (4–9). TG Time.
9*a* TG Forbear.
b Ezek. 18:23 (23–24).
c TG Repent.
10*a* TG Day of the Lord.
b TG Jesus Christ, Second Coming.
c Ps. 102:26 (25–26); Isa. 51:6.
d TG World, End of.
e TG Earth, Destiny of.
11*a* 3 Ne. 27:27.
b 1 Pet. 1:15.
12*a* D&C 35:15; 49:23.
b TG Haste.
c Heb. 9:28; Rev. 1:7; D&C 39:23.
d D&C 45:30.
13*a* TG Heaven.
b TG Earth, Renewal of; Millennium.
c Ether 13:9.
d TG Righteousness.
14*a* D&C 88:63; 101:38. TG Dedication; Diligence.
b D&C 38:31.
15*a* GR count, regard.
b TG Forbear.

and unstable [a]wrest, as *they do* also
the other [b]scriptures, unto their own
destruction.
17 Ye therefore, beloved, [a]seeing
ye know *these things* before, beware
lest ye also, being [b]led [c]away with
the error of the wicked, fall from
your own [d]steadfastness.
18 But grow in [a]grace, and *in* the
knowledge of our Lord and Saviour
Jesus Christ. To him *be* glory both
now and for ever. Amen.

THE FIRST EPISTLE GENERAL OF JOHN

CHAPTER 1

The Saints gain fellowship with God by obedience—We must confess our sins to gain forgiveness.

[a]THAT which was from the
[b]beginning, which we have
heard, which we have seen
with our eyes, which we have looked
upon, and our hands have handled,
of the [c]Word of life;
2 (For the life was manifested, and
we have seen *it*, and bear witness,
and [a]shew unto you that [b]eternal
life, which was with the Father, and
was manifested unto us;)
3 That which we have [a]seen and
heard declare we unto you, that ye
also may have fellowship with us:
and truly our [b]fellowship *is* with
the [c]Father, and with his Son Jesus
Christ.
4 And these things [a]write we unto
you, that your joy may be full.
5 This then is the message which
we have heard of him, and declare
unto you, that God is [a]light, and in
him is no [b]darkness at all.
6 If we say that we have fellowship
with him, and [a]walk in [b]darkness,
we lie, and do not the truth:
7 But if we [a]walk in the light, as he
is in the light, we have fellowship
one with another, and the [b]blood
of Jesus Christ his Son [c]cleanseth
us from all sin.
8 If we say that we have [a]no [b]sin,
we [c]deceive ourselves, and the truth
is not in us.
9 If we [a]confess our sins, he is

16*a* GR twist, distort. 1 Ne. 13:29 (24–29); Alma 13:20; D&C 10:63.
b TG Scriptures, Preservation of.
17*a* JST 2 Pet. 3:17 . . . seeing ye know before *the things which are coming,* beware lest . . .
b 2 Ne. 28:14 (3–14).
c TG Apostasy of the Early Christian Church.
d TG Steadfastness.
18*a* TG Grace.

[1 JOHN]

1 1*a* JST 1 Jn. 1:1 *Brethren, this is the testimony which we give of* that which was from the beginning . . .
b John 1:2 (1–4, 14).
c TG Jesus Christ, Messenger of the Covenant.
2*a* GR declare, announce, bring tidings.
b John 17:3; 1 Jn. 5:20.
3*a* TG Witness.
b TG Fellowshipping.
c Moses 6:68.
4*a* TG Scriptures, Writing of.
5*a* John 8:12. TG God, Perfection of; Light [noun].
b TG Darkness, Spiritual; Walking in Darkness.
6*a* TG Walking in Darkness.
b 2 Ne. 15:20.
7*a* TG Walking with God.
b Acts 20:28; Rev. 7:14; D&C 29:17. TG Blood, Symbolism of.
c Rev. 12:11 (10–12); D&C 50:28. TG Jesus Christ, Atonement through.
8*a* Prov. 30:20.
b TG Sin.
c TG Lying.
9*a* TG Confession; Repent.

faithful and [b]just to [c]forgive us *our*
sins, and to [d]cleanse us from all unrighteousness.
10 If we say that we have [a]not
sinned, we make him a liar, and his
word is not in us.

CHAPTER 2

Christ is our Advocate with the Father—We know God by obedience—Love not the world—Anti-Christs will come in the last days.

MY little children, these things write
I unto you, that ye sin not. [a]And if
any man sin, we have an [b]advocate
with the Father, Jesus Christ the
righteous:
2 And he is the [a]propitiation for
our sins: and not for ours only, but
also for *the sins of* the whole [b]world.
3 And hereby we do know that
we know him, if we [a]keep his commandments.
4 He that saith, I know him, and
keepeth not his [a]commandments, is
a [b]liar, and the truth is not in him.
5 But whoso [a]keepeth his word, in
him verily is the love of God perfected: hereby know we that we are
[b]in him.
6 He that saith he [a]abideth in him
ought himself also so to [b]walk, even
as he walked.
7 [a]Brethren, I write no new commandment unto you, but an old
commandment which ye had from
the beginning. The old commandment is the word which ye have
heard from the beginning.
8 Again, a new commandment
I write unto you, [a]which thing is
true in him and in you: because
the [b]darkness is [c]past, and the true
[d]light now shineth.
9 He that saith he is in the light,
and hateth his brother, is in darkness even until now.
10 He that [a]loveth his [b]brother
abideth in the light, and there is
none occasion of stumbling in him.
11 But he that hateth his brother is
in darkness, and [a]walketh in darkness, and knoweth not whither he
goeth, because that darkness hath
blinded his eyes.
12 I [a]write unto you, little [b]chil-
dren, because your sins are forgiven
you [c]for his [d]name's sake.
13 I write unto you, fathers, because ye have known him *that is*
from the beginning. I write unto
you, young men, because ye have
overcome the wicked one. I write
unto you, little children, because
ye have known the Father.
14 I have written unto you, fathers,
because ye have known him *that is*
from the beginning. I have written
unto you, young men, because ye

9*b* TG God, Justice of; Justice.
c TG Forgive.
d TG Purification; Purity.
10*a* Prov. 28:13.
2 1*a* JST 1 Jn. 2:1 . . . *But* if any man sin *and repent,* we have an advocate . . .
b GR intercessor, helper, comforter. TG Jesus Christ, Authority of; Jesus Christ, Relationships with the Father; Salvation, Plan of.
2*a* TG Jesus Christ, Atonement through; Jesus Christ, Redeemer; Jesus Christ, Savior; Redemption; Remission of Sins.
b Alma 11:41 (40–41); D&C 21:9; 76:41 (41–43).
3*a* 1 Jn. 3:22 (22–24); 5:3 (2–3).
4*a* 1 Jn. 3:6.
b TG Lying.
5*a* TG Obedience.
b 2 Cor. 5:17.
6*a* John 15:4.
b Matt. 11:29; 2 Ne. 31:12 (12–13); Moro. 7:4 (3–4); D&C 19:23.
7*a* JST 1 Jn. 2:7 Brethren, I write *a* new commandment unto you, but *it is the same* commandment which ye had from the beginning . . .
8*a* JST 1 Jn. 2:8 . . . which thing *was of old ordained of God; and* is true in him, and in you . . .
b TG Darkness, Spiritual.
c GR passing away.
d 2 Ne. 3:5; D&C 50:24.
10*a* D&C 95:12. TG Family, Love within; Love.
b TG Brotherhood and Sisterhood.
11*a* TG Walking in Darkness.
12*a* TG Scriptures, Writing of.
b Mosiah 5:7; Moses 6:52.
c GR because of, through His name.
d 1 Sam. 12:22; Ps. 23:3; Acts 4:12; 1 Ne. 20:9.

are strong, and the word of God
abideth in you, and ye have overcome the wicked one.
15 Love not the [a]world, neither the
things *that are* in the [b]world. If any
man love the world, the [c]love of the
Father is not in him.
16 For all that *is* in the world, the
[a]lust of the flesh, and the lust of the
eyes, and the [b]pride of life, is not
of the Father, but is of the [c]world.
17 And the [a]world [b]passeth away,
and the lust thereof: but he that
doeth the [c]will of God [d]abideth
for ever.
18 Little children, it is the last time:
and as ye have heard that [a]antichrist
shall come, even now are there many
[b]antichrists; whereby we know that
it is the last time.
19 They went out from us, but
they were not of us; for if they had
been of us, they would *no doubt* have
continued with us: but *they went
out*, that they might be made manifest that they were not all of us.
20 But ye have an [a]unction from the
[b]Holy One, and ye know all things.
21 I have not written unto you
because ye know not the truth,
but because ye know it, and that no
lie is of the truth.
22 Who is a [a]liar but he that denieth that Jesus is the Christ? He is
[b]antichrist, that denieth the Father
and the Son.
23 Whosoever denieth the Son, the
same hath not the Father: [*but*] *he
that [a]acknowledgeth the Son hath the
Father also.*
24 Let that therefore abide in you,
which ye have heard from the beginning. If that which ye have heard
from the [a]beginning shall remain
in you, ye also shall continue in the
Son, and in the Father.
25 And this is the [a]promise that he
hath promised us, *even* [b]eternal life.
26 These *things* have I written unto
you concerning them that [a]seduce
you.
27 But the anointing which ye have
received of him abideth in you, and
ye need not that any man [a]teach you:
but as the same [b]anointing [c]teacheth
you of all things, and is truth, and
is no lie, and even as it hath taught
you, ye shall abide in him.
28 And now, little children, abide
in him; that, when he shall appear, we may have confidence, and
not be ashamed before him at his
coming.
29 If ye know that he is righteous,
ye know that every one that doeth
[a]righteousness is [b]born of him.

CHAPTER 3

The sons of God will become like Christ—Love for others is required to gain eternal life—Obedience ensures us an answer to our prayers.

BEHOLD, what manner of [a]love the
Father hath bestowed upon us, that
we should be called the [b]sons of
God: therefore the [c]world knoweth
us not, because it knew him not.
2 Beloved, now are we the [a]sons
of God, and it doth not yet appear
what we shall be: but we know that,
when he shall [b]appear, we shall be

15*a* TG World.
b TG Worldliness.
c D&C 95:12.
16*a* TG Chastity; Lust; Sensuality.
b GR haughtiness, ostentation. TG Pride.
c Mark 7:21 (21–22).
17*a* 1 Cor. 7:31 (29–31).
b TG World, End of.
c TG God, Will of.
d Ps. 125:1; 3 Ne. 14:21.
18*a* TG Antichrist; False Prophets.
b TG Apostasy of the Early Christian Church.
20*a* GR anointing.
b TG Holiness.
22*a* Alma 5:39 (38–40).
b TG Antichrist.
23*a* John 14:7.
24*a* 2 Jn. 1:6.
25*a* D&C 88:4. TG Promise.
b John 17:3 (2–3); 2 Ne. 31:20.
26*a* GR deceive, lead astray, cause to wander.
27*a* D&C 43:15.
b TG Anointing.
c John 6:45; 1 Thes. 4:9.
29*a* TG Righteousness.
b TG Man, New, Spiritually Reborn.
3 1*a* TG God, Love of.
b GR children, people. Isa. 56:5.
c TG World.
2*a* GR children, people. TG Sons and Daughters of God.
b Col. 3:4. TG God, Body of, Corporeal Nature.

[c]like him; for we shall [d]see him as
he is.
3 And every man that hath this
[a]hope in him [b]purifieth himself,
even as he is [c]pure.
4 Whosoever committeth sin [a]trans-
gresseth also the law: for [b]sin is the
transgression of the law.
5 And ye know that he was manifested to take away our [a]sins; and
in him is no sin.
6 Whosoever abideth in him [a]sin-
neth not: [b]whosoever sinneth hath
not seen him, neither [c]known him.
7 Little children, let no man deceive you: he that doeth righteousness is righteous, even as he is righteous.
8 He that [a]committeth [b]sin is of
the devil; for the devil [c]sinneth
from the beginning. For this purpose the Son of God was manifested,
that he might destroy the works of
the [d]devil.
9 Whosoever is [a]born of God [b]doth
not commit sin; for his seed remaineth in him: and he cannot sin,
because he is born of God.
10 In this the children of God are
[a]manifest, and the [b]children of the
devil: whosoever doeth not [c]righ-
teousness is not of God, neither he
that loveth not his brother.
11 For this is the [a]message that ye
heard from the beginning, that we
should love one another.
12 Not as [a]Cain, *who* was of that
wicked one, and slew his brother.
And wherefore slew he him? Because his own works were evil, and
his brother's righteous.
13 Marvel not, my brethren, if the
world hate you.
14 We know that we have passed
from death unto [a]life, because we
love the [b]brethren. He that [c]loveth
not *his* brother abideth in [d]death.
15 Whosoever [a]hateth his brother
is a murderer: and ye know that no
[b]murderer hath eternal life abiding
in him.
16 Hereby perceive we the [a]love *of*
[b]*God*, because he laid down his life
for us: and we ought to lay down
our lives for the brethren.
17 But whoso hath this world's
good, and seeth his [a]brother have
[b]need, and [c]shutteth up his bowels
of [d]*compassion* from him, how dwelleth the love of God in him?
18 My little children, let us not love
in word, [a]neither in tongue; but in
[b]deed and in truth.
19 And hereby we know that we
are of the truth, and shall assure
our hearts before him.

2*c* Alma 5:19 (14, 19); Moro. 7:48 (47–48). TG Eternal Life; Man, Potential to Become like Heavenly Father; Resurrection.
d Job 19:26 (25–27). TG God, Privilege of Seeing.
3*a* TG Hope; Motivations.
b TG Chastity; Purification; Purity.
c 2 Cor. 5:21; 1 Pet. 1:16 (15–19); 2 Ne. 31:5 (5–7).
4*a* TG Transgress.
b TG Sin.
5*a* TG Forgive; Jesus Christ, Atonement through; Jesus Christ, Redeemer.
6*a* TG Sin.
b JST 1 Jn. 3:6 . . . whosoever *continueth in sin* hath not seen . . .
c 1 Jn. 2:4.
8*a* JST 1 Jn. 3:8 . . . *continueth in* sin . . .
b TG Sin.
c Gen. 3:1.
d TG Devil.
9*a* TG Man, New, Spiritually Reborn.
b JST 1 Jn. 3:9 . . . doth not *continue in* sin; for *the Spirit of God* remaineth in him; and he cannot *continue in* sin, because he is born of God, *having received that holy Spirit of promise.*
10*a* GR conspicuous, apparent.
b John 8:44; Acts 13:10.
c Matt. 7:20.
11*a* GR precept, doctrine.
12*a* Jude 1:11 (7–13).
14*a* John 5:24.
b 1 Cor. 8:12; 1 Tim. 6:2; D&C 45:5; 108:7. TG Brotherhood and Sisterhood.
c TG Love.
d TG Death, Spiritual, First.
15*a* Ps. 109:5 (3–5). TG Hate.
b TG Life, Sanctity of; Murder.
16*a* John 10:15 (14–15); 15:13; 1 Ne. 11:22 (22, 25).
b JST 1 Jn. 3:16 . . . *Christ* . . .
17*a* 1 Jn. 4:20 (20–21).
b Luke 3:11.
c GR is hardhearted, void of compassion. TG Hardheartedness.
d Mosiah 4:22 (22–25). TG Compassion.
18*a* JST 1 Jn. 3:18 . . . neither in tongue *only* . . .
b TG Good Works.

20 For if our heart condemn us,
God is greater than our heart, and
[a]knoweth all things.
21 Beloved, if our heart condemn
us not, *then* have we [a]confidence
toward God.
22 And whatsoever we [a]ask, we
receive of him, because we [b]keep
his [c]commandments, and do those
things that are pleasing in his sight.
23 And this is his [a]command-
ment, That we should [b]believe on
the [c]name of his Son Jesus Christ,
and [d]love one another, as he gave
us commandment.
24 And he that keepeth his commandments [a]dwelleth in him, and
he in him. And hereby we know
that he [b]abideth in us, by the [c]Spirit
which he hath given us.

CHAPTER 4

Try the spirits—God is love and dwells in those who love Him.

BELOVED, believe not every [a]spirit,
but [b]try the [c]spirits whether they
are of God: because many [d]false
prophets are gone out into the world.
2 Hereby [a]know ye the [b]Spirit of
God: Every spirit that confesseth
that Jesus Christ is come in the
[c]flesh is of God:
3 And every spirit that confesseth
not that Jesus Christ is come in the
flesh is [a]not of God: and this is that
spirit of [b]antichrist, whereof ye have
heard that it should come; and even
now already is it in the world.
4 Ye are of God, little children,
and have overcome them: because
greater is he that is in you, than he
that is in the world.
5 They are of the [a]world: therefore
speak they of the world, and the
world heareth them.
6 We are of God: he that knoweth
God [a]heareth us; he that is not of
God heareth not us. Hereby [b]know
we the [c]spirit of truth, and the spirit
of [d]error.
7 Beloved, let us [a]love one another:
for [b]love is of God; and every one
that loveth is [c]born of God, and
knoweth God.
8 He that loveth not [a]knoweth not
God; for God is love.
9 In this was manifested the love
of God toward us, because that God
sent his only begotten Son into the
world, that we might [a]live through
him.
10 Herein is love, not that we loved
God, but that he [a]loved us, and [b]sent
his Son *to be* the [c]propitiation for
our sins.
11 Beloved, if God so loved us, we
ought also to love one another.
12 [a]No man hath [b]seen God at any
time. If we love one another, [c]God

20*a* TG God, Intelligence of.
21*a* Alma 5:27.
22*a* TG Prayer.
b 1 Jn. 2:3.
c TG Good Works.
23*a* TG Commandments of God.
b TG Faith.
c 2 Ne. 25:20; Mosiah 3:17; D&C 11:30; 20:29. TG Jesus Christ, Taking the Name of.
d TG Family, Love within.
24*a* John 6:56; Rom. 8:9; 1 Cor. 2:16; 2 Cor. 13:5; 1 Jn. 4:13 (7–21).
b John 14:23.
c 1 Cor. 2:10; 1 Thes. 4:8.
4 1*a* Moro. 7:12 (12–17).
b GR test, prove by trial, discern. 1 Thes. 5:21; D&C 11:12 (12–14); 50:31 (1–3, 31–35); 129:9 (1–9).
c TG Spirits, Evil or Unclean.
d TG Apostasy of the Early Christian Church; False Prophets.
2*a* TG Discernment, Spiritual.
b TG God, Spirit of.
c TG Flesh and Blood.
3*a* D&C 50:32.
b TG Antichrist.
5*a* TG Worldliness.
6*a* John 8:47; 13:20; D&C 1:38 (14, 37–38); 29:7; 84:36 (35–39).
b TG Discernment, Spiritual.
c TG Holy Ghost, Mission of.
d GR deception, wandering, sin.
7*a* TG Love.
b TG God, Love of.
c TG Man, New, Spiritually Reborn.
8*a* John 17:3.
9*a* John 3:16.
10*a* 2 Thes. 2:16.
b TG Jesus Christ, Authority of.
c TG Jesus Christ, Atonement through; Jesus Christ, Redeemer.
12*a* JST 1 Jn. 4:12 No man hath seen God at any time, *except them who believe . . .*
b D&C 93:1; 110:2 (1–3); Abr. 3:11 (11–12); JS—H 1:17 (16–17).
c 2 Cor. 13:5.

[d]dwelleth in us, and his love is perfected in us.
13 Hereby know we that we [a]dwell
in him, and he in us, because he
hath given us of his Spirit.
14 And we have seen and do [a]tes-
tify that the Father [b]sent the Son *to*
be the [c]Saviour of the [d]world.
15 Whosoever shall [a]confess that
Jesus is the Son of God, God dwelleth in him, and he in God.
16 And we have known and believed the love that God hath to us.
God is love; and he that [a]dwelleth
in love dwelleth in God, and God
in him.
17 Herein is our love made perfect,
that we may have boldness in the
day of judgment: because as he [a]is,
so are we in this world.
18 There is no [a]fear in [b]love; but
perfect [c]love casteth out fear: because fear hath [d]torment. He that
feareth is not made perfect in love.
19 We [a]love him, because he first
loved us.
20 If a man say, I love God, and
[a]hateth his [b]brother, he is a [c]liar: for
he that loveth not his [d]brother whom
he hath seen, how can he love God
whom he hath not [e]seen?
21 And this commandment have
we from him, That he who [a]loveth
God love his brother also.

CHAPTER 5

Saints are born of God through belief in Christ—Water, blood, and the Spirit testify of Christ—Belief in Christ is required in order to gain eternal life.

WHOSOEVER believeth that Jesus is
the Christ is born of God: and every
one that loveth him that begat loveth
him also that is begotten of him.
2 By this we know that we [a]love
the [b]children of God, when we love
God, and keep his commandments.
3 For this is the [a]love of God, that
we [b]keep his commandments: and
his commandments are not [c]grievous.
4 For whatsoever is [a]born of God
[b]overcometh the world: and this is
the [c]victory that overcometh the
world, *even* our faith.
5 Who is he that [a]overcometh the
world, but he that believeth that
Jesus is the Son of God?
6 This is he that [a]came by water
and blood, *even* Jesus Christ; not by
water only, but by water and blood.
And it is the [b]Spirit that beareth
[c]witness, because the Spirit is truth.
7 For there are three that bear
record in heaven, the [a]Father, the
Word, and the Holy Ghost: and these
three are [b]one.
8 And there are three that bear
witness in earth, the [a]Spirit, and
the water, and the [b]blood: and these
three agree in one.
9 If we receive the [a]witness of men,
the [b]witness of God is greater: for
this is the [c]witness of God which he
hath testified of his Son.

12*d* 1 Cor. 2:16.
13*a* 1 Jn. 3:24.
14*a* TG Witness.
b TG Jesus Christ, Authority of.
c TG Jesus Christ, Savior.
d D&C 66:1.
15*a* TG Testimony.
16*a* D&C 42:45.
17*a* TG Jesus Christ, Exemplar.
18*a* Philip. 1:14 (12–17); D&C 50:41 (41, 42). TG Courage; Fearful.
b TG Family, Love within.
c TG Love.
d GR correction, punishment.
19*a* TG Love.
20*a* TG Family, Love within; Hate.
b TG Brotherhood and Sisterhood.
c TG Lying.
d 1 Jn. 3:17 (10–18).
e TG God, Privilege of Seeing.
21*a* TG Fellowshipping; Love.
5 2*a* TG Family, Love within.
b TG Sons and Daughters of God.
3*a* TG God, the Standard of Righteousness.
b 1 Jn. 2:3.
c GR burdensome, oppressive. Matt. 11:30.
4*a* Rom. 12:2 (1–2).
b Rev. 3:21; D&C 64:2.
c 1 Cor. 15:57.
5*a* Rev. 2:7 (1–7).
6*a* TG Jesus Christ, Condescension of.
b D&C 1:39.
c TG Holy Ghost, Mission of.
7*a* TG Godhead.
b TG Unity.
8*a* Moses 6:59 (59–60).
b TG Blood, Symbolism of.
9*a* D&C 6:23 (22–24).
b TG Witness.
c TG Witness of the Father.

10 He that [a]believeth on the Son of
God hath the [b]witness in himself: he
that believeth not God hath made
him a liar; because he believeth not
the [c]record that God gave of his Son.
11 And this is the record, that God
hath given to us [a]eternal life, and
this [b]life is in his Son.
12 He that hath the Son hath life;
and he that hath not the Son of God
hath not life.
13 These things have I [a]written
unto you that believe on the name
of the Son of God; that ye may know
that ye have eternal [b]life, and that
ye may believe on the name of the
Son of God.
14 And this is the confidence that
we have in him, that, if we ask any
thing according to his [a]will, he
[b]heareth us:
15 And if we know that he hear
us, whatsoever we [a]ask, we know
that we have the petitions that we
[b]desired of him.
16 If any man see his brother sin a
sin *which is* not unto death, he shall
ask, and he shall give him life for
them that sin not unto death. There
is a sin unto death: I do not say that
he shall pray for it.
17 All unrighteousness is [a]sin: and
there is a [b]sin not unto death.
18 We know that whosoever is
[a]born of God [b]sinneth not; but he
that is begotten of God [c]keepeth himself, and that [d]wicked one toucheth
him not.
19 *And* we know that we are of
[a]God, and the whole [b]world lieth
in [c]wickedness.
20 And we know that the Son of
God is come, and hath given us an
understanding, that we may know
him that is true, and we are in him
that is true, *even* in his Son Jesus
Christ. This is the true God, and
[a]eternal life.
21 Little children, keep yourselves
from idols. Amen.

THE SECOND EPISTLE OF

JOHN

John rejoices because the children of the elect lady are true and faithful.

THE elder unto the elect lady
and her children, whom I love
in the truth; and not I only,
but also all they that have known
the truth;
2 For the truth's sake, which dwelleth in us, and shall be with us for
ever.
3 Grace be with you, mercy, *and*
peace, from God the Father, and
from the Lord Jesus Christ, the Son
of the Father, in truth and love.
4 I rejoiced greatly that I found of

10*a* TG Faith.
b TG Testimony.
c GR testimony, witness.
11*a* TG Eternal Life.
b John 1:4; 2 Tim. 1:10.
13*a* John 20:31. TG Record Keeping.
b 2 Ne. 31:20.
14*a* TG God, Will of.
b Ps. 4:1 (1, 3).
15*a* TG Prayer.
b Ps. 145:19.
17*a* TG Sin.
b D&C 64:7.
18*a* TG Man, New, Spiritually Reborn.
b JST 1 Jn. 5:18 . . . *continueth not in sin;* but he that is begotten of God *and* keepeth himself, that wicked one *overcometh* him not.
c GR guards, shields.
d James 1:27 (22–27).
19*a* TG Called of God.
b D&C 84:49 (49–53).
c TG Wickedness.
20*a* 1 Jn. 1:2.

thy children walking in truth, as
we have received a commandment
from the Father.
5 And now I beseech thee, lady, not
as though I wrote a new commandment
unto thee, but that which we
had from the beginning, that we
love one another.
6 And this is [a]love, that we [b]walk
after his commandments. This is
the commandment, That, as ye
have heard from the [c]beginning, ye
should walk in it.
7 For many [a]deceivers are entered
into the world, who confess
not that Jesus Christ is come in
the flesh. This is a deceiver and an
[b]antichrist.
8 Look to yourselves, that we lose
not those things which we have
[a]wrought, but that we receive a
full reward.
9 Whosoever transgresseth, and
abideth not in the doctrine of Christ,
hath not God. He that abideth in the
doctrine of Christ, he hath both the
Father and the Son.
10 If there come any unto you, and
bring not this doctrine, receive him
not into *your* [a]house, neither bid
him God speed:
11 For he that biddeth him God
speed is [a]partaker of his evil deeds.
12 Having many things to write
unto you, I would not [a]*write* with
paper and ink: but I trust to come
unto you, and speak face to face,
that our joy may be full.
13 The children of thy elect sister
greet thee. Amen.

THE THIRD EPISTLE OF JOHN

John commends Gaius for his help to those who love the truth.

THE elder unto the wellbeloved
Gaius, whom I love in
the truth.
2 Beloved, I wish above all things
that thou mayest prosper and be in
health, even as thy soul prospereth.
3 For I rejoiced greatly, when the
brethren came and testified of the
truth that is in thee, even as thou
walkest in the truth.
4 I have no greater [a]joy than to
hear that my [b]children [c]walk in
truth.
5 Beloved, thou doest faithfully
whatsoever thou doest to the [a]brethren,
and to [b]strangers;
6 Which have borne witness of thy
charity before the church: whom if
thou bring forward on their journey
after a godly sort, thou shalt
do well:
7 Because that for his name's sake
they went forth, taking nothing of
the Gentiles.
8 We therefore ought to receive
such, that we might be fellowhelpers
to the truth.
9 I wrote unto the church: but
Diotrephes, who loveth to have the

1 6*a* TG Family, Love within.
b TG Walking with God.
c 1 Jn. 2:24.
7*a* TG Deceit.
b TG Antichrist.
8*a* GR performed, acquired.
10*a* 1 Cor. 5:11.
11*a* 1 Tim. 5:22.
12*a* TG Scriptures, Writing of.

[3 JOHN]
1 4*a* TG Joy.
b 1 Jn. 5:21.
c TG Walking with God.
5*a* D&C 84:88 (88–92).
b TG Stranger.

[a]preeminence among them, [b]receiv-
eth us not.
10 Wherefore, if I come, I will remember his deeds which he doeth,
[a]prating against us with malicious
words: and not content therewith,
neither doth he himself receive the
brethren, and forbiddeth them that
would, and casteth *them* out of the
church.
11 Beloved, follow not that which
is evil, but that which is good. He
that doeth [a]good is of God: but
he that doeth evil hath not seen
God.
12 Demetrius hath good report of
all *men*, and of the truth itself: yea,
and we *also* bear record; and ye know
that our [a]record is true.
13 I had many things to write, but
I will not with ink and pen [a]write
unto thee:
14 But I trust I shall shortly see
thee, and we shall speak face to face.
Peace *be* to thee. *Our* friends salute
thee. Greet the friends by name.

THE GENERAL EPISTLE OF

JUDE

Contend for the faith—Some angels kept not their first estate—Michael disputed about the body of Moses—Enoch prophesied of the Second Coming—Mockers will come in the last days.

[a]JUDE, the [b]servant of Jesus Christ,
and brother of James, to them
that are sanctified by God the
Father, and preserved in Jesus
Christ, *and* called:
2 Mercy unto you, and peace, and
love, be multiplied.
3 Beloved, when I gave all diligence
to [a]write unto you of the common
[b]salvation, it was needful for me to
write unto you, and exhort *you* that
ye should [c]earnestly [d]contend for
the faith which was once delivered
unto the saints.
4 For there are certain [a]men crept
in unawares, who were before of
old ordained to this condemnation,
[b]ungodly men, turning the grace of
our God into [c]lasciviousness, and
[d]denying the only Lord God, and
our Lord Jesus Christ.
5 I will therefore put you in remembrance, though ye once knew
this, how that the Lord, having
[a]saved the people out of the land of
Egypt, afterward [b]destroyed them
that [c]believed not.
6 And the [a]angels which kept not

9*a* TG Unrighteous Dominion.
b TG Apostasy of the Early Christian Church.
10*a* Num. 16:3.
11*a* Moro. 7:12.
12*a* GR witness, testimony.
13*a* TG Scriptures, Writing of.

[JUDE]

1 1*a* JST Jude 1:1 Jude, the servant *of God, called* of Jesus Christ, and brother of James; to them *who* are sanctified *of* the Father; and preserved in Jesus Christ;
b TG Servant.
3*a* TG Scriptures, Lost.
b 2 Ne. 2:4; 26:33; A of F 1:3.
c TG Zeal.
d Philip. 1:27; D&C 112:5.
4*a* 2 Pet. 2:19; D&C 29:45; JS—H 1:19.
b TG Godliness.
c GR licentiousness.
d TG Apostasy of the Early Christian Church.
5*a* 1 Cor. 10:5 (5, 9).
b Deut. 1:35.
c TG Unbelief.
6*a* TG Angels; Death, Spiritual, First; Devil; Sons of Perdition; Spirits, Evil or Unclean.

their [b]first [c]estate, but left their
own habitation, he hath reserved in
everlasting chains under darkness
unto the [d]judgment of the great day.
7 Even as [a]Sodom and Gomorrha,
and the cities about them in like
manner, giving themselves over
to [b]fornication, and going after
[c]strange flesh, are set forth for an
[d]example, suffering the [e]vengeance
of eternal fire.
8 Likewise also these [a]*filthy* dream-
ers [b]defile the flesh, despise dominion, and speak evil of dignities.
9 Yet [a]Michael the [b]archangel,
when contending with the devil he
disputed about the body of [c]Moses,
durst not bring against him a railing accusation, but said, The Lord
rebuke thee.
10 But these speak evil of those
things which they know not: but
what they know naturally, as brute
beasts, in those things they corrupt
themselves.
11 Woe unto them! for they have
gone in the way of [a]Cain, and ran
greedily after the error of [b]Balaam
for reward, and [c]perished in the
gainsaying of Core.
12 These are spots in your feasts
of charity, when they feast with
you, feeding themselves without
fear: [a]clouds *they are* without water,
carried about of winds; trees whose
fruit withereth, without fruit, twice
dead, plucked up by the roots;
13 Raging waves of the sea, foaming out their own shame; wandering [a]stars, to whom is reserved the
blackness of darkness for ever.
14 And [a]Enoch also, the seventh
from Adam, prophesied of these,
saying, Behold, the Lord [b]cometh
with ten thousands of his [c]saints,
15 To [a]execute [b]judgment upon
all, and to convince all that are
ungodly among them of all their
ungodly deeds which they have ungodly committed, and of all their
hard [c]*speeches* which ungodly sinners have spoken against him.
16 These are [a]murmurers, com-
plainers, walking after their own
[b]lusts; and their mouth [c]speaketh
great swelling *words*, having men's
persons in admiration because of
[d]advantage.
17 But, beloved, remember ye the
words which were spoken before
of the apostles of our Lord Jesus
Christ;
18 How that they told you there
should be [a]mockers in the [b]last time,
who should [c]walk after their own
ungodly lusts.
19 These be they who [a]separate
themselves, sensual, having not the
[b]Spirit.
20 But ye, beloved, [a]building up
yourselves on your most holy faith,
praying in the Holy Ghost,
21 Keep yourselves in the love of
God, looking for the mercy of our
Lord Jesus Christ unto eternal life.
22 And of some have [a]compassion,
making a difference:
23 And others save with fear,

6*b* TG Man, Antemortal Existence of.
c Abr. 3:26 (24–28).
d TG Judgment, the Last.
7*a* Gen. 19:24; 2 Pet. 2:6 (1–9).
b TG Fornication.
c TG Homosexual Behavior.
d TG Example.
e D&C 76:105. TG Punish.
8*a* The Greek text omits "filthy."
b TG Pollution.
9*a* TG Adam.
b TG Angels.
c TG Translated Beings.
11*a* Gen. 4:5 (1–15); 1 Jn. 3:12.
b 2 Pet. 2:18.
c JST Jude 1:11 . . . *shall perish* . . . Num. 16.
12*a* 2 Pet. 2:17.
13*a* TG Astronomy.
14*a* Gen. 5:23; Heb. 11:5 (5–6); Moses 6:27 (27–65). TG Scriptures, Lost.
b 1 Thes. 4:17 (13–18); Moses 7:65 (62–66). TG Jesus Christ, Second Coming.
c TG Saints.
15*a* TG Jesus Christ, Authority of.
b TG Accountability; Jesus Christ, Judge.
c Ps. 139:20 (17–24).
16*a* TG Murmuring.
b TG Lust.
c 2 Pet. 2:18 (10–19).
d GR profit, gain.
18*a* TG Apostasy of Individuals; Mocking.
b TG Last Days.
c TG Walking in Darkness.
19*a* Deut. 13:13; Judg. 20:13.
b TG Holy Ghost, Loss of.
20*a* D&C 21:2.
22*a* TG Compassion.

pulling *them* out of the [a]fire; hating even the [b]garment spotted by the flesh.
24 Now unto him that is able to keep you from falling, and to present
you [a]faultless before the presence of his glory with exceeding joy,
25 To the only wise God our Saviour, *be* glory and majesty, dominion and power, both now and ever. Amen.

THE REVELATION

OF ST JOHN THE DIVINE

CHAPTER 1

Christ chooses some as kings and priests unto God—Christ will come again—John sees the risen Lord.

[a]THE [b]Revelation of Jesus Christ, which God gave unto him, to shew unto his [c]servants things which must [d]shortly come to pass; and he sent and signified *it* by his [e]angel unto his servant John:
2 Who bare record of the word of God, and of the testimony of Jesus Christ, and of all things that he saw.
3 [a]Blessed *is* he that [b]readeth, and they that hear the words of this prophecy, and keep those things which are written therein: for the [c]time *is* at hand.
4 JOHN to the [a]seven churches which are in Asia: Grace *be* unto you, and peace, from him which [b]is, and which was, and
which is to come; and from the seven [c]Spirits which are before his throne;
5 And from Jesus Christ, *who is* the faithful witness, *and* the [a]first begotten of the dead, and the prince of the kings of the earth. Unto him that loved us, and [b]washed us from our sins in his own [c]blood,
6 And hath made us [a]kings and [b]priests unto God and his Father; to him *be* [c]glory and [d]dominion for ever and ever. Amen.
7 Behold, he [a]cometh with clouds; and every eye shall [b]see him, and they *also* which pierced him: and all [c]kindreds of the earth shall [d]wail because of him. Even so, Amen.
8 I am [a]Alpha and Omega, the [b]beginning and the ending, saith the Lord, which is, and which was, and which is to come, the [c]Almighty.
9 I John, who also am your brother, and companion in tribulation, and

23*a* Amos 4:11; Mal. 4:1.
b D&C 36:6.
24*a* Rev. 14:4 (2–5).

[REVELATION]

1 1*a* JST Rev. 1:1–8 (Appendix).
b 1 Ne. 14:21 (18–27). TG Revelation.
c TG Servant.
d Rev. 22:6 (6–16); D&C 88:79.
e Rev. 19:10 (6–10).
3*a* Rev. 22:7 (7, 18–19).
b TG Scriptures, Study of.
c D&C 34:7.
4*a* D&C 77:5.
b TG Jesus Christ, Jehovah.
c Rev. 3:1; 4:5.
5*a* TG Jesus Christ, Resurrection.
b TG Jesus Christ, Redeemer.
c TG Blood, Symbolism of.
6*a* TG Priesthood, Authority; Salvation, Plan of.
b D&C 76:56 (50–60). TG Priest, Aaronic Priesthood. BD Priests.
c TG Celestial Glory.
d GR might, power.
7*a* 1 Thes. 2:19; 3:13; Heb. 9:28; 2 Pet. 3:12; Rev. 22:12.
b TG Jesus Christ, Second Coming.
c D&C 45:53 (49, 53).
d Matt. 24:30.
8*a* D&C 35:1.
b D&C 38:1.
c Mosiah 3:5. TG God, Power of.

in the kingdom and [a]patience of
Jesus Christ, was in the isle that
is called Patmos, for the word of
God, and for the testimony of Jesus
Christ.
10 I was in the Spirit on the [a]Lord's
[b]day, and heard behind me a great
[c]voice, as of a trumpet,
11 Saying, I am Alpha and Omega,
the [a]first and the last: and, What
thou seest, [b]write in a book, and send
it unto the seven churches which
are in Asia; unto Ephesus, and unto
Smyrna, and unto Pergamos, and
unto [c]Thyatira, and unto Sardis,
and unto Philadelphia, and unto
[d]Laodicea.
12 And I turned to see the voice
that spake with me. And being
turned, I saw seven golden [a]candle-
sticks;
13 And in the midst of the seven
candlesticks *one* like unto the [a]Son
of man, [b]clothed with a garment
down to the foot, and girt about the
paps with a golden girdle.
14 His head and *his* hairs *were* white
like wool, as white as snow; and his
[a]eyes *were* as a flame of [b]fire;
15 And his feet like unto fine
brass, as if they burned in a furnace; and his [a]voice as the sound
of many waters.
16 And he had in his right hand
seven stars: and out of his mouth
went a sharp twoedged [a]sword: and
his [b]countenance *was* as the [c]sun
shineth in his strength.
17 And when I [a]saw him, I fell at
his feet as dead. And he laid his
right hand upon me, saying unto me,
Fear not; I am the first and the last:
18 I *am* he that [a]liveth, and was
[b]dead; and, behold, I am alive for
[c]evermore, Amen; and have the [d]keys
of [e]hell and of death.
19 [a]Write the things which thou
hast seen, and the things which
are, and the things which shall be
hereafter;
20 The mystery of the seven stars
which thou sawest in my right hand,
and the seven golden candlesticks.
The seven [a]stars are the [b]angels of
the seven churches: and the seven
[c]candlesticks which thou sawest are
the seven churches.

CHAPTER 2

He who overcomes will gain eternal life, avoid the second death, inherit the celestial kingdom, and rule many kingdoms.

UNTO the [a]angel of the church of
Ephesus [b]write; These things saith
he that holdeth the seven stars in
his right hand, who walketh in the
midst of the seven golden candlesticks;
2 I [a]know thy works, and thy labour, and thy patience, and how
thou canst not bear them which
are evil: and thou hast tried them
which say they are [b]apostles, and
are not, and hast found them liars:

9*a* TG Patience.
10*a* TG Sabbath.
b TG Jesus Christ, Types of, in Memory.
c D&C 29:4.
11*a* TG Jesus Christ, Firstborn.
b TG Scriptures, Writing of.
c Rev. 2:18.
d Col. 2:1; 4:15 (12–16).
12*a* Ex. 25:31.
13*a* TG Jesus Christ, Son of Man.
b Dan. 10:5.
14*a* Rev. 2:18; D&C 110:3.
b TG Jesus Christ, Glory of.
15*a* Ezek. 1:24; 43:2; D&C 110:3; 133:22.
16*a* Rev. 2:12 (12–17).
b D&C 110:3.
c JS—H 1:16 (16–17).
17*a* TG God, Privilege of Seeing; Jesus Christ, Appearances, Postmortal.
18*a* TG Jesus Christ, Resurrection; Resurrection.
b TG Jesus Christ, Death of.
c TG Immortality.
d TG Jesus Christ, Authority of.
e TG Hell.
19*a* TG Record Keeping.
20*a* Rev. 3:1.
b JST Rev. 1:20 . . . *servants* . . . Rev. 2:18.
c Ex. 37:17; Zech. 4:2 (1–14); Rev. 2:5.
2 1*a* JST Rev. 2:1 . . . *servant* . . . (Note: JST uses "servant" in place of "angel" in vv. 1, 8, 12, and 18.)
b TG Scriptures, Writing of.
2*a* TG God, Omniscience of.
b D&C 64:39 (38–39). TG Apostasy of the Early Christian Church.

3 And hast borne, and hast patience, and for my name's sake hast
laboured, and hast not fainted.
4 Nevertheless I have *somewhat*
against thee, because thou hast left
thy first [a]love.
5 Remember therefore from
whence thou art fallen, and repent,
and do the first works; or else I will
come unto thee quickly, and will
remove thy [a]candlestick out of his
place, except thou [b]repent.
6 But this thou hast, that thou hat-
est the deeds of the [a]Nicolaitans,
which I also hate.
7 He that hath an ear, let him
hear what the [a]Spirit saith unto the
churches; To him that [b]overcometh
will I give to eat of the [c]tree of life,
which is in the midst of the [d]para-
dise of God.
8 And unto the angel of the church
in Smyrna write; These things saith
the first and the last, which was
dead, and is alive;
9 I know thy works, and tribulation, and poverty, (but thou art
rich) and *I know* the [a]blasphemy
of them which say they are Jews,
and are not, but *are* the synagogue
of Satan.
10 Fear none of those things which
thou shalt [a]suffer: behold, the devil
shall cast *some* of you into prison,
that ye may be [b]tried; and ye shall
have tribulation ten days: be thou
faithful unto [c]death, and I will [d]give
thee a [e]crown of life.
11 He that hath an ear, let him
hear what the Spirit saith unto the
churches; He that overcometh shall
not be hurt of the second [a]death.
12 And to the angel of the church
in Pergamos write; These things
saith he which hath the sharp [a]sword
with two edges;
13 I know thy works, and where
thou dwellest, *even* where Satan's
seat *is:* and thou holdest fast my
name, and hast not denied my faith,
even in those days wherein Anti-
pas *was* my faithful [a]martyr, who
was slain among you, where Satan
dwelleth.
14 But I have a few things against
thee, because thou hast there them
that hold the doctrine of [a]Balaam,
who taught Balac to cast a stumblingblock before the children of
Israel, to eat things sacrificed unto
idols, and to commit [b]fornication.
15 So hast thou also them that
hold the doctrine of the Nicolaitans,
which thing I hate.
16 Repent; or else I will come unto
thee quickly, and will fight against
them with the sword of my mouth.
17 He that hath an ear, let him
hear what the Spirit saith unto the
churches; To him that [a]overcometh
will I give to eat of the hidden
[b]manna, and will give him a [c]white
[d]stone, and in the stone a new [e]name
written, which no man knoweth
saving he that receiveth *it*.
18 And unto the [a]angel of the
church in [b]Thyatira write; These
things saith the Son of God, who
hath his [c]eyes like unto a flame of
fire, and his feet *are* like fine brass;
19 I know thy works, and charity,
and [a]service, and faith, and thy patience, and thy works; and the last
to be more than the first.

4*a* D&C 4:2 (1–7).
5*a* Rev. 1:20. TG Apostasy of the Early Christian Church.
b TG Repent.
6*a* TG Secret Combinations.
7*a* TG Holy Ghost, Gifts of.
b 1 Jn. 5:5 (1–5); Rev. 2:26; 21:7.
c Gen. 2:9; Rev. 22:2 (1–16); 1 Ne. 8:10 (10–12).
d TG Paradise.
9*a* TG Blaspheme.
10*a* TG Suffering.
b TG Test.
c D&C 6:13; 31:13. TG Martyrdom.
d TG God, Gifts of.
e D&C 20:14. TG Reward.
11*a* TG Death, Spiritual, Second.
12*a* Heb. 4:12; Rev. 1:16.
13*a* TG Martyrdom.
14*a* 2 Pet. 2:15 (10–22).
b TG Sexual Immorality.
17*a* Rom. 6:22 (11–22); 12:21 (4–21).
b TG Bread of Life; Jesus Christ, Types of, in Anticipation.
c D&C 130:11 (10–11).
d TG Urim and Thummim.
e Isa. 62:2; 65:15; Rev. 19:12 (12–16). TG Name.
18*a* Rev. 1:20.
b Rev. 1:11.
c Rev. 1:14; D&C 110:3 (2–3).
19*a* TG Service.

20 Notwithstanding I have a few
things against thee, because thou
sufferest that woman Jezebel, which
calleth herself a prophetess, to teach
and to seduce my servants to commit fornication, and to eat things
sacrificed unto idols.
21 And I gave her space to repent
of her fornication; and she repented
not.
22 Behold, I will cast her [a]into a
bed, and them that commit [b]adul-
tery with her into great tribulation,
except they repent of their deeds.
23 And I will kill her children with
death; and all the churches shall
know that I am he which [a]searcheth
the [b]reins and hearts: and I will give
unto every one of you according to
your works.
24 But unto you I say, and unto
the rest in Thyatira, as many as
have not this doctrine, and which
have not known the depths of Satan, as they speak; I will put upon
you none other burden.
25 But that which ye have *already*
[a]hold fast till I come.
26 [a]And he that [b]overcometh, and
keepeth my works unto the end,
to him will I give [c]power over the
nations:
27 And he shall rule them with a
[a]rod of iron; as the [b]vessels of a potter shall they be broken to shivers:
even as I received of my Father.
28 And I will give him the morning [a]star.
29 He that hath an ear, let him
hear what the Spirit saith unto the
churches.

CHAPTER 3

He who overcomes will retain his name in the book of life, reach godhood, and be with Jesus as He is with the Father.

[a]AND unto the [b]angel of the church
in Sardis write; These things saith
he that hath the seven [c]Spirits of
God, and the seven [d]stars; I [e]know
thy works, that thou hast a name
that thou livest, and art [f]dead.
2 [a]Be watchful, and strengthen
the things which remain, that are
ready to die: for I have not found
thy works perfect before God.
3 Remember therefore how thou
hast received and heard, and hold
fast, and repent. If therefore thou
shalt not [a]watch, I will come on thee
as a [b]thief, and thou shalt not know
what hour I will come upon thee.
4 Thou hast a few names even in
Sardis which have not [a]defiled their
garments; and they shall [b]walk with
me in [c]white: for they are [d]worthy.
5 He that [a]overcometh, the same
shall be clothed in [b]white [c]raiment;
and I will not [d]blot out his name
out of the [e]book of life, but I will
[f]confess his name before my Father,
and before his angels.
6 He that hath an ear, let him
hear what the Spirit saith unto the
churches.
7 And to the angel of the church

22*a* JST Rev. 2:22 . . . into *hell,* and them . . .
b TG Adulterer.
23*a* TG God, Omniscience of.
b GR (from Hebrew) desires and thoughts.
25*a* 2 Ne. 31:20.
26*a* JST Rev. 2:26–27 (Appendix). 1 Ne. 11:25.
b Rev. 2:7; 3:5.
c Ps. 49:14; Mal. 4:3 (2–3).
27*a* Ps. 2:9; 1 Ne. 11:25.
b Ps. 31:12; D&C 76:33 (31–33).
28*a* 2 Pet. 1:19; Rev. 22:16 (6–16).
3 1*a* JST Rev. 3:1 And unto the *servant* of the church in Sardis, write; These things saith he *who* hath the seven *stars, which are* the seven *servants of God;* I know thy . . .
b Rev. 1:20.
c Rev. 1:4.
d Rev. 1:20 (16, 20).
e TG God, Omniscience of.
f Eph. 2:1.
2*a* JST Rev. 3:2 Be watchful *therefore,* and strengthen *those who* remain, *who* are ready to die . . .
3*a* D&C 39:23. TG Watch.
b Luke 21:35; Rev. 16:15.
4*a* TG Sacrilege.
b TG Walking with God.
c Rev. 6:11.
d TG Worthiness.
5*a* Rev. 2:26; D&C 76:60. TG Salvation.
b TG Remission of Sins.
c GR clothing.
d TG Book of Life.
e TG Record Keeping.
f GR acknowledge, praise.

in Philadelphia write; These things
saith he that is holy, he that is true,
he that hath the [a]key of David, he
that openeth, and no man shutteth; and shutteth, and no man
openeth;
8 I know thy works: behold, I have
set before thee an open door, and
no man can shut it: for thou hast
a little strength, and hast kept my
word, and hast not denied my name.
9 Behold, I will make them of the
synagogue of Satan, which say they
are Jews, and are not, but do lie;
behold, I will make them to come
and [a]worship before thy feet, and
to know that I have loved thee.
10 Because thou hast kept the word
of my patience, I also will [a]keep
thee from the hour of [b]temptation,
which shall come upon all the world,
to try them that dwell upon the
earth.
11 Behold, I come [a]quickly: hold
that fast which thou hast, that no
man take thy crown.
12 Him that overcometh will I make
a pillar in the temple of my God,
and he shall go no more out: and I
will write upon him the [a]name of
my God, and the name of the city
of my God, *which is* [b]new Jerusalem,
which cometh down out of heaven
from my God: and *I will write upon
him* my new name.
13 He that hath an ear, let him
hear what the Spirit saith unto the
churches.
14 And unto the angel of the church
of the Laodiceans write; These things
saith the Amen, the [a]faithful and
true witness, the [b]beginning of the
[c]creation of God;
15 I know thy [a]works, that thou art
neither cold nor hot: I would thou
wert cold or hot.
16 So then because thou art [a]luke-
warm, and neither cold nor hot, I
will [b]spue thee out of my mouth.
17 Because thou sayest, I am [a]rich,
and increased with goods, and
have need of nothing; and knowest not that thou art wretched, and
miserable, and poor, and blind,
and naked:
18 I [a]counsel thee to buy of me
[b]gold tried in the fire, that thou
mayest be rich; and white raiment,
that thou mayest be clothed, and
that the shame of thy nakedness do
not appear; and anoint thine eyes
with eyesalve, that thou mayest see.
19 As many as I love, I rebuke and
[a]chasten: be zealous therefore, and
repent.
20 Behold, I stand at the door, and
knock: if any man hear my voice,
and [a]open the door, I will [b]come in
to him, and will sup with him, and
he with me.
21 To him that [a]overcometh will I
grant to [b]sit with me in my [c]throne,
even as I also overcame, and am set
down with my Father in his throne.
22 He that hath an ear, let him
hear what the Spirit saith unto the
churches.

CHAPTER 4

John sees the celestial earth, the throne of God, and all created things worshipping the Lord.

AFTER this I looked, and, behold, a
door *was* opened in heaven: and the
first voice which I heard *was* as it
were of a trumpet talking with me;
which said, Come up hither, and I

7*a* TG Priesthood, Keys of; Sealing.
9*a* Isa. 49:23; 60:14. TG Worship.
10*a* TG Refuge.
b TG Temptation; Test.
11*a* D&C 87:8.
12*a* Rev. 14:1; 22:4 (1–5).
b TG Jerusalem, New; Zion.
14*a* Jer. 42:5.
b TG Jesus Christ, Firstborn.
c TG Creation.
15*a* Isa. 66:18.
16*a* TG Apathy; Apostasy of the Early Christian Church.
b GR vomit.
17*a* TG Treasure.
18*a* TG Counsel.
b Matt. 13:46 (44–46); D&C 6:7.
19*a* GR instruct, admonish. TG Chastening.
20*a* D&C 88:63.
b John 14:23 (23–25).
21*a* 1 Jn. 5:4 (4–5).
b D&C 6:30.
c Matt. 25:21. TG Exaltation; Man, Potential to Become like Heavenly Father; Salvation, Plan of.

will [a]shew thee things which must
be hereafter.
2 And immediately I was in the
spirit: and, behold, a throne was set
in heaven, and *one* sat on the throne.
3 And he that sat was to look upon
like a jasper and a sardine stone:
and *there was* a [a]rainbow round
about the throne, in sight like unto
an emerald.
4 [a]And round about the throne *were*
four and twenty [b]seats: and upon
the seats I saw four and twenty [c]el-
ders sitting, clothed in white raiment; and they had on their heads
crowns of gold.
5 And out of the throne proceeded
lightnings and thunderings and
voices: and *there were* seven lamps
of fire burning before the throne,
which are the [a]seven [b]Spirits of God.
6 And before the throne *there was* a
[a]sea of glass like unto crystal: [b]and in
the midst of the throne, and round
about the throne, *were* four [c]beasts
full of eyes before and behind.
7 And the first beast *was* like a
lion, and the second beast like a calf,
and the third beast had a face as a
man, and the fourth beast *was* like
a flying eagle.
8 And the four beasts had each of
them six wings about *him;* and *they
were* full of eyes within: and they
rest not day and night, saying, Holy,
holy, holy, [a]Lord God [b]Almighty,
which was, and is, and is to come.
9 And when those beasts give glory
and honour and thanks to him that
sat on the throne, who liveth for
ever and ever,
10 The four and twenty elders fall
down before him that sat on the
throne, and worship him that liveth for ever and ever, and cast their
crowns before the throne, saying,
11 Thou art worthy, O Lord, to receive glory and honour and power:
for thou hast [a]created all things,
and [b]for thy pleasure they are and
were created.

CHAPTER 5

John sees the book sealed with seven seals, and he sees those people redeemed out of every nation—He hears every creature praising God and the Lamb.

AND I saw in the right hand of him
that sat on the throne a book [a]writ-
ten within and on the backside,
[b]sealed with seven [c]seals.
2 And I saw a strong angel pro-
claiming with a loud voice, Who is
[a]worthy to open the book, and to
loose the seals thereof?
3 And no man in heaven, nor in
earth, neither under the earth, was
able to open the book, neither to
look thereon.
4 And I wept much, because no
man was found worthy to open
and to read the book, neither to
look thereon.
5 And one of the elders saith unto
me, Weep not: behold, the [a]Lion
of the tribe of [b]Juda, the [c]Root of
David, hath prevailed to open the
book, and to loose the seven seals
thereof.
6 And I beheld, and, lo, in the midst
of the throne and of the four beasts,
and in the midst of the elders, stood
a [a]Lamb as it had been slain, [b]having

---

4 1*a* TG Revelation.
3*a* Ezek. 1:28.
4*a* JST Rev. 4:4 And *in the midst of* the throne . . .
b GR thrones.
c D&C 77:5.
5*a* JST Rev. 4:5 . . . seven *servants* . . .
b Ezek. 1:13; Rev. 1:4.
6*a* Ezek. 1:22; D&C 77:1. TG Earth, Destiny of.
b JST Rev. 4:6 . . . and in the midst of the throne *were the four and twenty elders;* and round about . . .
c D&C 77:2. TG Cherubim; Symbolism.
8*a* Isa. 6:3 (2–3); Ezek. 1:28 (9–11, 28).
b TG God, Power of.
11*a* TG Jesus Christ, Creator.
b GR through, on account of Thy will.
5 1*a* Ezek. 2:9 (9–10).
b D&C 77:6.
c TG Seal.
2*a* TG Worthiness.
5*a* Gen. 49:9.
b TG Israel, Judah, People of.
c Isa. 11:10; Rev. 22:16 (6–16).
6*a* TG Jesus Christ, Types of, in Anticipation.
b JST Rev. 5:6 . . . having *twelve* horns and *twelve* eyes, which are the *twelve servants* of God, sent forth into all the earth.

seven horns and seven eyes, which
are the seven Spirits of God sent
forth into all the earth.
7 And he came and took the book
out of the right hand of him that
sat upon the throne.
8 And when he had taken the book,
the four beasts and four *and* twenty
elders fell down before the Lamb,
having every one of them harps, and
golden vials full of [a]odours, which
are the [b]prayers of saints.
9 And they [a]sung a new song, saying, Thou art worthy to take the
book, and to open the seals thereof:
for thou wast slain, and hast [b]re-
deemed us to God by thy blood out
of every [c]kindred, and tongue, and
people, and nation;
10 And hast made us unto our God
kings and [a]priests: and we shall
reign on the earth.
11 And I beheld, and I heard the
voice of many angels round about
the throne and the beasts and the
elders: and the number of them was
ten thousand times ten thousand,
and [a]thousands of thousands;
12 Saying with a loud voice, Worthy is the [a]Lamb that was slain to
receive [b]power, and riches, and [c]wis-
dom, and strength, and honour, and
glory, and blessing.
13 And every [a]creature which is in
heaven, and on the earth, and under the earth, and such as are in the
sea, and all that are in them, heard
I saying, Blessing, and honour, and
glory, and [b]power, *be* unto him that
sitteth upon the throne, and unto
the Lamb for ever and ever.
14 And the four beasts said, Amen.
And the four *and* twenty elders fell
down and worshipped him that liveth for ever and ever.

CHAPTER 6

Christ opens the six seals, and John sees the events therein—In the fifth seal, he sees the Christian martyrs; and in the sixth, he sees the signs of the times.

[a]AND I saw when the Lamb opened
one of the [b]seals, and I heard, as it
were the noise of thunder, one of the
four [c]beasts saying, Come and see.
2 And I saw, and behold a white
horse: and he that sat on him had
a bow; and a crown was given unto
him: and he went forth conquering,
and to conquer.
3 And when he had opened the
[a]second seal, I heard the second
beast say, Come and see.
4 And there went out another horse
that was red: and *power* was given to
him that sat thereon to take [a]peace
from the earth, and that they should
kill one another: and there was given
unto him a great sword.
5 And when he had opened the
third seal, I heard the third beast
say, Come and see. And I beheld,
and lo a black horse; and he that
sat on him had a pair of balances
in his hand.
6 And I heard a voice in the midst
of the four beasts say, A measure of
wheat for a penny, and three measures of barley for a penny; and *see*
thou hurt not the oil and the wine.
7 And when he had opened the
fourth seal, I heard the voice of the
fourth beast say, Come and see.
8 And I looked, and behold a pale
horse: and his name that sat on him
was Death, and Hell followed with
him. And power was given unto
them over the fourth part of the
earth, to kill with [a]sword, and with
hunger, and with death, and with
the beasts of the earth.

8*a* GR incense.
b 1 Chr. 23:13; Ps. 141:2; Rev. 8:4 (3–4).
9*a* TG Singing.
b TG Jesus Christ, Redeemer; Redemption.
c Rev. 7:9.
10*a* TG Priest, Aaronic Priesthood. BD Priests.
11*a* Dan. 7:10.
12*a* TG Jesus Christ, Lamb of God.
b TG Jesus Christ, Authority of.
c TG God, Wisdom of.
13*a* D&C 88:104.
b TG Jesus Christ, Power of.
6 1*a* JST Rev. 6:1 And I saw when the Lamb opened one of the seals, *one of the four beasts*, and I heard . . .
b TG Seal.
c TG Cherubim.
3*a* D&C 77:7; Moses 8:28 (22, 28–29).
4*a* D&C 1:35.
8*a* Ezek. 5:17; 14:21; 33:27.

9 And when he had opened the
fifth seal, I saw under the [a]altar
the souls of them that were [b]slain
for the word of God, and for the
testimony which they held:
10 And they cried with a loud
voice, saying, How long, O Lord,
holy and true, dost thou not judge
and [a]avenge our blood on them that
dwell on the earth?
11 And [a]white [b]robes were given
unto every one of them; and it was
said unto them, that they should
[c]rest yet for a little season, until
their fellowservants also and their
brethren, that should be killed as
they *were*, should be fulfilled.
12 And I beheld when he had
opened the [a]sixth seal, and, lo,
there was a great [b]earthquake; and
the [c]sun became [d]black as sackcloth of hair, and the moon became
as [e]blood;
13 And the stars of heaven fell
unto the earth, even as a fig tree
casteth her [a]untimely figs, when she
is shaken of a mighty wind.
14 [a]And the heaven departed as a
[b]scroll when it is rolled together; and
every [c]mountain and island were
moved out of their places.
15 And the [a]kings of the earth, and
the great men, and the rich men, and
the chief captains, and the mighty
men, and every bondman, and every
free man, hid themselves in the [b]dens
and in the rocks of the mountains;
16 And said to the [a]mountains and
rocks, Fall on us, and hide us from
the face of him that sitteth on the
throne, and from the wrath of the
Lamb:
17 For the great [a]day of his wrath
is come; and who shall be able to
[b]stand?

CHAPTER 7

John also sees in the sixth seal the Restoration of the gospel, the sealing of the 144,000, and the hosts of the exalted from all nations.

AND after these things I saw four
[a]angels standing on the four corners of the earth, holding the four
[b]winds of the earth, that the wind
should not blow on the earth, nor
on the sea, nor on any tree.
2 And I saw another angel [a]ascend-
ing from the east, having the [b]seal
of the living God: and he cried with
a loud voice to the four angels, to
whom it was given to hurt the earth
and the sea,
3 Saying, [a]Hurt not the earth, neither the sea, nor the trees, till we
have [b]sealed the [c]servants of our
God in their foreheads.
4 And I heard the number of them
which were sealed: *and there were*
sealed an [a]hundred *and* forty *and*
four thousand of all the [b]tribes of
the children of [c]Israel.
5 Of the tribe of [a]Juda *were* sealed
twelve thousand. Of the tribe of
[b]Reuben *were* sealed twelve thousand. Of the tribe of Gad *were* sealed
twelve thousand.
6 Of the tribe of Aser *were* sealed
twelve thousand. Of the tribe of

9*a* D&C 135:7.
b TG Martyrdom; Persecution.
10*a* Deut. 32:43.
11*a* Rev. 3:4.
b TG Apparel.
c TG Paradise.
12*a* D&C 77:10. TG Last Days.
b Rev. 16:18.
c TG World, End of.
d Matt. 24:29; D&C 45:42.
e Joel 2:31; D&C 88:87.
13*a* IE figs that ripen late, hanging on the tree even into the winter.
14*a* JST Rev. 6:14 And the *heavens opened* as a scroll *is opened* when it is rolled together; and every mountain, and island, *was* moved out of *its place.*
b Isa. 34:4; D&C 88:95.
c Rev. 16:20 (17–21).
15*a* TG Kings, Earthly.
b Isa. 2:19.
16*a* Hosea 10:8; Luke 23:30 (27–31).
17*a* TG Day of the Lord; Jesus Christ, Second Coming.
b Ps. 76:7.

7 1*a* D&C 77:8.
b Ezek. 37:9; Dan. 11:4.
2*a* D&C 77:9.
b TG Seal.
3*a* Rev. 9:4.
b Rev. 22:4 (1–5).
c TG High Priest, Melchizedek Priesthood; Servant.
4*a* D&C 77:11.
b TG Israel, Twelve Tribes of.
c D&C 77:9. TG Israel, Blessings of.
5*a* TG Israel, Judah, People of.
b Ezek. 48:31 (6–7, 31).

Nepthalim *were* sealed twelve thousand. Of the tribe of Manasses *were*
sealed twelve thousand.
7 Of the tribe of Simeon *were* sealed
twelve thousand. Of the tribe of
Levi *were* sealed twelve thousand.
Of the tribe of Issachar *were* sealed
twelve thousand.
8 Of the tribe of Zabulon *were*
sealed twelve thousand. Of the tribe
of [a]Joseph *were* sealed twelve thousand. Of the tribe of Benjamin *were*
sealed twelve thousand.
9 After this I beheld, and, lo, a
great multitude, which no man
could number, of all nations, and
[a]kindreds, and people, and tongues,
stood before the throne, and before
the Lamb, clothed with white robes,
and [b]palms in their hands;
10 And cried with a loud voice,
saying, Salvation to our God which
sitteth upon the throne, and unto
the Lamb.
11 And all the angels stood round
about the throne, and *about* the elders and the four [a]beasts, and fell
before the throne on their faces,
and worshipped God,
12 Saying, Amen: Blessing, and
glory, and wisdom, and thanksgiving, and honour, and power, and
might, *be* unto our God for ever and
ever. Amen.
13 And one of the elders answered,
saying unto me, What are these
which are arrayed in white robes?
and whence came they?
14 And I said unto him, Sir, thou
knowest. And he said to me, These
are they which came [a]out of great
[b]tribulation, and have [c]washed their
robes, and made them [d]white in the
[e]blood of the [f]Lamb.
15 Therefore are they before the
throne of God, and serve him day
and night in his [a]temple: and he that
[b]sitteth on the throne shall [c]dwell
among them.
16 They shall hunger no more, neither [a]thirst any more; neither shall
the [b]sun light on them, nor any heat.
17 For the Lamb which is in the
midst of the throne shall feed them,
and shall lead them unto living
fountains of [a]waters: and God shall
wipe away all [b]tears from their eyes.

CHAPTER 8

John sees fire and desolation poured out during the seventh seal and preceding the Second Coming.

AND when he had [a]opened the [b]sev-
enth seal, there was [c]silence in heav-
en about the space of half an hour.
2 And I saw the seven angels which
stood before God; and to them were
given seven [a]trumpets.
3 And another angel came and
stood at the altar, having a golden
censer; and there was given unto
him much [a]incense, that he should
offer *it* with the prayers of all saints
upon the golden altar which was
before the throne.
4 And the smoke of the incense,
which came with the [a]prayers of the
saints, ascended up before God out
of the angel's hand.
5 And the angel took the censer,
and filled it with fire of the altar,
and [a]cast *it* into the earth: and there
were [b]voices, and thunderings, and
lightnings, and an earthquake.
6 And the seven angels which had
the seven [a]trumpets prepared themselves to sound.
7 The first angel sounded, and there
followed hail and [a]fire mingled with

8*a* TG Israel, Joseph, People of.
9*a* Rev. 5:9.
b Ezek. 41:18 (18–19).
11*a* TG Cherubim.
14*a* TG Peace of God.
b TG Tribulation.
c 3 Ne. 27:19. TG Purity; Wash.
d TG Remission of Sins.
e 1 Jn. 1:7.
f TG Jesus Christ, Lamb of God.
15*a* TG Temple.
b Ps. 47:8; D&C 88:13.
c TG God, Presence of.
16*a* Isa. 49:10.
b Ps. 121:6.
17*a* TG Living Water.
b Rev. 21:4.
8 1*a* D&C 77:13.
b TG Jesus Christ, Second Coming; Sabbath.
c TG Silence.
2*a* D&C 77:12.
3*a* Lev. 16:13 (12–13); Num. 16:40 (36–40).
4*a* Rev. 5:8.
5*a* Ezek. 10:2.
b D&C 88:90.
6*a* D&C 77:12.
7*a* Ex. 9:24 (22–25).

blood, and they were cast upon
the earth: and the third part of
trees was burnt up, and all green
grass was burnt up.
8 And the second angel sounded,
and as it were a great mountain
burning with fire was cast into the
sea: and the third part of the sea
became [a]blood;
9 And the third part of the creatures which were in the sea, and
had life, died; and the third part of
the ships were destroyed.
10 And the third angel sounded,
and there [a]fell a great star from
heaven, burning as it were a lamp,
and it fell upon the third part of
the rivers, and upon the fountains
of waters;
11 And the name of the star is
called Wormwood: and the third part
of the waters became wormwood;
and many men died of the waters,
because they were made bitter.
12 And the fourth angel sounded,
and the third part of the sun was
smitten, and the third part of
the moon, and the third part of the
stars; so as the third part of them
was darkened, and the day shone
not for a third part of it, and the
night likewise.
13 And I beheld, and heard an
[a]angel flying through the midst of
heaven, saying with a loud voice,
[b]Woe, woe, woe, to the inhabiters
of the earth by reason of the other
voices of the trumpet of the three
angels, which are yet to sound!

CHAPTER 9

John also sees the wars and plagues poured out during the seventh seal and before the Lord comes.

AND the fifth angel sounded, and
I saw a star fall from heaven unto
the earth: [a]and to him was given the
key of the [b]bottomless [c]pit.
2 And he opened the bottomless
pit; and there arose a smoke out of
the pit, as the smoke of a great furnace; and the sun and the air were
darkened by reason of the smoke
of the pit.
3 And there came out of the smoke
locusts upon the earth: and unto
them was given power, as the scorpions of the earth have power.
4 And it was commanded them that
they should not hurt the grass of the
earth, neither any green thing, neither any tree; but only those [a]men
which have not the [b]seal of God in
their foreheads.
5 And to them it was given that
they should not kill them, but
that they should be tormented five
months: and their torment *was*
as the torment of a scorpion, when
he striketh a man.
6 And in those days shall men seek
[a]death, and shall not find it; and
shall desire to die, and death shall
flee from them.
7 And the shapes of the locusts
were like unto horses prepared unto
battle; and on their heads *were* as
it were crowns like gold, and their
faces *were* as the faces of men.
8 And they had hair as the hair of
women, and their teeth were as *the*
[a]*teeth* of lions.
9 And they had breastplates, as
it were breastplates of iron; and
the sound of their wings *was* as the
[a]sound of chariots of many horses
running to battle.
10 And they had tails like unto
scorpions, and there were stings in
their tails: and their power *was* to
hurt men five months.
11 And they had a king over them,
which is the angel of the bottomless
pit, whose name in the Hebrew
tongue *is* Abaddon, but in the Greek
tongue hath *his* name Apollyon.
12 One woe is past; *and*, behold,
there come two woes more hereafter.
13 And the sixth angel sounded,

8*a* TG Blood, Symbolism of.
10*a* Isa. 14:12.
13*a* D&C 88:92.
b Hel. 7:22; D&C 5:5.
9 1*a* JST Rev. 9:1 . . . and to *the angel* was given the key of the bottomless pit.
b GR pit of the abyss.
c Rev. 20:1.
4*a* Rev. 7:3.
b TG Seal.
6*a* Job 3:21; Jer. 8:3.
8*a* Joel 1:6.
9*a* Joel 2:5.

and I heard a voice from the four
horns of the golden altar which is
before God,
14 Saying to the sixth angel which
had the trumpet, Loose the four angels which are bound [a]in the great
river Euphrates.
15 And the four angels were loosed,
which were prepared for an hour,
and a day, and a month, and a year,
for to slay the third part of men.
16 And the [a]number of the army
of the horsemen *were* two hundred
thousand thousand: and I heard the
number of them.
17 And thus I saw the horses in the
vision, and them that sat on them,
having breastplates of fire, and of
jacinth, and brimstone: and the
heads of the horses *were* as the heads
of lions; and out of their mouths issued fire and smoke and brimstone.
18 By these three was the third
part of men killed, by the fire, and
by the smoke, and by the brimstone,
which issued out of their mouths.
19 For their power is in their
mouth, and in their tails: for their
tails *were* like unto serpents, and had
heads, and with them they do hurt.
20 And the rest of the men which
were not killed by these plagues yet
repented not of the works of their
hands, that they should not worship devils, and idols of gold, and
silver, and brass, and stone, and of
wood: which neither can see, nor
hear, nor walk:
21 Neither repented they of their
[a]murders, nor of their [b]sorceries,
nor of their fornication, nor of their
thefts.

CHAPTER 10

John seals up many things relative to the last days—He is commissioned to participate in the restoration of all things.

AND I saw another mighty angel
come down from heaven, clothed
with a cloud: and a rainbow *was*
upon his head, and his face *was* as
it were the sun, and his feet as pillars of fire:
2 And he had in his hand a little
[a]book open: and he set his right
foot upon the sea, and *his* left *foot*
on the earth,
3 And cried with a loud voice, as
when a lion roareth: and when he
had cried, seven thunders uttered
their voices.
4 And when the seven thunders
had uttered their voices, I was about
to write: and I heard a voice from
heaven saying unto me, Seal up
those things which the seven thunders uttered, and write them not.
5 And the angel which I saw [a]stand
upon the sea and upon the earth
lifted up his hand to heaven,
6 And [a]sware by him that liveth for
ever and ever, who created heaven,
and the things that therein are,
and the earth, and the things that
therein are, and the sea, and the
things which are therein, that there
should be [b]time no longer:
7 But in the days of the voice of
the seventh angel, when he shall
begin to sound, the [a]mystery of God
should be finished, as he hath declared to his servants the prophets.
8 And the voice which I heard
from heaven spake unto me again,
and said, Go *and* take the little book
which is open in the hand of the
angel which standeth upon the sea
and upon the earth.
9 And I went unto the angel, and
said unto him, Give me the little
book. And he said unto me, Take
it, and eat it up; and it shall make
thy belly bitter, but it shall be in
thy mouth sweet as honey.
10 And I took the little book out
of the angel's hand, and [a]ate it up;
and it was in my mouth sweet as
honey: and as soon as I had eaten
it, my belly was bitter.

14*a* JST Rev. 9:14 . . . in the *bottomless pit*.
16*a* Joel 1:6.
21*a* TG Murder.
b TG Sorcery.
10 2*a* Ezek. 2:9 (9–10).
5*a* D&C 88:110.
6*a* Dan. 12:7.
b TG Time.
7*a* TG Mysteries of Godliness.
10*a* Jer. 15:16; Ezek. 2:8; 3:3 (1–3); D&C 77:14.

11 And he said unto me, Thou
must prophesy [a]again before many
peoples, and nations, and tongues,
and kings.

CHAPTER 11

In the last days, two prophets will be slain in Jerusalem—After 3½ days, they will be resurrected—Christ will reign over all the earth.

AND there was given me a [a]reed like
unto a rod: [b]and the angel stood, saying, Rise, and [c]measure the temple
of God, and the [d]altar, and them
that worship therein.
2 But the court which is without
the temple leave out, and measure it
not; for it is given unto the Gentiles:
and the [a]holy city shall they tread
under foot forty *and* two months.
3 And I will give [a]*power* unto my two
[b]witnesses, and they shall prophesy
a thousand two hundred *and* threescore days, clothed in sackcloth.
4 These are the two olive trees,
and the two candlesticks standing
before the God of the earth.
5 And if any man will hurt them,
fire proceedeth out of their mouth,
and devoureth their enemies: and
if any man will hurt them, he must
in this manner be killed.
6 These have power to shut heaven,
that it rain not in the days of their
prophecy: and have power over waters to [a]turn them to blood, and to
smite the earth with all [b]plagues,
as often as they will.
7 And when they shall have finished their testimony, the beast that
ascendeth out of the bottomless pit
shall make war against them, and
shall [a]overcome them, and [b]kill
them.
8 And their dead bodies *shall lie* in
the street of the great city, which
spiritually is called Sodom and
Egypt, where also our Lord was
[a]crucified.
9 And they of the people and kindreds and tongues and nations shall
see their dead bodies three days and
an half, and shall not suffer their
dead bodies to be put in graves.
10 And they that dwell upon the
earth shall rejoice over them, and
make merry, and shall send gifts
one to another; because these two
prophets tormented them that dwelt
on the earth.
11 And after three days and an half
the Spirit of life from God entered
into them, and they stood upon their
feet; and great fear fell upon them
which saw them.
12 And they heard a great voice
from heaven saying unto them,
Come up hither. And they ascended
up to heaven in a cloud; and their
enemies beheld them.
13 And the same hour was there
a great [a]earthquake, and the tenth
part of the city fell, and in the
earthquake were slain of men seven
thousand: and the remnant were affrighted, and gave glory to the God of
heaven.
14 The second woe is past; *and,* behold, the third woe cometh quickly.
15 And the seventh angel sounded;
and there were great voices in
heaven, saying, The [a]kingdoms of
this world are become *the* [b]*kingdoms*
of our Lord, and of his [c]Christ; and
he shall [d]reign for ever and ever.
16 And the four and twenty elders,
which sat before God on their seats,
fell upon their faces, and worshipped God,

11*a* John 21:22 (20–25).
11 1*a* Ezek. 45:1.
b The Greek text omits "and the angel stood."
c Ezek. 40:3.
d Ex. 30:1; Ezek. 41:22.
2*a* Neh. 11:1.
3*a* The Greek text omits "power."
b Isa. 51:19 (19–20); Zech. 4:14 (11–14); 2 Ne. 8:19 (18–20); D&C 77:15. TG Last Days; Witness.
6*a* Ex. 7:17 (17–21).
b TG Plague.
7*a* TG Apostasy of the Early Christian Church.
b TG Martyrdom.
8*a* TG Jesus Christ, Crucifixion of.
13*a* Rev. 16:18 (18–19); D&C 88:89 (87–90).
15*a* TG Kings, Earthly.
b TG Kingdom of God, on Earth.
c Dan. 7:13 (9–14).
d TG Jesus Christ, Millennial Reign.

17 Saying, We give thee thanks, O Lord God [a]Almighty, which art, and wast, and art to come; because thou hast taken to thee thy great power, and hast reigned.

18 And the nations were angry, and thy wrath is come, and the time of the dead, that they should be [a]judged, and that thou shouldest give reward unto thy servants the prophets, and to the saints, and them that fear thy name, small and great; and shouldest destroy them which [b]destroy the earth.

19 And the temple of God was opened in heaven, and there was seen in his temple the [a]ark of his testament: and there were lightnings, and voices, and thunderings, and an earthquake, and great [b]hail.

CHAPTER 12

John sees the imminent apostasy of the Church—He also sees the War in Heaven in the beginning when Satan was cast out—He sees the continuation of that war on earth.

[a]AND there appeared a great wonder in heaven; a [b]woman clothed with the sun, and the moon under her feet, and upon her head a crown of twelve stars:

2 And she being with [a]child cried, travailing in birth, and pained to be delivered.

3 And there appeared another wonder in heaven; and behold a great red dragon, having seven heads and ten horns, and seven crowns upon his heads.

4 And his tail drew the [a]third part of the stars of heaven, and did cast them to the earth: and the dragon stood before the woman which was ready to be delivered, for to devour her child as soon as it was born.

5 And she brought forth a man child, who was to rule all nations with a [a]rod of iron: and her child was caught up unto God, and *to* his throne.

6 And the [a]woman fled into the wilderness, where she hath a place prepared of God, that they should feed her there a thousand two hundred *and* threescore days.

7 And there was [a]war in heaven: [b]Michael and his [c]angels fought against the dragon; and the [d]dragon fought and his angels,

8 And prevailed not; neither was their place found any more in [a]heaven.

9 And the great dragon was [a]cast out, that old serpent, called the [b]Devil, and Satan, which deceiveth the whole world: he was cast out into the earth, and his angels were cast out with him.

10 And I heard a loud [a]voice saying in heaven, Now is come salvation, and [b]strength, and the kingdom of our God, and the [c]power of his Christ: for the [d]accuser of our brethren is cast down, which accused them before our God day and night.

11 And they [a]overcame him by the blood of the Lamb, and by the word of their [b]testimony; and they loved not their lives unto the [c]death.

12 Therefore rejoice, *ye* heavens, and ye that dwell in them. Woe to the inhabiters of the earth and of the sea! for the devil is come down unto you, having great wrath, because he

17*a* TG God, Power of.
18*a* Dan. 7:10; D&C 29:13.
b GR corrupt, waste, pervert.
19*a* TG Ark of the Covenant.
b Ezek. 13:13; Rev. 16:21; D&C 29:16.
12 1*a* JST Rev. 12:1–17 (Appendix). Note the changed sequence of verses in the JST.
b D&C 5:14.
2*a* Isa. 66:7 (7–9).
4*a* D&C 29:36 (36–38). TG Sons of Perdition.
5*a* 1 Ne. 11:25.
6*a* Amos 8:11 (11–12); D&C 33:5; 86:3.
7*a* TG Council in Heaven; Rebellion; War.
b TG Adam; Man, Antemortal Existence of.
c TG Angels.
d TG Devil.
8*a* TG Death, Spiritual, First.
9*a* 2 Ne. 9:9 (8–9).
b TG Devil.
10*a* TG God, Manifestations of.
b TG Strength.
c TG Jesus Christ, Authority of.
d Isa. 29:20; D&C 88:124.
11*a* John 16:33; 1 Jn. 1:7.
b TG Testimony.
c TG Martyrdom.

knoweth that he hath but a short
time.
13 And when the dragon saw that
he was cast unto the earth, he [a]per-
secuted the woman which brought
forth the man *child*.
14 And to the woman were given
two wings of a great eagle, that she
might fly into the wilderness, into
her place, where she is nourished
for a time, and times, and half a
time, from the face of the serpent.
15 And the serpent cast out of his
mouth water as a flood after the
woman, that he might cause her to
be carried away of the flood.
16 And the earth helped the woman,
and the earth opened her mouth,
and swallowed up the flood which
the dragon cast out of his mouth.
17 And the [a]dragon was wroth
with the woman, and went to make
[b]war with the remnant of her seed,
which keep the commandments of
God, and have the testimony of Jesus
Christ.

CHAPTER 13

John sees fierce-looking beasts that represent degenerate earthly kingdoms controlled by Satan—The devil works miracles and deceives men.

[a]AND I stood upon the sand of the
sea, and saw a beast rise up out of
the [b]sea, having seven heads and
ten horns, and upon his horns ten
crowns, and upon his heads the
name of blasphemy.
2 And the beast which I saw was
like unto a leopard, and his feet
were as *the feet* of a bear, and his
mouth as the mouth of a lion: and
the dragon gave him his [a]power,
and his seat, and great authority.
3 And I saw one of his heads as
it were wounded to death; and his
deadly wound was healed: and all
the world wondered after the beast.
4 And they worshipped the dragon
which gave power unto the [a]beast:
and they [b]worshipped the beast,
saying, Who *is* like unto the beast?
who is able to make war with him?
5 And there was given unto him a
[a]mouth speaking great things and
[b]blasphemies; and power was given
unto him to continue forty *and* two
months.
6 And he opened his mouth in blasphemy against God, to blaspheme
his [a]name, and his tabernacle, and
them that dwell in heaven.
7 And it was given unto him to
make war with the saints, and to
overcome them: and [a]power was
given him over all kindreds, and
tongues, and nations.
8 And all that dwell upon the earth
shall worship him, whose names are
not written in the [a]book of life of
the [b]Lamb slain from the [c]founda-
tion of the world.
9 If any man have an ear, let him
hear.
10 He that leadeth into captivity
shall go into captivity: he that [a]kil-
leth with the sword must be killed
with the sword. Here is the [b]patience
and the faith of the [c]saints.
11 And I beheld another beast
coming up out of the earth; and he
had two horns like a lamb, and
he spake as a dragon.
12 And he exerciseth all the power
of the first beast before him, and
causeth the earth and them which
dwell therein to worship the first
beast, whose deadly wound was
healed.
13 And he doeth great wonders, so
that he maketh fire come down from

13*a* Dan. 7:25; 12:7; D&C 10:32; 132:57.
17*a* TG Devil, Church of.
b Dan. 7:21.
13 1*a* JST Rev. 13:1 And I *saw another sign, in the likeness of the kingdoms of the earth;* a beast rise up out of the sea, *and he stood upon the sand of the sea,* having seven heads . . .
b Dan. 7:3 (3–7).
2*a* Luke 4:6.
4*a* TG Babylon.
b TG Worship.
5*a* Dan. 7:8.
b TG Blaspheme; False Doctrine.
6*a* TG Name.
7*a* TG False Priesthoods.
8*a* TG Book of Life.
b TG Jesus Christ, Lamb of God.
c TG Foreordination.
10*a* TG Blood, Shedding of; Retribution.
b TG Patience.
c TG Saints.

heaven on the earth in the sight
of men,
14 And [a]deceiveth them that dwell
on the earth by *the means of* those
[b]miracles which he had power to do
in the sight of the beast; saying to
them that dwell on the earth, that
they should make an image to the
beast, which had the wound by a
sword, and did live.
15 And he had power to give life
unto the image of the beast, that
the image of the beast should both
speak, and cause that as many as
would not worship the image of the
beast should be killed.
16 And he causeth all, both small
and great, rich and poor, free and
bond, to receive a mark in their
right hand, or in their foreheads:
17 And that no man might buy or
sell, save he that had the mark, or
the name of the beast, or the number of his name.
18 Here is [a]wisdom. Let him that
hath understanding count the number of the beast: for it is the number of a man; and his number *is* Six
hundred threescore *and* six.

CHAPTER 14

The Lamb will stand upon Mount Zion—The gospel will be restored in the last days by angelic ministry—The Son of Man will harvest the earth.

AND I looked, and, lo, a [a]Lamb stood
on the mount [b]Sion, and with him
an hundred forty *and* four thousand,
having his Father's [c]name written
in their foreheads.
2 And I heard a voice from heaven,
as the voice of many waters, and as
the voice of a great thunder: and I
heard the voice of harpers harping
with their harps:
3 And they sung as it were a new
[a]song before the throne, and before the four beasts, and the elders:
and no man could learn that song
but the hundred *and* forty *and* four
thousand, which were redeemed
from the earth.
4 These are they which were not
defiled with [a]women; for they are
virgins. These are they which follow
the Lamb whithersoever he goeth.
These were [b]redeemed from among
men, *being* the firstfruits unto God
and to the Lamb.
5 And in their mouth was found
no [a]guile: for they are without fault
before the throne of God.
6 And I saw another [a]angel fly
in the midst of heaven, having the
[b]everlasting [c]gospel to [d]preach unto
them that dwell on the earth, and
to every [e]nation, and kindred, and
tongue, and people,
7 Saying with a loud voice, [a]Fear
God, and give glory to him; for the
hour of his [b]judgment is come: and
[c]worship [d]him that made [e]heaven,
and earth, and the sea, and the fountains of waters.
8 And there followed another angel, saying, [a]Babylon is [b]fallen, is
fallen, that great [c]city, because she
made all nations drink of the wine
of the wrath of her [d]fornication.
9 And the third angel followed
them, saying with a loud voice, If
any man worship the beast and his
image, and receive *his* mark in his
forehead, or in his hand,
10 The same shall drink of the wine

14*a* Matt. 24:24; Rev. 19:20; 2 Ne. 28:21 (6–21); D&C 52:14.
b TG Miracle.
18*a* D&C 10:34 (34–35); 57:9.
14 1*a* D&C 133:18.
b TG Zion.
c Rev. 3:12; 22:4 (1–5). TG Name.
3*a* TG Singing.
4*a* TG Woman.
b GR purchased, ransomed, redeemed. Jude 1:24; D&C 43:29; 77:5.
5*a* TG Guile.
6*a* D&C 133:36. TG Angels.
b D&C 79:1.
c D&C 27:16. TG Book of Mormon; Gospel; Restoration of the Gospel.
d TG Missionary Work.
e TG Nations.
7*a* D&C 88:104. TG Reverence.
b TG Judgment, the Last.
c TG Worship.
d TG God, Creator.
e Neh. 9:6.
8*a* Isa. 21:9. TG Babylon.
b D&C 88:105.
c Rev. 17:18.
d D&C 88:94.

of the wrath of God, which is [a]poured out without mixture into the cup of his [b]indignation; and he shall be tormented with fire and brimstone in the presence of the holy angels, and in the presence of the Lamb:

11 And the smoke of their torment ascendeth up for ever and ever: and they have no rest day nor night, who worship the beast and his image, and whosoever receiveth the mark of his name.

12 Here is the [a]patience of the saints: here *are* they that keep the commandments of God, and the faith of Jesus.

13 And I heard a voice from heaven saying unto me, Write, [a]Blessed *are* the [b]dead which [c]die in the Lord from henceforth: Yea, saith the Spirit, that they may [d]rest from their labours; and their works do follow them.

14 And I looked, and behold a white cloud, and upon the cloud *one* sat like unto the [a]Son of man, having on his head a golden crown, and in his hand a sharp sickle.

15 And another angel came out of the temple, crying with a loud voice to him that sat on the cloud, [a]Thrust in thy sickle, and [b]reap: for the time is come for thee to reap; for the [c]harvest of the earth is [d]ripe.

16 And he that sat on the cloud thrust in his sickle on the earth; and the earth was reaped.

17 And another angel came out of the temple which is in heaven, he also having a sharp sickle.

18 And another angel came out from the altar, which had power over fire; and cried with a loud cry to him that had the sharp sickle, saying, Thrust in thy sharp sickle, and gather the clusters of the [a]vine of the earth; for her grapes are fully ripe.

19 And the angel thrust in his sickle into the earth, and gathered the vine of the earth, and cast *it* into the great [a]winepress of the wrath of God.

20 And the winepress was trodden without the city, and blood came out of the winepress, even unto the horse bridles, by the space of a thousand *and* six hundred furlongs.

CHAPTER 15

Exalted Saints praise God in celestial glory forever.

AND I saw another sign in heaven, great and marvellous, seven angels having the seven last [a]plagues; for in them is filled up the wrath of God.

2 And I saw as it were a [a]sea of [b]glass mingled with fire: and them that had gotten the victory over the beast, and over his image, and over his mark, *and* over the number of his name, stand on the sea of glass, having the harps of God.

3 And they [a]sing the song of Moses the servant of God, and the song of the Lamb, saying, [b]Great and marvellous *are* thy works, Lord God Almighty; [c]just and true *are* thy ways, thou King of [d]saints.

4 Who shall not fear thee, O Lord, and glorify thy [a]name? for *thou* only *art* holy: for all nations shall come and worship before thee; for thy judgments are made manifest.

5 And after that I looked, and, behold, the temple of the tabernacle of the [a]testimony in heaven was opened:

6 And the seven angels came out of the temple, having the seven [a]plagues, clothed in pure and white

10*a* D&C 115:6.
b TG God, Indignation of.
12*a* TG Patience.
13*a* 1 Ne. 22:22 (22–23); D&C 88:26 (25–29); Moses 7:63 (1–66).
b TG Death; Spirits, Disembodied.
c D&C 42:44; 59:2.
d TG Paradise; Rest.
14*a* TG Jesus Christ, Son of Man.
15*a* D&C 31:5.
b D&C 12:4.
c TG Harvest.
d D&C 18:6.
18*a* TG Vineyard of the Lord.
19*a* Isa. 63:3 (3–4); Joel 3:13; Rev. 19:15; D&C 88:106.
15 1*a* TG Plague.
2*a* D&C 130:7 (1–11).
b TG Earth, Destiny of.
3*a* TG Singing.
b D&C 76:114.
c TG God, Justice of; Justice.
d TG Saints.
4*a* Ps. 99:3.
5*a* TG Testimony.
6*a* TG Last Days.

linen, and having their breasts
girded with golden girdles.
7 And one of the four beasts gave
unto the seven angels seven golden
vials full of the wrath of God, who
liveth for ever and ever.
8 And the temple was filled with
smoke from the glory of God, and
from his power; and no man was
able to enter into the temple, till
the seven plagues of the seven angels were fulfilled.

CHAPTER 16

God pours out plagues upon the wicked—The nations assemble for Armageddon—Christ comes, islands flee, and mountains cease.

AND I heard a great voice out of
the temple saying to the seven angels, Go your ways, and pour out
the vials of the wrath of God upon
the earth.
2 And the first went, and poured
out his vial upon the earth; and
there fell a [a]noisome and grievous
sore upon the men which had the
mark of the beast, and *upon* them
which worshipped his image.
3 And the second angel poured out
his vial upon the sea; and it became
as the blood of a dead *man:* and every living soul died in the sea.
4 And the third angel poured out
his vial upon the rivers and fountains of waters; and they became
blood.
5 And I heard the angel of the waters say, Thou art righteous, O Lord,
which art, and wast, and shalt be,
because thou hast [a]judged thus.
6 For they have [a]shed the [b]blood
of saints and prophets, and thou
hast given them blood to drink; for
they are [c]worthy.
7 And I heard another out of
the altar say, Even so, Lord God
Almighty, true and righteous *are*
thy judgments.
8 And the fourth angel poured out
his vial upon the sun; and power
was given unto him to scorch men
with fire.
9 And men were scorched with
great heat, and [a]blasphemed the
name of God, which hath power over
these plagues: and they repented
not to give him glory.
10 And the fifth angel poured out
his vial upon the seat of the beast;
and his kingdom was full of [a]dark-
ness; and they gnawed their tongues
for pain,
11 And blasphemed the God of
heaven because of their [a]pains and
their sores, and repented not of
their deeds.
12 And the sixth angel poured out
his vial upon the great river Euphrates; and the water thereof was dried
up, that the way of the kings of the
east might be prepared.
13 And I saw three unclean spirits
like frogs *come* out of the mouth of
the dragon, and out of the mouth
of the beast, and out of the mouth of
the [a]false prophet.
14 For they are the [a]spirits of [b]dev-
ils, working [c]miracles, *which* go forth
unto the kings of the earth and of
the whole world, to gather them to
the [d]battle of that great day of God
Almighty.
15 Behold, I come as a [a]thief.
Blessed *is* he that [b]watcheth, and
keepeth his garments, lest he walk
naked, and they see his shame.
16 And he gathered them together
into a place called in the Hebrew
tongue [a]Armageddon.
17 And the seventh angel poured
out his vial into the air; and there
came a great voice out of the temple
of heaven, from the throne, saying,
It is done.

---

16 2*a* GR bad, evil.
5*a* TG Jesus Christ, Judge.
6*a* TG Prophets, Rejection of.
b TG Martyrdom.
c GR deserving.
9*a* TG Blaspheme.
10*a* TG Darkness, Spiritual.
11*a* TG Pain.
13*a* TG Antichrist; False Prophets.
14*a* D&C 50:1.
b Matt. 24:24; 2 Ne. 9:9 (8–12).
c TG Miracle.
d Rev. 17:14.
15*a* Luke 21:35; Rev. 3:3.
b D&C 49:7 (5–9); 106:5 (4–5). TG Watch.
16*a* Ezek. 38:16 (15–16); Joel 3:14 (9–14); Zech. 14:2 (2–5); Luke 21:20 (20–24).

18 And there were voices, and
thunders, and lightnings; and there
was a great [a]earthquake, such as
was not since men were upon the
earth, so mighty an earthquake, *and*
so great.
19 And the great city was divided
into three parts, and the cities of
the nations fell: and great [a]Babylon
came in remembrance before God,
to give unto her the cup of the wine
of the fierceness of his [b]wrath.
20 And every island fled away,
and the [a]mountains were not found.
21 And there fell upon men a great
[a]hail out of heaven, *every stone* about
the weight of a talent: and men blasphemed God because of the plague
of the hail; for the plague thereof
was exceeding great.

CHAPTER 17

John is shown that Babylon the great, the mother of harlots and abominations, has become established throughout the earth.

AND there came one of the seven
angels which had the seven vials,
and talked with me, saying unto me,
Come hither; I will shew unto thee
the [a]judgment of the great [b]whore
that sitteth upon many [c]waters:
2 With whom the kings of the earth
have committed fornication, and
the [a]inhabitants of the earth have
been made drunk with the wine of
her [b]fornication.
3 So he carried me away in the
spirit into the wilderness: and I
saw a woman sit upon a scarlet
coloured beast, full of [a]names of
blasphemy, having seven heads and
ten horns.
4 And the woman was arrayed
in purple and scarlet colour, and
decked with gold and precious stones
and pearls, having a golden cup in
her hand [a]full of abominations and
[b]filthiness of her fornication:
5 And upon her forehead *was* a
name written, [a]MYSTERY, [b]BABYLON THE GREAT, THE [c]MOTHER
OF HARLOTS AND ABOMINATIONS OF THE EARTH.
6 And I saw the woman drunken
with the [a]blood of the saints, and with
the blood of the [b]martyrs of Jesus:
and when I saw her, I wondered
with great [c]admiration.
7 And the angel said unto me,
Wherefore didst thou marvel? I will
tell thee the mystery of the woman,
and of the beast that carrieth her,
which hath the seven heads and
ten horns.
8 The beast that thou sawest was,
and is not; and shall ascend out of
the bottomless pit, and go into [a]perdition: and they that dwell on the
earth shall wonder, whose names
were not written in the [b]book of life
from the foundation of the world,
when they behold the beast that
was, and is not, and yet is.
9 And here *is* the [a]mind which
hath wisdom. The seven heads are
seven mountains, on which the
woman sitteth.
10 And there are seven [a]kings: five
are fallen, and one is, *and* the other is
not yet come; and when he cometh,
he must continue a short space.
11 And the beast that was, and
is not, even he is the eighth, and is
of the seven, and goeth into perdition.
12 And the ten [a]horns which thou

18*a* Dan. 12:1; Rev. 6:12; 11:13 (13–14).
19*a* TG Babylon.
b TG God, Indignation of.
20*a* Isa. 64:1; Rev. 6:14 (12–17); D&C 133:22 (1–42).
21*a* Ex. 9:18 (13–35); Josh. 10:11; Ezek. 13:13; 38:22; Rev. 11:19; Mosiah 12:6; D&C 29:16.
17 1*a* Rev. 18:3 (3–9); 19:2.
b TG Devil, Church of.
c Jer. 51:13.
2*a* Isa. 24:6.
b 1 Ne. 14:13 (9–13).
3*a* TG Name.
4*a* D&C 10:21.
b TG Filthiness.
5*a* TG Secret Combinations.
b TG Babylon.
c D&C 88:94.
6*a* Rev. 18:24 (22–24).
b TG Martyrdom.
c GR astonishment, wonder.
8*a* TG Death, Spiritual, Second; Hell.
b Ps. 139:16.
9*a* TG Mind.
10*a* TG Kings, Earthly.
12*a* Dan. 7:24.

sawest are ten kings, which have received no kingdom as yet; but receive power as kings one hour with the beast.

13 These have one mind, and shall give their power and strength unto the beast.

14 These shall make [a]war with the Lamb, and the Lamb shall overcome them: for he is [b]Lord of lords, and [c]King of kings: and they that are with him *are* called, and chosen, and faithful.

15 And he saith unto me, The waters which thou sawest, where the whore sitteth, are peoples, and multitudes, and nations, and tongues.

16 And the ten horns which thou sawest upon the beast, these shall hate the [a]whore, and shall make her desolate and naked, and shall eat her flesh, and [b]burn her with fire.

17 For God hath put in their hearts to fulfil his will, and to agree, and [a]give their kingdom unto the beast, until the [b]words of God shall be fulfilled.

18 And the woman which thou sawest is that great [a]city, which reigneth over the kings of the earth.

CHAPTER 18

The Saints are called out of Babylon lest they partake of her sins—She falls and is lamented by her supporters.

AND after these things I saw another angel come down from heaven, having great power; and the earth was [a]lightened with his glory.

2 And he cried mightily with a strong voice, saying, [a]Babylon the great is fallen, is fallen, and is become the habitation of devils, and the [b]hold of every foul spirit, and a [c]cage of every unclean and hateful bird.

3 For all nations have drunk of the wine of the wrath of her [a]fornication, and the kings of the earth have committed [b]fornication with her, and the merchants of the earth are waxed rich through the [c]abundance of her delicacies.

4 And I heard another voice from heaven, saying, [a]Come [b]out of her, my people, that ye be not partakers of her [c]sins, and that ye receive not of her plagues.

5 For her [a]sins have reached unto heaven, and God hath remembered her iniquities.

6 [a]Reward her even as she rewarded you, and double unto her double according to her works: in the cup which she hath filled fill to her double.

7 How much she hath glorified herself, and lived [a]deliciously, so much torment and sorrow give her: for she saith in her heart, I sit a queen, and am no widow, and shall see no sorrow.

8 Therefore shall her [a]plagues come in one day, death, and mourning, and famine; and she shall be utterly [b]burned with fire: for strong *is* the Lord God who [c]judgeth her.

9 And the kings of the earth, who have committed fornication and lived deliciously with her, shall [a]bewail her, and lament for her, when they shall see the [b]smoke of her burning,

10 Standing afar off for the fear of her torment, saying, Alas, alas, that great city Babylon, that mighty city! for in one hour is thy judgment come.

14*a* Rev. 16:14.
b Deut. 10:17; Rev. 19:16 (11–16). TG Jesus Christ, Lord; Jesus Christ, Power of.
c Dan. 2:47; 1 Tim. 6:15.
16*a* 1 Ne. 22:13 (13–14).
b Rev. 18:8 (6–18).
17*a* Dan. 8:24.
b D&C 1:37.
18*a* Rev. 14:8.
18 1*a* Ezek. 43:2.
2*a* TG Babylon.
b GR ward, prison.
c GR ward, prison.
3*a* Rev. 17:1 (1–2); D&C 35:11.
b Isa. 23:17.
c GR power of her wantonness.
4*a* Zech. 2:7.
b Gen. 19:14.
c Isa. 52:11.
5*a* Jer. 51:9 (8–9).
6*a* D&C 1:9. TG Retribution.
7*a* GR wantonly, riotously.
8*a* TG Plague.
b Rev. 17:16; D&C 64:24; 86:7.
c TG Jesus Christ, Judge.
9*a* Jer. 51:8.
b Gen. 19:28.

11 And the merchants of the earth
shall weep and mourn over her; for
no man buyeth their merchandise
any more:
12 The merchandise of gold, and
silver, and precious stones, and of
pearls, and fine linen, and purple,
and silk, and scarlet, and all thy-
ine wood, and all manner vessels
of ivory, and all manner vessels of
most precious wood, and of brass,
and iron, and marble,
13 And cinnamon, and odours, and
ointments, and frankincense, and
wine, and oil, and fine flour, and
wheat, and beasts, and sheep, and
horses, and chariots, and [a]slaves,
and souls of men.
14 And the fruits that thy soul
[a]lusted after are departed from thee,
and all things which were dainty and
goodly are departed from thee, and
thou shalt find them no more at all.
15 The merchants of these things,
which were made rich by her, shall
stand afar off for the fear of her torment, weeping and wailing,
16 And saying, Alas, alas, that great
city, that was clothed in fine linen,
and purple, and scarlet, and decked
with gold, and precious stones, and
pearls!
17 For in one hour so great riches
is come to nought. And every ship-
master, and all the company in ships,
and sailors, and as many as trade
by sea, stood afar off,
18 And cried when they saw the
smoke of her burning, saying, What
city is like unto this great city!
19 And they cast [a]dust on their
heads, and cried, weeping and wailing, saying, Alas, alas, that great
city, wherein were made rich all
that had ships in the sea by reason
of her costliness! for in one hour is
she made desolate.
20 Rejoice over her, *thou* heaven,
and *ye* holy apostles and prophets;
for God hath avenged you on her.
21 And a mighty angel took up a
stone like a great millstone, and cast
it into the sea, saying, Thus with
violence shall that great city [a]Bab-
ylon be thrown down, and shall be
found no more at all.
22 And the voice of harpers, and
musicians, and of pipers, and trum-
peters, shall be heard no more at all
in thee; and no craftsman, of whatsoever craft *he be*, shall be found
any more in thee; and the sound of
a millstone shall be heard no more
at all in thee;
23 And the light of a candle shall
shine no more at all in thee; and
the [a]voice of the bridegroom and
of the bride shall be heard no more
at all in thee: for thy merchants
were the great men of the earth; for
by thy [b]sorceries were all nations
deceived.
24 And in her was found the [a]blood
of prophets, and of saints, and of
all that were slain upon the earth.

CHAPTER 19

The marriage supper of the Lamb is made ready—The testimony of Jesus is the spirit of prophecy—Christ is King of Kings and Lord of Lords.

AND after these things I heard a great
voice of much people in heaven, saying, Alleluia; Salvation, and glory,
and honour, and power, unto the
Lord our God:
2 For true and righteous *are* his
[a]judgments: for he hath [b]judged the
great [c]whore, which did corrupt the
earth with her fornication, and hath
avenged the blood of his servants
at her hand.
3 And again they said, Alleluia.
And her [a]smoke rose up for ever
and ever.
4 And the four and twenty elders
and the four [a]beasts fell down and
worshipped God that sat on the
throne, saying, Amen; Alleluia.

13*a* TG Slavery.
14*a* TG Lust.
19*a* Ezek. 27:30.
21*a* TG Babylon; Devil, Church of.
23*a* Jer. 7:34.
b TG Sorcery.
24*a* Rev. 17:6 (1–18); 2 Ne. 27:4 (3–4); 28:10; Morm. 8:27 (27, 40–41).
19 2*a* TG Jesus Christ, Judge.
b Rev. 17:1 (1–2).
c D&C 29:21.
3*a* Gen. 19:28.
4*a* TG Cherubim.

5 And a voice came out of the throne, saying, Praise our God, all ye his servants, and ye that fear him, both small and great.

6 And I heard as it were the voice of a great multitude, and as the voice of many waters, and as the voice of mighty thunderings, saying, Alleluia: for the Lord [a]God [b]omnipotent reigneth.

7 Let us be glad and rejoice, and give honour to him: for the [a]marriage of the [b]Lamb is come, and his wife hath made herself ready.

8 And to her was granted that she should be arrayed in fine linen, clean and white: for the fine [a]linen is the [b]righteousness of saints.

9 And he saith unto me, Write, Blessed *are* they which are called unto the [a]marriage [b]supper of the [c]Lamb. And he saith unto me, These are the true sayings of God.

10 And I [a]fell at his feet to [b]worship him. And he said unto me, See *thou do it* not: I am thy [c]fellowservant, and of thy brethren that have the testimony of Jesus: worship God: for the [d]testimony of Jesus is the spirit of [e]prophecy.

11 And I saw heaven opened, and behold a white horse; and he that sat upon him *was* called Faithful and True, and in righteousness he doth [a]judge and make [b]war.

12 His [a]eyes *were* as a flame of fire, and on his head *were* many crowns; and he had a [b]name written, that no man knew, but he himself.

13 And he *was* [a]clothed with a vesture dipped in blood: and his [b]name is called The [c]Word of God.

14 And the armies *which were* in heaven followed him upon white horses, [a]clothed in fine linen, white and clean.

15 [a]And out of his mouth goeth a sharp sword, that with it he should smite the nations: and he shall [b]rule them with a rod of iron: and he treadeth the [c]winepress of the fierceness and wrath of Almighty God.

16 And he hath on *his* vesture and on his thigh a name written, [a]KING OF KINGS, AND [b]LORD OF LORDS.

17 And I saw an angel standing in the sun; and he cried with a loud voice, saying to all the fowls that fly in the midst of heaven, Come and gather yourselves together unto the supper of the great God;

18 That ye may eat the flesh of kings, and the flesh of captains, and the flesh of mighty men, and the flesh of horses, and of them that sit on them, and the flesh of all [a]*men, both* free and bond, both small and great.

19 And I saw the beast, and the kings of the earth, and their armies, gathered together to make war against him that sat on the horse, and against his army.

6*a* Dan. 2:47.
b TG Jesus Christ, Power of.
7*a* Isa. 54:5; Matt. 22:2 (2–14); Luke 5:34; Rev. 21:2.
b TG Jesus Christ, Lamb of God.
8*a* Matt. 22:11 (11–14); 1 Ne. 12:10 (10–11).
b Alma 5:27.
9*a* D&C 58:11.
b Luke 14:15; 22:30.
c TG Jesus Christ, Lamb of God.
10*a* Rev. 22:8.
b TG Worship.
c Acts 10:26; Rev. 1:1 (1–6).
d TG Testimony.
e TG Prophecy.
11*a* TG Jesus Christ, Judge.
b TG War.
12*a* TG God, Manifestations of.
b Rev. 2:17 (12–17).
13*a* Isa. 63:2 (2–3); D&C 133:48 (48–51).
b TG Name.
c Moses 1:32 (32–33). TG Jesus Christ, Messenger of the Covenant.
14*a* TG Clothing.
15*a* JST Rev. 19:15 And out of his mouth *proceedeth the word of God, and* with it he *will* smite the nations; and he *will* rule them with *the word of his mouth;* and he treadeth the winepress *in* the fierceness and wrath of Almighty God. Isa. 11:4.
b TG Jesus Christ, Authority of.
c Isa. 63:3 (3–4); Rev. 14:19 (17–20); D&C 88:106.
16*a* TG Jesus Christ, Second Coming.
b Deut. 10:17; Rev. 17:14.
18*a* JST Rev. 19:18 . . . *who fight against the Lamb,* both *bond and* free, both small and great.

20 And the beast was taken, and
with him the [a]false prophet that
wrought [b]miracles before him, with
which he [c]deceived them that had
received the mark of the beast, and
them that worshipped his image.
These both were cast alive into a
[d]lake of [e]fire burning with brimstone.
21 And the remnant were slain
[a]with the sword of him that sat upon
the horse, which *sword* proceeded
out of his mouth: and all the fowls
were filled with their flesh.

CHAPTER 20

Satan is bound during the Millennium—The Saints will then live and reign with Christ—The dead stand before God and are judged out of the books according to their works.

AND I saw an [a]angel come down
from heaven, having the key of the
bottomless [b]pit and a great chain
in his hand.
2 And he laid hold on the dragon,
that old [a]serpent, which is the [b]Devil,
and Satan, and [c]bound him a thousand years,
3 And cast him into the bottomless
pit, and shut him up, and set a seal
upon him, that he should deceive the
[a]nations no more, till the thousand
years should be fulfilled: and after
that he must be [b]loosed a little season.
4 And I saw thrones, and they sat
upon them, and [a]judgment was given
unto them: and *I saw* the souls of
them that were beheaded for the
witness of Jesus, and for the word of
God, and which had not worshipped
the beast, neither his image, neither
had received *his* mark upon their
foreheads, or in their hands; and
they lived and [b]reigned with Christ
a [c]thousand years.
5 But the rest of the [a]dead lived
not again until the thousand years
were finished. This *is* the first resurrection.
6 [a]Blessed and holy *is* he that hath
part in the [b]first [c]resurrection: on
such the [d]second death hath no
power, but they shall be [e]priests of
God and of Christ, and shall reign
with him a thousand years.
7 And when the [a]thousand years
are expired, [b]Satan shall be loosed
out of his prison,
8 And shall go out to deceive the
nations which are in the four quarters of the earth, [a]Gog and Magog,
to gather them together to battle:
the number of whom *is* as the sand
of the sea.
9 And they went up on the breadth
of the earth, and compassed the
camp of the saints about, and the
beloved city: and fire came down
from God out of heaven, and devoured them.
10 And the [a]devil that deceived
them was [b]cast into the lake of [c]fire
and brimstone, where the beast and
the false prophet *are*, and shall be
tormented day and night for ever
and ever.
11 And I saw a great white throne,
and him that sat on it, from whose
face the [a]earth and the heaven fled

20*a* TG Antichrist; False Prophets.
b TG Miracle.
c Rev. 13:14 (11–18).
d Matt. 8:12; 13:42; D&C 112:24. TG Hell.
e Dan. 7:11.
21*a* JST Rev. 19:21 . . . with the *word* of him that sat upon the horse, which *word* proceeded out of his mouth . . .
20 1*a* TG Angels.
b Rev. 9:1; D&C 76:48.
2*a* Isa. 27:1.
b TG Devil.
c D&C 84:100.
3*a* TG Nations.
b D&C 43:31.
4*a* Dan. 7:22; 1 Cor. 6:2; 3 Ne. 27:27; D&C 20:13 (5–15); 75:21 (21–22).
b TG Jesus Christ, Millennial Reign.
c TG Millennium.
5*a* D&C 43:18; 88:101. TG Spirits, Disembodied.
6*a* JST Rev. 20:6 Blessed and holy *are they who have* part in the first resurrection . . .
b D&C 63:18.
c TG Resurrection.
d TG Death, Spiritual, Second.
e TG Priest, Aaronic Priesthood; Priest, Melchizedek Priesthood. BD Priests.
7*a* TG Jesus Christ, Millennial Reign.
b TG Devil.
8*a* Gen. 10:2 (2–3); Ezek. 38:2.
10*a* D&C 28:11.
b D&C 19:3.
c Dan. 7:11; D&C 76:36.
11*a* D&C 29:24 (24–25).

away; and there was found no [b]place
for them.
12 And I saw the [a]dead, small and
great, [b]stand before God; and the
[c]books were opened: and another
book was opened, which is *the* [d]*book*
of life: and the dead were [e]judged
out of those things which were
written in the books, according to
their [f]works.
13 And the sea gave up the dead
which were in it; and [a]death and
[b]hell delivered up the dead which
were in them: and they were judged
every man according to their
works.
14 And [a]death and [b]hell were cast
into the lake of fire. This is the [c]sec-
ond death.
15 And whosoever was not found
written in the book of life was cast
into the lake of fire.

CHAPTER 21

Those who overcome will be sons of God—The earth attains its celestial glory.

AND I saw a [a]new [b]heaven and a new
[c]earth: for the first heaven and the
first [d]earth were passed away; and
there was no more sea.
2 And I John saw the holy city, [a]new
[b]Jerusalem, coming down from God
out of heaven, prepared as a [c]bride
adorned for her husband.
3 And I heard a great voice out of
heaven saying, Behold, the tabernacle of God *is* with men, and he will
[a]dwell with them, and they shall be
his people, and [b]God himself shall
be with them, *and be* their God.
4 And God shall wipe away all tears
from their eyes; and there shall be
no more [a]death, neither [b]sorrow, nor
crying, neither shall there be any
more [c]pain: for the former things
are passed away.
5 And he that sat upon the throne
said, Behold, I make all things [a]new.
And he said unto me, [b]Write: for
these [c]words are true and faithful.
6 And he said unto me, It is done.
[a]I am [b]Alpha and Omega, the beginning and the end. I will give unto
him that is athirst of the fountain
of the [c]water of life freely.
7 He that [a]overcometh shall [b]in-
herit [c]all things; and I will be his
God, and he shall be my [d]son.
8 But the fearful, and [a]unbelieving,
and the abominable, and [b]murder-
ers, and [c]whoremongers, and [d]sor-
cerers, and idolaters, and all [e]liars,
shall have their part in the lake
which burneth with fire and brimstone: which is the [f]second [g]death.
9 And there came unto me one of
the seven angels which had the seven
vials full of the seven last [a]plagues,
and talked with me, saying, Come
hither, I will shew thee the bride,
the Lamb's wife.
10 And he carried me away in the
spirit to a great and high [a]mountain,
and shewed me that great city, the

11*b* Dan. 2:35 (31–36).
12*a* Alma 11:44 (43–44). TG Death.
b TG Resurrection.
c Dan. 7:10.
d TG Book of Life.
e D&C 137:9. TG Accountability; Judgment, the Last.
f TG Good Works.
13*a* 2 Tim. 1:10.
b TG Hell; Spirits in Prison.
14*a* 1 Cor. 15:26 (26, 54).
b TG Damnation.
c TG Death, Spiritual, Second.
21 1*a* TG Celestial Glory.
b TG Heaven.
c TG Earth, Destiny of; Earth, Renewal of.
d TG World, End of.
2*a* TG Zion.
b TG Jerusalem, New.
c Matt. 22:2 (2–14); Luke 5:34; Rev. 19:7 (7–9).
3*a* TG God, Presence of.
b Ezek. 48:35.
4*a* Rev. 7:17.
b TG Mourning; Sorrow.
c TG Pain.
5*a* 2 Cor. 5:17; D&C 130:5–9.
b TG Scriptures, Writing of.
c D&C 1:37.
6*a* TG Jesus Christ, Jehovah.
b D&C 45:7.
c TG Living Water.
7*a* Rev. 2:7; D&C 76:60 (58–60).
b TG Exaltation.
c Ps. 84:11. TG Eternal Life.
d TG Sons and Daughters of God.
8*a* TG Stiffnecked.
b TG Murder.
c TG Adulterer; Chastity.
d TG Sorcery.
e TG Lying.
f TG Hell.
g TG Death, Spiritual, Second.
9*a* TG Plague.
10*a* Ezek. 40:2; Moses 1:1.

holy [b]Jerusalem, descending out of
heaven from God,
11 Having the [a]glory of God: and
her light *was* like unto a stone most
precious, even like a jasper stone,
clear as crystal;
12 And had a wall great and high,
and had twelve [a]gates, and at the gates
twelve angels, and names written
thereon, which are *the names* of the
twelve tribes of the children of Israel:
13 On the east three gates; on the
north three gates; on the south three
gates; and on the west three gates.
14 And the wall of the city had
twelve foundations, and in them
the names of the twelve apostles
of the Lamb.
15 And he that talked with me
had a golden reed to measure the
city, and the gates thereof, and the
wall thereof.
16 And the city lieth foursquare,
and the [a]length is as large as the
breadth: and he measured the city
with the reed, twelve thousand [b]fur-
longs. The length and the breadth
and the height of it are equal.
17 And he measured the wall
thereof, an hundred *and* forty *and*
four cubits, *according to* the measure
of a man, that is, of the angel.
18 And the building of the wall
of it was *of* jasper: and the city *was*
pure gold, like unto clear glass.
19 And the foundations of the wall
of the city *were* garnished with all
manner of precious stones. The first
foundation *was* jasper; the second,
sapphire; the third, a chalcedony;
the fourth, an emerald;
20 The fifth, sardonyx; the sixth,
sardius; the seventh, chrysolite; the
eighth, beryl; the ninth, a topaz; the
tenth, a chrysoprasus; the eleventh,
a jacinth; the twelfth, an amethyst.
21 And the twelve gates *were* twelve
pearls; every several gate was of one
pearl: and the street of the city *was*
pure [a]gold, as it were transparent
[b]glass.
22 And I saw no temple therein:
for the Lord God [a]Almighty and the
Lamb are the [b]temple of it.
23 And the city had no need of
the [a]sun, neither of the moon, to
shine in it: for the glory of God did
lighten it, and the [b]Lamb *is* the [c]light
thereof.
24 And the nations of them which
are saved shall [a]walk in the light of
it: and the [b]kings of the [c]earth do
bring their glory and honour into it.
25 And the [a]gates of it shall not be
shut at all by day: for there shall be
no night there.
26 And they shall bring the glory
and honour of the nations into it.
27 And there shall in no wise enter into it any thing that [a]defileth,
neither *whatsoever* worketh abomination, or *maketh* a lie: but they
which are written in the Lamb's
[b]book of life.

CHAPTER 22

The Saints will reign in celestial splendor—Christ will come, and men will be judged—Blessed are they who keep His commandments.

AND he shewed me a pure river of
[a]water of life, clear as crystal, pro-
ceeding out of the throne of God
and of the Lamb.
2 In the midst of the street of it, and
on either side of the river, *was there*
the [a]tree of [b]life, which bare twelve
manner of fruits, *and* yielded her
fruit every month: and the [c]leaves
of the tree *were* for the healing of
the nations.

10*b* Moses 7:63 (21, 62–64).
11*a* Ezek. 43:2 (1–6).
12*a* Ezek. 48:31.
16*a* Ezek. 40:5.
b GR stadia. A stadium was about 607 English feet, or 185.2 meters.
21*a* D&C 137:4 (2–4).
b TG Earth, Destiny of.
22*a* TG God, Power of.
b TG Temple.
23*a* Isa. 60:19; Rev. 22:5.
b TG Jesus Christ, Lamb of God.
c TG Jesus Christ, Light of the World.
24*a* TG Walking with God.
b TG Kings, Earthly.
c Isa. 49:22; 60:5.
25*a* Isa. 60:11.
27*a* D&C 76:112 (81–112).
b TG Book of Life.
22 1*a* Ezek. 47:1; Joel 3:18; Zech. 14:8.
2*a* Gen. 2:9; Rev. 2:7 (1–7); 1 Ne. 8:10 (1–11).
b TG Immortality.
c Ezek. 47:12.

3 And there shall be no more
[a]curse: but the [b]throne of God and
of the [c]Lamb shall be in it; and his
servants shall serve him:
4 And they shall [a]see his [b]face; and
his [c]name *shall be* in their foreheads.
5 And there shall be no night there;
and they need no candle, neither
light of the [a]sun; for the Lord God
giveth them [b]light: and they shall
[c]reign [d]for ever and ever.
6 And he said unto me, These sayings *are* faithful and [a]true: and the
Lord God of the holy prophets sent
his angel to shew unto his servants
the things which must [b]shortly be
done.
7 Behold, I [a]come quickly: [b]blessed
is he that keepeth the [c]sayings of
the prophecy of this book.
8 And I John saw these things, and
heard *them*. And when I had heard
and seen, I [a]fell down to worship
before the feet of the angel which
shewed me these things.
9 Then saith he unto me, See *thou*
do it not: for I am thy fellowservant,
and of thy brethren the prophets,
and of them which keep the sayings
of this book: worship God.
10 And he saith unto me, Seal not
the sayings of the prophecy of this
book: for the time is at hand.
11 He that is [a]unjust, let him be
[b]unjust still: and he which is [c]filthy,
let him be filthy still: and he that is
righteous, let him be righteous still:
and he that is holy, let him be holy
still.
12 And, behold, I [a]come quickly;
and my [b]reward *is* with me, to give
every man according as his [c]work
shall be.
13 I am Alpha and Omega, the
beginning and the end, the [a]first
and the last.
14 Blessed *are* they that [a]do his
[b]commandments, that they may
have right to the tree of life, and
may enter in through the gates into
the city.
15 For without *are* dogs, and [a]sor-
cerers, and [b]whoremongers, and
[c]murderers, and idolaters, and whosoever loveth and maketh a [d]lie.
16 I Jesus have sent mine [a]angel
to testify unto you these things in
the churches. I am the [b]root and the
offspring of David, *and* the bright
and morning [c]star.
17 And the Spirit and the bride
say, [a]Come. And let him that heareth
say, Come. And let him that is athirst
come. And whosoever will, let him
take the [b]water of life freely.
18 For I testify unto every man that
heareth the words of the prophecy
of this book, If any man shall [a]add
unto these things, God shall add unto
him the [b]plagues that are written
in this book:
19 And if any man shall take away
from the words of the book of this
prophecy, God shall take away his

3*a* TG Curse; Earth, Curse of.
b Jer. 3:17; Joel 3:21 (18–21); Zech. 2:10 (10–12).
c TG Jesus Christ, Lamb of God.
4*a* TG God, Privilege of Seeing.
b John 14:3; 1 Thes. 4:17; D&C 38:8 (7–8). TG God, Body of, Corporeal Nature.
c Rev. 3:12 (7–13); 7:3 (2–8); 14:1 (1–5).
5*a* Isa. 60:19; Rev. 21:23.
b TG Earth, Destiny of.
c Matt. 25:34. TG Eternal Life; Kingdom of God, on Earth.
d D&C 132:20.
6*a* D&C 68:34.
b Rev. 1:1 (1–6); D&C 88:79.
7*a* D&C 51:20.
b Rev. 1:3 (1–6).
c D&C 58:2.
8*a* Rev. 19:10.
11*a* Alma 41:13 (10–15).
b Dan. 12:10.
c TG Filthiness.
12*a* 1 Thes. 2:19; 3:13; Rev. 1:7.
b TG Reward.
c Alma 41:13.
13*a* TG God, Eternal Nature of.
14*a* TG Obedience.
b TG Good Works.
15*a* TG Sorcery; Telestial Glory.
b TG Adulterer; Whore.
c TG Murder.
d TG Lying.
16*a* TG Angels.
b Isa. 53:2; Rev. 5:5 (1–14).
c 2 Pet. 1:19; Rev. 2:28.
17*a* Moro. 10:32 (30–33).
b TG Living Water.
18*a* Deut. 4:2 (2–3); 3 Ne. 11:40 (39–40); D&C 20:35 (35–36). TG Scriptures, Preservation of.
b TG Plague.

part out of the [a]book of life, and out
of the holy city, and *from* the things
which are written in this book.
20 He which testifieth these things
saith, Surely I [a]come quickly. Amen.
Even so, come, Lord Jesus.
21 The [a]grace of our [b]Lord Jesus
Christ *be* with you all. Amen.

19*a* TG Book of Life.
20*a* D&C 33:18; 35:27.
21*a* Rom. 16:24 (20–24).
b TG Jesus Christ, Lord.

THE END

APPENDIX

JOSEPH SMITH TRANSLATION

SELECTIONS FROM THE JOSEPH SMITH TRANSLATION OF THE BIBLE

Following are selected portions of the Joseph Smith Translation of the King James Version of the Bible (JST). The Lord inspired the Prophet Joseph Smith to restore truths to the King James Bible text that had become lost or changed since the original words were written. These restored truths clarified doctrine and improved scriptural understanding.

Because the Lord revealed to Joseph certain truths that the original authors had once recorded, the Joseph Smith Translation is unlike any other Bible translation in the world. In this sense, the word *translation* is used in a broader and different way than usual, for Joseph's translation was more revelation than literal translation from one language into another.

Joseph Smith's translation of the King James Bible has connections with or is mentioned in several sections of the Doctrine and Covenants (see sections 37, 45, 73, 76, 77, 86, 91, and 132). Also, the book of Moses and Joseph Smith—Matthew are excerpts from the Joseph Smith Translation.

For more information about the Joseph Smith Translation, see "Joseph Smith Translation (JST)" in the Bible Dictionary.

The following illustration shows a sample selection from the Joseph Smith Translation:

This reference in bold type is the passage in Joseph Smith's translation of the King James Bible. Because his translation restored words to the Bible text, the verse numbers may differ from the edition you are using.

JST, Matthew 4:1, 5–6, 8–9. Compare Matthew 4:1, 5–6, 8–9; similar changes were made in Luke 4:2, 5–11

This cross-reference indicates the passage in your Bible you should compare to Joseph Smith's translation.

Jesus is led by the Spirit, not by Satan.

This statement explains what doctrine Joseph Smith clarified with his translation.

1 Then *Jesus was* led up of the
Spirit, into the wilderness, to
be *with God.*
5 Then *Jesus was taken* up into
the holy city, and *the Spirit* setteth him on *the* pinnacle of the
temple.
6 *Then the devil came unto him*
and said, If thou be the Son of
God, cast thyself down, for it is
written, He shall give his angels
charge concerning thee, and in
their hands they shall bear thee
up, lest at any time thou dash
thy foot against a stone.
8 *And* again, *Jesus was in the*
Spirit, and it taketh him up
into an exceeding high mountain, and showeth him all the
kingdoms of the world and the
glory of them.
9 And *the devil came unto him*
again, and said, All these things
will I give *unto* thee, if thou wilt
fall down and worship me.

This is the text as Joseph Smith translated it. (Italics have been added to show differences from the King James Version wording.)

JST, Genesis 1:1–8:18. Compare Genesis 1:1–6:13

This text of the Bible was restored by Joseph Smith and is published in the Pearl of Great Price as Selections from the Book of Moses.

JST, Genesis 9:4–6. Compare Genesis 8:20–22

After the Flood, Noah asks the Lord not to curse the earth again.

4 And Noah builded an altar unto the Lord, and took of every clean beast, and of every clean fowl, and offered burnt offerings on the altar; *and gave thanks unto the Lord, and rejoiced in his heart.*
5 *And the Lord spake unto Noah, and he blessed him.* And *Noah* smelled a sweet savor, and *he* said in his heart;
6 *I will call on the name of the Lord, that he* will not again curse the ground any more for man's sake, for the imagination of man's heart is evil from his youth; *and that he* will *not* again smite any more every thing living, as *he* hath done, while the earth remaineth;

JST, Genesis 9:10–15. Compare Genesis 9:4–9

Man is accountable for shedding the blood of animals and of men. God establishes with Noah and his sons the same covenant He made with Enoch.

10 But, *the blood of all* flesh *which I have given you for meat, shall be shed upon the ground, which taketh life thereof, and the blood* ye shall not eat.
11 And surely, *blood shall not be shed, only for meat, to save your lives; and the blood* of every beast will I require *at your hands.*
12 *And* whoso sheddeth man's blood, by man shall his blood be shed; *for man shall not shed the blood of man.*
13 *For a commandment I give,* that every man's brother *shall preserve* the life of man, for in *mine own* image *have* I made man.
14 *And a commandment I give unto you,* Be ye fruitful and multiply; bring forth abundantly on the earth, and multiply therein.
15 And God spake unto Noah, and to his sons with him, saying, And I, behold, I *will* establish my covenant with you, *which I made unto your father Enoch, concerning* your seed after you.

JST, Genesis 9:21–25. Compare Genesis 9:16–17

God sets the rainbow in heaven as a reminder of His covenant to Enoch and to Noah. In the last days the general assembly of the Church of the Firstborn will join the righteous on earth.

21 And the bow shall be in the cloud; and I will look upon it, that I may remember the everlasting covenant, *which I made unto thy father Enoch; that, when men should keep all my commandments, Zion should again come on the earth, the city of Enoch which I have caught up unto myself.*
22 *And this is mine everlasting covenant, that when thy posterity shall embrace the truth, and look upward, then shall Zion look downward, and all the heavens shall shake with gladness, and the earth shall tremble with joy;*
23 *And the general assembly of the church of the firstborn shall come down out of heaven, and possess the earth, and shall have place until the end come. And this is mine everlasting covenant, which I made with thy father Enoch.*
24 *And the bow shall be in the cloud, and I will establish my covenant unto thee, which I have made* between *me* and *thee, for* every living creature of all flesh that *shall be* upon the earth.
25 And God said unto Noah, This is the token of the covenant which I have established between me and *thee; for* all flesh that *shall be* upon the earth.

JST, Genesis 14:25–40. Compare Genesis 14:18–20

Melchizedek blesses Abram. Melchizedek's great ministry and the powers and blessings of the Melchizedek Priesthood are described.

25 *And Melchizedek lifted up his*
voice and blessed Abram.
26 *Now Melchizedek was a man*
of faith, who wrought righteousness;
and when a child he feared God,
and stopped the mouths of lions, and
quenched the violence of fire.
27 *And thus, having been approved*
of God, he was ordained an high
priest after the order of the covenant
which God made with Enoch,
28 *It being after the order of the*
Son of God; which order came, not
by man, nor the will of man; neither
by father nor mother; neither by be-
ginning of days nor end of years; but
of God;
29 *And it was delivered unto men*
by the calling of his own voice, ac-
cording to his own will, unto as
many as believed on his name.
30 *For God having sworn unto*
Enoch and unto his seed with an oath
by himself; that every one being or-
dained after this order and calling
should have power, by faith, to break
mountains, to divide the seas, to dry up
waters, to turn them out of their course;
31 *To put at defiance the armies of*
nations, to divide the earth, to break
every band, to stand in the presence
of God; to do all things according to
his will, according to his command,
subdue principalities and powers;
and this by the will of the Son of God
which was from before the founda-
tion of the world.
32 *And men having this faith, com-*
ing up unto this order of God, were
translated and taken up into heaven.
33 *And now, Melchizedek was*
a priest of this order; therefore he
obtained peace in Salem, and was
called the Prince of peace.
34 *And his people wrought righ-*
teousness, and obtained heaven, and
sought for the city of Enoch which
God had before taken, separating it
from the earth, having reserved it
unto the latter days, or the end of
the world;
35 *And hath said, and sworn with*
an oath, that the heavens and the earth
should come together; and the sons of
God should be tried so as by fire.
36 *And this Melchizedek, having*
thus established righteousness, was
called the king of heaven by his people,
or, in other words, the King of peace.
37 *And he lifted up his voice, and*
he blessed Abram, being the high
priest, and the keeper of the storehouse
of God;
38 *Him whom God had appointed*
to receive tithes for the poor.
39 *Wherefore, Abram paid unto*
him tithes of all that he had, of all
the riches which he possessed, which
God had given him more than that
which he had need.
40 *And it came to pass, that* God
blessed Abram, and gave unto him
riches, and honor, and lands for an
everlasting possession; according to
the covenant which he had made,
and according to the blessing where-
with Melchizedek had blessed him.

JST, Genesis 15:9–12. Compare Genesis 15:1–6

Abraham learns of the Resurrection and sees a vision of Jesus' mortal ministry.

9 *And Abram said, Lord God, how*
wilt thou give me this land for an ev-
erlasting inheritance?
10 *And the Lord said, Though thou*
wast dead, yet am I not able to give
it thee?
11 *And if thou shalt die, yet thou*
shalt possess it, for the day cometh,
that the Son of Man shall live; but
how can he live if he be not dead? he
must first be quickened.
12 *And it came to pass, that Abram*
looked forth and saw the days of the
Son of Man, and was glad, and his
soul found rest, and he believed in
the Lord; and *the Lord* counted it
unto him for righteousness.

JST, Genesis 17:3–12. Compare Genesis 17:3–12

The people fail to obey the gospel ordinances, including baptism. God explains to Abraham the covenant of circumcision and the age of accountability of children.

3 And *it came to pass, that* Abram
fell on his face, *and called upon the name of the Lord.*
4 And God talked with him, saying, *My people have gone astray from my precepts, and have not kept mine ordinances, which I gave unto their fathers;*
5 *And they have not observed mine anointing, and the burial, or baptism wherewith I commanded them;*
6 *But have turned from the commandment, and taken unto themselves the washing of children, and the blood of sprinkling;*
7 *And have said that the blood of the righteous Abel was shed for sins; and have not known wherein they are accountable before me.*
8 *But* as for *thee*, behold, *I will make* my covenant with thee, and thou shalt be a father of many nations.
9 *And this covenant I make, that thy children may be known among all nations.* Neither shall thy name any more be called Abram, but thy name shall be called Abraham; for, a father of many nations have I made thee.
10 And I will make thee exceedingly fruitful, and I will make nations of thee, and kings shall come of thee, *and of thy seed.*
11 And I will establish *a covenant of circumcision with thee, and it shall be* my covenant between me and thee, and thy seed after thee, in their generations; *that thou mayest know forever that children are not accountable before me until they are eight years old.*
12 *And thou shalt observe to keep all my covenants wherein I covenanted with thy fathers; and thou shalt keep the commandments which I have given thee with mine own mouth, and I will be a God unto thee and thy seed after thee.*

JST, Genesis 17:23–24. Compare Genesis 17:17–18

Abraham rejoices at the prophecy of Isaac's birth and prays for Ishmael.

23 Then Abraham fell on his face
and *rejoiced*, and said in his heart, *There* shall a child be born unto him that is an hundred years old, and Sarah that is ninety years old *shall bear.*
24 And Abraham said unto God, Oh that Ishmael might live *uprightly* before thee!

JST, Genesis 19:9–15. Compare Genesis 19:8–10

Lot resists the wickedness of Sodom, and angels protect him.

9 And they said *unto him*, Stand
back. *And they were angry with him.*
10 And they said *among themselves*, This one *man* came in to sojourn *among us*, and he will needs *now make himself to be* a judge; now we will deal worse with *him* than with them.
11 *Wherefore they said unto the man, We will have the men, and thy daughters also; and we will do with them as seemeth us good.*
12 *Now this was after the wickedness of Sodom.*
13 And Lot said, Behold now, I have two daughters which have not known man; let me, I pray you, *plead with my brethren that I may not* bring them out unto you; and ye *shall not* do unto them as seemeth good in your eyes;
14 *For God will not justify his servant in this thing; wherefore, let me plead with my brethren, this once only, that* unto these men ye do nothing, *that they may have peace in my house;* for therefore came they under the shadow of my roof.
15 *And they were angry with Lot* and came near to break the door, but the *angels of God, which were holy men,* put forth their hand and

pulled Lot into the house unto them, and shut the door.

JST, Genesis 21:31–32. Compare Genesis 21:32–34

Abraham worships the everlasting God.

31 Then Abimelech, and Phicol, the chief captain of his hosts, rose up, *and they planted a grove in Beer-sheba, and called there on the name of the Lord;* and they returned unto the land of the Philistines.

32 And Abraham *worshiped the everlasting God, and* sojourned in the land of the Philistines many days.

JST, Genesis 48:5–11. Compare Genesis 48:5–6

Ephraim and Manasseh become tribes of Israel. Just as ancient Joseph saved his family temporally, his descendants will save Israel spiritually in the latter days.

5 And now, of thy two sons, Ephraim and Manasseh, which were born unto thee in the land of Egypt, before I came unto thee into Egypt; *behold, they* are mine, *and the God of my fathers shall bless them; even* as Reuben and Simeon they *shall be blessed, for they are* mine; *wherefore they shall be called after my name. (Therefore they were called Israel.)*

6 And thy issue which thou begettest after them, shall be thine, and shall be called after the name of their brethren in their inheritance, *in the tribes; therefore they were called the tribes of Manasseh and of Ephraim.*

7 *And Jacob said unto Joseph, When the God of my fathers appeared unto me in Luz, in the land of Canaan; he sware unto me, that he would give unto me, and unto my seed, the land for an everlasting possession.*

8 *Therefore, O my son, he hath blessed me in raising thee up to be a servant unto me, in saving my house from death;*

9 *In delivering my people, thy brethren, from famine which was sore in the land; wherefore the God of thy fathers shall bless thee, and the fruit of thy loins, that they shall be blessed above thy brethren, and above thy father's house;*

10 *For thou hast prevailed, and thy father's house hath bowed down unto thee, even as it was shown unto thee, before thou wast sold into Egypt by the hands of thy brethren; wherefore thy brethren shall bow down unto thee, from generation to generation, unto the fruit of thy loins forever;*

11 *For thou shalt be a light unto my people, to deliver them in the days of their captivity, from bondage; and to bring salvation unto them, when they are altogether bowed down under sin.*

JST, Genesis 50:24–38. Compare Genesis 50:24–26; 2 Nephi 3:4–22

Joseph in Egypt prophesies of Moses freeing Israel from Egyptian bondage; of a branch of Joseph's descendants being led to a faraway land, where they will be remembered in the covenants of the Lord; of God calling a latter-day prophet named Joseph to join the records of Judah and of Joseph; and of Aaron serving as a spokesman for Moses.

24 And Joseph said unto his brethren, I die, *and go unto my fathers; and I go down to my grave with joy. The God of my father Jacob be with you, to deliver you out of affliction in the days of your bondage; for the Lord hath visited me, and I have obtained a promise of the Lord, that out of the fruit of my loins, the Lord God will raise up a righteous branch out of my loins; and unto thee, whom my father Jacob hath named Israel, a prophet; (not the Messiah who is called Shilo;) and this prophet shall deliver my people out of Egypt in the days of thy bondage.*

25 *And it shall come to pass that they shall be scattered again; and a branch shall be broken off, and shall be carried into a far country; nevertheless they shall be remembered in the covenants of the Lord, when the Messiah cometh; for he shall be*

made manifest unto them in the lat-
ter days, in the Spirit of power; and
shall bring them out of darkness into
light; out of hidden darkness, and out
of captivity unto freedom.
26 *A seer shall the Lord my God*
raise up, who shall be a choice seer
unto the fruit of my loins.
27 *Thus saith the Lord God of*
my fathers unto me, A choice seer
will I raise up out of the fruit of thy
loins, and he shall be esteemed highly
among the fruit of thy loins; and unto
him will I give commandment that he
shall do a work for the fruit of thy
loins, his brethren.
28 *And he shall bring them to the*
knowledge of the covenants which
I have made with thy fathers; and
he shall do whatsoever work I shall
command him.
29 *And I will make him great in*
mine eyes, for he shall do my work;
and he shall be great like unto him
whom I have said I would raise up
unto you, to deliver my people, O
house of Israel, out of the land of
Egypt; for a seer will I raise up to
deliver my people out of the land of
Egypt; and he shall be called Moses.
And by this name he shall know that
he is of thy house; for he shall be
nursed by the king's daughter, and
shall be called her son.
30 *And again, a seer will I raise up*
out of the fruit of thy loins, and unto
him will I give power to bring forth
my word unto the seed of thy loins;
and not to the bringing forth of my
word only, saith the Lord, but to the
convincing them of my word, which
shall have already gone forth among
them in the last days;
31 *Wherefore the fruit of thy loins*
shall write, and the fruit of the loins
of Judah shall write; and that which
shall be written by the fruit of thy
loins, and also that which shall be
written by the fruit of the loins of
Judah, shall grow together unto the
confounding of false doctrines, and
laying down of contentions, and
establishing peace among the fruit
of thy loins, and bringing them to
a knowledge of their fathers in the
latter days; and also to the knowledge
of my covenants, saith the Lord.
32 *And out of weakness shall he*
be made strong, in that day when
my work shall go forth among all
my people, which shall restore them,
who are of the house of Israel, in the
last days.
33 *And that seer will I bless, and*
they that seek to destroy him shall
be confounded; for this promise I
give unto you; for I will remember
you from generation to generation;
and his name shall be called Joseph,
and it shall be after the name of his
father; and he shall be like unto you;
for the thing which the Lord shall
bring forth by his hand shall bring
my people unto salvation.
34 *And the Lord sware unto Joseph*
that he would preserve his seed for-
ever, saying, I will raise up Moses,
and a rod shall be in his hand, and
he shall gather together my people,
and he shall lead them as a flock,
and he shall smite the waters of the
Red Sea with his rod.
35 *And he shall have judgment,*
and shall write the word of the Lord.
And he shall not speak many words,
for I will write unto him my law by
the finger of mine own hand. And I
will make a spokesman for him, and
his name shall be called Aaron.
36 *And it shall be done unto thee*
in the last days also, even as I have
sworn. Therefore, Joseph said unto
his brethren, God will surely visit
you, and bring you out of this land,
unto the land which he sware unto
Abraham, and unto Isaac, and to
Jacob.
37 And Joseph *confirmed many*
other things unto his brethren, and
took an oath of the children of Israel, saying unto them, God will
surely visit you, and ye shall carry
up my bones from hence.
38 So Joseph died *when he was*
an hundred and ten years old; and
they embalmed him, and *they* put
him in a coffin in Egypt; *and he*
was kept from burial by the children
of Israel, that he might be carried up
and laid in the sepulchre with his

father. And thus they remembered the oath which they sware unto him.

JST, Exodus 4:21. Compare Exodus 4:21; 7:3, 13; 9:12; 10:1, 20, 27; 11:10; 14:4, 8, 17; Deuteronomy 2:30

The Lord is not responsible for Pharaoh's hardness of heart. See also JST, Exodus 7:3, 13; 9:12; 10:1, 20, 27; 11:10; 14:4, 8, 17; each reference, when correctly translated, shows that Pharaoh hardened his own heart.

21 And the Lord said unto Moses, When thou goest to return into Egypt, see that thou do all those wonders before Pharaoh, which I have put in thine hand, *and I will prosper thee;* but *Pharaoh* will harden his heart, *and* he *will* not let the people go.

JST, Exodus 4:24–27. Compare Exodus 4:24–27

When the Lord threatens to kill Moses for not circumcising his son, Zipporah saves his life by performing the ordinance herself. Moses confesses his sin.

24 And it came to pass, *that the Lord appeared unto him as he was in* the way, *by* the inn. *The Lord was angry with Moses, and his hand was about to fall upon him,* to kill him; *for he had not circumcised his son.*
25 Then Zipporah took a sharp stone and *circumcised* her son, and cast *the stone* at his feet, and said, Surely *thou art* a bloody husband unto me.
26 *And the Lord spared Moses and* let him go, *because Zipporah, his wife, circumcised the child. And* she said, Thou art a bloody husband. *And Moses was ashamed, and hid his face from the Lord, and said, I have sinned before the Lord.*
27 And the Lord said unto Aaron, Go into the wilderness to meet Moses, and he went and met him, in the mount of God; *in the mount where God appeared unto him;* and *Aaron* kissed him.

JST, Exodus 18:1. Compare Exodus 18:1

Jethro is a high priest.

1 When Jethro, the *high priest* of Midian, Moses' father-in-law, heard of all that God had done for Moses, and for Israel his people, and that the Lord had brought Israel out of Egypt;

JST, Exodus 22:18. Compare Exodus 22:18

Murderers shall not live.

18 Thou shalt not suffer a *murderer* to live.

JST, Exodus 32:14. Compare Exodus 32:14

The Lord will spare the Israelites who will repent.

14 And the Lord *said unto Moses, If they will repent* of the evil which *they have done, I will spare them, and turn away my fierce wrath; but, behold, thou shalt execute judgment upon all that will not repent of this evil this day. Therefore, see thou do this thing that I have commanded thee, or I will execute all that which I had* thought to do unto *my* people.

JST, Exodus 33:20, 23. Compare Exodus 33:20, 23

No sinful man can see God's face and live.

20 And he said *unto Moses,* Thou canst not see my face *at this time, lest mine anger be kindled against thee also, and I destroy thee, and thy people;* for there shall no man *among them* see me *at this time,* and live, *for they are exceeding sinful. And no sinful man hath at any time, neither shall there be any sinful man at any time, that shall see my face and live.*
23 And I will take away mine hand, and thou shalt see my back parts, but my face shall not be seen, *as at other times; for I am angry with my people Israel.*

JST, Exodus 34:1–2, 14. Compare Exodus 34:1–2, 14; D&C 84:21–26

God again writes the law on tablets of stone prepared by Moses but takes the Melchizedek Priesthood and its ordinances away from the children of Israel. He gives them the law of carnal commandments instead.

1 And the Lord said unto Moses, Hew thee two *other* tables of stone, like unto the first, and I will write upon *them also,* the words *of the law, according as they were written at the* first *on the* tables which thou brakest; *but it shall not be according to the first, for I will take away the priesthood out of their midst; therefore my holy order, and the ordinances thereof, shall not go before them; for my presence shall not go up in their midst, lest I destroy them.*

2 *But I will give unto them the law as at the first, but it shall be after the law of a carnal commandment; for I have sworn in my wrath, that they shall not enter into my presence, into my rest, in the days of their pilgrimage. Therefore do as I have commanded thee,* and be ready in the morning, and come up in the morning unto mount Sinai, and present thyself there to me, in the top of the mount.

Jehovah is one name by which the Old Testament people know the Lord Jesus Christ.

14 For thou shalt worship no other god; for the Lord, whose name is *Jehovah,* is a jealous God.

JST, Deuteronomy 10:2. Compare Deuteronomy 10:2

On the first set of tablets God reveals the everlasting covenant of the holy priesthood.

2 And I will write on the tables the words that were *on* the first tables, which thou brakest, *save the words of the everlasting covenant of the holy priesthood,* and thou shalt put them in the ark.

JST, 1 Samuel 16:14–16, 23. Compare 1 Samuel 16:14–16, 23; similar changes were made to 1 Samuel 18:10 and 19:9

The evil spirit that comes upon Saul is not from the Lord.

14 But the Spirit of the Lord departed from Saul, and an evil spirit *which was not of* the Lord troubled him.

15 And Saul's servants said unto him, Behold now, an evil spirit *which is not of* God troubleth thee.

16 Let our lord now command thy servants, which are before thee, to seek out a man, who is a cunning player on a harp; and it shall come to pass, when the evil spirit, *which is not of* God, is upon thee, that he shall play with his hand, and thou shalt be well.

23 And it came to pass, when the evil spirit, *which was not of* God, was upon Saul, that David took a harp, and played with his hand; so Saul was refreshed, and was well, and the evil spirit departed from him.

JST, 2 Samuel 12:13. Compare 2 Samuel 12:13

David's grievous sin is not put away by God.

13 And David said unto Nathan, I have sinned against the Lord. And Nathan said unto David, The Lord also hath *not* put away thy sin *that* thou shalt not die.

JST, 1 Chronicles 21:15. Compare 1 Chronicles 21:15

God stops an angel from destroying Jerusalem.

15 And God sent an angel unto Jerusalem to destroy it. *And the angel stretched forth his hand unto Jerusalem to destroy it; and God said to the angel, Stay now thine hand, it is enough; for* as he was destroying, the Lord beheld *Israel, that* he repented him of the evil; *therefore the Lord stayed* the angel that destroyed, *as he* stood

by the threshing floor of Ornan, the Jebusite.

JST, 2 Chronicles 18:22. Compare 2 Chronicles 18:22

The Lord does not put a lying spirit into the mouths of prophets.

22 Now therefore, behold, the Lord hath *found* a lying spirit in the mouth of these thy prophets, and the Lord hath spoken evil against thee.

JST, Psalm 11:1–5. Compare Psalm 11:1–5

In the last days the righteous will flee to the mountain of the Lord. When the Lord comes, He will destroy the wicked and redeem the righteous.

1 *In that day thou shalt come,* O *Lord; and* I will put my trust *in thee. Thou shalt say unto thy people, for mine ear hath heard thy voice; thou shalt say unto every* soul, Flee unto *my* mountain; *and the righteous shall flee like* a bird *that is let go from the snare of the fowler.*
2 For the wicked bend their bow; lo, they make ready their arrow upon the string, that they may privily shoot at the upright in heart, *to destroy their foundation.*
3 *But* the foundations *of the wicked shall* be destroyed, *and* what can *they* do?
4 *For* the Lord, *when he shall come into* his holy temple, *sitting upon God's* throne in heaven, his eyes *shall pierce the wicked.*
5 Behold his eyelids *shall* try the children of men, *and he shall redeem the righteous, and they shall be tried.* The Lord *loveth* the righteous, but the wicked, and him that loveth violence, his soul hateth.

JST, Psalm 14:1–7. Compare Psalm 14:1–7

The Psalmist sees the loss of truth in the last days and looks forward to the establishment of Zion.

1 The fool hath said in his heart, *There is no man that hath seen God. Because he showeth himself not unto us, therefore* there is no God. *Behold,* they are corrupt; they have done abominable works, *and none of them* doeth good.
2 *For* the Lord looked down from heaven upon the children of men, *and by his voice said unto his servant, Seek ye among the children of men,* to see if there *are* any that *do* understand God. *And he opened his mouth unto the Lord, and said, Behold, all these who say they are thine.*
3 *The Lord answered, and said,* They are all gone aside, they are together become filthy, *thou canst behold* none *of them* that *are doing* good, no, not one.
4 *All they have for their teachers are* workers of iniquity, *and there is* no knowledge *in them. They are they* who eat up my people. They eat bread and call not upon the Lord.
5 They *are* in great fear, for God *dwells* in the generation of the righteous. *He is the counsel of the poor, because they are ashamed of the wicked, and flee unto the Lord, for their refuge.*
6 *They are ashamed of* the counsel of the poor because the Lord is his refuge.
7 Oh that *Zion were established out of heaven,* the salvation of Israel. O *Lord, when wilt thou establish Zion?* When the Lord bringeth back the captivity of his people, Jacob shall rejoice, Israel shall be glad.

JST, Psalm 24:7–10. Compare Psalm 24:7–10

The King of Glory will redeem His people at His coming.

7 Lift up your heads, O ye *generations of Jacob;* and be ye lifted up; *and* the Lord strong and mighty; the Lord mighty in battle, who is the king of glory, *shall establish you forever.*
8 *And he will roll away the heavens; and will come down to redeem*

his people; to make you an everlasting name; to establish you upon his everlasting rock.

9 Lift up your heads, O ye *generations of Jacob;* lift up *your heads,* ye everlasting *generations,* and the *Lord of hosts, the king of kings;*

10 *Even* the king of glory shall come *unto you; and shall redeem his people, and shall establish them in righteousness.* Selah.

JST, Psalm 109:4. Compare Psalm 109:4

We are to pray for our adversaries.

4 *And, notwithstanding* my love, they are my adversaries; *yet* I *will continue in* prayer *for them.*

JST, Isaiah 29:1–8. Compare Isaiah 29:1–8

The messages formerly preached in Jerusalem by ancient prophets will in the latter days be preached from the Book of Mormon, which came forth "out of the ground."

1 Woe to Ariel, to Ariel, the city where David dwelt! add ye year to year; let them kill sacrifices.

2 Yet I will distress Ariel, and there shall be heaviness and sorrow; *for thus hath the Lord said unto me,* It shall be unto Ariel;

3 *That* I *the Lord* will camp against *her* round about, and will lay siege against *her* with a mount, and I will raise forts against *her.*

4 And *she shall* be brought down, and *shall* speak out of the ground, and *her* speech shall be low out of the dust; and *her* voice shall be as of one that hath a familiar spirit, out of the ground, and *her* speech shall whisper out of the dust.

5 Moreover the multitude of *her* strangers shall be like small dust, and the multitude of the terrible ones shall be as chaff that passeth away; yea, it shall be at an instant suddenly.

6 *For they shall* be visited of the Lord of hosts with thunder, and with earthquake, and great noise, with storm and tempest, and the flame of devouring fire.

7 And the multitude of all the nations that fight against Ariel, even all that fight against her and her munition, and that distress her, shall be as a dream of a night vision.

8 *Yea,* it shall *be unto them even* as *unto* a hungry man *who* dreameth, and behold, he eateth, but he awaketh and his soul is empty; or *like unto* a thirsty man *who* dreameth, and behold, he drinketh, but he awaketh, and behold, he is faint, and his soul hath appetite. *Yea, even* so shall the multitude of all the nations be that fight against mount Zion.

JST, Isaiah 42:19–23. Compare Isaiah 42:19–22

The Lord sends His servant to teach those who have chosen not to see or hear the truth; those who listen and obey will be made perfect.

19 *For I will send my servant unto you who are blind; yea, a messenger to open the eyes of the blind, and unstop the ears of the deaf;*

20 *And they shall be made perfect notwithstanding their blindness, if they will hearken unto the messenger,* the Lord's servant.

21 *Thou art a people,* seeing many things, but thou observest not; opening the ears *to hear, but thou* hearest not.

22 The Lord is *not* well pleased *with such a people, but* for his righteousness' sake he will magnify the law and make it honorable.

23 *Thou art* a people robbed and spoiled; *thine enemies,* all of them, *have* snared *thee* in holes, and they *have hid thee* in prison houses; they *have taken thee* for a prey, and none delivereth; for a spoil, and none saith, Restore.

JST, Jeremiah 26:13. Compare Jeremiah 26:13

The Lord does not repent; men repent.

13 Therefore now, amend your

ways and your doings, and obey the voice of the Lord your God, *and repent,* and the Lord will *turn away* the evil that he hath pronounced against you.

JST, Amos 7:3. Compare Amos 7:3

The Lord does not repent; men repent.

3 *And* the Lord *said, concerning Jacob, Jacob shall repent* for this, *therefore I will not utterly destroy him,* saith the Lord.

JST, Matthew 3:4–6. Compare Matthew 2:4–6

The prophets foretold that Bethlehem would be the place of the Messiah's birth.

4 And when he had gathered all the chief priests, and scribes of the people together, he demanded of them, *saying, Where is the place that is written of by the prophets, in which* Christ should be born? *For he greatly feared, yet he believed not the prophets.*
5 And they said unto him, *It is written by the prophets, that he should be born* in Bethlehem of Judea, for thus *have they said,*
6 *The word of the Lord came unto us, saying,* And thou Bethlehem, *which lieth* in the land of Judea, *in thee shall be born a prince, which* art not the least among the princes of Judea; for out of thee shall come *the Messiah,* who shall *save* my people Israel.

JST, Matthew 3:24–26. Compare Matthew 2:23

Jesus grows up and waits on the Lord before beginning His ministry.

24 *And it came to pass that Jesus grew up with his brethren, and waxed strong, and waited upon the Lord for the time of his ministry to come.*
25 *And he served under his father, and he spake not as other men, neither could he be taught; for he needed not that any man should teach him.*
26 *And after many years, the hour of his ministry drew nigh.*

JST, Matthew 3:34–36. Compare Matthew 3:8–9

Those who rejected the message of John the Baptist rejected Christ. God can make covenant people of those not of Israel.

34 *Why is it that ye receive not the preaching of him whom God hath sent? If ye receive not this in your hearts, ye receive not me; and if ye receive not me, ye receive not him of whom I am sent to bear record; and for your sins ye have no cloak.*
35 *Repent, therefore, and* bring forth fruits meet for repentance;
36 And think not to say within yourselves, *We are the children of Abraham, and we only have power to bring seed unto our father Abraham;* for I say unto you that God is able of these stones to raise up children *into* Abraham.

JST, Matthew 3:38–40. Compare Matthew 3:11–12

John the Baptist testifies that Jesus has power to baptize with the Holy Ghost and fire.

38 I indeed baptize you with water, *upon your* repentance; *and when he of whom I bear record cometh, who is* mightier than I, whose shoes I am not worthy to bear, *(or whose place I am not able to fill,) as I said, I indeed baptize you before he cometh, that when he cometh he may* baptize you with the Holy Ghost and fire.
39 *And it is he of whom I shall bear record,* whose fan *shall be* in his hand, and he will thoroughly purge his floor, and gather his wheat into the garner; but *in the fullness of his own time* will burn up the chaff with unquenchable fire.
40 *Thus came John, preaching and baptizing in the river of Jordan; bearing record, that he who was coming after him had power to baptize with the Holy Ghost and fire.*

JST, Matthew 3:43–46. Compare Matthew 3:15–17

John baptizes Jesus by immersion, sees the Holy Ghost descending like a dove, and hears the Father's voice.

43 And Jesus, answering, said unto him, Suffer *me to be baptized of thee,* for thus it becometh us to fulfill all righteousness. Then he suffered him.

44 *And John went down into the water and baptized him.*

45 And Jesus when he was baptized, went up straightway out of the water; *and John saw,* and lo, the heavens were opened unto him, and he saw the Spirit of God descending like a dove and lighting upon *Jesus.*

46 And lo, *he heard* a voice from heaven, saying, This is my beloved Son, in whom I am well pleased. *Hear ye him.*

JST, Matthew 4:1, 5–6, 8–9. Compare Matthew 4:1, 5–6, 8–9; similar changes were made in Luke 4:2, 5–11

Jesus is led by the Spirit, not by Satan.

1 Then *Jesus was* led up of the Spirit, into the wilderness, to be *with God.*

5 Then *Jesus was taken* up into the holy city, and *the Spirit* setteth him on *the* pinnacle of the temple.

6 *Then the devil came unto him and said,* If thou be the Son of God, cast thyself down, for it is written, He shall give his angels charge concerning thee, and in their hands they shall bear thee up, lest at any time thou dash thy foot against a stone.

8 *And* again, *Jesus was in the Spirit, and it* taketh him up into an exceeding high mountain, and showeth him all the kingdoms of the world and the glory of them.

9 And *the devil came unto him again, and said,* All these things will I give *unto* thee, if thou wilt fall down and worship me.

JST, Matthew 4:11. Compare Matthew 4:11

Jesus sends angels to minister to John the Baptist.

11 *And now Jesus knew that John was cast into prison, and he sent angels,* and, behold, *they* came and ministered unto him.

JST, Matthew 4:18. Compare Matthew 4:19

Old Testament prophets speak of Jesus.

18 And he *said* unto them, *I am he of whom it is written by the prophets;* follow me, and I will make you fishers of men.

JST, Matthew 4:22. Compare Matthew 4:23

Jesus heals people among those who believe on His name.

22 And Jesus went about all Galilee teaching in their synagogues, and preaching the gospel of the kingdom; and healing all manner of sickness, and all manner of *diseases* among the people *which believed on his name.*

JST, Matthew 5:21. Compare Matthew 5:19

Whoso keeps the commandments and teaches others to do the same will be saved.

21 Whosoever, therefore, shall break one of these least commandments, and shall teach men so *to do, he shall in no wise be saved in the kingdom of heaven;* but whosoever shall do and teach *these commandments of the law until it be fulfilled,* the same shall be called great, *and shall be saved* in the kingdom of heaven.

JST, Matthew 6:14. Compare Matthew 6:13; similar changes were made in Luke 11:4

The Lord does not lead us into temptation.

14 And *suffer* us not *to be led* into temptation, but deliver us from evil.

JST, Matthew 6:22. Compare Matthew 6:22

If our eyes are single to the glory of God, our whole bodies will be filled with light.

22 The light of the body is the eye; if therefore thine eye be single *to the glory of God*, thy whole body shall be full of light.

JST, Matthew 6:25–27. Compare Matthew 6:25; 10:10

Jesus warns His disciples of the difficulty of their work but promises that He will prepare the way and that Heavenly Father will provide for them.

25 *And, again, I say unto you, Go ye into the world, and care not for the world; for the world will hate you, and will persecute you, and will turn you out of their synagogues.*
26 *Nevertheless, ye shall go forth from house to house, teaching the people; and I will go before you.*
27 *And your heavenly Father will provide for you, whatsoever things ye need for food, what ye shall eat; and for raiment, what ye shall wear or put on.*

JST, Matthew 6:38. Compare Matthew 6:33

We should seek first to build the kingdom of God.

38 *Wherefore, seek not the things of this world* but seek ye first *to build up* the kingdom of God, and *to establish* his righteousness, and all these things shall be added unto you.

JST, Matthew 7:1–2. Compare Matthew 7:1–2

Judge not unrighteously.

1 *Now these are the words which Jesus taught his disciples that they should say unto the people.*
2 Judge not *unrighteously*, that ye be not judged; *but judge righteous judgment.*

JST, Matthew 7:4–8. Compare Matthew 7:3–5

Jesus teaches His disciples to confront scribes, Pharisees, priests, and Levites because of their hypocrisy.

4 *And again, ye shall say unto them, Why is it that thou* beholdest the mote that is in thy brother's eye, but considerest not the beam that is in thine own eye?
5 Or how wilt thou say to thy brother, Let me pull out the mote out of thine eye; *and canst not behold* a beam in thine own eye?
6 *And Jesus said unto his disciples, Beholdest thou the scribes, and the Pharisees, and the priests, and the Levites? They teach in their synagogues, but do not observe the law, nor the commandments; and all have gone out of the way, and are under sin.*
7 *Go thou and say unto them, Why teach ye men the law and the commandments, when ye yourselves are the children of corruption?*
8 *Say unto them,* Ye hypocrites, first cast out the beam out of thine own eye; and then shalt thou see clearly to cast out the mote out of thy brother's eye.

JST, Matthew 7:9–11. Compare Matthew 7:6

Jesus teaches His disciples to preach repentance and not to share the mysteries of the kingdom with the world.

9 *Go ye into the world, saying unto all, Repent, for the kingdom of heaven has come nigh unto you.*
10 *And the mysteries of the kingdom ye shall keep within yourselves; for it is not meet to* give that which is holy unto the dogs; neither cast ye your pearls *unto* swine, lest they trample them under their feet.
11 *For the world cannot receive that which ye, yourselves, are not able to bear; wherefore ye shall not give your pearls unto them, lest they* turn again and rend you.

JST, Matthew 7:12–17. Compare Matthew 7:7–8

Jesus teaches His disciples that the Father gives revelation to all who ask.

12 *Say unto them, Ask of God;* ask, and it shall be given you; seek, and ye shall find; knock, and it shall be opened unto you.

13 For everyone that asketh, receiveth; and he that seeketh, findeth; and unto him that knocketh, it shall be opened.

14 *And then said his disciples unto him, They will say unto us, We ourselves are righteous, and need not that any man should teach us. God, we know, heard Moses and some of the prophets; but us he will not hear.*

15 *And they will say, We have the law for our salvation, and that is sufficient for us.*

16 *Then Jesus answered, and said unto his disciples, Thus shall ye say unto them,*

17 *What man among you, having a son, and he shall be standing out, and shall say, Father, open thy house that I may come in and sup with thee, will not say, Come in, my son; for mine is thine, and thine is mine?*

JST, Matthew 9:18–21. Compare Matthew 9:16–17

Jesus rejects the baptism of the Pharisees; it has no value because they do not accept Him. He proclaims that He is the one who gave the law of Moses.

18 *Then said the Pharisees unto him, Why will ye not receive us with our baptism, seeing we keep the whole law?*

19 *But Jesus said unto them, Ye keep not the law. If ye had kept the law, ye would have received me, for I am he who gave the law.*

20 *I receive not you with your baptism, because it profiteth you nothing.*

21 *For when that which is new is come, the old is ready to be put away.*

JST, Matthew 11:13–15. Compare Matthew 11:10–11, 13–14

John the Baptist is the Elias who would come to prepare the way for the Savior.

13 *But the days will come, when the violent shall have no power;* for all the prophets and the law prophesied *that it should be thus* until John.

14 *Yea, as many as have prophesied have foretold of these days.*

15 And if ye will receive it, *verily, he was the* Elias, *who* was for to come *and prepare all things.*

JST, Matthew 12:37–38. Compare Matthew 12:43–44; see also JST, Luke 12:9–12

Whosoever speaks against the Holy Ghost will not be forgiven.

37 *Then came some of the scribes and said unto him, Master, it is written that, Every sin shall be forgiven; but ye say, Whosoever speaketh against the Holy Ghost shall not be forgiven. And they asked him, saying, How can these things be?*

38 *And he said unto them,* When the unclean spirit is gone out of a man, he walketh through dry places, seeking rest and findeth none; *but when a man speaketh against the Holy Ghost,* then he saith, I will return into my house from whence I came out; and when he is come, he findeth *him* empty, swept and garnished; *for the good spirit leaveth him unto himself.*

JST, Matthew 13:39–44. Compare Matthew 13:39–42; see also D&C 86:1–7

Before the end of the world (the destruction of the wicked), messengers sent of heaven will gather the righteous from among the wicked.

39 The harvest is the end of the world, *or the destruction of the wicked.*

40 The reapers are the angels, *or the messengers sent of heaven.*

41 As, therefore, the tares are gathered and burned in the fire, so shall it be in the end of this world, *or the destruction of the wicked.*

42 *For in that day, before* the Son

of man shall *come, he* shall send forth his angels *and messengers of heaven.*

43 And they shall gather out of his kingdom all things that offend, and them which do iniquity, and shall cast them *out among the wicked; and* there shall be wailing and gnashing of teeth.

44 *For the world shall be burned with fire.*

JST, Matthew 16:25–29. Compare Matthew 16:24–26

Jesus explains what it means "to take up one's cross": to deny all ungodliness and every worldly lust and to keep His commandments.

25 Then said Jesus unto his disciples, If any man will come after me, let him deny himself, and take up his cross and follow me.

26 *And now for a man to take up his cross, is to deny himself all ungodliness, and every worldly lust, and keep my commandments.*

27 *Break not my commandments for to save your lives;* for whosoever will save his life *in this world,* shall lose it *in the world to come.*

28 And whosoever will lose his life *in this world,* for my sake, shall find it *in the world to come.*

29 *Therefore, forsake the world, and save your souls;* for what is a man profited, if he shall gain the whole world, and lose his own soul? Or what shall a man give in exchange for his soul?

JST, Matthew 17:10–14. Compare Matthew 17:11–13

Jesus teaches of two Eliases—one to prepare and another to restore.

10 And Jesus answered and said unto them, Elias truly shall first come, and restore all things, *as the prophets have written.*

11 *And again* I say unto you that Elias has come already, *concerning whom it is written, Behold, I will send my messenger, and he shall prepare the way before me;* and they knew him not, and have done unto him, whatsoever they listed.

12 Likewise shall also the Son of man suffer of them.

13 *But I say unto you, Who is Elias? Behold, this is Elias, whom I send to prepare the way before me.*

14 Then the disciples understood that he spake unto them of John the Baptist, *and also of another who should come and restore all things, as it is written by the prophets.*

JST, Matthew 18:11. Compare Matthew 18:11; see also Moroni 8

Little children have no need of repentance.

11 For the Son of man is come to save that which was lost, *and to call sinners to repentance; but these little ones have no need of repentance, and I will save them.*

JST, Matthew 19:13. Compare Matthew 19:13

Little children will be saved.

13 Then were there brought unto him little children, that he should put his hands on them and pray. And the disciples rebuked them, *saying, There is no need, for Jesus hath said, Such shall be saved.*

JST, Matthew 21:33. Compare Matthew 21:32–33

Man must repent before he can believe in Christ.

33 *For he that believed not John concerning me, cannot believe me, except he first repent.*

JST, Matthew 21:47–56. Compare Matthew 21:45–46

Jesus declares that He is the chief cornerstone. The gospel is offered to the Jews and then to the Gentiles. The wicked will be destroyed when Jesus returns.

47 And when the chief priests and Pharisees had heard his parables, they perceived that he spake of them.

48 *And they said among themselves, Shall this man think that he*

alone can spoil this great kingdom? And they were angry with him.

49 But when they sought to lay hands on him, they feared the multitude, because they *learned that the multitude* took him for a prophet.

50 *And now his disciples came to him, and Jesus said unto them, Marvel ye at the words of the parable which I spake unto them?*

51 *Verily, I say unto you, I am the stone, and those wicked ones reject me.*

52 *I am the head of the corner. These Jews shall fall upon me, and shall be broken.*

53 *And the kingdom of God shall be taken from them, and shall be given to a nation bringing forth the fruits thereof; (meaning the Gentiles.)*

54 *Wherefore, on whomsoever this stone shall fall, it shall grind him to powder.*

55 *And when the Lord therefore of the vineyard cometh, he will destroy those miserable, wicked men, and will let again his vineyard unto other husbandmen, even in the last days, who shall render him the fruits in their seasons.*

56 *And then understood they the parable which he spake unto them, that the Gentiles should be destroyed also, when the Lord should descend out of heaven to reign in his vineyard, which is the earth and the inhabitants thereof.*

JST, Matthew 23:6. Compare Matthew 23:9

He who is in heaven is our creator.

6 And call no *one* your *creator* upon the earth, or *your heavenly Father*; for one is your *creator and heavenly* Father, *even he who* is in heaven.

JST, Matthew 26:22, 24–25. Compare Matthew 26:26–28; JST, Mark 14:20–25

Jesus first breaks the sacramental bread then blesses it. The sacrament is in remembrance of Jesus' body and blood.

22 And as they were eating, Jesus took bread and *brake* it, and *blessed* it, and gave to *his* disciples, and said, Take, eat; this is *in remembrance of* my body *which I give a ransom for you.*

24 For this is *in remembrance of* my blood of the new testament, which is shed for *as* many *as shall believe on my name*, for the remission of *their* sins.

25 *And I give unto you a commandment, that ye shall observe to do the things which ye have seen me do, and bear record of me even unto the end.*

JST, Matthew 27:3–6. Compare Matthew 27:3–5; Acts 1:18

Judas's death is described.

3 Then Judas, *who* had betrayed him, when he saw that he was condemned, repented himself, and brought again the thirty pieces of silver to the chief priests and elders,

4 Saying, I have sinned in that I have betrayed the innocent blood.

5 And they said *unto him,* What is that to us? See thou to *it; thy sins be upon thee.*

6 And he cast down the pieces of silver in the temple, and departed, and went, and hanged himself *on a tree. And straightway he fell down, and his bowels gushed out, and he died.*

JST, Mark 2:26–27. Compare Mark 2:27–28

The Son of Man is Lord of the Sabbath because He made the Sabbath day.

26 *Wherefore the Sabbath was given unto man for a day of rest; and also that man should glorify God, and not that man should not eat;*

27 *For the Son of man made the Sabbath day,* therefore the Son of man is Lord also of the Sabbath.

JST, Mark 3:21–25. Compare Mark 3:28–30

Jesus will forgive all sinners who repent except those who blaspheme against the Holy Ghost.

21 *And then came certain men unto him, accusing him, saying,* Why do *ye receive sinners, seeing thou makest thyself the Son of God.*

22 *But he answered them and said,* Verily I say unto you, All sins *which men have committed, when they repent,* shall be forgiven *them; for I came to preach repentance* unto the sons of men.

23 And blasphemies, wherewith soever they shall blaspheme, *shall be forgiven them that come unto me, and do the works which they see me do.*

24 *But there is a sin which shall not be forgiven.* He that shall blaspheme against the Holy Ghost, hath never forgiveness; but is in danger of *being cut down out of the world. And they shall inherit* eternal damnation.

25 *And this he said unto them* because they said, He hath an unclean spirit.

JST, Mark 7:10–12. Compare Mark 7:10

Jesus condemns those who reject the prophets and do not obey the law of Moses.

10 *Full well is it written of you, by the prophets whom ye have rejected.*

11 *They testified these things of a truth, and their blood shall be upon you.*

12 Ye *have kept not the ordinances of God;* for Moses said, Honor thy father and thy mother; and whoso curseth father or mother, let him die the death *of the transgressor, as it is written in your law; but ye keep not the law.*

JST, Mark 8:37–38. Compare Mark 8:35

Whoever is willing to die for Jesus' sake will receive salvation.

37 For whosoever will save his life, shall lose it; *or whosoever will save his life, shall be willing to lay it down for my sake; and if he is not willing to lay it down for my sake, he shall lose it.*

38 But whosoever shall *be willing to* lose his life for my sake, and the gospel, the same shall save it.

JST, Mark 8:42–43. Compare Mark 8:38

People who are ashamed of Christ have no part in the first resurrection, but those willing to die for Christ will come with Him in His glory.

42 *And they shall not have part in that resurrection when he cometh.*

43 *For verily I say unto you, That he shall come; and he that layeth down his life for my sake and the gospel's, shall come with him, and shall be clothed with his glory in the cloud, on the right hand of the Son of man.*

JST, Mark 9:3. Compare Mark 9:4

John the Baptist is on the Mount of Transfiguration.

3 And there appeared unto them Elias with Moses, *or in other words, John the Baptist and Moses;* and they were talking with Jesus.

JST, Mark 9:40–48. Compare Mark 9:43–48

Jesus compares cutting off an offending hand or foot to discontinuing associations that may lead one astray.

40 *Therefore,* if thy hand offend thee, cut it off; *or if thy brother offend thee and confess not and forsake not, he shall be cut off.* It is better for thee to enter into life maimed, than having two hands, to go into hell.

41 *For it is better for thee to enter into life without thy brother, than for thee and thy brother to be cast into hell;* into the fire that never shall be quenched, where their worm dieth not, and the fire is not quenched.

42 And *again,* if thy foot offend thee, cut it off; *for he that is thy standard, by whom thou walkest, if he become a transgressor, he shall be cut off.*

43 It is better for thee, to enter halt into life, than having two feet to be cast into hell; into the fire that never shall be quenched.

44 *Therefore, let every man stand or fall, by himself, and not for another; or not trusting another.*

45 *Seek unto my Father, and it shall be done in that very moment what ye shall ask, if ye ask in faith, believing that ye shall receive.*

46 And if thine eye *which seeth for thee, him that is appointed to watch over thee to show thee light, become a transgressor and* offend thee, pluck *him* out.

47 It is better for thee to enter into the kingdom of God, with one eye, than having two eyes to be cast into hell fire.

48 *For it is better that thyself should be saved, than to be cast into hell with thy brother,* where their worm dieth not, and where the fire is not quenched.

JST, Mark 12:32. Compare Mark 12:27

God is not a God of the dead, because He raises the dead from their graves.

32 He is not *therefore* the God of the dead, but the God of the living; *for he raiseth them up out of their graves.* Ye therefore do greatly err.

JST, Mark 14:20–26. Compare Mark 14:22–25

Jesus institutes the sacrament in remembrance of His body and blood.

20 And as they did eat, Jesus took bread and blessed it, and brake, and gave to them, and said, Take *it, and* eat.

21 *Behold, this is for you to do in remembrance of my body; for as oft as ye do this ye will remember this hour that I was with you.*

22 And he took the cup, and when he had given thanks, he gave it to them; and they all drank of it.

23 And he said unto them, This is *in remembrance of* my blood which is shed for many, *and the new testament which I give unto you; for of me ye shall bear record unto all the world.*

24 *And as oft as ye do this ordinance, ye will remember me in this hour that I was with you and drank with you of this cup, even the last time in my ministry.*

25 Verily I say unto you, *Of this ye shall bear record; for* I will no more drink of the fruit of the vine *with you,* until that day that I drink it new in the kingdom of God.

26 *And now they were grieved, and wept over him.*

JST, Mark 14:36–38. Compare Mark 14:32–34

At Gethsemane, even the Twelve do not fully grasp Jesus' role as the Messiah.

36 And they came to a place which was named Gethsemane, *which was a garden; and the disciples began to be sore amazed, and to be very heavy, and to complain in their hearts, wondering if this be the Messiah.*

37 *And Jesus knowing their hearts, said* to his disciples, Sit ye here, while I shall pray.

38 And he taketh with him, Peter, and James, and John, *and rebuked them,* and said unto them, My soul is exceeding sorrowful, *even* unto death; tarry ye here and watch.

JST, Mark 16:3–6. Compare Mark 16:4–7; Luke 24:2–4

Two angels greet the women at the tomb of the Savior.

3 *But* when they looked, they saw that the stone was rolled away, (for it was very great,) *and two angels sitting thereon,* clothed in long white *garments;* and they were affrighted.

4 *But the angels said* unto them, Be not affrighted; ye seek Jesus of Nazareth, *who* was crucified; he is risen; he is not here; behold the place where they laid him;

5 *And* go your way, tell his disciples and Peter, that he goeth before you into Galilee; there shall ye see him as he said unto you.

6 *And they, entering into the sepulcher, saw the place where they laid Jesus.*

JST, Luke 1:8. Compare Luke 1:8

Zacharias, John the Baptist's father, performs priesthood duties.

8 And while he executed the priest's office before God, in the order of his *priesthood,*

JST, Luke 2:46. Compare Luke 2:46

The doctors in the temple listen to Jesus and ask Him questions.

46 And it came to pass, after three days they found him in the temple, sitting in the midst of the doctors, *and they were* hearing *him,* and asking *him* questions.

JST, Luke 3:4–11. Compare Luke 3:4–6

Christ will come as prophesied to bring salvation to Israel and to the Gentiles. In the fulness of times, He will come again to judge the world.

4 As it is written in the book of the *prophet* Esaias; *and these are the words,* saying, The voice of one crying in the wilderness, Prepare ye the way of the Lord, and make his paths straight.
5 *For behold, and lo, he shall come, as it is written in the book of the prophets, to take away the sins of the world, and to bring salvation unto the heathen nations, to gather together those who are lost, who are of the sheepfold of Israel;*
6 *Yea, even the dispersed and afflicted; and also to prepare the way, and make possible the preaching of the gospel unto the Gentiles;*
7 *And to be a light unto all who sit in darkness, unto the uttermost parts of the earth; to bring to pass the resurrection from the dead, and to ascend up on high, to dwell on the right hand of the Father,*
8 *Until the fullness of time, and the law and the testimony shall be sealed, and the keys of the kingdom shall be delivered up again unto the Father;*
9 *To administer justice unto all; to come down in judgment upon all, and to convince all the ungodly of their ungodly deeds, which they have committed; and all this in the day that he shall come;*
10 *For it is a day of power; yea,* every valley shall be filled, and every mountain and hill shall be brought low; the crooked shall be made straight, and the rough ways made smooth;
11 And all flesh shall see the salvation of God.

JST, Luke 3:19–20. Compare Luke 3:10–13

The poor are cared for from the treasury's abundance. Publicans (tax collectors) should take no more than is appointed by law.

19 *For it is well known unto you, Theophilus, that after the manner of the Jews, and according to the custom of their law in receiving money into the treasury, that out of the abundance which was received, was appointed unto the poor, every man his portion;*
20 *And after this manner did the publicans also, wherefore John* said unto them, Exact no more than that which is appointed you.

JST, Luke 6:29–30. Compare Luke 6:29–30

Jesus teaches that it is better to endure persecution than to contend with an enemy.

29 And unto him who smiteth thee on the cheek, offer also the other; *or, in other words, it is better to offer the other, than to revile again.* And him who taketh away thy cloak, forbid not to take thy coat also.
30 *For it is better that thou suffer thine enemy to take these things, than to contend with him. Verily I say unto you, Your heavenly Father who seeth in secret, shall bring that wicked one into judgment.*

JST, Luke 9:24–25. Compare Luke 9:24–25

Gaining worldly wealth is not worth losing one's soul.

24 For whosoever will save his life, *must be willing to* lose it *for my sake; and* whosoever will *be willing to* lose his life for my sake, the same shall save it.

25 For what *doth it profit a man* if he gain the whole world, *and yet he receive him not whom God hath ordained, and he* lose *his own soul, and he* himself be *a* castaway?

JST, Luke 11:53. Compare Luke 11:52

The fulness of the scriptures is the key of knowledge.

53 Woe unto you, lawyers! For ye have taken away the key of knowledge, *the fullness of the scriptures;* ye *enter* not in yourselves *into the kingdom;* and *those who* were entering in, ye hindered.

JST, Luke 12:9–12. Compare Luke 12:9–10; see also JST, Matthew 12:37–38 and D&C 132:26–27

Jesus explains that blasphemy against the Holy Ghost will not be forgiven.

9 But he *who* denieth me before men, shall be denied before the angels of God.

10 *Now his disciples knew that he said this, because they had spoken evil against him before the people; for they were afraid to confess him before men.*

11 *And they reasoned among themselves, saying, He knoweth our hearts, and he speaketh to our condemnation, and we shall not be forgiven. But he answered them, and said unto them,*

12 Whosoever shall speak a word against the Son of man, *and repenteth,* it shall be forgiven him; but unto him *who* blasphemeth against the Holy Ghost, it shall not be forgiven him.

JST, Luke 12:41–57. Compare Luke 12:37–48

Jesus teaches that His servants must always be ready for His coming.

41 *For, behold, he cometh in the first watch of the night, and he shall also come in the second watch, and again he shall come in the third watch.*

42 *And verily I say unto you, He hath already come, as it is written of him; and again when* he shall come in the second watch, or come in the third watch, blessed are those servants *when he cometh, that he shall* find so *doing;*

43 *For the Lord of those servants shall gird himself, and make them to sit down to meat, and will come forth and serve them.*

44 *And now, verily I say these things unto you, that ye may know this, that the coming of the Lord is as a thief in the night.*

45 *And it is like unto a man who is an householder, who, if he watcheth not his goods, the thief cometh in an hour of which he is not aware, and taketh his goods, and divideth them among his fellows.*

46 *And they said among themselves,* If the good man of the house had known what hour the thief would come, he would have watched, and not have suffered his house to be broken through *and the loss of his goods.*

47 *And he said unto them, Verily I say unto you,* be ye therefore ready also; for the Son of man cometh at an hour when ye think not.

48 Then Peter said unto him, Lord, speakest thou this parable unto us, or unto all?

49 And the Lord said, *I speak unto those whom the Lord* shall make *rulers* over his household, to give *his children* their portion of meat in due season.

50 *And they said, Who then is that faithful and wise servant?*

51 *And the Lord said unto them, It is that servant who watcheth, to impart his portion of meat in due season.*

52 Blessed *be* that servant whom his *Lord* shall find, when he cometh, so doing.
53 Of a truth I say unto you, that he will make him ruler over all that he hath.
54 *But the evil servant is he who is not found watching. And if that servant is not found watching, he will* say in his heart, My Lord delayeth his coming; and shall begin to beat the menservants, and the maidens, and to eat, and drink, and to be drunken.
55 The *Lord* of that servant will come in a day he looketh not for, and at an hour when he is not aware, and will cut him *down,* and will appoint him his portion with the unbelievers.
56 And that servant who knew his *Lord's* will, and prepared not *for his Lord's coming,* neither did according to his will, shall be beaten with many stripes.
57 But he that knew not *his Lord's will,* and did commit things worthy of stripes, shall be beaten with few. For unto whomsoever much is given, of him shall much be required; and to whom *the Lord* has committed much, of him *will men* ask the more.

JST, Luke 14:35–37. Compare Luke 14:34

Those who know Moses and the prophets believe in Jesus.

35 *Then certain of them came to him, saying, Good Master, we have Moses and the prophets, and whosoever shall live by them, shall he not have life?*
36 *And Jesus answered, saying, Ye know not Moses, neither the prophets; for if ye had known them, ye would have believed on me; for to this intent they were written. For I am sent that ye might have life. Therefore I will liken it unto* salt *which* is good;
37 But if the salt *has* lost *its* savor, wherewith shall it be seasoned?

JST, Luke 16:16–23. Compare Luke 16:16–18

The law and the prophets testify of Jesus. The Pharisees seek to destroy the kingdom. Jesus introduces the parable of the rich man and Lazarus.

16 *And they said unto him, We have the law, and the prophets; but as for this man we will not receive him to be our ruler; for he maketh himself to be a judge over us.*
17 *Then said Jesus unto them,* The law and the prophets *testify of me; yea, and all the prophets who have written, even* until John, *have foretold of these days.*
18 Since that time, the kingdom of God is preached, and every man *who seeketh truth* presseth into it.
19 And it is easier for heaven and earth to pass, than for one tittle of the law to fail.
20 *And why teach ye the law, and deny that which is written; and condemn him whom the Father hath sent to fulfill the law, that ye might all be redeemed?*
21 *O fools! for you have said in your hearts, There is no God. And you pervert the right way; and the kingdom of heaven suffereth violence of you; and you persecute the meek; and in your violence you seek to destroy the kingdom; and ye take the children of the kingdom by force. Woe unto you, ye adulterers!*
22 *And they reviled him again, being angry for the saying, that they were adulterers.*
23 *But he continued, saying,* Whosoever putteth away his wife, and marrieth another, committeth adultery; and whosoever marrieth her who is put away from her husband, committeth adultery. *Verily I say unto you, I will liken you unto the rich man.*

JST, Luke 17:21. Compare Luke 17:20–21

The kingdom of God has already come.

21 Neither shall they say, Lo, here! or, Lo, there! For, behold,

the kingdom of God *has already come unto* you.

JST, Luke 17:36–40. Compare Luke 17:37

Jesus tells the parable of the eagles to explain the gathering of His Saints in the last days.

36 And they answered and said unto him, Where, Lord, *shall they be taken?*
37 And he said unto them, Wheresoever the body is *gathered; or, in other words, whithersoever the saints are gathered,* thither will the eagles be gathered together; *or, thither will the remainder be gathered together.*
38 *This he spake, signifying the gathering of his saints; and of angels descending and gathering the remainder unto them; the one from the bed, the other from the grinding, and the other from the field, whithersoever he listeth.*
39 *For verily there shall be new heavens, and a new earth, wherein dwelleth righteousness.*
40 *And there shall be no unclean thing; for the earth becoming old, even as a garment, having waxed in corruption, wherefore it vanisheth away, and the footstool remaineth sanctified, cleansed from all sin.*

JST, Luke 18:27. Compare Luke 18:27

Trusting in riches prevents a person from entering the kingdom of God.

27 And he said *unto them, It is impossible for them who trust in riches, to enter into the kingdom of God; but he who forsaketh the things which are of this world, it is* possible with God, *that he should enter in.*

JST, Luke 21:24–26. Compare Luke 21:25–26

Jesus speaks of some signs of His coming.

24 *Now these things he spake unto them, concerning the destruction of Jerusalem. And then his disciples asked him, saying, Master, tell us concerning thy coming?*
25 *And he answered them, and said, In the generation in which the times of the Gentiles shall be fulfilled,* there shall be signs in the sun, and in the moon, and in the stars; and upon the earth distress of nations with perplexity, *like* the sea and the waves roaring. *The earth also shall be troubled, and the waters of the great deep;*
26 Men's hearts failing them for fear, and for looking after those things which are coming on the earth. For the powers of heaven shall be shaken.

JST, Luke 21:32. Compare Luke 21:32

All will be fulfilled when the times of the Gentiles are fulfilled.

32 Verily I say unto you, this generation, *the generation when the times of the Gentiles be fulfilled,* shall not pass away till all be fulfilled.

JST, Luke 23:35. Compare Luke 23:34

Jesus asks forgiveness for the Roman soldiers who are crucifying Him.

35 Then said Jesus, Father, forgive them; for they know not what they do *(Meaning the soldiers who crucified him,)* and they parted his raiment and cast lots.

JST, Luke 24:2–4. Compare Luke 24:2–5

The women see two angels at Jesus' sepulcher.

2 And they found the stone rolled away from the sepulcher, *and two angels standing by it in shining garments.*
3 And they entered *into the sepulcher,* and *not finding* the body of the Lord Jesus, they were much perplexed thereabout;
4 And were *affrighted,* and bowed down their faces to the earth. *But behold the angels* said unto them,

Why seek ye the living among the
dead?

JST, John 1:1–34. Compare John 1:1–34

The gospel of Jesus Christ has been preached from the beginning. John the Baptist is the Elias who prepares the way for Christ, and Jesus Christ is the Elias who restores all things and through whom salvation comes.

1 In the beginning was the *gospel*
preached through the Son. And the
gospel was the word, and the *word*
was with *the Son, and the Son was*
with God, and the *Son* was *of* God.
2 The same was in the begin-
ning with God.
3 All things were made by him;
and without him was not anything made which was made.
4 In him was *the gospel,* and *the*
gospel was the life, and the life was
the light of men;
5 And the light shineth *in the*
world, and the *world perceiveth* it
not.
6 There was a man sent from
God, whose name was John.
7 The same came *into the world*
for a witness, to bear witness of
the *light, to bear record of the gos-*
pel through the Son, unto all, that
through him *men* might believe.
8 He was not that *light,* but *came*
to bear witness of that *light,*
9 Which was the true *light,*
which lighteth every man *who*
cometh into the world;
10 *Even the Son of God.* He *who* was
in the world, and the world was
made by him, and the world knew
him not.
11 He came unto his own, and
his own received him not.
12 But as many as received him,
to them gave he power to become
the sons of God; *only* to them who
believe on his name.
13 *He was* born, not of blood,
nor of the will of the flesh, nor of
the will of man, but of God.
14 And the *same word* was made
flesh, and dwelt among us, and we
beheld his glory, the glory as of
the Only Begotten of the Father,
full of grace and truth.
15 John *bear* witness of him, and
cried, saying, This *is* he of whom
I spake; He who cometh after me,
is preferred before me; for he was
before me.
16 *For in the beginning was the*
Word, even the Son, who is made
flesh, and sent unto us by the will of
the Father. And as many as believe
on his name shall receive of his full-
ness. And of his fullness have all
we received, *even immortality and*
eternal life, through his grace.
17 For the law was given *through*
Moses, but *life* and truth came
through Jesus Christ.
18 *For the law was after a carnal*
commandment, to the administration
of death; but the gospel was after
the power of an endless life, through
Jesus Christ, the Only Begotten Son,
who is in the bosom of the Father.
19 *And* no man hath seen God
at any time, *except he hath borne*
record of the Son; for except it is
through him no man can be saved.
20 And this is the record of
John, when the Jews sent priests
and Levites from Jerusalem, to ask
him; Who art thou?
21 And he confessed, and denied not *that he was Elias;* but confessed, *saying;* I am not the Christ.
22 And they asked him, *saying;*
How then art thou Elias? And he
said, I am not *that Elias who was*
to restore all things. And they asked
him, saying, Art thou that prophet?
And he answered, No.
23 Then said they unto him,
Who art thou? that we may give
an answer to them that sent us.
What sayest thou of thyself?
24 He said, I am the voice of one
crying in the wilderness, Make
straight the way of the Lord, as
saith the prophet Esaias.
25 And they who were sent were
of the Pharisees.
26 And they asked him, and said
unto him; Why baptizest thou
then, if thou be not the Christ, nor

Elias *who was to restore all things,*
neither that prophet?
27 John answered them, saying;
I baptize with water, but there
standeth one among you, whom
ye know not;
28 He it is *of whom I bear record.*
He is that prophet, even Elias, who,
coming after me, is preferred before me, whose shoe's latchet I am
not worthy to unloose, *or whose*
place I am not able to fill; for he shall
baptize, not only with water, but with
fire, and with the Holy Ghost.
29 The next day John seeth Jesus
coming unto him, and said; Behold the Lamb of God, who taketh
away the sin of the world!
30 *And John bare record of him*
unto the people, saying, This is he
of whom I said; After me cometh
a man who is preferred before me;
for he was before me, and I knew
him, *and* that he should be made
manifest to Israel; therefore am I
come baptizing with water.
31 And John bare record, saying; *When he was baptized of me,*
I saw the Spirit descending from
heaven like a dove, and it abode
upon him.
32 And I knew him; *for* he who
sent me to baptize with water, the
same said unto me; Upon whom
thou shalt see the Spirit descending, and remaining on him, the
same is he who baptizeth with the
Holy Ghost.
33 And I saw, and bare record
that this is the Son of God.
34 *These things were done in Beth-*
abara, beyond Jordan, where John
was baptizing.

JST, John 1:42. Compare John 1:42

Cephas means "seer" or "stone."

42 And he brought him to Jesus.
And when Jesus beheld him, he
said, Thou art Simon, the son of
Jona, thou shalt be called Cephas,
which is, by interpretation, *a seer,*
or a stone. And they were fishermen.
And they straightway left all, and fol-
lowed Jesus.

JST, John 4:1–4. Compare John 4:1–2

The Pharisees desire to kill Jesus. He performs some baptisms, but His disciples perform more.

1 When therefore the Pharisees
had heard that Jesus made and
baptized more disciples than John,
2 *They sought more diligently some*
means that they might put him to
death; for many received John as a
prophet, but they believed not on Jesus.
3 *Now the Lord knew this,* though
he himself baptized not *so many as*
his disciples;
4 *For he suffered them for an exam-*
ple, preferring one another.

JST, John 4:26. Compare John 4:24

God promises His Spirit to true believers.

26 *For unto such hath* God *prom-*
ised his Spirit. And they *who* worship him, must worship in spirit
and in truth.

JST, John 6:44. Compare John 6:44

The Father's will is that all receive Jesus. Those who do the will of Jesus will be raised in the resurrection of the just.

44 No man can come unto me,
except *he doeth the will of my*
Father *who* hath sent me. *And this*
is the will of him who hath sent me,
that ye receive the Son; for the Father
beareth record of him; and he who re-
ceiveth the testimony, and doeth the
will of him who sent me, I will raise
up *in the resurrection of the just.*

JST, John 13:8–10. Compare John 13:8–10

Jesus washes the feet of the Apostles to fulfill the law of the Jews.

8 Peter saith unto him, Thou *needest not to* wash my feet. Jesus answered him, If I wash thee not, thou hast no part with me.

9 Simon Peter saith unto him, Lord, not my feet only, but also my hands and my head.

10 Jesus saith to him, He that *has* washed *his hands and his head,* needeth not save to wash his feet, but is clean every whit; and ye are clean, but not all. *Now this was the custom of the Jews under their law; wherefore, Jesus did this that the law might be fulfilled.*

JST, John 14:30. Compare John 14:30

The prince of darkness, or Satan, is of this world.

30 Hereafter I will not talk much with you; for the prince *of darkness, who is* of this world, cometh, *but* hath *no power over me, but he hath power over you.*

JST, Acts 9:7. Compare Acts 9:7; 22:9

Those who are with Paul at his conversion see the light, but they do not hear the voice or see the Lord.

7 And *they who were journeying* with him *saw indeed the light, and were afraid; but they heard not the voice of him who spake to him.*

JST, Acts 22:29–30. Compare Acts 22:29–30

The chief captain loosed Paul from his bands.

29 Then straightway they departed from him which should have examined him, and the chief captain also was afraid after he knew that he was a Roman, because he had bound him, *and he loosed him from his bands.*

30 On the morrow, because he would have known the certainty wherefore he was accused of the Jews, *he* commanded the chief priests and all their council to appear, and brought Paul down, and set him before them.

JST, Romans 3:5–8. Compare Romans 3:5–8

Paul teaches that a person cannot do evil to bring about good.

5 But if *we remain in* our unrighteousness *and* commend the righteousness of God, *how dare* we say, God is unrighteous who taketh vengeance? (I speak as a man *who fears God,*)

6 God forbid; for then how shall God judge the world?

7 For if the truth of God hath more abounded through my lie, *(as it is called of the Jews,)* unto his glory; why yet am I also judged as a sinner? and not *received? Because* we *are* slanderously reported;

8 And some affirm that we say, *(whose damnation is just,)* Let us do evil that good may come. *But this is false.*

JST, Romans 4:2–5. Compare Romans 4:2–5

Man can only be saved by the grace of Jesus Christ, not by works related to observance of the law of Moses.

2 For if Abraham were justified by *the law of* works, he hath to glory *in himself;* but not *of* God.

3 For what saith the scripture? Abraham believed God, and it was counted unto him for righteousness.

4 Now to him *who is justified by the law of works,* is the reward reckoned, not of grace, but of debt.

5 But to him that *seeketh not to be justified by the law of works,* but believeth on him who justifieth *not* the ungodly, his faith is counted for righteousness.

JST, Romans 4:16. Compare Romans 4:16

Both faith and works, through grace, are necessary for salvation.

16 Therefore *ye are justified* of

faith *and works, through* grace, to the end the promise might be sure to all the seed; not to *them* only *who are* of the law, but to *them* also *who are* of the faith of Abraham; who is the father of us all,

JST, Romans 7:5–27. Compare Romans 7:5–25

Only Christ has power to permanently change men's souls for good.

5 For when we were in the flesh, the motions of sin, which were *not according to* the law, did work in our members to bring forth fruit unto death.

6 But now we are delivered from the law wherein we were held, *being dead to the law,* that we should serve in newness of spirit, and not in the oldness of the letter.

7 What shall we say then? Is the law sin? God forbid. Nay, I had not known sin, but by the law; for I had not known lust, except the law had said, Thou shalt not covet.

8 But sin, taking occasion by the commandment, wrought in me all manner of concupiscence. For without the law sin was dead.

9 For *once* I was alive without *transgression of* the law, but when the commandment *of Christ* came, sin revived, and I died.

10 And *when I believed not* the commandment *of Christ which came,* which was ordained to life, I found *it condemned me* unto death.

11 For sin, taking occasion, *denied* the commandment, *and* deceived me; and by it *I was slain.*

12 *Nevertheless, I found* the law *to be* holy, and the commandment *to be* holy, and just, and good.

13 Was then that which is good made death unto me? God forbid. But sin, that it might appear sin by that which is good working death in me; that sin, by the commandment, might become exceeding sinful.

14 For we know that the *commandment* is spiritual; but *when I was under the law,* I *was yet* carnal, sold under sin.

15 *But now I am spiritual;* for that which *I am commanded to do, I do; and that which I am commanded not to allow,* I allow not.

16 For what I *know is not right, I would* not *do; for that which is sin,* I hate.

17 If then I do *not* that which I would not *allow,* I consent unto the law, that it is good; *and I am not condemned.*

18 Now then, it is no more I that do *sin;* but I *seek to subdue that* sin which dwelleth in me.

19 For I know that in me, that is, in my flesh, dwelleth no good thing; for to will is present with me, *but to* perform that which is good I find not, *only in Christ.*

20 For the good that I would *have done when under the law, I find not to be good; therefore,* I do *it* not.

21 But the evil which I would not *do under the law, I find to be good;* that, I do.

22 Now if I do that, *through the assistance of Christ,* I would not *do under the law, I am not under the law; and* it is no more *that I seek to do wrong,* but *to subdue* sin that dwelleth in me.

23 I find then *that under the* law, that when I would do good evil *was* present with me; for I delight in the law of God after the inward man.

24 *And now* I see another law, *even the commandment of Christ, and it is imprinted in my mind.*

25 *But* my members *are* warring against the law of my mind, and bringing me into captivity to the law of sin which is in my members.

26 *And if I subdue not the sin which is in me, but with the flesh serve the law of sin;* O wretched man that I am! who shall deliver me from the body of this death?

27 I thank God through Jesus Christ our Lord, *then, that so* with

the mind I myself serve the law of God.

JST, Romans 8:8. Compare Romans 8:8

Those who follow after the ways of the flesh cannot please God.

8 So then they that are *after* the flesh cannot please God.

JST, Romans 8:29–30. Compare Romans 8:29–30

Jesus Christ sanctifies the righteous in preparation for their salvation.

29 For *him* whom he did fore-
know, he also did predestinate to
be conformed to *his own* image,
that he might be the firstborn
among many brethren.
30 Moreover, *him* whom he did
predestinate, *him* he also called;
and *him* whom he called, *him* he
also *sanctified;* and *him* whom he
sanctified, him he also glorified.

JST, Romans 13:6–7. Compare Romans 13:6–7

Those who honor civil authorities make their honor to God greater and more perfect.

6 For, for this cause pay ye *your*
consecrations also *unto them;* for
they are God's ministers, attending
continually upon this very thing.
7 *But first,* render to all their
dues, *according to custom,* tribute
to whom tribute, custom to whom
custom, *that your consecrations may
be done in* fear *of him* to whom
fear *belongs, and in* honor *of him* to
whom honor *belongs.*

JST, 1 Corinthians 7:1–2, 5, 26, 29–33, 38. Compare 1 Corinthians 7:1–2, 5, 26, 29–38

Paul teaches that marriage is desirable. Those called as missionaries, however, serve God better if they remain single during their ministry.

1 Now concerning the things
whereof ye wrote unto me, *saying,*
It is good for a man not to touch
a woman.
2 Nevertheless, *I say,* to avoid
fornication, let every man have
his own wife, and let every woman
have her own husband.
5 *Depart* ye not one *from* the
other, except it be with consent for a time, that ye may give
yourselves to fasting and prayer;
and come together again, that
Satan tempt you not for your
incontinency.
26 I suppose therefore that this
is good for the present distress, for
a man so to *remain that he may do
greater good.*
29 But *I speak unto you who are
called unto the ministry. For* this I say,
brethren, the time *that remaineth* is
but short, *that ye shall be sent forth
unto the ministry. Even* they who
have wives, *shall* be as though they
had none; *for ye are called and chosen
to do the Lord's work.*
30 And *it shall be with them* who
weep, as though they wept not;
and them who rejoice, as though
they rejoiced not, and them who
buy, as though they possessed not;
31 And them who use this world,
as not *using* it; for the fashion of
this world passeth away.
32 But *I would, brethren, that ye
magnify your calling.* I would have
you without carefulness. For he
who is unmarried, careth for the
things that belong to the Lord,
how he may please the Lord; *therefore he prevaileth.*
33 But he who is married, careth for the things that are of the
world, how he may please his
wife; *therefore there is a difference,
for he is hindered.*
38 So then he that giveth *himself*
in marriage doeth well; but he
that giveth *himself* not in marriage
doeth better.

JST, 1 Corinthians 15:40. Compare 1 Corinthians 15:40

There are three degrees of glory in the Resurrection.

40 Also celestial bodies, and bodies terrestrial, *and bodies telestial;* but the glory of the celestial, one; and the terrestrial, another; *and the telestial, another.*

JST, 2 Corinthians 5:16. Compare 2 Corinthians 5:16

Paul counsels Saints not to live after the manner of the flesh.

16 Wherefore, henceforth *live* we no *more* after the flesh; *yea, though we once lived after the flesh, yet since* we have known Christ, now henceforth *live* we no more *after the flesh.*

JST, Galatians 3:19–20. Compare Galatians 3:19–20

Moses is the mediator of the first covenant, or the law. Jesus Christ is the mediator of the new covenant.

19 Wherefore then, *the law* was added because of transgressions, till the seed should come to whom the promise was made *in the law given to Moses, who* was ordained by *the hand of* angels *to be* a mediator *of this first covenant, (the law.)*
20 Now *this* mediator *was* not a mediator of *the new covenant; but there is one mediator of the new covenant, who is Christ, as it is written in the law concerning the promises made to Abraham and his seed. Now Christ is the mediator of life; for this is the promise which God made unto Abraham.*

JST, Ephesians 4:26. Compare Ephesians 4:26

Unrighteous anger is sin.

26 *Can ye be* angry, and *not sin?* let not the sun go down upon your wrath;

JST, Colossians 2:21–22. Compare Colossians 2:20–23

The commandments of men might have value in teaching such things as self-discipline, but they neither honor God nor save man.

21 *Which are after the doctrines and commandments of men, who teach you to* touch not, taste not, handle not; *all those things* which are to perish with the using?
22 Which things have indeed a show of wisdom in will worship, and humility, and neglecting the body *as to the satisfying the flesh,* not in any honor to *God.*

JST, 1 Thessalonians 4:15. Compare 1 Thessalonians 4:15

Those righteous people who are alive at the coming of the Lord will have no advantage over the righteous dead.

15 For this we say unto you by the word of the Lord, that *they who* are alive *at* the coming of the Lord, shall not prevent them *who remain unto the coming of the Lord, who* are asleep.

JST, 2 Thessalonians 2:2–3, 7–9. Compare 2 Thessalonians 2:2–9

Satan will cause a falling away or apostasy before the Lord returns.

2 That ye be not soon shaken in mind, or be troubled *by letter, except ye receive it from us;* neither by spirit, nor by word, as that the day of Christ is at hand.
3 Let no man deceive you by any means; for there *shall* come a falling away first, and that man of sin be revealed, the son of perdition;
7 For the mystery of iniquity doth already work, *and he it is who now worketh, and Christ suffereth him to work,* until *the time is fulfilled that* he *shall* be taken out of the way.
8 And then shall that wicked *one* be revealed, whom the Lord shall consume with the spirit of his mouth, and shall destroy with the brightness of his coming.
9 *Yea, the Lord, even Jesus,* whose coming is *not until* after *there cometh a falling away, by* the working of Satan with all power, and signs and lying wonders,

JST, 1 Timothy 2:4. Compare 1 Timothy 2:4

Christ is the Only Begotten Son and Mediator.

4 Who *is willing to* have all men to be saved, and to come unto the knowledge of the truth *which is in Christ Jesus, who is the Only Begotten Son of God, and ordained to be a Mediator between God and man; who is one God, and hath power over all men.*

JST, 1 Timothy 3:15–16. Compare 1 Timothy 3:15–16

The Church is founded on the central principle that Jesus became mortal, taught the gospel, and returned to His Father. Note: The subtle change in the following verses emphasizes that the "pillar and ground of the truth" is Jesus Christ.

15 But if I tarry long, that thou mayest know how thou oughtest to behave thyself in the house of God, which is the church of the living God.

16 The pillar and ground of the truth *is,* (and without controversy, great is the mystery of godliness,) God was manifest in the flesh, justified in the Spirit, seen of angels, preached unto the Gentiles, believed on in the world, received up into glory.

JST, 1 Timothy 6:15–16. Compare 1 Timothy 6:15–16

Those who have the light of immortality (the gospel) dwelling in them can see Jesus.

15 Which in his times he shall show, who is the blessed and only Potentate, the King of kings, and Lord of lords, *to whom be honor and power everlasting;*

16 *Whom no man hath seen, nor can see, unto whom no man can approach, only he who hath the light and the hope of immortality dwelling in him.*

JST, Hebrews 1:6–7. Compare Hebrews 1:6–7

Angels are ministering spirits.

6 And again, when he bringeth in the first begotten into the world, he saith, And let all the angels of God worship him, *who maketh his ministers as a flame of fire.*

7 And of the angels he saith, *Angels are ministering spirits.*

JST, Hebrews 4:3. Compare Hebrews 4:3

Those who harden their hearts will not be saved; those who repent will enter into the Lord's rest.

3 For we who have believed do enter into rest, as he said, As I have sworn in my wrath, If they *harden their hearts* they shall *not* enter into my rest; *also, I have sworn, If they will not harden their hearts, they shall enter into my rest;* although the works of God were *prepared, (or finished,)* from the foundation of the world.

JST, Hebrews 6:1–10. Compare Hebrews 6:1–10

The principles of Christ's doctrine lead to perfection.

1 Therefore *not* leaving the principles of the doctrine of Christ, let us go on unto perfection; not laying again the foundation of repentance from dead works, and of faith toward God.

2 Of the doctrine of baptisms, of laying on of hands, and of the resurrection of the dead, and of eternal judgment.

3 And *we will go on unto perfection* if God permit.

4 For *he hath made it* impossible for those who were once enlightened, and have tasted of the heavenly gift, and were made partakers of the Holy Ghost,

5 And have tasted the good word of God, and the powers of the world to come,

6 If they shall fall away, to *be renewed* again unto repentance; seeing they crucify unto themselves the Son of God afresh, and put him to an open shame.

7 For *the day cometh that* the earth

which drinketh in the rain that cometh oft upon it, and bringeth forth herbs meet for them *who dwelleth thereon,* by whom it is dressed, *who now* receiveth blessings from God, *shall be cleansed with fire.*
8 *For* that which beareth thorns and briers is rejected, and is nigh unto cursing; *therefore they who bring not forth good fruits, shall be cast into the fire; for their* end is to be burned.
9 But, beloved, we are persuaded *of* better things of you, and things that accompany salvation, though we thus speak.
10 For God is not unrighteous, *therefore he will not* forget your work and labor of love, which ye have showed toward his name, in that ye have ministered to the saints, and do minister.

JST, Hebrews 7:3. Compare Hebrews 7:3

Melchizedek was a priest after the order of the Son of God. All those who receive this priesthood can become like the Son of God.

3 *For this Melchizedek was ordained a priest after the order of the Son of God, which order was* without father, without mother, without descent, having neither beginning of days, nor end of life. *And all those who are ordained unto this priesthood are* made like unto the Son of God, *abiding* a priest continually.

JST, Hebrews 7:19–21. Compare Hebrews 7:19–21

The law prepared people for Jesus, who is "the surety of a better testament."

19 For the law *was administered without an oath and* made nothing perfect, but *was only* the bringing in of a better hope; by the which we draw nigh unto God.
20 Inasmuch as *this high priest was* not without an oath, *by so much was Jesus made the surety of a better testament.*
21 (For those priests were made without an oath; but this with an oath by him that said unto him, The Lord sware and will not repent, Thou art a priest forever after the order of Melchizedek;)

JST, Hebrews 7:25–26. Compare Hebrews 7:26–27

Jesus offers Himself as a sinless sacrifice for our sins.

25 For such an high priest became us, who is holy, harmless, undefiled, separate from sinners, and made *ruler over* the heavens;
26 *And not* as those high priests *who* offered up sacrifice *daily,* first for *their* own sins, and then for the *sins of the people;* for *he needeth not offer sacrifice for his own sins, for he knew no sins; but for the sins of the people. And* this he did once, when he offered up himself.

JST, Hebrews 11:1. Compare Hebrews 11:1

Faith is the assurance of things hoped for.

1 Now faith is the *assurance* of things hoped for, the evidence of things not seen.

JST, Hebrews 11:35. Compare Hebrews 11:35

The faithful who are tortured for Christ obtain the First Resurrection.

35 Women received their dead raised to life again; and others were tortured, not accepting deliverance; that they might obtain *the first* resurrection;

JST, James 1:2. Compare James 1:2

Afflictions, not temptations, help to sanctify us.

2 My brethren, count it all joy when ye fall into *many afflictions;*

JST, James 2:1. Compare James 2:1

Members should not regard one person more highly than another.

1 My brethren, *ye cannot* have

the faith of our Lord Jesus Christ, the Lord of glory, *and yet have* respect *to* persons.

JST, James 2:14–21. Compare James 2:14–22

Faith without works is dead and cannot save.

14 What profit *is it,* my brethren, *for* a man *to* say he hath faith, and hath not works? can faith save him?
15 Yea, a man may say, *I will show thee I have faith without works; but I say,* Show me thy faith without works, and I will show thee my faith by my works.
16 *For* if a brother or sister be naked and destitute, and one of you say, Depart in peace, be warmed and filled; notwithstanding *he* give not those things which are needful to the body; what profit *is your faith unto such?*
17 Even so faith, if it *have* not works is dead, being alone.
18 *Therefore* wilt thou know, O vain man, that faith without works is dead *and cannot save you?*
19 Thou believest there is one God; thou doest well; the devils also believe, and tremble; *thou hast made thyself like unto them, not being justified.*
20 Was not Abraham our father justified by works, when he had offered Isaac his son upon the altar?
21 Seest thou how *works* wrought with his *faith,* and by works was faith made perfect?

JST, 1 Peter 3:20. Compare 1 Peter 3:20

Some of the spirits in prison were unrighteous in the days of Noah.

20 *Some of whom* were disobedient *in the days of Noah, while* the long-suffering of God waited, while the ark was preparing, wherein few, that is, eight souls were saved by water.

JST, 1 Peter 4:6. Compare 1 Peter 4:6

The gospel is preached to those who are dead.

6 *Because of this, is* the gospel preached to them *who* are dead, that they might be judged according to men in the flesh, but live *in the spirit* according to *the will of* God.

JST, 1 Peter 4:8. Compare 1 Peter 4:8

Charity prevents us from sinning.

8 And above all things have fervent charity among yourselves; for charity *preventeth a* multitude of sins.

JST, 2 Peter 3:3–13. Compare 2 Peter 3:3–13

In the last days, many people will deny the Lord Jesus Christ. When He comes, many natural calamities will happen. If we endure in righteousness, we will receive a new earth.

3 Knowing this first, that *in the last days* there shall come scoffers, walking after their own lusts.
4 *Denying the Lord Jesus Christ,* and saying, Where is the promise of his coming? for since the fathers fell asleep, all things *must* continue as they *are, and have continued as they are* from the beginning of the creation.
5 For this they willingly are ignorant of, that *of old* the heavens, and the earth standing *in the water* and out of the water, *were created by the word of God;*
6 *And by the word of God,* the world that then was, being overflowed with water perished;
7 But the heavens, and the earth which are now, are kept in store *by the same word,* reserved unto fire against the day of judgment and perdition of ungodly men.
8 But *concerning the coming of the Lord,* beloved, *I would not have you* ignorant of this one thing, that one day is with the Lord as

a thousand years, and a thousand
years as one day.
9 The Lord is not slack concerning his promise *and coming,* as some men count slackness; but long-suffering *toward us,* not willing that any should perish, but that all should come to repentance.
10 But the day of the Lord will come as a thief in the night, in the which the heavens shall *shake, and the earth also shall tremble, and the mountains shall melt, and* pass away with a great noise, and the elements shall *be filled* with fervent heat; the earth also *shall be filled,* and the *corruptible* works *which* are therein shall be burned up.
11 *If* then all these things shall be *destroyed,* what manner of persons ought ye to be in holy *conduct* and godliness,
12 Looking *unto,* and *preparing for the day of* the coming of the *Lord* wherein the *corruptible things of the* heavens being on fire, shall be dissolved, and the *mountains* shall melt with fervent heat?
13 Nevertheless, *if we shall endure,* we *shall be kept* according to his promise. *And we* look for *a* new heavens, and a new earth wherein dwelleth righteousness.

JST, 1 John 2:1. Compare 1 John 2:1

Christ is our advocate with the Father if we repent.

1 My little children, these things write I unto you, that ye sin not. *But* if any man sin *and repent,* we have an advocate with the Father, Jesus Christ the righteous;

JST, 1 John 3:9. Compare 1 John 3:9

Whoever is born of God does not continue in sin.

9 Whosoever is born of God doth not *continue in* sin; for *the Spirit of God* remaineth in him; and he cannot *continue in* sin, because he is born of God, *having received that holy Spirit of promise.*

JST, 1 John 4:12. Compare 1 John 4:12

Only men who believe in God can see Him.

12 No man hath seen God at any time, *except them who believe.* If we love one another, God dwelleth in us, and his love is perfected in us.

JST, Revelation 1:1–8. Compare Revelation 1:1–8

John the Apostle receives the prophecies in the book of Revelation. He is visited by Jesus Christ and by an angel.

1 The Revelation of *John, a servant of God,* which *was given* unto him *of Jesus Christ,* to show unto his servants things which must shortly come to pass, *that* he sent and signified by his angel unto his servant John,
2 Who *bore* record of the word of God, and of the testimony of Jesus Christ, and of all things that he saw.
3 Blessed *are they* who read, and they who hear *and understand* the words of this prophecy, and keep those things which are written therein, for the time *of the coming of the Lord draweth nigh.*
4 *Now this is the testimony of* John to *the seven servants who are over* the seven churches in Asia. Grace unto you, and peace from him *who* is, and *who* was, and *who* is to come; *who hath sent forth his angel from* before his throne, *to testify unto those who are the seven servants over the seven churches.*
5 *Therefore, I, John,* the faithful witness, *bear record of the things which were delivered me of the angel,* and from Jesus Christ the first begotten of the dead, and the *Prince* of the kings of the earth.
6 *And* unto him who loved us, *be glory; who* washed us from our sins in his own blood, and hath made us kings and priests unto God, his Father. To him be glory and dominion, forever and ever. Amen.

7 *For* behold, he cometh *in the* clouds *with ten thousands of his saints in the kingdom, clothed with the glory of his Father.* And every eye shall see him; and they who pierced him, and all kindreds of the earth shall wail because of him. Even so, Amen.

8 *For he saith,* I am Alpha and Omega, the beginning and the ending, the Lord, *who* is, and *who* was, and *who* is to come, the Almighty.

JST, Revelation 2:22. Compare Revelation 2:22

The wicked are cast into hell.

22 Behold, I will cast her into *hell,* and them that commit adultery with her into great tribulation, except they repent of their deeds.

JST, Revelation 2:26–27. Compare Revelation 2:26–27

Those who overcome the world by obedience to Christ's commandments will rule kingdoms in the world to come with faith, equity, and justice.

26 And *to him who* overcometh, and keepeth my *commandments* unto the end, will I give power over *many kingdoms;*

27 And he shall rule them with *the word of God; and they shall be in his hands* as the vessels *of clay in the hands* of a potter; *and he shall govern them by faith, with equity and justice,* even as I received of my Father.

JST, Revelation 5:6. Compare Revelation 5:6

Twelve servants of God are sent to all the earth.

6 And I beheld, and, lo, in the midst of the throne and of the four beasts, and in the midst of the elders, stood a Lamb as it had been slain, having *twelve* horns and *twelve* eyes, which are the *twelve servants* of God, sent forth into all the earth.

JST, Revelation 12:1–17. Compare Revelation 12:1–17

John explains the symbols of the woman, the child, the rod of iron, the dragon, and Michael. The war that began in heaven is continued on the earth. Note the changed sequence of verses in the JST.

1 And there appeared a great *sign* in heaven, *in the likeness of things on the earth;* a woman clothed with the sun, and the moon under her feet, and upon her head a crown of twelve stars.

2 And *the woman* being with child, cried, travailing in birth, and pained to be delivered.

3 *And she brought forth a man child, who was to rule all nations with a rod of iron; and her child was caught up unto God and his throne.*

4 And there appeared another *sign* in heaven; and behold, a great red dragon, having seven heads and ten horns, and seven crowns upon his heads. And his tail drew the third part of the stars of heaven, and did cast them to the earth. And the dragon stood before the woman which was delivered, *ready* to devour her child *after* it was born.

5 And the woman fled into the wilderness, where she *had* a place prepared of God, that they should feed her there a thousand two hundred and threescore *years.*

6 And there was war in heaven; Michael and his angels fought against the dragon; and the dragon and his angels *fought against Michael;*

7 And *the dragon* prevailed not *against Michael, neither the child, nor the woman which was the church of God, who had been delivered of her pains, and brought forth the kingdom of our God and his Christ.*

8 Neither was *there* place found in heaven *for* the great dragon, *who* was cast out; that old serpent called the devil, and *also called* Satan, which deceiveth the whole world; he was cast out into the earth; and his angels were cast out with him.

9 And I heard a loud voice saying
in heaven, Now is come salvation,
and strength, and the kingdom
of our God, and the power of his
Christ;
10 For the accuser of our brethren is cast down, which accused
them before our God day and
night.
11 *For* they *have overcome* him
by the blood of the Lamb, and by
the word of their testimony; *for*
they loved not their own lives, *but*
kept the testimony even unto death.
Therefore, rejoice O heavens, and
ye that dwell in them.
12 *And after these things I heard*
another voice saying, Woe to the inhabiters of the earth, *yea,* and *they*
who dwell upon the islands of the
sea! for the devil is come down
unto you, having great wrath, because he knoweth that he hath
but a short time.
13 *For* when the dragon saw
that he was cast unto the earth,
he persecuted the woman which
brought forth the man-child.
14 *Therefore,* to the woman were
given two wings of a great eagle,
that she might *flee* into the wilderness, into her place, where she
is nourished for a time, and times,
and half a time, from the face of
the serpent.
15 And the serpent casteth out
of his mouth water as a flood
after the woman, that he might
cause her to be carried away of
the flood.
16 And the earth *helpeth* the
woman, and the earth *openeth*
her mouth, and *swalloweth* up the
flood which the dragon *casteth* out
of his mouth.
17 *Therefore,* the dragon was
wroth with the woman, and went
to make war with the remnant
of her seed, which keep the commandments of God, and have the
testimony of Jesus Christ.

JST, Revelation 19:15, 21.
Compare Revelation 19:15, 21

God uses the word of Christ to smite the nations.

15 And out of his mouth *pro-*
ceedeth the word of God, and with it
he *will* smite the nations; and he
will rule them with *the word of his*
mouth; and he treadeth the winepress *in* the fierceness and wrath
of Almighty God.
21 And the remnant were slain
with the *word* of him that sat
upon the horse, which *word* proceeded out of his mouth; and
all the fowls were filled with
their flesh.